BASIC COMPUTER ARCHITECTURE

SMRUTI R. SARANGI

White Falcon Publishing

www.whitefalconpublishing.com

Basic Computer Architecture
Smruti R. Sarangi

www.whitefalconpublishing.com

Requests for permission should be addressed to
srsarangi@cse.iitd.ac.in

ISBN - 978-1-63640-303-8

Preface

1. Organization of the Book

This book is meant for early-stage undergraduate students from the Computer Science, Electronics, and Electrical Engineering streams. A basic understanding of C/Java programming and digital logic is required. The rest of the book is self-contained. A chapter-wise description follows.

Chapter 1 provides a general introduction to computer architecture, and then proposes the notion of an instruction set architecture. We ponder on the question of completeness of an ISA by taking recourse to results developed by the founder of computer science, Alan Turing. We show how modern computers have descended from the ideas of Alan Turing and other theoretical computer scientists of his time. We conclude the chapter by noting that computers are information processing machines, where information is presented to them in the form of executable programs, and data.

The book is subsequently divided into three parts. The first part comprises of chapters 2-5. It describes the software interface of a processor. The second part (chapters 6-9) contains chapters that describe the design of a processor. The last part (chapters 10-12) looks at the design of a full system inclusive of complex memory systems, multiple processors, and the I/O subsystem. We have two appendices in the book. Appendix A describes the design of a few contemporary Intel, ARM, and AMD processors. We describe both low power processors for mobile applications, as well as server class processors. Appendix B is devoted to the study of the NVIDIA TESLA graphics processor.

We start part I by describing the methods to represent information in chapter 2, "The Language of Bits". In this chapter, we look at representing integers, real numbers, and pieces of text using a sequence of zeros and ones (known as bits). There are several interesting theoretical results in this section in the design of number systems, and the relative power of different representations. We shall cover these in detail, and also discuss the IEEE 754 format for representing real numbers (also known as floating-point numbers). We conclude this chapter with a discussion of the ASCII and Unicode formats for representing pieces of text.

Chapter 3 is devoted to the study of assembly languages, and the design of a novel assembly language called *SimpleRisc*. We introduce 21 *SimpleRisc* instructions along with their machine encoding and semantics, and further supplement the chapter with a wealth of solved examples that show how to solve a variety of problems using the *SimpleRisc* assembly language.

Chapters 4 and 5 describe two real world assembly languages namely ARM and x86. These languages are used by an overwhelming majority of processors as of 2013. We describe the semantics of most of the commonly used instructions, discuss their machine encodings, and show examples for solving some common programming problems in assembly language. In both these chapters, we have made an effort to discuss the intricacies of the assembly languages in great detail such that students can start serious system programming after going through them.

Part II contains 4 chapters. Chapters 6 and 7 describe the design of the basic elements of a processor such as logic elements, memory elements, and functional units for arithmetic and logical operations. Chapters 8 and 9 describe the design of a processor in great detail.

Chapter 6 gives a brief introduction to digital circuits. We discuss the physics of transistors, logic gates, combinational circuits, flip-flops, sequential circuits, memory cells, and programmable logic arrays. The aim of this chapter is to provide the reader with a basic understanding of the operation of digital circuits, and also provide any relevant background that is deemed necessary. Note that this chapter takes a rather cursory view of digital circuits, and the reader is advised to consult a textbook on digital electronics for a more thorough treatment of this subject. This chapter can be used by students to recapitulate their knowledge, or by readers who simply wish to get a broad overview of digital circuits.

Chapter 7 builds on chapter 2. It explains the basics of computer arithmetic. We start out with a thorough discussion on adders. Here also, we establish a connection with theoretical computer science, and use a computational complexity theory based approach for evaluating the time and space complexity of different adders. This formalism helps us in comparing different designs very intuitively. The chapter starts with simple adders such as Ripply carry adders, and gradually introduces more complex designs such as the carry select, and carry lookahead adders. We subsequently, describe algorithms for integer multiplication and division. In specific the Wallace tree multipler, restoring and non-restoring algorithms are covered. Sections 7.4-7.6 describe algorithms for adding and multiplying floating-point numbers. We conclude with two algorithms for floating-point division that are asymptotically much faster than integer division namely the Goldschmidt algorithm, and the Newton-Raphson method.

Chapter 8 describes the implementation of a complete *SimpleRisc* processor with the basic elements that we have presented in Chapters 6 and 7. We present two design styles in this chapter. The first design has a hardwired control unit, and the second design has a microprogrammed control unit. We discuss both the designs at the level of logic gates, and wires, and explain the different design choices in great detail. We show how the microprogrammed processor can be used to implement complex instructions, or implement instructions in the ISA in a different way.

Chapter 9 introduces advanced processors. We discuss methods to improve the performance of our basic hardwired processor. In this context, we discuss pipelining extensively. In specific, we discuss pipeline hazards, interlocks, software solutions, forwarding, and support for interrupts/exceptions. Subsequently, Chapter 9 presents a theoretical framework for estimating the performance of pipelined processors. In modern processors, power and temperature considerations are very important. Hence, we found it apt to introduce basic power and temperature models, and introduce the ED^2 metric to connect energy consumption and performance. The chapter ends with a study of advanced features in processors such as superscalar execution, out-of-order execution, and VLIW processors in Section 9.11.

Part III introduces full system design. A full system contains a complex memory hierarchy, multiple processors, and storage elements.

Chapter 10 discusses the memory system. We make an effort to give a mathematical flavor to this chapter by introducing the notions of stack distance and address distance. We subsequently, use these metrics to argue that we need a multilevel memory system with caches. The first part of this chapter (Sections 10.1 and 10.2) discusses the design of caches in detail including their structure, replacement policies, and their basic operations. The second part of this chapter (Sections 10.3 and 10.4) describes the entire memory system, virtual memory, and the memory management unit.

Chapter 11 introduces multiprocessor systems. It is assumed that most readers would not have a background of parallel programming. Hence, we felt it necessary to introduce the basics of parallel programming in Sections 11.1 and 11.2. In specific, we discuss shared memory and message passing based programs. In Section 11.4, we discuss MIMD machines. We first discuss the logical view of memory in Sections 11.4.1-11.4.3. Readers will learn about coherence and memory consistency in these machines. Henceforth, we describe methods to enforce coherence and consistency in Sections 11.4.4-11.4.7. Subsequently, we discuss multithreaded and vector processors. We conclude the chapter in Section 11.6 with a discussion on interconnection networks.

The last chapter of the book (chapter 12) discusses I/O protocols and storage devices. We introduce a novel 4 layered taxonomy of the functions of an I/O system. Sections 12.2-12.6 discuss the standards, conventions, and protocols in each layer. We then move on to discuss the detailed implementation of five state of the art I/O protocols (PCI Express, SAS, SATA, USB, and FireWire) in Section 12.7. Section 12.8 discusses a host of storage technologies such as hard drives, RAID disks, optical drives, and flash drives.

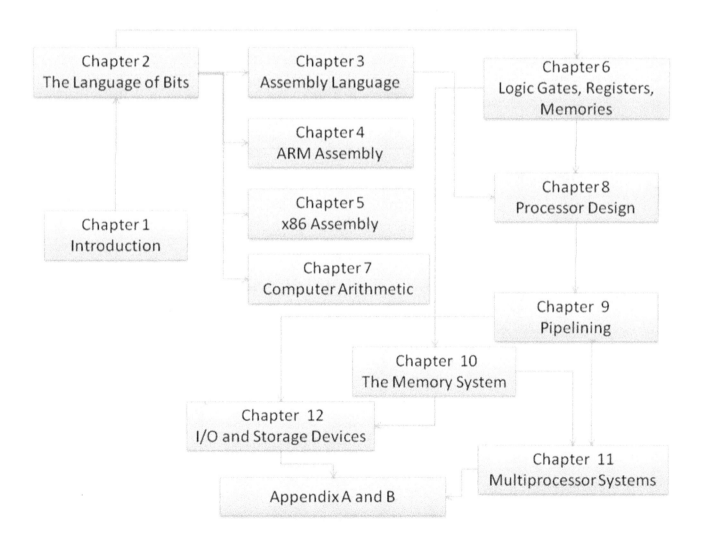

2. How to use the book?

(i) Guidelines for instructors, (ii) Guidelines for students

(i) Guidelines for instructors

Instructors who wish to use this book as a textbook in a computer architecture course can follow one of the several course plans that we shall describe next.

Course Type	Chapters	Remarks
Light (1 semester)	1, 2, 3, 8, 9, 10	Skip * marked sections, skip Sections 8.4-8.8, 9.8, 9.10, 9.11
Moderate (1 semester)	1, 2, 3, (4 or 5), 6.4, 7, 8, 9, 10, 12	Skip * marked sections, skip Sections 7.6, 9.11, 12.7. Cover chapters 4 or 5 only if there is enough time.
Heavy (1 semester)	1, 2, 3, (4 or 5), 6.4, 7, 8, 9, 10, 11, 12, Appendices	Skip Sections 9.11, 11.4, 12.7.2, 12.7.3, 12.7.5. Cover at least one chapter (4 or 5).
Heavy with gifted students (1 semester)	1, 2, 3, 6, 7, 8, 9, 10, 11, 12, Appendices	Cover chapter 4 or 5 in extra classes (if required). Pay special attention to Chapters 2.3, 7, 9, and 11.4.
Two-semester course	Sem I: 1, 2, 3, 4, 5, 6.4, 7	Cover chapter 6 in detail if students do not have prior to exposure to digital logic. In Chapter 9, it might not be necessary to cover Sections 9.8 and 9.11 in most courses.
	Sem II: 8, 9, 10, 11, 12, Appendices	

(ii) Guidelines for students

It is important to read the material in a chapter thoroughly and solve the exercises at the back of the chapter. Additionally, for the chapters on assembly language, hands-on experience with programming in assembly language is required. Just reading the text is not sufficient. It is necessary to gain proficiency by writing long and complex assembly programs. Secondly, for the sections on processor design, the student is encouraged to try to design a processor using either the Logisim toolkit or a hardwire description language such as Verilog or VHDL. This will give the student a practical feel for the area, and she will genuinely appreciate the nuances and tradeoffs in designing processors. Try to solve the design problems at the end of the chapter. These are meant to provide a holistic perspective to the student.

3. Supplementary Material

All the supplementary material is provided on the website of the book:

https://www.cse.iitd.ac.in/~srsarangi/archbooksoft.html

1. Slides: PowerPoint slides for all the chapters are available to both instructors and students on the book's website. Instructors can use this material for teaching in classes, and students can use the slides as important learning aids. The slides will continue to get updated. Students/instructors are advised to check on a regular basis for updates.
2. Solution manual: This will be available to instructors only on request. Instructors need to contact the author.
3. YouTube videos: The links to YouTube videos for all the chapters are there on the website of the book.
4. Link to all the software.
   a. emuArm: This is a graphical user interface based emulator for the ARM instruction set. It can be used to run and debug programs in the ARM assembly language. It has been especially designed for educational purposes.
   b. emuSimpleRisc: It is designed on the lines of emuArm for the *SimpleRisc* instruction set. It can be used to write, debug, and analyse *SimpleRisc* assembly programs in a graphical environment.
   c. SimpleRisc interpreter: We include a batch mode interpreter for *SimpleRisc* in C, along with a set of test programs. The interpreter can be used to quickly and run test assembly programs.
   d. Logisim model of the *SimpleRisc* processor: We include a full hardware model of the hardwired (non-pipelined) *SimpleRisc* processor in the Logisim framework. The users can run and edit the circuit using the popular Logisim tool.
   e. VHDL model of the *SimpleRisc* processor: We also include a VHDL model of the *SimpleRisc* processor along with its associated documentation. It can be simulated on any VHDL emulator such as GNU HDL, or on commercial EDA software.
   f. RISC-V emulator: It emulates the behavior of RISC-V programs. 32 and 64-bit RISC-V instructions are supported.

Trademark Attributions

ARM, AMBA, Cortex, and Thumb are registered trademarks of ARM Limited*(or its subsidiaries) in the EU and/or elsewhere. All rights reserved.*

NEON is a trademark of ARM Limited(or its subsidiaries) in the EU and/or elsewhere. All rights reserved.

Intel, Intel Xeon, Itanium, and Pentium are registered trademarks of Intel Corporation in the U.S and/or other countries.

Intel Atom, Intel Core i3, Intel Core i5, Intel Core i7, and MMX are trademarks of Intel Corporation in the U.S and/or other countries.

Microsoft, and Windows are registered trademarks of Microsoft Corporation in the United States and/or other countries.

Inkscape is a trademark of the Software Freedom Conservancy.

SPARC is a registered trademark of SPARC International, Inc. Products bearing SPARC trademarks are based on an architecture developed by Sun Microsystems, Inc.

Sun, Sun Microsystems, Solaris, and Java are trademarks or registered trademarks of Sun Microsystems, Inc. in the U.S. and certain other countries

IBM, Power, Power7, and PowerPC are registered trademarks of the International Business Machines Corporation in the U.S. and/or other countries.

Wikipedia is a registered trademark of the Wikimedia Foundation, Inc., a non-profit organization.

PCI Express is a registered trademark of the PCI-SIG.

NVIDIA, GeForce and Tesla are trademarks and/or registered trademarks of NVIDIA Corporation in the U.S. and/or other countries.

Apple, FireWire, iPad, iPod, iPhone, Mac, Macintosh, Mac OS, OS X, are trademarks of Apple Inc., registered in the U.S. and other countries.

AMD, 3dNow!, AMD-K6, AMD-K8 are trademarks of Advanced Micro Devices, Inc.

HyperTransport is a trademark of the Hypertransport Consortium.

InfiniBand is a registered trademark of the InfiniBand Trade Association.

Myrinet is a registered trademark of Myricom, Inc.

Contents

1

Introduction to Computer Architecture

Welcome to the exciting world of **computer architecture**. Computer architecture is the study of computers. We shall study the basic design principles of computers in this book including the basic technologies, algorithms, design methodologies and future trends.

The field of computer architecture is a very fast moving field, and every couple of years there are a plethora of new inventions. Fifty years ago, the existence of computers was almost unknown to the common man. Computers were visible only in large financial institutions or in top universities. However, today billions of people all over the world have access to some form of computing device. They use it actively, and have found a place for it in their daily activities. Such kind of an epic transformation in the use, and ubiquity of computers has made the field of computer architecture extremely interesting.

In this chapter, we shall present an overview of computer architecture from an academic standpoint, and explain the major principles behind today's computers. We shall observe that there are two perspectives in computer architecture. We can look at computer architecture from the point of view of software applications. This point of view is sometimes referred to as *architecture* in literature. It is very important for students of computer architecture to study computer architecture from the viewpoint of a software designer because they need to know about the expectations of software writers from hardware. Secondly, it is also important for software writers to know about computer architecture because they can tailor their software appropriately to make it more efficient. In the case of system software such as operating systems and device drivers, it is absolutely essential to know the details of the architecture because the design of such kind of software is very strongly interlinked with low level hardware details.

The other perspective is the point of view of hardware designers. Given the software interface, they need to design hardware that is compatible with it and also implement algorithms that make the system efficient in terms of performance and power. This perspective is also referred to as *organisation* in literature.

Definition 1

Architecture *The view of a computer presented to software designers.*

Organisation *The actual implementation of a computer in hardware.*

Computer architecture is a beautiful amalgam of software concepts and hardware concepts. We design hardware to make software run efficiently. Concomitantly, we also design software keeping in mind the interface and constraints presented by hardware. Both the perspectives run hand in hand. Let us start out by looking at the generic definition of a *computer*.

1.1   What is a Computer?

Let us now answer the following questions.

Question 1
What is a computer?
What it can do, and what it cannot do?
How do we make it do intelligent things?

Let us start out with some basic definitions. The first question that we need to answer is – What is a computer? Well to answer this question, we just need to look all around us. We are surrounded by computers. Nowadays, computers are embedded in almost any kind of device such as mobile phones, tablets, mp3 players, televisions, dvd players, and obviously desktops and laptops. What is common between all of these devices? Well, each one of them has a computer that performs a specific task. For example, the computer in a mp3 player can play a song, and the computer in a dvd player can play a movie. It is absolutely not necessary that the mp3 player and dvd player contain different types of computers. In fact, the odds are high that both the devices contain the same type of computer. However, each computer is programmed differently, and processes different kinds of **information**. An mp3 player processes music files, and a dvd player processes video files. One can play a song, while the other can play a video.

Using these insights, let us formally define a computer in Definition 2.

Definition 2
A computer is a general purpose device that can be programmed to process information, and yield meaningful results.

Note that there are three important parts to the definition as shown in Figure 1.1 – the computer, information store, and the program. The computer takes as an input a program, and in response performs a set of operations on the information store. At the end it yields meaningful results. A typical program contains a set of instructions that tell the computer regarding the operations that need to be performed on the information store. The *information store* typically contains numbers and pieces of text that the program can use. Let us consider an example.

Example 1
Here is a snippet of a simple C program.

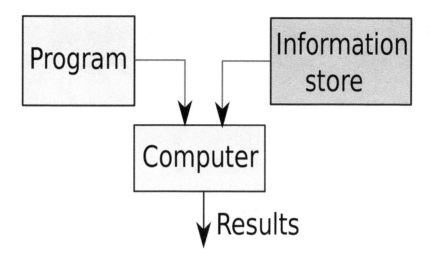

Figure 1.1: A basic computer

```
1: a = 4;
2: b = 6;
3: c = a + b;
4: print c
```

A computer will produce the output - 10. This C program contains four statements. Here, each statement can conceptually be treated as an instruction. Each statement instructs the computer to do something. Statements 1 and 2 instruct the computer to assign the variables a and b, the values 4 and 6 respectively. Statement 3 instructs the computer to add a and b, and assign the result to variable c. Finally, statement 4 instructs the computer to print the value of c (output of the program).

Given the fact that we have defined a computer as a sophisticated device that follows the instructions in a program to produce an output, let us see how it can be built. Modern day computers are made of silicon based transistors and copper wires to connect them. However, it is absolutely not necessary that computers need to be built out of silicon and copper. Researchers are now looking at building computers with electrons (quantum computers), photons(optical computers), and even DNA. If we think about it, our own brains are extremely powerful computers themselves. They are always in the process of converting thoughts(program) into action(output).

1.2 Structure of a Typical Desktop Computer

Let us now open the lid of a desktop computer, and see what is inside (shown in Figure 1.2). There are three main parts of a typical desktop computer – CPU (Central Processing Unit), Main Memory, and Hard Disk. The CPU is also referred to as the *processor* or simply *machine* in common parlance. We will use the terms interchangeably in this book. The CPU is the main part of the computer that takes a program as input, and executes it. It is the brain of the computer. The main memory is used to store data that a program might need during its execution (information store). For example, let us say that we want to recognise all the faces in an image. Then the image will be stored in main memory. There is some limited storage on the

Figure 1.2:

processor itself. However, we shall discuss this aspect later. When we turn off the power, the processor and main memory lose all their data. However, the hard disk represents permanent storage. We do not expect to lose our data when we shut down the system. This is because all our programs, data, photos, videos, and documents are safely backed up in the hard disk.

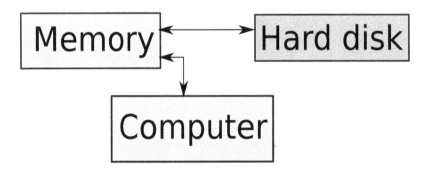

Figure 1.3: Block diagram of a simple computer

Figure 1.3 shows a simplistic block diagram of the three components. Along with these main components, there are a host of peripheral components that are connected to the computer. For example, the keyboard and mouse are connected to a computer. They take inputs from the user and communicate them to programs running on the processor. Similarly, to show the output of a program, the processor typically sends the output data to a monitor that can graphically display the result. It is also possible to print the result using a printer. Lastly the computer can be connected to other computers through the network. A revised block diagram with all the peripherals is shown in Figure 1.4.

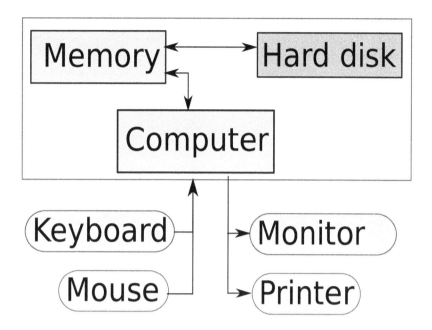

Figure 1.4: Block diagram of a simple computer with peripherals

In this book, we will mainly study the processor. The processor has the central responsibility of executing programs, communicating with the main memory, hard disk, and peripherals. It is the only active unit in our entire system. The others are passive and only respond to requests. They do not have any computational capability of their own.

1.3   Computers are Dumb Machines

Irrespective of the underlying technology, a fundamental concept that we need to understand is that a computer is fundamentally a *dumb* machine. Unlike our brains, it is not endowed with abstract thought, reason, and conscience. At least at the moment, computers cannot take very sophisticated decisions on their own. All they can do is execute a program. Nonetheless, the reason computers are so powerful is because they are extremely good at executing programs. They can execute billions of basic instructions per second. This makes them dumb yet very fast. A comparison of the computer with the human brain is shown in Table 1.1.

Feature	Computer	Our Brilliant Brain
Intelligence	Dumb	Intelligent
Speed of basic calculations	Ultra-fast	Slow
Can get tired	Never	After some time
Can get bored	Never	Almost always

Table 1.1: Computer vs the brain

If we combine the processing power of computers, with intelligent programs written by the human brain, we have the exquisite variety of software available today. Everything from operating systems to word processors to computer games is written this way.

The basic question that we need to answer is :

Question 2
How, do we make a dumb machine do intelligent things?

Computers are these tireless machines that can keep on doing calculations very quickly without ever complaining about the monotonicity of the work. As compared to computers, our brains are creative, tire easily, and do not like to do the same thing over and over again. To combine the best of both worlds, our brains need to produce computer programs that specify the set of tasks that need to be performed in great detail. A computer can then process the program, and produce the desired output by following each instruction in the program.

Hence, we can conclude that we should use the creative genius of our brains to write programs. Each program needs to contain a set of basic instructions that a computer can process. Henceforth, a computer can produce the desired output. An *instruction* is defined as a basic command that can be given to a computer.

1.4   The Language of Instructions

We observe that to communicate with a computer, we need to speak its language. This language consists of a set of basic instructions that the computer can understand. The computer is not smart enough to process instructions such as, "calculate the distance between New Delhi and the North Pole". However, it can do simple things like adding two numbers. This holds for people as well. For example, if a person understands only Spanish, then there is no point speaking to her in Russian. It is the responsibility of the person who desires to communicate to arrange for a translator. Likewise, it is necessary to convert high level thoughts and concepts to basic instructions that are machine understandable.

Programmers typically write programs in a high level language such as C or Java^{TM}. These languages contain complex constructs such as structures, unions, switch-case statements, classes and inheritance. These concepts are too complicated for a computer to handle. Hence, it is necessary to pass a C or C++ program through a dedicated program called a *compiler* that can convert it into a sequence of basic instructions. A compiler effectively removes the burden of creating machine (computer) readable code from the programmer. The programmer can concentrate only on the high level logic. Figure 1.5 shows the flow of actions. The first step is to write a program in a high level language (C or C++). Subsequently, the second step involves compiling it. The compiler takes the high level program as input, and produces a program containing machine instructions. This program is typically called an *executable* or *binary*. Note, that the compiler itself is a program consisting of basic machine instructions.

Figure 1.5:   Write-compile-execute

Let us now come to the semantics of instructions themselves. The same way that any language has a finite number of words, the number of basic instructions/rudimentary commands that a processor can support have to be finite. This set of instructions is typically called the **instruction set**. Some examples of basic instructions are: add, subtract, multiply, logical or, and logical not. Note that each instruction needs to work on a set of variables and constants, and finally save the result in a variable. These variables are not programmer defined variables; they are internal locations within the computer. We define the term instruction set architecture as:

Definition 3

The semantics of all the instructions supported by a processor is known as the instruction set architecture (ISA). This includes the semantics of the instructions themselves, along with their operands, and interfaces with peripheral devices.

The instruction set architecture is the way that software perceives hardware. We can think of it as the list of basic functions that the hardware exports to the external world. It is the, "language of the computer". For example, Intel and AMD CPUs use the x86 instruction set, IBM processors use the PowerPC® instruction set, HP processors use the PA-RISC instruction set, and the ARM processors use the ARM® instruction set (or variants of it such as Thumb-1 and Thumb-2). It is thus not possible to run a binary compiled for an Intel system on an ARM based system. The instruction sets are not compatible. However, in most cases it is possible to reuse the C program. To run a C program on a certain architecture, we need to procure a compiler for that specific architecture, and then appropriately compile the C program.

1.5   Instruction Set Design

Let us now begin the difficult process of designing an instruction set for a processor. We can think of an instruction set as a legal contract between software and hardware. Both sides need to implement their side of the contract. The software part needs to ensure that all the programs that users write can be successfully and efficiently translated to basic instructions. Likewise, hardware needs to ensure that all the instructions in the instruction set are efficiently implementable. On both sides we need to make reasonable assumptions. An ISA needs to have some necessary properties and some desirable properties for efficiency. Let us first look at a property, which is absolutely necessary.

1.5.1   Complete - The ISA should be able to Implement all User Programs

This is an absolutely necessary requirement. We want an ISA to be able to represent all programs that users are going to write for it. For example, if we have an ISA with just an ADD instruction, then we will not be able to subtract two numbers. To implement loops, the ISA should have some method to re-execute the same piece of code over and over again. Without this support *for* and *while* loops in C programs will not work. Note that for general purpose processors, we are looking at all possible programs. However, a lot of processors for embedded devices have limited functionality. For example, a simple processor that does string processing does not require support for floating point numbers (numbers with a decimal point). We need to note that different processors are designed to do different things, and hence their ISAs can be different. However, the bottom line is that any ISA should be *complete* in the sense that it should be able to express all the programs in machine code that a user intends to write for it.

Let us now explore the desirable properties of an instruction set.

1.5.2   Concise – Limited Size of the Instruction Set

We should ideally not have a lot of instructions. We shall see in Chapter 8 that it takes a fairly non-trivial amount of hardware to implement an instruction. Implementing a lot of instructions will unnecessarily increase the number of transistors in the processor and increase its complexity. Consequently, most instruction sets have somewhere between 64 to 1000 instructions. For example, the MIPS instruction set contains 64 instructions, whereas the Intel x86 instruction set has roughly a 1000 instructions as of 2012. Note that 1000 is considered a fairly large number for the number of instructions in an ISA.

1.5.3   Generic – Instructions should Capture the Common Case

Most of the common instructions in programs are simple arithmetic instructions such as add, subtract, multiply, divide. The most common logical instructions are logical and, or, exclusive-or, and not. Hence, it makes sense to dedicate an instruction to each of these common operations.

It is not a good idea to have instructions that implement a very rarely used computation. For example, it might not make sense to implement an instruction that computes $sin^{-1}(x)$. It is possible to provide dedicated library functions that compute $sin^{-1}(x)$ using existing mathematical techniques such as Taylor series expansion. Since this function is rarely used by most programs, they will not be adversely affected if this function takes a relatively long time to execute.

1.5.4   Simple – Instructions should be Simple

Let us assume that we have a lot of programs that add a sequence of numbers. To design a processor especially tailored towards such programs, we have several options with regards to the add instruction. We can implement an instruction that adds two numbers, or we can also implement an instruction that can take a list of operands, and produce the sum of the list. There is clearly a difference in complexity here, and we cannot say which implementation is faster. The former approach requires the compiler to generate more instructions; however, each add operation executes quickly. The latter approach generates a fewer number of instructions; but, each instruction takes longer to execute. The former type of ISA is called a *Reduced Instruction Set*, and the latter ISA type is called a *Complex Instruction Set*. Let us give two important definitions here.

Definition 4
A reduced instruction set computer (RISC) implements simple instructions that have a simple and regular structure. The number of instructions is typically a small number (64 to 128). Examples: ARM, IBM PowerPC, HP PA-RISC

Definition 5
A complex instruction set computer (CISC) implements complex instructions that are highly irregular, take multiple operands, and implement complex functionalities. Secondly, the number of instructions is large (typically 500+). Examples: Intel x86, VAX

The RISC vs CISC debate used to be a very contentious issue till the late nineties. However, since then designers, programmers, and processor vendors have been tilting towards the RISC design style. The consensus seems to be go for a small number of relatively simple instructions that have a regular structure and format. It is important to note that this point is still debatable as CISC instructions are sometimes preferable for certain types of applications. Modern processors typically use a hybrid approach where they have simple, as well as some complicated instructions. However, under the hood CISC instructions are translated into RISC instructions. Hence, we believe that the scale tilts slightly more towards RISC instructions. We shall thus consider it a desirable property to have *simple* instructions.

Important Point 1

An ISA needs to be complete, concise, generic, and simple. It is necessary to be complete, whereas the rest of the properties are desirable (and sometimes debatable).

Way Point 1

We have currently considered the following concepts.

- *Computers are dumb yet ultra-fast machines.*

- *Instructions are basic rudimentary commands used to communicate with the processor. A computer can execute billions of instructions per second.*

- *The compiler transforms a user program written in a high level language such as C to a program consisting of basic machine instructions.*

- *The instruction set architecture(ISA) refers to the semantics of all the instructions supported by a processor.*

- *The instruction set needs to be complete. It is desirable if it is also concise, generic, and simple.*

Let us subsequently look at the conditions that ensure the completeness of an ISA. We will then try to create a concise, simple, and generic ISA in Chapter 3.

1.6 How to Ensure that an ISA is Complete?

This is a very interesting, difficult, and theoretically profound question. The problem of finding if a given ISA is complete for a given set of programs, is a fairly difficult problem, and is beyond the scope of the book. The general case is far more interesting. We need to answer the question:

Question 3

Given an ISA, can it represent all possible programs?

We will need to take recourse to theoretical computer science to answer this question. Casual readers can skip Sections 1.6.1 to 1.6.6 without any loss in continuity. They can directly proceed to Section 1.6.7, where we summarise the main results.

1.6.1   Towards a Universal ISA*

Let us try to answer Question 3. Assume that we are given an ISA that contains the basic instructions add, and multiply. Can we use this ISA to run all possible programs? The answer is no, because we cannot subtract two numbers using the basic instructions that we have. If we add the subtract instruction to our repertoire of instructions, can we compute the square root of a number? Even if we can, is it guaranteed that we can do all types of computations? To answer such vexing questions we need to first define a *universal machine*.

Definition 6

A machine that can execute any program is known as a universal *machine.*

It is a machine that can execute all programs. We can treat each basic action of this machine as an instruction. Thus the set of actions of a universal machine is its ISA, and this ISA is complete. Consequently, when we say that an ISA is complete, it is the same as saying that we can build a universal machine exclusively based on the given ISA. Hence, we can solve the problem of completeness of an ISA by solving the problem of designing universal machines. They are dual problems. It is easier to reason in terms of universal machines. Hence, let us delve into this problem.

Computer scientists started pondering at the design of universal machines at the beginning of the 20th century. They wanted to know what is computable, and what is not, and the power of different classes of machines. Secondly, what is the form of a theoretical machine that can compute the results of all possible programs? These fundamental results in computer science form the basis of today's modern computer architectures.

Alan Turing was the first to propose a universal machine that was extremely simple and powerful. This machine is aptly named after him, and is known as the *Turing* machine. This is merely a theoretical entity, and is typically used as a mathematical reasoning tool. It is possible to create a hardware implementation of a Turing machine. However, this would be extremely inefficient, and require a disproportionate amount of resources. Nonetheless, Turing machines form the basis of today's computers and modern ISAs are derived from the basic actions of a Turing machine. Hence, it is very essential for us to study its design. Note that we provide a very cursory treatment in this book. Interested readers are requested to take a look at the seminal text on the theory of computation by Hopcroft, Motwani and Ulmann [Hopcroft et al., 2006].

1.6.2   Turing Machine*

The general structure of a Turing machine is shown in Figure 1.6. A Turing machine contains an infinite tape that is an array of cells. Each cell can contain a symbol from a finite alphabet. There is a special symbol $ that works as a special marker. A dedicated tape head points to a cell in the infinite tape. There is a small piece of storage to save the current state among a finite set of states. This storage element is called a *state register*.

The operation of the Turing machine is very simple. In each step, the tape head reads the symbol in the current cell, its current state from the state register, and looks up a table that contains the set of actions for each combination of symbol and state. This dedicated table is called a *transition function table* or *action table*. Each entry in this table specifies three things – whether to move the tape head one step to the left or right, the next state, and the symbol that should be written in the current cell. Thus, in each step, the tape head can overwrite the value of the cell, change its state in the state register and move to a new cell. The only constraint is that the new cell needs to be to the immediate left or right of the current cell. Formally, its format is $(state, symbol) \rightarrow (\{L, R\}, new\_state, new\_symbol)$. L stands for left, and R stands for right.

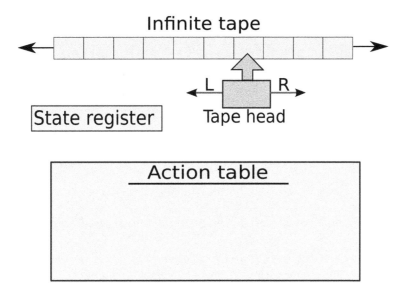

Figure 1.6: A Turing machine

This seemingly abstract and obscure computing device is actually very powerful. Let us explain with examples. See Examples 2, 3, and 4. In all the cases, we assume that the input is demarcated by the special marker symbol $.

Example 2

Design a Turing machine to increment a number by 1.

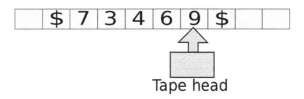

Answer: *Each cell contains a single digit. The number is demarcated at both ends by the special marker $. Lastly, the tape head points to the unit's digit.*

We first define four states (S_0, S_1): pre-exit and exit. The computation is over when the Turing machine reaches the exit state. The states S_0 and S_1 represent the value of the carry, 0 or 1, respectively. The state register is initialised to S_1 since we are incrementing the number by 1. In other words, we can assume that the starting value of the carry digit is equal to 1.

At each step, the tape head reads the current digit, d, and the value of the carry, c, from the state register. For each combination of d, and c, the action table contains the next state (new value of carry), and the result digit. The tape head always moves to the left. For example, if $(d, c) = (9, 1)$, then we are effectively adding $(9 + 1)$. The next state is equal to S_1 (output carry), the Turing machine writes 0 in the current cell, and the tape head moves to the cell on the left.

The only special case arises when the computation is ending. When the tape head encounters the $ symbol, then it looks at the value of the carry. If it is equal to 0, then it leaves the value untouched and *moves to the* exit *state. If it is equal to 1, then it moves to the* pre-exit *state, writes 1 to the cell, and moves to the left. Subsequently, it writes $ to the cell under the tape head, and then moves to the* exit *state.*

Example 3

Design a Turing machine to find out if a string is of the form $aaa \ldots abb \ldots bb$.

Answer: *Let us define two states* (S_a, S_b), *and two special states –* exit *and* error. *If the state becomes equal to* exit *or* error, *then the computation stops. The Turing machine can start scanning the input from right to left as Example 2. It starts in state* S_b. *The action table is as follows:*

$(S_b, b) \to (L, S_b, b)$
$(S_b, a) \to (L, S_a, a)$
$(S_b, \$) \to (L, error, \$)$
$(S_a, b) \to (L, error, b)$
$(S_a, a) \to (L, S_a, a)$
$(S_a, \$) \to (L, exit, \$)$

Example 4

Design a Turing machine to find out if a string of characters is a palindrome. A palindrome is a word that reads the same forward and backwards. Example: civic, rotator, rotor. Furthermore, assume that each character is either 'a' or 'b'.

Answer: *Let us assume that the Turing machine starts at the rightmost character in the* begin *state. Let us consider the case when the symbol under the tape head is a in the* begin *state. The machine enters the state* L_a*(move left, starting symbol is a) and replaces a with $. Now it needs to see if the leftmost character is a. Hence, the tape head moves towards the left until it encounters $. It then enters the* $Rcheck_a$ *state. It moves one cell to the right and checks if the symbol is equal to a. If it is a, then the string might be a palindrome. Otherwise, it is definitely not a palindrome and the procedure can terminate by entering the* error *state. The tape head again rewinds by moving all the way to the right and starts at the cell, which is to the immediate left of the starting cell in the previous round. The same algorithm is performed iteratively till either an error is encountered or all the symbols are replaced with $.*

If the starting symbol was b, the procedure would have been exactly the same albeit with a different set of states – L_b *and* $Rcheck_b$. *The action table is shown below.*

$(begin, \$) \rightarrow (L, exit, \$)$	
$(begin, a) \rightarrow (L, L_a, \$)$	
$(L_a, a) \rightarrow (L, L_a, a)$	$(begin, b) \rightarrow (L, L_b, \$)$
$(L_a, b) \rightarrow (L, L_a, b)$	$(L_b, a) \rightarrow (L, L_b, a)$
$(L_a, \$) \rightarrow (R, Rcheck_a, \$)$	$(L_b, b) \rightarrow (L, L_b, b)$
$(Rcheck_a, a) \rightarrow (R, Rmove, \$)$	$(L_b, \$) \rightarrow (R, Rcheck_b, \$)$
$(Rcheck_a, b) \rightarrow (R, error, \$)$	$(Rcheck_b, a) \rightarrow (R, error, \$)$
$(Rmove, a) \rightarrow (R, Rmove, a)$	$(Rcheck_b, b) \rightarrow (R, Rmove, \$)$
$(Rmove, b) \rightarrow (R, Rmove, b)$	
$(Rmove, \$) \rightarrow (L, begin, \$)$	

In these examples we have considered three simple problems and designed Turing machines from them. We can immediately conclude that designing Turing machines for even simple problems is difficult, and cryptic. The action table can contain a lot of states, and quickly blow out of size. However, the baseline is that it is possible to solve complex problems with this simple device. It is in fact possible to solve all kinds of problems such as weather modelling, financial calculations, and solving differential equations with this machine!

Definition 7

Church-Turing thesis: Any real-world computation can be translated into an equivalent computation involving a Turing machine. (source: Wolfram Mathworld)

This observation is captured by the **Church-Turing thesis**, which basically says that all functions that are computable by any physical computing device are computable by a Turing machine. In lay man's terms, any program that can be computed by deterministic algorithms on any computer known to man, is also computable by a Turing machine.

This thesis has held its ground for the last half century. Researchers have up till now not been able to find a machine that is more powerful than a Turing machine. This means that there is no program that can be computed by another machine, and not by a Turing machine. There are some programs that might take forever to compute on a Turing machine. However, they would also take infinite time on all other computing machines. We can extend the Turing machine in all possible ways. We can consider multiple tapes, multiple tape heads, or multiple tracks in each tape. It can be shown that each of these machines is as powerful as a simple Turing machine.

1.6.3   Universal Turing Machine*

The Turing machine described in the Section 1.6.2 is not a universal machine. This is because it contains an action table, which is specific to the function being computed by the machine. A true universal machine will have the same action table, symbols, and also the same set of states for every function. We can make a universal Turing machine, if we can design a Turing machine that can simulate another Turing machine. This Turing machine will be generic and will not be specific to the function that is being computed.

Let the Turing machine that is being simulated be called $\mathcal{M}$, and the universal Turing machine be called $\mathcal{U}$. Let us first create a generic format for the action table of $\mathcal{M}$, and save it in a designated location on the tape of $\mathcal{U}$. This *simulated action table* contains a list of actions, and each action requires the five parameters – old state, old symbol, direction(left or right), new state, new symbol. We can use a common set of basic symbols that can be the 10 decimal digits (0-9). If a function requires more symbols then we can consider one symbol to be contained in a set of contiguous cells demarcated by special delimiters. Let such a symbol be called a *simulated symbol*. Likewise, the state in the simulated action table can also be encoded as a decimal number. For the direction, we can use 0 for left, and 1 for right. Thus a single action table entry might look something like (@1334@34@0@1335@10@). Here the '@' symbol is the delimiter. This entry is saying that we are moving from state 1334 to 1335 if symbol 34 is encountered. We move left (0), and write a value of 10. Thus, we have found a way of encoding the action table, set of symbols, and states of a Turing machine designed to compute a certain function.

Similarly, we can designate an area of the tape to contain the state register of $\mathcal{M}$. We call this the simulated state register. Let the tape of $\mathcal{M}$ be given a dedicated space in the tape of $\mathcal{U}$, and let us call this space the *work area*.

The organisation is shown in Figure 1.7.

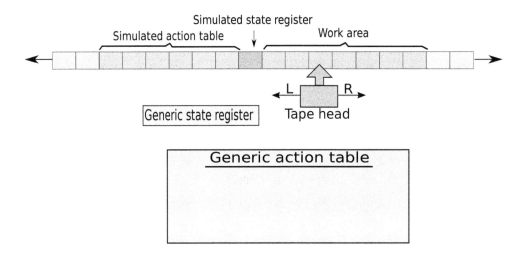

Figure 1.7: Layout of a universal Turing machine

The tape is thus divided into three parts. The first part contains the simulated action table, the second part contains the simulated state register, and the last part contains the work area that contains a set of simulated symbols.

The universal Turing machine($\mathcal{U}$) has a very simple action table and set of states. The idea is to find the right entry in the simulated action table that matches the value in the simulated state register and simulated symbol under the tape head. Then the universal Turing machine needs to carry out the corresponding action by moving to a new simulated state, and overwriting the simulated symbol in the work area if required.

The devil is in the details. For doing every basic action, $\mathcal{U}$ needs to do tens of tape head movements. The details are given in Hopcroft, Motwani, and Ulmann [Hopcroft et al., 2006]. However, the conclusion is that we can construct a universal Turing machine.

Important Point 2
It is possible to construct a universal Turing machine that can simulate any other Turing machine.

Turing Completeness

Since the 1950s, researchers have devised many more types of hypothetical machines with their own sets of states and rules. Each of these machines have been proven to be at most as powerful as the Turing machine. There is a generic name for all machines and computing systems that are as expressive and powerful as a Turing machine. Such systems are said to be *Turing complete*. Any universal machine and ISA is thus Turing complete.

Definition 8

Any computing system that is equivalent to a Turing machine is said to be Turing complete.

We thus need to prove that an ISA is complete or universal if it is Turing complete.

1.6.4 A Modified Universal Turing Machine*

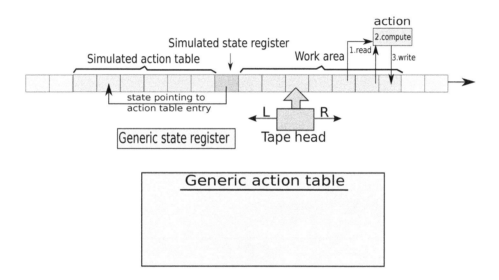

Figure 1.8: A modified universal Turing machine

Let us now consider a variant of a universal Turing machine (see Figure 1.8) that is more amenable to practical implementations. Let it have the following features. Note that such a machine has been proven to be Turing complete.

1. The tape is semi-infinite (extends to infinity in only one direction).

2. The simulated state is a pointer to an entry in the simulated action table.

3. There is one unique entry in the simulated action table for each state. While looking up the simulated action table, we do not care about the symbol under the tape head.

4. An action directs the tape head to visit a set of locations in the work area, and based on their values computes a new value using a simple arithmetical function. It writes this new value into a new location in the work area.

5. The default next state is the succeeding state in the action table.

6. An action can also arbitrarily change the state if a symbol at a certain location on the tape is less than a certain value. Changing the state means that the simulated tape head will start fetching actions from a new area in the simulated action table.

This Turing machine suggests a machine organisation of the following form. There is a large array of instructions (action table). This array of instructions is commonly referred to as the *program*. There is a state register that maintains a pointer to the current instruction in the array. We can refer to this register as the *program counter*. It is possible to change the program counter to point to a new instruction. There is a large work area, where symbols can be stored, retrieved and modified. This work area is also known as the *data* area. The instruction table (program) and the work area (data) were saved on the tape in our modified Turing machine. In a practical machine, we call this infinite tape as the *memory*. The memory is a large array of memory cells, where a memory cell contains a basic symbol. A part of the memory contains the program, and another part of it contains data.

Definition 9

The memory in our conceptual machine is a semi-infinite array of symbols. A part of it contains the program consisting of basic instructions, and the rest of it contains data. Data refers to variables and constants that are used by the program.

Furthermore, each instruction can read a set of locations in the memory, compute a small arithmetic function on them, and write the results back to the memory. It can also jump to any other instruction depending on values in the memory. There is a dedicated unit to compute these arithmetic functions, write to memory, and jump to other instructions. This is called the *CPU*(Central Processing Unit). Figure 1.9 shows a conceptual organisation of this machine.

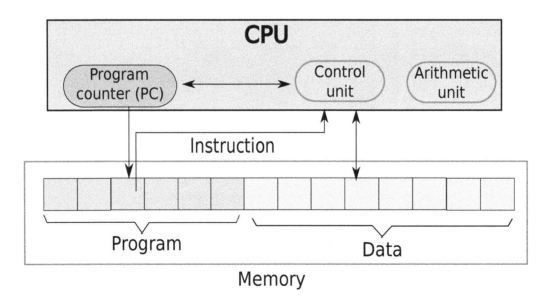

Figure 1.9: A basic instruction processing machine

Interested readers might want to prove the fact that this machine is equivalent to a Turing machine. It is not very difficult to do so. We need to note that we have captured all aspects of a Turing machine: state transition, movement of the tape head, overwriting symbols, and decisions based on the symbol under the tape head. We shall see in Section 1.7.2 that such a machine is very similar to the Von Neumann machine. Von Neumann machines form the basis of today's computers. Readers can also refer to books on computational complexity.

Important Point 3

Figure 1.9 represents a universal machine that can be practically designed.

1.6.5   Single Instruction ISA*

Let us now try to design an ISA for our modified Turing machine. We shall see that it is possible to have a complete ISA that contains just a single instruction. Let us consider an instruction that is compatible with the modified Turing machine and has been proven to be Turing complete.

```
sbn a, b, c
```

sbn stands for subtract and branch if negative. Here, a, and b are memory locations. This instruction subtracts b from a, saves the results in a, and if $a < 0$, it jumps to the instruction at location c in the instruction table. Otherwise, the control transfers to the next instruction. For example, we can use this instruction to add two numbers saved in locations a and b. Note that *exit* is a special location at the end of the program.

```
1: sbn temp, b, 2
2: sbn a, temp, exit
```

Here, we assume that the memory location *temp* already contains the value 0. The first instruction saves $-b$ in *temp*. Irrespective of the value of the result it jumps to the next instruction. Note that the identifier (*number* :) is a sequence number for the instruction. In the second instruction we compute $a = a + b = a - (-b)$. Thus, we have successfully added two numbers. We can now use this basic piece of code to add the numbers from 1 to 10. We assume that the variable *counter* is initialised to 9, *index* is initialised to 10, *one* is initialised to 1, and *sum* is initialised to 0.

```
1: sbn temp, temp, 2    // temp = 0
2: sbn temp, index, 3   // temp = -1 * index
3: sbn sum, temp, 4     // sum += index
4: sbn index, one, 5    // index -= 1
5: sbn counter, one, exit  // loop is finished, exit
6: sbn temp, temp, 7    // temp = 0
7: sbn temp, one, 1     // (0 - 1 < 0), hence goto 1
```

We observe that this small sequence of operations runs a *for* loop. The exit condition is in line 5, and the loop back happens in line 7. In each iteration it computes – $sum+ = index$.

There are many more similar single instruction ISAs that have been proven to be complete such as subtract and branch if less than equal to, reverse subtract and skip if borrow, and a computer that has generic memory move operations. The interested reader can refer to the book by Gilreath and Laplante [Gilreath and Laplante, 2003].

1.6.6 Multiple Instruction ISA*

Writing a program with just a single instruction is very difficult, and programs tend to be very long. There is no reason to be stingy with the number of instructions. We can make our life significantly easier by considering a multitude of instructions. Let us try to break up the basic *sbn* instructions into several instructions.

Arithmetic Instructions We can have a set of arithmetic instructions such as add, subtract, multiply and divide.

Move Instructions We can have move instructions that move values across different memory locations. They should allow us to also load constant values into memory locations.

Branch Instructions We require branch instructions that change the program counter to point to new instructions based on the results of computations or values stored in memory.

Keeping these basic tenets in mind, we can design many different types of complete ISAs. The point to note is that we definitely need three types of instructions – arithmetic (data processing), move (data transfer), and branch (control).

Important Point 4

In any instruction set, we need at least three types of instructions:

1. *We need arithmetic instructions to perform operations such as add, subtract, multiply, and divide. Most instruction sets also have specialised instructions in this category to perform logical operations such as logical OR and NOT.*

2. *We need data transfer instructions that can transfer values between memory locations and can load constants into memory locations.*

3. *We need branch instructions that can start executing instructions at different points in the program based on the values of instruction operands.*

1.6.7 Summary of Theoretical Results

Let us summarise the main results that we have obtained from our short discussion on theoretical computer science.

1. The problem of designing a complete ISA is the same as that of designing a *universal machine*. A universal machine can run any program. We can map each instruction in the ISA to an action in this universal machine. A universal machine is the most powerful computing machine known to man. If a universal machine cannot compute the result of a program because it never terminates (infinite loop), then all other computing machines are also guaranteed to fail for this program.

2. Universal machines have been studied extensively in theoretical computer science. One such machine is the Turing machine named after the father of computer science – Alan Turing.

3. The Turing machine is a very abstract computing device, and is not amenable to practical implementations. A practical implementation will be very slow and consume a lot of resources. However, machines equivalent to it can be much faster. Any such machine, ISA, and computing system that is equivalent to a Turing machine is said to be *Turing complete*.

4. We defined a modified Turing machine that is Turing complete in Section 1.6.4. It has the structure shown in Figure 1.10. Its main parts and salient features are as follows.

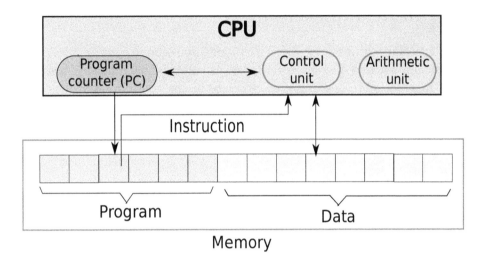

Figure 1.10: A basic processing machine

(a) It contains a dedicated *instruction table* that contains a list of instructions.

(b) It has a *program counter* that keeps track of the current instruction that is being executed. The program counter contains a pointer to an entry in the instruction table.

(c) It has a semi-infinite array of storage locations that can save symbols belonging to a finite set. This array is known as the *memory*.

(d) The memory contains the instruction table (also referred to as the *program*), and contains a data area. The *data* area saves all the variables and constants that are required by the program.

(e) Each instruction can compute the result of a simple arithmetic function using values stored at different memory locations. It can then save the result in another memory location.

(f) The machine starts with the first instruction in the program, and then by default, after executing an instruction, the machine fetches the next instruction in the instruction table.

(g) It is possible for an instruction to direct the machine to fetch a new instruction from an arbitrary location in the instruction table based on the value stored in a memory location.

5. A simple one instruction ISA that is compatible with our modified Turing machine, contains the single instruction *sbn* (subtract the values of two memory locations, and branch to a new instruction if the result is negative).

6. We can have many Turing complete ISAs that contain a host of different instructions. Such ISAs will need to have the following types of instructions.

Arithmetic Instructions Add, subtract, multiply and divide. These instructions can be used to simulate logical instructions such as OR and AND.

Move Instructions Move values across memory locations, or load constants into memory.

Branch Instructions Fetch the next instruction from a new location in the instruction table, if a certain condition on the value of a memory location holds.

1.7 Design of Practical Machines

A broad picture of a practical machine has emerged from our discussion in Section 1.6.7. We have summarised the basic structure of such a machine in Figure 1.10. Let us call this machine as the *concept* machine. Ideas similar to our concept machine were beginning to circulate in the computer science community after Alan Turing published his research paper proposing the Turing machine in 1936. Several scientists got inspired by his ideas, and started pursuing efforts to design practical machines.

1.7.1 Harvard Architecture

One of the earliest efforts in this direction was the Harvard Mark-I. The Harvard architecture is very similar to our concept machine shown in Figure 1.10. Its block diagram is shown in Figure 1.11. There are separate structures for maintaining the instruction table and the memory. The former is also known as *instruction memory* because we can think of it as a specialised memory tailored to hold only instructions. The latter holds data values that programs need. Hence, it is known as the *data memory*. The engine for processing instructions is divided into two parts – control and ALU. The job of the control unit is to fetch instructions, process them, and co-ordinate their execution. ALU stands for arithmetic-logic-unit. It has specialised circuits that can compute arithmetic expressions or logical expressions (AND/OR/NOT etc.).

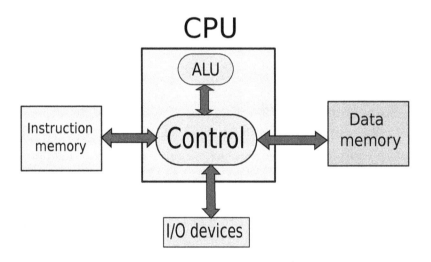

Figure 1.11: The Harvard architecture

Note that every computer needs to take inputs from the user/programmer and needs to finally communicate results back to the programmer. This can be done through a multitude of methods. Today we use a keyboard and monitor. Early computers used a set of switches and the final result was printed out on a piece of paper.

1.7.2 Von Neumann Architecture

John von Neumann proposed the Von Neumann architecture for general purpose Turing complete computers. Note that there were several other scientists such as John Mauchly and J. Presper Eckert who independently developed similar ideas. Eckert and Mauchly designed the first general purpose Turing complete computer(with one minor limitation) called ENIAC (Electronic Numerical Integrator and Calculator) based on this architecture in 1946. It was used to compute artillery firing tables for the US army's ballistic research laboratory. This computer was later succeeded by the EDVAC computer in 1949, which was also used by the US army's ballistics research laboratory.

The basic Von Neumann architecture, which is the basis of ENIAC and EDVAC is shown in Figure 1.12. This is pretty much the same as our concept machine. The instruction table is saved in memory. The processing engine that is akin to our modified Turing machine is called the CPU (central processing unit). It contains the program counter. Its job is to fetch new instructions, and execute them. It has dedicated functional units to calculate the results of arithmetic functions, load and store values in memory locations, and compute the results of branch instructions. Lastly, like the Harvard architecture, the CPU is connected to the I/O subsystem.

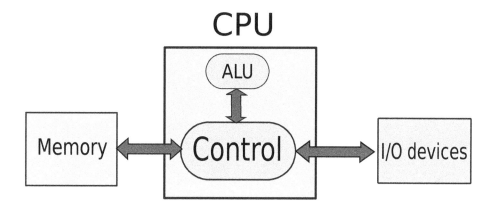

Figure 1.12: Von Neumann architecture

The path breaking innovation in this machine was that the instruction table was stored in memory. It was possible to do so by encoding every instruction with the same set of symbols that are normally stored in memory. For example, if the memory stores decimal values, then each instruction needs to be encoded into a string of decimal digits. A Von Neumann CPU needs to decode every instruction. The crux of this idea is that instructions are treated as regular data(memory values). We shall see in later chapters that this simple idea is actually a very powerful tool in designing elegant computing systems. This idea is known as the **stored program concept**.

Definition 10

Stored-program concept: A program is stored in memory and instructions are treated as regular memory values.

The stored program concept tremendously simplifies the design of a computer. Since memory data and instructions are conceptually treated the same way, we can have one unified processing system and memory system that treats instructions and data the same way. From the point of view of the CPU, the program counter points to a generic memory location whose contents will be interpreted as that of an encoded instruction. It is easy to store, modify, and transmit programs. Programs can also dynamically change their behavior during runtime by modifying themselves and even other programs. This forms the basis of today's complex compilers that convert high level C programs into machine instructions. Furthermore, a lot of modern systems such as the Java virtual machine dynamically modify their instructions to achieve efficiency.

Lastly, astute readers would notice that a Von Neumann machine or a Harvard machine do not have an infinite amount of memory like a Turing machine. Hence, strictly speaking they are not exactly equivalent to a Turing machine. This is true for all practical machines. They need to have finite resources. Nevertheless, the scientific community has learnt to live with this approximation.

1.7.3   Towards a Modern Machine with Registers and Stacks

Many extensions to the basic Von-Neumann machine have been proposed in literature. In fact this has been a hot field of study for the last half century. We discuss three important variants of Von Neumann machines that augment the basic model with registers, hardware stacks, and accumulators. The register based design is by far the most commonly used today. However, some aspects of stack based machines and accumulators have crept into modern register based processors also. It would be worthwhile to take a brief look at them before we move on.

Von-Neumann Machine with Registers

The term "register machine" refers to a class of machines that in the most general sense contain an unbounded number of named storage locations called registers. These registers can be accessed randomly, and all instructions use register names as their operands. The CPU accesses the registers, fetches the operands, and then processes them. However, in this section, we look at a hybrid class of machines that augment a standard Von Neumann machine with registers. A register is a storage location that can hold a symbol. These are the same set of symbols that are stored in memory. For example, they can be integers.

Let us now try to motivate the use of registers. The memory is typically a very large structure. In modern processors, the entire memory can contain billions of storage locations. Any practical implementation of a memory of this size is fairly slow in practice. There is a general rule of thumb in hardware, "large is slow, and small is fast." Consequently, to enable fast operation, every processor has a small set of registers that can be quickly accessed. The number of registers is typically between 8 and 64. Most of the operands in arithmetic and branch operations are present in these registers. Since programs tend to use a small set of variables repeatedly at any point of time, using registers saves many memory accesses. However, it sometimes becomes necessary to bring in memory locations into registers or writeback values in registers to memory locations. In those cases, we use dedicated *load* and *store* instructions that transfer values between memory and registers. Most programs have a majority of pure register instructions. The number of load and store instructions are typically about a third of the total number of executed instructions.

Let us give an example. Assume that we want to add the cubes of the numbers in the memory locations b and c, and we want to save the result in the memory location a. A machine with registers would need the following instructions. Assume that $r1$, $r2$, and $r3$ are the names of registers. Here, we are not using any specific ISA (the explanation is generic and conceptual).

```
1: r1 = mem[b]    // load b
2: r2 = mem[c]    // load c
3: r3 = r1 * r1   // compute b^2
4: r4 = r1 * r3   // compute b^3
5: r5 = r2 * r2   // compute c^2
```

```
6: r6 = r2 * r5   // compute c^3
7: r7 = r4 + r6   // compute b^3 + c^3
4: mem[a] = r7    // save the result
```

Here, *mem* is an array representing memory. We need to first load the values into registers, then perform arithmetic computations, and then save the result back in memory. We can see in this example that we are saving on memory accesses by using registers. If we increase the complexity of the computations, we will save on even more memory accesses. Thus, our execution with registers will get even faster. The resulting processor organisation is shown in Figure 1.13.

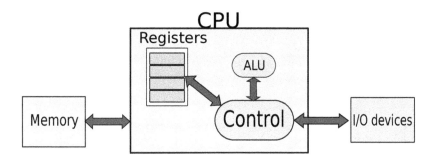

Figure 1.13: Von Neumann machine with registers

Von-Neumann Machine with a Hardware Stack

A stack is a standard data structure that obeys the semantics – last in, first out. Readers are requested to lookup a book on data structures such as [Lafore, 2002] for more information. A stack based machine has a stack implemented in hardware.

First, it is necessary to insert values from the memory into the stack. After that arithmetic functions operate on the top k elements of the stack. These values get replaced by the result of the computation. For example, if the stack contains the values 1 and 2 at the top. They get removed and replaced by 3. Note that here arithmetic operations do not require any operands. If an add operation takes two operands, then they do not need to be explicitly specified. The operands are implicitly specified as the top two elements in the stack. Likewise, the location of the result also does not need to be specified. It needs to be inserted at the top of the stack. Even though, generating instructions for such a machine is difficult and flexibility is an issue, the instructions can be very compact. Most instructions other than load and store do not require any operands. We can thus produce very dense machine code. Systems in which the size of the program is an issue can use a stack based organisation. They are also easy to verify since they are relatively simpler systems.

A stack supports two operations – *push* and *pop*. *Push* pushes an element to the top of the stack. *Pop* removes an element from the top of the stack. Let us now try to compute $w = x + y/z - u * v$ using a stack based Von Neumann machine, we have:

```
1: push u      // load u
2: push v      // load v
3: multiply    // u*v
4: push z      // load y
5: push y      // load z
6: divide      // y/z
```

```
7: subtract    // y/z - u*v
8: push x      // load x
9: add         // x + y/z - u*v
10: pop w      // store result in w
```

It is clearly visible that scheduling a computation to work on a stack is difficult. There will be many redundant loads and stores. Nonetheless, for machines that are meant to evaluate long mathematical expressions, and machines for which program size is an issue, typically opt for stacks. There are few practical implementations of stack based machines such as Burroughs Large Systems, UCSD Pascal, and HP 3000 (classic). The Java language assumes a hypothetical stack based machine during the process of compilation. Since a stack based machine is simple, Java programs can virtually run on any hardware platform. When we run a compiled Java program, then the Java Virtual Machine(JVM) dynamically converts the Java program into another program that can run on a machine with registers.

Accumulator based Machines

Accumulator based machines use a single register called an *accumulator*. Each instruction takes a single memory location as an input operand. For example, an *add* operation adds the value in the accumulator to the value in the memory address and then stores the result back in the accumulator. Early machines in the fifties that could not accommodate a register file used to have accumulators. Accumulators were able to reduce the number of memory accesses and speed up the program.

Some aspects of accumulators have crept into the Intel x86 set of processors that are the most commonly used processors for desktops and laptops as of 2012. For multiplication and division of large numbers, these processors use the register *eax* as an accumulator. For other generic instructions, any register can be specified as an accumulator.

1.8   The Road Ahead

We have outlined the structure of a modern machine in Section 1.7.3, which broadly follows a Von Neumann architecture, and is augmented with registers. Now, we need to proceed to build it. As mentioned at the outset, computer architecture is a beautiful amalgam of software and hardware. Software engineers tell us **what to build?** Hardware designers tell us **how to build?**

Let us thus first take care of the requirements of software engineers. Refer to the roadmap of chapters in Figure 1.14. The first part of the book will introduce computer architecture from the point of view of system software designers and application developers. Subsequently, we shall move on to designing processors, and lastly, we shall look at building a full systems of processors, memory elements, and I/O cum storage devices.

1.8.1   Representing Information

In modern computers, it is not possible to store numbers or pieces of text directly. Today's computers are made of transistors. A transistor can be visualised as a basic switch that has two states – on and off. If the switch is on, then it represents 1, otherwise it represents 0. Every single entity inclusive of numbers, text, instructions, programs, and complex software needs to be represented using a sequence of 0s and 1s. We have only two basic symbols that we can use namely 0 and 1. A variable/value that can either be 0 or 1, is known as a *bit*. Most computers typically store and process a set of 8 bits together. A set of 8 bits is known as a *byte*. Typically, a sequence of 4 bytes is known as a *word*.

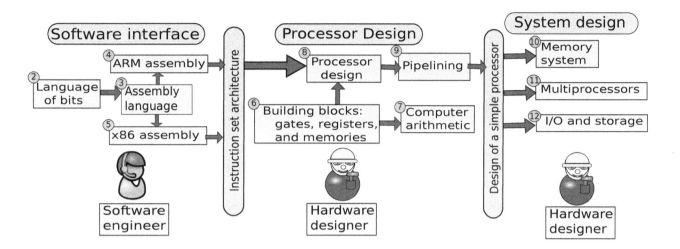

Figure 1.14: Roadmap of chapters

Definition 11

bit *A value that can either be 0 or 1.*

byte *A sequence of 8 bits.*

word *A sequence of 4 bytes.*

We can thus visualise all the internal storage structures of a computer such as the memory or the set of registers as a large array of switches as shown in Figure 1.15. In Chapter 2, we shall study the language of bits. We shall see that using bits it is possible to express logical concepts, arithmetic concepts (integer and real numbers), and pieces of text.

This chapter is a prerequisite for the next chapter on **assembly language**. Assembly language is a textual representation of an ISA. It is specific to the ISA. Since an instruction is a sequence of 0s and 1s, it is very difficult to study it in its bare form. Assembly language gives us a good handle to study the semantics of instructions in an ISA. Chapter 3 introduces the general concepts of assembly language and serves as a common introduction to the next two chapters that delve into the details of two very popular real world ISAs – ARM and x86. We introduce a simple ISA called *SimpleRisc* in Chapter 3. Subsequently, in Chapter 4 we introduce the ARM ISA, and in Chapter 5 we briefly cover the x86 ISA. Note that it is not necessary to read both these chapters. After reading the introductory chapter on assembly language and obtaining an understanding of the *SimpleRisc* assembly language, the interested reader can read just one chapter to deepen her knowledge about a real world ISA. At this point, the reader should have a good knowledge of what needs to be built.

1.8.2 Processing Information

In this part, we shall actually build a basic computer. Chapter 6 will start out with the basic building blocks of a processor – logic gates, registers, and memories. Readers who have already taken a digital design

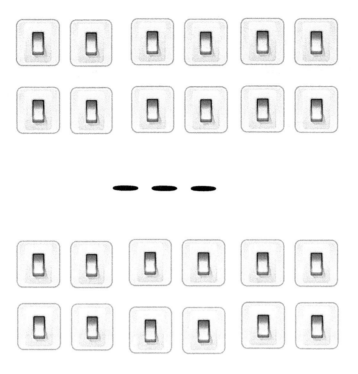

Figure 1.15: Memory – a large array of switches

course can skip this chapter. Chapter 7 deals with computer arithmetic. It introduces detailed algorithms for addition, subtraction, multiplication, and division for both integers as well as real numbers. Most computers today perform very heavy numerical computations. Hence, it is necessary to obtain a firm understanding of how numerical operations are actually implemented, and get an idea of the tradeoffs of different designs.

After these two chapters, we would be ready to actually design a simple processor in Chapter 8. We shall assemble a simple processor part by part, and then look at two broad design styles – hardwired, and micro-programmed. Modern processors are able to process many instructions simultaneously, and have complex logic for taking the dependences across instructions into account. The most popular technique in this area is known as *pipelining*. We shall discuss pipelining in detail in Chapter 9.

1.8.3 Processing More Information

By this point, we would have gotten a fair understanding of how simple processors are designed. We shall proceed to optimise the design, add extra components, and make a full system that can support all the programs that users typically want to run. We shall describe three subsystems –

Memory System We shall see in Chapter 10 that it is necessary to build a fast and efficient memory system, because it is a prime driver of performance. To build a fast memory system, we need to introduce many new structures and algorithms.

Multiprocessors Nowadays, vendors are incorporating multiple processors on a single chip. The future belongs to multiprocessors. The field of multiprocessors is very extensive and typically forms the core of an advanced architecture course. In this book, we shall provide a short overview of multiprocessors in Chapter 11.

I/O and Storage In Chapter 12, we shall look at methods to interface with different I/O devices, especially storage devices such as the hard disk. The hard disk saves all our programs and data when the computer is powered off, and it also plays a crucial role in supplying data to our programs during their operations. Hence, it is necessary to study the structure of the hard disk, and optimise it for performance and reliability.

1.9 Summary and Further Reading

1.9.1 Summary

Summary 1

1. *A computer is a dumb device as compared to the human brain. However, it can perform routine, simple and monotonic tasks, very quickly.*

2. *A computer is defined as a device that can be programmed to process information.*

3. *A* program *consists of basic instructions that need to be executed by a computer.*

4. *The semantics of all the instructions supported by a computer is known as the instruction set architecture (ISA).*

5. *Ideally, an ISA should be complete, concise, simple, and generic.*

6. *An ISA is complete, if it is equivalent to an universal Turing machine.*

7. *A practical implementation of any complete ISA requires:*

    (a) *A memory to hold instructions and data.*
    (b) *A CPU to process instructions and perform arithmetic and logical operations.*
    (c) *A set of I/O devices for communicating with the programmer.*

8. *Harvard and Von Neumann architectures are practical implementations of complete ISAs, and are also the basis of modern computers.*

9. *Modern processors typically have a set of registers, which are a set of named storage locations. They allow the processor to access data quickly by avoiding time consuming memory accesses.*

10. *Some early processors also had a stack to evaluate arithmetic expressions, and had accumulators to store operands and results.*

1.9.2 Further Reading

The field of computer architecture is a very exciting and fast moving field. The reader can refer to the books by Jan Bergstra [Bergstra and Middelburg, 2012] and Gilreath [Gilreath and Laplante, 2003] to learn more about the theory of instruction set completeness and classes of instructions. The book on formal languages by by Hopcroft, Motwani, and Ulmann [Hopcroft et al., 2006] provides a good introduction to Turing machines and theoretical computer science in general. To get a historical perspective, readers can refer to the original reports written by Alan Turing [Carpenter and Doran, 1986] and John von Neumann [von Neumann, 1945].

Exercises

Processor and Instruction Set

Ex. 1 — Find out the model and make of at least 5 processors in devices around you. The devices can include desktops, laptops, cell phones, and tablet PCs.

Ex. 2 — Make a list of peripheral I/O devices for computers. Keyboards are mice are common devices. Search for uncommon devices. (HINT: joysticks, game controllers, fax machines)

Ex. 3 — What are the four properties of an instruction set?

Ex. 4 — Design an instruction set for a simple processor that needs to perform the following operations:
1. Add two registers
2. Subtract two registers

Ex. 5 — Design an instruction set for a simple processor that needs to perform the following operations:
1. Add two registers
2. Save a register to memory
3. Load a register from memory
4. Divide a value in a register by two

Ex. 6 — Design an instruction set to perform the basic arithmetic operations – add, subtract, multiply, and divide. Assume that all the instructions can have just one operand.

* Ex. 7 — Consider the *sbn* instruction that subtracts the second operand from the first operand, and branches to the instruction specified by the label (third operand), if the result is negative. Write a small program using only the *sbn* instruction to compute the factorial of a positive number.

* Ex. 8 — Write a small program using only the *sbn* instruction to test if a number is prime.

Theoretical Aspects of an ISA*

Ex. 9 — Explain the design of a modified Turing machine.

Ex. 10 — Prove that the *sbn* instruction is Turing complete.

Ex. 11 — Prove that a machine with memory load, store, branch, and subtract instructions is Turing complete.

** Ex. 12 — Find out other models of universal machines from the internet and compare them with Turing Machines.

Practical Machine Models

Ex. 13 — What is the difference between the Harvard architecture and Von Neumann architecture?

Ex. 14 — What is a register machine?

Ex. 15 — What is a stack machine?

Ex. 16 — Write a program to compute $a + b + c - d$ on a stack machine.

Ex. 17 — Write a program to compute $a + b + (c - d) * 3$ on a stack machine.

Ex. 18 — Write a program to compute $(a + b/c) * (c - d) + e$ on a stack machine.

** **Ex. 19 —** Try to search the internet, and find answers to the following questions.

1. When is having a separate instruction memory more beneficial?
2. When is having a combined instruction and data memory more beneficial?

Part I

Architecture: Software Interface

2
The Language of Bits

A computer does not understand words or sentences like human beings. It understands only a sequence of 0s and 1s. We shall see in the rest of this book that it is very easy to store, retrieve and process billions of 0s and 1s. Secondly, existing technologies to implement computers using silicon transistors are very compatible with the notion of processing 0s and 1s. A basic silicon transistor is a *switch* that can set the output to a logical 0 or 1, based on the input. The silicon transistor is the basis of all the electronic computers that we have today right from processors in mobile phones to processors in supercomputers. Some early computers made in the late nineteenth century processed decimal numbers. They were mostly mechanical in nature. It looks like for the next few decades, students of computer architecture need to study the language of 0s and 1s in great detail.

Now, let us define some simple terms. A variable that can be either 0 or 1, is called a *bit*. A set of 8 bits is called a *byte*.

Definition 12
Bit: *A variable that can have two values: 0 or 1.*

Definition 13
Byte: *A sequence of 8 bits.*

In this chapter, we shall look at expressing different concepts in terms of bits. The first question is, " what can we do with our notion of bits?". Well it turns out that we can do everything that we could have done if our basic circuits were able to process normal decimal numbers. We can divide the set of operations into two major types – logical and arithmetic. *Logical* operations express concepts of the form, "the red light is on AND the yellow light is on", or "the bank account is closed if the user is inactive AND the account is a current account." Arithmetic operations refer to operations such as addition, multiplication, subtraction, and division.

We shall first look at logical operations using bits in Section 2.1. Then, we shall look at methods to represent positive integers using 0s and 1s in Section 2.2. A representation of a number using 0s and 1s is also known as a *binary* representation. We shall then look at representing negative integers in Section 2.3, representing floating point numbers(numbers with a decimal point) in Section 2.4, and representing regular text in Section 2.5. Arithmetic operations using binary values will be explained in detail in Chapter 7.

Definition 14

Representation of numbers or text using a sequence of 0s and 1s is known as a binary *representation.*

2.1   Logical Operations

Binary variables (0 or 1) were first described by George Boole in 1854. He used such variables and their associated operations to describe logic in a mathematical sense. He defined a full algebra consisting of simple binary variables, along with a new set of operators, and basic operations. In the honour of George Boole, a binary variable is also known as a *Boolean* variable, and an algebraic system of Boolean variables is known as *Boolean algebra*.

Historical Note 1

George Boole(1815 – 1864) was a professor of mathematics at Queen's college, Cork, Ireland. He proposed his theory of logic in his book – An Investigation of the Laws of Thought, on Which are Founded the Mathematical Theories of Logic and Probabilities. During his lifetime, the importance of his work was not recognised. It was only in 1937 that Claude Shannon observed that it is possible to describe the behavior of electronic digital circuits using Boole's system.

Definition 15

Boolean variable *A variable that can take only two values – 0 or 1.*

Boolean algebra *An algebraic system consisting of Boolean variables and some special operators defined on them.*

2.1.1   Basic Operators

A simple Boolean variable can take two values – 0 or 1. It corresponds to two states of a system. For example, it can represent the fact that a light bulb is off(0) or on(1). It is easy to represent a Boolean variable in an electronic circuit. If the voltage on a wire is 0, then we are representing a logical 0. If the voltage is equal to the supply voltage V_{dd}, then we are representing a logical 1. We shall have an opportunity to read more about electronic circuits in Chapter 6.

Let us consider a simple Boolean variable, A. Let us assume that A represents the fact that a light bulb is on. If $A = 1$, then the bulb is on, else it is off. Then the logical complement or negation of A, represented by $\overline{A}$, represents the fact that the bulb is off. If $\overline{A} = 1$, then the bulb is off, otherwise, it is on. The logical complement is known as the NOT operator. Any Boolean operator can be represented by the means of a *truth table*, which lists the outputs of the operator for all possible combinations of inputs. The truth table for the NOT operator is shown in Table 2.1.

A	$\overline{A}$
0	1
1	0

Table 2.1: Truth table for the NOT operator

Let us now consider multiple Boolean variables. Let us consider the three bulbs in a typical traffic light – red, yellow, green. Let their states at a given time t be represented by the Boolean variables – R, Y, and G – respectively. At any point of time, we want one and only one of the lights to be on. Let us try to represent the first condition (one light on) symbolically using Boolean logic. We need to define the OR operator that represents the fact that either of the operands is equal to 1. For example, A OR B, is equal to 1, if $A = 1$ or $B = 1$. Two symbols for the OR operator are used in literature – '+' and '$\vee$'. In most cases '+' is preferred. The reader needs to be aware that '+' is not the same as the addition operator. The correct connotation for this operator needs to be inferred from the context. Whenever, there is a confusion, we will revert to the $\vee$ operator in this book. By default, we will use the '+' operator to represent Boolean OR. Thus, condition 1 is: $R + Y + G = 1$. The truth table for the OR operator is shown in Table 2.2.

A	B	A OR B
0	0	0
0	1	1
1	0	1
1	1	1

Table 2.2: Truth table for the OR operator

A	B	A AND B
0	0	0
0	1	0
1	0	0
1	1	1

Table 2.3: Truth table for the AND operator

Now, let us try to formalise condition 2. This states that only one light needs to be on. We can alternatively say that it is not possible to find a pair of bulbs that are on together. We need to define a new operator called the AND operator (represented by '.' or '$\wedge$'). A AND B is equal to 1, when both A and B are 1. The truth table for the AND operator is shown in Table 2.3. Now, $R.Y$ represents the fact that both the red and yellow bulbs are on. This is not possible. Considering all such pairs, we have condition 2 as: $R.Y + R.G + G.Y = 0$. This formula represents the fact that no two pairs of bulbs are on simultaneously.

We thus observe that it is possible to represent complex logical statements using a combination of Boolean variables and operators. We can say that NOT, AND, and OR, are basic operators. We can now derive a set of operators from them.

2.1.2 Derived Operators

Two simple operators namely NAND and NOR are very useful. NAND is the logical complement of AND (truth table in Table 2.4) and NOR is the logical complement of OR (truth table in Table 2.5).

A	B	A NAND B
0	0	1
0	1	1
1	0	1
1	1	0

A	B	A NOR B
0	0	1
0	1	0
1	0	0
1	1	0

Table 2.4: Truth table for the NAND operator   Table 2.5: Truth table for the NOR operator

NAND and NOR are very important operators because they are known as *universal operators*. We can use just the NAND operator or just the NOR operator to construct any other operator. For more details the reader can refer to Kohavi and Jha [Kohavi and Jha, 2009].

Let us now define the XOR operator that stands for exclusive-or. A XOR B is equal to 1, when $A = 1, B = 0$, or $A = 0, B = 1$. The truth table is shown in Table 2.6. They symbol for XOR is $\oplus$. The reader can readily verify that $A \oplus B = A.\overline{B} + \overline{A}.B$ by constructing truth tables.

A	B	A XOR B
0	0	0
0	1	1
1	0	1
1	1	0

Table 2.6: Truth table for the XOR operator

2.1.3 Boolean Algebra

Given Boolean variables and basic operators, let us define some rules of Boolean algebra.

NOT Operator

Let us look at some rules governing the NOT operator.

1. **Definition:** $\overline{0} = 1$, and $\overline{1} = 0$ – This is the definition of the NOT operator.

2. **Double negation:** $\overline{\overline{A}} = A$ – The NOT of (NOT of A) is equal to A itself.

OR and AND Operators

1. **Identity:** $A + 0 = A$, and $A.1 = A$ – If we compute the OR of a Boolean variable, A, with 0, or AND with 1, the result is equal to A.

2. **Annulment:** $A + 1 = 1$, and $A.0 = 0$ – If we compute A OR 1, then the result is always equal to 1. Similarly, A AND 0, is always equal to 0 because the value of the second operand determines the final result.

3. **Idempotence:** $A + A = A$, and $A.A = A$ – The result of computing the OR or AND of A with itself, is A.

4. **Complementarity:** $A + \overline{A} = 1$, and $A.\overline{A} = 0$ – Either $A = 1$, or $\overline{A} = 1$. In either case $A + \overline{A}$ will have one term, which is 1, and thus the result is 1. Similarly, one of the terms in $A.\overline{A}$ is 0, and thus the result is 0.

5. **Commutativity:** $A.B = B.A$, and $A + B = B + A$ – The order of Boolean variables does not matter.

6. **Associativity:** $A + (B + C) = (A + B) + C$, and $A.(B.C) = (A.B).C$ – We are free to parenthesise expressions containing only OR or AND operators in any way we choose.

7. **Distributivity:** $A.(B + C) = A.B + A.C$, and $A + B.C = (A + B).(A + C)$ – We can use this law to open up a parenthesis and simplify expressions.

We can use these rules to manipulate expressions containing Boolean variables in a variety of ways. Let us now look at a basic set of theorems in Boolean algebra.

2.1.4 De Morgan's Laws

There are two De Morgan's laws that can be readily verified by constructing truth tables for the LHS and RHS.

$$\overline{A + B} = \overline{A}.\overline{B} \tag{2.1}$$

The NOT of $(A + B)$ is equal to the AND of the complements of A and B.

$$\overline{AB} = \overline{A} + \overline{B} \tag{2.2}$$

The NOT of $(A.B)$ is equal to the OR of the complements of A and B.

Example 5
Prove the consensus theorem: $X.Y + \overline{X}.Z + Y.Z = X.Y + \overline{X}.Z$.
Answer:

$$\begin{aligned}
X.Y + \overline{X}.Z + Y.Z &= X.Y + \overline{X}.Z + (X + \overline{X}).Y.Z \\
&= X.Y + \overline{X}.Z + X.Y.Z + \overline{X}.Y.Z \\
&= X.Y.(1 + Z) + \overline{X}.Z.(1 + Y) \\
&= X.Y + \overline{X}.Z
\end{aligned} \tag{2.3}$$

Example 6
Prove the theorem: $(X + Z).(\overline{X} + Y) = X.Y + \overline{X}.Z$.
Answer:

$$
\begin{aligned}
(X + Z).(\overline{X} + Y) &= X.\overline{X} + X.Y + Z.\overline{X} + Z.Y \\
&= 0 + X.Y + \overline{X}.Z + Y.Z \\
&= X.Y + \overline{X}.Z + Y.Z \\
&= X.Y + \overline{X}.Z \quad (see\ Example\ 5)
\end{aligned}
\tag{2.4}
$$

2.1.5 Logic Gates

Let us now try to implement circuits to realise complex Boolean formulae. We will discuss more about this in Chapter 6. We shall just provide a conceptual treatment in this section. Let us define the term "logic gate" as a device that implements a Boolean function. It can be constructed from silicon, vacuum tubes, or any other material.

Definition 16
A logic gate is a device that implements a Boolean function.

Given a set of logic gates, we can design a circuit to implement any Boolean function. The symbols for different logic gates are shown in Figure 2.1.

2.1.6 Implementing Boolean Functions

Let us now consider a generic boolean function $f(A, B, C \ldots)$. To implement it we need to create a circuit out of logic gates. Our aim should be to minimise the number of gates to save area, power, and time. Let us first look at a brute force method of implementing any Boolean function.

Simple Method

We can construct the truth table of the function, and then try to realise it with an optimal number of logic gates. The reason we start from a truth table is as follows. In some cases, the Boolean function that we are trying to implement might not be specified in a concise form. It might be possible to simplify it significantly. Secondly, using truth tables ensures that the process can be automated. For example, let us consider the following truth table of some function, f. We show only those lines that evaluate to 1.

A	B	C	Result
1	1	0	1
1	1	1	1
1	0	1	1

Let us consider the first line. It can be represented by the Boolean function $A.B.\overline{C}$. Similarly, the second and third lines can be represented as $A.B.C$ and $A.\overline{B}.C$ respectively. Thus, the function can be represented as:

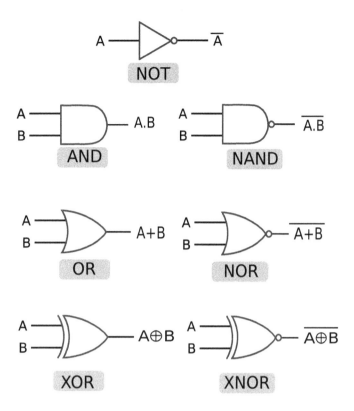

Figure 2.1: List of logic gates

$$f(A, B, C) = A.B.\overline{C} + A.B.C + A.\overline{B}.C \tag{2.5}$$

We see that we have represented the function as an OR function of several terms. This representation is known as a *sum-of-products* representation, or a representation in the *canonical form*. Each such term is known as a *minterm*. Note that in a minterm, each variable appears only once. It is either in its original form or in its complemented form.

Definition 17

Let us consider a Boolean function f with n arguments.

minterm *A* minterm *is an AND function on all n Boolean variables, where each variable appears only once (either in its original form or in its complemented form). A minterm corresponds to one line in the truth table, whose result is 1.*

Canonical representation *It is a Boolean formula, which is equivalent to the function f. It computes an OR operation of a set of minterms.*

To summarise, to implement a truth table, we first get a list of minterms that might evaluate to a logical 1 (*true*), then create a canonical representation, and then realise it with logic gates. To realise the canonical representation using logic gates, we need to realise each minterm separately, and then compute an OR operation.

This process works, but is inefficient. The formula: $A.B.\overline{C} + A.B.C + A.\overline{B}.C$, can be simplified as $A.B + A.\overline{B}.C$. Our simple approach is not powerful enough to simplify this formula.

Karnaugh Maps

Instead of directly converting the canonical representation into a circuit, let us build a structure called a *Karnaugh map*. This is a rectangular grid of cells, where each cell represents one minterm. To construct a Karnaugh map, let us first devise a method of numbering each minterm. Let us first represent all minterms such that the order of variables in them is the same (original or complemented). Second, if a variable is not complemented, then let us represent it by 1, otherwise, let us represent it by 0. Table 2.7 shows the representation of all the possible 8 minterms in a three variable function.

Minterm	Representation
$\overline{A}.\overline{B}.\overline{C}$	000
$\overline{A}.\overline{B}.C$	001
$\overline{A}.B.\overline{C}$	010
$A.\overline{B}.\overline{C}$	100
$\overline{A}.B.C$	011
$A.\overline{B}.C$	101
$A.B.\overline{C}$	110
$A.B.C$	111

Table 2.7: Representation of minterms

Now, given the representation of a minterm we use some bits to specify the row in the Karnaugh map, and the rest of the bits to specify the column. We number the rows and columns such that adjacent rows or columns differ in the value of only one variable. We treat the last row, and the first row as adjacent, and likewise, treat the first and last columns as adjacent. This method of numbering ensures that the difference in representation across any two adjacent cells (same row, or same column) in the Karnaugh map is in only one bit. Moreover, this also means that the corresponding minterms differ in the value of only one variable. One minterm contains the variable in its original form, and the other contains it in its complemented form.

Now, let us proceed to simplify or minimise the function. We construct the Karnaugh map as shown in Figure 2.2 for our simple function $f(A, B, C) = A.B.\overline{C} + A.B.C + A.\overline{B}.C$. We mark all the cells(minterms) that are 1 using a dark colour. Let us consider the first minterm, $A.B.\overline{C}$. Its associated index is 110. We thus, locate the cell 110 in the Karnaugh map, and mark it. Similarly, we mark the cells for the other minterms – $A.B.C(111)$, and $A.\overline{B}.C(101)$. We see that we have three marked cells. Furthermore, since adjacent cells differ in the value of only one variable, we can combine them to a single Boolean expression. In Figure 2.2, we try to combine the cells with indices 110, and 111. They differ in the value of the Boolean variable, C. After combining them, we have the boolean expression: $A.B.\overline{C} + A.B.C = A.B$. We have thus replaced two minterms by a smaller yet equivalent Boolean expression. We were able to combine the two adjacent cells, because they represented a logical OR of the Boolean expressions, which had the variable C in both its original and complemented form. Hence, the function f gets minimised to $A.B + A.\overline{B}.C$.

Instead of combining, two cells in the same column, let us try to combine two cells in the same row as shown in Figure 2.3. In this case, we combine the minterms, $A.B.C$, and $A.\overline{B}.C$. Since the variable B is present in both its original and complemented forms, we can eliminate it. Thus, the Boolean expression denoting the combination of the cells is $A.C$. Hence, function f is equal to $A.C + A.B.\overline{C}$. We can readily verify that both the representations for $f – (A.C + A.B.\overline{C})$ and $(A.B + A.\overline{B}.C)$, are equivalent and optimal

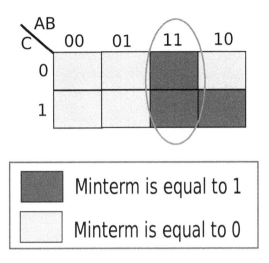

Figure 2.2: Karnaugh Map for $f(A, B, C) = A.B.\overline{C}(110) + A.B.C(111) + A.\overline{B}.C(101)$

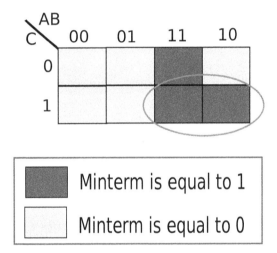

Figure 2.3: Karnaugh Map for $f(A, B, C) = A.B.\overline{C}(110) + A.B.C(111) + A.\overline{B}.C(101)$

in terms of the number of Boolean terms.

Note that we cannot arbitrarily draw rectangles in the Karnaugh map. They cannot include any minterm that evaluates to 0 in the truth table. Secondly, the size of each rectangle needs to be a power of 2. This is because to remove n variables from a set of m minterms, we need to have all combinations of the n variables in the rectangle. It thus needs to have 2^n minterms.

To minimise a function, we need to draw rectangles that are as large as possible. It is possible that two rectangles might have an overlap. However, one rectangle should not be a strict subset of the other.

2.1.7   The Road Ahead

Way Point 2

- *Boolean algebra is a symbolic algebra that uses Boolean variables, which can be either 0 or 1.*

- *The basic Boolean operators are AND, OR, and NOT.*

- *These operators are associative, commutative, and reflexive.*

- *NAND, NOR, XOR are very useful Boolean operators.*

- *De Morgan's laws help convert an expression with an AND operator, to an expression that replaces it with an OR operator.*

- *A logic gate is a physical realisation of a simple Boolean operator or function.*

- *Our aim is to minimise the number of logic gates while designing a circuit for a Boolean function.*

- *One effective way of minimising the number of logic gates is by using Karnaugh maps.*

Up till now, we have learnt about the basic properties of Boolean variables, and a simple method to design efficient circuits to realise Boolean functions. An extensive discussion on Boolean logic or optimal circuit synthesis is beyond the scope of this book. Interested readers can refer to seminal texts by Zvi Kohavi [Kohavi and Jha, 2009] and [Micheli, 1994].

Nevertheless, we are at a position to appreciate the nature of Boolean circuits. Up till now, we have not assigned a meaning to sets of bits. We shall now see that sequences of bits can represent integers, floating point numbers, and strings(pieces of text). Arithmetic operations on such sequences of bits are described in detail in Chapter 7.

2.2   Positive Integers

2.2.1   Ancient Number Systems

Ever since man developed higher intelligence, he has faced the need to count. For numbers from one to ten, human beings can use their fingers. For example, the little finger of the left hand can signify one, and the little finger of the right hand can signify ten. However, for counting numbers greater than ten, we need to figure out a way for representing numbers. In the ancient world, two number systems prevailed – the Roman numerals used in ancient Rome, and the Indian numerals used in the Indian subcontinent.

The Roman numerals used the characters – I, II ... X, for the numbers 1 ... 10 respectively. However, there were significant issues for representing numbers greater than ten. For example, to represent 50, 100, 500, and 1000, Romans used the symbols L, C, D, and M respectively. To represent a large number, the Romans represented it as a sequence of symbols. The number 204 can be represented as CCIV (C + C + IV = 100 + 100 + 4). Hence, to derive the real value of a number, we need to scan the number from left to right, and keep on adding the values. To make things further complicated, there is an additional rule that if a smaller number is preceded by a larger value, then we need to subtract it from the total sum. Note that there is no notion of negative numbers, and zero in this number system. Furthermore, it is extremely difficult to represent large numbers, and perform simple operations such as addition and multiplication.

The ancient Indians used a number system that was significantly simpler, and fundamentally more powerful. The Arabs carried the number system to Europe sometime after seventh century AD, and thus this number system is popularly known as the *Arabic* number system. The magic tricks used by ancient Indian mathematicians are the number '0', and the place value system. The Indian mathematicians used a sequence of ten symbols including zero, as the basic alphabet for numbers. Figure 2.4 shows ten symbols obtained in the Bakhshali manuscript obtained in the north west frontier province of modern Pakistan (dated seventh century AD). Each such symbol is known as a 'digit'.

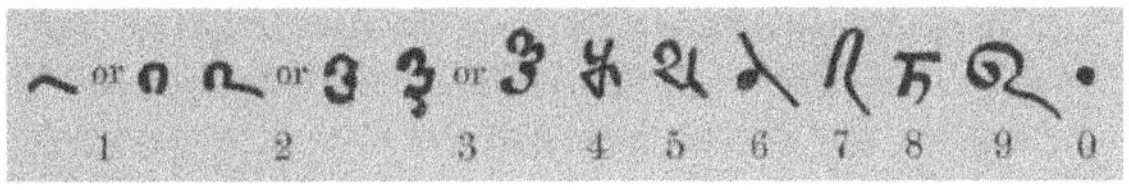

Figure 2.4: Numerals from the Bakhshali Manuscript (source Wikipedia®) This article uses material from the Wikipedia article "Bakhshali Manuscript" [bak,], which is released under the Creative Commons Attribution-Share-Alike License 3.0 [ccl,]

Every number was represented as a sequence of digits. Each digit represents a number between zero and nine. The first problem is to represent a number that is greater than nine by one unit. This is where we use the place value system. We represent it as 10. The left most number, 1, is said to be in the ten's place, and the right most number, 0, is in the unit's place. We can further generalise this representation to any two digit number of the form, x_2x_1. The value of the number is equal to $10 \times x_2 + x_1$. As compared to the Roman system, this representation is far more compact, and can be extended to represent arbitrarily large integers.

A number of the form $x_n x_{n-1} \ldots x_1$ is equal to $x_n \times 10^{n-1} + x_{n-1} \times 10^{n-1} + \ldots + x_1 = \sum_{i=1}^{n} x_i 10^{i-1}$. Each decimal digit is multiplied with a power of 10, and the sum of the products is equal to the value of the number. As we have all studied in elementary school, this number system makes the job of addition, multiplication, and subtraction substantially easier. In this case, the number '10', is known as the *base* of the number system.

Historical Note 2

The largest number known to ancient Indian mathematicians was 10^{53} [ind,].

Let us now ponder about a basic point. Why did the Indians choose ten as the base. They had the liberty to choose any other number such as seven or eight or nine. The answer can be found by considering the most basic form of counting again, i.e., with fingers. Since human beings have ten fingers, they use them to count till one to ten, or from zero to nine. Hence, they were naturally inclined to use ten as the base.

Let us now move to a planet, where aliens have seven fingers. It would not be surprising to see them use a base seven number system. In their world, a number of the form, 56, would actually be $7 \times 5 + 6$ in our number system. We thus observe that it is possible to generalise the concept of a *base*, and it is possible to represent any number in any base. We introduce the notation 3243_{10}, which means that the number 3243 is being represented in base 10.

Example 7

The number 1022_8 is equal to : $8^3 + 0 + 2*8^1 + 2 = 530_{10}$.

2.2.2   Binary Number System

What if we consider a special case? Let us try to represent numbers in base 2. The number 7_{10} can be represented as 111_2, and 12_{10} is equal to 1100_2. There is something interesting about this number system. Every digit is either 0 or 1. As we shall see in Chapters 6 and 7, computers are best suited to process values that are either 0 or 1. They find it difficult to process values from a larger set. Hence, representing numbers in base 2 should be a natural fit for computers. We call this a *binary number system* (see Definition 18). Likewise, a number system that uses a base of 10, is known as a *decimal* number system.

Definition 18

- *A number system based on Indian numerals that uses a base equal to 2, is known as a **binary** number system.*

- *A number system based on Indian numerals that uses a base equal to 10, is known as a **decimal** number system.*

Formally, any number A can be represented as a sequence of n binary digits:

$$A = \sum_{i=1}^{n} x_i 2^{i-1} \tag{2.6}$$

Here, $x_1 \ldots x_n$ are binary digits (0 or 1). We represent a number as a sum of the powers of 2, as shown in Equation 2.6. The coefficients of the equation, are the binary digits. For example, the decimal number 23 is equal to $(16 + 4 + 2 + 1) = 1 \times 2^4 + 0 \times 2^3 + 1 \times 2^2 + 1 \times 2 + 1$. Thus, its binary representation is 10111.

Let us consider some more examples, as shown in Table 2.8.

Number in decimal	Number in binary
5	101
100	1100100
500	111110100
1024	10000000000

Table 2.8: Examples of binary numbers

Example 8

Convert the decimal number 27 to binary.

Answer: $27 = \underbrace{16}_{1} + \underbrace{8}_{1} + \underbrace{0}_{0} + \underbrace{2}_{1} + \underbrace{1}_{1} = 11011_2$

Let us now define two more terms, the most significant bit (MSB), and the least significant bit (LSB). The LSB is the rightmost bit, and the MSB is the leftmost bit.

Definition 19

- *MSB (Most Significant Bit) : The leftmost bit of a binary number. For example the MSB of 1110 is 1.*

- *LSB (Least Significant Bit) : The rightmost bit of a binary number. For example the LSB of 1110 is 0.*

Hexadecimal and Octal Numbers

If we have a 32-bit number system, then representing each number in binary will take 32 binary digits (0/1). For the purposes of explanation, this representation is unwieldy. We can thus make our representation more elegant by representing numbers in base 8 or base 16. We shall see that there is a very easy method of converting numbers in base 8, or base 16, to base 2.

Numbers represented in base 8 are known as *octal numbers*. They are traditionally represented by adding a prefix, '0'. The more popular representation is the hexadecimal number system. It uses a base equal to 16. We shall use the hexadecimal representation extensively in this book. Numbers in this format are prefixed by '0x'. Secondly, the word 'hexadecimal' is popularly abbreviated as 'hex'. Note that we require 16 hex digits. We can use the digits 0-9 for the first ten digits. The next six digits require special characters. These six characters are typically – A (10), B(11), C(12), D(13), E(14), and F(15). We can use the lower case versions of ABCDEF also.

To convert a binary number (A) to a hexadecimal number, or do the reverse, we can use the following relationship:

$$
\begin{aligned}
A &= \sum_{i=1}^{n} x_i 2^{i-1} \\
&= \sum_{j=1}^{n/4} (2^3 \times x_{4(j-1)+4} + 2^2 \times x_{4(j-1)+3} + 2^1 \times x_{4(j-1)+2} + x_{4(j-1)+1}) \times 2^{4(j-1)} \\
&= \sum_{j=1}^{n/4} \underbrace{(2^3 \times x_{4(j-1)+4} + 2^2 \times x_{4(j-1)+3} + 2^1 \times x_{4(j-1)+2} + x_{4(j-1)+1})}_{y_j} \times 2^{4(j-1)} \\
&= \sum_{j=1}^{n/4} y_j 16^{(j-1)}
\end{aligned}
\tag{2.7}
$$

We can thus represent the number (A) in base 16 (hexadecimal notation) by creating groups of four consecutive binary digits. The first group is comprised of the binary digits $x_4 x_3 x_2 x_1$, the second group is comprised of $x_8 x_7 x_6 x_5$ and so on. We need to convert each group of 4 binary digits, to represent a hexadecimal digit (y_j). Similarly, for converting a number from hex to binary, we need to replace each hex digit with a sequence of 4 binary digits. Likewise, for converting numbers from binary to octal and back, we need to consider sequences of 3 binary digits.

Example 9

Convert 110001010_2 to the octal format.

Answer: $\underbrace{110}_{6}\,\underbrace{001}_{1}\,\underbrace{010}_{2} \to 0612$

Example 10

Convert 110000101011 to the hexadecimal format.

Answer: $\underbrace{1100}_{C}\,\underbrace{0010}_{2}\,\underbrace{1011}_{B} \to 0xC2B$

2.2.3 Adding Binary Numbers

Adding binary numbers is as simple as adding decimal numbers. For adding decimal numbers, we start from the rightmost position and add digit by digit. If the sum exceeds 10, then we write the unit's digit at the respective position in the result, and carry the value at the ten's place to the next position in the result. We can do something exactly similar for binary numbers.

Let us start out by trying to add two 1-bit binary numbers, A and B. Table 2.9 shows the different combinations of numbers and results. We observe that for two bits, a carry is generated only when the input operands are both equal to 1. This carry bit needs to be added to the bits in the higher position. At that position, we need to add three bits – two input operand bits and a carry bit. This is shown in Figure 2.5. In this figure, the input operand bits are designated as A and B. The input carry bit is designated as C_{in}. The result will have two bits in it. The least significant bit (right most bit) is known as the *sum*, and the output carry is referred to as C_{out}.

Table 2.10 shows the results for the different combinations of input and carry bits.

A	B	$(A+B)_2$
0	0	00
0	1	01
1	0	01
1	1	11

Table 2.9: Addition of two binary bits

Let us now try to add two n-bit binary numbers. Our addition needs to proceed exactly the same ways as decimal numbers. We add the values at a position, compute the result, and carry a value to the next (more significant) position. Let us explain with an example (see Example 11).

Example 11

Add the two binary numbers, 1011 and 0011.

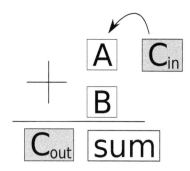

Figure 2.5: Addition of two binary bits and a carry bit

A	B	C_{in}	Sum	C_{out}
0	0	0	0	0
0	1	0	1	0
1	0	0	1	0
1	1	0	0	1
0	0	1	1	0
0	1	1	0	1
1	0	1	0	1
1	1	1	1	1

Table 2.10: A truth table that represents the addition of three bits

Answer: *The process of addition is shown in the figure, and the values of the intermediate values of the carry bits are shown in shaded boxes. Let us now verify if the result of the addition is correct. The two numbers expressed in the decimal number system are 11 and 3. 11 + 3 = 14. The binary representation of 14 is 1110. Thus, the computation is correct.*

$$
\begin{array}{r}
\boxed{0}\ \boxed{1}\ \boxed{1} \\
1\ 0\ 1\ 1 \\
+\ 0\ 0\ 1\ 1 \\
\hline
1\ 1\ 1\ 0
\end{array}
$$

2.2.4   Sizes of Integers

Note that up till now we have only considered positive integers. We shall consider negative integers in Section 2.3. Such positive integers are known as *unsigned* integers in high level programming languages such as C or C++. Furthermore, high level languages define three types of unsigned integers – short (2 bytes), int (4 bytes), long long int (8 bytes). A *short unsigned* integer is represented using 16 bits. Hence, it can represent all the integers from 0 to $2^{16} - 1$ (for a proof, see Example 12). Likewise, a regular 32-bit unsigned integer can represent numbers from 0 till $2^{32} - 1$. The ranges of each data type are given in Table 2.11.

Example 12

Calculate the range of unsigned 2-byte short integers.

Answer: *A short integer is represented by 16 bits. The smallest short integer is represented by 16 zeros. It has a decimal value equal to 0. The largest short integer is represented by all 1s. Its value, V, is equal to $2^{15} + \ldots + 2^0 = 2^{16} - 1$. Hence, the range of unsigned short integers is 0 to $2^{16} - 1$.*

Example 13

Calculate the range of an n-bit integer.

Answer: *0 to $2^n - 1$.*

Example 14

We need to represent a set of decimal numbers from 0 till $m - 1$. What is the minimum number of binary bits that we require?

Answer: *Let us assume that we use n binary bits. The range of numbers that we can represent is 0 to $2^n - 1$. We note that $2^n - 1$ needs to be at least as large as m. Thus, we have:*

$$2^n - 1 \geq m - 1$$
$$\Rightarrow 2^n \geq m$$
$$\Rightarrow n \geq log_2(m)$$
$$\Rightarrow n \geq \lceil log_2(m) \rceil$$

Hence, the minimum number of bits that we require is $\lceil log_2(m) \rceil$.

Data Type	Size	Range
unsigned short int	2 bytes	0 to $2^{16} - 1$
unsigned int	4 bytes	0 to $2^{32} - 1$
unsigned long long int	8 bytes	0 to $2^{64} - 1$

Table 2.11: Ranges of unsigned integers in C/C++

Important Point 5

For the more mathematically inclined, we need to prove that for a n bit integer, there is a one to one mapping between the set of n bit binary numbers, and the decimal numbers, 0 to $2^n - 1$. In other words, every n bit binary number has a unique decimal representation. We leave this as an exercise for the reader.

2.3 Negative Integers

We represent a negative decimal number by adding a '-' sign before it. We can in principle do the same with a binary number, or devise a better representation.

Let us consider the generic problem first. For a number system comprising of a set of numbers, $\mathcal{S}$ (both positive and negative), we wish to create a mapping between each number in $\mathcal{S}$, and a sequence of zeros and ones. A sequence of zeros and ones can alternatively be represented as an unsigned integer. Thus, putting it formally, we propose to devise a method for representing both positive and negative integers as a function $\mathcal{F} : \mathcal{S} \rightarrow \mathcal{N}$ that maps a set of numbers, $\mathcal{S}$, to a set of unsigned integers, $\mathcal{N}$. Let us define the function $SgnBit(u)$ of a number, u. It is equal to 1 when u is negative, and equal to 0 when u is positive or zero. Secondly, unless specified otherwise, we assume that all our numbers require n bits per storage in the next few subsections.

2.3.1 Sign-Magnitude based Representation

We can reserve a bit for representing the sign of a number. If it is equal to 0, then the number is positive, else it is negative. This is known as the *sign-magnitude* representation. Let us consider an n bit integer. We can use the MSB as the designated signed bit, and use the rest of the number to represent the number's magnitude. The magnitude of a number is represented using $n-1$ bits. This is a simple and intuitive representation. In this representation, the range of the magnitude of a n bit integer is from 0 till $2^{n-1} - 1$. Hence, the number system has a range equal to $\pm(2^{n-1} - 1)$. Note that there are two zeros – a positive zero$(00\ldots0)$ and a negative zero$(10\ldots0)$.

Formally, the mapping function – $\mathcal{F}(u)$ – where u is a number in the range of the number system, is shown in Equation 2.8.

$$\mathcal{F}(u) = SgnBit(u) \times 2^{n-1} + \mid u \mid \tag{2.8}$$

For example, if we consider a 4-bit number system, then we can represent the number -2 as 1010_2. Here, the MSB is 1 (represents a negative number), and the magnitude of the number is 010, which represents 2.

The issues with this system are that it is difficult to perform arithmetic operations such as addition, subtraction, and multiplication. For example in our 4-bit number system, -2 + 2, can be represented as $1010 + 0010$. If we naively do simple unsigned addition, then the result is 1100, which is actually -6. This is the wrong result. We need to use a more difficult approach to add numbers.

2.3.2 The 1's Complement Approach

For positive numbers, let us use the same basic scheme that assigns the MSB to a dedicated sign bit, which is 0 in this case. Moreover, let the rest of the $(n-1)$ bits represent the number's magnitude. For a negative number, -u$(u \geq 0)$, let us simply flip all the bits of +u. If a bit is 0, we replace it by 1, and vice versa. Note that this operation flips the sign bit also, effectively negating the number. The number system can represent numbers between $\pm(2^{n-1}-1)$ like the sign-magnitude system.

Formally, the mapping function $\mathcal{F}$ is defined as:

$$\mathcal{F}(u) = \begin{cases} u & u \geq 0 \\ \sim (\mid u \mid) \text{ or } (2^n - 1 - \mid u \mid) & u < 0 \end{cases} \tag{2.9}$$

Note that a bitwise complement($\sim$) is the same as subtracting the number from $11\ldots1$ $(2^n - 1)$.

Let us consider some examples with a 4-bit number system. We represent the number 2 as 0010. Here the sign bit is 0, signifying that it is a positive number. To compute -2, we need to flip each bit. This process yields 1101. Note that the sign bit is 1 now.

The 1's complement approach also suffers from similar deficiencies as the sign magnitude scheme. First, there are two representations for zero. There is a positive zero - 0000, and a negative zero - 1111.

Second, adding two numbers is difficult. Let us try to add 2 and -2. 2 + (-2) = 0010 + 1101. Using simple binary addition, we get 1111, which is equal to 0(negative zero). Hence, in this case simple binary addition works. However, now let us try to add 1 to -0. We have: -0 + 1 = 1111 + 0001 = 0000. This leads to a mathematical contradiction. If we add one to zero, the result should be one. However, in this case, it is still zero! This means that we need to make the process of addition more sophisticated. This will slow down the process of addition and make it more complex.

2.3.3   Bias-based Approach

Let us adopt a different approach now. Let us assume that the unsigned representation of a number $(\mathcal{F}(u))$ is given by:

$$\mathcal{F}(u) = u + bias \tag{2.10}$$

Here, $bias$ is a constant.

Let us consider several examples using a 4-bit number system. The range of unsigned numbers is from 0 to 15. Let the bias be equal to 7. Then, the actual range of the number system is from -7 to +8. Note that this method avoids some pitfalls of the sign-magnitude and 1's complement approach. First, there is only one representation for 0. In this case it is 0111. Second, it is possible to use standard unsigned binary addition to add two numbers with a small modification.

Let us try to add 2 and -2. 2 is represented as +9 or 1001_2. Likewise, -2, is represented as +5, or 0101_2. If we add 2 and -2, we are in effect adding the unsigned numbers 5 and 9. 5 + 9 = 14. This is not the right answer. The right answer should be 0, and it should be represented as 0111 or +7. Nonetheless, we can get the right answer by subtracting the bias, i.e., 7. 14 - 7 = 7. Hence, the algorithm for addition is to perform simple binary unsigned addition, and then subtract the bias. Performing simple binary subtraction is also easy (need to add the bias). Hence, in the case of addition, for two numbers, u and v, we have:

$$\mathcal{F}(u + v) = \mathcal{F}(u) + \mathcal{F}(v) - bias \tag{2.11}$$

However, performing binary multiplication is difficult. The bias values will create issues. In this case, if the real value of a number is A, we are representing it as $A + bias$. If we multiply A and B naively, we are in effect multiplying $A + bias$ and $B + bias$. To recover the correct result, AB, from $(A + bias) \times (B + bias)$ is difficult. We desire an even simpler representation.

2.3.4   The 2's Complement Method

Here are the lessons that we have learnt from the sign-magnitude, 1's complement, and bias based approaches.

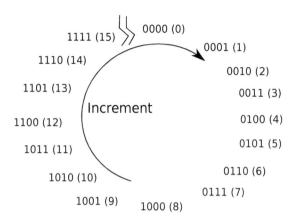

Figure 2.6: Unsigned 4-bit binary numbers

1. We need a representation that is simple.

2. We would ideally like to perform signed arithmetic operations, using the same kind of hardware that is used for unsigned numbers.

3. It is not desirable to have two representations for zero. The number zero, should have a single representation.

Keeping all of these requirements in mind, the 2's complement system was designed. To motivate this number system, let us consider a simple 4-bit number system, and represent the numbers in a circle. Let us first consider unsigned numbers. Figure 2.6 shows the numbers presented in a circular fashion. As we proceed clockwise, we increment the number, and as we proceed anti-clockwise, we decrement the number. This argument breaks at one point as shown in the figure. This is between 15 and 0. If we increment 15, we should get 16. However, because of the limited number of bits, we cannot represent 16. We can only capture its four low order bits which are 0000. This condition is also called an overflow. Likewise, we can also define the term, *underflow*, that means that a number is too small to be represented in a given number system (see Definition 20). In this book, we shall sometimes use the word "overflow" to denote both overflow as well as underflow. The reader needs to infer the proper connotation from the context.

Definition 20

overflow *An* overflow *occurs when a number is too large to be represented in a given number system.*

underflow *An* underflow *occurs when a number is too small to be represented in a given number system.*

Let us now take a look at these numbers slightly differently as shown in Figure 2.7. We consider the same circular order of numbers. However, after 7 we have -8 instead of +8. Henceforth, as we travel clockwise, we effectively increment the number. The only point of discontinuity is between 7 and -8. Let us call this point of discontinuity as the "break point". This number system is known as the 2's complement number system. We shall gradually refine the definition of a 2's complement number to make it more precise and generic.

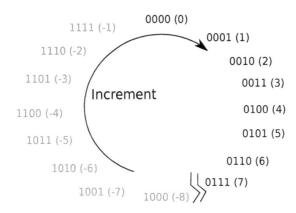

Figure 2.7: Signed 4-bit binary numbers

Definition 21

The point of discontinuity in the number circle is called the break point.

Let us now try to understand what we have achieved through this procedure. We have 16 numbers in the circle, and we have assigned each one of them to numbers from -8 to +7. Each number is represented by a 4-bit value. We observe that incrementing a signed number, is tantamount to incrementing its unsigned 4-bit representation. For example, -3 is represented as 1101. If we increment, -3, we get -2, which is represented as 1110. We also observe that $1101 + 1 = 1110$.

Let us now try to formalise the pattern of numbers shown in the circle in Figure 2.7. First, let us try to give the circular representation a name. Let us call it a **Number Circle**. In a number circle, we observe that for numbers between 0 and 7, their representation is the same as their unsigned representation. The MSB is 0. For numbers between -8 and -1, the MSB is 1. Secondly, the representation of a negative number, -u $(u \geq 0)$, is the same as the unsigned representation for $16 - u$.

Definition 22

The steps for creating a n bit number circle are:

1. *We start by writing 0 at the top. Its representation is a sequence of n zeros.*

2. *We proceed clockwise and add the numbers 1 to $(2^{n-1} - 1)$. Each number is represented by its n bit unsigned representation. The MSB is 0.*

3. *We introduce a break point after $2^{n-1} - 1$.*

4. *Then next number is -2^{n-1} represented by 1 followed by $n - 1$ zeros.*

5. *We then proceed clockwise incrementing both the numbers, and their unsigned representations by 1 till we reach 0.*

We can generalise the process of creating a number circle, to create a n bit number circle (see Definition 22). To add a positive number, A, to a number B, we need to proceed A steps in the clockwise direction from B. If A is negative, then we need to proceed A steps in the anti-clockwise direction. Note that moving k steps in the clockwise direction is the same as moving $2^n - k$ steps in the anti-clockwise direction. This magical property means that subtracting k is the same as adding $2^n - k$. Consequently, every subtraction can be replaced by an addition. Secondly, a negative number, $-u$, is located in the number circle by moving $|u|$ steps anti-clockwise from 0, or alternatively, $2^n - |u|$ steps clockwise. Hence, the number circle assigns the unsigned representation $2^n - |u|$, to a negative number of the form $-u$ ($u \geq 0$).

Succinctly, a number circle can be described by Equation 2.12. This number system is called a *2's complement number system*.

$$\mathcal{F}(u) = \begin{cases} u & 0 \leq u \leq 2^{n-1} - 1 \\ 2^n - |u| & -2^{n-1} \leq u < 0 \end{cases} \tag{2.12}$$

Properties of the 2's Complement Representation

1. There is one unique representation for 0, i.e., $000\ldots0$.

2. The MSB is equal to the sign bit ($SgnBit(u)$).
   Proof: Refer to the number circle. A negative number's unsigned representation is greater than or equal to 2^{n-1}. Hence, its MSB is 1. Likewise all positive numbers are less than 2^{n-1}. Hence, their MSB is 0.

3. **Negation Rule**: $\mathcal{F}(-u) = 2^n - \mathcal{F}(u)$
   Proof: If $u \geq 0$, then $\mathcal{F}(-u) = 2^n - u = 2^n - \mathcal{F}(u)$ according to Equation 2.12. Similarly, if $u < 0$, then $\mathcal{F}(-u) = |u| = 2^n - (2^n - |u|) = 2^n - \mathcal{F}(u)$.

4. Every number in the range $[-2^{n-1}, 2^{n-1} - 1]$ has a unique representation.
   Proof: Every number is a unique point on the number circle.

5. **Addition Rule**:

$$\mathcal{F}(u + v) \equiv \mathcal{F}(u) + \mathcal{F}(v) \tag{2.13}$$

For the sake of brevity, we define the $\equiv$ operator. ($a \equiv b$) means that ($a \mod 2^n = b \mod 2^n$). Recall that the modulo (mod) operator computes the remainder of a division, and the remainder is assumed to be always non-negative, and less than the divisor. The physical significance of (mod 2^n) is that we consider the n LSB bits. This is always the case because we have a n bit number system, and in all our computations we only keep the n LSB bits, and discard the rest of the bits if there are any. In our number circle representation, if we add or subtract 2^n to any point (i.e. move 2^n hops clockwise or anti-clockwise), we arrive at the same point. Hence, $a \equiv b$ implies that they are the same point on the number circle, or their n LSB bits are the same in their binary representation.

Proof: Let us consider the point u on the number circle. Its binary representation is $\mathcal{F}(u)$. Now, if we move v points, we arrive at $u + v$. If v is positive, we move v steps clockwise; otherwise, we move v steps anticlockwise. The binary representation of the new point is $\mathcal{F}(u + v)$.

We can interpret the movement on the number circle in another way. We start at u. We move $\mathcal{F}(v)$ steps clockwise. If $v \geq 0$, then $v = \mathcal{F}(v)$ by Equation 2.12, hence we can conclude that we arrive at $u + v$. If $v < 0$, then $\mathcal{F}(v) = 2^n - |v|$. Now, moving $|v|$ steps anticlockwise is the same as moving $2^n - |v|$ steps clockwise. Hence, in this case also we arrive at $u + v$, which has a binary representation equal to $\mathcal{F}(u+v)$. Since, each step moved in a clockwise direction is equivalent to incrementing the binary representation by 1, we can conclude that the binary representation of the destination is equal to: $\mathcal{F}(u) + \mathcal{F}(v)$. Since, we only consider, the last n bits, the binary representation is equal to $(\mathcal{F}(u) + \mathcal{F}(v)) \mod 2^n$. Hence, $\mathcal{F}(u+v) \equiv \mathcal{F}(u) + \mathcal{F}(v)$.

6. **Subtraction Rule**

$$\mathcal{F}(u-v) \equiv \mathcal{F}(u) + (2^n - \mathcal{F}(v)) \tag{2.14}$$

Proof: We have:

$$\begin{aligned}
\mathcal{F}(u-v) &\equiv \mathcal{F}(u) + \mathcal{F}(-v) \quad \text{(addition rule)} \\
&\equiv \mathcal{F}(u) + 2^n - \mathcal{F}(v) \quad \text{(negation rule)}
\end{aligned} \tag{2.15}$$

7. **Loop Rule**: $\mathcal{F}(u) \equiv 2^n + \mathcal{F}(u)$
   Proof: After moving 2^n points on the number circle, we come back to the same point.

8. **Multiplication Rule**: (assuming no overflows)

$$\mathcal{F}(u \times v) \equiv \mathcal{F}(u) \times \mathcal{F}(v) \tag{2.16}$$

Proof: If u and v are positive, then this statement is trivially true. If u and v are negative, then we have, $u = -|u|$ and $v = -|v|$:

$$\begin{aligned}
\mathcal{F}(u) \times \mathcal{F}(v) &\equiv (2^n - \mathcal{F}(|u|)) \times (2^n - \mathcal{F}(|v|)) \\
&\equiv 2^{n+1} - 2^n(\mathcal{F}(|u|) + \mathcal{F}(|v|) + \mathcal{F}(|u|) \times \mathcal{F}(|v|) \\
&\equiv \mathcal{F}(|u|) \times \mathcal{F}(|v|) \\
&\equiv \mathcal{F}(|u| \times |v|) \\
&\equiv \mathcal{F}(u \times v)
\end{aligned} \tag{2.17}$$

Now, let us assume that u is positive and v is negative. Thus, $u = |u|$ and $v = -|v|$. We have:

$$\begin{aligned}
\mathcal{F}(u) \times \mathcal{F}(v) &\equiv \mathcal{F}(u) \times (2^n - \mathcal{F}(|v|)) \\
&\equiv 2^n \mathcal{F}(u) - \mathcal{F}(u) \times \mathcal{F}(|v|) \\
&\equiv -\mathcal{F}(u) \times \mathcal{F}(|v|) \quad \text{(loop rule)} \\
&\equiv -(\mathcal{F}(u \times |v|)) \quad (u \geq 0, |v| \geq 0) \\
&\equiv 2^n - \mathcal{F}(u \times |v|) \quad \text{(loop rule)} \\
&\equiv \mathcal{F}(-(u \times (|v|))) \quad \text{(negation rule)} \\
&\equiv \mathcal{F}(u \times (-|v|)) \\
&\equiv \mathcal{F}(u \times v)
\end{aligned} \tag{2.18}$$

Likewise, we can prove the result for a negative u and positive v. We have thus covered all the cases.

We thus observe that the 2's complement number system, and the number circle based method make the process of representing both positive and negative numbers easy. It has a unique representation for zero. It is easy to compute its sign. We just need to take a look at the MSB. Secondly, addition, subtraction, and multiplication on signed numbers is as simple as performing the same operations on their unsigned representations.

Example 15
Add 4 and -3 using a 4-bit 2's complement representation.

Answer: *Let us first try to add it graphically. We can start at 4 and move 3 positions anti-clockwise. We arrive at 1, which is the correct answer. Let us now try a more conventional approach. 4 is represented as 0100, -3 is represented as 1101. If we add, 0100 and 1101 using a regular unsigned binary adder, the result is 10001. However, we cannot represent 5 bits in our simple 4-bit system. Hence, the hardware will discard the fifth bit, and report the result as 0001, which is the correct answer.*

Computing the 2's Complement Representation

Let us now try to explore the methods to compute a 2's complement representation. For positive numbers it is trivial. However, for negative numbers of the form, -u ($u \geq 0$), the representation is $2^n - u$. A simple procedure is outlined in Equation 2.19.

$$
\begin{aligned}
2^n - u &= (2^n - 1 - u) + 1 \\
&= (\sim u) + 1
\end{aligned}
\tag{2.19}
$$

According to Equation 2.9, we can conclude that $(2^n - 1 - u)$ is equivalent to flipping every bit, or alternatively computing $\sim u$. Hence, the procedure for negating a number in the 2's complement system, is to first compute its 1's complement, and then add 1.

The Sign Extension Trick

Let us assume that we want to convert a number's representation from a 16-bit number system to a 32-bit number system. If the number is positive, then we just need to prefix it with 16 zeros. Let us consider the case when it is negative. Let the number again be of the form, -u ($u \geq 0$). Its representation in 16 bits is $\mathcal{F}_{16}(u) = 2^{16} - u$. Its representation using 32 bits is $\mathcal{F}_{32}(u) = 2^{32} - u$.

$$
\begin{aligned}
\mathcal{F}_{32}(u) &= 2^{32} - u \\
&= (2^{32} - 2^{16}) + (2^{16} - u) \\
&= \underbrace{11\ldots1}_{16}\underbrace{00\ldots0}_{16} + \mathcal{F}_{16}(u)
\end{aligned}
\tag{2.20}
$$

For a negative number, we need to prepend it with 16 ones. By combining both the results, we conclude that to convert a number from a 16-bit representation to a 32-bit representation, we need to prepend it with 16 copies of its sign bit(MSB).

Range of the 2's Complement Number System

The range of the number system is from -2^{n-1} to $2^{n-1} - 1$. There is one extra negative number, -2^{n-1}.

Checking if a 2's Complement Addition has Resulted in an Overflow

Let us outline the following theorem for checking if a 2's complement addition results in an overflow.

Theorem 2.3.4.1 *Let us consider an addition operation, where both the operands are non-zero. If the signs of the operands are different, then we can never have an overflow. However, if the signs of the operands are the same, and the result has an opposite sign or is zero, then the addition has led to an overflow.*

Proof: Let us consider the number circle, and an addition operation of the form $A+B$. Let us first locate point A. Then, let us move B steps clockwise if B is positive, or B steps anti-clockwise if B is negative. The final point is the answer. We also note that if we cross the break point (see Definition 21), then there is an overflow, because we exceed the range of the number system. Now, if the signs of A and B are different, then we need to move a minimum of $2^{n-1}+1$ steps to cross the break point. This is because we need to move over zero (1), the break point(1), and the set of all the positive numbers ($2^{n-1} - 1$), or all the negative numbers (2^{n-1}). Since, we have 1 less positive number, we need to move at least $2^{n-1} - 1 + 1 + 1 = 2^{n-1} + 1$ steps. Since B is a valid 2's complement number, and is in the range of the number system, we have $\mid B \mid < 2^{n-1}+1$. Hence, we can conclude that after moving B steps, we will never cross the break point, and thus an overflow is not possible.

Now, let us consider the case in which the operands have the same sign. In this case, if the result has an opposite sign or is zero, then we are sure that we have crossed the break point. Consequently, there is an overflow. It will never be the case that there is an overflow and the result has the same sign. For this to happen, we need to move at least $2^{n-1} + 1$ steps (cross over 0, the break point, and all the positive/negative numbers). Like the earlier case, this is not possible.

Alternative Interpretation of 2's Complement

Theorem 2.3.4.2 *A signed n bit number, A, is equal to $(A_{1...n-1} - A_n 2^{n-1})$. A_i is the ith bit in A's 2's complement binary representation (A_1 is the LSB, and A_n is the MSB). $A_{1...j}$ is a binary number containing the first j digits of A's binary 2's complement representation.*

Proof: Let us consider a 4-bit representation. -2 is represented as 1110_2. The last $n-1$ digits are 110_2. This is equal to 6 in decimal. The MSB represents 1000_2 or 8. Indeed -2 = 6 - 8.

If $A > 0$, then $A_n = 0$, and the statement of the theorem is trivially true. Let us consider the case when $A < 0$. Here, $A_n = 1$. We observe that $A_{1...n} = 2^n - |A| = 2^n + A$ since A is negative. Thus, $A = A_{1...n} - 2^n$.

$$
\begin{aligned}
A &= A_{1...n} - 2^n \\
&= (A_{1...n-1} + A_n 2^{n-1}) - 2^n \\
&= (A_{1...n-1} + 2^{n-1}) - 2^n \quad (A_n = 1) \\
&= A_{1...n-1} - 2^{n-1}
\end{aligned}
\tag{2.21}
$$

∎

2.4   Floating Point Numbers

Floating Point Numbers are numbers that contain a decimal point. Examples are: 3.923, -4.93, 10.23e-7 (10.23×10^{-7}). Note that the set of integers are a subset of the set of floating point numbers. An integer such as 7 can be represented as 7.0000000. We shall describe a method to represent floating point numbers in the binary format in this section.

In specific, we shall describe the IEEE 754 [Kahan, 1996] standard for representing floating point numbers. We shall further observe that representing different kinds of floating point numbers is slightly complicated, and requires us to consider many special cases. To make our life easy, let us first slightly simplify the problem and consider representing a set of numbers known as *fixed point numbers*.

2.4.1   Fixed Point Numbers

A fixed point number has a fixed number of digits after the decimal point. For example, any value representing money typically has two digits after the decimal point for most currencies in the world. In most cases, there is no reason for having more than three digits after the decimal point. Such numbers can be represented in binary easily.

Let us consider the case of values representing a monetary amount. These values will only be positive. A value such as 120.23 can be represented in binary as the binary representation of 12023. Here, the implicit assumption is that there are two digits after the decimal point. It is easy to add two numbers using this notation. It is also easy to subtract two numbers as long as the result is positive. However, multiplying or dividing such numbers is difficult.

2.4.2   Generic Form of Floating Point Numbers

Unlike fixed point numbers, there can potentially be many more digits after the decimal point in floating point numbers. We need a more generic representation. Let us first look at how we represent floating point numbers in a regular base 10 number system. For simplicity, let us limit ourselves to positive floating point numbers in this section.

Representing Floating Point Numbers in Base-10

Examples of positive floating point numbers in base 10 are: 1.344, 10.329, and 2.338. Alternatively, a floating point number, A, can be expanded according to Equation 2.22.

$$A = \sum_{i=-n}^{n} x_i 10^i \tag{2.22}$$

For example, $1.344 = 1 \times 10^0 + 3 \times 10^{-1} + 4 \times 10^{-2} + 4 \times 10^{-3}$. The coefficient x_i can vary from 0 to 9. Let us try to use the basic idea in this equation to create a similar representation for floating point numbers in base 2.

Representing Floating Point Numbers in Binary

Let us try to extend the expansion shown in Equation 2.22 to expand positive floating point numbers in base 2. A is a positive floating point number. We can try to expand A as:

$$A = \sum_{i=-n}^{n} x_i 2^i \tag{2.23}$$

Here, x_i is either 0 or 1. Note that the form of Equation 2.23 is exactly the same as Equation 2.22. However, we have changed the base from 10 to 2.

We have negative exponents from -1 to $-n$, and non-negative exponents from 0 to n. The negative exponents represent the **fractional part** of the number, and the non-negative exponents represent the **integer part** of the number. Let us show a set of examples in Table 2.12. We show only non-zero co-coefficients for the sake of brevity.

Number	Expansion
0.375	$2^{-2} + 2^{-3}$
1	2^0
1.5	$2^0 + 2^{-1}$
2.75	$2^1 + 2^{-1} + 2^{-2}$
17.625	$2^4 + 2^0 + 2^{-1} + 2^{-3}$

Table 2.12: Representation of floating point numbers

We observe that using Equation 2.23, we can represent a lot of floating point numbers exactly. However, there are a lot of numbers such as 1.11, which will potentially require an infinite number of terms with negative exponents. It is not possible to find an exact representation for it using Equation 2.23. However, if n is large enough, we can reduce the error between the actual number and the represented number to a large extent.

Let us now try to represent a positive floating point number in a binary format using Equation 2.23. There are two parts in a positive floating point number – integer part and fractional part. We represent the integer part using a standard binary representation. We represent the fractional part also with a binary representation of the form: $x_{-1}x_{-2} \ldots x_{-n}$. Lastly, we put a '.' between the integer and fractional parts.

Number	Expansion	Binary Representation
0.375	$2^{-2} + 2^{-3}$	0.011
1	2^0	1.0
1.5	$2^0 + 2^{-1}$	1.1
2.75	$2^1 + 2^{-1} + 2^{-2}$	10.11
17.625	$2^4 + 2^0 + 2^{-1} + 2^{-3}$	10001.101

Table 2.13: Representation of floating point numbers in binary

Table 2.13 shows the binary representation of numbers originally shown in Table 2.12.

Normal Form

Let us take a look at Table 2.13 again. We observe that there are a variable number of binary bits before and after the decimal point. We can limit the number of bits before and after the decimal point to L_i and L_f respectively. By doing so, we can have a binary representation for a floating point number that requires $L_i + L_f$ bits – L_i bits for the integer part, and L_f bits for the fractional part. The fractional part is traditionally known as the *mantissa*, whereas the entire number (both integer and fraction) is known as the *significand*. If we wish to devote 32 bits for representing a floating point number, then the largest number that we can represent is approximately $2^{16} = 65,536$ (if $L_i = L_f$), which is actually a very small number for most practical purposes. We cannot represent large numbers such as 2^{50}.

Let us thus, slightly modify our generic form to expand the range of numbers that we can represent. We start out by observing that 101110 in binary can be represented as 1.01110×2^5. The number 1.01110 is the *significand*. As a convention, we can assume that the first binary digit in the significand is 1, and the decimal point is right after it. Using this notation, we can represent all floating point numbers as:

$$A = P \times 2^X, \quad (P = 1 + M, 0 \le M < 1, X \in \mathbf{Z}) \tag{2.24}$$

Definition 23

Significand *It is the part of the floating point number that just contains its digits. The decimal point is somewhere within the significand. The significand of 1.3829×10^3 is 1.3829.*

Mantissa *It represents the fractional part of the significand. The mantissa of 1.3829×10^3 is 0.3829.*

$\mathbf{Z}$ is the set of integers, P is the significand, M is the mantissa, and X is known as the exponent. This representation is slightly more flexible. It allows us to specify large exponents, both positive as well as negative. Lastly, let us try to create a generic form for both positive and floating point numbers by introducing a sign bit, S. We show the resulting form in Equation 2.25 and refer to it as the *normal form* henceforth.

$$A = (-1)^S \times P \times 2^X, \quad (P = 1 + M, 0 \le M < 1, X \in \mathbf{Z}) \tag{2.25}$$

If $S = 0$, the number is positive. If $S = 1$, the number is negative.

2.4.3 IEEE 754 Format for Representing Floating Point Numbers

Let us now try to represent a floating point number using a sequence of 32 bits. We shall describe the IEEE 754 format, which is the de facto standard for representing floating point numbers in binary.

Let us start with the normal form as shown in Equation 2.25. We observe that there are three variables in the equation: S(sign bit), M(mantissa), and X(exponent). Since all significands have 1 as their first digit, there is no need to explicitly represent it. We can assume that we have a 1 by default as the MSB of the significand, and we need to just represent the L_f bits of the mantissa. Secondly, since we are representing all our numbers in binary, the base is 2, and this can be assumed to be the default value. The IEEE 754 format thus proposes to apportion 32 bits as shown in Figure 2.8.

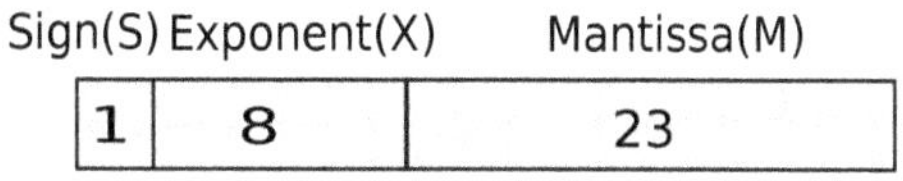

Sign(S)	Exponent(X)	Mantissa(M)
1	8	23

Figure 2.8: IEEE 754 format for representing 32-bit floating point numbers

The format allocates 1 bit for the sign bit, 8 bits for the exponent, and 23 bits for the mantissa. The exponent can be positive, negative or zero. The point to note here is that the exponent is not represented in the 2's complement notation. It is represented using the biased representation (see Section 2.3.3). The exponent(X) is represented by a number, E, where:

$$E = X + bias \tag{2.26}$$

In this case, the *bias* is equal to 127. Thus, if the exponent is equal 10, it is represented as 137. If the exponent is -20, it is represented as 107. E is an unsigned number between 0 and 255. 0 and 255 are reserved for special values. The valid range for E for **normal** floating point numbers is 1 to 254. Thus, the exponent can vary from -126 to 127. We can represent the normal form for IEEE 754 numbers as:

$$A = (-1)^S \times P \times 2^{E-bias}, \quad (P = 1 + M, 0 \leq M < 1, 1 \leq E \leq 254) \tag{2.27}$$

Example 16

Find the smallest and largest positive normal floating point numbers.
Answer:

- *The largest positive normal floating point number is* $1.\underbrace{11\ldots1}_{23} \times 2^{127}$.

$$1.\underbrace{11\ldots1}_{23} = 1 + \sum_{i=-1}^{-23} 2^i$$

$$= \sum_{i=0}^{-23} 2^i$$

$$= 2^1 - 2^{-23}$$

$$= 2 - 2^{-23}$$

The result is equal to $(2 - 2^{-23}) \times 2^{127} = 2^{128} - 2^{104}$.

- *The smallest positive normal floating point number is* $1.00\ldots0 \times 2^{-126} = 2^{-126}$.

Example 17

What is the range of normal floating point numbers.
Answer: $\pm(2^{128} - 2^{104})$.

Special Numbers

We reserved two values of E, 0 and 255, to represent special numbers.

If (E=255), then we can represent two kinds of values: ∞ and NAN (Not a number). We need to further look at the mantissa(M). If ($M = 0$), then the number represents $\pm\infty$ depending on the sign bit. We can get ∞ as a result of trying to divide any non-zero number by 0, or as the result of other mathematical operations. The point to note is that the IEEE 754 format treats infinities separately.

If we divide 0/0 or try to compute $sin^{-1}(x)$ for $x > 1$, then the result is invalid. An invalid result is known as a *NAN*. Any mathematical operation involving a NAN has as its result a NAN. Even $NAN - NAN = NAN$. If $M \neq 0$, then the represented number is a NAN. In this case the exact value of M is not relevant.

E	M	Value
255	0	∞ if $S = 0$
255	0	$-\infty$ if $S = 1$
255	$\neq 0$	NAN (Not a number)
0	0	0
0	$\neq 0$	Denormal number

Table 2.14: Special floating point numbers

Now, let us take a look at the case, when $E = 0$. If M is also 0, then the number represented is 0. Note that there are two 0s in the IEEE 754 format – a positive zero and a negative zero. Ideally implementations of this format are supposed to treat both the zeros as the same. However, this can vary depending upon the processor vendor.

The last category of numbers are rather special. They are called **denormal numbers**. We shall discuss them separately in Section 2.4.4.

2.4.4 Denormal Numbers

We have seen in Example 16 that the smallest positive normal floating point number is 2^{-126}. Let us consider a simple piece of code.

```
f = 2^(-126);
g = f / 2;
if (g == 0)
        print ("error");
```

Sadly, this piece of code will compute g to be 0 as per our current understanding. The reason for this is that f is the smallest possible positive number that can be represented in our format. g can thus not be represented, and most processors will round g to 0. However, this leads to a mathematical fallacy. The IEEE 754 protocol designers thus tried to avoid situations like this by proposing the idea of denormal numbers. Denormal numbers have a slightly different form as given by Equation 2.28.

$$A = (-1)^S \times P \times 2^{-126}, \quad (P = 0 + M, 0 \leq M < 1) \tag{2.28}$$

Note the differences with Equation 2.25. The implicit value of 1 is not there any more. Instead of $(P = 1 + M)$, we have $(P = 0 + M)$. Secondly, there is no room to specify any exponent. This is because $E=0$. The default exponent is -126. We can view denormal numbers as an extension of normal floating point numbers on both sides (smaller and larger). Refer to Figure 2.9.

Example 18
Find the smallest and largest positive denormal numbers.
Answer:

- *The smallest positive denormal number is $0.\underbrace{00\ldots0}_{22}1 \times 2^{-126} = 2^{-149}$.*

- *The largest possible denormal number is $0.\underbrace{11\ldots1}_{23} \times 2^{-126} = 2^{-126} - 2^{-149}$.*

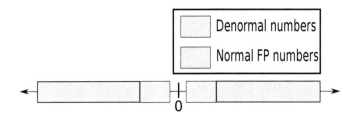

Figure 2.9: Denormal numbers on a conceptual number line (not drawn to scale)

- *Note that the largest denormal number $(2^{-126} - 2^{-149})$ is smaller than the smallest positive normal number (2^{-126}). This justifies the choice of 2^{-126} as the default exponent for denormal numbers.*

Example 19
Find the ranges of denormal numbers.
Answer:

- *For positive denormal numbers, the range is $[2^{-149}, 2^{-126} - 2^{-149}]$.*

- *For negative denormal numbers, the range is $[-(2^{-126} - 2^{-149}), -2^{-149}]$.*

By using denormal numbers we will not get a wrong answer if we try to divide 2^{-126} by 2, and then compare it with 0. Denormal numbers can thus be used as a buffer such that our normal arithmetic operations do not give unexpected results. In practice, incorporating denormal numbers in a floating point unit is difficult and they are very slow to process. Consequently, a lot of small embedded processors do not support denormal numbers. However, most modern processors running on laptops and desktops have full support for denormal numbers.

2.4.5 Double Precision Numbers

We observe that by using 32 bits, the largest number that we can represent is roughly 2^{128}, which is approximately 10^{38}. We might need to represent larger numbers, especially while studying cosmology. Secondly, there are only 23 bits of precision (mantissa is 23 bits long). If we are doing highly sensitive calculations, then we might need more bits of precision. Consequently, there is a IEEE 754 standard for **double precision** numbers. These numbers require 64 bits of storage. They are represented by the *double* datatype in C or Java.

64 bits are apportioned as follows:

The mantissa is now 52 bits long. We have 11 bits for representing the exponent. The bias is equal to 1023, and the range of the exponent is from -1022 to 1023. We can thus represent many more numbers that are much larger, and we have more bits in the mantissa for added precision. The format and semantics of $\pm\infty$, zero, NAN, and denormal numbers remains the same as the case for 32 bits.

Field	Size(bits)
S	1
E	11
M	52

2.4.6 Floating Point Mathematics

Because of limited precision, floating point formats do not represent most numbers accurately. This is because, we are artificially constraining ourselves to expressing a generic real number as a sum of powers of 2, and restricting the number of mantissa bits to 23. It is possible that some numbers such as 1/7 can be easily represented in one base (base 7), and can have inexact representations in other bases (base 2). Furthermore, there are a large set of numbers that cannot be exactly represented in any base. These are *irrational numbers* such as $\sqrt{2}$ or π. This is because a floating point representation is a rational number that is formed out of repeatedly adding fractions. It is a known fact that rational numbers cannot be used to represent numbers such as $\sqrt{2}$. Leaving theoretical details aside, if we have a large number of mantissa bits, then we can get arbitrarily close to the actual number. We need to be willing to sacrifice a little bit of accuracy for the ease of representation.

Floating point math has some interesting and unusual properties. Let us consider the mathematical expression involving two positive numbers A and B: $A + B - A$. We would ideally expect the answer to be non-zero. However, this need not be the case. Let us consider the following code snippet.

```
A = 2^(50);
B = 2^(10);
C = (B + A) - A;
```

Due to the limited number of mantissa bits (23), there is no way to represent $2^{50} + 2^{10}$. If the dominant term is 2^{50}, then our flexibility is only limited to numbers in the range $2^{50\pm23}$. Hence, a processor will compute $A + B$ equal to A, and thus C will be 0. However, if we slightly change the code snippet to look like:

```
A = 2^(50);
B = 2^(10);
C = B + (A - A);
```

C is computed correctly in this case. We thus observe that the order of floating point operations is very important. The programmer has to be either smart enough to figure out the right order, or we need a smart compiler to figure out the right order of operations for us. As we see, floating point operations are clearly not associative. The proper placement of brackets is crucial. However, floating point operations are commutative ($A + B = B + A$).

Due to the inexact nature of floating point mathematics, programmers and compilers need to pay special attention while dealing with very large or very small numbers. As we have also seen, if one expression contains both small and large numbers, then the proper placement of brackets is very important.

2.5 Strings

A string data type is a sequence of characters in a given language such as English. For example, "test", is a string of four characters. We need to derive a bitwise representation for it, the same way we devised a representation for integers. Traditionally, characters in the English language are represented using the ASCII character set. Hence, we shall describe it first.

2.5.1   ASCII Format

ASCII stands for "American Standard Code for Information Interchange". It is a format that assigns a 7 bit binary code for each English language character including punctuation marks. Most languages that use the ASCII format, use 8 bits to represent each character. One bit(MSB) is essentially wasted.

The ASCII character set defines 128 characters. The first 32 characters are reserved for control operations, especially for controlling the printer. For example, the zeroth character is known as the null character. It is commonly used to terminate strings in the C language. Similarly, there are special characters for backspace(8), line feed(10), and escape(27). The common English language characters start from 32 onwards. First, we have punctuation marks and special characters, then we have 26 capital letters, and finally 26 small letters. We show a list of ASCII characters along with their decimal encodings in Table 2.15.

Character	Code	Character	Code	Character	Code
a	97	A	65	0	48
b	98	B	66	1	49
c	99	C	67	2	50
d	100	D	68	3	51
e	101	E	69	4	52
f	102	F	70	5	53
g	103	G	71	6	54
h	104	H	72	7	55
i	105	I	73	8	56
j	106	J	74	9	57
k	107	K	75	!	33
l	108	L	76	#	35
m	109	M	77	$	36
n	110	N	78	%	37
o	111	O	79	&	38
p	112	P	80	(	40
q	113	Q	81	)	41
r	114	R	82	*	42
s	115	S	83	+	43
t	116	T	84	,	44
u	117	U	85	.	46
v	118	V	86	;	59
w	119	W	87	=	61
x	120	X	88	?	63
y	121	Y	89	@	64
z	122	Z	90	∧	94

Table 2.15: ASCII Character Set

Since ASCII can represent only 128 symbols, it is suitable only for English. However, we need an encoding for most of the languages in the world such as Arabic, Russian, French, Spanish, Swahili, Hindi, Chinese,

Thai, and Vietnamese. The Unicode format was designed for this purpose. The most popular Unicode standard until recently was UTF-8.

2.5.2 UTF-8

UTF (Universal character set Transformation Format - 8 bit) can represent every character in the Unicode character set. The *Unicode* character set assigns a unsigned binary number to each character of most of the world's writing systems. UTF-8 encodes 1,112,064 characters defined in the Unicode character set. It uses 1-6 bytes for this purpose.

UTF-8 is compatible with ASCII. The first 128 characters in UTF-8 correspond to the ASCII characters. When using ASCII characters, UTF-8 requires just one byte. It has a leading 0. However, the first byte can contain extra information such as the total number of bytes. This is encoded by having leading ones followed by a zero in the first byte. For example, if the first byte is of the form 11100010, then it means that the character contains 3 bytes. Each continuation byte begins with 10. Most of the languages that use variants of the Roman script such as French, German, and Spanish require 2 bytes in UTF-8. Greek, Russian (Cyrillic), Hebrew, and Arabic, also require 2 bytes.

UTF-8 is a standard for the world wide web. Most browsers, applications, and operating systems are required to support it. It is by far the most popular encoding as of 2012.

2.5.3 UTF-16 and UTF-32

UTF-8 has been superseded by UTF-16, and UTF-32. UTF-16 uses either 2 byte or 4 byte encodings to represents all the Unicode characters. It is primarily used by Java and the Windows operating system. UTF-32 encodes all characters using exactly 32 bits. It is rarely used since it is an inefficient encoding.

2.6 Summary and Further Reading

2.6.1 Summary

Summary 2

1. *In computer architecture, we represent information using the* language of bits. *A bit can either take the value of 0 or 1. A sequence of 8 bits is called a byte.*

2. *A variable representing a bit is also called a Boolean variable, and an algebra on such Boolean variables is known as Boolean algebra.*

3. (a) *The basic operators in Boolean algebra are logical OR, AND, and NOT.*

   (b) *Some derived operators are NAND, NOR, and XOR.*

   (c) *We typically use the De Morgan's laws (see Section 2.1.4) to simplify Boolean expressions.*

4. *Any Boolean expression can be represented in a canonical form as a logical OR of minterms. It can then be minimised using Karnaugh Maps.*

5. *We can represent positive integers in a binary representation by using a sequence of bits. In this case, we represent a number, A, as $x_n x_{n-1} \ldots x_1$, where $A = \sum_{i=1}^{n} x_i 2^{i-1}$.*

---

6. *The four methods to represent a negative integer are:*

   (a) *Sign Magnitude based Method*

   (b) *The 1's Complement Method*

   (c) *Bias based Method*

   (d) *The 2's Complement Method*

7. *The 2's complement method is the most common. Its main properties are as follows:*

   (a) *The representation of a positive integer is the same as its unsigned representation with a leading 0 bit.*

   (b) *The representation of a negative integer $(-u)$ is equal to $2^n - u$, in an n bit number system.*

   (c) *To convert an m-bit 2's complement number to an n-bit 2's complement number, where $n > m$, we need to extend its sign by $n - m$ places.*

   (d) *We can quickly compute the 2's complement of a negative number of the form $-u$ $(u \geq 0)$, by computing the 1's complement of u (flip every bit), and then adding 1.*

   (e) *Addition, subtraction, and multiplication (ignoring overflows) of integers in the 2's complement representation can be done by assuming that the respective binary representations represent unsigned numbers.*

8. *Floating point numbers in the IEEE 754 format are always represented in their normal form.*

   (a) *A floating point number, A, is equal to*

   $$A = (-1)^S \times P \times 2^X$$

   S is the sign bit, P is the significand, and X is the exponent.

   (b) *We assume that the significand is of the form $1 + M$, where $0 \leq M < 1$. M is known as the mantissa.*

9. *The salient points of the IEEE 754 format are as follows:*

   (a) *The MSB is the sign bit.*

   (b) *We have a 8 bit exponent that is represented using the biased notation (bias equal to 127).*

   (c) *We do not represent the leading bit (equal to 1) in the significand. We represent the mantissa using 23 bits.*

   (d) *The exponents, 0 and 255, are reserved for special numbers – denormal numbers, NAN, zero, and $\pm\infty$.*

10. *Denormal numbers are a special class of floating point numbers, that have a slightly different normal form.*
    $$A = (-1)^S \times P \times 2^{-126}, (0 \leq P < 1, P = 0 + M)$$

11. *Floating point arithmetic is always approximate; hence, arithmetic operations can lead to mathematical contradictions.*

12. *We represent pieces of text as a contiguous sequence of characters. A character can either be encoded in the 7 bit ASCII format, or in the Unicode formats that use 1-4 bytes per character.*

2.6.2   Further Reading

Boolean algebra is a field of study by itself. Boolean formulae, logic, and operations form the basis of modern computer science. We touched upon some basic results in this chapter. The reader should refer to [Kohavi and Jha, 2009] for a detailed discussion on Boolean logic, Karnaugh Maps, and a host of other advanced techniques to minimise the number of terms in Boolean expressions. For Boolean logic and algebra, the reader can also consult [Gregg, 1998, Patt and Patel, 2003, Whitesitt, 2010] The next step for the reader is to read more about the synthesis and optimisation of large digital circuits. The book by Giovanni de Michel [Micheli, 1994] can be a very helpful reference in this regard. Number systems such as 2's complement naturally lead to computer arithmetic where we perform complex operations on numbers. The reader should consult the book by Zimmermann [Brent and Zimmermann, 2010]. For learning more about the representation of characters, and strings, especially in different languages, we refer the reader to the unicode standard [uni,].

Exercises

Boolean Logic

Ex. 1 — A, B, C and D are Boolean variables. Prove the following results:

a) $A.B + \overline{A}.B + \overline{B}.C + \overline{B}.\overline{C} = 1$

b) $(\overline{A} + \overline{B}).(\overline{A} + B).(A + \overline{B}.D + C) = \overline{A}.\overline{B}.D + \overline{A}.C$

c) $\overline{\overline{A.\overline{B}} + \overline{B}.C} = A.\overline{C} + B$

d) $A.\overline{B} + \overline{A}.\overline{B} + A.\overline{B}.C.D = \overline{B}$

Ex. 2 — Construct a circuit to compute the following functions using only NOR gates.

a) $\overline{A}$

b) $A + B$

c) $A.B$

d) $A \oplus B$

Ex. 3 — Construct a circuit to compute the following functions using only NAND gates.

a) $\overline{A}$

b) $A + B$

c) $A.B$

d) $A \oplus B$

** **Ex. 4** — Prove that any Boolean function can be realised with just NAND or NOR gates. [HINT: Use the idea of decomposing a function into its set of minterms.]

Ex. 5 — Why are the first and last rows or columns considered to be adjacent in a Karnaugh Map?

Ex. 6 — Minimise the following Boolean functions using a Karnaugh Map.

a) $ABC + AB\overline{C} + \overline{A}BC$

b)$ABCD + A\overline{BC}D + A\overline{D}$

* Ex. 7 — Consider the Karnaugh map of the function $A_1 \oplus A_2 \ldots \oplus A_n$. Prove that it looks like a chess board. Why cannot we minimise this expression further?

Integer Number Systems

Ex. 8 — Convert the following 8 bit binary numbers in 1's complement form to decimal.

a) 01111101

b) 10000000

c) 11111111

d) 00000000

e) 11110101

Ex. 9 — Convert the following unsigned numbers (in the given base) to decimal:

a) $(243)_5$

b) $(77)_8$

c) $(FFA)_{16}$

d) $(100)_4$

e) $(55)_6$

Ex. 10 — Do the following calculations on unsigned binary numbers and write the result as an unsigned binary number.

a) $1100110101 + 1111001101$

b) $110110110 + 10111001$

c) $11101110 - 111000$

d) $10000000 - 111$

Ex. 11 — What are the pros and cons of the 1's complement number system?

Ex. 12 — What are the pros and cons of the sign-magnitude number system?

Ex. 13 — What is a number circle? How is it related to the 2's complement number system?

Ex. 14 — What does the point of discontinuity on the number circle signify?

Ex. 15 — Why is moving k steps on the number circle in a clockwise direction equivalent to moving $2^n - k$ steps in an anti-clockwise direction? Assume that the number circle contains 2^n nodes.

Ex. 16 — What are the advantages of the 2's complement notation over other number systems?

Ex. 17 — Outline a method to quickly compute the 2's complement of a number.

Ex. 18 — Prove the following result in your own words:

$$\mathcal{F}(u - v) \equiv \mathcal{F}(u) + (2^n - \mathcal{F}(v)) \tag{2.29}$$

Ex. 19 — Let us define *sign contraction* to be the reverse of sign extension. What are the rules for converting a 32-bit number to a 16-bit number by using sign contraction? Can we do this conversion all the time without losing information?

Ex. 20 — What are the conditions for detecting an overflow while adding two 2's complement numbers?

Floating Point Number System

Ex. 21 — Describe the IEEE 754 format.

Ex. 22 — Why do we avoid representing the bit to the left of the decimal point in the significand?

Ex. 23 — Define denormal numbers. How do they help to extend the range of normal floating point numbers?

Ex. 24 — In the standard form of a denormal number, why is the exponent term equal to 2^{-126}? Why is it not equal to 2^{-127}?

Ex. 25 — Convert the following floating point numbers into the IEEE 32-bit 754 format. Write your answer in the hexadecimal format.

   a) $-1 * (1.75 * 2^{-29} + 2^{-40} + 2^{-45})$

   b) 52

Ex. 26 — What is the range of positive and negative denormal floating point numbers numbers?

Ex. 27 — What will be the output of the following C code snippet assuming that the fractions are stored in an IEEE 32-bit 754 format:

```
float a=pow(2,-50);
float b=pow(2,-74);
float d=a;
for(i=0; i<100000; i++)
{
        d=d+b;
}
if(d>a)
        printf("%d",1);
else
        printf("%d",2);
```

Ex. 28 — We claim that the IEEE 754 format represents real numbers approximately. Is this statement correct?

* Ex. 29 — Prove that it is not possible to exactly represent $\sqrt{2}$ even if we have an indefinitely large number of bits in the mantissa.

* Ex. 30 — How does having denormal numbers make floating point mathematics slightly more intuitive?

* Ex. 31 — What is the correct way for comparing two floating point numbers for equality?

** **Ex. 32** — Assume that the exponent e is constrained to lie in the range $0 \leq e \leq X$ with a bias of q, and the base is b. The significand is p digits in length. Use an IEEE 754 like encoding. However, you need to devote one digit to store the value to the left of the decimal point in the significand.

a) What are the largest and smallest positive values that can be written in normal form.

b) What are the largest and smallest positive values that can be written in denormal form.

* **Ex. 33** — Most of the floating point numbers cannot be represented accurately in hardware due to the loss of precision. However, if we choose some other representation, we can represent certain kinds of floating point numbers without error.

a) Give a representation for storing rational numbers accurately. Devise a normal form for it.

b) Can other floating point numbers such as $\sqrt{2}$ be represented in a similar way?

Ex. 34 — Design a floating point representation, for a base 3 system on the lines of the IEEE 754 format.

Strings

Ex. 35 — Convert the string "459801" to ASCII. The ASCII representation of 0 is 0x30. Assume that all the numbers are represented in the ASCII format in sequence.

Ex. 36 — Find the Unicode representation for characters in a non-English language, and compare it with the ASCII encoding.

Design Problems

Ex. 37 — In this section, we have minimised Boolean expressions using Karnaugh maps. We solved all our examples manually. This method is not scalable for expressions containing hundreds of variables. Study automated techniques for minimising Boolean expressions such as the Quinn-McCluskey tabulation method. Write a program to implement this method.

3

Assembly Language

Assembly language can broadly be defined as a textual representation of machine instructions. Before building a processor, we need to know about the semantics of different machine instructions, and a rigorous study of assembly language will be of benefit in this regard. An assembly language is specific to an ISA and compiler framework; hence, there are many flavors of assembly languages. In this chapter we shall describe the broad principles underlying different variants of assembly languages, some generic concepts and terms. We will subsequently design our own assembly language, *SimpleRisc* . It is a simple RISC ISA with a few instructions. Subsequently, in Chapter 8, we will design a processor that fully implements this ISA. Thus, the plan for this chapter is as follows. We shall first convince ourselves of the need for assembly language in Section 3.1 from the point of view of both software developers and hardware designers. Then we shall proceed to discuss the generic semantics of assembly languages in Section 3.2. Once, we have a basic understanding of assembly languages, we shall design our own assembly language, *SimpleRisc* , in Section 3.3, and then design a method to encode it using a sequence of 32 bits in Section 3.3.14.

Subsequently, in Chapter 4 we shall describe the ARM assembly language that is meant for ARM based processors, and in Chapter 5, we shall describe the x86 assembly language meant for Intel/AMD processors. In these two chapters, these machine specific assembly languages will be covered in great detail. This chapter is introductory, and creates the framework for a more serious study of different instruction sets and assembly languages.

3.1 Why Assembly Language

3.1.1 Software Developer's Perspective

A human being understands natural languages such as English, Russian, and Spanish. With some additional training a human can also understand computer programming languages such as C or Java. However, a computer is a dumb machine as mentioned in Chapter 1. It is not smart enough to understand commands in a human language such as English, or even a programming language such as C. It only understands zeros and ones. Hence, to program a computer it is necessary to give it a sequence of zeros and ones. Indeed some of the early programmers used to program computers by turning on or off a set of switches. Turning on a switch corresponded to a 1, and turning it off meant a 0. However, for today's massive multi-million line programs, this is not a feasible solution. We need a better method.

Consequently, we need an automatic converter that can convert programs written in high level languages such as C or Java to a sequence of zeros and ones known as *machine code*. Machine code contains a set of instructions known as *machine instructions*. Each machine instruction is a sequence of zeros and ones, and instructs the processor to perform a certain action. A program that can convert a program written in a high level language to machine code is called a *compiler*(see Figure 3.1).

Definition 24

- *A high level programming language such as C or Java uses fairly complex constructs and statements. Each statement in these languages typically corresponds to a multitude of basic machine instructions. These languages are typically independent of the processor's ISA.*

- *A compiler is an executable program that converts a program written in a high level language to a sequence of machine instructions that are encoded using a sequence of zeros and ones.*

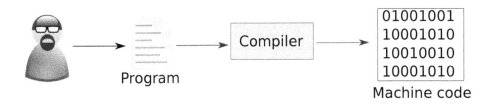

Figure 3.1: The compilation process

Note that the compiler is an executable program that typically runs on the machine that it is supposed to generate machine code for. A natural question that can arise is – who wrote the first compiler? See Trivia 1.

Trivia 1 *Who Wrote the First Compiler? If a programmer wrote the compiler in a high level language such as C or Java, then she must have needed a compiler to compile it into machine code. However, she did not have a compiler with her at that point of time, because she was in the process of building one! Since she did not have a compiler, while building the compiler, how did she ultimately build it? This is an example of a* chicken and egg problem. *The classic chicken and egg problem poses a simple yet vexing question – did the chicken come first or the egg come first? However, the chicken and egg problem has a solution that can be explained in terms of evolution. Scientists believe that early organisms reproduced by replication. At some point of time, due to a genetic mutation, an organism started to lay eggs. These organisms perpetuated, and started reproducing by only laying eggs. They evolved into all kinds of birds and reptiles, including chickens.*

We can explain this conundrum in a similar manner. The early programmers wrote simple compilers using machine instructions. A primitive compiler is just a sequence of zeros and ones. The early programmers then used these primitive compilers to compile programs. A special class of such programs were compilers themselves. They were written in high level languages and were better in terms of features, functionality and even performance. These first generation compilers were then used to create second generation compilers, and this process has continued till date. Nowadays, if a new processor is being developed, then it is not necessary to follow this procedure. Programmers, use another set of programs called cross compilers. *A cross compiler runs on an existing processor, and produces an executable using the machine instructions of the new processor that is being developed. Once the new processor is ready, this program can be moved to the new processor and executed directly. It is thus possible to develop a large range of software including compilers for processors with new instruction sets. Hence, most modern day programmers do not have to write programs using raw machine instructions.*

Definition 25

A cross compiler *is a program that runs on machine A, and generates machine code for machine B. It is possible that B has a different ISA.*

Given the ubiquity of compilers, almost all programs are written in high level languages and compilers are used to convert them to machine code. However, there are important exceptions to this rule. Note that the role of a compiler is two fold. First, it needs to correctly translate a program in a high level language to machine instructions. Second, it needs to produce efficient machine code that does not take a lot of space, and is fast. Consequently, algorithms in compilers have become increasingly complicated over the years. However, it is not always possible to meet these requirements. For example, in some scenarios, compilers might not be able to produce code that is fast enough, or has a certain kind of functionality that the programmer desires. Let us elaborate further. Algorithms in compilers are limited by the amount of analysis that they can perform on the program. For example, we do not want the process of compilation to be extremely slow. A lot of the problems in the area of compilers are computationally difficult to solve and are thus time consuming. Secondly, the compiler is not aware of the broad patterns in the code. For example, it is possible that a certain variable might only take a restricted set of values, and on the basis of this, it might be possible to optimise the machine code further. It is hard for a compiler to figure this out. However, smart programmers can sometimes produce machine code that is more optimal than a compiler because they are aware of some broad patterns of execution, and their brilliant brains can outsmart compilers.

Secondly, it is also possible that a processor vendor might add new instructions in their ISA. In this case, compilers meant for older versions of the processor might not be able to leverage the new instructions. It will be necessary to add them manually in programs. Continuing this argument further, we observe that popular compilers such as gcc (GNU compiler collection) are fairly generic. They do not use all possible machine instructions that a processor provides while generating machine code. Typically, a lot of the missed out instructions are required by operating systems and device drivers (programs that interface with devices such as the printer, and scanner). These software programs require these instructions because they need low level access to the hardware. Consequently, system programmers have a strong incentive to occasionally bypass the compiler.

In all of these situations, it is necessary for programmers to manually embed a sequence of machine instructions in a program. As mentioned, there are two primary reasons for doing so – efficiency and extra functionality. Hence, from the point of view of system software developers, it is necessary to know about machine instructions such that they can be more productive in their job.

Now, our aim is to insulate modern day programmers from the intricate details of zeros and ones. Ideally, we do not want our programmers to program by manually turning on and off switches as was done fifty years ago. Consequently, a low level language called *assembly language* was developed (see Definition 26).

Assembly language is a human readable form of machine code. Each assembly language statement typically corresponds to one machine instruction. Furthermore, it eases the burden on the programmer significantly by not forcing her to remember the exact sequence of zeros/ones that are needed to encode an instruction.

Definition 26

- *A low level programming language uses simple statements that correspond to typically just one machine instruction. These languages are specific to the ISA.*

- *The term "assembly language" refers to a family of low level programming languages that are specific to each ISA. They have a generic structure that consists of a sequence of assembly statements. Typically, each assembly statement has two parts – (1) an instruction code that is a mnemonic for a basic machine instruction, and (2) and a list of operands.*

From a practical standpoint, it is possible to write stand alone assembly programs and convert them to executables using a program called an *assembler*(Definition 27). Alternatively, it is also possible to embed snippets of assembly code in high level languages such as C or C++. The latter is more common. A compiler ensures that it is able to compile the combined program into machine code. The benefits of assembly languages are manifold. Since each line in assembly code corresponds to one machine instruction, it is as expressive as machine code. Because of this one to one mapping, we do not sacrifice efficiency by writing programs in assembly. Secondly, it is a human readable and elegant form of textually representing machine code. It makes it significantly easier to write programs using it, and it is also possible to cleanly embed snippets of assembly code in software written in high level languages such as C. The third advantage of assembly language is that it defines a level of abstraction over and above real machine code. It is possible that two processors might be compatible with the same variant of assembly language, but actually have different machine encodings for the same instruction. In this case, assembly programs will be compatible across both of these processors.

Definition 27
An assembler is an executable program that converts an assembly program into machine code.

Example 20
The core engines of high performance 3D games need to be optimised for speed as much as possible [Phelps and Parks, 2004]. Most compilers fail to produce code that runs fast enough. It becomes necessary for programmers to manually write sequences of machine instructions.

Example 21
Vranas et. al. [Vranas et al., 2006] describe a high performance computing application to study the

structure of an atomic nucleus. Since the computational requirements are high, they needed to run their program on a supercomputer. They observed that the core of the program lies in a small set of functions that are just 1000 lines long. They further observed that compilers were not doing a good in job in optimising the output machine code. Consequently, they decided to write the important functions in assembly code, and obtained record speedups on a supercomputer. Durr et. al. [Durr et al., 2009] subsequently used this framework to accurately calculate the mass of a proton and a neutron from first principles. The results were in complete agreement with experimentally observed values.

3.1.2 Hardware Designer's Perspective

The role of hardware designers is to design processors that can implement all the instructions in the ISA. Their main aim is to design an efficient processor that is optimal with regards to area, power efficiency, and design complexity. From their perspective, the ISA is the crucial link between software and hardware. It answers the basic question for them – "what to build?" Hence, it is very essential for them to understand the precise semantics of different instruction sets such that they can design processors for them. As mentioned in Section 3.1.1, it is cumbersome to look at instructions as merely a sequence of zeros and ones. They can gain a lot by taking a look at the textual representation of a machine instruction, which is an assembly instruction.

An assembly language is specific to an instruction set and an assembler. In this chapter, we use the assembly language format of the popular GNU assembler [Elsner and Fenlason, 1994] to explain the syntax of a typical assembly language file. Note that other systems have similar formats, and the concepts are broadly the same.

3.2   The Basics of Assembly Language

3.2.1   Machine Model

Let us reconsider the basic abstract machine model explained in Chapter 1. We had finished the chapter by describing a form of the Harvard and Von Neumann machines with registers. Assembly languages do not see the instruction memory and data memory as different entities. They assume an abstract Von Neumann machine augmented with registers.

Refer to Figure 3.2 for a pictorial representation of the machine model. The program is stored in a part of the main memory. The central processing unit (CPU) reads out the program instruction by instruction, and executes the instructions appropriately. The program counter keeps track of the memory address of the instruction that a CPU is executing. We typically refer to the program counter using the acronym – PC. Most instructions are expected to get their input operands from registers. Recall that every CPU has a fixed number of registers (typically < 64). However, a large number of instructions, can also get their operands from the memory directly. It is the job of the CPU to co-ordinate the transfers to and from the main memory and registers. Secondly, the CPU also needs to perform all the arithmetic/logical calculations, and liaise with external input/output devices.

Most flavors of assembly language assume this abstract machine model for a majority of their statements. However, since another aim of using assembly language is to have more fine grained and intrusive control of hardware, there are a fair number of assembly instructions that are cognisant of the internals of the processor. These instructions typically modify the behaviour of the processor by changing the behaviour of some key internal algorithms; they modify built-in parameters such as power management settings, or read/write some

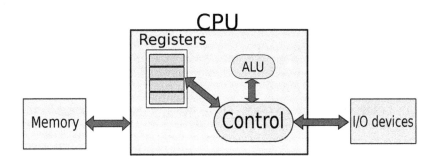

Figure 3.2: The Von Neumann machine with registers

internal data. Finally, note that the assembly language does not distinguish between machine independent and machine dependent instructions.

View of Registers

Every machine has a set of registers that are visible to the assembly programmer. ARM has 16 registers, x86 (32-bit) has 8 registers, and x86_64 (64 bits) has 16 registers. The registers have names. ARM names them $r0 \ldots r15$, and x86 names them $eax, ebx, ecx, edx, esi, edi, ebp$, and esp. A register can be accessed using its name.

In most ISAs, a return address register is used for function calls. Let us assume that a program starts executing a function. It needs to remember the memory address that it needs to come back to after executing the function. This address is known as the *return address*. Before jumping to the starting address of a function, we can save the value of the return address in this register. The return statement can simply be implemented by copying the value saved in the return address register to the PC. The return address register is visible to the programmer in assembly languages such as ARM and MIPS. However, x86 does not use a return address register. It uses another mechanism called a stack, which we shall study in Section 3.3.10.

In an ARM processor, the PC is visible to the programmer and it is the last register ($r15$). It is possible to read the value of the PC, as well as set its value. Setting the value of the PC means that we want to branch to a new location within the program. However, in x86, the program counter is implicit, and is not visible to the programmer.

3.2.2   View of Memory

In Section 1.6.7, we explained the concept of a memory in an abstract machine. The memory can be thought of as one large array of bytes. Each byte has a unique address, which is essentially its location in the array. The address of the first byte is 0, the address of the second byte is 1, and so on. Note that the finest granularity at which we can access memory is at the level of a byte. We do not have a method to uniquely address a given bit. The address is a 32-bit unsigned integer in 32-bit machines and it is a 64-bit unsigned integer in 64-bit machines.

Now, in a Von Neumann machine, we assume that the program is stored in memory as a sequence of bytes, and the program counter points to the next instruction that is going to be executed.

Assuming that memory is one large array of bytes is fine, if all our data items are only one byte long. However, languages such as C and Java have data types of different sizes – char (1 byte), short (2 bytes), integer (4 bytes), and long integer (8 bytes). For a multi-byte data type it is necessary to find a representation for it in memory. There are two possible ways of representing a multibyte data type in memory – *little endian* and *big endian*. Secondly, we also need to find methods to represent arrays or lists of data in memory.

Little Endian and Big Endian Representations

Let us consider the problem of storing an integer in locations 0-3. Let the integer be 0x87654321. It can be broken into four bytes – 87, 65, 43, and 21. One option is to store the most significant byte, 87, in the lowest memory address 0. The next location can store 65, then 43, and then 21. This is called the *big endian* representation because we are starting from the position of the most significant byte. In comparison, we can save the least significant byte first in location 0, and then continue to save the most significant byte in location 3. This representation is called *little endian*. Figure 3.3 shows the difference.

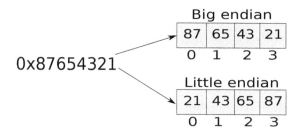

Figure 3.3: Big endian and little endian representations

There is as such no reason to prefer one representation over the other. It depends on the convention. For example, x86 processors use the little endian format. Early versions of ARM processors used to be little endian. However, now they are bi-endian. This means an ARM processor can work as both a little endian and a big endian machine depending on the settings set by the user. Traditionally, IBM® POWER® processors, and Sun® SPARC® processors have been big endian.

Representing Arrays

An array is a linearly ordered set of objects, where an object can be a simple data type such as an integer or character, or can be a complex data type also.

```
int a[100];
char c[100];
```

Let us consider a simple array of integers, a. If the array has 100 entries, then the total size of the array in memory is equal to $100 \times 4 = 400$ bytes. If the starting memory location of the array is *loc*. Then $a[0]$ is stored in the locations $(loc+0), (loc+1), (loc+2), (loc+3)$. Note that there are two methods of saving the data – big endian and little endian. The next array entry, $a[1]$, is saved in the locations $(loc+4) \ldots (loc+7)$. By continuing the argument further, we note that the entry $a[i]$ is saved in the locations – $(loc+4 \times i) \ldots (loc+4 \times i+3)$.

Most programming languages define multidimensional arrays of the form:

```
int a[100][100];
char c[100][100];
```

They are typically represented as regular one dimensional arrays in memory. There is a mapping function between the location in a multidimensional array and an equivalent 1-dimensional array. Let us consider Example 22. We can extend the scheme to consider multidimensional arrays of dimensions greater than 2.

Example 22
Consider a multidimensional array: $a[100][100]$. Map each entry (i,j) to an entry in a 1-D array: $b[10000]$.

Answer: *Let us assume that each entry (i,j), is in a (row,column) format. Let us try to save the array in row-major fashion. We save the first row in contiguous locations, then the second row and so on. The starting entry of each row is equal to $100 \times i$. Within each row the offset for column j is equal to j. Thus we can map (i,j) to the entry: $(100 \times i + j)$ in the array b.*

We observe that a two-dimensional array can be saved as a one dimensional array by saving it in row-major fashion. This means that data is saved row wise. We save the first row, then the second row, and so on. Likewise, it is also possible to save a multidimensional array in column major fashion, where the first column is saved, then the second column and so on.

Definition 28

row major *In this representation, an array is saved row wise in memory.*

column major *In this representation, an array is saved column wise in memory.*

3.2.3 Assembly Language Syntax

In this section, we shall describe the syntax of assembly language. The exact syntax of an assembly file is dependent on the assembler. Different assemblers can use different syntax, even though they might agree on the basic instructions, and their operand formats. In this chapter, we explain the syntax of the GNU family of assembly languages. They are designed for the GNU assembler, which is a part of the GNU compiler collection (gcc). Like all GNU software, this assembler and the associated compiler is freely available for most platforms. As of 2012, the assembler is available at [gnu.org,]. In this section, we shall provide a brief overview of the format of assembly files. For additional details refer to the official manual of the GNU assembler [Elsner and Fenlason, 1994]. Note that other assemblers such as NASM, and MASM, have their own formats. However, the overall structure is not conceptually very different from what we shall describe in this section.

Assembly Language File Structure

An assembly file is a regular text file, and it has a (.s) suffix. The reader can quickly generate an assembly file for a C program (test.c), if she has the gcc (GNU Compiler) installed. It can be generated by issuing the following command.

```
gcc -S test.c
```

The generated assembly file will be named test.s. GNU assembly files have a very simple structure, as shown in Figure 3.4. They contain a list of sections. Examples of different sections are text (actual program),

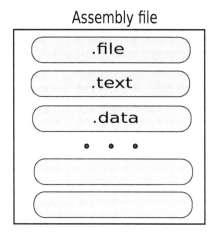

Figure 3.4: Assembly language file structure

data (data with initialised values), and bss (common data that is initialised to 0). Each section starts with a section heading, which is the name of the section prefixed by the '.' symbol. For example, the text section starts with the line ".text". Thereafter, there is a list of assembly language statements. Each statement is typically terminated by the newline character. Likewise, the data section contains a list of data values. An assembly file begins with the file section that contains a line of the form – ".file <name of the file> ". When we are generating an assembly file from a C program using the gcc compiler, the name of the file in the .file section is typically the same as our original C program (test.c). The text section is mandatory, and the rest of the sections are optional. There might be one or more data sections. It is also possible to define new sections using the .section directive. In this book, we primarily concentrate on the text section because we are interested in learning about the nature of the instruction set. Let us now look at the format of assembly statements.

Basic Statements

A bare bones assembly language statement specifies an assembly instruction and has two parts – the instruction and its list of operands, as shown in Figure 3.5. The instruction is a textual identifier of the actual machine instruction. The list of operands contains the value or location of each operand. The value of an operand is a numeric constant. It is also known as an *immediate* value. The operand locations can either be register locations or memory locations.

Figure 3.5: Assembly language statement

Definition 29
In computer architecture, a constant value specified in an instruction is also known as an immediate.

Now, let us consider an example.

```
add r3, r1, r2
```

In this ARM assembly statement, the *add* instruction is specifying the fact that we wish to add two numbers and save the result in some pre-specified location. The format of the add instruction in this case is as follows: $< instruction > < destination\,register > < operand\,register\,1 > < operand\,register\,2 >$. The name of the instruction is *add*, the destination register is $r3$, the operand registers are $r1$ and $r2$. The detailed steps of the instruction are as follows:

1. Read the value of register $r1$. Let us refer to the value as v_1.

2. Read the value of register $r2$. Let us refer to the value as v_2.

3. Compute $v_3 = v_1 + v_2$.

4. Save v_3 in register $r3$

Let us now give an example of two more instructions that work in a similar fashion(see Example 23).

Example 23
sub r3, r1, r2
mul r3, r1, 3

The *sub* instructions subtracts two numbers stored in registers, and the *mul* instruction multiplies a number stored in the register, $r1$, with the numeric constant, 3. Both the instructions save the result in the register, $r3$. Their mode of operation is similar to the *add* instruction. Moreover, the arithmetic instructions – *add*, *sub*, and *mul* – are also known as data processing instructions. There are several other classes of instructions such as data transfer instructions that load or store values from memory, and control instructions that implement branching.

Generic Statement Structure

The generic structure of an assembly statement is shown in Figure 3.6. It consists of three fields namely a label (identifier of the instruction), the key (an assembly instruction, or a directive to the assembler), and a comment. All three of these fields are optional. However, any assembly statement needs to have at least one of these fields.

A statement can optionally begin with a label. A *label* is a textual identifier for the statement. In other words, a label uniquely identifies an assembly statement in an assembly file. Note that we are not allowed to repeat labels in the same assembly file. We shall find labels to be very useful while implementing branch instructions.

Definition 30
A label in an assembly file uniquely identifies a given point or data item in the assembly program.

An example of a label is shown in Example 24. Here the name of the label is "label1", and it is succeeded by a colon. After the label we have written an assembly instruction and given it a list of operands. A label can consist of valid alpha-numeric characters $[a-z][A-Z][0-9]$ and the symbols '.', '_', and '$'. Typically, we cannot start a label with a digit. After specifying a label we can keep the line empty, or we can specify a key (part of an assembly statement). If the key begins with a '.', then it is an assembler directive, which is valid for all computers. It directs the assembler to perform a certain action. This action can include starting a new section, or declaring a constant. The directive can also take a list of arguments. If the key begins with a letter, then it is a regular assembly instruction.

Example 24
label1: add r1, r2, r3

After the label, assembly instruction, and list of operands, it is possible to optionally insert comments. The GNU assembler supports two types of comments. We can insert regular C or Java style comments enclosed between /* and */. It is also possible to have a small single line comment by preceding the comment with the '@' character in ARM assembly.

Example 25

```
label1: add r1, r2, r3 @ Add the values in r2 and r3
label2: add r3, r4, r5 @ Add the values in r4 and r5
add r5, r6, r7          /* Add the values in r6 and r7 */
```

Let us not slightly amend our statement regarding labels. It is possible that an assembly statement only contains a label, and does not contain a key. In this case, the label essentially points to an empty statement, which is not very useful. Hence, the assembler assumes that in such a case a label points to the nearest succeeding assembly statement that contains a key.

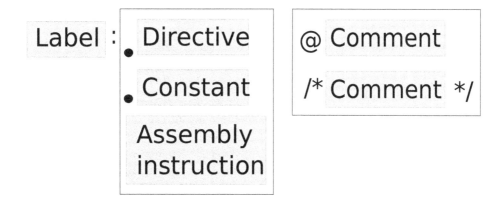

Figure 3.6: Generic Structure of an assembly statement

3.2.4 Types of Instructions

Classification by Functionality

The four major types of instructions are as follows:

1. **Data Processing Instructions:** Data processing instructions are typically arithmetic instructions such as add, subtract, and multiply, or logical instructions that compute bitwise or, and exclusive or. Comparison instructions also belong to this family.

2. **Data Transfer Instructions:** These instructions transfer values between two locations. A location can be a register or a memory address.

3. **Branch Instructions:** Branch instructions help the processor's control unit to jump to different parts of the program based on the values of operands. They are useful in implementing *for* loops and *if-then-else* statements.

4. **Exception Generating Instructions:** These specialised instructions help transfer control from a user level program to the operating system.

In this book we shall cover data processing, data transfer, and control instructions.

Classification based on the Number of Operands

As mentioned in Section 3.2.3, all assembly language statements in the GNU assembler have the same structure. They start with the name of the instruction, and are succeeded by a list of operands. We can classify instructions based on the number of operands that they require. If an instruction requires n operands, then we typically say that it is in the n-address format. For example, an instruction that does not require any operands is a 0-address format instruction. If it requires 3 operands, then it is a 3-address format instruction.

Definition 31

If an instruction requires n operands (including source and destination), then we say that it is a n-address format instruction.

In ARM most of the data processing instructions are in the 3-address format, and data transfer instructions are in the 2-address format. However, in x86 most of the instructions are in the 2-address format. The first question that comes to our mind is what is the logic of having a 3-address format instruction versus having a 2-address format instruction? There must be some tradeoff here.

Let us outline some general rules of thumb. If an instruction has more operands then it will require more bits to represent the instruction. Consequently, we will require more resources to store, and handle instructions. However, there is a flip side to this argument. Having more operands will also make the instruction more generic and flexible. It will make the life of compiler writers and assembly programmers much easier, because it will be possible to do more things with an instruction that uses more operands. The reverse logic applies to instructions that take less operands. They take less space to store, and are less flexible. Let us consider an example. Assume that we are trying to add two numbers, 3 and 5, to produce a result, 8.

An ARM instruction for addition would look like this:

```
add r3, r1, r2
```

This instruction adds the contents of registers, $r1(3)$, and $r2(5)$, and saves it in $r3(8)$. However, an x86 instruction would look like this:

```
add edx, eax
```

Here, we assume that *edx* contains 3, and *eax* contains 5. The addition is performed, and the result, 8, is stored back in *edx*. Thus, in this case the x86 instruction is in the 2-address format because the destination register is the same as the first source register.

When we describe the details of the ARM and x86 instruction sets in Chapters 4 and 5, we shall see many more examples of instructions that have different address formats. We will be able to appreciate the tradeoffs of having different address formats in all their glory.

3.2.5   Types of Operands

Let us now look at the different types of operands. The method of specifying and accessing an operand in an assembly statement is known as the **addressing mode**.

Definition 32

The method of specifying and accessing an operand in an assembly statement is known as the addressing mode.

The simplest way of specifying an operand is by embedding its value in the instruction. Most assembly languages allow the user to specify the values of integer constants as an operand. This addressing mode is known as the *immediate* addressing mode. This method is very useful for initialising registers or memory locations, or for performing arithmetic operations.

Once the requisite set of constants have been loaded into registers and memory locations, the program needs to proceed by operating on registers and memory locations. There are several addressing modes in this space. Before introducing them, let us introduce some extra terminology in the form of the *register transfer notation*.

Register Transfer Notation

This notation allows us to specify the semantics of instructions and operands. Let us look at the various methods to represent the basic actions of instructions.

$$r1 \leftarrow r2$$

This expression has two register operands $r1$, and $r2$. $r1$ is the destination register, and $r2$ is the source register. We are transferring the contents of register $r2$ to register $r1$.

We can specify an add operation with a constant as follows:

$$r1 \leftarrow r2 + 4$$

We can also specify operations on registers using this notation. We are adding the contents of $r2$ and $r3$ and saving the result in $r1$.

$$r1 \leftarrow r2 + r3$$

It is also possible to represent memory accesses using this notation.

$$r1 \leftarrow [r2]$$

In this case the memory address is saved in $r2$. The processor hardware fetches the memory address in $r2$, accesses the location, fetches the contents of the memory location, and saves the data item in $r1$. Let us assume that the value in $r2$ is 100. In this case the processor accesses memory with address 100, fetches the integer saved in locations (100-103), and saves it in $r1$. By default we assume that we are loading and saving integers.

We can also specify a more complicated memory address of the form:

$$r1 \leftarrow [r2 + 4]$$

Here, the memory address is equal to the contents of the register $r2$ plus 4. We fetch the integer starting at the contents of this memory address, and save it in the register $r1$.

Generic Addressing Modes for Operands

Let us represent the value of an operand as V. In the subsequent discussion, we use expressions such as $V \leftarrow r1$. This does not mean that we have a new storage location called V. It basically means that the value of an operand is specified by the RHS (right hand side). Let us briefly take a look at some of the most commonly used addressing modes with examples.

immediate $V \leftarrow imm$
> Uses the constant imm as the value of the operand.

register $V \leftarrow r1$
> In this addressing mode, the processor uses the value contained in a register as the operand.

register-indirect $V \leftarrow [r1]$
> The register saves the address of the memory location that contains the value.

base-offset $V \leftarrow [r1 + offset]$
> $offset$ is a constant. The processor fetches the base memory address from $r1$, adds the constant $offset$ to it, and accesses the new memory location to fetch the value of the operand. The $offset$ is also known as the *displacement*.

base-index $V \leftarrow [r1 + r2]$
> $r1$ is the base register, and $r2$ is the index register. The memory address is equal to $(r1 + r2)$.

base-index-offset $V \leftarrow [r1 + r2 + offset]$
> The memory address that contains the value is $(r1 + r2 + offset)$, where $offset$ is a constant.

memory-direct $V \leftarrow addr$
> The value is contained in memory starting from address $addr$. $addr$ is a constant. In this case the memory address is directly embedded in the instruction.

memory-indirect $V \leftarrow [[r1]]$
> The value is present in a memory location, whose address is contained in the memory location, M. Furthermore, the address of M is contained in the register, $r1$.

PC-relative $V \leftarrow [PC + offset]$

Here, $offset$ is a constant. The memory address is computed to be $PC + offset$, where PC represents the value contained in the PC. This addressing mode is useful for branch instructions.

Let us introduce a new term called the *effective memory address* by considering the base-offset addressing mode. The memory address is equal to the contents of the base register plus the offset. The computed memory address is known as the *effective memory address*. We can similarly define the effective address for other addressing modes in the case of memory operands. .

Definition 33

The memory address specified by an operand is known as the effective memory address.

3.3 *SimpleRisc*

In this book, we shall introduce a simple, generic, complete and concise RISC ISA called *SimpleRisc* . The assembly language of *SimpleRisc* has just 21 instructions, and captures most of the features of full scale assembly languages. We will use *SimpleRisc* to demonstrate the flavour of different types of assembly programs, and also design a processor for the *SimpleRisc* ISA in Chapter 8. We shall assume that *SimpleRisc* assembly follows the GNU assembly format, and we shall only describe the text section in this book.

Before proceeding further, let us take a tour of different instruction sets, and take a look at their properties.

3.3.1 Different Instruction Sets

In Chapter 1, we looked at properties of different instruction sets including necessary, and desirable properties. In this book, we shall describe two real instruction sets namely the *ARM* instruction set and x86 instruction set. ARM stands for "Advanced RISC Machines". It is an iconic company based out of Cambridge, UK. As of 2012, around 90% of mobile devices including the Apple iPhone, and iPad, run on ARM based processors. Similarly, as of 2012, more than 90% of the desktops and laptops run on Intel or AMD based x86 processors. ARM is a RISC instruction set, and x86 is a CISC instruction set.

There are many other instruction sets tailored for a wide variety of processors. Another popular instruction set for mobile computers is the MIPS instruction set. MIPS based processors are also used in a wide variety of processors used in automobiles, and industrial electronics.

For large servers, typically IBM (PowerPC), Sun (now Oracle)(UltraSparc), or HP (PA-RISC) processors are used. Each of these processor families has its own instruction set. These instruction sets are typically RISC instruction sets. Most ISAs share simple instructions such as add, subtract, multiply, shifts, and load/store instructions. However, beyond this simple set, they use a large number of more specialised instructions. As we shall see in the next few chapters, choosing the right set of instructions in an ISA is dependent on the target market of the processor, the nature of the workload, and many design time constraints. Table 3.1 shows a list of popular instruction sets. The *SimpleRisc* ISA is conceptually the closest to ARM and MIPS; however, it has some significant differences also.

3.3.2 Model of the *SimpleRisc* Machine

SimpleRisc assumes that we have 16 registers numbered $r0 \ldots r15$. The first 14 registers are general purpose registers, and can be used for any purpose within the program. Register $r14$ is known as the stack pointer.

ISA	Type	Year	Vendor	Bits	Endianness	Registers
VAX	CISC	1977	DEC	32	little	16
SPARC	RISC	1986	Sun	32	big	32
	RISC	1993	Sun	64	bi	32
PowerPC	RISC	1992	Apple,IBM,Motorola	32	bi	32
	RISC	2002	Apple,IBM	64	bi	32
PA-RISC	RISC	1986	HP	32	big	32
	RISC	1996	HP	64	big	32
m68000	CISC	1979	Motorola	16	big	16
	CISC	1979	Motorola	32	big	16
MIPS	RISC	1981	MIPS	32	bi	32
	RISC	1999	MIPS	64	bi	32
Alpha	RISC	1992	DEC	64	bi	32
x86	CISC	1978	Intel,AMD	16	little	8
	CISC	1985	Intel,AMD	32	little	8
	CISC	2003	Intel,AMD	64	64 little	16
ARM	RISC	1985	ARM	32	bi (little default)	16
	RISC	2011	ARM	64	bi (little default)	31

Table 3.1: List of instruction sets

We shall also refer to it as *sp*. Register $r15$ is known as the return address register, and it will also be referred as *ra*. We shall discuss *sp* and *ra*, when we discuss how to implement functions in *SimpleRisc* . Each register is 32 bits wide. We assume a special internal register called *flags*, which is not visible to the programmer. It contains two fields *flags.E*(equal) and *flags.GT*(greater than). E is set to 1 if the result of a comparison is equality, and GT is set to 1 if a comparison concludes that the first operand is greater than the second operand. The default values of both the fields are 0.

Each instruction is encoded into a 32-bit value, and it requires 4 bytes of storage in memory.

SimpleRisc assumes a memory model similar to the Von Neumann machine augmented with registers as described in Section 1.7.3. The memory is a large array of bytes. A part of it saves the program and the rest of the memory is devoted to storing data. We assume that multibyte data types such as integers are saved in the little endian format.

3.3.3   Register Transfer Instruction – *mov*

The *mov* instruction is a 2-address format instruction that can transfer values from one register to another, or can load a register with a constant. Our convention is to always have the destination register at the beginning. Refer to Table 3.2. The size of the signed immediate operand is limited to 16 bits. Hence, its range is between -2^{15} to $2^{15} - 1$.

Semantics	Example	Explanation
mov *reg*, (*reg*/*imm*)	mov r1, r2	$r1 \leftarrow r2$
	mov r1, 3	$r1 \leftarrow 3$

Table 3.2: Semantics of the *mov* instruction

3.3.4 Arithmetic Instructions

SimpleRisc has 6 arithmetic instructions – *add*, *sub*, *mul*, *div*, *mod*, and *cmp*. The connotations of *add*, *sub*, and *mul* are self explanatory (also see Table 3.3). For arithmetic instructions, we assume that the first operand in the list of operands is the destination register. The second operand is the first source operand, and the third operand is the second source operand. The first and second operands need to be registers, whereas the last operand (second source register) can be an immediate value.

Semantics	Example	Explanation
add *reg, reg, (reg/imm)*	add r1, r2, r3	$r1 \leftarrow r2 + r3$
	add r1, r2, 10	$r1 \leftarrow r2 + 10$
sub *reg, reg, (reg/imm)*	sub r1, r2, r3	$r1 \leftarrow r2 - r3$
mul *reg, reg, (reg/imm)*	mul r1, r2, r3	$r1 \leftarrow r2 \times r3$
div *reg, reg, (reg/imm)*	r1, r2, r3	$r1 \leftarrow r2/r3$ (quotient)
mod *reg, reg, (reg/imm)*	mod r1, r2, r3	$r1 \leftarrow r2 \bmod r3$ (remainder)
cmp *reg, (reg/imm)*	cmp r1, r2	set flags

Table 3.3: Semantics of arithmetic instructions in *SimpleRisc*

Example 26
Write assembly code in SimpleRisc to compute: 31 * 29 - 50, and save the result in r4.
Answer:

```
———————————————————— SimpleRisc ————————————————————
mov r1, 31
mov r2, 29
mul r3, r1, r2
sub r4, r3, 50
```

The *div* instruction divides the first source operand by the second source operand, computes the quotient, and saves it in the destination register. For example it will compute 30/7 to be 4. The *mod* instruction computes the remainder of a division. For example, it will compute 30 *mod* 7 as 2.

Example 27
Write assembly code in SimpleRisc to compute: 31 / 29 - 50, and save the result in r4.
Answer:

```
———————————————————— SimpleRisc ————————————————————
mov r1, 31
mov r2, 29
div r3, r1, r2
sub r4, r3, 50
```

The *cmp* instruction is a 2-address instruction that takes two source operands. The first source operand needs to be a register, and the second one can be an immediate or a register. It compares both the operands by subtracting the second from the first. If the operands are equal, or in other words the result of the subtraction is zero, then it sets $flags.E$ to 1. Otherwise $flags.E$ is set to 0. If the first operand is greater than the second operand, then the result of the subtraction will be positive. In this case, the cmp instruction sets $flags.GT$ to 1, otherwise it sets it to 0. We will require these flags when we implement branch instructions.

3.3.5 Logical Instructions

SimpleRisc has three logical instructions – *and*, *or*, and *not*. *and* and *or* are 3-address instructions. They compute the bitwise AND and OR of two values respectively. The *not* instruction is a 2-address instruction that computes the bitwise complement of a value. Note that the source operand of the *not* instruction can be an immediate or a register. Refer to Table 3.4.

Semantics	Example	Explanation
and *reg*, *reg*, (*reg/imm*)	and r1, r2, r3	$r1 \leftarrow r2 \wedge r3$
or *reg*, *reg*, (*reg/imm*)	or r1, r2, r3	$r1 \leftarrow r2 \vee r3$
not *reg*, (*reg/imm*)	not r1, r2	$r1 \leftarrow \sim r2$
$\wedge$ bitwise AND, $\vee$ bitwise OR, $\sim$ logical complement		

Table 3.4: Semantics of logical instructions in *SimpleRisc*

Example 28

Compute $\overline{(a \vee b)}$. Assume that a is stored in $r0$, and b is stored in $r1$. Store the result in $r2$.
Answer:

──────────────────── SimpleRisc ────────────────────
```
or r3, r0, r1
not r2, r3
```

3.3.6 Shift Instructions – *lsl*, *lsr*, *asr*

SimpleRisc has three types of shift instructions *lsl* (logical shift left), *lsr* (logical shift right), and *asr* (arithmetic shift right). Each of these instructions are in the 3-address format. The first source operand points to the source register, and the second source operand contains the shift amount. The second operand can either be a register or an immediate value.

The *lsl* instruction shifts the value in the first source register to the left Similarly, *lsr*, shifts the value in the first source register to the right. Note that it is a logical right shift. This means that it fills all the MSB positions with zeros. In comparison, *asr*, performs an arithmetic right shift. It fills up all the MSB positions with the value of the previous sign bit. Semantics of shift instructions are shown in Table 3.5.

3.3.7 Data Transfer Instructions: *ld* and *st*

SimpleRisc has two data transfer instructions – load(*ld*) and store(*st*). The load instructions loads values from memory into registers, and the store instruction saves values in registers to memory locations. Examples and semantics are shown in Table 3.6.

Semantics	Example	Explanation
lsl *reg, reg, (reg/imm)*	lsl r3, r1, r2	$r3 \leftarrow r1 \ll r2$ (shift left)
	lsl r3, r1, 4	$r3 \leftarrow r1 \ll 4$ (shift left)
lsr *reg, reg, (reg/imm)*	lsr r3, r1, r2	$r3 \leftarrow r1 \ggg r2$ (shift right logical)
	lsr r3, r1, 4	$r3 \leftarrow r1 \ggg 4$ (shift right logical)
asr *reg, reg, (reg/imm)*	asr r3, r1, r2	$r3 \leftarrow r1 \gg r2$ (arithmetic shift right)
	asr r3, r1, 4	$r3 \leftarrow r1 \gg 4$ (arithmetic shift right)

Table 3.5: Semantics of shift instructions in *SimpleRisc*

Semantics	Example	Explanation
ld *reg, imm[reg]*	ld r1, 12[r2]	$r1 \leftarrow [r2 + 12]$
st *reg, imm[reg]*	st r1, 12[r2]	$[r2 + 12] \leftarrow r1$

Table 3.6: Semantics of load-store instructions in *SimpleRisc*

Let us consider the load instruction: *ld* $r1, 12[r2]$. Here, we are computing the memory address as the sum of the contents of $r2$ and the number 12. The *ld* instructions accesses this memory address, fetches the stored integer and stores it in $r1$. We assume that the computed memory address points to the first stored byte of the integer. Since we assume a little endian representation, the memory address contains the LSB. The details are shown in Figure 3.7(a).

The store operation does the reverse. It stores the value of $r1$ into the memory address $(r2 + 12)$. Refer to Figure 3.7(b).

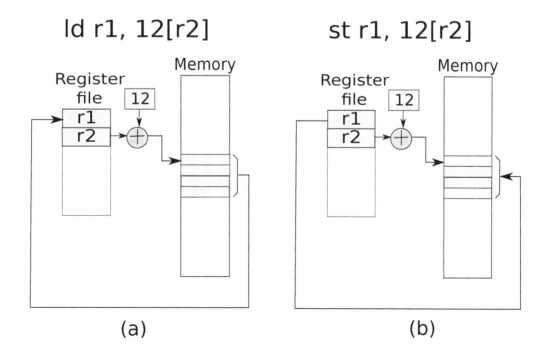

Figure 3.7: Load and store operations in *SimpleRisc*

3.3.8 Unconditional Branch Instructions

SimpleRisc has one unconditional branch instruction, *b*, which makes the program counter jump to the address corresponding to a label in the code. It takes a single operand, which is a label in the program. Its semantics is shown in Table 3.7.

Semantics	Example	Explanation
b *label*	b .foo	branch to .foo

Table 3.7: Semantics of unconditional branch instructions in *SimpleRisc*

Let us explain its operation with the help of a simple example, as shown below.

```
add r1, r2, r3
b .foo
...
...
.foo:
        add r3, r1, r4
```

In this example, we add the values of $r2$, and $r3$, and then save the result in $r1$. After that, the processor jumps to the code pointed to by the label, *.foo*. It proceeds to execute the code after the label, *.foo*. It starts out by executing the instruction $add\ r3, r1, r4$. It then proceeds to execute subsequent instructions.

3.3.9 Conditional Branch Instructions

SimpleRisc has two conditional branch instructions – *beq* and *bgt*. Real world instruction sets typically have more branch instructions. Nonetheless, at the cost of code size, these two instructions are sufficient for implementing all types of branches.

The *beq* instruction stands for "branch if equal". This means that if any preceding *cmp* instruction has set the E flag, then the PC will branch to the label specified in this instruction. Otherwise, the branch is said to fail, and the processor will proceed to execute the instruction after the branch. Similarly, the *bgt* instruction stands for "branch if greater than". This branch instruction bases its outcome on the value of the GT flag. It if is set to 1, then it branches to the label specified in the branch instruction, otherwise the processor executes the next instruction after the branch. Refer to Table 3.8.

Semantics	Example	Explanation
beq *label*	beq .foo	branch to .foo if $flags.E = 1$
bgt *label*	bgt .foo	branch to .foo if $flags.GT = 1$

Table 3.8: Semantics of ranch instructions in *SimpleRisc*

Example 29

Write an iterative program to compute the factorial of a number stored in r0. Assume that the number is greater than 2. Save the result in r1.

Answer: *Let us first take a look at a small C program to compute the factorial of the variable num.*

```C
                              ─────── C ───────
int prod = 1;
int idx;
for(idx = num; idx > 1; idx --) {
        prod = prod * idx
}
```

Let us now try to convert this program to SimpleRisc .

```SimpleRisc
                         ─────── SimpleRisc ───────
mov r1, 1              /* prod = 1 */
mov r2, r0            /* idx = num */
.loop:
        mul r1, r1, r2  /* prod = prod * idx */
        sub r2, r2, 1   /* idx = idx - 1 */
        cmp r2, 1       /* compare (idx, 1) */
        bgt .loop       /* if (idx > 1) goto .loop*/
```

Example 30 *Write an assembly program to find out if the number stored in r1 is a prime number. Assume that it is greater than 3. Save the Boolean result in r0.*

Answer:

```SimpleRisc
                         ─────── SimpleRisc ───────
    mov r2, 2
.loop:
    mod r3, r1, r2    @ divide number by r2
    cmp r3, 0         @ compare the result with 0
    beq .notprime     @ if the result is 0, not prime
    add r2, r2, 1     @ increment r2
    cmp r1, r2        @ compare r2 with the number
    bgt .loop         @ iterate if r2 is smaller

mov r0, 1             @ number is prime
b .exit               @ exit

.notprime:
    mov r0, 0         @ number is not prime

.exit:
```

Example 31 *Write an assembly program to find the least common multiple (LCM) of two positive numbers stored in r1 and r2. Save the result in r0.*

Answer:

```
————————————————————————————————— SimpleRisc —————
@ let the numbers be A(r1) and B(r2)

@ iterate
    mov r3, 1          @ idx = 1
    mov r4, r1         @ L = A

.loop:
    mod r5, r4, r2     @ L = A % B
    cmp r5, 0          @ compare mod with 0
    beq .lcm           @ LCM found (L is the LCM)
    add r3, r3, 1      @ increment idx
    mul r4, r1, r3     @ L = A * idx
    b .loop

.lcm:
    mov r0, r4         @ result is equal to L
```

3.3.10 Functions

Now, that we have seen generic instructions, operands, and addressing modes, let us come to one of the most advanced features in high level programming languages that makes their structure extremely modular namely *functions* (also referred to as subroutines or procedures in some languages). If the same piece of code is used at different points in a program, then it can be encapsulated in a function. The following example shows a function in C to add two numbers.

```
int addNumbers(int a, int b) {
        return (a+b);
}
```

Calling and Returning from Functions

Let us now go over the basic requirements to implement a simple function. Let us assume that an instruction with address A *calls* a function foo. After executing function foo, we need to come back to the instruction immediately after the instruction at A. The address of this instruction is $A + 4$ (if we assume that the instruction at A is 4 bytes long). This process is known as *returning from a function*, and the address $(A+4)$ is known as the *return address*.

Definition 34
Return address: It is the address of the instruction that a process needs to branch to after executing a function.

Thus, there are two fundamental aspects of implementing a function. The first is the process of invoking or calling a function, and the second aspect deals with returning from a function.

Let us consider the process of calling a function in bit more detail. A function is essentially a block of assembly code. Calling a function is essentially making the PC point to the start of this block of code. We have already seen a method to implement this functionality when we discussed branch instructions. We can associate a label with every function. The label should be associated with the first instruction in a function. Calling a function is as simple as branching to the label at the beginning of a function. However, this is only a part of the story. We need to implement the return functionality as well. Hence, we cannot use an unconditional branch instruction to implement a function call.

Let us thus propose a dedicated function call instruction that branches to the beginning of a function, and simultaneously saves the address that the function needs to return to (referred to as the return address). Let us consider the following C code, and assume that each C statement corresponds to one line of assembly code.

```
a = foo(); /* Line 1 */
c = a + b; /* Line 2 */
```

In this small code snippet, we use a function call instruction to call the *foo* function. The return address is the address of the instruction in Line 2. It is necessary for the call instruction to save the return address in a dedicated storage location such that it can be retrieved later. Most RISC instruction sets (including *SimpleRisc*) have a dedicated register known as the return address register to save the return address. The return address register gets automatically populated by a function *call* instruction. When we need to return from a function, we need to branch the address contained in the return address register. In *SimpleRisc* , we devote register 15 to save the return address, and refer to it as *ra*.

What happens if *foo* calls another function? In this case, the value in *ra* will get overwritten. We will look at this issue later. Let us now consider the problem of passing arguments to a function, and getting return values back.

Passing Arguments and Return Values

Assume that a function *foo* invokes a function *foobar*. *foo* is called the *caller*, and *foobar* is called the *callee*. Note that the caller-callee relationships are not fixed. It is possible for *foo* to call *foobar*, and also possible for *foobar* to call *foo* in the same program. The caller and callee are decided for a single function call based on which function is invoking the other.

Definition 35

caller *A function, foo, that has called another function, foobar.*

callee *A function, foobar, that has been called by another function, foo.*

Both the caller and the callee see the same view of registers. Consequently, we can pass arguments through the registers, and likewise pass the return values through registers also. However, there are several issues in this simple idea as we enumerate below (Assume that we have 16 registers).

1. A function can take more than 16 arguments. This is more than the number of general purpose registers that we have. Hence, we need to find a extra space to save the arguments.

Figure 3.8: Function *foo* as a black box.

2. A function can return a large amount of data, for example, a large structure in C. It might not be possible for this piece of data to fit in registers.

3. The callee might overwrite registers that the caller might require in the future.

We thus observe that passing arguments and return values through registers works only for simple cases. It is not a very flexible and generic solution. Nonetheless, there are two requirements that emerge from our discussion.

Space Problem We need extra space to send and return more arguments.

Overwrite Problem We need to ensure that the callee does not overwrite the registers of the caller.

To solve both the problems, we need to take a deeper look at how functions really work. We can think of a function – *foo* – as a black box to begin with. It takes a list of arguments and returns a set of values. To perform its job, *foo* can take one nano-second, or one week, or even one year. *foo* might call other functions to do its job, send data to I/O devices, and access memory locations. Let us visualise the function, *foo*, in Figure 3.8.

To summarise, a generic function processes the arguments, reads and writes values from memory and I/O devices if required, and then returns the result. Regarding memory and I/O devices, we are not particularly concerned at this point of time. There is a large amount of memory available, and space is not a major constraint. Reading and writing I/O devices is also typically not associated with space constraints. The main issue is with registers, because they are in short supply.

Let us solve the **space problem** first. We can transfer values through both registers and memory. For simplicity, if we need to transfer a small amount of data, we can use registers, otherwise we can transfer them through memory. Similarly, for return values, we can transfer values through memory. We are not limited by space constraints if we use memory to transfer data. However, this approach suffers from lack of flexibility. This is because there has to be strict agreement between the caller and the callee regarding the memory locations to be used. Note that we cannot use a fixed set of memory locations, because it is possible for the callee to recursively call itself.

```
───────────────────────── recursive function call ─────────────────────────
foobar() {
    ...
    foobar();
    ...
}
```

An astute reader might argue that it is possible for the callee to read the arguments from memory and transfer them to some other temporary area in memory and then call other functions. However, such approaches are not elegant and not very efficient also. We shall look at more elegant solutions later.

Hence, at this point, we can conclude that we have solved the space problem partially. If we need to transfer a few values between the caller and the callee or vice versa, we can use registers. However, if the arguments/return values do not fit in the set of available registers, then we need to transfer them through memory. For transferring data through memory, we need an elegant solution that does not require a strict agreement between the caller and the callee regarding the memory locations used to transfer data. We shall consider such solutions in Section 3.3.10.

Definition 36
The notion of saving registers in memory and later restoring them is known as register spilling.

To solve the **overwrite problem**, there are two solutions. The first is that the caller can save the set of registers it requires in a dedicated location in memory. It can later retrieve its set of registers after the callee finishes, and returns control to the caller. The second solution is for the callee to save and restore the registers that it will require. Both the approaches are shown in Figure 3.9. This method of saving the values of registers in memory, and later retrieving them is known as *spilling*.

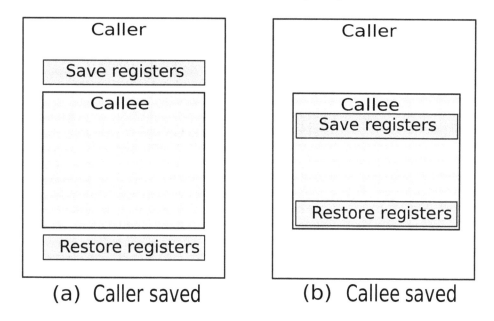

Figure 3.9: Caller saved and callee saved registers

Here, we have the same problem again. Both the caller and the callee need to have a strict agreement on the locations in memory that need to be used. Let us now try to solve both the problems together.

The Stack

We simplified the process of passing arguments to and from a function, and saving/restoring the registers using dedicated locations in memory. However, this solution was found to be inflexible and it can be quite complex to implement for large real world programs. To simplify this idea, let us find a pattern in function calls.

A typical C or Java program starts with the *main* function. This function then calls other functions, which might in turn call other functions, and finally the execution terminates when the main function exits. Each function defines a set of local variables and performs a computation on these variables and the function arguments. It might also call other functions. Finally, the function returns a value and rarely a set of values (structure in C). Note that after a function terminates, the local variables, and the arguments are not required anymore. Hence, if some of these variables or arguments were saved in memory, we need to reclaim the space. Secondly, if the function has spilled registers, then these memory locations also need to be freed after it exits. Lastly, we note that if the callee calls another function, then it will need to save the value of the return address register in memory. We will need to free this location also after the function exits.

It is best to save all of these pieces of information contiguously in a single region of memory. This is known as the *activation block* of the function. Figure 3.10 shows the memory map of the activation block.

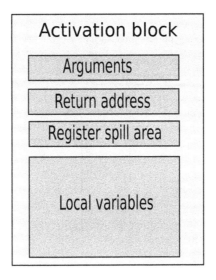

Figure 3.10: Activation block

The activation block contains the arguments, return address, register spill area (for both caller saved and callee saved schemes), and the local variables. Once a function terminates, it is possible to get rid of the activation block entirely. If a function wants to return some values, then it can either do so using registers. However, if it wants to return a large structure, then it can write it into the activation block of the caller. The caller can supply a location within its activation block where this data can be written. We shall see that it is possible to do this more elegantly. Prior to explaining how this can be done, we need to look at how to arrange activation blocks in memory.

We can have one memory region where all the activation blocks are stored in contiguous regions. Let us consider an example. Let us assume that function *foo* calls function *foobar*, which in turn calls *foobarbar*. Figure 3.11(a) - (d) show the state of memory at four points – (a) just before calling *foobar*, (b) just before calling *foobarbar*, (c) after calling *foobarbar*, (d) just after *foobarbar* returns.

We observe that there is a last in first out behavior in this memory region. The function that was invoked the last is the first function to finish. Such kind of a last in-first out structure is traditionally known as a *stack* in computer science. Hence, the memory region dedicated to saving activation blocks is known as the *stack*. Traditionally, the stack has been considered to be downward growing (growing towards smaller memory addresses). This means that the activation block of the main function starts at a very high location and new activation blocks are added just below (towards lower addresses) existing activation blocks. Thus the top of the stack is actually the smallest address in the stack, and the bottom of the stack is the largest

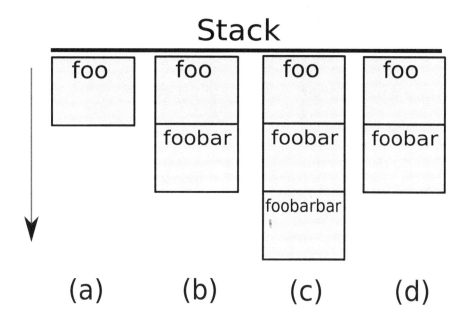

Figure 3.11: The state of the stack after several function calls

address. The top of the stack represents the activation block of the function that is currently executing, and the bottom of the stack represents the initial main function.

Definition 37

The stack *is a memory region that saves all the activation blocks in a program.*

- *It is traditionally considered to be downward growing.*

- *Before calling a function, we need to push its activation block to the stack.*

- *When a function finishes execution, we need to pop its activation block off the stack.*

Definition 38

The stack pointer register maintains a pointer to the top of the stack.

Most architectures save a pointer to the top of the stack in a dedicated register called the *stack pointer*. This register is $r14$ in *SimpleRisc* . It is also called *sp*. Note that for a lot of architectures, the stack is a purely software structure. For them, the hardware is not aware of the stack. However, for some architectures such as x86, hardware is aware of the stack and uses it to push the return address or the values of other registers. However, even in this case the hardware is not aware of the contents of each activation block. The structure is decided by the assembly programmer or the compiler. In all cases, the compiler needs to explicitly add assembly instructions to manage the stack.

Creating a new activation block for the callee involves the following steps.

1. Decrement the stack pointer by the size of the activation block.

2. Copy the values of the arguments.

3. Initialise any local variables by writing to their corresponding memory locations if required.

4. Spill any registers (store to the activation block) if required.

It is necessary to destroy the activation block upon returning from a function. This can be trivially done by adding the size of the activation block to the stack pointer.

By using a stack, we have solved all of our problems. The caller and the callee cannot overwrite each other's local variables. The local variables are saved in the activation blocks, and two activation blocks do not overlap. Along with variables it is possible to stop the callee from overwriting the caller's registers by explicitly inserting instructions to save registers in the activation blocks. There are two methods of achieving this – caller-saved scheme and callee-saved scheme. Secondly, there is no need to have an explicit agreement regarding the memory area that will be used to pass arguments. The stack can be used for this purpose. The caller can simply push the arguments on the stack. These arguments will get pushed into the callee's activation block, and the callee can easily use them. Similarly, while returning from a function the callee can pass return values through the stack. It needs to first destroy its activation block by decrementing the stack pointer, and then it can push the return values on the stack. The caller will be aware of the semantics of the callee, and thus after the callee returns it can assume that its activation block has been effectively enlarged by the callee. The additional space is consumed by the return values.

3.3.11   Function Call/Return Instructions

SimpleRisc has two instructions for functions – *call* and *ret*. The *call* instructions takes a single argument – the label of the first instruction of the function. It transfers control to the label and saves the return address in register ra. The *ret* instructions transfers the contents of ra to the PC. It is a 0-address instruction because it does not require any operands. Table 3.9 shows the semantics of these instructions. In Table 3.9, we assume that the *address* method provides the address of the first instruction of the *foo* function. Secondly, the return address is equal to $PC + 4$ because we assume that each instruction is 4 bytes long. *call* and *ret* can be thought of as *branch* instructions because they change the value of the PC. However, they are not dependent on any condition such as the value stored in a register. Hence, these instructions can conceptually be considered to be *unconditional branch instructions*.

Semantics	Example	Explanation
call *label*	call .foo	$ra \leftarrow PC + 4$; $PC \leftarrow address(.foo)$;
ret	ret	$PC \leftarrow ra$

Table 3.9: Semantics of function call/return instructions in *SimpleRisc*

Example 32
Write a function in SimpleRisc that adds the values in registers r0, and r1, and saves the result in r2.
Answer:

```SimpleRisc
.foo:
        add r2, r0, r1
        ret
```

Example 33

Write a function, foo, in SimpleRisc that adds the values in registers r0, and r1, and saves the result in r2. Then write another function that invokes this function. The invoking function needs to first set r0 to 3, r1 to 5, and then invoke foo. After foo returns, it needs to add 10 to the result of foo, and finally save the sum in r3.

Answer:

```SimpleRisc
.foo:
        add r2, r0, r1
        ret

.main:
        mov r0, 3
        mov r1, 5
        call .foo
        add r3, r2, 10
```

Example 34

Write a recursive function to compute the factorial of 10 that is initially stored in r0. Save the result in r1.

Answer: *Let us first take a look at a small C program to compute the factorial of the variable num.*

```C
int factorial(int num) {
        if (num <= 1) return 1;
        return num * factorial(num - 1);
}
void main() {
        int result = factorial(10);
}
```

Let us now try to convert this program to SimpleRisc .

```SimpleRisc
.factorial:
    cmp r0, 1          /* compare (1,num) */
    beq .return
```

```
        bgt .continue
        b .return

.continue:
        sub sp, sp, 8    /* create space on the stack */
        st r0, [sp]      /* push r0 on the stack */
        st ra, 4[sp]     /* push the return address register */
        sub r0, r0, 1    /* num = num - 1 */
        call .factorial  /* result will be in r1 */
        ld r0, [sp]      /* pop r0 from the stack */
        ld ra, 4[sp]     /* restore the return address */
        mul r1, r0, r1   /* factorial(n) = n * factorial(n-1) */
        add sp, sp, 8    /* delete the activation block */
        ret
.return:
        mov r1, 1
        ret

.main:
        mov r0, 10
        call .factorial
```

This example uses the stack to save and restore the value of r0. In this case, the caller saves and restores its registers.

3.3.12 The *nop* Instruction

Let us now add an instruction called *nop* that does nothing. Unlike other instructions, we do not need a table explaining the semantics of the instruction, because it does absolutely nothing!!!

Question 4 *Why on earth would we add an instruction that does not do anything?*

We will justify the need to have a nop instruction in our portfolio of instructions in Chapter 9. We shall see that it is important to have an instruction that does not do anything to ensure correctness in execution. Let us for the time being bear with this extra instruction that does not seem to have any purpose. The reader will definitely appreciate the need for this instruction in Chapter 9, when we discuss pipelining.

3.3.13 Modifiers

Let us now consider the problem of loading a 32-bit constant into a register. The following code snippet shows us how to load the constant $0xFB12CDEF$.

```
/* load the upper two bytes */
mov r0, 0xFB12
lsl r0, r0, 16

/* load the lower two bytes with 0x CD EF */
mov r1, 0x CDEF
lsl r1, r1, 16
lsr r1, r1, 16 /* top 16 bits are zeros */

/* load all the four bytes */
add r0, r0, r1
```

This problem requires 6 instructions. The reader needs to note that loading constants is a common operation in programs. Hence, let us devise a mechanism to speedup the process, and load a constant in a register in two operations. Most assemblers provide directives to directly load constants. Nevertheless, these directives need to get translated into a basic sequence of assembly instructions. Thus directives do not fundamentally solve of our problem of loading constants into registers of memory locations efficiently.

We shall achieve this by using *modifiers*. Let us assign a modifier, 'u', or 'h', to an ALU instruction other than shift instructions. By default, we assume that when we load a 16-bit immediate into a 32-bit register, the processor automatically performs sign extension. This means that it sets each of the 16 MSB bits to the sign of the immediate. This preserves the value of the immediate. For example, if our immediate is equal to -2, then its hexadecimal representation is 0x FF FE. If we try to store it in a register, then in effect, we are storing – 0x FF FF FF FE.

Let us have two additional modes. Let us add the suffix 'u' to an instruction to make it interpret the immediate as an unsigned number. For example, the instruction *movu r0, 0x FEAB*, will load 0x 00 00 FE AB into register r0. This suffix allows us to specify 16-bit unsigned immediate values. Secondly, let us add the suffix 'h' to an instruction to instruct it to load the 16-bit immediate into the upper half of a register. For example, *movh r0, 0x FEAB*, effectively loads 0x FE AB 00 00, into *r0*. We can use modifiers with all ALU instructions, with the exception of shift instructions.

Let us now consider the previous example of loading a 32-bit constant into a register. We can implement it with two instructions as follows:

```
movh r0, 0xFB12      /* r0 = 0xFB 12 00 00 */
addu r0, r0, 0xCDEF  /* r0 = r0 + 0x00 00 CD EF */
```

By using modifiers, we can load constants in 2 instructions, rather than 6 instructions. Furthermore, it is possible to create generic routines using modifiers that can set the value of any single byte in a 4 byte register. These routines will require a lesser number of instructions due to the use of modifiers.

3.3.14   Encoding the *SimpleRisc* Instruction Set

Let us now try to encode each instruction to a 32-bit value. We observe that we have instructions in 0,1,2 and 3 address formats. Secondly, some of the instructions take immediate values. Hence, we need to divide 32 bits into multiple fields. Let us first try to encode the type of instruction. Since there are 21 instructions, we require 5 bits to encode the instruction type. The code for each instruction is shown in Table 3.10. We can use the five most significant bits in a 32-bit field to specify the instruction type. The code for an instruction is also known as its *opcode*.

Definition 39
An opcode *is a unique identifier for each machine instruction.*

Instruction	Code	Instruction	Code	Instruction	Code
add	00000	not	01000	beq	10000
sub	00001	mov	01001	bgt	10001
mul	00010	lsl	01010	b	10010
div	00011	lsr	01011	call	10011
mod	00100	asr	01100	ret	10100
cmp	00101	nop	01101		
and	00110	ld	01110		
or	00111	st	01111		

Table 3.10: List of instruction opcodes

Now, let us try to encode each type of instruction starting from 0-address instructions.

Encoding 0-Address Instructions

The two 0-address instructions that we have are *ret*, and *nop*. The opcode is specified by the five most significant bits. In this case it is equal to 10100 for *ret*, and 10010 for *b* (refer to Table 3.10). Their encoding is shown in Figure 3.12. We only need to specify the 5 bit opcode in the MSB positions. The rest of the 27 bits are not required.

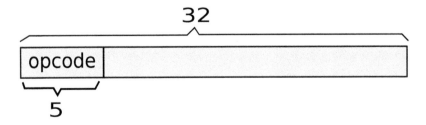

Figure 3.12: Encoding the *ret* instruction

Encoding 1-Address Instructions

The 1-address instructions that we have are *call*, *b*, *beq*, and *bgt*. In *SimpleRisc* assembly, they take a label as an argument. While encoding the instruction we need to specify the address of the label as the argument. The address of a label is the same as the address of the instruction that it is pointing to. If the line after the label is empty, then we need to consider the next assembly statement that has an instruction.

These four instructions require 5 bits for their opcode. The remaining 27 bits can be used for the address. Note that a memory address is 32 bits long. Hence, we cannot cover the address space with 27 bits. However, we can make two key optimisations. The first is that we can assume PC-relative addressing. We can assume that the 27 bits specify an offset (both positive and negative) with respect to the current PC. The branch statements in modern programs are generated because of *for/while* loops or *if-statements*. For these constructs the branch target is typically within a range of several hundred instructions. If we have 27 bits to specify the offset, and we assume that it is a 2's complement number, then the maximum offset in any direction (positive or negative) is 2^{26}. This is more than sufficient for almost all programs.

There is another important observation to be made. An instruction takes 4 bytes. If we assume that all instructions are aligned to 4-byte boundaries, then all starting memory addresses of instructions will be a multiple of 4. Hence, the least two significant binary digits of the address will be 00. There is no reason for wasting bits in trying to specify them. We can assume that the 27 bits specify the offset of the address of the memory word (in units of 4-byte memory words) that contains the instruction. With this optimisation, the offset from the PC in terms of bytes becomes 29 bits. This number should suffice for even the largest programs. Just in case, there is a pathological example, in which the branch target is more than 2^{28} bytes away, then the assembler needs to chain the branches such that one branch will call another branch and so on. However, this would be a very rare case. The encoding for these instructions is shown in Figure 3.13.

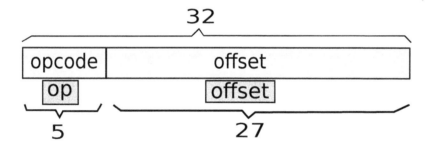

Figure 3.13: Encoding of 1-address instructions(*branch* format)

Note that the 1-address instruction format finds a use for the unused bits in the 0-address format. We can think of the 0-address format for the *ret* instruction as a special case of the 1-address format. Let us refer to the 1-address format as the *branch* format. Let us name the fields in this format. Let us call the opcode portion of the format as *op*, and the offset as *offset*. The *op* field contains the bits in positions 28-32, and the offset field contains the bits in positions 1-27.

Encoding 3-Address Instructions

Let us consider 3-address instructions first, and then look at other types of instructions. The 3-address instructions in *SimpleRisc* are *add*, *sub*, *mul*, *div*, *mod*, *and*, *or*, *lsl*, *lsr*, and *asr*.

Let us consider a generic 3-address instruction. It has a destination register, one input source register, and a second source operand that can either be a register or an immediate. We need to devote one bit to find out if the second source operand is a register or an immediate. Let us call this the *I* bit and specify it just after the opcode in the instruction. If $I = 1$, then the second source operand is an immediate. If $I = 0$, the second source operand is a register.

Let us now consider the case of 3-address registers that have their second source operand as a register($I = 0$). Since we have 16 registers, we require 4 bits to uniquely specify each register. Register ri can be encoded as the unsigned 4-bit binary equivalent of i. Hence, to specify the destination register and two input source registers, we require 12 bits. The structure is shown in Figure 3.14. Let us call this instruction format as the *register* format. Like the *branch* format let us name the different fields – *op* (opcode, bits: 28-32), I (immediate present, bits:27), rd (destination register, bits: 23-26), $rs1$ (source register 1, bits: 19-22), and $rs2$ (source register 2, bits:15-18).

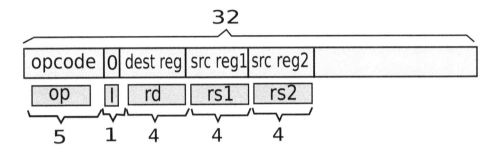

Figure 3.14: Encoding 3-address instructions with register operands (*register* format)

Now, if we assume that the second source operand is an immediate, then we need to set I to 1. Let us calculate the number of bits we have left for specifying the immediate. We have already devoted 5 bits for the opcode, 1 bit for the I bit, 4 bits for the destination register, and 4 bits for the first source register. In all, we have expended 14 bits. Hence, out of 32 bits, we are left with 18 bits, and we can use them to specify the immediate.

We propose to divide the 18 bits into two parts – 2 bits (modifier) + 16 bits (constant part of the immediate). The two modifier bits can take three values – 00 (default), 01 ('u'), and 10 ('h'). The remaining 16 bits are used to specify a 16-bit 2's complement number when we are using default modifiers. For the u and h modifiers, we assume that the 16-bit constant in the immediate field is an unsigned number. In the rest of this book, we assume that the immediate field is 18 bits long with a modifier part, and a constant part. The processor internally expands the immediate to a 32-bit value, in accordance with the modifiers.

This encoding is shown in Figure 3.15. Let us call this instruction format as the *immediate* format. Like the *branch* format let us name the different fields – *op* (opcode, bits: 28-32), I (immediate present, bits:27), rd (destination register, bits: 23-26), $rs1$ (source register 1, bits: 19-22), and imm (immediate, bits:1-18).

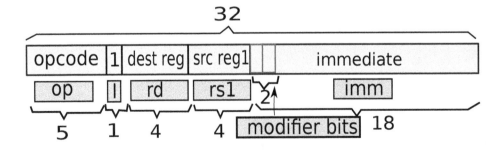

Figure 3.15: Encoding 3-address instructions with an immediate source operand (*immediate* format)

Example 35
Encode the instruction: sub r1, r2, 3.

Answer: *Let us encode each field of the instruction. We have:*

Field	Encoding
sub	00001
I	1
r1	0001
r2	0010
3	11

Thus, the binary encoding is (spaces added for readability): 00001 1 0001 0010 00 0000 0000 0000 0011. When we convert to hex, we get: 0x0C480003.

Encoding *cmp*, *not*, and *mov*

The *cmp* instruction has two source operands. The second source operand can be a register or an immediate. We will use the standard 3-address *register* or *immediate* formats for encoding the *cmp* instruction. The destination register field will remain empty. See Figure 3.16. One of our aims in designing the encoding is to keep things as simple and regular as possible such that the processor can decode the instruction very easily. We could have designed a separate encoding for a 2-address instruction such as *cmp*. However, the gains would have been negligible, and by sticking to a fixed format, the processor's instruction decode logic becomes more straight forward.

The *not* and *mov* instructions have one destination register, and one source operand. This source operand can be either an immediate or a register. Hence, we can treat the source operand of these instructions as the second source operand in the 3-address format, and keep the field for the first source register empty for both of these instructions. The format is shown in Figure 3.16.

Load and Store Instructions

In *SimpleRisc* the instructions – *ld* and *st* – are 2-address instructions. The second operand points to a memory address. It uses a base-offset addressing mode. There is a base register, and an integer offset.

For a load instruction, there are three unique pieces of information that need to be encoded: destination register, base register, and offset. In this case, we propose to use the three address *immediate* format. The *I* bit is set to 1, because we need to specify an offset. The first source register represents the base register, and the immediate represents the offset. Note that this encoding follows our principle of regularity and simplicity. Our aim is to reuse the 3-address *register* and *immediate* formats for as many instructions as possible.

Now, let us look at store instructions. Store instructions are slightly special in the sense that they do not have a destination register. The destination of a store instruction is a memory location. This information cannot be encoded in the *immediate* format. However, for reasons of simplicity, we still want to stick to the formats that we have defined. We need to take a crucial design decision here by answering Question 5.

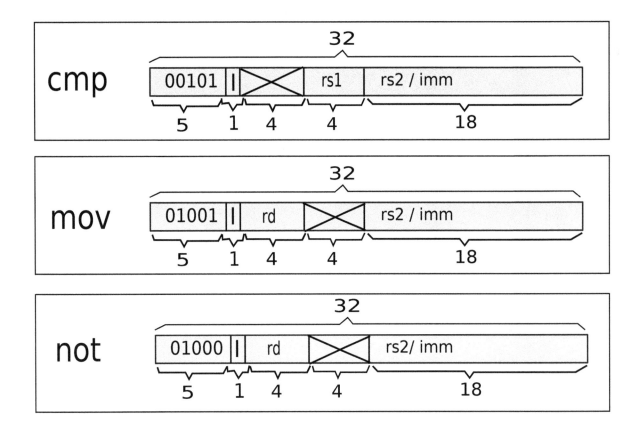

Figure 3.16: *cmp*, *not*, and *mov* instructions

Question 5
Should we define a new instruction format for the store instruction?

Let us adjudge this case in the favor of not introducing a new format. Let us try to reuse the *immediate* format. The *immediate* format has four fields – *op*, *rd*, *rs1*, and *imm*. The opcode field (*op*) need not be touched. We can assume that the format of the store instruction is: st rd, imm[rs1]. In this case, the field *rd* represents the register to be stored. Like the load instruction we can keep the base register as *rs1*, and use the *imm* field to specify the offset. We break the pattern we have been following up till now by saving a source register in *rd*, which is meant to save a destination register. However, we were compelled to do this at the cost of not introducing a new instruction format. Such design tradeoffs need to be made continuously. We have to always balance the twin objectives of elegance and efficiency. It is sometimes not possible to choose the best of both worlds. In this case, we have gone for efficiency, because introducing a new instruction format for just one instruction is overkill.

To conclude, figure 3.17 shows the encoding for load and store instructions.

Example 36
Encode the instruction: st r8, 20[r2].

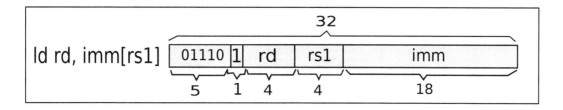

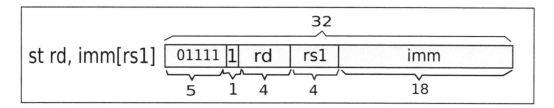

Figure 3.17: Encoding of load and store instructions

Answer: *Let us encode each field of the instruction. We have:*

Field	Encoding
st	*01111*
I	*1*
r8	*1000*
r2	*0010*
20	*0001 0100*

Thus, the binary encoding is (spaces added for readability): 01111 1 1000 0010 00 0000 0000 0001 0100. When we convert to hex, we get: 0x7E080014.

Summary of Instruction Formats

In the last few subsections, we have described a method to encode an instruction into a sequence of bits (machine code). A compiler can use this method to translate a program written in a high level language to machine code, and thus create an executable program. It is now the job of the processor to execute this program by reading the instructions one by one. We have substantially made our life easy by assuming that each instruction is exactly 4 bytes long. The processor simply needs to start at the starting address of the program in memory and fetch one instruction after the other. If an instruction is a branch, then the processor needs to evaluate the branch condition, and jump to the branch target. The part of the processor that is primarily concerned about the details of the ISA is the *decode* logic or the *decoder*. It is the role of the decoder to understand and decode an instruction. While designing an encoding for an ISA, creating a simple and efficient instruction decoder was our prime objective.

To decode a *SimpleRisc* instruction, the first task is to find the instruction format. We have defined three formats – *branch*, *immediate*, and *register*. Let us refer to Table 3.10. The six *branch* format instructions are *call*, *ret*, *beq*, *bgt*, *b*, and *nop*. Recall that we encode both 0 and 1-address format instructions in the *branch* format.

The opcodes of all the five branch instructions (*b*, *beq*, *bgt*, *call*, *ret*) have 1 as their most significant bit,

Format	Definition				
branch	*op* (28-32)	*offset* (1-27)			
register	*op* (28-32)	*I* (27)	*rd* (23-26)	*rs1* (19-22)	*rs2* (15-18)
immediate	*op* (28-32)	*I* (27)	*rd* (23-26)	*rs1* (19-22)	*imm* (1-18)
op → opcode, *offset* → branch offset, *I* → immediate bit, *rd* → destination register					
rs1 → source register 1, *rs2* → source register 2, *imm* → immediate operand					

Table 3.11: Summary of instruction formats

whereas all other instructions have a 0 in their most significant position. Hence, for a decoder to find out if an instruction is a branch is very easy. It just needs to take a look at the three most significant bit of the opcode. It should be 1. Moreover, to find out if an instruction is a *nop*, the decoder needs to compare it with 01101, which requires a small circuit.

If an instruction is not in the *branch* format, then it must be in the *immediate* or *register* format. This can be quickly decided by taking a look at the *I* bit. If it is 1, then the instruction is in the *immediate* format, otherwise it is in the *register* format. The formats are summarised in Table 3.11.

Lessons Learnt

Now that we have designed a small instruction set of our own, looked at sample programs, and encoded our instructions, we are all set to design a processor for our *SimpleRisc* ISA. It needs to decode every single instruction, and execute it accordingly. Before proceeding further, let us look back at how we designed our ISA, and how should ISAs be designed in general.

1. The first step in designing an ISA is to study the workload that the ISA is being designed for. In the case of *SimpleRisc* , we wanted to use it for running general purpose programs. This meant that *SimpleRisc* needed to be simple, concise, generic, and complete as outlined in Chapter 1. However, for different target workloads, the requirements might be very different.

2. After studying the workload, we need to next decide on the number of instructions that we need to have. Unless there are compelling requirements otherwise, it is not advisable to have more than 64-128 instructions. More than 128 instructions will make the instruction decoder very complex. It will also complicate the design of the processor.

3. After finalising the number of instructions, we need to finalise the different types of instructions. If we are designing an ISA for extensive numerical computation, then we should have many arithmetic operations. If we are designing an ISA for processing text, then we should have many instructions that can process strings (pieces of text). In the case of *SimpleRisc* we devoted 6 instructions to arithmetic operations, 3 instructions to shift operations, 3 instructions to logical operations, 3 instructions to data transfer, 5 instructions to branch operations, and designated 1 instruction as no-op (no operation). We chose this distribution because we expect to run a lot of general purpose programs that will have complex arithmetical and logical constructs. We could have very well gotten rid of an instruction such as *mod* and replaced it with a sophisticated branch instruction, if we wanted to look at programs that will have a lot of branches. These subtle tradeoffs need to be evaluated thoroughly.

4. Once, we have finalised the broad types of instructions and the distribution of instructions across these types, we come to the actual instructions themselves. In this case also, we want to make the common case fast. For example, there is no point in having a division instruction in programs that do not have

divisions operations. Secondly, we need to decide the format of each instruction in terms of the number and type of operands. For example, in *SimpleRisc* , all our arithmetic operations are in the 3-address format. If there is a requirement from the side of processor designers that they want to reduce the number of registers, then we can opt for the 2-address format. Alternatively, if we want to process a massive amount of information in one go such as add a list of 10 numbers, then we can even have a 11-address format instruction.

5. Once the format of the instruction is decided, we need to decide on the different addressing modes. This decision has many ramifications. For example, if we allow the register-indirect addressing mode in arithmetic instructions, then we need to add additional hardware to access the memory and fetch the operand values. On the other hand, if we have a register-only addressing mode for arithmetic instructions, then their implementation will be fast. However, the flip side is that we will need more registers, and more dedicated load-store instructions to access memory. This tradeoff needs to be kept in mind.

6. Once we have designed the set of instructions, we need to decide a proper encoding for it. The main aim should be to reduce the work of the instruction decoder. It is best to have a small set of generic instruction formats that the decoder can quickly discern. We need to balance elegance and efficiency such that the decoder can be simple yet efficient.

3.4   Summary and Further Reading

3.4.1   Summary

Summary 3

1. *Assembly language is a textual representation of machine instructions. Each statement in an assembly language program typically corresponds to one machine instruction.*

2. *An assembler is a program that converts an assembly language program to machine code.*

3. *An assembly language is specific to an ISA and an assembler.*

4. *Assembly language is a vital tool for writing efficient programs, and for designing the core routines of operating systems, and device drivers.*

5. *Hardware designers learn assembly languages to understand the semantics of an ISA. It tells them what to build.*

6. *An assembly language program typically assumes a Von Neumann machine augmented with a finite set of registers.*

7. *A typical GNU assembly file contains a list of sections. Two important sections are text and data. The text section contains the assembly statements that correspond to machine code. The data section holds data and constants that the program will need during its operation.*

8. *A typical assembly statement contains an optional label to uniquely identify it, an instruction with a set of operands, and an optional comment. Instead of an instruction, it can also contain a directive that is a command to the assembler.*

9. *There are typically four types of generic assembly instructions:*

   (a) *Data processing instructions – arithmetic and logical*

   (b) *Data transfer instructions – move, load, and store*

   (c) *Branch instructions – branch, function call, return*

   (d) *Exception generating instructions – transfer control to the operating system*

   An assembly language for a specific ISA also contains some machine specific instructions also that are mainly used to set its configuration or invoke some special feature.

10. *The semantics of operands is also known as the addressing mode.*

11. *The main addressing modes are immediate (specify constant in instruction), register-direct (specify the register's name in the instruction), register-indirect (a register contains the memory address), and base-offset (the offset is added to the memory location in the base register).*

12. *We designed the SimpleRisc assembly language that contains 21 instructions. It is a complete RISC ISA.*

13. *We designed an encoding for each SimpleRisc instruction. We broadly defined three instruction formats*

    branch Contains a 5 bit opcode and 27 bit offset.

    register Encodes a 3-address instruction with two register source operands and one register destination operand.

    immediate Encodes a 3-address instruction that has an immediate as one of the operands.

In this chapter we have looked at the generic principles underlying different flavors of assembly language. We constructed a small assembly language of our own for the *SimpleRisc* ISA, and proceeded to encode it. This information is sufficient to design a basic processor for *SimpleRisc* in Chapter 8. However, we would like to strongly advise the reader to at least study one of the chapters on real world assembly languages – either ARM (Chapter 4) or x86 (Chapter 5). Studying a real language in all its glory will help the reader deepen her knowledge, and she can appreciate all the tricks that are required to make an ISA expressive.

3.4.2   Further Reading

Instruction set design and the study of assembly languages are very old fields. Readers should refer to classic computer architecture textbooks by Henessey and Patterson [Henessey and Patterson, 2010], Morris Mano [Mano, 2007], and William Stallings [Stallings, 2010] to get a different perspective. For other simple instruction sets such as *SimpleRisc* , readers can read about the MIPS [Farquhar and Bunce, 2012], and Sparc [Paul, 1993] instruction sets. Their early variants are simple RISC instruction sets with up to 64 instructions, and a very regular structure. Along with the references that we provide, there are a lot of excellently written tutorials and guides on the web for different ISAs.

Since the last 10 years, a trend has started to move towards virtual instruction sets. Programs compiled for these instruction sets need to be compiled once again on a real machine such that the virtual instruction set can be translated to a real instruction set. The reasons for doing so shall be described in later chapters. The Java language uses a virtual instruction set. Details can be found in the book by Meyer et. al. [Downing and Meyer, 1997]. Readers can also refer to a highly cited research paper that proposes the LLVA [Adve et al., 2003] virtual instruction set.

Exercises

Assembly Language Concepts

Ex. 1 — What is the advantage of the register-indirect addressing mode over the memory-direct addressing mode?

Ex. 2 — When is the base-offset addressing mode useful?

Ex. 3 — Consider the base-scaled-offset addressing mode, which directs the hardware to automatically multiply the offset by 4. When is this addressing mode useful?

Ex. 4 — Which addressing modes are preferable in a machine with a large number of registers?

Ex. 5 — Which addressing modes are preferable in a machine with very few registers?

Ex. 6 — Assume that we are constrained to have at the most two operands per instruction. Design a format for arithmetic instructions such as add and multiply in this setting.

Assembly Programming

Ex. 7 — Write simple assembly code snippets in *SimpleRisc* to compute the following:

  i) $a + b + c$

  ii) $a + b - c/d$

  iii) $(a + b) * 3 - c/d$

  iv) $a/b - (c * d)/3$

  v) $(a \ll 2) - (b \gg 3)$ ($(\ll$ (left shift logical), $\gg$ (left shift arithmetic))

Ex. 8 — Write a program to load the value $0xFFEDFC00$ into $r0$. Try to minimise the number of instructions.

Ex. 9 — Write an assembly program to set the 5th bit of register $r0$ to the value of the 3rd bit of $r1$. Keep the rest of the contents of $r0$ the same. The convention is that the LSB is the first bit, and the MSB is the 32nd bit. (Use less than or equal to 5 *SimpleRisc* assembly statements)

Ex. 10 — Write a program in *SimpleRisc* assembly to convert an integer stored in memory from the little endian to the big endian format.

Ex. 11 — Write a program in *SimpleRisc* assembly to compute the factorial of a positive number using an iterative algorithm.

Ex. 12 — Write a program in *SimpleRisc* assembly to find if a number is prime.

Ex. 13 — Write a program in *SimpleRisc* assembly to test if a number is a perfect square.

Ex. 14 — Given a 32-bit integer in $r3$, write a *SimpleRisc* assembly program to count the number of 1 to 0 transitions in it.

* **Ex. 15** — Write a program in *SimpleRisc* assembly to find the smallest number that is a sum of two different pairs of cubes. [Note: 1729 is the Hardy-Ramanujan number. $1729 = 12^3 + 1^3 = 10^3 + 9^3$].

Ex. 16 — Write a *SimpleRisc* assembly program that checks if a 32-bit number is a palindrome. Assume that the input is available in $r3$. The program should set $r4$ to 1 if it is a palindrome, otherwise $r4$ should contain a 0. A palindrome is a number which is the same when read from both sides. For example, 1001 is a 4-bit palindrome.

Ex. 17 — Design a *SimpleRisc* program that examines a 32-bit value stored in $r1$ and counts the number of contiguous sequences of 1s. For example, the value:

$$0111000100011110110001110000111111$$

contains six sequences of 1s. Write the result in $r2$.

** **Ex. 18** — Write a program in *SimpleRisc* assembly to subtract two 64-bit numbers, where each number is stored in two registers.

** **Ex. 19** — In some cases, we can rotate an integer to the right by n positions (less than or equal to 31) so that we obtain the same number. For example: a 8-bit number 11011011 can be right rotated by 3 or 6 places to obtain the same number. Write an assembly program to *efficiently* count the number of ways we can rotate a number to the right such that the result is equal to the original number.

** **Ex. 20** — A number is known as a cubic Armstrong number if the sum of the cubes of the decimal digits is equal to the number itself. For example, 153 is a cubic Armstrong number ($153 = 1^3 + 5^3 + 3^3$). You are given a number in register, $r0$, and it is known to be between 1 and 1 million. Can you write a piece of assembly code in *SimpleRisc* to find out if this number is a cubic Armstrong number. Save 1 in $r1$ if it is a cubic Armstrong number; otherwise, save 0.

*** **Ex. 21** — Write a *SimpleRisc* assembly language program to find the greatest common divisor of two binary numbers u and v. Assume the two inputs (positive integers) to be available in $r3$ and $r4$. Store the result in $r5$. [HINT: The gcd of two even numbers u and v is $2 * gcd(u/2, v/2)$]

Instruction Set Encoding

Ex. 22 — Encode the following *SimpleRisc* instructions:

   i) *sub sp, sp, 4*
   ii) *mov r4, r5*
   iii) *addu r4, r4, 3*
   iv) *ret*
   v) *ld r0, [sp]*
   vi) *st r4, 8[r9]*

Design Problems

Ex. 23 — Design an emulator for the *SimpleRisc* ISA. The emulator reads an assembly program line by line, checks each assembly statement for errors, and executes it. Furthermore, define two assembler directives namely *.print*, and *.encode* to print data on the screen. The *.print* directive takes a register or memory location as input. When the emulator encounters the *.print* directive, it prints the value in the register or memory location to the screen. Similarly, when the emulator encounters the *.encode* directive it prints the 32-bit encoding of the instruction on the screen. Additionally, it needs to also execute the instruction.

4

ARM® Assembly Language

In this chapter, we will study the ARM instruction set. As of 2012, this instruction set is the most widely used instruction set in smart phones, and tablets. It has more than 90% market share[1] in this space. ARM processors are also one of the most popular processors in hard disk drives, and set top boxes for televisions. Hence, for any student of computer architecture it is very important to learn about the ARM instruction set because it will prove to be useful in programming the mobile and handheld devices of the future.

The ARM instruction set is a 32-bit instruction set. This means that the sizes of all registers are 32 bits, and the size of the memory address is equal to 32 bits. It is a RISC instruction set with a very regular structure. Each instruction is encoded into a string of exactly 32 bits like *SimpleRisc* . All arithmetic and logical operations, use only register operands, and lastly all the communication between registers and memory happens through two data transfer instructions – load and store.

4.1 The ARM® Machine Model

ARM assembly language assumes a machine model similar to that explained in Section 3.2.1 for *SimpleRisc* . For the register file, it assumes that there are 16 registers that are visible to the programmer at any point of time. All the registers in ARM are 32 bits or 4 bytes wide.

The registers are numbered from $r0$ to $r15$. Registers $r11 \ldots r15$ are known by certain mnemonics also as shown in Table 4.1. $r11$ is the frame-pointer. It points to the top of the activation block. $r12$ is a scratch register that is not meant to be saved by the caller or the callee. $r13$ is the stack pointer. It is important to understand that $r11$ and $r12$ are assigned a special connotation by the GNU compiler collection. They are not assigned special roles by the ARM ISA.

Let us differentiate between generic registers and registers with special roles. Registers $r0 \ldots r12$ are generic. The programmer and the compiler can use them in any way they like. However, the registers $r13(\text{sp})$, $r14(\text{lr})$ and $r15(\text{pc})$ have special roles. *sp* is the stack pointer, *lr* is the return address register, and *pc* is the program counter. In this chapter, we shall use the little endian version of the ARM ISA, and we shall describe the syntax of the assembly language used by the GNU ARM Assembler [arm, 2000].

---

[1]Most of the ARM code running on processors is actually written in the Thumb-2 ARM ISA. The Thumb-2 ISA is essentially a recoding (or a simpler variant) of the ISA presented in this chapter. Hence, it is necessary for readers to get a thorough understanding of the material that follows.

Register	Abbrv.	Name
$r11$	fp	frame pointer
$r12$	ip	intra-procedure-call scratch register
$r13$	sp	stack pointer
$r14$	lr	link register
$r15$	pc	program counter

Table 4.1: Registers with special names in ARM

4.2 Basic Assembly Instructions

4.2.1 Simple Data Processing Instructions

Register Transfer Instructions

The simplest type of assembly instructions transfer the value of one register into another, or store a constant in a register. There are two instructions in this class – *mov* and *mvn*. Their semantics are shown in Table 4.2. Note that we always prefix an immediate with '#' in ARM assembly.

Semantics	Example	Explanation
mov *reg*, (*reg/imm*)	mov r1, r2	r1 ← r2
	mov r1, #3	r1 ← 3
mvn *reg*, (*reg/imm*)	mvn r1, r2	r1 ← ∼ r2
	mvn r1, #3	r1 ← ∼ 3

Table 4.2: Semantics of the move instructions

The register based *mov* instruction simply moves the contents of $r2$ to register $r1$. Alternatively, it can store an immediate in a register. In Table 4.2, the *mvn* instruction flips every bit in the 32-bit register $r2$, and then transfers the contents of the result to $r1$. The ∼ symbol represents logical complement. For example, the complement of the 4-bit binary value, 0110, is 1001. The *mov* and *mvn* instructions take two inputs. These instructions are examples of 2-address format instructions in ARM.

Arithmetic Instructions

The simplest instructions in this class are *add*, *sub*, *rsb* (reverse subtract). Their semantics are given in Table 4.3. The second operand can also be an immediate.

Semantics	Example	Explanation
add *reg*, *reg*, (*reg/imm*)	add r1, r2, r3	r1 ← r2 + r3
sub *reg*, *reg*, (*reg/imm*)	sub r1, r2, r3	r1 ← r2 - r3
rsb *reg*, *reg*, (*reg/imm*)	rsb r1, r2, r3	r1 ← r3 - r2

Table 4.3: Semantics of add and subtract instructions

Example 37

Write an ARM assembly program to compute: 4+5 - 19. Save the result in r1.

Answer: *Simple yet suboptimal solution.*

```
mov r1, #4
mov r2, #5
add r3, r1, r2
mov r4, #19
sub r1, r3, r4
```

Optimal solution.

```
mov r1, #4
add r1, r1, #5
sub r1, r1, #19
```

Logical Instructions

Semantics	Example	Explanation
and reg, reg, (reg/imm)	and r1, r2, r3	r1 ← r2 AND r3
eor reg, reg, (reg/imm)	eor r1, r2, r3	r1 ← r2 XOR r3
orr reg, reg, (reg/imm)	orr r1, r2, r3	r1 ← r2 OR r3
bic reg, reg, (reg/imm)	bic r1, r2, r3	r1 ← r2 AND (∼ r3)

Table 4.4: Semantics of logical instructions

ARM's bitwise logical instructions are shown in Table 4.4. *and* computes a bit-wise AND, *eor* computes an exclusive OR, *orr* computes a regular bit-wise OR, and the *bic*(bit-clear) instruction clears off the bits in $r2$ that are specified in $r3$. Like arithmetic instructions, the second operand can be an immediate.

Example 38

Write an ARM assembly program to compute: $\overline{A \vee B}$, where A and B are 1 bit Boolean values. Assume that $A = 0$ and $B = 1$. Save the result in r0.

Answer:

```
mov r0, #0x0
orr r0, r0, #0x1
mvn r0, r0
```

Multiplication Instructions

We shall introduce four multiply instructions with varying degrees of complexity. The fundamental issue with multiplication is that if we are multiplying two 32-bit numbers, then the result will require 64 bits. The reason is that the largest unsigned 32-bit number is $2^{32} - 1$. Consequently, when we try to square this number, our result is approximately 2^{64}. We would thus need a maximum of 64 bits.

ARM has two 32-bit multiplication instructions that truncate the result to 32 bits – *mul* and *mla*. They ignore the rest of the bits. *mul* multiplies the values in two registers and stores the result in a third register. *mla* (multiply and accumulate) is in the 4-address format. It multiplies the values of two registers, and adds the result to the value stored in a third register (see Table 4.5). The advantage of the *mla* instruction is that it makes it possible to represent code sequences of the form $(d = a + b * c)$ with one instruction. Such instructions are extremely useful when it comes to implementing linear algebra kernels such as matrix multiplication.

Semantics	Example	Explanation
mul *reg, reg, reg*	mul r1, r2, r3	r1 $\leftarrow$ r2 $\times$ r3
mla *reg, reg, reg, reg*	mla r1, r2, r3, r4	r1 $\leftarrow$ r2 $\times$ r3 + r4
smull *reg, reg, reg, reg*	smull r0, r1, r2, r3	$\underbrace{r1\ r0}_{64} \leftarrow$ r2 $\times_{signed}$ r3
umull *reg, reg, reg, reg*	umull r0, r1, r2, r3	$\underbrace{r1\ r0}_{64} \leftarrow$ r2 $\times_{unsigned}$ r3

Table 4.5: Semantics of multiply instructions

In this chapter, we shall introduce two instructions that store the entire 64-bit result in two registers. The *smull* and *umull* instructions perform signed and unsigned multiplication respectively on two 32-bit values to produce a 64-bit result. Their semantics is shown in Table 4.5. $r0$ contains the lower 32 bits, and $r1$ contains the upper 32 bits.

For all the multiply instructions that we have introduced, all the operands need to be registers. Secondly, the first source register, should not be the same as the destination register.

Example 39
Compute $12^3 + 1$, and save the result in r3.
Answer:

```
/* load test values */
mov r0, #12
mov r1, #1


/* perform the logical computation */
mul r4, r0, r0        @ 12*12
mla r3, r4, r0, r1    @ 12*12*12 + 1
```

Division Instructions

Newer versions of the ARM ISA have introduced two integer division instructions, *sdiv* and *udiv*. The former is used for signed division and the latter is used for unsigned division (see Table 4.6). Both of them compute the quotient. The remainder can be computed by subtracting the product of the dividend and the quotient from the dividend.

Semantics	Example	Explanation
sdiv *reg, reg, reg*	sdiv r1, r2, r3	r1 ← r2 ÷ r3 (signed)
udiv *reg, reg, reg*	udiv r1, r2, r3	r1 ← r2 ÷ r3 (unsigned)

Table 4.6: Semantics of divide instructions

4.2.2 Advanced Data-Processing Instructions

Let us consider the generic format of 3-address data-processing instructions.

```
instruction <destination register> <register operand 1> <operand 2>
```

Likewise, the generic format for 2 address data processing instructions is

```
instruction <register operand 1> <operand 2>
```

Up till now, we have been slightly quiet about $< operand\ 2 >$. It can be a register operand, an immediate, or a special class of operands called – *shifter operands*. The first two classes are intuitive. Let us describe shifter operands in this section. Their generic format is shown in Figure 4.1.

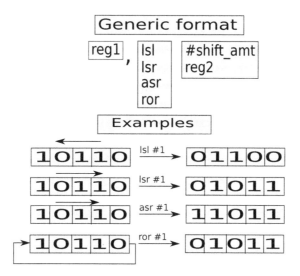

Figure 4.1: Format of shifter operands

A shifter operand contains two parts. This first part is a register, and the latter part specifies an operation to be performed on the value in the register. The ARM instruction set defines four such operations – *lsl* (logical shift left), *lsr* (logical shift right), *asr* (arithmetic shift right), and *ror* (rotate right). These operations are collectively called shift and rotate instructions.

Shift and Rotate Instructions

A logical left shift operation is shown in Figure 4.1. In this example, we are shifting the value 10110 one place to the left. We need to shift in an extra 0 at the LSB position. The final result is equal to 01100. A left shift operation is present in most programming languages including C and Java. It is denoted by the following symbol: $\ll$. Note that shifting a word (4 byte number) by k positions to the left is equivalent to multiplying it by 2^k. This is in fact a quick way of multiplying a number by a power of 2.

Let us now consider the right shift operation. Unlike the left shift operation, this operation comes in two variants. Let us first consider the case of unsigned numbers. Here, we treat a word as a sequence of 32 bits. In this case, if we shift the bits 1 position to the right, we fill the MSB with a 0. This operation is known as – logical shift right (see Figure 4.1). Note that shifting a number right by k places is usually the same as dividing it by 2^k. The right shift operation in C or Java is $\gg$.

If we consider a signed number, then we need to use the arithmetic right shift (*asr*) operation. This operation preserves the sign bit. If we shift a number right using *asr* by one position, then we fill the MSB with the previous value of the MSB. This ensures that if we shift a negative number to the right, the number still remains negative. In a four bit number system, if we shift 1010 to the right by 1 place using *asr*, then we get 1101. The original number is -6, and the shifted number is equal to -3. We thus see that arithmetic right shift divides a signed number by a power of two. Note that using the right shift operations for odd numbers is tricky. Let us consider the representation of -5 in a 4-bit number system. It is 1011. After performing an arithmetic right shift, the result is equal to 1101, which is equal to -3 in decimal. Whether we consider -5/2 = -3 as a correct answer or not depends on the semantics of the programming language.

The right rotate operation performs a right shift on the number. However, it fills the MSB with the number shifted out from the rightmost end. In Figure 4.1, if we right rotate 10110, we get 01011. In this case we have moved the previous LSB (0) to the new MSB. Note that ror (right rotate) by 32 positions gives us the original value. ARM provides a special connotation for *ror #0*. It performs a right shift. It moves the value of the carry flag to the MSB, and then sets the shifted out LSB to the carry flag. This is also referred to as the *rrx* operation. This operation does not take any arguments.

Using Shifter Operands

A shifter operand of the form – r1, lsl #2 – means that we shift the value in r1 by 2 places to the left. Note that the value in r1 is not affected in this process. Likewise, an operand of the form – r1, lsr r3 – means that we shift the value in r1 to the right by the value specified in r3. We can now use the shifter operand as a valid second operand. See examples 40, and 41.

Example 40

Write ARM assembly code to compute: r1 = r2 / 4. Assume that the number stored in r1 is divisible by 4.

Answer:

```
mov r1, r2, asr #2
```

Example 41

Write ARM assembly code to compute: r1 = r2 + r3 × 4.

Answer:

```
add r1, r2, r3, lsl #2
```

Addressing Modes

We have now seen different formats of operands. An operand can either be a register, an immediate, or a shifted register.

We have up till now seen three addressing modes:

1. register addressing mode: Example, $r1$, $r2$, $r3$

2. immediate addressing mode: Example, #1, #2

3. scaled-register addressing mode: Example, $(r1, lsl \; \#2)$, $(r1, lsl \; r2)$

4.2.3 Compare Instructions

ARM has four compare instructions – *cmp*, *cmn*, *tst*, and *teq* – in the 2-address format. These instructions compare the values in the two registers and save some properties of the result of the comparison in a dedicated internal register called the *CPSR* register. Other instructions base their behavior based on the values saved in the CPSR register. This is similar to the *flags* register in *SimpleRisc* .

The *CPSR* register

The CPSR (Current Program Status Register) maintains some state regarding the execution of the program. It is a 32-bit register like the other registers, and is usually used implicitly. In this book, we are concerned with four bits that it stores in the positions [29-32]. They are N(Negative), Z(Zero), C(Carry), and V(Overflow). These four bits are known as *condition code flags*, or simply *flags*. It is similar to the *flags* register in *SimpleRisc* .

There are two sets of instructions that can set CPSR flags. The first set comprises of compare instructions, and the second set includes flag setting variants of generic instructions. In either case, the rules for setting the flags are as follows:

N (Negative) This flag is set if the result is a 2's complement based signed integer. It is set to 1 if the result is negative, and 0 if it is non-negative.

Z (Zero) This flag is set to 1 if the result is zero. In a comparison operation, if the operands are equal, then this flag is also set to 1.

C (Carry) • For an addition, the C bit is set to 1 if the result produced a carry. This can happen when there was an overflow while adding the unsigned numbers. For example, if we add -1(1111_2) and -2(1110_2), then the result is -3(1101_2), and there is a carry out at the MSB. Note that there is no real overflow, because -3 can be represented in the number system. However, if the numbers are treated as unsigned numbers, then there is an *unsigned overflow*. Consequently, we can also say that the carry bit is set if there is an unsigned overflow.

- For a subtraction, the carry bit is set to 0 if there is an unsigned underflow. For example, if we try to compute $0 - 1$, then there is no real overflow/underflow. However, $0000_2 - 0001_2$ will lead to an unsigned underflow. This basically means that when we subtract these two numbers, we will need to borrow a bit. In this case, we set the C flag to 0. Otherwise, we set it to 1.

- For logical shift operations, C is equal to the last bit shifted out of the result value.

V (Overflow) V is set to 1 when an actual signed overflow/underflow occurs. Note that in the rest of the book, we might casually refer to both overflow and underflow as just *overflow*.

Compare Instructions

ARM has four compare instructions – *cmp*, *cmn*, *tst* and *teq*. All four of them update the CPSR flags. Let us consider the *cmp* instruction. It is a 2-address instruction that takes two inputs. It essentially subtracts their values and sets the appropriate flags. For example, if the values are equal, then the zero flag is set. Later instructions can take some decisions based on these flags. For example, they might decide if they need to branch, or perform a certain computation based on the value of the zero flag. We show the semantics of all four compare instructions in Table 4.7.

Semantics	Example	Explanation
cmp *reg, (reg/imm)*	cmp r1, r2	Set flags after computing (r1 - r2)
cmn *reg, (reg/imm)*	cmn r1, r2	Set flags after computing (r1 + r2)
tst *reg, (reg/imm)*	tst r1, r2	Set flags after computing (r1 AND r2)
teq *reg, (reg/imm)*	teq r1, r2	Set flags after computing (r1 XOR r2)

Table 4.7: Semantics of compare instructions

cmn computes the flags after adding the register values, *tst* computes a bitwise AND of the two operands and then sets the flags, and *teq* tests for equality by computing an XOR (exclusive or) of the operands. For this set of instructions, the second operand can be an immediate also. Note that the compare instructions, are not the only instructions that can set the flags. Let us discuss a generic class of instructions that can set the CPSR flags.

4.2.4 Instructions that Set CPSR Flags – The 'S' Suffix

Normal instructions such as *add* and *sub* do not set the CPSR flags. However, it is possible to make any data processing instruction set the flags by adding the suffix - 's' - to it. For example, the *adds* and *subs* instructions do the regular jobs of addition and subtraction respectively, and additionally also set the CPSR flags. The rules for setting the flags are given in Section 4.2.3. Let us now see how we can use these flags.

4.2.5 Data Processing Instructions that use CPSR Flags

There are three simple data processing instructions that use the CPSR flags in their computation. They are *sbc*, *rsc*, and *adc*.

Let us now motivate this section with an example. Our basic ARM instruction format does not support 64-bit registers. Consequently, if we desire to implement the *long* data type that uses 64 bits, we need to use two registers. Let us assume that one long value is present in registers, $r2$, and $r1$. Here, $r2$ contains the upper 32 bits, and $r1$ contains the lower 32 bits. Let the second long value be present in registers $r4$, and

$r3$. Let us now try to add these two long values to produce a 64-bit result, and save it in registers, $r6$ and $r5$. See Example 42.

Example 42

Add two long values stored in r2,r1 and r4,r3.

Answer:

```
adds r5, r1, r3
adc  r6, r2, r4
```

The (adds) instruction adds the values in r1 and r3. adc(add with carry) adds r2, r4, and the value of the carry flag. This is exactly the same as normal addition.

Example 43 shows how to subtract the values.

Example 43

Subtract two long values stored in r2,r1 and r4,r3.

Answer:

```
subs r5, r1, r3
sbc  r6, r2, r4
```

subs subtracts the value of r3 from the value in r1. sbc(subtract with carry) subtracts the value in r4 from the value in r2. Additionally, if the previous instruction resulted in a borrow (carry equal to 0), then it also subtracts the carry bit. This is the same as normal subtraction.

We list the semantics of the instructions in Table 4.8. Note that in the case of a subtraction the carry flag is set to 0, when there is a borrow. The *NOT* operation flips a 0 to 1, and vice versa. Lastly, *rsc* stands for – *reverse subtract with carry*.

Semantics	Example	Explanation
adc *reg, reg, reg*	adc r1, r2, r3	r1 = r2 + r3 + Carry_Flag
sbc *reg, reg, reg*	sbc r1, r2, r3	r1 = r2 - r3 - NOT(Carry_Flag)
rsc *reg, reg, reg*	rsc r1, r2, r3	r1 = r3 - r2 - NOT(Carry_Flag)

Table 4.8: Semantics of *adc*, *sbc*, and *rsc* instructions

4.2.6 Simple Branch Instructions

An ISA with just data processing instructions is very weak. We need branch instructions such that we can implement if-statements and for-loops. ARM programs primarily use three branch instructions to do most of their work. They are: *b, beq, bne*. Their semantics are given in Table 4.9.

Semantics	Example	Explanation
b *label*	b .foo	Jump unconditionally to label .foo
beq *label*	beq .foo	Branch to .foo if the last flag setting instruction has resulted in an equality and (Z flag is 1)
bne *label*	bne .foo	Branch to .foo if the last flag setting instruction has resulted in an inequality and (Z flag is 0)

Table 4.9: Semantics of simple branch instructions

Example 44
Write an ARM assembly program to compute the factorial of a positive number (> 1) stored in r0. Save the result in r1.
Answer:

```
───────────────────────── C ─────────────────────────
int val = get_input();
int idx;
int prod = 1;
for (idx = 1; idx <= val ;
     idx++) {
     prod = prod * idx;
}
```

```
──────────────────────── ARM assembly ────────────────────────
    mov r1, #1        /* prod = 1 */
    mov r3, #1        /* idx = 1 */
.loop:
    mul r1, r3, r1    /* prod = prod * idx */
    cmp r3, r0        /* compare idx, with the input (num) */
    add r3, r3, #1    /* idx ++ */
    bne .loop         /* loop condition */
```

Let us now see, how we can use the power of branches to write some powerful programs. Let us consider the factorial function. In Example 44, we show a small program to compute the factorial of a natural number. $r3$ is a counter that is initialised to 0. We keep on incrementing it till it matches $r0$. $r1$ represents the product. We iteratively multiply the value of $r3$ with $r1$. At the end of the set of iterations, $r1$ contains the factorial of the value given in $r0$.

Example 45

Write an assembly program to find out if a natural number stored in r0 is a perfect square. Save the Boolean result in r1.

Answer:

```
1  mov r1, #0 /* result initialised to false */
2  mov r2, #1 /* counter */
3  .loop:
4          mul r3, r2, r2
5          cmp r3, r0
6          beq .square
7          add r2, r2, #1
8          cmp r2, r0
9          bne .loop
10
11         b .exit    /* number is not a square */
12 .square:
13         mov r1, #1 /* number is a square */
14 .exit:
```

Let us show the example of another program to test if a number is a perfect square (see Example 45). $r1$ contains the result of the operation. If the number is a perfect square we set $r1$ to 1, else we set $r1$ to 0. The main loop is between lines 3 and 9. Here, we increment the value of $r2$ iteratively, and test if its square equals $r0$. If it does, we jump to .square, set $r1$ to 1, and jump to .exit. Here, we print the value (code not shown), and exit the program. We assume a hypothetical label – .exit – that is present at the end of the program (also shown in the code). The exit condition of the loop is Line 9, where we consider the result of the comparison of $r2$ and $r0$. If $r2$ is equal to $r0$, then $r0$ cannot contain a perfect square because $r0$ is at least equal to 2 at the end of any iteration.

4.2.7 Branch and Link Instruction

We can use the simple branch instructions to implement *for* loops and *if* statements. However, we need a stronger variant of the branch instruction to implement function calls. Function calls are different than regular branches because we need to remember the point in the program that the function needs to return to. ARM provides the *bl* (branch-and-link) instruction for this purpose. The semantics of this instruction is shown in Table 4.10.

Semantics	Example	Explanation
bl *label*	bl .foo	(1) Jump unconditionally to the function at .foo
		(2) Save the next PC (PC + 4) in the *lr* register

Table 4.10: Semantics of the branch and link instruction

The *bl* instruction jumps to the function that begins at the specified label. Note that in the ARM ISA, there is no special way for designating the start of a function. Any instruction can in principle be the start of a function. In ARM assembly, the starting instruction of a function needs to have a label assigned to it. Along with branching to the given label, the *bl* instruction also saves the value of the return address, which is equal to the current PC plus 4, into the *lr* register (*r14*). We need to add 4 over here because the size of an instruction in ARM is exactly equal to 4 bytes.

Once a function starts executing, it is expected that it will preserve the value of the return address saved in the *lr* register unless it invokes other functions. If a function invokes other functions, it needs to spill and restore registers as mentioned in Section 3.3.10. When we wish to return from a function, we need to move the value in the *lr* register to the *pc* register (*r15*). The PC will point to the instruction at the return address and execution will proceed from that point.

Example 46
Example of an assembly program with a function call.

```
───────────────────── C ─────────────────────
int foo() {
    return 2;
}
void main() {
        int x = 3;
        int y = x + foo();
}
```

```
───────────────────── ARM assembly ─────────────────────
foo:
    mov r0, #2
    mov pc, lr

main:
    mov r1, #3      /* x = 3 */
    bl foo          /* invoke foo */
                    /*  y = x + foo() */
    add r2, r0, r1
```

Let us take a look at Example 46. In this example, we consider a simple piece of C code that calls a function *foo* that returns a constant value of 2. It adds the return value to the variable *x* to produce *y*.

In the equivalent ARM code, we define two labels – *foo* and *main*. We assume that execution starts from the *main* label. We map *x* to *r1*, and set its value equal to 3. Then, we call the function *foo*. In it we set the value of register *r0* to 2, and return by moving the value in the *lr* register to the PC. When the program returns, it begins execution at the subsequent line in the main function. The register *r0* maintains its value equal to 2 across functions. We add the value in *r1* to the value in *r0* to produce the value for *y*. It is saved in *r2*.

Nowadays, there is a simpler method is used to return from a function. We can use the *bx* instruction that jumps to an address contained in a register (semantics shown in Figure 4.11).

Semantics	Example	Explanation
bx *reg*	bx r2	(1) Jump unconditionally to the address contained in register, r2

Table 4.11: Semantics of the *bx* instruction

We can simplify the assembly code in Example 46 as follows.

```
──────────────────────── ARM assembly ────────────────────────
foo:
    mov r0, #2
    bx lr

main:
    mov r1, #3        /* x = 3 */
    bl foo            /* invoke foo */
                      /*  y = x + foo() */
    add r2, r0, r1
```

4.2.8   Conditional Instructions

Now, that we have a fairly good idea of basic branch instructions, let us elaborate some special features of ARM assembly. These features help make the process of coding very efficient. Let us consider the instructions *beq* and *bne* again. We note that they are variants of the basic *b* instruction. They are distinguished by their suffixes – *eq* and *ne*. The former denotes equality, and the latter denotes inequality. These suffixes are known as *condition codes*

ARM Condition Codes

Let us first consider the list of *condition codes* shown in Table 4.12. There are 16 condition codes in ARM. Each condition code has a unique number, and suffix. For example, the condition code with suffix *eq* has a number equal to 0. Every condition code is associated with a unique condition. For example, *eq* is associated with equality. To test if the condition holds, the ARM processor takes a look at the CPSR flags. The last column in Table 4.12 shows the values of the flags that need to be set for the condition to hold.

The *eq* and *ne* conditions can be tested by considering the Z(zero) flag alone. The expectation is that an earlier *cmp* or *subs* instruction would have set these flags. If the comparison resulted in an equality, then the Z flag would be set to 1.

As described in Section 4.2.3, if a subtraction of unsigned numbers leads to a borrow, then the carry flag is set to 0. This condition is also known as an unsigned underflow. If there is no borrow, then the carry flag is set to 1. Consequently, if the comparison between unsigned numbers concludes that the first number is greater than or equal to the second number, then the C(carry flag) needs to be set to 1. Likewise, if the carry flag is set to 0, then we can say that the first operand is smaller than the second operand (unsigned comparison). These two conditions are captured by the *hs* and *lo* condition codes respectively.

The next four condition codes check if a number is positive or negative, and if there has been an overflow. These conditions can be trivially evaluated by considering the values of N(negative) and V(overflow) flags respectively. *hi* denotes unsigned higher. In this case, we need to additionally test the Z flag. Likewise for *ls* (unsigned lower or equal), we need to test the Z flag, along with the C flag.

Number	Suffix	Meaning	Flag State
0	eq	equal	Z = 1
1	ne	not equal	Z = 0
2	cs/hs	carry set/ unsigned higher or equal	C = 1
3	cc/lo	carry clear/ unsigned lower	C = 0
4	mi	negative/ minus	N = 1
5	pl	positive or zero/ plus	N = 0
6	vs	overflow	V = 1
7	vc	no overflow	V = 0
8	hi	unsigned higher	$(C = 1) \land (Z = 0)$
9	ls	unsigned lower or equal	$(C = 0) \lor (Z = 1)$
10	ge	signed greater than or equal	N = 0
11	lt	signed less than	N = 1
12	gt	signed greater than	$(Z = 0) \land (N = 0)$
13	le	signed less than or equal	$(Z = 1) \lor (N = 1)$
14	al	always	
15	–	reserved	

Table 4.12: Condition codes

ARM has four condition codes for signed numbers – $ge(\geq)$, $le(\leq)$, $gt(>)$, and $lt(<)$. The ge condition code simply tests the N flag. It should be equal to 0. This means that a preceding cmp or $subs$ instruction has subtracted two numbers, where the first operand was greater than or equal to the second operand. For the gt instruction, we need to consider the Z flag also. In a similar manner, the less than condition codes – lt and le – work. The conditions for the flags are given in Table 4.12.

Note that for signed numbers, we have not considered the possibility of an overflow in Table 4.12. Theorem 2.3.4.1 outlines the precise conditions for detecting an overflow. We leave the process of augmenting the conditions to consider overflow as an exercise for the reader. Lastly, the al(always) condition code means that the instruction is not associated with any condition. It executes according to its default specification. Hence, it is not required to explicitly specify the al condition since it is the default.

Conditional Variants of Normal Instructions

Condition codes are not just restricted to branches. We can use condition codes with normal instructions such as add and sub also. For example, the instruction $addeq$ performs an addition if the Z flag in the $flags$ register is set to true. It means that the last time that the flags were set (most likely by a cmp instruction), the instruction must have concluded an equality. However, if the last comparison instruction concluded that its operands are unequal, then the ARM processor treats the $addeq$ instruction as a nop instruction (no operation). We shall see in Chapter 9 that by using such conditional instructions, we can increase the performance of an advanced processor. Let us consider an example that uses the $addeq$ instruction.

Example 47
Write a program in ARM assembly to count the number of 1s in a 32-bit number stored in r1. Save the result in r4.
Answer:

```
mov r2, #1 /* idx = 1 */
mov r4, #0 /* count = 0 */

/* start the iterations */
.loop:
        /* extract the LSB and compare */
        and r3, r1, #1
        cmp r3, #1

        /* increment the counter */
        addeq r4, r4, #1

        /* prepare for the next iteration */
        mov r1, r1, lsr #1
        add r2, r2, #1

        /* loop condition */
        cmp r2, #32
        ble .loop
```

4.2.9 Load-Store Instructions

Simple Load-Store Instructions

The simplest load and store instructions are *ldr* and *str* respectively. Here, is an example.

```
ldr r1, [r0]
```

This instruction directs the processor to load the value in register $r1$, from the memory location stored in $r0$, as shown in Figure 4.2.

Note that in this case, $r0$, contains the starting address of the data in memory. The *ldr* instructions loads 4 bytes in a register. If the value contained in $r0$ is v, then we need to fetch the bytes from v to $v + 3$. These 32 bits (4 bytes), are brought from memory and saved in register $r1$.

The *str* instruction performs the reverse process. It reads the value in a register and saves it in a memory location. An example is shown in Figure 4.3. Here $r0$ is known as the base register.

```
str r1, [r0]
```

Load-Store Instructions with an Offset

We can specify load and store instructions with a base register, and an optional offset. Let us consider:

```
ldr r1, [r0, #4]
```

Here, the memory address is equal to the value in $r0$ plus 4. It is possible to specify a register in place of an immediate operand.

ldr r1, [r0]

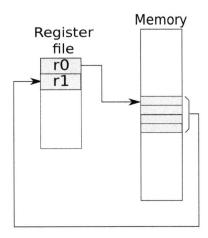

Figure 4.2: The *ldr* instruction

str r1, [r0]

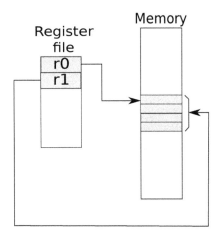

Figure 4.3: The *str* instruction

```
ldr r1, [r0, r2]
```

The memory address is equal to $r0 + r2$. In this expression, $r0$ and $r2$ refer to the values stored in them. We can alternatively state the operation in this program as: $r1 \leftarrow [r0 + r2]$ (see the register transfer notation defined in Section 3.2.5).

Table 4.13 shows the semantics of different types of load store instructions. The third column shows the *addressing mode*. The register $r2$ in this case is known as the index register because it contains a value that is added to the base register, and this value can be used as the index of an array (see Section 4.3.1). Note

Semantics	Example	Explanation	Addressing Mode
ldr *reg*, [*reg*]	ldr r1, [r0]	$r1 \leftarrow [r0]$	register-indirect
ldr *reg*, [*reg, imm*]	ldr r1, [r0, #4]	$r1 \leftarrow [r0 + 4]$	base-offset
ldr *reg*, [*reg, reg*]	ldr r1, [r0, r2]	$r1 \leftarrow [r0 + r2]$	base-index
ldr *reg*, [*reg, reg*, shift *imm*]	ldr r1, [r0, r2, lsl #2]	$r1 \leftarrow [r0 + r2 \ll 2]$	base-scaled-index
str *reg*, [*reg*]	str r1, [r0]	$[r0] \leftarrow r1$	register-indirect
str *reg*, [*reg, imm*]	str r1, [r0, #4]	$[r0 + 4] \leftarrow r1$	base-offset
str *reg*, [*reg, reg*]	str r1, [r0, r2]	$[r0 + r2] \leftarrow r1$	base-index
str *reg*, [*reg, reg*, shift *imm*]	str r1, [r0, r2, lsl #2]	$[r0 + r2 \ll 2] \leftarrow r1$	base-scaled-index

Table 4.13:   Load and store instruction semantics

that some authors call the base-offset mode as also the *displacement* addressing mode.

Load-Store instructions for Bytes and Half-Words

The *ldr* and *str* instructions load/store 4 bytes of data. However, it is possible to also load and store 1 and 2 bytes of data. 2 bytes is also known as a half-word, where a word is equal to 4 bytes.

Semantics	Example	Explanation
ldrb *reg*, [*reg, imm*]	ldrb r1, [r0, #2]	$r1 \leftarrow [r0 + 2]$ (1 unsigned byte)
ldrh *reg*, [*reg, imm*]	ldrh r1, [r0, #2]	$r1 \leftarrow [r0 + 2]$ (2 unsigned bytes)
ldrsb *reg*, [*reg, imm*]	ldrsb r1, [r0, #2]	$r1 \leftarrow [r0 + 2]$ (1 signed byte)
ldrsh *reg*, [*reg, imm*]	ldrsh r1, [r0, #2]	$r1 \leftarrow [r0 + 2]$ (2 signed bytes)
strb *reg*, [*reg, imm*]	strb r1, [r0, #2]	$[r0 + 2] \leftarrow r1$ (1 unsigned byte)
strh *reg*, [*reg, imm*]	strh r1, [r0, #2]	$[r0 + 2] \leftarrow r1$ (2 unsigned bytes)

Table 4.14:   Load and store instructions for bytes and half-words in the base-offset addressing mode

Table 4.14 shows the load and store instructions for bytes and half words using the base-offset addressing mode. *ldrb* loads an unsigned byte to a register. It places the byte in the least significant 8 bits. The rest of the 24 bits are set to 0. *ldrh* similarly loads an unsigned half-word (16 bits). *ldrsb*, and *ldrsh* load a signed byte and half-word respectively. They extend the sign of the operand (see Section 2.3.4) to make it fit in 32 bits. This is done by replicating the MSB. *strb* and *strh* store an unsigned byte in memory. Note that unlike loads, there are no ARM instructions to extend the sign of the operand while saving it in memory.

4.3   Advanced Features

We are in a good point to take a look at some of the advanced features in the ARM instruction set. Up till now, we have taken a look at basic instructions that allow us to implement simple data types in a high level language such as C or Java. We can translate simple programs that contain integers into assembly code, compute the results of mathematical functions, load and store values from memory. However, there are other high level features such as functions, arrays, and structures that are present in high level languages. They shall require special support at the assembly level for creating efficient implementations.

By no means has the process of programming language development stopped. We expect that over the next few decades, there will be many new kinds of programming languages. They will make the process of programming easier for more programmers, and it should be easier to leverage novel features of futuristic hardware. This would require extra instructions and support at the level of assembly programs. This is thus an evolving field, and deserves a thorough study.

4.3.1 Arrays

Array Specific Features

Note that the starting memory location of entry i is equal to the base address of the array plus $4i$ in an array with word (4 byte) sized elements. In a high level language, the programmer always specifies the index in an array, and relies on the compiler to multiply the index by 4. ARM assembly provides nice features to multiply i by 4 by using the *lsl* instruction. This feature can be embedded in load-store instructions.

```
ldr r0, [r1, r2, lsl #2]
```

In this case the base address is stored in register, $r1$, and the offset is equal to $r2 << 2 = 4*r2$. The advantage here is that we do not need a separate instruction to multiply the index by 4. We have already seen this optimisation in Section 4.2.2. However, there are other optimisations that can make our life easier. Let us consider array accesses in a loop as shown in Example 48.

Example 48 *Convert the following C program to a program to ARM assembly. Assume that the base address of the array is stored in $r0$.*

———————————————————————————— C ————————————————————————————
```
void addNumbers(int a[100]) {
    int idx;
    int sum = 0;
    for (idx = 0; idx < 100; idx++){
        sum = sum + a[idx];
    }
}
```

Answer:
——————————————————————— ARM assembly ———————————————————————
```
1  /* base address of array a in r0 */
2  mov r1, #0   /* sum = 0 */
3  mov r2, #0   /* idx = 0 */
4
5  .loop:
6      ldr r3, [r0, r2, lsl #2]
7      add r2, r2, #1   /* idx ++ */
8      add r1, r1, r3   /* sum += a[idx] */
9      cmp r2, #100     /* loop condition */
10     bne .loop
```

There is a scope for added efficiency here. We note that Lines 6 and 7 form a standard pattern. Line 6 reads the array entry, and Line 7 increments the index. Almost all sequential array accesses follow a similar pattern. Hence, it makes sense to have one instruction that simplifies this process.

The ARM architecture adds two extra addressing modes for the load and store instructions to achieve this. They are called *pre-indexed* and *post-indexed* with auto-update. In the pre-indexed addressing mode (with auto-update), the base address is updated first, and then the effective memory address is computed. In a post-indexed scheme, the base address is updated after the effective address is computed.

The pre-indexed addressing mode with auto-update is implemented by adding a '!' sign after the address.

```
────────────────────── Examples of the pre-indexed addressing mode ──────────────────────
ldr r3, [r0, #4]!          /*  r3 = [r0+4]; r0 = r0 + 4*/
ldr r3, [r0, r1, lsl #2]! /* r3 = [r0 + r1 << 2];
                                r0 = r0 + r1 << 2;  */
```

The post-indexed addressing mode is implemented by encapsulating the base address within '[' and ']', and writing the offset arguments separated by commas after it.

```
────────────────────── Examples of the post-indexed addressing mode ──────────────────────
ldr r3, [r0], #4           /* r3 = [r0], r0 = r0 + 4 */
ldr r3, [r0], r1, lsl #2  /* r3 = [r0], r0 = r0 + r1 << 2 */
```

Let us now see, how we can slightly make our *addNumbers* slightly more intuitive. The modified ARM code is shown in Example 49.

Example 49

Convert the assembly code shown in Example 48 to use the post indexed addressing mode.
Answer:

```
──────────────────────── ARM assembly ────────────────────────
1 /* base address of array a in r0 */
2     mov r1, #0        /* sum = 0 */
3     add r4, r0, #400  /* address of a[100]*/
4 .loop:
5         ldr r3, [r0], #4
6     add r1, r1, r3    /* sum += a[idx] */
7     cmp r0, r4
8     bne .loop
```

We have eliminated the index variable saved in $r2$. It is not required anymore. We directly update the base address in Line 5. For the loop exit condition, we compute the first address beyond the end of the array in Line 3. We compare the base address with this illegal address in Line 7, and then if they are unequal we keep iterating.

Example 48 contains 5 lines in the loop, whereas the code in Example 49 contains 4 lines in the loop. We have thus shown that it is possible to reduce the code size (of the loop) by 20% using post-indexed addressing, and increase performance too since most cores do not impose additional time overheads when auto-update addressing modes are used.

Structures

Implementing structures is very similar to implementing arrays. Let us look at a typical structure in C.

```
struct Container {
    int a;
    int b;
    char c;
    short int d;
    int e;
};
```

We can treat each structure as an array. Consequently, a structure will have a base address and each element of the structure will have an offset. Unlike an array, different elements in a structure can have different sizes, and thus they are not constrained to start with offsets that are multiples of the word size.

Type	Element	Offset
int	a	0
int	b	4
char	c	8
short int	d	10
int	e	12

Table 4.15: Elements in the structure and their offsets

Table 4.15 shows the offsets for different elements within a structure (as generated by the GNU ARM compiler). We need to note that compilers for the ARM architecture impose additional constraints. They pad variable addresses, and align them with 2 byte or 4 byte boundaries as shown in Table 4.15 The rules for variable alignment are described in detail in the ARM architecture manual [arm, 2000]. In a similar fashion it is possible to implement more high level data structures such as unions and classes. The interested reader is referred to a book on compilers.

4.3.2 Functions

Let us now use two sophisticated ARM instructions for spilling and restoring registers in the stack. They can be used to implement both caller saved and callee saved functions.

Instructions for Spilling and Restoring Registers

Let us now describe two instructions to use the stack for saving and restoring a set of registers – $ldmfd$ and $stmfd$. These registers load and store multiple registers in a memory region such as the stack. For brevity, we do not consider generic memory regions in this book. We limit our discussion to the stack. $ldmfd$ and $stmfd$ instructions take a base register (e.g., stack pointer), and set of registers as arguments. They load or store the set of registers in the memory region pointed to by the base register. Note that the order of the registers does not matter. The registers are always rearranged in ascending order.

Let us consider an example using the store instruction, $stmfd$.

```
stmfd sp!, {r2,r3,r1,r4}
```

The $stmfd$ instruction assumes a downward growing stack, and it also assumes that the stack pointer points to the starting address of the value at the top of the stack. Recall that the top of the stack in a downward growing stack is defined as the starting address of the last value pushed on the stack. In this case the registers are processed in ascending order – $r1$, $r2$, $r3$, $r4$. Secondly memory addresses are also

Instruction	Semantics
ldmfd sp!, {list of registers }	Pop the stack and assign values to registers in ascending order. Update the value of sp.
stmfd sp!, {list of registers }	Push the registers on the stack in descending order. Update the value of sp.

Table 4.16: Semantics of the $ldmfd$ and $stmfd$ instructions

accessed in ascending order. Consequently $r1$ will be saved in $sp - 16$, $r2$ in $sp - 12$, $r3$ in $sp - 8$, and $r4$ in $sp - 4$. Alternatively, we can explain this instruction by observing that registers are pushed into the stack in descending order. We use the '!' suffix with the base address register to instruct the processor to update the value of the stack pointer after the execution of the instruction. In this case, we set sp equal to $sp - 16$.

There is a variant of this instruction that does not set the stack pointer to the starting address of the memory region used to save registers. An example with this variant is:

```
stmfd sp, {r2,r3,r1,r4}
```

Note that this variant is rarely used in practice, especially when the base register is sp.

Similarly, the $ldmfd$ instruction loads a set of values starting at the stack pointer, and then updates the stack pointer. Akin to the $stmfd$ instruction, we use the '!' suffix to use the base register auto update feature.

```
ldmfd sp!, {r2,r3,r1,r4}
```

For example, in this case we set $r1 = [sp]$, $r2 = [sp+4]$, $r3 = [sp+8]$, and $r4 = [sp+12]$. In other words, we iteratively pop the stack and assign the values to registers in ascending order. The $ldmfd$ instruction also has a variant that does not update the base register. We simply need to delete the '!' suffix after the base register.

```
ldmfd sp, {r2,r3,r1,r4}
```

The semantics of these instructions are shown in Table 4.16.

Let us conclude this section with an example. We show a recursive power function in C that takes two arguments x and n, and computes x^n.

Example 50

Write a function in C and implement it in ARM assembly to compute x^n, where x and n are natural numbers. Assume that x is passed through $r0$, n through $r1$, and the return value is passed back to the original program via $r0$. ***Answer:***

——————————————————————————— C ———————————————————————————

```
int power(int x, int n) {
        if (n == 0)
                return 1;
        int y = x * power(x, n-1);
```

```
        return y;
}
```

When we compile this function to ARM assembly, we get:

```
──────────────────────────────── ARM assembly ────────────────────────────────
 1  power:
 2      cmp r1, #0              /* compare n with 0  */
 3      moveq r0, #1           /* return 1 */
 4      bxeq pc, lr            /* return */
 5
 6      stmfd sp!, {r4, lr}    /* save r4 and lr */
 7      mov r4, r0             /* save x in r4 */
 8      sub r1, r1, #1         /* n = n - 1 */
 9      bl power               /* recursively call power */
10      mul r0, r4, r0         /* power(x,n) = x * power(x,n-1) */
11      ldmfd sp!, {r4, pc}    /* restore r4 and return */
```

We first compare n with 0. If n is equal to 0, then we need to return 1 (Line 3). We subsequently, return from the function. Note the use of the instruction moveq here.

However, if $n \neq 0$, then we need to make a recursive function call to evaluate x^{n-1}. We start out by saving register r4, and the return address (lr) on the stack in Line 6 using the stmfd instruction. We save the value of r0 in r4 because it will get overwritten by the recursive call to the power function. Subsequently, we decrement r1 that contains the value of n, and then we call the power function recursively in Line 10. The result of the power function is assumed to be present in r0. We multiply this result with the value of x (stored in r4) in Line 10.

We simultaneously do two operations in Line 11. We load the value of r4, and pc from the stack. We first read the first operand, r4, which was saved on the stack by the corresponding stmfd instruction in Line 6. The second operand saved on the stack was the return address. We read this value and save it in pc. Effectively, we are executing the instruction mov pc, lr, *and we are thus returning from the function. Hence, after executing Line 11, we start executing instructions from the return address of the function.*

The *ldm* and *stm* instructions can also assume an upward growing stack. The interested reader can refer to the ARM manual [arm, 2000] for a thorough explanation.

4.4   Encoding the Instruction Set

Let us now see how to convert ARM assembly instructions to a sequence of 0s and 1s. Each ARM instruction is represented using 32 bits. We need to encode the instruction type, values of conditional fields, register numbers, and immediate operands using these 32 bits only.

Let us take a look at the generic format of ARM instructions. For every instruction we need to initially encode at least two pieces of information – condition codes (see Table 4.12), and the format of the instruction (data processing, branch, load/store, or others). Table 4.12 defines 15 conditions on each instruction. It will take 4 bits to represent this information.

> **Important Point 6**
> *To uniquely encode a set of n elements, we need at least $\lceil log_2(n) \rceil$ bits. We can assign each element a number between 0 and $n-1$. We can represent these numbers in the binary format. The number of bits required is equal to the number of bits needed to represent the largest number, $n-1$. If we have $log_2(n)$ bits, then the largest number that we can represent is $2^{log_2(n)} - 1 = n - 1$. However, $log_2(n)$ might be a fraction. Hence, we need to use $\lceil log_2(n) \rceil$ bits.*

ARM has four types of instructions – data processing (add/ subtract/ multiply/ compare), load/store, branch, and miscellaneous. We need 2 bits to represent this information. These bits determine the type of the instruction. Figure 4.4 shows the generic format for instructions in ARM.

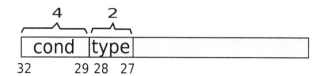

Figure 4.4: Generic format of an ARM instruction

4.4.1   Data Processing Instructions

The type field is equal to 00 for data processing instructions. The rest of the 26 bits need to contain the instruction type, special conditions, and registers. Figure 4.5 shows the format for data processing instructions.

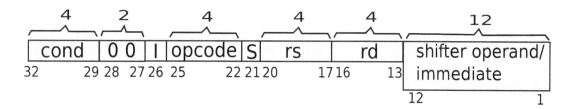

Figure 4.5: Format of the data processing instruction

The 26th bit is called the I (immediate) bit. It is similar to the I bit in *SimpleRisc* . If it is set to 1, then the second operand is an immediate, otherwise, it is a register. Since ARM has 16 data processing instructions, we require 4 bits to represent them. This information is saved in bits 22-25. The 21st bit saves the S bit. If it is turned on, then the instruction will set the CPSR (see Section 4.2.4).

The rest of the 20 bits save the input and output operands. Since ARM has 16 registers, we require 4 bits to encode a register. Bits 17-20 save the identifier of the first input operand (rs), which needs to be a register. Bits 13-16 save the identifier of the destination register (rd).

Bits 1-12 are used to save the immediate value or the shifter operand. Let us see how to make best use of these 12 bits.

Encoding Immediate Values

ARM supports 32-bit immediate values. However, we observe that we have only 12 bits to encode them. Hence, we cannot possibly encode all the 2^{32} possible values. We need to choose a meaningful subset of them. The idea is to encode a subset of 32-bit values using 12 bits. The hardware is expected to decode these 12 bits, and expand them to 32 bits while processing the instruction.

Now, 12 bits is a rather unwieldy value. Neither is it 1 byte nor is it 2 bytes. Hence, it was necessary to come up with a very ingenious solution. The idea is to split the 12 bits into two parts – a 4-bit constant (*rot*), and an 8 bit payload (*payload*) (see Figure 4.6).

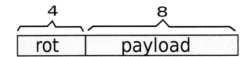

Figure 4.6: Format of the immediate

Let the actual number that is encoded in these 12 bits be n. We have:

$$n = payload \ ror \ (2 \times rot)$$

The actual number n is obtained by right rotating the payload by 2 times the value in the *rot* field. Let us now try to understand the logic of doing so.

The final number n is a 32-bit value. A naive solution would have been to use the 12 bits to specify the least significant bits of n. The higher order bits could be 0. However, programmers tend to access data and memory in terms of bytes. Hence, 1.5 bytes is of no use to us. A better solution is to have a 1 byte payload and place it in any location in the 32-bit field. The rest of the 4 bits are used for this purpose. They can encode a number from 0 to 15. The ARM processor doubles this value to consider all even numbers between 0 and 30. It right rotates the payload by this amount. The advantage of doing so is that it is possible to encode a wider set of numbers. For all of these numbers, there are 8 bits that correspond to the payload, and the rest of the 24 bits are all zeros. The *rot* bits just determine which 8 bits in a 32-bit field are occupied by the payload.

Let us consider a set of examples.

Example 51
Encode the decimal number 42.
Answer: *42 in the hex format is 0x2A, or alternatively 0x00 00 00 2A. There is no right rotation involved. Hence, the immediate field is 0x02A.*

Example 52
Encode the number 0x2A 00 00 00.
Answer: *This number is obtained by right rotating 0x2A by 8 places. Note that we need to right rotate by 4 places to move a hex digit by one position. We need to now divide 8 by 2, to get 4. Thus, the encoded format for this number is 0x42A.*

Example 53

Encode 0x 00 00 2A 00.

Answer: *The first step is to count the number of right rotations. We observe that the number 0x2A has been rotated to the right by 24 positions. We now proceed to divide 24 by 2 to obtain 12. Thus, the encoded format of the number is 0xC2A.*

Example 54

Encode the number 0x 00 02 DC 00 as an ARM immediate.

Answer: *The first part is to figure out the payload. The payload is – 10 1101 11 – in binary. This is equal to 0xB7. The next step is to figure out the rotation. Let us simplify the task by observing that right rotating by n places is the same as left rotating by $32 - n$ places. Let us concentrate on 0xC00. This is equal to 110000000000 in binary. The rightmost 1 is now at the 11th position. It has moved 10 places from the 1st position. Thus the number has been rotated to the left by 10 places. It has been rotated to the right by 22 places. $22/2 = 11(0xB)$. Hence, the encoded number is 0xBB7.*

The reader needs to understand that this encoding is supposed to be done by the assembler or the compiler. The user simply needs to only use values in her assembly code that can be encoded as an ARM immediate. For example, a number like -1 cannot be encoded as an ARM immediate. It is 0xFF FF FF FF. The payload is greater than 8 bits. Ideally, an instruction of the form: $add\ r1, r1, \# - 1$ is wrong. Some assemblers will try to fix the problem by changing the instruction to $sub\ r1, r1, \#1$. However, all assemblers are not smart enough to figure this out. If the user wishes to uses a value that cannot be encoded in ARM's 12 bit format, then the user (or the program loader) needs to load it byte by byte in a register, and use the register as an operand.

Encoding the Shifter Operand

We have 12 bits to encode the shifter operand. Figure 4.7 shows the scheme for encoding it. A shifter operand is of the form: rt (lsl|lsr|asr|ror) (shift reg/ shift imm.)

The first four bits (1-4) encode the id of the register *rt*. The next bit determines the nature of the shift argument (immediate or register). If it is 0 then the argument is an immediate, otherwise it is a register. Bits 6 and 7 specify the type of the shift (also see Figure 4.7(c)). For example, the type can be *lsl* (logical shift left). It can also be *lsr* (logic shift right), *asr* (arithmetic shift right), or *ror* (right rotate). If we are shifting by an immediate value, then bits 8-12 specify a 32-bit value called a *shift immediate*. Otherwise, if we are shifting by a value in a register, then bits 9-12 specify the id of the register.

Let us consider an instruction of the form: $add\ r3, r1, r2$. In this case, the second operand is $r2$. We can think of $r2$ as actually a shifter operand where it is being left shifted by 0. Hence, to encode we need to set the shift type to *lsl* (00), set the argument to immediate (0), and set the shift immediate to 00000. We thus see that specifying a register as the second argument is easy. It is a special case of a shifter operand, and we just need to set bits 5-12 as 0.

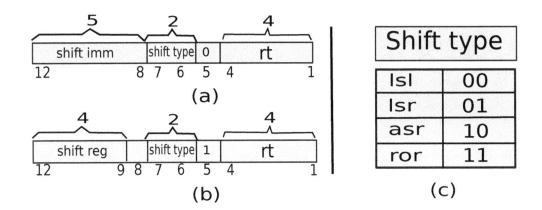

Figure 4.7: Format of the shifter operand

4.4.2 Load-Store Instructions

A simple load or store instruction can be represented as : (ldr | str) rd, [rs, (immediate/shifter operand)].
We require additional syntax for pre and post-indexed addressing (see Section 4.3.1). The format for the
encoding of load and store instructions is shown in Figure 4.8.

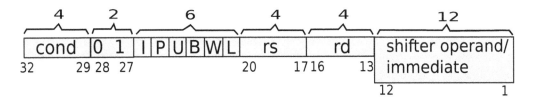

Figure 4.8: Format of the load/store instructions

The semantics of the bits I, P, U, B, W, and L is shown in Table 4.17. In this case, the I bit has reverse
semantics as compared to the case of data processing instructions. If it is 1, then the last 12 bits represent
a shifter operand, otherwise they represent an immediate value. P represents the advanced addressing mode
– pre or post, and W determines if the advanced addressing mode is used or a simple addressing mode is
used. We can either add the offset from the base register or we can subtract it from the base register. This
is specified by the U bit. The B bit determines the granularity of the transfer – byte level or word level.
Lastly, the L bit determines if the instruction is a load or a store.

These six bits $IPUBWL$ capture all the different variants of the load and store instructions. The rest of
the format is the same as the data processing instruction other than the encoding of immediates. Immediates
in memory instructions do not follow the (rot+payload) format. The 12 bit immediate fields represents an
unsigned number between 0 and 4095.

We thus observe that like *SimpleRisc* , the designers of the ARM instruction set have tried to stick to
the same instruction format with minor variations..

Question 6 *What is the necessity for having the U bit?*

Answer: *Negative numbers such as -4 or -8 cannot be represented in ARM's 12 bit format for specifying*

Bit	Value	Semantics
I	0	last 12 bits represent an immediate value
	1	last 12 bits represent a shifter operand
P	0	post-indexed addressing
	1	pre-indexed addressing
U	0	subtract offset from base
	1	add offset to base
B	0	transfer word
	1	transfer byte
W	0	do not use pre or post indexed addressing
	1	use pre or post indexed addressing
L	0	store to memory
	1	load from memory

Table 4.17: Semantics of I, P, U, B, W, and L bits

offsets in memory instructions. However, we might need to use addresses with a negative displacement, especially when they are relative to the frame pointer or the stack pointer. The U bit allows us to represent an immediate such as -4 as +4. It additionally instructs the processor to subtract the displacement from the base register.

4.4.3   Branch Instructions

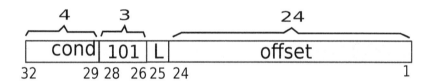

Figure 4.9: Format of the branch and branch-and-link instructions

Figure 4.9 shows the format of the branch (*b*) and the branch-and-link (*bl*) instructions. If the L(link) bit is equal to 1, then the instruction is *bl*, otherwise it is just *b*. The instruction contains a 24-bit signed offset. The ARM processor first shifts the offset by 2 bits. This is because each instruction is 32 bits or 4 bytes long, and additionally the hardware expects instructions to be stored at 4 byte boundaries. Therefore, the starting address of each instruction will contain two zeros in its two least significant positions. Hence, there is no necessity to waste two bits in the encoding for saving these two zeros. The next step is to extend the sign of this shifted offset to 32 bits. Lastly, the hardware computes the branch target by adding the shifted and sign-extended offset to the PC plus 8 bytes.

The interesting thing to note is that we are adding the sign-extended shifted offset to PC+8, not the PC. We shall see in Chapter 9 that the reason for doing this is to simplify the hardware. The format for branches is different from the format used to encode data transfer and data processing instructions. This is because more bits have used to encode the displacement. We had followed a similar approach in *SimpleRisc* also. However, we need to note that having a new format is not a very bad thing if it is simple as is the case for a branch.

4.5   Summary and Further Reading

4.5.1   Summary

Summary 4

1. The ARM ISA is a simple 32-bit RISC ISA.

   (a) It uses 16 registers $r0 \ldots r15$.

   (b) The return address register is known as lr (link register), and it is $r14$.

   (c) The PC is visible to the programmer. It is register $r15$.

   (d) All the instructions are encoded using 32 bits.

2. Data processing instructions accept register operands, and at most one immediate operand. They are 3-address instructions.

3. ARM has a set of compare instructions that can set flags in the CPSR register. Additionally, it is possible to instruct a standard data processing instruction to set the CPSR flags by adding the suffix 's' to it.

4. ARM supports conditional instructions that either execute or not depending upon the values of the CPSR flags. They can be created by appending a condition code to a regular data processing or branch instruction. There are 15 such condition codes. Examples of some condition codes are: gt (greater than), and eq (equal).

5. ARM has two variants of branch instructions.

   (a) It has simple branch instructions that branch to another instruction.

   (b) It has branch-and-link instructions that additionally save the return address in the link register lr.

6. ARM supports both the base-index and base-offset addressing modes for load and store instructions. It has additional support for shifting the index register by treating it as a shifter operand.

7. ARM supports complex addressing modes such as pre-indexed and post-indexed addressing. These addressing modes update the base register.

8. ARM also has support for loading and storing bytes and half-words (2 bytes).

9. The instruction set encoding for data processing instructions is as follows:

   (a) Condition code (4 bits)

   (b) Instruction type (2 bits)

   (c) Second operand: immediate or register (1 bit)

(d) *Opcode (4 bits)*

(e) *S bit (should the CPSR flags be set) (1 bit)*

(f) *Source register1 (4 bits)*

(g) *Destination register (4 bits)*

(h) *Immediate or shifter operand (12 bits)*

10. *The data transfer instructions do not have the S bit. They instead have extra bits to encode the type of load/store instructions, and the addressing mode.*

11. *The branch instructions have an L bit to specify if the return address needs to be saved or not. They use PC-relative addressing and have a 24-bit signed offset. Like SimpleRisc , the hardware assumes that instructions are aligned to 4 byte boundaries, and treats this offset as a distance in terms of memory words. It thus left shifts the offset by 2 positions.*

4.5.2   Further Reading

We have presented an overview of the major features of ARM's assembly language. The reader can refer to ARM's assembly language manual [arm, 2000] for more details.

We have deliberately left out some advanced features. A subset of ARM cores support Thumb-1 and Thumb-2 instructions. These instructions are based on a subset of general purpose instructions and have implicit operands. They are used to decrease the size of compiled code. Some ARM processors have extensive support for floating point instructions (VFP instruction set), and SIMD instructions (execute an instruction on multiple integers/floating point numbers in one go). However, we have not discussed these extensions for the sake of brevity. Some other sophisticated features of ARM processors are security extensions that prevent malicious programs or users from stealing data. Since 2013 ARM processors (conforming to the ARMv8-A architecture) have started using a new 64-bit ARM ISA called A64. The reader can refer to the books by Joseph Yiu [Yiu, 2011, Yiu, 2009], William Hohl [Hohl, 2009], and J. R. Gibson [Gibson, 2011] for a detailed discussion on the ARM instruction set and its latest extensions. Needless to say the reader can always find up to date documentation at ARM's web site http://www.arm.com.

Exercises

Basic ARM Instructions

Ex. 1 — Translate the following code in C to the ARM instruction set using a minimum number of instructions. Assume the variables a, b, c, d and e are 32-bit integers and stored in $r0$, $r1$, $r2$, $r3$ and $r4$ respectively.

(a) `a=a+b+c+d+e;`

(b) `a=b+c;`
   `d=a+b;`

(c) `a=b+c+d;`
   `a=a+a;`

(d) a=2*a+b+c+d;

(e) a=b+c+d;
    a=3*a;

Ex. 2 — Translate the following pieces of code from the ARM assembly language to a high level language. Assume that the variables a, b, c, d and e (containing integers) are stored in the registers $r0$, $r1$, $r2$, $r3$ and $r4$ respectively.

(a)
```
add r0, r0, r1
add r0, r0, r2
add r0, r0, r3
```

(b)
```
orr r0, r0, r1, lsl #1
and r1, r0, r1, lsr #1
```

(c)
```
add r0, r1, r2
rsb r1, r0, r2
```

(d)
```
add r0, r1, r2
add r0, r3, r4
add r0, r0, r1
```

(e)
```
mov r0 #1, lsl #3
mov r0, r0, lsr #1
```

Ex. 3 — Answer the following:

(a) Write the smallest possible ARM assembly program to load the constant 0xEFFFFFF2 into register $r0$.

(*b) Write the smallest possible ARM assembly program to load the constant 0xFFFD67FF into register $r0$.

* **Ex. 4** — Using valid ARM assembly instructions, load the constant, 0xFE0D9FFF, into register $r0$. Try do to it with a minimum number of instructions. DO NOT use pseudo-instructions or assembler directives.

Ex. 5 — Can you give a generic set of ARM instructions or a methodology using which you can load any 32-bit immediate value into a register? Try to minimise the number of instructions.

Ex. 6 — Convert the following C program to ARM assembly. Store the integer, i, in register $r0$. Assume that the starting address of array a is saved in register $r1$, and the starting address of array b is saved in register $r2$.

```
int i;
int b[500];
int a[500];
for(i=0; i < 500; i++) {
    b[i] = a[a[i]];
}
```

** **Ex. 7** — Consider the instruction, *mov lr, pc*. Why does this instruction add 8 to the PC, and use that value to set the value of *lr*? When is this behaviour helpful?

Assembly Language Programming

- For all the questions below, assume that two specialised functions, $\_div$ and $\_mod$, are available. The $\_div$ function divides the contents of $r1$ by the contents of $r2$, and saves the result in $r0$. Similarly, the $\_mod$ function is used to divide $r1$ by $r2$, and save the remainder in $r0$. Note that in this case both the functions perform integer division.

Ex. 8 — Write an ARM assembly language program to compute the 2's complement of a number stored in $r0$.

Ex. 9 — Write an ARM assembly language program that subtracts two 64-bit integers stored in four registers.
Assumptions:

- Assume that you are subtracting $A - B$
- A is stored in register, $r4$ and $r5$. The MSB is in $r4$, and the LSB is in $r5$.
- B is stored in register, $r6$ and $r7$. The MSB is in $r6$, and the LSB is in $r7$.
- Place the final result in $r8$(MSB), and $r9$(LSB).

Ex. 10 — Write an assembly program to add two 96-bit numbers A and B using the minimum number of instructions. A is stored in three registers $r2$, $r3$ and $r4$ with the higher byte in $r2$ and the lower byte in $r4$. B is stored in registers $r5$, $r6$ and $r7$ with the higher byte in $r5$ and the lower byte in $r7$. Place the final result in $r8$(higher byte), $r9$ and $r10$(lower byte).

Ex. 11 — Write an ARM assembly instruction code to count the number of 1's in a 32-bit number.

Ex. 12 — Given a 32-bit integer in $r3$, write an ARM assembly program to count the number of 1 to 0 transitions in it.

* **Ex. 13** — Write an ARM assembly program that checks if a 32-bit number is a palindrome. Assume that the input is available in $r3$. The program should set $r4$ to 1 if it is a palindrome, otherwise $r4$ should have 0. A palindrome is a number which is the same when read from both sides. For example, 1001 is a 4-bit palindrome.

Ex. 14 — Design an ARM Assembly Language program that will examine a 32-bit value stored in $r1$ and count the number of contiguous sequences of 1s. For example, the value:

$$01110001000111101100011100011111$$

contains six sequences of 1s. Write the final value in register $r2$. Use conditional instructions as much as possible.

** **Ex. 15** — In some cases, we can rotate an integer to the right by n positions (less than or equal to 31) so that we obtain the same number. For example: an 8-bit number 01010101 can be right rotated by 2, 4, or 6 places to obtain the same number. Write an ARM assembly program to *efficiently* count the number of ways we can rotate a number to the right such that the result is equal to the original number.

Ex. 16 — Write an ARM assembly program to load and store an integer from memory, where the memory saves it in the big endian format.

Ex. 17 — Write an ARM assembly program to find out if a number is prime using a recursive algorithm.

* Ex. 18 — Suppose you decide to take your ARM device to some place with a high amount of radiation, which can cause some bits to flip, and consequently corrupt data. Hence, you decide to store a single bit checksum, which stores the parity of all the other bits, at the least significant position of the number (essentially you can now store only 31 bits of data in a register). Write an ARM assembly program, which adds two numbers taking care of the checksum. Assume that no bits flip while the program is running.

* Ex. 19 — Let us encode a 16-bit number by using 2 bits to represent 1 bit. We shall represent logical 0 by 01, and logical 1 by 10. Now let us assume that a 16-bit number is encoded and stored in a 32-bit register $r3$. Write a program in ARM assembly to convert it back into a 16-bit number, and save the result in $r4$. Note that 00 and 11 are invalid inputs and indicate an error. The program should set $r5$ to 1 in case of an error; otherwise, $r5$ should be 0.

** Ex. 20 — Write an ARM assembly program to convert a 32-bit number to its 12 bit immediate form, if possible, with first 4 bits for rotation and next 8 bits for the payload. If the conversion is possible, set $r4$ to 1 and store the result in $r5$, otherwise, $r4$ should be set to 0. Assume that the input number is available in register $r3$.

** Ex. 21 — Suppose you are given a 32-bit binary number. You are told that the number has exactly one bit equal to 1; the rest of the bits are 0. Provide a fast algorithm to find the location of that bit. Implement the algorithm in ARM assembly. Assume the input to be available in $r9$. Store the result in $r10$.

*** Ex. 22 — Write an ARM assembly language program to find the greatest common divisor of two binary numbers u and v. Assume the two inputs (positive integers) to be available in $r3$ and $r4$. Store the result in $r5$. [HINT: The gcd of two even numbers u and v is $2 * gcd(u/2, v/2)$]

ARM Instruction Encoding

Ex. 23 — How are immediate values encoded in the ARM ISA?

Ex. 24 — Encode the following ARM instructions. Find the opcodes for instructions from the ARM architecture manual [arm, 2000].

   i) add r3, r1, r2

   ii) ldr r1, [r0, r2]

   iii) str r0, [r1, r2, lsl #2]

Design Problems

Ex. 25 — Run your ARM programs on an ARM emulator such as the QEMU (www.qemu.org) emulator, or *arm-elf-run* (available at www.gnuarm.com).

5

x86 Assembly Language

In this chapter, we shall study the basics of the x86 family of assembly languages. They are primarily used in Intel and AMD processors, which have an overwhelmingly large market share in the desktop, laptop, and low end server markets. They are steadily making deep inroads into the middle and high end server markets as well as the smart phone market. Hence, it is essential for the reader to have a good understanding of this important class of assembly languages. At this stage we expect the reader to have a basic understanding of assembly language from Chapter 3.

5.1 Overview of the x86 Family of Assembly Languages

5.1.1 Brief History

Let us start out by noting that x86 is not one language; it is actually a family of assembly languages with a very interesting history. Intel released the 8086 microprocessor in 1978, and called it 8086. It was Intel's first 16-bit microprocessor. This microprocessor proved to be very successful in the market, and succeeded in displacing other 8-bit competitors at that time. This motivated Intel to continue this line of processors. Intel then designed the 80186 and 80286 processors in 1982. 80186 was aimed at the embedded processor market, and 80286 was aimed at desktops. Both of them were fairly successful and helped establish Intel processors firmly in the desktop market. Those days IBM was the biggest vendor of PCs (personal computers), and most IBM PCs used Intel processors. The rapid proliferation of PCs led Intel to release two more processors, 80386 and 80486, in 1985 and 1989 respectively. These were 32-bit processors. Note that as Intel moved from 8086 to 80486, it continuously added more and more instructions to the instruction set. However, it also maintained backward compatibility. This means that any program meant to run on a 8086 machine, could also run on a 80486 machine. Secondly, it also maintained a consistent assembly language format for this family of processors whose name ended with "86". Over time this family of processors came to be known as "x86".

Gradually, other companies started using the x86 instruction set. Most notably, AMD (Advanced Micro Devices) started designing and selling x86 based processors. AMD released the K5, K6, and K7 processors in the mid nineties based on the 32-bit x86 instruction set. It also introduced the x86_64 instruction set in 2003, which was a 64-bit extension to the standard 32-bit x86 Intel ISA. Many other vendors such as VIA, and Transmeta also started manufacturing x86 based processors starting from 2000.

Each vendor has historically taken the liberty to add new instructions to the base x86 instruction set. For example, Intel has proposed many extensions over the years such as Intel® MMX^{TM}, SSE1, SSE2, SSE3, and SSE4. The number of x86 instructions are more than 900 as of 2012. Similarly, AMD introduced the 3D Now!^{TM}instruction set, and VIA introduced its custom extensions. The rich history of x86 processors has led to many different extensions of the basic instruction set, and there are numerous assemblers that have their unique syntax. Almost all x86 vendors today support hundreds of instructions. Current 64-bit Intel processors support 16-bit, and 32-bit code that dates way back to the original 8086.

If we try to classify the entire family tree of x86 ISAs, we can broadly divide them as 16-bit, 32-bit, and 64-bit instruction sets. 16-bit instruction sets are rarely used nowadays. 32-bit instruction sets are extremely popular in the smart phone, embedded, and laptop/netbook markets. The 64-bit ISAs (also known as the x86-64 ISA) are mainly meant for workstation class desktop/laptops and servers. Other than minor syntactic differences the assembly languages for these instruction sets are mostly the same. Hence, learning one ISA is sufficient. In this book, we try to strike a compromise between embedded processors, laptops, desktops, smart phones, and high end servers. We thus focus on the 32-bit x86 ISA because in our opinion it falls in the middle of the usage spectrum of the x86 ISA. We shall mention the minor syntactic differences with other flavours of x86 whenever the need arises.

5.1.2   Main Features of the x86 ISA

Before delving into the details of the 32-bit x86 ISA, let us list some of its main features.

1. It is a CISC ISA. Instructions have varying lengths, and operands also do not have a fixed length.

2. There are at least 300 scalar instructions, and this number is increasing every year.

3. Almost all the instructions can have a memory operand. In fact, most instructions allow a source, and a destination memory operand.

4. Most of the x86 instructions are in the 2-address format. For example, the assembly instruction to add two registers *eax*, and *ebx*, is *add eax, ebx*. Here, we add the contents of the *eax*, and *ebx* registers, and save the results in the *eax* register.

5. x86 has many complicated addressing modes for memory operands. Along with the traditional base-offset addressing mode, it supports base-index and base-index-offset addressing modes.

6. It does not have a return address register. Function call and return instructions, save and retrieve the return address from the stack.

7. Like ARM and *SimpleRisc* , x86 has a *flags* register that saves the outcome of the last comparison. The *flags* register is used by conditional branch instructions.

8. Unlike *SimpleRisc* , x86 instructions do not see an unified view of instruction and data memory. The x86 memory is *segmented*. This means that instructions and data reside in different memory regions (known as *segments*). x86 machines restrict the segments that an instruction can access.

It is true that the x86 architecture is a CISC instruction set, and it has hundreds of opcodes and many addressing modes. Nevertheless, we are sure that at the end of this chapter, the reader will concur with us that the x86 instruction set is in reality a fairly simple instruction set, is easy to understand, and is very elegant. A conventional argument supporting the case of RISC ISAs is that the hardware is simpler, and more efficient. Consequently, in modern Intel/AMD processors (Pentium® 4 onwards), the x86 instructions are internally translated into RISC instructions, and the entire processor is essentially a RISC processor. We can thus get the best of both worlds.

5.2   x86 Machine Model

5.2.1   Integer Registers

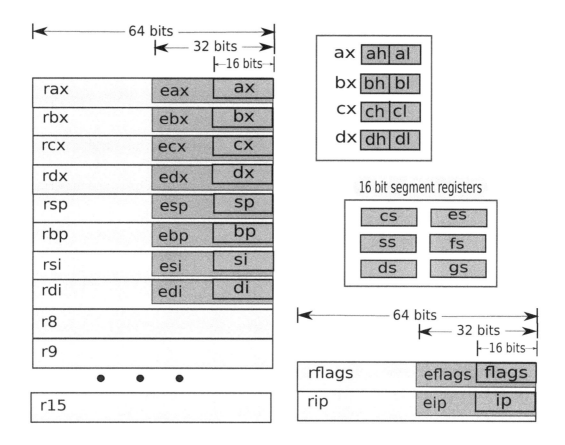

Figure 5.1: The x86 register set

Figure 5.1 shows the x86 register set. The 16 and 32-bit x86 ISAs have 8 general purpose registers. These registers have an interesting history. The original 8080 microprocessor designed forty years ago had seven 8-bit general purpose registers namely a, b, c, d, e, f and g. In the late seventies, x86 designers decided to create a 16-bit processor called 8086. They decided to keep four registers (a, b, c, and d), and suffixed them with the 'x' tag ('x' for extended). Thus, the four general purpose registers got renamed to ax, bx, cx, and dx. Additionally, the designers of the 8086 machine decided to retain some 16-bit registers namely the stack pointer (sp), and the register to save the PC (ip). The designers also introduced three extra registers in their design – bp (base pointer), si (starting index), and di (destination index). The intention of adding the bp register was to save the value of the stack pointer at the beginning of a function. Compilers are expected to set sp equal to bp at the end of the function. This operation destroys the stack frame of the callee function. The registers si, and di are used by the rep instruction that repeats a certain operation. Typically, a single rep instruction is equivalent to a simple for loop. Thus, the 8086 processor had eight 16-bit general purpose registers – ax, bx, cx, dx, sp, bp, si, and di. It was further possible to access the two bytes (lower and upper) in the registers ax – dx. For example, the lower byte in the ax register can be addressed as al, and the upper byte can be addressed as ah. 16-bit x86 instructions can use combinations of 8-bit and 16-bit operands.

The 8086 processor had two special purpose registers. The first register called ip contained the PC. The PC is typically not accessible to programmers on x86 machines (unlike the ARM ISA). The second special purpose register is the *flags* register that saves the results of the last comparison (similar to the *flags* register in ARM and *SimpleRisc*). The *flags* register is used by subsequent conditional branch instructions to compute the outcome of the branch.

In the might eighties, when Intel decided to extend the 8086 design to support 32-bit registers, it decided to keep the same set of registers (8 general purpose + *ip* + *flags*), and similar nomenclature. However, it extended their names by adding an 'e' prefix. Thus in a 32-bit machine, register *eax* is the 32-bit version of *ax*. To maintain backward compatibility with the 8086, the lower 16 bits of *eax* can be addressed as *ax* (if we wish to use 16-bit operands). Furthermore, the two bytes in *ax* can be addressed as *ah* and *al* (similar to 8086). As shown in Figure 5.1, the names were changed for all the other registers also. Notably, in a 32-bit machine, the stack pointer is stored in *esp*, the PC is stored in *eip*, and the *flags* are stored in the *eflags* register.

There are many advantages to this strategy. The first is that 8086 code can run on a 32-bit x86 processor seamlessly. All of its registers are defined in the 32-bit ISA. This is because each 16-bit register is represented by the lower 16 bits of a 32-bit register. Hence, there are no issues with backward compatibility. Secondly, we do not need to add new registers, because we simply extend each 16-bit register with 16 additional bits. We refer to the new register with a new name (16-bit name prefixed with 'e').

Exactly the same pattern was followed while extending the x86 ISA to create the 64-bit x86-64 ISA. The first letter was replaced from 'e' to 'r' to convert a 32-bit register to a 64-bit register. For example, the register *rax* is the 64-bit version of *eax*. Its lower 32 bits can be addressed as *eax*. The connotation of *ax*, *ah*, and *al* remains the same as before. Additionally, the x86-64 ISA introduced 8 more general purpose registers namely *r8 – r15*. However, their subfields cannot be addressed directly. The 64-bit PC is saved in the *rip* register, and the flags are stored in the *rflags* register.

The *eflags* register

Let us now quickly discuss the structure of the *eflags* register. Like ARM and x86, the *eflags* register contains a set of fields, where each field or bit indicates the status of execution of the instruction that last set it. Table 5.1 lists some of the most commonly used fields in the *eflags* register, along with their semantics.

Field	Condition	Semantics
OF	Overflow	Set on an overflow
CF	Carry flag	Set on a carry or borrow
ZF	Zero flag	Set when the result is a 0, or the comparison leads to an equality
SF	Sign flag	Sign bit of the result

Table 5.1: Fields in the *eflags* register

5.2.2   Floating Point Registers

The floating point instructions in x86 have a dual view of the floating point register file. They can either see them as normal registers or as a set of registers organised as a stack. Let us elaborate.

To start out, x86 defines 8 floating point registers named: *st0 ... st7*. These are 80-bit registers, The x86 floating point format has a 64-bit mantissa, and a 15-bit exponent. It is thus more precise than double precision numbers. The registers *st0* to *st7* are organised as a stack. Here, *st0* is the top of the stack, and *st7* is the bottom of the stack as shown in Figure 5.2. Additionally, x86 has a tag register that maintains the status of each register in the stack. The tag register has 8 fields (1 field for 1 register). Each field contains 2 bits. If the value of these bits is 00, then the corresponding register contains valid data. If the value is 01, then the register contains a 0, and if it is 11, then the register is empty. 10 is reserved for special purposes. We shall refer to the stack of registers, as *the floating point stack*, or simply *the FP stack*.

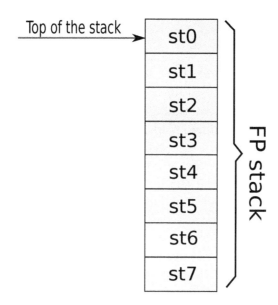

Figure 5.2: The x86 floating point register stack

The registers *st*0 to *st*7 are positions on the FP stack. *st*0 is always the top of the stack, and *st*7 is always the bottom of the stack. If we push a data item on to the FP stack, then the contents of each register get transferred to the register below it. If the stack is full (means that *st*7 contains valid data), then a stack overflow occurs. This situation needs to be avoided. Most floating point instructions operate on data values saved at the top of the stack. They pop the source operands, and push the destination operand.

5.2.3 View of Memory

Let us now describe the functionality of the segment registers (see Figure 5.1), and the view of memory. x86 instructions can have two views of memory. The first view is like ARM and *SimpleRisc* , which views memory as one large array of bytes that stores both code and data. This is known as the *linear memory model*. In comparison, the *segmented memory model* views memory as consisting of fixed size segments, where each segment is tailored to store one kind of data such as code, stack data, or heap data (for dynamically allocated data structures). We shall not discuss the linear model of memory because we have seen it before in Chapter 3. Let us discuss the segment registers, and the segmented memory model in this section.

Definition 40

Linear Memory Model *A linear memory model views the entire memory as one large array of bytes that saves both code and data.*

> **Segmented Memory Model** *A* segmented memory model *views the memory as a sequence of multiple fixed size segments. Code, data, and the stack have their own segments.*

The Segmented Memory Model

Let us define the term *address space* as the set of all memory addresses accessible to a program. The aim of the segmented memory model is to divide the address space into separate smaller address spaces. Each address space can be specialised to store a specific type of information such as code or data.

There are two reasons for using segmentation. The first is historical. In the early days different parts of a program were physically saved at different locations. The code was saved on punch cards, and the memory data was stored in DRAM memories. Hence, it was necessary to partition the address space among the devices that stored all the information that a program required (code, static data, dynamic data). This reason is not valid anymore. Nowadays, all the information a program requires is typically stored at the same place. However, we still need segmentation to enforce security. Hackers and viruses typically try to change the code of a program and insert their own code. Thus a normal program can exhibit malicious behaviour and can corrupt data, or transfer sensitive data to third parties. To ensure added protection, the code region is saved in a code segment. Most systems do not allow normal store instructions to modify the code segment. We can similarly partition the data segments for different classes of data. In Section 10.4.6, we will have a more thorough discussion on this topic.

Segmentation in x86

The 8086 designers had 6 segment registers that stored the most significant 16 bits of the starting location of the segment. The remaining bits were assumed to be all zeros. The *cs* register stored the upper 16 bits of the starting location of the code segment. Similarly, the *ds* register stored the upper 16 bits of the starting location for the data segment, and the *ss* register stored the corresponding set of bits for the stack segment. The *es* (extra segment), *fs*, and *gs* registers could be used to store information for additional user defined segments. Till date all x86 processors have preserved this model (see Figure 5.1). The contents of instructions are saved in the code segment, and the data that a program accesses is saved in the data segment. In most small programs, the stack and data segments are the same. In 8086 processors the memory address was 20 bits wide. Hence, to obtain the final address also known as the *linear address*, the 8086 processor first shifted the contents of the segment register 4 positions to the left to obtain the starting location of the segment. It then added this address with the memory address specified by the instruction. We can think of the memory address specified by an instruction as an offset in the segment, where the starting memory location of the segment is indicated by the appropriate segment register.

This strategy served the needs of the 8086 designers well. However, this strategy is not suitable for 32 and 64-bit machines. In this case, the memory addresses are 32 and 64 bits wide respectively. Thus, the segment registers need to be wider. In the interest of backward compatibility, designers did not touch the segment registers. They just changed the semantics of its contents for newer processors. Instead of saving the upper 16 bits of the starting location of a segment, the registers now contain a segment id. The *segment id* uniquely identifies a segment across all the programs running in a system. To get the starting location, 32/64-bit x86 processors, lookup a segment descriptor table with 13 bits (bits 4 to 16) of the segment id. 13 bits can specify 8192 entries, which is more than sufficient for all the programs in the system.

Modern x86 processors have two kinds of segment descriptor tables namely the local descriptor table (LDT), and the global descriptor table (GDT). The LDT is typically local to a process (running instance of a program) and contains the details of the segments for that process. The LDT is normally not used nowadays because programs do not use a lot of segments. In comparison there is only one system level GDT. The GDT can contain up to 8191 entries (the first entry is reserved). Each entry in the GDT contains the starting address of the segment, the size of the segment, and the privileges required to access the segment. Every memory access needs to go through the GDT for fetching the starting address of the segment. This unnecessarily lengthens the critical path of a memory request, and creates contention at the GDT. To make the access to the GDT faster, modern processors have a small structure called a *segment descriptor cache* that stores a few entries of the GDT that are relevant to the currently executing process. The descriptor cache typically stores the details of all the segments that the frequently running processes use. This strategy ensures that we do not need to access the GDT on every memory access. The small and fast descriptor cache is sufficient. After accessing the descriptor cache, or the GDT, x86 processors get the starting address of the segment. They subsequently generate the memory address by adding the address specified in the instruction with the starting address of the segment. This address is then passed on to the memory system.

Definition 41

Process *It is defined as the running instance of a program. For example, if we run two copies of a program, then we create two processes.*

LDT (Local Descriptor Table) *The LDT is a per process table that saves the description of all the segments that a process uses. The LDT is indexed by a segment id, and contains the starting address of the segment, and the privileges required to access it. It is not used very frequently in modern systems.*

GDT (Global Descriptor Table) *The GDT is similar to the LDT. However, it is a system wide table that is shared by all the processes running on a machine.*

Now, that we have discussed the view of the register files, and the memory system, let us describe the addressing modes.

5.2.4 Addressing Modes

Addressing Modes for Specifying Immediates

The best thing about x86 is that there are no size restrictions on immediates. Immediates can be as large as the size of the register. For example, in a 32-bit system, the size of the immediate can be as large as 32 bits. Depending upon the assembly language, we can specify immediates in the hex format (0x...), binary format (e.g., 10101b), or in decimal. Most of the time programmers prefer the hex or decimal formats. For hexadecimal numbers most assemblers allow us to specify the number with the standard 0x prefix. Additionally, we can specify a number with the h/H suffix. For example, $21H$ is the same as $0x21$. For negative numbers, we need to simply put a '-' before the number.

Addressing Modes for Specifying Registers

All registers in x86 are addressed by their names. For example, the general purpose registers on a 32-bit machine are addressed as *eax, ebx ... edi*, according to the rules mentioned in Section 5.2.1. We can use 16-bit register names in 32-bit mode, and we can use 16 and 32-bit register addressing in 64-bit mode. Note that we cannot do the reverse. For example, we cannot use 64-bit register names in 32-bit mode.

Addressing Modes for Memory Operands

x86 supports a variety of addressing modes for main memory. In specific, it supports the register-indirect, base-offset, base-index, and base-index-offset addressing modes as mentioned in Section 3.2.5. In addition, it also supports a new addressing mode called the base-scaled-index-offset addressing mode that scales the index by a constant factor. Let us elaborate.

$$
address = \underbrace{\begin{bmatrix} cs: \\ ds: \\ ss: \\ es: \\ fs: \\ gs: \end{bmatrix} \begin{bmatrix} eax \\ ebx \\ ecx \\ edx \\ esp \\ ebp \\ esi \\ edi \end{bmatrix}}_{base} + \underbrace{\begin{bmatrix} \begin{pmatrix} eax \\ ebx \\ ecx \\ edx \\ ebp \\ esi \\ edi \end{pmatrix} \times \underbrace{\begin{bmatrix} 1 \\ 2 \\ 4 \\ 8 \end{bmatrix}}_{scale} \end{bmatrix}}_{index} + \underbrace{[displacement]}_{offset} \tag{5.1}
$$

Equation 5.1 shows the generic format of a memory address in the 32-bit version of x86. The interesting aspect of x86 memory addressing is that all of these fields are optional. Hence, it is possible to have a large number of addressing modes.

Let us first consider the addressing modes that require a base register. With the base register, we can optionally specify a segment register. If we do not specify a segment register, then the hardware assumes default segments (ds for data, ss for stack, and cs for code). We can subsequently specify an index. The index is contained in another register (excluding esp). We can optionally multiply the index with a power of 2 (1, 2, 4, or 8). Lastly, we can specify a 32-bit offset known as the *displacement*. The memory address is computed using Equation 5.1.

Now, let us look at addressing modes that do not require a base register. We can just use an index register and optionally scale it by 1, 2, 4, or 8. For example, we can specify that we want to access the memory address equal to $2 \times ecx$. This approach uses the scaled-index addressing mode. We can optionally add a fixed offset (known as the displacement) to the address.

Lastly, it is possible to specify the entire 32-bit address in the displacement field, and not specify any register at all. This approach is typically used in the operating system code to directly operate on memory addresses. Regular assembly programmers need to strictly avoid such direct memory addressing because most of the time we are not aware of the exact memory addresses. For example, the starting address of the stack pointer is typically allocated at run time in modern systems, and tends to vary across runs. Secondly, this is not a portable and elegant approach. It is only meant for operating system writers.

Let us explain with examples (see Table 5.2).

Definition 42
In the x86 ISA, the fixed offset used while specifying the effective address of a memory operand, is known as the displacement.

Memory operand	Value of the address (in register transfer notation)	Addressing mode
[eax]	eax	register-indirect
[eax + ecx*2]	eax + 2 * ecx	base-scaled-index
[eax + ecx*2 - 32]	eax + 2 * ecx - 32	base-scaled-index-offset
[edx - 12]	edx - 12	base-offset
[edx*2]	edx * 2	scaled-index
[0xFFE13342]	0xFFE13342	memory-direct

Table 5.2: Example of memory operands

5.2.5 x86 Assembly Language

There are various x86 assemblers such as MASM [mas,], NASM [nas,], and the GNU assembler [gx8,]. In this book, we shall present code snippets that have been tested with the NASM assembler. The popular NASM assembler is freely available at [nas,], and is known to work on a variety of platforms including Windows® , Mac OS X, and different flavours of Linux. Note that we shall mostly avoid using NASM specific features, and we shall keep the presentation of assembly code very generic. Our assembly codes should be compatible with any assembler that supports the Intel format for x86 assembly. The only major feature of NASM that we shall use is that comments begin with a ';' character.

Let us now describe the structure of an assembly language statement in the Intel format. Its generic structure is as follows.

```
——————————————————— Structure of an Assembly Statement ———————————————————
<label>: <assembly instruction> ; <comment>
```

For an assembly instruction, the label and the comment are optional. Alternatively, we can just have a label or a comment, or a combination of both in a single line. In our code, we shall use labels starting with a '.'. However, labels can start with regular alphabets and other special characters also. For a detailed description readers can refer to the NASM documentation.

Each x86 assembly instruction has an opcode followed by a set of operands.

```
——————————————————— x86 Assembly Instruction ———————————————————
<opcode>
<opcode> <operand1>
<opcode> <operand1>, <operand2>
```

An overwhelming majority of x86 instructions are in the 0, 1 and 2-address formats. 0-address format instructions like *nop* instructions in *SimpleRisc* do not require any operands. 1-address format instructions have a single source operand. In this case the destination operand is equal to the source operand. For example, the instruction *not eax* computes the bitwise complement of *eax*, and saves the result in *eax*. In two operand instructions, the first operand is the first source operand and also the destination operand. The second operand is the second source operand. For example, *add eax, ebx*, adds the contents of *eax* and *ebx*, and subsequently saves the result in *eax*.

The source operands can be register, memory, or immediate operands. However, both the sources cannot be memory operands. Needless to say the destination operand cannot be an immediate operand. When a single operand is both the source and destination, both the rules apply.

5.3   Integer Instructions

5.3.1   Data Transfer Instructions

The *mov* Instruction

Semantics	Example	Explanation
mov (reg/mem), (reg/mem/imm)	mov eax, ebx	eax ← ebx

Table 5.3: Semantics of the *mov* instruction

The *mov* instruction is a very simple yet versatile instruction in the x86 ISA. It moves the contents of the second operand, into the first operand. The second operand can be a register, a memory location, or an immediate. The first operand can be a register or a memory location (Table 5.3 shows the semantics). The reader needs to note that both the operands cannot be memory locations.

We thus do not need any dedicated load/store instructions in x86. The *mov* instruction can achieve the function of loading and storing memory values because it accepts memory operands. The *mov* instruction can also transfer values between registers (similar to *SimpleRisc* and ARM). Thus, we have fused the functionality of three RISC instructions into one CISC instruction. Let us consider some examples.

Example 55
Write an x86 assembly instruction to set the value of ebx to -17.
Answer:

```
mov ebx, -17
```

Example 56
Write an x86 assembly instruction to load ebx with the contents of (esp - eax*4 -12).
Answer:

```
mov ebx, [esp - eax*4 -12]
```

Example 57
Write an x86 assembly instruction to store the contents of edx in (esp - eax*4 -12). ***Answer:***

```
mov [esp - eax*4 -12], edx
```

***movsx,* and *movzx* Instructions**

The simple *mov* instruction assumes that the sizes of the operands are the same (16, or 32, or 64 bits). However, sometimes we face the need for saving a smaller register or memory operand in a larger register.

Semantics	Example	Explanation
movsx *reg*, (*reg/mem*)	movsx eax, bx	eax ← sign_extend(bx), the second operand is either 8 or 16 bits
movzx *reg*, (*reg/mem*)	movsx eax, bx	eax ← zero_extend(bx), the second operand is either 8 or 16 bits

Table 5.4: Semantics of the *movsx*, and *movzx* instructions

For example, if we save the 16 bit register *ax* in *ebx* then we need we have two options. We can either extend the sign of the input operand, or pad it with 0s. The *movsx* instruction (see Table 5.4) copies a smaller register or memory operand to a larger register and extends its sign. For example, the following code snippet extends the sign of *bx* (from 16 to 32 bits), and saves the results in *eax*.

```
movsx eax, bx   ; eax = sign_extend(bx)
```

The *movzx* instruction is defined on the same lines. However, instead of performing a sign extension, it pads the MSB bits with 0s.

```
movzx eax, bx   ; eax = bx (unsigned)
```

The Atomic Exchange (*xchg*) Instruction

Semantics	Example	Explanation
xchg (*reg/mem*), (*reg/mem*)	xchg eax, [eax + edi]	swap the contents of eax and [eax + edi] atomically

Table 5.5: Semantics of the *xchg* instruction

The *xchg* instruction swaps the contents of the first and second operands. Here, also we cannot have two memory operands. This instruction ensures that before the operation is done, no other operation can read temporary values. For example, if we are swapping the values of *eax*, and the memory operand [*ebx*], there might be an intermediate point in the execution where the contents of *eax* are updated, but the contents of [*ebx*] are not updated. The x86 processor does not allow other threads (sub-programs that share the address space) to read the contents of [*ebx*] at this point. It makes other conflicting instructions in other execution threads wait till the *xchg* instruction completes. This property is known as *atomicity*. An instruction is *atomic* if it appears to execute instantaneously. Most of the time, atomic instructions such as *xchg* are used for implementing data structures that are shared across multiple threads. The reader should read Chapter 11 for a detailed discussion on parallel software that uses multiple threads.

Definition 43
An instruction is atomic *if it appears to execute instantaneously.*

Example 58
Write a function to swap the contents of eax, and [esp].

Answer:

```
xchg eax, [esp]
```

---

push **and** *pop* **Instructions**

Semantics	Example	Explanation
push (*reg/mem/imm*)	push ecx	temp ← ecx; esp ← esp - 4; [esp] ← temp
pop (*reg/mem*)	pop ecx	temp ← [esp]; esp ← esp + 4; ecx ← temp

Table 5.6: Semantics of the *push* and *pop* instructions

The x86 architecture is explicitly aware of the stack. It has two dedicated instructions for saving and retrieving operands off the stack. The *push* instruction pushes data on the stack. In specific, the *push* instruction can push the contents of a register, memory location, or immediate on the stack. It has just one source operand. Its operation is shown in Table 5.6. Conceptually, it first saves the value of the first operand as a temporary value *temp*. Then, it decrements the stack pointer, and transfers the temporary value to the top of the stack. In a 32-bit system, we decrement the stack pointer by 4. When we are pushing a register, the processor knows its size based on the name of the register. For example, if the name of the register is *ax*, its size is 16 bits, and if the name of the register is *eax*, its size is 32 bits. However, if we are pushing a memory operand or a constant, the assembler cannot determine the size of the operand. We might be intending to push 2 bytes, 4 bytes, or 8 bytes on the stack. In this case, it is necessary to indicate the size of the operand to the assembler such that it can generate appropriate binary code. In the NASM assembler, we specify this information as follows:

```
push dword [esp]
```

The modifier *dword* (double word) represents the fact that we need to push 4 bytes on the stack. The starting address of the 4 bytes is stored in *esp*. Table 5.7 shows the list of modifiers for different sized data types.

Modifier	Size
byte	8 bits
word	16 bits
dword	32 bits
qword	64 bits

Table 5.7: Modifiers in the NASM assembler

For pushing in the value of immediate values, NASM assumes they are by default 32 bits long (if we are running NASM in 32-bit mode). We can override this setting by specifying a size modifier (word,dword,...) in the instruction.

On the same lines we can define a *pop* instruction as shown in Table 5.6. Conceptually, the pop instruction saves the top of the stack in a temporary location. It then proceeds to increment the stack pointer by 4 (in the case of 32 bits), and then it saves the temporary value in the destination. The destination can either be a register or a memory location. The *push* and *pop* instructions thus make working with the stack very easy in x86 assembly programs.

Example 59 *What is the final value of ebx?*

```
mov eax, 10
push eax
mov ebx, [esp]
```

Answer: 10

Example 60
What is the final value of ebx?

```
mov ebp, esp
mov eax, 10
mov [esp], eax
push dword [esp]
mov ebx, [ebp-4]
```

Answer: *Note that ebp and esp are initially the same. After we push a value to the stack, esp gets decremented by 4. Hence, the new location of the top of the stack is equal to ebp − 4. Since we push the value of eax (10) to the top of the stack using the push instruction, the value of ebx is equal to 10.*

Example 61 *What is the final value of ebx?*

```
mov eax, 17
push eax
pop dword [esp]
mov dword ebx, [esp]
```

Answer: 17

5.3.2 ALU Instructions

Let us now discuss the rich set of ALU instructions that x86 processors support.

Add and Subtract Instructions

Semantics	Example	Explanation
add (reg/mem), (reg/mem/imm)	add eax, ebx	eax ← eax + ebx
sub (reg/mem), (reg/mem/imm)	sub eax, ebx	eax ← eax - ebx
adc (reg/mem), (reg/mem/imm)	adc eax, ebx	eax ← eax + ebx + (carry bit)
sbb (reg/mem), (reg/mem/imm)	sbb eax, ebx	eax ← eax - ebx - (carry bit)

Table 5.8: Semantics of add and subtract instructions

Table 5.8 shows the add and subtract operations that are typically used in x86 processors. The basic add and subtract instructions add the values of the first and second operands, and treat the first operand also as the destination operand. They set the carry and overflow fields of the *eflags* register. The *adc* instruction adds its two source operands, and also adds the value of the carry bit. Similarly, the *sbb* instruction subtracts the second operand from the first, and then subtracts the carry bit from the result. We can use the *adc* and *sbb* instructions to add or subtract very large integers (refer to Example 62 and Example 63). In these examples, we first operate on the lower bytes. While operating on the higher bytes we need to take the carry generated by adding or subtracting the lower bytes into account. We use the *adc* and *sbb* instructions respectively for this purpose.

Example 62
Write an x86 assembly program to add two 64-bit numbers. The first number is stored in the registers ebx, and eax, where ebx stores the higher byte, and eax stores the lower byte. The second number is stored in edx, and ecx. Save the result in ebx (higher byte), and eax(lower byte).
Answer:

```
add eax, ecx
adc ebx, edx
```

Example 63
Write an x86 assembly program to subtract two 64-bit numbers. The first number is stored in the registers ebx, and eax, where ebx stores the higher byte, and eax stores the lower byte. The second number is stored in edx, and ecx. Subtract the second number from the first number. Save the result in ebx (higher byte), and eax(lower byte).

Answer:

```
sub eax, ecx
sbb ebx, edx
```

Semantics	Example	Explanation
inc (*reg/mem*)	inc edx	edx ← edx + 1
dec (*reg/mem*)	dec edx	edx ← edx - 1
neg (*reg/mem*)	neg edx	edx ← -1 * edx

Table 5.9: Semantics of *inc*, *dec*, and *neg* instructions

inc, *dec*, and *neg* Instructions

Table 5.9 shows the semantics of increment (*inc*), decrement (*dec*), and negate (*neg*) instructions. The *inc* instruction, adds 1 to the source operand. In this case also the source and destination operands are the same. Similarly, the *dec* instruction subtracts 1 from the source operand, which is also the destination operand. Note that the operand can either be a register or a memory location. The *neg* instruction computes the negative of the value stored in the first operand (register or memory). Let us consider an example (see Example 64).

Example 64
Write an x86 assembly code snippet to compute eax = -1 * (eax + 1).
Answer:

```
inc eax
neg eax
```

The Compare(*cmp*) Instruction

Semantics	Example	Explanation
cmp (*reg/mem*), (*reg/mem/imm*)	cmp eax, [ebx + 4]	compare the values in eax, and [ebx+4], and set the flags
cmp (*reg/mem*), (*reg/mem/imm*)	cmp ecx, 10	compare the contents of ecx with 10, and set the flags

Table 5.10: Semantics of the *cmp* instructions

Table 5.10 shows the *cmp* (compare) instruction. It compares two operands and sets the values of the flags. It performs the comparison by subtracting the value of the second operand from the first operand. It is conceptually a subtract instruction that does not have a destination operand.

Multiplication and Division Instructions

Table 5.11 shows the signed multiplication and division instructions in x86. They are known as *imul* and *idiv* respectively. The unsigned variants of the instructions are known as *mul* and *div*. They have exactly the same semantics as their signed counterparts. The signed instructions are more generic. Hence, we only discuss their operation in this section.

Semantics	Example	Explanation
imul (*reg*/*mem*)	imul ecx	edx:eax ← eax * ecx
imul *reg*, (*reg*/*mem*)	imul ecx, [eax + 4]	ecx ← ecx * [eax + 4]
imul *reg*, (*reg*/*mem*), *imm*	imul ecx, [eax + 4], 5	ecx ← [eax + 4] * 5
idiv (*reg*/*mem*)	idiv ebx	Divide (edx:eax) by the contents of ebx; eax contains the quotient, and edx contains the remainder.

Table 5.11: Semantics of the *imul* and *idiv* instructions

The *imul* instruction has three variants. The 1-address format variant has 1 source operand, which can either be a register or a memory address. This source operand is multiplied with the contents of *eax*. Note that when we multiply two 32-bit numbers, we require at most 64 bits to save the result (see Section 7.2.1). Hence, to avoid overflows, the processor saves the results in the register pair (*edx*,*eax*). *edx* contains the upper 32 bits, and *eax* contains the lower 32 bits of the final product. The 2-address format version is similar to other ALU instructions that we have studied. It multiplies the first and second source operands, and saves the result in the destination register (which is the first operand). Note that in this variant of the multiply instruction, the destination is always a register, and the result is truncated to fit in the register. The *imul* instruction has another variant that requires 3 operands. Here, it multiplies the contents of the second and third operands and stores the product in the register specified by the first operand. For this variant of the *imul* instruction, the first operand needs to be a register, the second operand can be a register or memory location, and the third operand needs to be an immediate value.

The *idiv* instruction takes just 1 operand (register or memory). It divides the contents of the register pair (*edx*:*eax*) by the contents of the operand. It saves the quotient in *eax*, and the remainder in *edx*. Note that the remainder has the same sign as the dividend. A subtle point should be noted here. While using a positive dividend that fits in 32 bits, we need to explicitly set *edx* to 0, and for a negative dividend that fits in 32 bits, we need to explicitly set *edx* to -1 (for sign extension).

Let us consider a set of examples.

Example 65
Write an assembly code snippet to multiply 3 with -17, and save the result in eax.

Answer:

```
mov ebx, 3
imul eax, ebx, -17
```

Example 66
Write an assembly code snippet to compute k^3, where k is the content of ecx, and save the result in eax.

Answer:

```
mov eax, ecx
imul ecx
imul ecx
```

Example 67
Write an assembly code snippet to divide -50 by 3. Save the quotient in eax, and remainder in edx.

Answer:

```
mov edx, -1
mov eax, -50
mov ebx, 3
idiv ebx
```

At the end eax contains -16, and edx contains -2.

Logical Instructions

Semantics	Example	Explanation
and (reg/mem), (reg/mem/imm)	and eax, ebx	eax ← eax AND ebx
or (reg/mem), (reg/mem/imm)	or eax, ebx	eax ← eax OR ebx
xor (reg/mem), (reg/mem/imm)	xor eax, ebx	eax ← eax XOR ebx
not (reg/mem)	not eax	eax ← ∼ eax

Table 5.12: Semantics of *and, or, xor,* and *not* instructions

Table 5.12 shows the semantics of four commonly used logical operations. *and, or,* and *xor* instructions have exactly the same format as *add* and *sub* instructions, and most of the other 2-address format instructions. They compute the bitwise AND, OR, and exclusive OR of the first two operands respectively. The *not* instruction computes the 1's complement (flips each bit) of the source operand, which is also the destination operand (format is similar to other 1-address format instructions such as *inc, dec,* and *neg*).

Shift Instructions

Semantics	Example	Explanation
sar (reg/mem), imm	sar eax, 3	eax ← eax ⋙ 3
shr (reg/mem), imm	shr eax, 3	eax ← eax ≫ 3
sal/shl (reg/mem), imm	sal eax, 2	eax ← eax ≪ 2

Table 5.13: Semantics of shift instructions

Table 5.13 shows the semantics of shift instructions. *sar* (shift arithmetic right) performs an arithmetic right shift by replicating the sign bit. *shr* (shift logical right), shifts the first operand to the right. Instead of replicating the sign bit, it fills the MSB bits with 0s. *sal* and *shl* are the same instruction. They perform a left shift. Recall that we do not have an arithmetic left shift operation. Let us consider some examples.

Example 68
What is the final value of eax?

```
mov eax, 0xdeadbeef
sal eax, 4
```

Answer: | *0xeadbeef0* |

Example 69 *What is the final value of eax?*

```
mov eax, 0xdeadbeef
sar eax, 4
```

Answer: | *0xfdeadbee* |

Example 70 *What is the final value of eax?*

```
mov eax, 0xdeadbeef
shr eax, 4
```

Answer: | *0xdeadbee* |

5.3.3   Branch/ Function Call Instructions

Conditional and Unconditional Branch Instructions

Semantics	Example	Explanation
jmp ⟨*label*⟩	jmp .foo	jump to .foo
j ⟨*condcode*⟩	j ⟨*condcode*⟩ .foo	jump to .foo if the ⟨*condcode*⟩ condition is satisfied

Table 5.14: Semantics of branch instructions

Condition code	Meaning
o	Overflow
no	No overflow
b	Below (unsigned less than)
nb	Not below (unsigned greater than or equal to)
e/z	Equal or zero
ne/nz	Not equal or not zero
be	Below or equal (unsigned less than or equal)
s	Sign bit is 1 (negative)
ns	Sign bit is 0 (0 or positive)
l	Less than (signed less than)
le	Less than or equal (signed)
g	Greater than (signed)
ge	Greater than or equal (signed)

Table 5.15: Condition codes in x86

Table 5.14 shows the semantics of branch instructions. *jmp* is an unconditional branch instruction that branches to a label. The assembler internally replaces the label by the PC of the label. x86 defines a series of branch instructions with the *j* prefix. These are conditional branch instructions. The *j* prefix is followed by the branch condition. The conditions are shown in Table 5.15. For example, the instruction *je* means jump if equal. If the last comparison has resulted in an equality, then the processor branches to the label; otherwise, it executes the next instruction. If the condition is not satisfied, the conditional branch is equivalent to a *nop* instruction.

Now that we have introduced branch instructions, we can implement complex algorithms using loops. Let us look at a couple of examples. We would like to advise the reader at this point that the best method to learn assembly language is by actually writing assembly programs. No amount of theoretical reading can substitute for actual practice.

Example 71

Write a program in x86 assembly to add the numbers from 1 to 10.

Answer:

```
————————————————————— x86 assembly code ——————————————
1  mov eax, 0   ; sum = 0
2  mov ebx, 1   ; idx = 1
3  .loop:
4          add eax, ebx ; sum += idx
5          inc ebx      ; idx ++
6          cmp ebx, 10  ; compare idx and 10
7          jle .loop    ; jump if idx <= 10
```

Here, we store the running sum in eax and the index in ebx. In Line 4, we add the index to the sum. We subsequently, increment the index, and compare it with 10 in Line 6. If it is less than or equal to 10, then we continue iterating. eax contains the final value.

Example 72

Write a program in x86 assembly to test if a number stored in eax is prime. Save the result in eax. If the number is prime, set eax to 1, otherwise set it to 0. Assume that the number in eax is greater than 10.

Answer:

```
                              ─── x86 assembly code ───
 1     mov ebx, 2        ; starting index
 2     mov ecx, eax      ; ecx contains the original number
 3 .loop:
 4     mov edx, 0        ; required for correct division
 5     idiv ebx
 6     cmp edx, 0        ; compare the remainder
 7     je .notprime      ; number is composite
 8     inc ebx
 9     mov eax, ecx      ; set the value of eax again
10     cmp ebx, eax      ; compare the index and the number
11     jl .loop
12
13     ; end of the loop
14     mov eax, 1        ; number is prime
15     jmp .exit         ; exit
16
17 .notprime:
18     mov eax, 0
19 .exit:
```

In this algorithm, we keep on dividing the input (stored in eax) by a monotonically increasing index. If the remainder is equal to 0 in any iteration, then the number is composite (non prime). Otherwise, the number is prime. In specific, we perform the division in Line 5, and jump to the label .notprime if the remainder (stored in edx) is 0. Otherwise, we increment the index in ebx, and keep iterating. Note that in each iteration, we need to set the values of eax and edx because they are overwritten by the idiv instruction.

Example 73

Write a program in x86 assembly to find the factorial of a number stored in eax. Save your result in ecx. You can assume that the number is greater than 10.

Answer:

```
                              ─── x86 assembly code ───
 1     mov ebx, 2        ; idx = 2
 2     mov ecx, 1        ; prod = 1
 3
 4 .loop:
 5     imul ecx, ebx     ; prod *= idx
 6     inc ebx           ; idx++
```

```
7       cmp ebx, eax    ; compare num (number) and idx
8       jle .loop       ; jump to .loop if idx <= num
```

In Line 2, we initialise the product to 1. Subsequently, we multiply the index with the product in Line 5. We then increment the index, and compare it with the input stored in eax. We keep on iterating till the index is less than or equal to the input.

Function Call and Return Instructions

Semantics	Example	Explanation
call ⟨label⟩	call .foo	Push the return address on the stack. Jump to the label .foo.
ret	ret	Return to the address saved on the top of the stack, and pop the entry

Table 5.16: Semantics of the function call and return instructions

Unlike ARM and *SimpleRisc* , x86 does not have a return address register. The *call* instruction pushes the return address on the stack, and jumps to the beginning of the function as explained in Table 5.16. Similarly, the *ret* instruction jumps to the entry at the top of the stack. The entry at the top of the stack needs to contain the return address. The *ret* instruction subsequently pops the stack and removes the return address. Let us now consider a set of examples.

Example 74

Write a recursive function to compute the factorial of a number (≥ 1) stored in eax. Save the result in ebx.

Answer:

```
                          ──────── x86 assembly code ────────
1  factorial:
2       mov ebx, 1       ; default return value
3       cmp eax, 1       ; compare num (input) with 1
4       je .return       ; return if input is equal to 1
5
6       ; recursive step
7       push eax         ; save input on the stack
8       dec eax          ; num--
9       call factorial   ; recursive call
10      pop eax          ; retrieve input
11      imul ebx, eax    ; prod = prod * num
12
13 .return:
14      ret              ; return
```

In the factorial function, we assume that the input (num) is stored in eax. We first compare the input with 1. If it is equal to 1, then we return 1 (Lines 2 to 4). However, if the input is greater than 1, then we save the input by pushing it to the stack (7). Subsequently, we decrement it and recursively call the factorial function in Line 9. The result of the recursive call is stored in ebx. To compute the result (in ebx), we multiply ebx with num (stored in eax) in Line 11.

In Example 74 we pass arguments through registers. We use the stack to only store values that are overwritten by the callee function. Let us now use the stack to pass arguments to the factorial function (see Example 75)

Example 75

Write a recursive function to compute the factorial of a number (≥ 1) stored in eax. Save the result in ebx. Use the stack to pass arguments.

Answer:

```
                              ─── x86 assembly code ───
1
2  factorial:
3      mov eax, [esp+4] ; get the value of eax from the stack
4      mov ebx, 1        ; default return value
5      cmp eax, 1        ; compare num (input) with 1
6      je .return        ; return if input is equal to 1
7
8      ; recursive step
9      push eax          ; save eax on the stack
10     dec eax           ; num--
11     push eax          ; push the argument
12     call factorial    ; recursive call
13     pop eax           ; pop the argument
14     pop eax           ; retrieve the value of eax
15     imul ebx, eax     ; prod = prod * num
16
17 .return:
18     ret               ; return
```

Here, we use the stack to pass arguments. Since the stack pointer gets automatically decremented by 4 after a function call, the argument eax is available at [esp+4] because we push it on the stack just before we call the function. To call the factorial function again, we push eax on the stack, and then pop it out after the function returns.

Let us now assume that we have a lot of arguments. In this case, we need to push and pop a lot of arguments from the stack. It is possible that we might lose track of the order of push and pop operations, and bugs might be introduced in our program. Hence, if we have a lot of arguments, it is a better idea to create space in the stack by subtracting the estimated size of the activation block from the stack pointer and moving data between the registers and stack using regular *mov* instructions. Let us now modify our factorial example to use *mov* instructions instead of push and pop instructions (see Example 76).

Example 76

Write a recursive function to compute the factorial of a number (≥ 1) stored in eax. Save the result in ebx. Use the stack to pass arguments. Avoid push and pop instructions.

Answer:

```
———————————————————— x86 assembly code ————————————————————
1  factorial:
2      mov eax, [esp+4]   ; get the value of eax from the stack
3      mov ebx, 1         ; default return value
4      cmp eax, 1         ; compare num (input) with 1
5      jz .return         ; return if input is equal to 1
6
7      ; recursive step
8      sub esp, 8         ; create space on the stack
9      mov [esp+4], eax   ; save the input eax on the stack
10     dec eax            ; num--
11     mov [esp], eax     ; push the argument
12     call factorial     ; recursive call
13     mov eax, [esp+4]   ; retrieve eax
14     imul ebx, eax      ; prod = prod * num
15     add esp, 8         ; restore the stack pointer
16
17 .return:
18     ret                ; return
```

In this example, we have avoided push and pop instructions altogether. We instead create space on the stack by subtracting 8 bytes from esp in Line 8. We use 4 bytes to save the input (in eax) for later use. We use the rest of the 4 bytes to send the argument to the recursive function call. After the function returns, we retrieve the value of eax from the stack in Line 13. Lastly, we restore the stack pointer in Line 15.

However, this method is also not suitable for large functions in complex programming languages such as C++. In a lot of C++ functions, we dynamically allocate space on the stack. In such cases, most of the time, we do not know the size of the activation block (see Section 3.3.10) of a function in advance. Hence, deallocating an activation block becomes difficult. We need to dynamically keep track of the size of the activation block of the function. This introduces additional complexity, and additional code. It is a better idea to save the value of *esp* in a dedicated register at the beginning of a function. At the end of the function, we can transfer the saved value in the register to *esp*. This strategy effectively destroys the activation block. Most of the time, we use the *ebp* (base pointer) register to save the value of *esp* at the beginning of a function. This register is also referred to as the *frame pointer*. Now, it is possible that a called function might follow the same strategy, and overwrite the value of *ebp* set by the caller. Thus, in this case, *ebp* needs to be a callee saved register. If an invoked function overwrites the value of *ebp*, it needs to ensure that by the time it returns to the caller, the value of *ebp* is restored. By using the base pointer, we do not need to explicitly remember the size of the activation block. We dynamically allocate data structures on the stack.

Let us augment our running example with this feature (see Example 77).

Example 77

Write a recursive function to compute the factorial of a number (≥ 1) stored in eax. Save the result in ebx. Use the stack to pass arguments. Avoid push and pop instructions. Secondly, use the ebp register to store the value of the stack pointer.

Answer:

```
                              ─── x86 assembly code ───
 1  factorial:
 2       mov eax, [esp+4]    ; get the value of eax from the stack
 3
 4       push ebp            ; save ebp
 5       mov ebp, esp        ; save the stack pointer
 6
 7       mov ebx, 1          ; default return value
 8       cmp eax, 1          ; compare num (input) with 1
 9       je .return          ; return if input is equal to 1
10
11       ; recursive step
12       sub esp, 8          ; create space on the stack
13       mov [esp+4], eax    ; save input on the stack
14       dec eax             ; num--
15       mov [esp], eax      ; push the argument
16       call factorial      ; recursive call
17       mov eax, [esp+4]    ; retrieve input
18       imul ebx, eax       ; prod = prod * num
19
20  .return:
21               mov esp, ebp     ; restore the stack pointer
22               pop ebp          ; restore ebp
23               ret              ; return
```

Here, we save the old value of ebp on the stack, and set its new value to the stack pointer in Lines 4 and 5, respectively. At the end of the function, we restore the values of esp and ebp in Lines 21 and 22.

Stack Management Instructions – *enter* **and** *leave*

The four extra lines added in Example 77 are fairly generic, and are typically a part of most large functions. Programmers can add them if they are writing assembly code, or compilers can add them during automatic code generation. In either case, using the base pointer is a very convenient mechanism to manage the stack, and to destroy the activation block. Since these set of instructions are so commonly used, the designers of the x86 ISA decided to dedicate two specialised instructions for this purpose. The *enter* instruction pushes the value of *ebp* on the stack, and sets its new value to be equal to the stack pointer. Additionally, it is also possible to set the initial size of the activation block. The first argument takes the size of the activation block. If we specify 32 as the first argument, then the *enter* instruction decrements *esp* by 32. Note that

Semantics	Example	Explanation
enter *imm*, 0	enter 32, 0	push ebp (push the value of *ebp* on the stack); mov ebp, esp (save the stack pointer in *ebp*); esp ← esp - 32
leave	leave	mov esp, ebp (restore the value of *esp*); pop ebp (restore the value of *ebp*)

Table 5.17: Semantics of the *enter* and *leave* instructions.

during the course of execution of the function, the size of the activation block might continue to vary. The second argument for the *enter* instruction corresponds to the nesting level of the function. We shall refrain from discussing it here. Interested readers can refer to the references mentioned at the end of the chapter. We shall simply use the value of 0 for the second argument.

The *leave* instruction performs the reverse set of computations. It first restores the value of *esp*, and then the value of *ebp* (see Table 5.17). Note that the *leave* instruction is meant to be invoked just before the *ret* instruction. We can thus augment Example 77 to use the *enter* and *leave* instructions (see Example 78). Secondly, we can omit the statement that subtracted 8 from *esp* (Line 12) in Example 77 because this functionality is now built in to the *enter* instruction.

Example 78

Write a recursive function to compute the factorial of a number (≥ 1) stored in eax. Save the result in ebx. Use the stack to pass arguments. Avoid push and pop instructions. Use the enter and leave instructions to buffer the values of ebp and esp.

Answer:

```
                           x86 assembly code
1
2  factorial:
3      mov eax, [esp+4]   ; get the value of eax from the stack
4
5      enter 8, 0         ; save ebp and esp, decrement esp by 8
6
7      mov ebx, 1         ; default return value
8      cmp eax, 1         ; compare num (input) with 1
9      je .return         ; return if the input is equal to 1
10
11     ; recursive step
12     mov [esp+4], eax   ; save input on the stack
13     dec eax            ; num--
14     mov [esp], eax     ; push the argument
15     call factorial     ; recursive call
16     mov eax, [esp+4]   ; retrieve input
17     imul ebx, eax      ; prod = prod * num
18
19 .return:
```

```
20    leave            ; load esp and ebp
21    ret              ; return
```

Lastly, we should mention that x86 processors have a *nop* instruction that does not do anything at all. It is mainly used for the purpose of ensuring correctness in modern processors (see Chapter 9), and for ensuring that blocks of code are aligned to 16 byte or 64 byte boundaries. We require the latter functionality for better behaviour at the level of the memory system.

5.3.4   Advanced Memory Instructions

String Instructions

Semantics	Example	Explanation
lea *reg, mem*	lea ebx, [esi + edi*2 + 10]	ebx ← esi + edi*2 + 10
stos(b/w/d/q)	stosd	[edi] ← eax; edi ← edi + 4 * $(-1)^{DF}$
lods(b/w/d/q)	lodsd	eax ← [esi]; esi ← esi + 4 * $(-1)^{DF}$
movs(b/w/d/q)	movsd	[edi] ← [esi] ; esi ← esi + 4 * $(-1)^{DF}$; edi ← edi + 4 * $(-1)^{DF}$
std	std	DF ← 1
cld	cld	DF ← 0
DF → Direction Flag		

Table 5.18: Semantics of advanced memory instructions

The *lea* instruction stands for *load effective address*. It has a register operand, and a memory operand. The role of the *lea* instruction is to copy the address of the memory operand (not its contents) to the register.

Let us now introduce a special set of instructions known as *string instructions*. We shall introduce the following instructions: *stos*, *lods*, and *movs*. The *stos* instruction transfers data from the *eax* register to the location specified by the *edi* register. It comes in four flavours depending upon the amount of data that we wish to transfer. It uses the 'b' suffix for 1 byte, 'w' for 2 bytes, 'd' for 4 bytes, and 'q' for 8 bytes. We show an example of the *stosd* instruction in Table 5.18. The *stosd* instruction transfers the contents of *eax* (4 bytes) to the memory address specified by *edi*. Subsequently, this instruction increments or decrements the contents of *edi* by 4 depending on the direction flag. The direction flag (DF) is a field in the *flags* register similar to zero, carry, and overflow. If the direction flag is set (equal to 1), then the *stos* instruction subtracts the size of the operand from the contents of *edi*. Conversely, if DF is equal to 0, then the *stos* instruction adds the size of the operand to *edi*.

We introduce two 0-address format instructions namely *std* and *cld* to set and reset the direction flag respectively.

The *lods* and *movs* set of instructions are defined in a similar manner. For example, the *lodsd* instruction transfers the contents of the memory location specified by *esi* to *eax*. It subsequently increments or decrements the contents of *esi* by the size of the operands based on the value of DF. The *movs* instruction combines the functionality of *lods* and *stos*. It first fetches a set of bytes from the memory address stored in *esi*. Subsequently, it writes the bytes to the memory address specified by *edi*. It increments or decrements *esi* and *edi* based on the value of the direction flag.

Trivia 2

The si register (16-bit version of esi) stands for the source index *register. Similarly, the di register stands for the* destination index *register.*

Let us now look at a set of examples.

Example 79 *What is the value of ebx?*

```
lea   edi, [esp+4]
mov   eax, 21
stosd                ; saves eax in [edi]
mov ebx, [esp+4]
```

Answer: *We save 21 (eax) in the memory address specified in edi by using the stosd instruction. This memory address is equal to (esp + 4). After executing the stosd instruction, we load the contents of this memory address into ebx. The result is equal to the value of eax seen by the stosd instruction, which is 21.*

Example 80 *What is the value of eax after executing this code snippet?*

```
lea   esi, [esp+4]
mov dword [esp+4], 19
lodsd    ; eax <-- [esi]
```

Answer: *Note the use of the modifier dword here. We need to use it because we are saving an immediate to a memory location, and we need to specify its size. The value of eax is equal to the value stored in [esp+4], which is 19.*

Example 81 *What is the value of eax after executing this code snippet?*

```
mov dword [esp+4], 192
lea   esi, [esp+4]
lea   edi, [esp+8]
movsd
mov eax, [esp+8]
```

Answer: *The movsd instruction transfer 4 bytes from the memory address specified in esi to the memory address specified in edi. Since we write 192 to the memory address specified in esi, we shall read back the same value in the last line.*

Instructions with the *rep* Prefix

The string instructions can additionally increment or decrement the values of *esi* and *edi*. We have not used this feature up till now. Let us use this feature to transfer an array of 10 integers from one location to another. This feature is very frequently used in modern processors to transfer large amounts of data between two locations.

Let us first show a conventional solution in Example 82.

Example 82 *Write a program to create a copy of a 10 element integer array. Assume that the starting address of the original array is stored in esi, and the starting address of the destination array is stored in edi.*

Answer:

```
mov ebx, 0                    ; initialise
.loop:
    mov edx, [esi+ebx*4]      ; transfer the contents
    mov [edi + ebx*4], edx
    inc ebx                   ; increment the index
    cmp ebx, 10               ; loop condition
    jne .loop
```

Example 83 *Write a program to create a copy of a 10 element integer array. Assume that the starting address of the original array is stored in esi, and the starting address of the destination array is stored in edi. Use the movsd instruction.*

Answer:

```
    cld               ; DF = 0
    mov ebx, 0        ; initialisation of the loop index
.loop:
    movsd             ; [edi] <-- [esi]
    inc ebx           ; increment the index
    cmp ebx, 10       ; loop condition
    jne .loop
```

As compared to Example 82, we reduce the number of instruction in the loop from 5 to 4.

In Example 83, we use the *movsd* instruction to replace a pair of load/store instructions with just one instruction. This reduces the number of instructions in the loop from 5 to 4. We were not able to get a bigger reduction because we still need to update the loop index, and compute the loop condition.

To make our code look even more elegant, the x86 ISA defines a *rep* prefix that can used with any string instruction. The *rep* prefix instructs the processor to execute a single string instruction n times, where n is the value stored in the *ecx* register. Every time the processor executes the string instruction, it decrements *ecx*. At the end, the value of *ecx* becomes 0. Its semantics is shown in Table 5.19.

Semantics	Example	Explanation
rep inst	rep movsd	val ← ecx; Execute the movsd instruction *val* times; ecx ← 0

Table 5.19: Semantics of *rep* instructions

Example 84 *Write a program to create a copy of a 10 element integer array. Assume that the starting address of the original array is stored in esi, and the starting address of the destination array is stored in edi. Use the rep prefix with the movsd instruction.*
Answer:

```
cld          ; DF = 0
mov ecx, 10  ; Set the count to 10
rep movsd    ; Execute movsd 10 times
```

The *rep* prefix thus allows us to fold an entire loop into just one instruction as shown in Example 84. The *rep* prefix is meant to be used with string instructions for copying large regions of data. It makes the code for operating on strings of data very compact and elegant. The *rep* instruction has two variants namely *repe*, and *repne*. These instructions use an additional termination condition, along with the value of *ecx*. Instructions prefixed with *repe* can also terminate when the *zero* flag becomes 0, and an instruction prefixed with *repne* also terminates when the *zero* flag becomes 1.

5.4 Floating Point Instructions

x86 has a large set of floating point instructions. Let us first give a historical perspective. The early 8086 processor, and many of its successors till the Intel 486 did not have a floating point unit in the processor. They used a separate co-processor chip called the x87 that provided floating point capability. However, after the release of Intel 486, the floating point unit has been an integral part of the x86 architecture. Hence, many features of the floating point ISA are artefacts of the older era, in which a floating point instruction was essentially a message to an external processing unit.

One of the direct consequences of such a design strategy is that there are no direct communication paths between integer registers, and floating point registers. Secondly, it is not possible to load an immediate into a floating point register by specifying its value in an instruction. We can only load the value of floating point registers via memory. For example, if we wish to store a floating point constant in a floating point register, then we need to first load the constant in memory. Subsequently, we need to issue a floating point load instruction to load the constant into a floating point register. Figure 5.3 shows a conceptual organisation of the x86 ISA. The integer instructions use the integer registers, and they have their own processor state. Likewise, the floating point instructions use their set of registers, and have their own state. Both the types of instructions, however, share the memory.

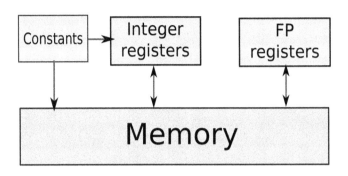

Figure 5.3: Conceptual organisation of the x86 ISA

Let us start by looking at methods to load values into the floating point registers. We shall refer to the floating point register stack as the FP stack and designate the floating point registers ($st0$ ... $st7$) as reg while describing the semantics of instructions. We shall also abbreviate floating point as FP for the sake of brevity.

5.4.1   Data Transfer Instructions

Load Instruction

Semantics	Example	Explanation
fld *mem*	fld dword [eax]	Pushes an FP number stored in [*eax*] to the FP stack
fld *reg*	fld st1	Pushes the contents of *st1* to the top of the stack
fild *mem*	fild dword [eax]	Pushes an integer stored in [*eax*] to the FP stack after converting it to a 32-bit floating point number

Table 5.20: Floating point load instructions

Table 5.20 shows the semantics of the floating point load instructions. The most commonly used floating point load instruction is the *fld* instruction. The first variant of the *fld* instruction can load a 32-bit floating point value from memory, and push it to the FP stack. We can use our standard addressing modes with integer registers as described in Section 5.2.4 for specifying an address in memory. The second variant can push the contents of an existing FP register on the FP stack. We can alternatively use the *fild* instruction that can read an integer from memory, convert it to floating point, and push it on the FP stack. Let us consider an example.

Example 85

Push the constant, 2.392, on the FP stack.

Answer: *We need to first define the constant 2.392 in the data section. In NASM, we do this as follows.*

```
section .data
      num: dd 2.392
```

We need to embed this code snippet at the beginning of the assembly file. Here, the declaration "section .data" means that we are declaring the data section. In the data section, we further declare a variable, num, that is a double word (32 bits, specified by dd), and its value is 2.392. Let us now push this value to the FP stack. We need to embed the following code snippet in the main assembly function.

```
fld dword [num]
```

The assembler treats num as a memory address. While generating code, it will replace it with its actual address. However, in an assembly program, we can seamlessly treat num as a valid memory address, and its contents can thus be represented as [num]. The fld instruction in this code snippet loads 32 bits (dword) from num to the top of the FP stack.

Exchange Instruction

Semantics	Example	Explanation
fxch *reg*	fxch st3	Exchange the contents of *st*0 and *st*3
fxch	fxch	Exchange the contents of *st*0 and *st*1

Table 5.21: Floating point exchange instructions

Table 5.21 shows the format of the floating point exchange instruction, $fxch$. It exchanges the contents of two floating point registers. The 1-address format $fxch$ instruction exchanges the contents of the register specified as the first operand and *st*0. If we do not specify any operands, then the processor exchanges *st*0 and *st*1 (the top of the stack, and the entry just below the top of the stack).

Store Instructions

Let us now look at the store instructions in Table 5.22. The format is similar to the floating point load instructions. We have three variants of the basic fst instruction. The first variant requires a single memory operand. It stores the contents of *st*0 in the memory location specified by the memory operand. The second variant requires a FP register operand and stores the contents of *st*0 in the FP register.

The third variant uses the 'p' suffix which is a generic suffix and is used by many other instructions also. The $fstp$ instruction initially saves the value contained in *st*0 in the memory location specified by the first

Semantics	Example	Explanation
fst *mem*	fst dword [eax]	[eax] ← st0
fst *reg*	fst st4	st4 ← st0
fstp *mem*	fstp dword [eax]	[eax] ← st0; pop the FP stack
fist *mem*	fist dword [eax]	[eax] ← int(st0)
fistp *mem*	fistp dword [eax]	[eax] ← int(st0); pop the FP stack

Table 5.22: Floating point store instructions

operand, and then pops the stack. Since the stack size is limited, it is often necessary to pop the stack to create more space. When we are storing *st0*, we are saving a copy of its contents in main memory. Hence, it makes sense to have a variant of the *fst* instruction that can free the entry from the stack by popping it.

x86 has additional support for conversion of floating point values to integers. We can use the *fist* instruction that first converts the contents of *st0* to a signed integer by rounding it and then saves it in the location specified by the memory operand. Note that we always use a modifier (byte/word/dword/qword) for memory operands such that we can specify the number of bytes that need to be transferred. The *fist* instruction also supports the 'p' suffix (see the semantics of the *fistp* instruction in Table 5.22).

Example 86
Transfer the contents of st0 to eax by converting the save FP number to an integer.
Answer:

```
fist dword[esp]
mov eax, [esp]
```

5.4.2   Arithmetic Instructions

Let us now consider arithmetic instructions. The floating point ISA in x86 has rich support for floating point operations, and is thus extensively used in numerical computing. Let us start with the basic floating point add instruction, and take a look at all of its variants.

Add Instruction

Semantics	Example	Explanation
fadd *mem*	fadd dword [eax]	st0 ← st0 + [eax]
fadd *reg, reg*	fadd st0, st1	st0 ← st0 + st1 (one of the registers has to be st0)
faddp *reg*	faddp st1	st1 ← st0 + st1; pop the FP stack
fiadd *mem*	fiadd dword [eax]	st0 ← st0 + float([eax])

Table 5.23: Floating point add instructions

The semantics of the floating point add instructions is shown in Table 5.23. The basic *fadd* instruction has two variants. The first variant uses a single memory operand. Here, we add the value of the floating point number contained in the memory location to the contents of $st0$. The result is also stored in $st0$. The second variant of the $fadd$ instruction uses two floating point registers as arguments. It adds the contents of the second register to the first register.

The $fadd$ instruction follows the same pattern as the floating point load and store instructions. It accepts the 'p' suffix. The $faddp$ instruction typically takes 1 argument, which is a register. We show an example of the instruction $faddp$ $st1$ in Table 5.23. Here, we add the contents of $st0$ to $st1$, and save the result in $st1$. Then, we pop the stack. For working with integers, we can use the $fiadd$ instruction that takes the address of an integer in memory. It adds this integer to $st0$, and saves the results in $st0$.

Subtraction, Multiplication, and Division Instructions

x86 defines subtraction, multiplication, and division instructions that have exactly the same format as the $fadd$ instructions, and all of its variants as shown in Table 5.23. Let us just show the basic form of each instruction that uses a single memory operand in Table 5.24.

Semantics	Example	Explanation
fsub mem	fsub dword [eax]	st0 ← st0 - [eax]
fmul mem	fmul dword [eax]	st0 ← st0 * [eax]
fdiv mem	fdiv dword [eax]	st0 ← st0 / [eax]

Table 5.24: Floating point subtract, multiply, and divide instructions

Example 87

Compute the arithmetic mean of two integers stored in eax and ebx. Save the result (in 64 bits) in $esp + 4$. Assume that the data section contains the integer, 2, in the memory address two.

Answer:

```
; load the inputs to the FP stack
mov [esp], eax
mov [esp+4], ebx
fild dword [esp]
fild dword[esp + 4]

; compute the arithmetic mean
fadd st0, st1
fdiv dword [two]

; save the result (converted to 64 bits) to [esp+4]
; use the qword identifier
fstp qword [esp + 4]
```

Semantics	Example	Explanation
fabs	fabs	$st0 \leftarrow |st0|$
fsqrt	fsqrt	$st0 \leftarrow \sqrt{st0}$
fcos	fcos	$st0 \leftarrow \cos(st0)$
fsin	fsin	$st0 \leftarrow \sin(st0)$

Table 5.25: Floating point instructions for special functions

5.4.3   Instructions for Special Functions

The greatness of the x86 ISA is that it supports trigonometric functions, and complex mathematical operations such as the square root, and log operations (not covered in this book). Table 5.25 shows the x86 instructions for computing the values of special functions. The *fabs* function computes the absolute value of *st0*, the *fsqrt* function computes the square root, the *fcos* and *fsin* functions compute the sine and cosine of the value stored in *st0* respectively. All of these instructions use *st0* as their default operand, and also write the result back to *st0*.

Example 88
Compute the geometric mean of two integers stored in eax and ebx. Save the result (in 64 bits) in esp+4.

Answer:

```
; load the inputs to the FP stack
mov [esp], eax
mov [esp+4], ebx
fild dword [esp]
fild dword[esp + 4]

; compute the geometric mean
fmul st0, st1
fsqrt

; save the result (converted to 64 bits) to [esp+4]
; use the qword identifier
fstp qword [esp + 4]
```

5.4.4   Compare Instruction

The x86 ISA has many compare instructions. In this section, we shall present only one compare instruction called *fcomi* that compares two floating point values saved in registers, and sets the *eflags* register. Table 5.26 shows the semantics of the *fcomi* instruction with and without the 'p' suffix. Once, the *eflags* register is set, we can use regular branch instructions for implementing control flow within the program. Note that in x86 we need to use the condition codes for unsigned comparison in this case. Most of the time programmers make the mistake of using the condition codes for signed comparison such as *l*, *le*, *g*, or *ge* for

Semantics	Example	Explanation
fcomi *reg, reg*	fcomi st0, st1	compare st0 and st1, and set the *eflags* register (first register has to be st0)
fcomip *reg, reg*	fcomi st0, st1	compare st0 and st1, and set the *eflags* register; pop the FP stack

Table 5.26: Floating point compare instructions

testing the results of floating point comparison. This leads to wrong results. We should instead use the a (above) and b (below) condition codes.

Let us now consider an example (Example 89) that computes the value of $sin(2\theta)$, and verifies if it is equal to $2sin(\theta)cos(\theta)$. The readers should recall from their high school trigonometry class that both these expressions are actually equal, and one can be derived from the other. Example 89 experimentally verifies this fact for any given value of θ. We compute the value of $sin(2\theta)$ and $2sin(\theta)cos(\theta)$, and compare them using *fcomi*. Note that floating point arithmetic is approximate (see Section 2.4.6). Hence, the correct way to compare floating point numbers is to first subtract them, compute the absolute value of the difference, and compare the difference with a threshold. The threshold is typically a small number (10^{-5} in our case). If the difference is less than a threshold, we can infer equality.

Example 89
Compare $sin(2\theta)$ and $2sin(\theta)cos(\theta)$. Verify that they have the same value for any given value of θ. Assume that theta is stored in the data section at the label theta, *and the threshold for floating point comparison is stored at label* threshold. *Save the result in eax (1 if equal, and 0 if unequal).*
Answer:

```
; compute sin(2*theta), and save in [esp]
fld dword [theta]
fadd st0   ; st0 = theta + theta
fsin
fstp dword [esp]

; compute (2*sin(theta)*cos(theta))
fld dword [theta]
fst st1
fsin
fxch
fcos        ; st0 = cos(theta)
fmul st1    ; st0 = sin(theta) * cos (theta)
fadd st0    ; st0 = 2 * st0

; compute the modulus of the difference
fld dword [esp]  ; load (sin(2*theta))
fsub st0, st1
fabs
```

```
; compare
fld dword [threshold]
fcomi st0, st1  ; compare
ja .equal
mov eax, 0
jmp .exit

.equal:
        mov eax, 1
.exit:
```

After the end of a function, it is time to clean up the floating point registers, and stack such that another function can use them. Let us conclude this section by taking a look at the cleanup instructions.

5.4.5 Stack Cleanup Instructions

Semantics	Example	Explanation
ffree *reg*	ffree st4	Free st4
finit	finit	Reset the status of the FP unit including the FP stack and registers

Table 5.27: Floating point stack cleanup instructions

Table 5.27 shows two instructions for cleaning up the FP stack. The $ffree$ instruction sets the status of the register specified as an operand to empty. Using $ffree$ to free all the registers is a quick solution. For freeing the entire stack we need to invoke the $ffree$ instruction iteratively. For deleting the entire FP stack, a cleaner solution is to use the $finit$ instruction that does not take any arguments. It resets the FP unit, frees all the registers, and resets the stack pointer. The $finit$ instruction ensures that an unrelated function can start from a clean state.

5.5 Encoding the x86 ISA

We have taken a look at a wide variety of x86 instructions, addressing modes, and instruction formats. It is truly a CISC instruction set. However, the process of encoding is more regular. Almost all the instructions follow a standard format. In the case of ARM and *SimpleRisc* , we described the process of encoding instructions in great detail. We shall refrain from doing this here for the sake of brevity. Secondly, an opcode in x86 typically has a variety of modes, and prefixes. We do not want to digress from the main theme of this book by describing x86 in such level of detail. Let us start out by looking at the broad structure of an encoded machine instruction.

5.5.1 High Level View of x86 Instruction Encoding

Figure 5.4 shows the structure of an encoded instruction in binary.

Prefix	Opcode	ModR/M	SIB	Displacement	Immediate
1-4 bytes (optional)	1-3 bytes	1 byte (optional)	1 byte (optional)	1/2/4 bytes (optional)	1/2/4 bytes (optional)

Figure 5.4: x86 binary instruction format

The first set of 1-4 bytes are used to encode the prefix of the instruction. The *rep* prefix is one such example of a prefix. There are many other kinds of prefixes that can be encoded in the first group of 1-4 bytes.

The next 1-3 bytes are used for encoding the opcode. Recall that the entire x86 ISA has hundreds of instructions. Secondly, the opcode also encodes the format of operands. For example, the *add* instruction can either have its first operand as a memory operand, or have its second operand as a memory operand. This information is also a part of the opcode.

The next two bytes are optional. The first byte is known as the ModR/M byte, which specifies the address of the source and destination registers, and the second byte is known as the SIB (scale-index-base) byte. This byte records the parameters for the base-scaled-index and base-scaled-index-offset addressing modes. A memory address might optionally have a displacement (also referred to as the offset in this book) that can be as large as 32 bits. We can thus optionally have 4 more bytes in an instruction to record the value of the displacement. Lastly, some x86 instructions accept an immediate as an operand. The immediate can also be as large as 32 bits. Hence, the last field, which is again optional, is used to specify an immediate operand.

Let us now discuss the ModR/M and SIB bytes in more detail.

ModR/M Byte

The ModR/M byte has three fields as shown in Figure 5.5.

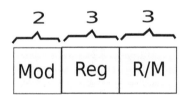

Figure 5.5: The ModR/M byte

The two MSB bits of the ModR/M byte contain the *Mod* field. The *Mod* field indicates the addressing mode of the instruction. It can take 4 values as shown in Table 5.28.

The *Mod* field indicates the addressing mode of one of the operands. It can either be a register or a memory operand. If it is a memory operand, then we have three options. We can either have no displacement (Mod = 00), a 8 bit displacement (Mod = 01), or a 32-bit displacement (Mod=10). If it is a register operand, then the Mod field has a value of 11.

The important point to note is that for all the memory address modes, if the R/M bits are equal to 100, then we need to use the information in the SIB byte for computing the effective memory address.

The *Reg* field encodes the second operand if it is a register. Since both the operands cannot be memory operands, we use the Mod and R/M bits for encoding one of the operands that might be a memory operand

Mod bits	Semantics
00	We use the register indirect addressing mode for one of the operands. When R/M = 100, we use the base-scaled-index addressing mode, and there is no displacement. The ids of the scale, index, and base are specified in the SIB byte. When R/M = 101, the memory address only consists of the displacement. The rest of the values of the R/M bits specify the id of the base register as shown in Table 5.29. Other than the case of R/M=101, the rest of the combinations of the R/M bits are not associated with a displacement (assumed to be 0).
01	We use a single byte signed displacement. If R/M = 100, then we get the ids of the base and index registers from the SIB byte.
10	We use a 4 byte signed displacement. If R/M = 100, then we get the ids of the base and index registers from the SIB byte.
11	Register direct addressing mode.

Register	Code
eax	000
ecx	001
edx	010
ebx	011
esp	100
ebp	101
esi	110
edi	111

Table 5.29: Register encoding

Table 5.28: Semantics of the Mod field

(source or destination), and use the *Reg* field for encoding the other operand, which has to be a register. The encoding for the registers is shown in Table 5.29.

For floating point instructions, the default register operand is always *st0*. Some instructions accept another FP register operand. For such instructions, we use register direct addressing (Mod = 11). We use the R/M bits for specifying the id of the additional FP register. We use 3 bits to encode the index of the register. For example, *st0* is encoded as 000, and *st6* is encoded as 110. For the rest of the instructions that either assume default operands, or have a single memory operand, we use the same format as defined for integer instructions.

SIB Byte

The SIB byte is used to specify the base and index registers (possibly with scaling). For example, it can be used to encode memory operands of the form [eax + ecx*4]. Recall that to use the SIB byte it is essential to set the Mod field in the ModR/M register to 100. This indicates to the processor that the SIB byte follows the ModR/M byte.

The structure of the SIB byte is shown in Figure 5.6.

Figure 5.6: The SIB byte

The SIB byte has three fields – *scale*, *index*, and *base*. The effective memory address (before considering the displacement) is equal to $base + index \times scale$. The *base* and *index* fields point to integer registers. Both of them are 3 bits each (can encode up to 8 registers), and use the encoding shown in Table 5.29. The two MSB bits are used to specify the scale. We can have four values for the scale in x86 instructions namely 1 (00), 2 (01), 4 (10), and 8 (11).

Rules for Encoding Memory Operands

Note that some rules need to be followed while encoding memory operands. The *esp* register cannot be an index, and if the value of the Mod field is 00, then *ebp* cannot be a valid *base* register. Recall that if we set the R/M bits to 101 (id of *ebp*), when the Mod field is 00, then the memory address is only a displacement. Or, in other words we can use memory direct addressing here by directly specifying its address.

If (Mod = 00), then in the SIB byte *ebp* cannot be a valid base register. If we specify the base register as *ebp* in the SIB byte, then the processor calculates the effective memory address based on the value of the scale and the index.

Example 90

Encode the instruction add ebx, [edx + ecx*2 + 32]. *Assume that the opcode for the add instruction is 0x03.*

Answer: *Let us calculate the value of the ModR/M byte. In this case, our displacement fits within 8 bits. Hence, we can set the Mod bits equal to 01 (corresponding to an 8 bit displacement). We need to use the SIB byte, because we have a scale, and an index. Thus, we set the R/M bits to 100. The destination register is ebx. Its code is 011 (according to Table 5.29). Thus, the ModR/M byte is 01011100 (equal to 0x5C).*

Now, let us calculate the value of the SIB byte. The scale is equal to 2. This is encoded as 01. The index is ecx (001), and the base is edx (010). Hence, the SIB byte is: 01 001 010 = 4A. The last byte is the displacement, which is equal to 0x20.

Thus, the encoding of the instruction is $\boxed{03\ 5C\ 4A\ 20}$ *in hex.*

5.6 Summary and Further Reading

5.6.1 Summary

Summary 5

1. *The x86 ISA is a family of CISC instruction sets that is primarily used by Intel and AMD processors.*

   (a) *The original x86 ISA used by 8086 processors used a 16-bit ISA.*

   (b) *Since the mid eighties, x86 processors have moved to the 32-bit ISA.*

   (c) *Finally, since 2003, most of the high end x86 architectures have moved to the 64-bit ISA.*

   (d) *The basic structures of all the ISAs is the same. There are minor differences in the syntax.*

2. *The 8 basic registers of the 16-bit x86 ISA are – ax, bx, cx, dx, sp, bp, si, and di. We use the 'e' prefix in 32-bit mode, and the 'r' prefix in 64-bit mode.*

3. *Additionally, the 16-bit x86 ISA has the ip register to save the program counter, and the flags register to save the results of the last comparison, and other fields that instructions may use.*

4. *The x86 ISA predominantly uses instructions in the 2-address format. The first operand is typically both the source, and the destination. Secondly, one of the operands can be a memory operand. It is thus possible to fetch the value of a memory location, operate on it, and write it back to memory, in the same instruction.*

5. *x86 processes see a segmented memory model. The entire memory space is partitioned into different segments. Instructions reside in the code segment by default, and data resides in the data or stack segments by default. It is in general not possible for instructions to access segments that they typically are not meant for. For example, it is in general not possible for a store instruction to change the contents of an instruction in the code segment.*

   (a) *In the 16-bit mode, the top 16 bits of the starting address of each segment are stored in a segment register.*

   (b) *The effective memory address specified by a memory instruction is added to the address contained in the segment register (after left shifting it by 4 positions) to compute the actual memory address.*

   (c) *In later ISAs (32 and 64-bit mode), the contents of segment registers are looked up in segment descriptor tables (referred to as the LDT and GDT) for obtaining the starting address of segments. To speed up memory accesses, processors typically use a small memory structure known as a segment descriptor cache that keeps the most recently used entries.*

6. *x86 integer instructions:*

   (a) *The mov instruction is one of the most versatile instructions. It can move values between two registers, or between registers and memory addresses. It can also be used to load immediates in registers or memory locations.*

   (b) *x86 defines a host of other arithmetic, and branch instructions.*

   (c) *String instructions are a unique feature of the x86 ISA. They can be used to transfer large amounts of data between memory locations. To compress an entire loop of string instructions into one instruction, we typically use the rep prefix that repeats a given instruction n times, where n is the value stored in the ecx register.*

7. *The x86 floating point registers can either be accessed as normal registers (st0 ... st7), or as values on a floating point stack. Most of the floating point instructions operate on st0, which is the top of the stack.*

8. *There is no direct way to load immediates into the FP registers. We need to first load them into memory, and then load them to the floating point stack. x86 has instructions for computing complex mathematical operations (such as square root), and trigonometric functions directly.*

9. *Encoding the x86 instruction set is relatively simpler, since the encoded form has a very regular structure.*

   (a) *We can optionally use 1-4 bytes to encode the prefix.*

   (b) *The opcode's encoding requires 1-3 bytes.*

   (c) *We can optionally use two additional bytes known as the ModR/M and SIB bytes to encode the address of operands (both register and memory).*

(d) *If the memory operand uses a displacement (offset), then we can add 1-4 bytes for encoding the displacement after the SIB byte.*

(e) *Lastly, the x86 ISA accepts 32-bit immediate values. Hence, we can use the last 1-4 bytes to specify the value of an immediate operand if required.*

5.6.2 Further Reading

The most accurate source of information is the x86 developer manuals released by Intel on their website [int, , INTEL, 2010].

For the sake of brevity, we have only discussed the popularly used instructions. However, there are many instructions in the x86 ISA that might prove to be useful in a specific set of scenarios, which we have not covered in this book. Intel's software developer manuals are always the best places to find this information. Secondly, we have only discussed the basic x86 ISA. The reader should definitely look at the extensions to the x86 ISA such as the MMX^{TM}, SSE, and 3d Now! (by AMD) extensions. These extensions add vector instructions, which can operate on arrays of data. These instructions are used in graphics, games, and scientific applications. The Intel AVX instruction set is the latest addition in the long line of x86 ISAs. It introduces 512 bit registers that can contain multiple integers. The interested reader should definitely take a look at this instruction set and try to write programs with it. In this book, we shall show an example using the SSE instruction set in Section 11.5.3.

The reader can additionally refer to books that describe the x86 instruction set in great detail, and have a wealth of solved examples. The following books [Cavanagh, 2013, Das, 2010, Kumar, 2003] are useful references in this regard.

Exercises

x86 Machine Model

Ex. 1 — What are the advantages of the segmented addressing mode? Why do modern x86 processors need the LDT and GDT tables?

Ex. 2 — Explain the memory addressing modes in x86.

Ex. 3 — Describe the floating point registers and the floating point stack in x86.

* **Ex. 4** — We can specify an entire 32-bit immediate in a single instruction in x86. Recall that this was not possible in ARM and *SimpleRisc* . What are the advantages and disadvantages of having this feature in the ISA?

* **Ex. 5** — We claim that using a stack based architecture makes the software very portable. It does not need to be aware of the number and semantics of registers in an ISA. Comment on this statement, and try to find other reasons for preferring a stack based machine.

** **Ex. 6** — Given an arithmetic expression containing floating point operands, how can we evaluate it using a floating point stack? What should be the order of loading and operating on operands? [HINT: A regular arithmetic operation such as – (1 + 2.5) * 3.9 – is called an infix expression. To evaluate expressions using a stack, we need to convert it into a postfix expression of the form – 1 2.5 + 3.9 *. Here, we first push 1 and 2.5 on the stack, add the result, push 3.9 on the stack, and multiply the first two entries. The reader should read more about postfix expressions in textbooks on discrete mathematics.]

Assembly Programming using Integer Instructions

Ex. 7 — Write x86 assembly code snippets to compute the following:

i) $a + b + c$

ii) $a + b - c/d$

iii) $(a + b) * 3 - c/d$

iv) $a/b - (c * d)/3$

v) $(a \ll 2) - (b \gg 3)$

Ex. 8 — Write an assembly program to convert an integer stored in memory from the little endian to the big endian format.

Ex. 9 — Compute the factorial of a positive number using an iterative algorithm.

Ex. 10 — Compute the factorial of a positive number using a recursive algorithm.

Ex. 11 — Write an assembly program to find if a number is prime.

Ex. 12 — Write an assembly program to test if a number is a perfect square.

Ex. 13 — Write an assembly program to test if a number is a perfect cube.

Ex. 14 — Given a 32-bit integer, count the number of 1 to 0 transitions in it.

Ex. 15 — Write an assembly program that checks if a 32-bit number is a palindrome. A palindrome is a number which is the same when read from both sides. For example, 1001 is a 4-bit palindrome.

Ex. 16 — Write an assembly program to examine a 32-bit value stored in *eax* and count the number of contiguous sequences of 1s. For example, the value:

$$01110001000111101100011100011111$$

contains six sequences of 1s. Write the final value in register *ebx*.

Ex. 17 — Write an assembly program to count the number of 1's in a 32-bit number.

* Ex. 18 — Write an assembly program to find the smallest number that is a sum of two different pairs of cubes. [Note: 1729 is known as the Hardy-Ramanujan number. $1729 = 12^3 + 1^3 = 10^3 + 9^3$].

** Ex. 19 — In some cases, we can rotate an integer to the right by n positions (less than or equal to 31) so that we obtain the same number. For example: a 8-bit number 01010101 can be right rotated by 2, 4, or 6 places to obtain the same number. Write an assembly program to *efficiently* count the number of ways we can rotate a number to the right such that the result is equal to the original number.

*** **Ex. 20** — Write an assembly language program to find the greatest common divisor of two binary numbers u and v. Assume the two inputs (positive integers) to be available in *eax* and *ebx*. Store the result in *ecx*. [HINT: The gcd of two even numbers u and v is $2 * gcd(u/2, v/2)$]

Ex. 21 — Write an assembly program that uses string instructions to set the value of a range of memory addresses to 0. Reduce the code size by using the *rep* prefix.

Assembly Programming using Floating Point Instructions

Ex. 22 — How do you load and store floating point numbers?

Ex. 23 — Write an assembly program to find the roots of the equation $x^2 - x - 1 = 0$. Recall that the roots of a quadratic equation of the form $ax^2 + bx + c$ are equal to $\frac{-b \pm \sqrt{b^2 - 4ac}}{2a}$.

Ex. 24 — Verify the following trigonometric identities for random values of θ using assembly programs. Use the *rdrand* instruction that loads a random 32-bit integer into a register.

S. No.	Identity
1	$sin^2(\theta) + cos^2(\theta) = 1$
2	$sin\left(\frac{\pi}{2} - \theta\right) = cos(\theta)$
3	$cos(\theta + \phi) = cos(\theta)cos(\phi) - sin(\theta)sin(\phi)$
4	$sin(\theta) + sin(\phi) = 2sin\left(\frac{\theta + \phi}{2}\right)cos\left(\frac{\theta - \phi}{2}\right)$

Ex. 25 — Assume that we have two arrays of 10 floating point numbers, where the starting addresses of the arrays are stored in *eax* and *ebx* respectively. Find the arithmetic mean (AM), geometric mean (GM), and harmonic mean (HM) using assembly routines. Verify that $AM \geq GM \geq HM$.

* **Ex. 26** — Let us compute the value of the constant e using an assembly program. Use the following mathematical expression.

$$e = 1 + \frac{1}{1!} + \frac{1}{2!} + \frac{1}{3!} + \frac{1}{4!} + \ldots + \frac{1}{10!}$$

** **Ex. 27** — For random values of θ show that the following identity holds:

$$sin(\theta) = \theta - \frac{\theta^3}{3!} + \frac{\theta^5}{5!} - \ldots$$

x86 ISA Encoding

Ex. 28 — What are the values of the SIB and ModR/M bytes for the instruction, *mov eax, [eax + ebx*4]*?

Ex. 29 — What are the values of the SIB, ModR/M, and displacement bytes for the instruction, *mov eax, [eax + ebx*4 + 32]*?

Ex. 30 — What is the value of the *ModR/M* byte when we need to specify a memory address that does not have any base or index registers? Assume that the value of the *reg* field is 000.

* **Ex. 31** — Assume that we have an instruction that has two operands: *eax* and [*ebp*]. How do we encode it (specify the values of the relevant bytes)?

* **Ex. 32** — What are the values of the SIB and ModR/M bytes for the instruction, *mov eax, [ebx*4]*?

Design Problems

Ex. 33 — Write an x86 assembly emulator that can read an assembly file, and execute each assembly instruction one by one.

Ex. 34 — Use the GNU compiler to generate an assembly file for a test program written in C using the command, *gcc -S -masm=intel*.

Part II

Organisation: Processor Design

6

Logic Gates, Registers, and Memories

We are ready to design a real computer now. Before we start, let us quickly take a glance at some of the main requirements and constraints for designing a computer as described in the last few chapters.

Way Point 3

- *A computer needs a central processing unit, set of registers, and a large amount of memory.*

- *A computer needs to support a complete, concise, generic, and simple instruction set.*

- *SimpleRisc is a representative instruction set. To implement it, we need to primarily have support for logical operations, arithmetic computations, register and memory accesses.*

Figure 6.1 shows a plan for the next few chapters. In this chapter, we shall look at designing simple circuits for logical operations, registers, and basic memory cells. We shall consider arithmetic units such as adders, multipliers, and dividers in Chapter 7, and subsequently combine the basic elements to form advanced elements such as the central processing unit, and an advanced memory system in Chapters 8, 9, and 10.

Before, we proceed further, let us warn the reader that this chapter is meant to give a brief introduction to the design and operation of logic circuits. This chapter takes a cursory look at digital logic, and focuses on introducing the broad ideas. A rigorous treatment of digital logic is beyond the scope of this book. The interested reader is referred to seminal texts on digital logic [Taub and Schilling, 1977, Lin, 2011, Wakerly, 2000]. This chapter is primarily meant for two types of readers. The first type of readers are expected to have taken an introductory course on digital logic, and they can use this chapter to refresh their knowledge. The second category of readers are presumed to have little or no background in digital electronics. We provide enough information for them to appreciate the nuances of digital circuits, and their operation. They can use this knowledge to understand the circuits required to perform computer arithmetic, and implement complex processors.

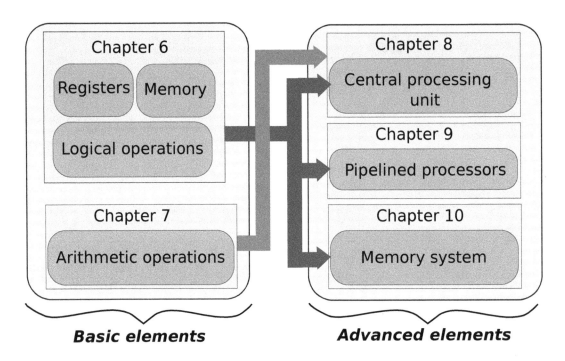

Figure 6.1: Plan for the next few chapters

For implementing logical operations such as bitwise AND, OR, shifts, and register/memory cells, we typically use silicon based circuits today. Note that this was not always the case. The earliest computers in the 19th century were made from mechanical parts. Till the sixties, they were made of vacuum tubes. It is only after the discovery of the transistor and integrated circuit technology that computer processors started getting manufactured using silicon. However, this might be a passing trend. It is perfectly possible in the future that we will have computers made of other materials.

6.1 Silicon based Transistors

Silicon is the 14th element in the periodic table. It has four valence electrons and belongs to the same group as carbon and germanium. However, it is less reactive than both.

Over 90% of the earth's crust consists of silicon based minerals. Silicon dioxide is the primary constituent of sand, and quartz. It is abundantly available, and is fairly inexpensive to manufacture.

Silicon has some interesting properties that make it the ideal substrate for designing circuits and processors. Let us consider the molecular structure of silicon. It has a dense structure, where each silicon atom is connected to four other silicon atoms, and the tightly connected set of silicon atoms are bound together to form a strong lattice. Other materials notably, diamond, have a similar crystalline structure. Silicon atoms are thus more tightly packed than most metals.

Due to the paucity of free electrons, silicon does not have very good electrical conduction properties. In fact it is midway between a good conductor, and an insulator. It is thus known as a *semiconductor*. It is possible to slightly modify its properties by adding some impurities in a controlled manner. This process is called *doping*.

Definition 44

A semiconductor has an electrical conductivity, which is midway between a good conductor and an insulator.

6.1.1 Doping

Typically, two types of impurities are added to silicon to modify its properties: *n-type* and *p-type*. N-type impurities typically consist of group V elements in the periodic table. Phosphorus is the most common n-type dopant. Arsenic is also occasionally used. The effect of adding a group V dopant with five valence electrons is that an extra electron gets detached from the lattice, and is available for conducting current. This process of doping effectively increases the conductivity of silicon.

Likewise, it is possible to add a group III element such as boron or gallium to silicon to create p-type doped silicon. This produces the reverse effect. It creates a void in the lattice. This void is also referred to as a *hole*. A hole denotes the absence of an electron. Like electrons, holes are free to move. Holes can also help in conducting current. Electrons have a negative charge, and holes are conceptually associated with a positive charge.

Now that we have created two kinds of semiconductor materials – n-type and p-type. Let us see what happens if we connect them to form a *p-n junction*.

Definition 45

- *A n-type semiconductor has group V impurities such as phosphorus and arsenic. Its primary charge carriers are electrons.*

- *A p-type semiconductor has group III impurities such as boron and gallium. Its primary charge carriers are holes. Holes have an effective positive charge.*

- *A p-n junction is formed when we place a p-type and n-type semiconductor side by side.*

6.1.2 P-N Junction

Let us consider a p-n junction as shown in Figure 6.2. The p-type region has an excess of holes and the n-type region has an excess of electrons. At the junction, some of the holes cross over and move to the n region because they are attracted by electrons. Similarly, some electrons cross over and get amassed on the side of the p region. This migration of holes and electrons is known as *diffusion*. The area around the junction that witnesses this migration is known as the *depletion region*. However, due to the migration of electrons and holes, an electric field is produced in the opposite direction of migration in the depletion region. This electric field induces a current known as the *drift* current. At steady state, the drift and diffusion currents balance each other, and thus there is effectively no current flow across the junction.

Now, let us see what will happen if we connect both sides of the p-n junction to a voltage source such as a battery. If we connect the *p* side to the positive terminal, and the n side to the negative terminal, then

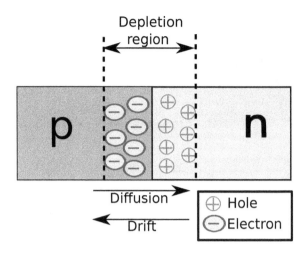

Figure 6.2: A P-N junction

this configuration is known as *forward bias*. In this case, holes flow from the p side of the junction to the n side, and electrons flow in the reverse direction. The junction thus conducts current.

If we connect the p side to the negative terminal and the n side to the positive terminal, then this configuration is known as *reverse bias*. In this case, holes and electrons are pulled away from the junction. Thus, there is no current flow across the junction and the p-n junction in this case does not conduct electricity.

A simple p-n junction as described is known as a *diode*. It conducts current in only one direction, i.e., when it is in forward bias.

Definition 46

A diode is an electronic device typically made of a single p-n junction that conducts current in only one direction.

6.1.3   NMOS Transistor

Now, let us connect two p-n junctions to each other as shown in Figure 6.3(a). This structure is known as an NMOS (Negative Metal-Oxide-Semiconductor) transistor. In this figure there is a central substrate of p type doped silicon. There are two small regions on both sides that contain n type doped silicon. These regions are known as the *drain* and *source* respectively. Note that since the structure is totally symmetric, any of these two regions can be designated as the source or the drain. The region in the middle of the source and drain is known as the *channel*. On top of the channel there is a thin insulating layer typically made of silicon dioxide(SiO_2) and it is covered by a metallic or polysilicon based conducting layer. This is known as the *gate*.

There are thus three terminals of a typical NMOS transistor – source, drain and gate. Each of them can be connected to a voltage source. We now have two options for the gate voltage – logical 1 (V_{dd} volts) or logical 0 (0 volts). If the voltage at the gate is logical 1 (V_{dd} volts), then the electrons in the channel get attracted towards the gate. In fact, if the voltage at the gate is larger that a certain *threshold voltage* (typically 0.15 V in current technologies), then a low resistance conducting path forms between the drain and the source due to the accumulation of electrons. Thus current can flow between the drain and the source. If

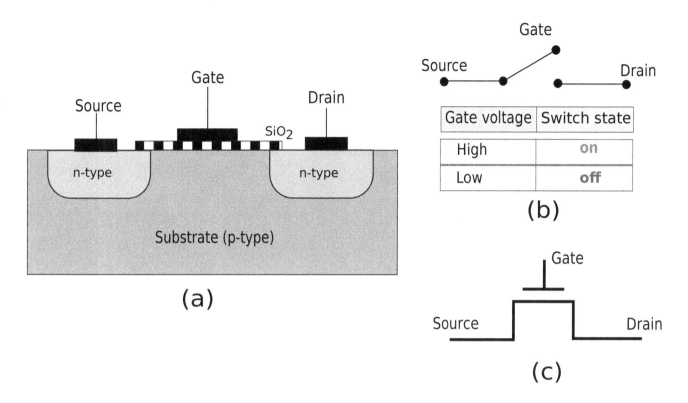

Figure 6.3: NMOS transistor

the effective resistance of the channel is $R_{channel}$, then we have $V_{drain} = IR_{channel} + V_{source}$. If the amount of current flow through the transistor is low, then V_{drain} is roughly equal to V_{source} because of the low channel resistance ($R_{channel}$). We can thus treat the NMOS transistor as a switch (see Figure 6.3(b)). It is turned on when the voltage of the gate is 1.

Now, if we set the voltage at the gate to 0, then a conducting path made up of electrons cannot form in the channel. Hence, the transistor will not be able to conduct current. It will be in the *off* state. In this case, the switch is turned off.

The circuit symbol for a NMOS transistor is shown in Figure 6.3(c).

6.1.4   PMOS Transistor

Like the NMOS transistor, we can have a PMOS transistor as shown in Figure 6.4(a). In this case, the source and drain are regions made up of p type silicon. The logic for the operation of the transistor is exactly the reverse of that of the NMOS transistor. In this case, if the gate is at logical 0, then holes get attracted to the channel and form a conducting path. Whereas, if the gate is at logical 1, then holes get repelled from the channel and do not form a conducting path.

The PMOS transistor can also be treated as a switch (see Figure 6.4(b)). It is turned on, when the gate voltage is 0, and it is turned off when the voltage at the gate is a logical 1. The circuit symbol of a PMOS transistor is shown in Figure 6.4(c).

6.1.5   A Basic CMOS based Inverter

Now, let us construct some basic circuits using NMOS and a PMOS transistors. When a circuit uses both these types of transistors, we say that it uses *CMOS* (combined mos) logic. The circuit diagram of an

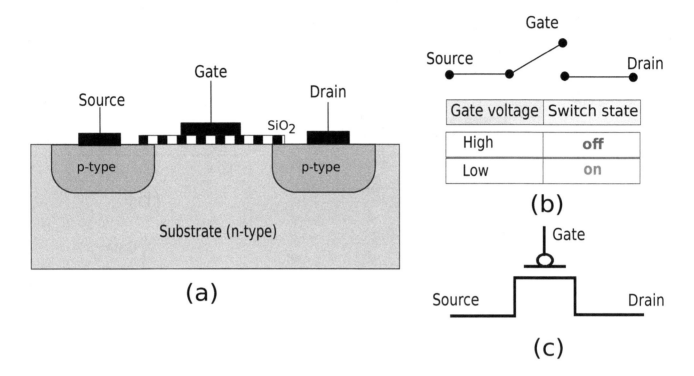

Figure 6.4: PMOS transistor

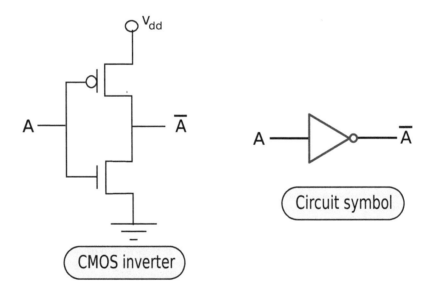

Figure 6.5: CMOS inverter

inverter using CMOS logic is shown in Figure 6.5. In this circuit, an NMOS transistor is connected between the ground and the output, and a PMOS transistor is connected between V_{dd} and the output. The input is fed to the gates of both the transistors.

If the input is a logical 0, then the PMOS transistor is switched on, and the NMOS transistor is switched off. In this case, the output is equal to 1. Likewise, if the input is a logical 1, then the NMOS transistor is switched on and the PMOS transistor is switched off. In this case the output is a logical 0. We thus see that this simple circuit inverts the value at the input. It can thus be used to implement the NOT operation.

The benefits of CMOS technology are manifold. Note that during steady state one of the transistors is in the off state. It thus does not conduct any current. A little amount of current can still leak through the transistors or flow through the output terminal. However, this is minimal. Hence, we can conclude that the power dissipation of a CMOS inverter at steady state is vanishingly small since power is equal to current multiplied by voltage. However, some power is dissipated, when the transistor switches its input value. In this case, both the transistors are on for a small amount of time. There is some current flow from V_{dd} to ground. Nonetheless, as compared to competing technologies, the power dissipated by a CMOS inverter is significantly lower and is thus amenable for use by today's processors that have more than a billion transistors.

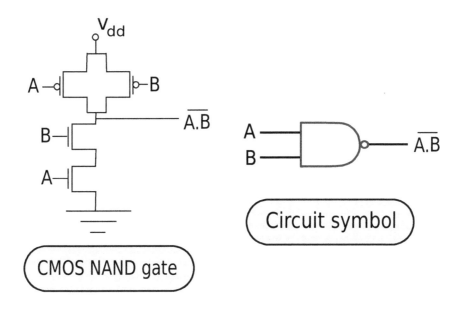

Figure 6.6: CMOS NAND gate

6.1.6 NAND and NOR Gates

Figure 6.6 shows how to construct a NAND gate in CMOS technology. The two inputs, A and B, are connected to the gates of each NMOS-PMOS pair. If both A and B are equal to 1, then the PMOS transistors will switch off, and both the NMOS transistors will conduct. This will set the output to a logical 0. However, if one of the inputs is equal to 0, then one of the NMOS transistors will turn off and one of the PMOS transistors will turn on. The output will thus get set to a logical 1.

Note that we use the '.' operator for the AND operation. This notation is very widely used in representing Boolean formulae. Likewise for the OR operation, we use the '+' sign.

Figure 6.7 shows how to construct a NOR gate. In this case, the two inputs, A and B, are also connected to the gates of each NMOS-PMOS pair. However, as compared to the NAND gate, the topology is different. If one of the inputs is a logical 1, then one of the NMOS transistors will turn on and one of the PMOS transistors will turn off. The output will thus get set to 0. If both the inputs are equal to 0, then both the NMOS transistors will shut off, and both the PMOS transistors will turn on. The output in this case will be equal to a logical 1.

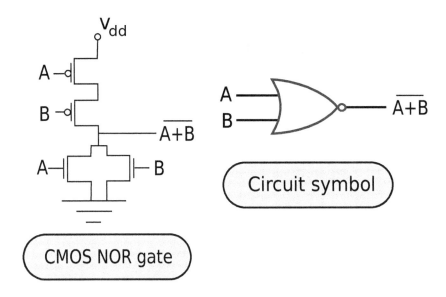

Figure 6.7: CMOS NOR gate

Now, that we have constructed a basic inverter, a NAND, and NOR gate using CMOS logic; we have the tools to construct any type of logic gate. This is because NAND and NOR gates are known as universal gates (see [Kohavi and Jha, 2009]). They can be used to construct any kind of logic gate and implement any logic function. In our circuits, we shall implement complex logic gates using AND, OR, NAND, NOR, XOR, and NOT gates. Other than AND and OR gates, we have described the construction of the rest of the four gates in this section. We can construct an AND gate by connecting the output of a NAND gate to a NOT gate. Similarly, we can construct an OR gate by connecting the output of a NOR gate to a NOT gate.

In the next section, we shall look at structures that compute complex functions on a set of Boolean input bits. We call such structures *combinational logic* structures because they decide if a certain set of input boolean bits belong to a set containing restricted combinations of bits. For example, a XOR gate produces 1 if the input bits are either 01 or 10. In this case the set $\mathcal{S}$ contains the combinations: $\{01, 10\}$. A XOR logic structure decides if the two input bits are in the set $\mathcal{S}$. If they are in the set, then it produces an output equal to 1, otherwise it produces 0.

6.2   Combinational Logic

6.2.1   XOR Gate

Let us implement the logic function for exclusive or (XOR). The truth table is shown in Table 6.1. We shall use the $\oplus$ operator for the XOR operation. An exclusive or operation returns a 1 if both the inputs are unequal, otherwise it returns a 0.

We observe that $A \oplus B = A.\overline{B} + \overline{A}.B$. The circuit for implementing a XOR gate is shown in Figure 6.8.

6.2.2   Decoder

A decoder takes as input a $log(n)$-bit binary number and has n outputs. Based on the input it sets one of the outputs to 1.

A	B	A ⊕ B
0	0	0
1	0	1
0	1	1
1	1	0

Table 6.1: The XOR operation

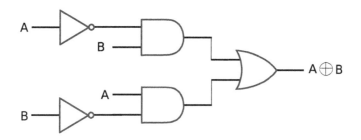

Figure 6.8: XOR gate

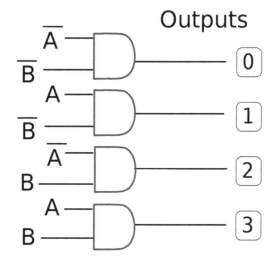

Figure 6.9: Design of a 2×4 decoder

Let us assume that n is a power of 2. Now any value from 0 to $n - 1$ can be encoded using $log(n)$ bits. Let us thus treat the input as a Boolean representation of one of the outputs $(0 \ldots (n - 1))$. For example, if the value of the $log(n)$-bit input is equal to i, then the ith output is set to 1. The rest of the outputs are set to 0. Decoders are extensively used in the design of memory cells and other combinational elements such as multiplexers and demultiplexers.

The design of the decoder is shown in Figure 6.9. We show the design of a 2×4 decoder that has two inputs and four outputs. Let the inputs be A and B. We generate all possible combinations: $\overline{AB}$, $\overline{A}B$, $A\overline{B}$, and AB. These Boolean combinations are generated by computing a logical NOT of A and B and then routing the values to a set of AND gates.

Let us now explain with an example. Assume that the input is equal to 10. This means that $B = 1$ and

$A = 0$. We need to set the 2nd output line to 1, and the rest to 0. The reader can verify that this is indeed happening (note that we are counting from 0). The AND gate corresponding to the 2nd output needs to compute $\overline{A}B$. In this case, it will be the only condition that evaluates to 1.

On similar lines, we can create a generic $log(n) \times n$ decoder.

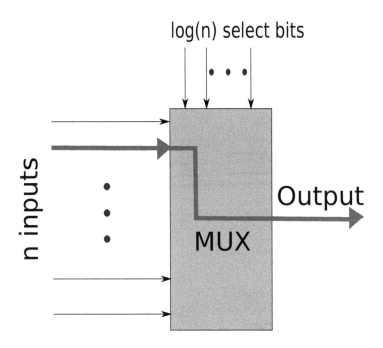

Figure 6.10: Block diagram of a multiplexer

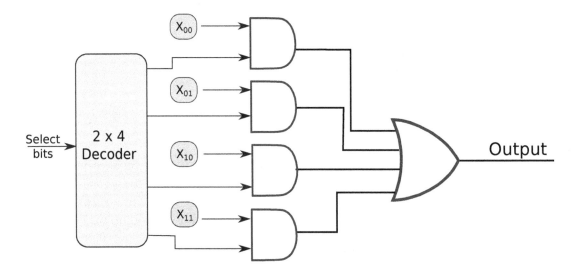

Figure 6.11: Design of a 4-input multiplexer

6.2.3 Multiplexer

The block diagram of a multiplexer is shown in Figure 6.10. It takes n input bits and $log(n)$ select bits, and based on the value of the select bits, chooses one input as the output (refer to the line with arrows in Figure 6.10). Multiplexers are heavily used in the design of processors, where we need to choose one output out of a set of inputs. A multiplexer is also known as a *mux*.

To choose 1 input out of n inputs, we need to specify the identifier of the input. Note that it takes $\lceil log(n) \rceil$ bits to identify any input uniquely (see Section 4.4). We can number each input using $\lceil log(n) \rceil$ binary bits. Each input thus has a unique representation. Now, if the select bits match the binary encoding of an input, then the input gets reflected at the output. For example, if the value of the select bits is i, then the value of the output is equal to the value of the ith input.

A multiplexer consists of three stages (see Figure 6.11). The first stage is a decoder that takes the $log(n)$ select bits as its input and sets one of the n output lines to a logical 1. Each output line is connected to an AND gate (second stage). Since only one of the output lines is set to 1, only the AND gate corresponding to that output is *enabled*. This means that the output of this gate is equal to the value of the other input.

In the example in Figure 6.11, the multiplexer has four inputs: X_{00}, X_{01}, X_{10}, and X_{11}. Each input is connected to an AND gate. If the select bits are equal to 01, then the AND gate corresponding to the input X_{01} is enabled by the decoder. Its output is equal to X_{01}. The outputs of the rest of the AND gates are a logical 0 because they are not enabled by the decoder: one of their inputs is a logical 0.

Finally, in the third stage, an OR gate computes the logical OR of all the outputs of the second stage. Note that for the OR gate, the inputs are $n - 1$ zeros and X_{BA}, where B and A are the values of the select bits, respectively. The final output is thus the value of the input that was selected, X_{BA}.

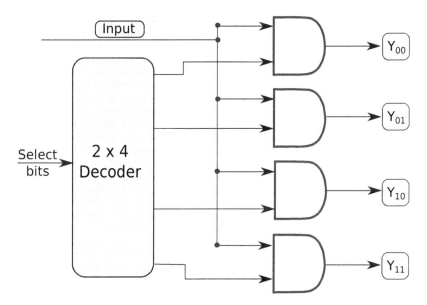

Figure 6.12: Design of a demultiplexer

6.2.4 Demultiplexer

A demultiplexer takes as input a $log(n)$-bit binary number, a 1-bit input, and transfers the input to one of n output lines. The block diagram is shown in Figure 6.12. Demultiplexers are used in the design of memory cells, where it is necessary for the input to reflect in exactly one of the output lines.

The operation is similar to that of a multiplexer. Instead of having multiple inputs, we have just 1 input. Like the case of the multiplexer, we first enable the appropriate AND gate with a decoder. Then the second stage consists of an array of AND gates, where each gate reflects the input bit at its output if it is *enabled* by the decoder. Recall that an AND gate is *enabled* if one of its inputs is a logical 1; in this case the output is equal to the value of the other input.

6.2.5 Encoder

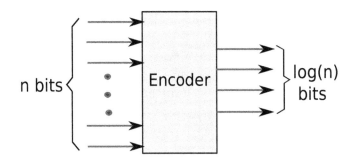

Figure 6.13: Block diagram of an n bit encoder

Let us now consider a circuit with the reverse logic as that of a decoder. Its block diagram is shown in Figure 6.13. The circuit has n inputs, and $log(n)$ outputs. One of the n inputs is assumed to be 1, and the rest are assumed to be 0. The output bits provide the binary encoding of the input that is equal to 1. For example in a 8 input, 3 output encoder, if the fifth line is equal to 1, then the output is equal to 100 (count starts from 0).

Let us construct a simple 4-2 encoder (4 inputs, 2 output bits). Let us number the bits X_0, X_1, X_2, and X_3. If bit X_A is equal to 1, then the output should be equal to the binary encoding of A. Let us designate the output as Y, with two bits Y_0, and Y_1. We have the following equations for Y_0, and Y_1.

$$Y_0 = X_1 + X_3 \tag{6.1}$$
$$Y_1 = X_2 + X_3 \tag{6.2}$$
$$\tag{6.3}$$

The intuition behind these equations is that the LSB of a 2-bit number is equal to 1, when it is equal to 01(1), or 11(3). The MSB is equal to 1, when it is equal to 10(2), or 11(3). We can extend this logic to create a generic n-log(n) bit encoder. The circuit diagram of a 4-2-bit encoder is shown in Figure 6.14.

Example 91
Write the equations for a 8-3 bit encoder. Assume that the inputs are $X_0 \ldots X_7$, and the outputs are Y_0, Y_1, and Y_2.
Answer:

$$Y_0 = X_1 + X_3 + X_5 + X_7 \tag{6.4}$$
$$Y_1 = X_2 + X_3 + X_6 + X_7 \tag{6.5}$$
$$Y_3 = X_4 + X_5 + X_6 + X_7 \tag{6.6}$$

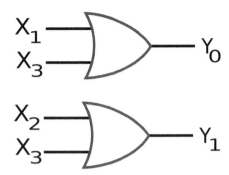

Figure 6.14: Circuit diagram of a 4-2-bit encoder

6.2.6   Priority Encoder

Let us now assume that we do not have the restriction that only one input line can be equal to 1. Let us assume that more than one inputs can be equal to 1. In this case, we need to report the binary encoding of the input line that has the highest index (priority). For example, if lines 3 and 5 and on, then we need to report the binary encoding of the 5th line. The block diagram remains the same as Figure 6.13.

However, the equations for computing the output change. For a 4-2-bit priority encoder, the equations are as follows.

$$Y_0 = X_1.\overline{X_2} + X_3 \tag{6.7}$$

$$Y_1 = X_2 + X_3 \tag{6.8}$$

Let us consider Y_0. If $X_3 = 1$, then $Y_0 = 1$, because X_3 has the highest priority. However, if $X_1 = 1$, then we cannot take a decision based on its value, because X_2, and X_3 might also be equal to 1. If $X_3 = 1$, then there is no issue, because it also sets the value of Y_0. However, if $X_3 = 0$, and $X_2 = 1$, then we need to disregard X_1. Hence, we need to compute $X_1.\overline{X_2} + X_3$ for Y_0. The equation for Y_1 remains the same (the reader should try to find the reason). The circuit diagram of a 4-2-bit encoder is shown in Figure 6.15.

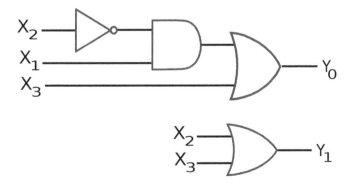

Figure 6.15: Circuit diagram of a 4-2-bit priority encoder

Example 92
Write the equations for a 8-3 bit priority encoder. Assume that the inputs are $X_0 \ldots X_7$, and the outputs are Y_0, Y_1, and Y_2.
Answer:

$$Y_0 = X_1.\overline{X_2}.\overline{X_4}.\overline{X_6} + X_3.\overline{X_4}.\overline{X_6} + X_5.\overline{X_6} + X_7 \tag{6.9}$$

$$Y_1 = X_2.\overline{X_4}.\overline{X_5} + X_3.\overline{X_4}.\overline{X_5} + X_6 + X_7 \tag{6.10}$$

$$Y_3 = X_4 + X_5 + X_6 + X_7 \tag{6.11}$$

6.3   Sequential Logic

We have looked at combinational logic circuits that compute different functions on bits. In this section, we shall look at saving bits for later use. These structures are known as sequential logic elements because the output is dependent on past inputs, which came earlier in the *sequence* of events. The basic idea in a logic gate was to modify the input values to get the desired outputs. In a combinational logic circuit, if the inputs are set to 0, then the outputs also get reset. To ensure that a circuit stores a value and maintains it for as long as the processor is powered on, we need to design a different kind of circuit that has some kind of "built-in memory". Let us start with formulating a set of requirements.

1. The circuit should be self-sustaining, and should maintain its values after the external inputs are reset. should not rely on external signals to maintain its stored elements.

2. There should be a method to read the stored value without destroying it.

3. There should be a method to set the stored value to either 0 or 1.

The best way to ensure that a circuit maintains its value is to create a feedback path, and connect the output back to the input. Let us take a look at the simplest logic circuit in this space: an SR latch.

6.3.1   SR Latch

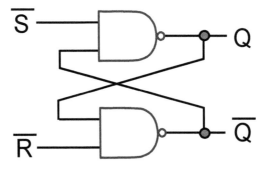

Figure 6.16: The SR latch

Figure 6.16 shows the SR latch. There are two inputs S(set) and R (reset). There are two outputs Q, and its complement $\overline{Q}$. Let us now analyse this circuit that contains two cross-coupled NAND gates. Note that if one of the inputs of a NAND gate is 0, then the output is guaranteed to be 1. However, if one of the inputs is 1, and the other input is A, then the output is $\overline{A}$.

Let us consider the case when, S=1 and R=0. One of the inputs($\overline{S}$) to the top NAND gate is 0. Thus, Q=1. The bottom NAND gate has two inputs $\overline{R} = 1$, and $Q = 1$. Thus, the output, $\overline{Q} = 0$. Similarly, if S=0 and R=1, then Q=0, and $\overline{Q} = 1$. The S input sets the bit in the latch, and the R bit resets it to 0. Let us now consider the case when both S and R are 0. In this case one of the inputs to both the NAND gates is 1. The top NAND gate's output is $\overline{\overline{Q}} = Q$, and the bottom NAND gate's output is $\overline{Q}$. Thus, the value is maintained and we have effectively achieved the objective of storing a bit.

Now, let us see what happens if we set both S and R to 1. In this case, $\overline{S} = 0$ and $\overline{R} = 0$. Thus, Q and $\overline{Q}$ are both equal to 1. In this case, $\overline{Q}$ is not the logical complement of Q. Now, let us say that S is set to 0. Then Q will become 0, and $\overline{Q}$ will become 1. Likewise, if R is set to 0, then Q will become 1, and $\overline{Q}$ will become 0. However, if both S and R simultaneously become 0, then we cannot predict the state of the latch before hand. This is because in practice, signal transitions are never perfectly simultaneous. A non-zero time lag between the transitions of both the inputs is almost always there. Hence, the circuit can see the following sequence of transitions in the SR bits: $11 \rightarrow 10 \rightarrow 00$, or $11 \rightarrow 01 \rightarrow 00$. For the former sequence, Q will be set to 1, and for the latter sequence Q will be set to 0. This is known as a *race* condition and causes unpredictable behaviour. Thus, we do not want to set both S and R to 1.

S	R	Q	$\overline{Q}$	Action
0	0	Q_{old}	$\overline{Q}_{old}$	maintain
1	0	1	0	set
0	1	0	1	reset
1	1	?	?	indeterminate

Table 6.2: State transition table for an SR latch

Table 6.2 shows the state transition table for the SR latch. Q_{old} and $\overline{Q}_{old}$ are the old values of Q and $\overline{Q}$ respectively. The main feature is that setting SR=00 maintains the value stored in the latch. During this period, we can read the value of the outputs infinitely often.

The main issues with the SR latch are as follows.

- S=1 and R=1 is an invalid input.

- We do not have a method of synchronising the transitions in the input and the output. Whenever the inputs change, the outputs also change. As we shall see in the next section, this is not desired behaviour.

6.3.2   The Clock

A typical processor contains millions or possibly billions of logic gates and thousands of latches. Different circuits take different amounts of time. For example, a multiplexer might take 1 ns, and a decoder might take 0.5 ns. Now, a circuit is ready to forward its outputs when it has finished computing them. If we do not have a notion of global time, it is difficult to synchronise the communication across different units, especially those that have variable latencies. Under such a scenario it is difficult to design, operate, and verify a processor. We need a notion of time. For example, we should be able to say that an adder takes two units of time. At the end of the two units, the data is expected to be found in latch X. Other units can then pick up the value from latch X after two units of time and proceed with their computation.

Let us consider the example of a processor that needs to send some data to the printer. Let us further assume that to communicate data, the processor sends a series of bits over a set of copper wires, the printer reads them, and then prints the data. The question is, when does the processor send the data? It needs to send the data, when it is done with the computation. The next question that we can ask is, "How does the processor know, when the computation is over?" It needs to know the exact delays of different units, and once the total duration of the computation has elapsed, it can write the output data to a latch and also set the voltages of the copper wires used for communication. Consequently, the processor does need a notion of time. Secondly, the designers need to tell the processor the time that different sub-units take. Instead of dealing with numbers like 2.34 ns, and 1.92 ns, it is much simpler to deal with integers such as 1, 2, and 3. Here, 1, 2, and 3, represent units of time. A unit of time can be any number such as 0.9333 ns.

Definition 47

clock signal *A periodic square wave that is sent to every part of a large circuit or processor.*

clock cycle *The period of a clock signal.*

clock frequency *The inverse of the clock cycle period.*

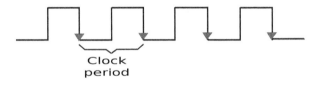

Figure 6.17: A Clock Signal

Hence, most digital circuits synchronise themselves with a *clock signal* that sends a periodic pulse to every part of the processor at exactly the same time. A clock signal is a square wave as shown in Figure 6.17; most of the time the clock signal is generated externally by a dedicated unit on the motherboard. Let us consider the point at which the clock signal transitions from 1 to 0 (downward/negative edge) as the beginning of a *clock cycle*. A clock cycle is measured from one downward edge of the clock to the next downward edge. The duration of a clock cycle is also known as a *clock period*. The inverse of a clock period is known as the *clock frequency*.

Important Point 7
A computer, laptop, tablet, or mobile phone typically has a line listing the frequency in its specifications. For example, the specifications might say that a processor runs at 3 GHz. Now we know that this number refers to the clock frequency.

The typical model of computation is as follows. The time required to perform all basic actions in a circuit is measured in terms of clock cycles. If a producer unit takes n clock cycles, then at the end of n clock cycles, it writes its value to a latch. Other consumer units are aware of this delay, and at the beginning of the $(n+1)^{th}$ clock cycle, they read the value from the latch. Since all the units explicitly synchronise with the clock, and the processor is aware of the delays of every unit, it is very easy to sequence the computation, communicate with I/O devices, avoid race conditions, debug and verify circuits. We can see that our simple example in which we wanted to send data to a printer can be easily solved by using a clock.

6.3.3 Clocked SR Latch

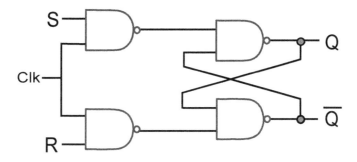

Figure 6.18: The Clocked SR latch

Figure 6.18 shows the SR latch augmented with two NAND gates that have the clock as one of the inputs. The other two inputs are the S and R bits respectively. If the clock is 0, then both the inputs to the cross-coupled NAND gates are 1. This maintains the previous value. If the clock is 1, then the inputs to the cross-coupled NAND gates are $\overline{S}$ and $\overline{R}$ respectively. These are the same inputs as the basic SR latch. The rest of the operation follows Table 6.2. Note that a clocked latch is typically referred to as a *flip-flop*.

Definition 48
Flip-flop : It is a clocked latch that can save a bit (0 or 1).

By using the clock, we have partially solved the problem of synchronising inputs and outputs. In this case, when the clock is 0, the outputs are unaffected by the inputs. When the clock is 1, the outputs are affected by the input. Such a latch is also called a *level sensitive latch*.

Definition 49
A level sensitive latch is dependent on the value of the clock signal – 0 or 1. Typically, it can read in new values, only when the clock is 1.

In a level sensitive latch, circuits have half a clock cycle to compute the correct outputs (when the clock is 0). When the clock is 1, the outputs are visible. It would be better to have one full clock cycle to compute the outputs. This would require an edge sensitive latch. An *edge sensitive* latch reflects the inputs at the output, only at the downward edge of the clock.

Definition 50
An edge sensitive latch reflects the inputs at the output only at a fixed clock edge, such as the downward edge (transition from 1 to 0).

Let us try to create an edge sensitive SR latch.

6.3.4 Edge Sensitive SR Flip-flop

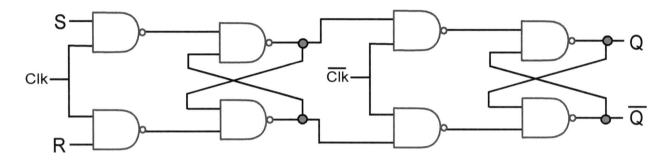

Figure 6.19: The clocked edge sensitive SR flip-flop

Figure 6.19 shows a clocked edge sensitive SR flip-flop. We connect two clocked SR flip-flops together. The only difference is that the second SR flip-flop uses the complement of the clock signal, $\overline{CLK}$. The first flip-flop is known as the *master*, and the second flip-flop is known as the *slave*. This flip-flop is also known as a master-slave SR flip-flop. Here, is how this circuit works.

Definition 51
A master-slave flip-flop contains two flip-flops that are connected to each other. The master's output is the slave's input. Typically, the slave uses a clock signal that is the logical complement of the master's clock.

Whenever the clock signal is high (1), the inputs (S and R) are read into the first SR flip-flop. When the clock signal becomes low (0), then the first flip-flop stops accepting new data; however, the second flip-flop takes the output of the first flip-flop and sets its output accordingly. Thus, new data arrives at the output terminals Q and $\overline{Q}$ when the clock transitions from 1 to 0 (downward clock edge). We thus have created a flip-flop that is edge sensitive.

However, some problems still remain. If both S and R are 1, then there might be a race condition, and the output can be unpredictable. This problem needs to be fixed. Let us first try to look at a complex solution that augments the clocked edge sensitive SR flip-flop, and then look at simpler solutions.

6.3.5 JK Flip-flop

Figure 6.20 shows a JK flip-flop. There are two minor differences as compared to the master-slave SR flip-flop. The first is that the inputs are now J and K, instead of S and R. The second is that Q and $\overline{Q}$ are now inputs to the input NAND gates ($N1$ and $N2$).

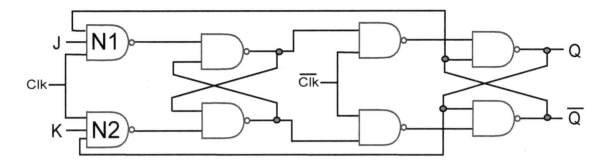

Figure 6.20: The JK flip-flop

Let us do a case by case analysis. Assume that the clock is high. If J and K are both 0, then the outputs of $N1$ and $N2$ are both 1 and the case is same as that for the master-slave SR flip-flop. The outputs are maintained. If J=1 and K=0, then we need to consider the value of $\overline{Q}$. If $\overline{Q} = 1$, then Q = 0, and the output of NAND gate N1 (see Figure 6.20) is 0. The outputs of the master flip-flop are therefore 1 and 0 respectively. The output of the slave after the downward/ negative clock edge will therefore be: $Q = 1, \overline{Q} = 0$.

Now, assume that $\overline{Q} = 0$, and Q=1. In this case, the outputs of both N1 and N2 are 1 and thus all the values are maintained. Hence, after the negative clock edge we have: Q=1, and $\overline{Q} = 0$. We can thus conclude, that if J=1 and K=0, Q=1, and $\overline{Q}$=0.

Similarly, if J=0 and K=1, we can prove that Q=0, and $\overline{Q}$=1.

Let us now consider the case when both J and K are 1. In this case the output of N1 is Q and the output of N2 is $\overline{Q}$. The output of the master flip-flop is equal to $\overline{Q}$ and Q respectively. After the negative clock edge the outputs will be: $Q = \overline{Q}_{old}$ and $\overline{Q} = Q_{old}$. Thus, the outputs will get toggled. We will not have a race condition anymore. Table 6.3 shows the state transition table for the JK flip-flop.

J	K	Q	$\overline{Q}$	Action
0	0	Q_{old}	$\overline{Q}_{old}$	maintain
1	0	1	0	set
0	1	0	1	reset
1	1	$\overline{Q}_{old}$	Q_{old}	toggle

Table 6.3: State transition table for a JK flip-flop

6.3.6 D Flip-flop

Instead of having a dedicated S(set) and R (reset) signal, we can make our life easy by making one the complement of the other. However, in this case, we will not have a method of maintaining the value. The input will get reflected at the output at every negative clock edge. In a lot of cases, this is sufficient and we do not need dedicated logic to either maintain or toggle the values. In this case, we can use the simplistic D flip-flop as shown in Figure 6.21. It is basically a SR flip-flop where R = $\overline{S}$.

Note that the second input (to the lower NAND gate) is equal to $\overline{D \wedge Clk}$. When Clk is equal to 1, the second input is equal to $\overline{D}$. When Clk is 0, the flip-flop maintains the previous values and does not accept new data.

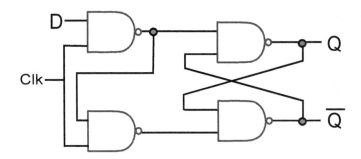

Figure 6.21: D flip-flop

6.3.7 Master-slave D Flip-flop

Akin to the JK flip-flop we can have a master-slave version of the D flip-flop.

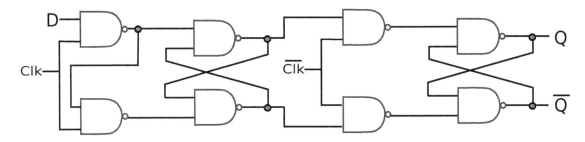

Figure 6.22: Master-slave D flip-flop

Figure 6.22 shows a master-slave version of the D flip-flop. We connect one D flip-flop to a SR flip-flop. Here, we do not need wires connecting the inputs with Q and $\overline{Q}$ because we are not interested in toggling the state. Secondly, we have avoided race conditions by not having the evil (1,1) input.

A master-slave flip-flop uses 8 NAND gates and 1 inverter for the clock. A master slave D flip-flop requires 34 transistors, and a master-slave JK flip-flop requires 38 transistors. This is a large expenditure for saving just 1 bit! We should be able to do better. We shall see in later sections that we can store a single bit with even 1 transistor. But the circuit will become extremely slow. We can thus conclude that flip-flops are inefficient as far as power and the transistor budget are concerned; however, they are very fast. If we need to save a lot of data and we are willing to sacrifice on time, then we should opt for SRAM and DRAM memories (described in Section 6.4).

6.3.8 Metastability

Up till now we have assumed that at the negative edge of a clock the input instantaneously reflects at the output. This high level assumption is however not strictly correct. Readers need to appreciate the fact that every digital circuit is at its core an analog circuit. Quantities like current and voltage take time to reach their optimal levels, and the circuit is sensitive to the voltage levels, and the timing of the inputs. The readers can refer to standard text books [Taub and Schilling, 1977] on digital design for a thorough explanation.

In this section, we shall take a look at one particular aspect of the analog nature of flip flops known as *metastability*. If there is a change in the input close to the negative clock edge, then the output becomes non-deterministic, and might even fluctuate or oscillate for some period of time. This phenomenon is known as *metastability*. To avoid such behaviour it is necessary to ensure that the input is stable (does not change) for t_{setup} units of time before the clock edge, and is also stable for t_{hold} units of time after the clock edge. This means that there is a window of time around the clock edge in which the input to the flip flop needs to remain stable. Only, in this case, we can guarantee the correct operation of a flip flop. This window of time in which we want the inputs to be stable is known as the *keep out* region.

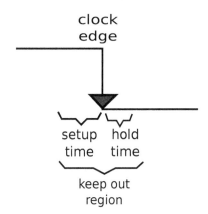

Figure 6.23: Setup time, hold time, and the keep out region

Let us now display these concepts graphically in Figure 6.23. We need to note that in practice, the setup time, and the hold time are small fractions of the total cycle time ($< 10\%$). Designers take special precautions to ensure that there are no transitions in the input in the keep out region. We shall see that this phenomenon has important implications when we discuss I/O circuits. These circuits have sophisticated delay elements that delay signals to keep transitions out of the keep out region.

6.3.9   Registers

Parallel In–Parallel Out

We can store n bit data by using a set of n master slave D flip flops. Each D flip flop is connected to an input line, and its output terminal is connected to an output line. Such an n bit structure is known as an n bit register. Here, we can load n bits in parallel, and also read out n bits in parallel at every negative clock edge. Hence, this structure is known as a parallel in–parallel out register. Its structure is shown in Figure 6.24.

Serial In – Parallel Out

Let us now consider a serial in–parallel out register as shown in Figure 6.25. Here, we have a single input that is fed into the leftmost D flip flop. Every cycle, the input moves to the adjacent flip flop on the right. Thus, to load n bits it will take n cycles. The first bit will get loaded into the leftmost flip flop in the first cycle, and it will take n cycles for it to reach the last flip flop. By that time, the rest of the $n-1$ flip flops will get loaded with the rest of the $n-1$ bits. We can then read out all the n bits in parallel (similar to the parallel in–parallel out register). This register is also known as a *shift register* and is used for implementing circuits used in high speed I/O buses.

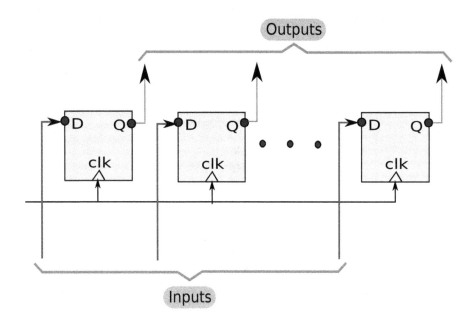

Figure 6.24: A parallel in–parallel out register

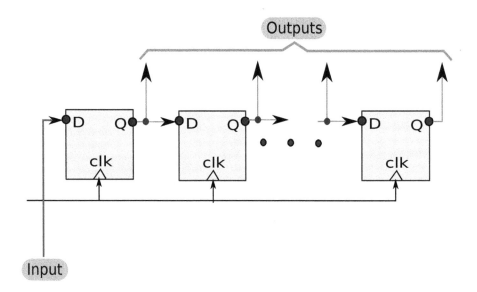

Figure 6.25: A serial in–parallel out register

6.4 Memories

6.4.1 Static RAM (SRAM)

SRAM Cell

SRAM refers to static random access memory. A basic SRAM cell contains two cross-coupled inverters as shown in Figure 6.26. In comparison, a basic SR flip-flop or a D flip-flop contains cross-coupled NAND gates. The design is shown in Figure 6.26.

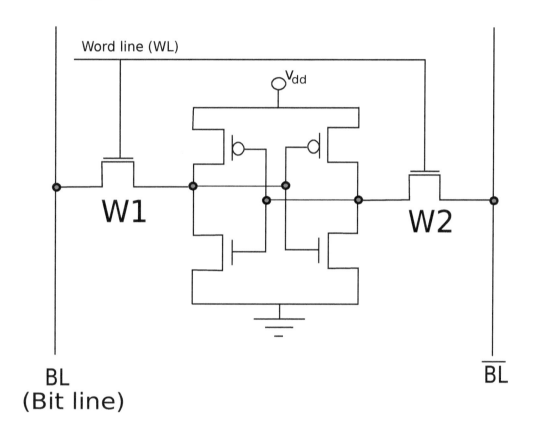

Figure 6.26: A 6 transistor SRAM cell

The core of the SRAM cell contains 4 transistors (2 in each inverter). This cross-coupled arrangement is sufficient to save a single bit (0 or 1). However, we need some additional circuitry to read and write values. At this point, the reader might be wondering if it is a bad idea to have cross-coupled inverters in a latch. They after all require fewer transistors. We shall see that the overheads of implementing the circuitry for reading and writing a SRAM cell are non-trivial. The overheads do not justify making a latch with a SRAM cell as its core.

The cross coupled inverters are connected to transistors on each side (W1, W2). The gates of W1 and W2 are connected to the same signal, known as the *word line*. The four transistors in the two inverters, W1, and W2, comprise the SRAM cell. It has six transistors in total. Now, if the voltage on the word line is low, then W1 and W2 are off. It is not possible to read or write the SRAM cell. However, if the signal on the word line is high, then W1 and W2 are on. It is possible to access the SRAM cell.

Now, the transistors, $W1$, and $W2$, are connected to copper wires on either side known as the bit lines. The bit lines are designed to carry complementary values. One of them is BL and the other is $\overline{BL}$. To write a value into the cell it is necessary to set the values of BL and $\overline{BL}$ to A and $\overline{A}$ respectively, where A is the value that we intend to write. To read a value, we need to turn the word line on and read the voltages of the bit lines.

Let us now delve slightly deeper into the operation of the SRAM cells. Note that SRAM cells are not solitary units like latches. They exist as a part of an array of SRAM cells. We need to consider the array of SRAM cells in entirety.

Array of SRAM Cells

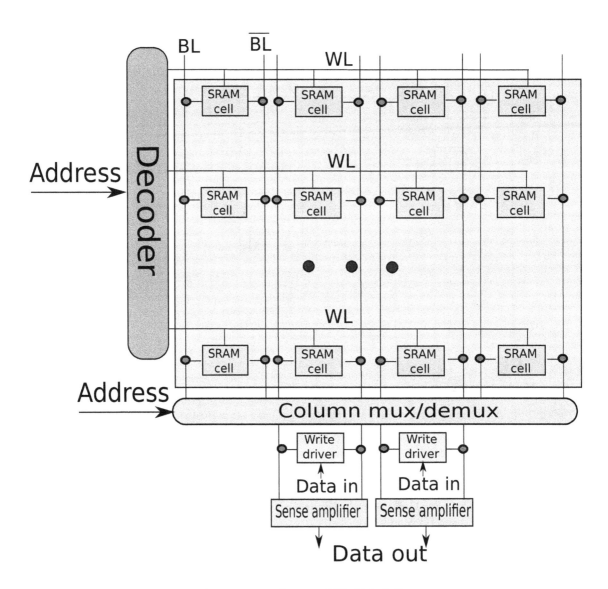

Figure 6.27: Array of SRAM Cells

Figure 6.27 shows a typical SRAM array. SRAM cells are laid out as a two dimensional matrix. All the SRAM cells in a row share the word line, and all SRAM cells in a column share a pair of bit lines. To activate a certain SRAM cell it is necessary to turn its associated word line on. This is done by a decoder. It takes a subset of address bits, and turns the appropriate word line on. A single row of SRAM cells might contain

100+ SRAM cells. Typically, we will be interested in the values of 32 SRAM cells (on a 32-bit machine). In this case the column mux/demux selects the bit lines belonging to the SRAM cells of interest. It uses a subset of the bits in the address as the column select bits. This design methodology is also known as 2.5D memory organisation.

As the size of the array grows it may become more asymmetric. This needs to be avoided, otherwise the capacitive loading on the word lines or bit lines will become prohibitive. Hence, columns need to become wider and the column mux/demux structure needs to be driven by a large column decoder.

The process of writing is easy. The strong write drivers need to set the values of BL and $\overline{BL}$. To write 1, BL needs to be driven to 1, and $\overline{BL}$ needs to be driven to 0. However, reading a value is slightly more difficult. The reason is that a SRAM cell needs to charge an entire bit line to the stored value such that it can be read. Since hundreds of SRAM cells are typically connected to a bit line, the bit line has a very high capacitance. Consequently, it will take a long time to charge/discharge the bit line to logical 0 or 1.

Hence, something smarter needs to be done. The read operation is divided into two phases. In the first phase, BL and $\overline{BL}$ are precharged to $V_{dd}/2$ volts. If the supply voltage is equal to 1 volt, then the bit lines are charged to 0.5 volts. This step is known as *pre-charging*. Subsequently, the SRAM cells of interest are accessed by setting the corresponding word line. The sense amplifiers simply monitor the difference in voltage between BL and $\overline{BL}$. The moment the absolute value of the difference exceeds a threshold, the result can be inferred. For example, if we are reading a logical 1, we need not wait for BL to reach 1, and $\overline{BL}$ to reach 0. If the voltage difference between BL and $\overline{BL}$ exceeds a threshold, then we can declare the result to be 1.

This method is very fast because of the following reasons. Pre-charging bit lines is very fast because there are dedicated pre-charge circuits that can pump a large amount of current into the bit lines to enable faster charging or discharging. After pre-charging inferring the stored value from the voltage swing between BL and $\overline{BL}$ is also very fast. This is because the threshold for the voltage swing is much lower as compared to the supply voltage. Given the high capacitance of bit lines, the time to charge/discharge bit lines is very crucial. Hence, if we reduce the amount of the voltage swing that is required to infer the value stored in the SRAM cell, it makes a significant difference.

We can justify the overhead of pre-charge circuits, write drivers, and sense amplifiers, if we have a large number of SRAM cells. Hence, SRAMs are suitable for structures such as register files and on-chip memories. They should not be used for storing a few bits; flip-flops are better choices.

6.4.2 Content Addressable Memory (CAM)

CAM Cell

In this section, we shall look at a special type of memory cell called a CAM (Content Addressable Memory) cell. First, consider an SRAM array. A typical SRAM array is a matrix of SRAM cells. Each row contains a vector of data. A given row is addressed or located by using a specific set of address bits. However, it is possible to locate a row using a different method. We can address a row by its content. For example, if each row contains 32 SRAM cells, then we can think of the contents of a row as a 32-bit number. We wish to address the row this 32-bit number. For example, if a row contains 0x AB 12 32 54, then we should be able to find the index of the row that contains this value. Such a memory is known as a CAM memory, and each basic cell is known as a CAM cell. A CAM memory is typically used to implement a hashtable(see [Cormen et al., 2009]) in hardware. A hashtable saves key-value pairs such as (name and address). We address a hashtable by its key, and read the value. It is a more flexible data structure than an array, because we are not limited to integer indices. We shall use CAM arrays to implement some memory structures in Chapter 10.

Let us take a look at a 10 transistor CAM cell in Figure 6.28. If the value stored in the SRAM cell, V, is not equal to the input bit, A_i, then we wish to set the value of the *match* line to 0. In the CAM cell, the

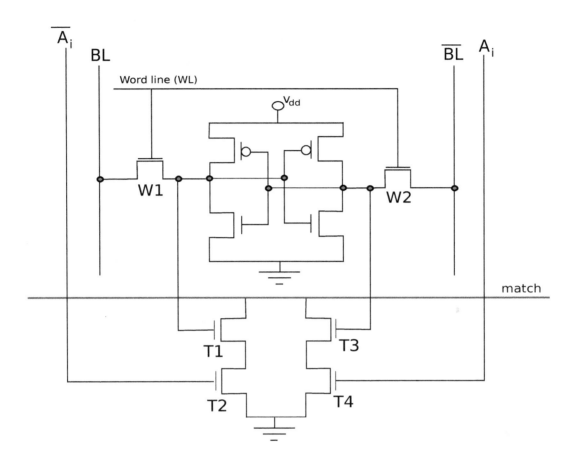

Figure 6.28:   A 10 Transistor CAM cell

upper half is a regular SRAM cell with 6 transistors. We have 4 extra transistors in the lower half. Let us now consider transistor $T1$. It is connected to a global *match* line, and transistor $T2$. $T1$ is controlled, by the value, V, which is stored in the SRAM cell, and $T2$ is controlled by $\overline{A_i}$. Let us assume that $V = \overline{A_i}$. If both of them are 1, then transistors $T1$, and $T2$ are in the ON stage, and there is a direct conducting path between the match line and ground. Thus, the value of the match line will get set to 0. However, if V and $\overline{A_i}$ are both 0, then the path through $T1$ and $T2$ is not conducting. But, in this case, the path through $T3$, and $T4$ becomes conducting, because the gates of these transistors are connected to $\overline{V}$, and A_i respectively. The input to both the gates is a logical 1. Thus, the match line will be pulled down to 0. The reader can conversely verify that if $V = A_i$, no conducting path is formed. Thus, a CAM cell drives the match line to a logical 0, if there is a mismatch between the value stored and the input bit, A_i.

Array of CAM Cells

Figure 6.29 shows an array of CAM cells. The structure is mostly similar to an SRAM array. We can address a row by its index, and perform a read/write access. Additionally, we can compare each row of the CAM cell with the input, A. If any row matches the input, then the corresponding match line will have a value of 1. We can compute a logical OR of all the match lines, and decide if we have a match in the CAM array or not. Additionally, we can connect all the match lines of the CAM array to a priority encoder to find the index of the row that matches the data.

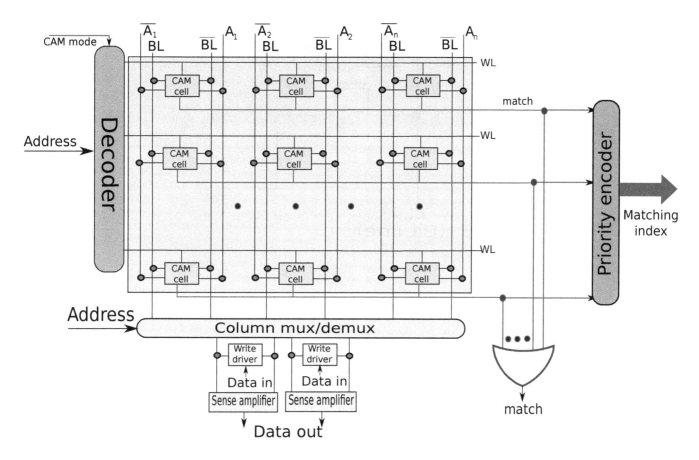

Figure 6.29:   Array of CAM Cells

6.4.3 Dynamic RAM (DRAM)

Let us now take a look at a memory technology that just uses one transistor to save a bit. It is thus very dense, area, and power efficient. However, it is also much slower than SRAMs and latches. It is suitable for large off-chip memories.

A basic DRAM(dynamic RAM) cell is shown in Figure 6.30. The gate of the single transistor is connected to the word line, which enables or disables it. One of the terminals is connected to a capacitor that stores charge. If the bit stored is a logical 1, then the capacitor is fully charged. Otherwise, it is not charged.

Thus, reading and writing values is very easy. We need to first set the word line such that the capacitor can be accessed. To read the value we need to sense the voltage on the bit line. If it is at ground potential, then the cell stores 0, else if it is close to the supply voltage, then the cell stores 1. Similarly, to write a value, we need to set the bit line (BL) to the appropriate voltage, and set the word line. The capacitor will get charged or discharged accordingly.

However, in the case of DRAMs, everything does not come for free. Let us assume that the capacitor is charged to a voltage equal to the supply voltage. In practice, the capacitor will gradually leak some charge through the dielectric, and the transistor. This current is very small, but the total loss of charge over a large duration of time can be significant and can ultimately discharge the capacitor. To prevent this, it is necessary to periodically refresh the value of a DRAM cell. We need to read it and write the data value back. This also needs to be done after a read operation because the capacitor loses some charge while charging the bit line. Let us now try to make an array of DRAM cells.

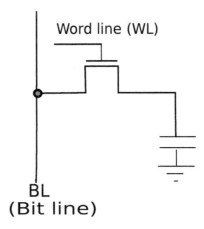

Figure 6.30: A DRAM cell

Array of DRAM Cells

We can construct an array of DRAM cells (see Figure 6.31) the same way that we created an array of SRAM cells. There are three differences. The first is that there is one bit line instead of two. Second, we also have a dedicated refresh circuit connected to the bit lines. This is used after read operations, and is also invoked periodically. Finally, in this case the sense amplifiers appear before the column mux/demux. The sense amplifiers additionally cache the data for the entire DRAM row (also called a DRAM *page*). They ensure that subsequent accesses to the same DRAM row are fast because they can be serviced directly from the sense amplifiers.

Let us now briefly discuss the timing aspects of modern DRAMs. In the good old days, DRAM memory was accessed asynchronously. This means that the DRAM modules did not make any timing guarantees. However, nowadays every DRAM operation is synchronised with a system clock. Hence, today's DRAM chips are synchronous DRAM chips (SDRAM chips). Figure 12.26 in Chapter 12 shows the timing diagram of a simple SDRAM chip for a read access.

Synchronous DRAM memories typically use the DDR4 or DDR5 standards as of today. DDR stands for *Double Data Rate*. Devices using the earliest standard, DDR1, send 8-byte data packets to the processor on both the rising and falling edges of the clock. This is known as *double pumped* operation. The peak data rate of DDR1 is 1.6 GB/s. Subsequent DDR generations extend DDR1 by transferring data at a higher frequency. For example, DDR2 has twice the data rate as DDR1 devices (3.2 GB/s). DDR3 further doubles the peak transfer rate by using a higher bus frequency, and has been in use since 2007 (peak rate of 6.4GB/s).

6.4.4 Read Only Memory (ROM)

Let us now consider simpler memory structures that are read-only in nature. We require read only memories that save data that should never be modified. This can include security information in smart phones, BIOS chips in the motherboards of processors, or the programs in some microcontrollers. We desire read only memory such that it is not possible for users to maliciously change the information stored in them. It turns that we can make simple modifications to our DRAM cell, and construct read only memories.

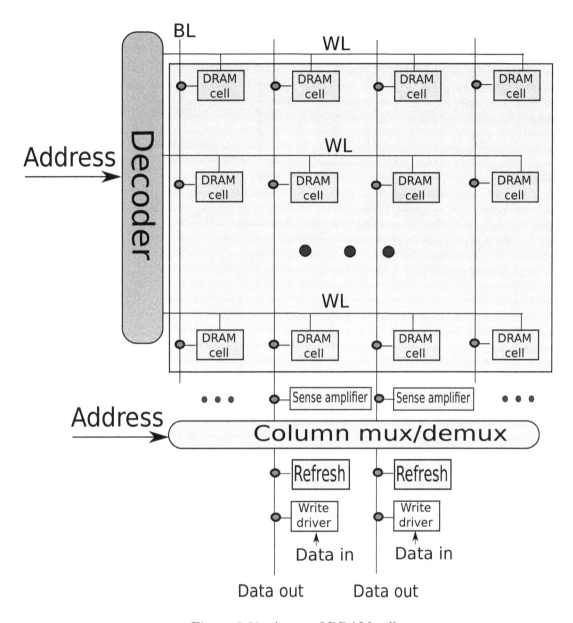

Figure 6.31: Array of DRAM cells

ROM Memories

The capacitor in a DRAM cell stores a logical bit. If it stores a logical 1, then the charge across the capacitor is equal to the supply voltage V_{dd}, and if it stores a logical 0, then the charge across the capacitor is 0V. Instead of having a capacitor, we can directly connect one end of the transistor to either ground or V_{dd} depending upon the bit that we wish to store. This can be done at the time of designing and manufacturing the chip. The ROM memory cell as shown in Figure 6.32 replaces the capacitor by a direct connection to V_{dd} or ground. A ROM array is similar to a DRAM array. However, it does not have write drivers, and refresh circuitry.

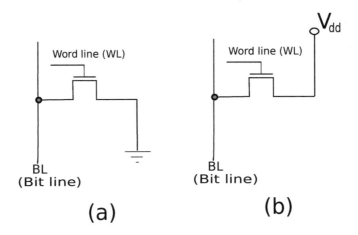

Figure 6.32: (a) ROM cell storing a logical 0, (b) ROM cell storing a logical 1

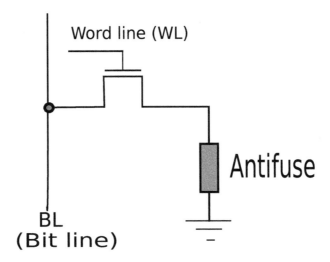

Figure 6.33: PROM Cell

PROM (Programmable ROM) Memories

Let us now look at a programmable ROM (PROM) cell that can be programmed only once to store either a 0 or 1. Typically vendors of PROM cells release PROM arrays to the market. They are then programmed by microprocessor vendors to hold a given set of data values. Note that once data has been written, we cannot make any further modifications. Hence, it acts like read only memory. A PROM cell is shown in Figure 6.33. We have a connection between the transistor and ground through an element known as an *antifuse*. An *antifuse* is the reverse of a conventional fuse. By default, an antifuse is a very weak conductor of current. However, when we transfer a large amount of current through the antifuse, it changes its structure and forms a conducting path. In the former case, the transistor is left floating, and it does not have the ability to drive the bit line to a logical 0. Hence, we can infer that the cell stores a logical 1. Once, the antifuse becomes conducting, the transistor (if enabled by the word line) can drive the bit line to a logical 0. Thus, in this case, the transistor stores a logical 0. A PROM cell based array is similar to an array of ROM cells. Each bit line is initially precharged. After enabling the word line, if the voltage at the sense amplifiers does not increase, then we can infer a logical 1. However, if the voltage keeps decreasing towards 0 V, then we can infer a logical 0.

We can build antifuses with a variety of materials. Dielectric antifuses use a thin layer of a sensitive material (silicon oxides) between two conducting wires. This thin layer breaks down and forms a conducting path upon the application of a large current pulse. In place of dielectrics we can use other materials such as amorphous silicon.

Read only memories are useful in a limited set of scenarios since their contents cannot be modified. We have two related sets of devices called EPROM (Erasable PROM), and EEPROM (Electrically Erasable PROM). Typically these memories are made of special transistors that allow charge storage in a structure known as a *floating gate*. EPROM memories could be erased by applying a strong ultraviolet light pulse to the floating gate. However, such memories are not used today, and have been superseded by flash memories that can be read, written, and erased electrically. Flash memories are explained in detail in Section 12.8.4.

6.4.5   Programmable Logic Arrays

It turns out that we can make a combinational logic circuit out of a memory cell similar to a PROM cell very easily. Such devices are known as *programmable logic arrays*, or PLAs. PLAs are used to implement complex logic functions consisting of tens or hundreds of minterms in practice. The advantage of a PLA over a hardwired circuit made up of logic gates is that a PLA is flexible. We can change the Boolean logic implemented by the PLA at run time. In comparison, a circuit made in silicon can never change its logic. Secondly, designing and programming a PLA is simpler, and there are a lot of software tools to design and work with PLAs. Lastly, a PLA can have multiple outputs, and it can thus implement multiple Boolean functions very easily. This additional flexibility comes at a cost, and the cost is **performance**.

Let us now consider an example. Let us assume that we wish to implement the Boolean function $(\overline{ABC} + AB)$ using a PLA. Let us break the Boolean expression into a set of minterms (see Section 2.1.6). We thus have:

$$\overline{ABC} + AB = \overline{ABC} + ABC + AB\overline{C} \tag{6.12}$$

Since, we have three variables (A, B, and C) here, we have 8 possible minterms. Let us thus have a PLA with 8 rows that generates the values of all the possible minterms. Let each row correspond to a minterm. Let us design the PLA in such a way that a row has an output equal to 1 if the corresponding minterm evaluates to 1. We can compute the result of the entire Boolean expression by computing the logical OR of the values of all the minterms that we are interested in. For this specific example ($\overline{ABC} + AB$), we are interested in 3 out of 8 minterms. Hence, we need a mechanism to filter these 3 minterms and compute a logical OR of their values.

Let us start out with the design of a PLA cell.

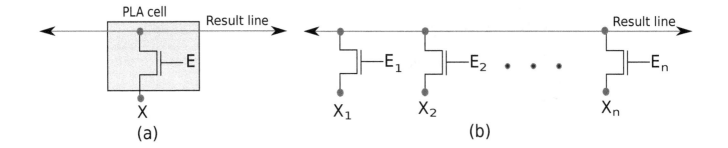

Figure 6.34: A PLA cell

PLA Cell

The PLA cell shown in Figure 6.34(a) is in principle similar to a basic PROM cell. If the value (E) at the gate is equal to 1, then the NMOS transistor is in the ON state. As a result of this, the voltage difference between the source and drain terminals of the NMOS transistor is very small. In other words, we can simplistically assume that the voltage of the result line is equal to the voltage of the signal, X. If ($E = 0$), the NMOS transistor is in the OFF state. The result line is floating, and it maintains its precharged voltage. In this case, we propose to infer a logical 1.

Let us now construct a row of PLA cells where each PLA cell is connected to an input wire at its source terminal as shown in Figure 6.34(b). The inputs are numbered $X_1 \ldots X_n$. The drains of all the NMOS transistors are connected to the result line. The gates of the transistors of the PLA cells are connected to a set of enable signals, $E_1 \ldots E_n$. If any of the enable signals is equal to 0, then that specific transistor is disabled, and we can think of it as being logically removed from the PLA array.

Let us consider all the PLA cells that are enabled (gate voltage is equal to a logical 1). If any of the source inputs ($X_1 \ldots X_n$) is equal to 0, then the voltage of the result line will be driven to 0. We assume that we precharge the result line to a voltage corresponding to logical 1 at the beginning. Now, if none of the input voltages is equal to 0, then the value of the result line will be equal to a logical 1. We can thus conclude that the Boolean function computed by a row of PLA cells is equal to $X_1.X_2.\ldots.X_n$ (assuming that all the cells are enabled). For example, if we want to compute the value of the minterm, $ABCD$, then we need to set $X_1 = A$, $X_2 = B$, $X_3 = C$, and $X_4 = D$. The Boolean value represented by the result line will be equal to $ABCD$.

In this manner, we can evaluate the values of all the minterms by connecting the source terminals of PLA cells to the input bits. Up till now we have not considered the case of Boolean variables in minterms in their complemented form such as $\overline{A}BC\overline{D}$. For the minterm, $\overline{A}BC\overline{D}$, we need to make the following connections. We need to connect 4 PLA cells to the result line, where their source terminals are connected to the signals $\overline{A}$, B, C, and $\overline{D}$ respectively. We need to generate, $\overline{A}$, and $\overline{D}$ by complementing the values of A and D using inverters.

Array of PLA Cells

Let us now create an array of PLA cells as shown in Figure 6.35. Each row corresponds to a minterm. For our 3 variable example, each row consists of 6 columns. We have 2 columns for each variable (original and complemented). For example, the first two columns correspond to A and $\overline{A}$ respectively. In any row, only one of these two columns contains a PLA cell. This is because A and $\overline{A}$ cannot both be true at the same time. In the first row, we compute the value of the minterm, $\overline{ABC}$. Hence, the first row contains PLA cells

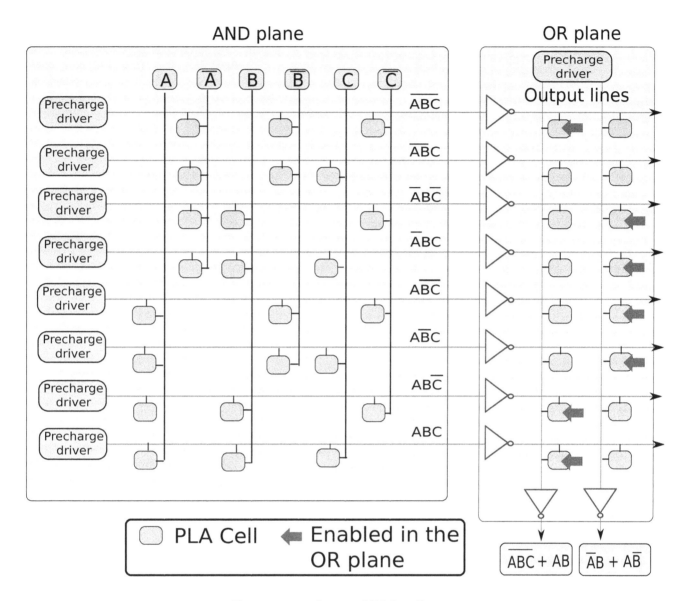

Figure 6.35: Array of PLA cells

in the columns corresponding to $\overline{A}$, $\overline{B}$, and $\overline{C}$. We make similar connections in the rest of the rows for the remaining minterms. This part of the PLA array is known as the AND plane because we are computing a logical AND of the values (original or complemented) of variables. The AND plane of the PLA array is independent of the Boolean functions that we wish to compute. Given the inputs, it calculates the value of all possible minterms.

Now, we need to compute the logical OR of the minterms that we are interested in. For example, in Equation 6.12, we are interested in the logical OR of 3 minterms. To compute the OR function, we use another PLA array known as the OR plane. However, there is a small problem here. A row of PLA cells is designed to compute a logical AND of all the inputs. We can use DeMorgan's theorem to compute the OR of inputs using a PLA array. Let us use the following relationship:

$$(X_1 + X_2 + \ldots X_n) = \overline{\overline{X_1 + X_2 + \ldots X_n}} = \overline{\overline{X_1}.\overline{X_2}.\ldots\overline{X_n}}$$

Thus, to compute the logical OR of $(X_1, X_2, \ldots X_n)$, we need to complement each input, compute the logical AND of all the complemented inputs, and compute the complement of the result. A similar computation needs to be performed in the OR plane of the PLA array. In Figure 6.35, we have inverters to compute the logical negation of each minterm. Then, we compute their logical AND using a column of PLA cells (similar to a row of PLA cells). In this case, only the PLA cells that correspond to minterms in the Boolean expression need to be enabled (shown as an arrow in Figure 6.35). The rest of the PLA cells in each column are disabled. Finally, we compute the logical negation of the result line, to get the value of the Boolean function.

Note that we can have multiple output lines in the OR plane, and thus we can compute the values of multiple Boolean functions in parallel. In Figure 6.35 we also compute the value of $A \oplus B = A.\overline{B} + \overline{A}.B$ in the second output line. For the result lines, and the output lines, we assume an array of sense amplifiers that perform appropriate voltage conversions. For the sake of simplicity, we do not show them in the figure.

The important point to remember here is that the OR plane is programmable. As shown in Figure 6.35, we compute the logical OR of a set of result lines by setting the gate voltage of the connecting PLA cell to a logical 1. At any point of time, we can change the connections to the output lines by changing the gate voltages, and we can thus change the Boolean expression that is computed by the PLA.

Way Point 4

- *We have assembled the arsenal required to implement circuits to perform complex arithmetic operations.*

- *Using our set of logic gates, flip-flops, memories, and arithmetic circuits(to be studied in Chapter 7), we are ready to implement a full fledged processor.*

6.5 Summary and Further Reading

6.5.1 Summary

Summary 6

1. *Modern processors use silicon based transistors. Silicon is a semi-conductor. However, its properties can be modified by adding impurities (known as doping) from the III, and V groups of the periodic table. If we add group III elements such as boron (p type), we remove a charge carrier from the silicon atom lattice, and thus create a hole. Similarly, if we add a group V element such as phosphorus (n type), then we introduce an additional electron to the lattice. In either case, we increase the conductivity of silicon.*

2. *We can create a p-n junction by juxtaposing p-type and n-type silicon structures. A p-n junction conducts when it is forward biased (the p side is connected to the higher voltage), and stops conducting when it is reverse biased.*

3. We can create an NMOS transistor by having two wells of n-type silicon in a p-type substrate. These wells are connected to electrical terminals, and are known as the source and drain. The area between the wells is known as the channel, and is separated from an electrical terminal (known as the gate) by a thin layer of silicon dioxide. When we apply a positive voltage (> threshold voltage) at the gate, the NMOS transistor can conduct current. Otherwise, it acts like an open circuit.

4. In comparison, the PMOS transistor has two p-type wells in an n-type substrate. It forms a conducting path, when the voltage at the gate is 0V.

5. We can use NMOS and PMOS transistors to implement a basic inverter, NAND, NOR, AND and OR gates.

6. We can use these basic gates to create a host of complex structures such as the XOR gate, multiplexer, decoder, encoder, and priority encoder.

7. By creating a feedback path between NAND or NOR gates, we can save a logical bit. This structure is known as a latch. If we enable and disable access to a latch based on the value of a clock signal, then the latch is known as a flip flop.

8. We have considered SR, JK, and D flip flops in this chapter. The SR flip flop does not have deterministic outputs for all combinations of input transitions.

9. We use a master slave design for JK, and D flip flops because we can make the inputs appear at the outputs almost instantaneously at the negative clock edge.

10. A set of flip flops can be used to make registers.

11. We use a cross coupled pair of inverters to make an SRAM cell. It is connected by two transistors (enabled by a word line) to a pair of bit lines. A sense amplifier monitors the difference in voltages across the pair of bit lines. Based on the sign of the difference, we can infer a logical 0 or 1.

12. In comparison, a DRAM cell uses a single transistor and a capacitor. It is a high density memory technology. However, we need to regularly refresh the value of DRAM cells to keep it operational.

13. We can modify the basic structure of a DRAM cell by creating hardwired connections between the transistor and the supply rails to implement read only memory. Programmable ROM (PROM) cells use an antifuse to create an alterable connection to V_{dd}.

14. We can create programmable logic arrays for computing the values of Boolean expressions by arranging PLA cells (similar to PROM cells) in an array. In the AND plane, each row computes the value of a minterm. In the OR plane, we compute a logical OR of all the minterms that form a part of the Boolean expression.

6.5.2   Further Reading

Semiconductors and electronic devices are thoroughly studied in advanced courses on semiconductor device physics. Readers can refer to the books by Sze [Sze and Ng, 2006], and Streetman [Streetman and Banerjee, 2005] for a deeper discussion on the physics of semiconductor devices. In advanced courses on semiconductor device physics, students typically study the basics of the operations of diodes, transistors, and other semiconductor devices from the point of view of quantum mechanics. After introducing semiconductor devices, we introduced combinational logic gates and sequential logic elements. The simple structures that we introduced in this chapter, are very commonly used. Students should however take a look at the following books [Lin, 2011, Wakerly, 2000, Dally and Poulton, 1998] for getting a thorough understanding of the devices, including their behaviour from the perspective of analog electronics. We lastly talk about memories. The book, "Introduction to VLSI Systems", by Ming Bo Lin [Lin, 2011] has a fairly in-depth coverage of memory structures. Memory technology, especially DRAM technology, is advancing very quickly. A host of standards, and design styles have evolved over the last decade. A lot of these trends are discussed in the book on memory systems by Jacob, Ng, and Wang [Jacob et al., 2007]. This book is also very useful for professionals who are looking to build commercial systems with state of the art memory technology.

Exercises

Transistors and Logic Gates

Ex. 1 — Describe the operation of a p-n junction.

Ex. 2 — Define drift and diffusion current.

Ex. 3 — Describe the operation of a NMOS transistor?

Ex. 4 — Draw the circuit of a CMOS inverter, NOR gate, and NAND gate.

Ex. 5 — Implement the AND, OR and NOT gates using NAND gates only.

Ex. 6 — Implement the AND, OR and NOT gates using NOR gates only.

Ex. 7 — Implement XOR and XNOR gates using NAND gates only.

Ex. 8 — Implement the following Boolean functions by using only AND, OR and NOT gates.
   (a) $\overline{A}.B + A.\overline{B} + \overline{A}.\overline{B}.\overline{C}$
   (b) $\overline{(A + B + C)}.(\overline{A}.\overline{B} + C)$
   (c) $\overline{(A + B).(\overline{C + D})}$
   (d) $\overline{A}.\overline{B}.\overline{C} + A.B.C + \overline{D}$

Ex. 9 — Answer Question 8 by using only NAND gates.

Combinational Logic and Sequential Logic

Ex. 10 — Draw the circuit diagram of a 3×8 decoder.

Ex. 11 — Draw the circuit diagram of a 8-3 bit encoder.

Ex. 12 — Draw the circuit diagram of a 8-3 bit priority encoder.

Ex. 13 — Suppose a poll has to be conducted with three entities A, B and C, each of which can either vote a 'yes' (encoded as 1) or a 'no' (encoded as 0). The final output is equal to the majority opinion. Draw a truth table of the system, simplify the function, and implement it using logic gates.

* **Ex. 14** — Most circuits in modern computers are built using NAND and NOR gates, because they are easy to build using CMOS technology. Suppose another technology in invented in the near future, which implements a new gate, X, very efficiently. X takes 3 inputs A, B and C and computes: $X(A, B, C) = A.B + \overline{C}$. Using only X gates and NOT gates, how will you implement the following function: $f(A, B, C) = A + B + C$?

** **Ex. 15** — Implement the following logic functions using a 4 to 1 multiplexer, and a single NOT gate.

(a) $AB + BC + AC$

(b) $\overline{A} + \overline{B} + \overline{C}$

(c) $A.\overline{B} + A.B.\overline{C}$

** **Ex. 16** — Is it possible to implement every 3 variable Boolean function with a 4 to 1 multiplexer, and a single NOT gate? Prove your answer.

Sequential Logic

Ex. 17 — What is the difference between a flip-flop and a latch?

Ex. 18 — Define the following terms:

i)Metastability

ii)*Keep out* region

iii)Setup time

iv)Hold time

Ex. 19 — Why do we wish to avoid the indeterminate state in an SR flip-flop?

Ex. 20 — What is the advantage of an edge sensitive flip-flop?

* **Ex. 21** — What is the fundamental advantage of a JK flip-flop over a D flip-flop?

Ex. 22 — Describe the design of registers in your own words.

Ex. 23 — An edge sensitive toggle flip-flop (or T flip-flop) has a single input T and toggles its state on a negative clock edge if $T = 1$. If $(T = 0)$, then it maintains its state. How will you construct an edge sensitive T flip-flop form an edge sensitive J-K flip-flop?

* **Ex. 24** — Can you create a negative edge triggered D flip-flop using 2 multiplexers, and a NOT gate?

Ex. 25 — Design a SR flip-flop with NOR gates.

* **Ex. 26** — Using two edge triggered D flip-flops, design a circuit that divides the frequency of the clock signal by 4.

** **Ex. 27** — Counters are essential components of any complex digital circuit. They are essentially sequential circuits which loop through a specific set of states. Design a counter which generates a sequence of numbers (in binary form) from 0 to 7 and cycles back again to 0. This is called a MOD 8 counter.

** **Ex. 28** — Using D flip-flops and logic gates, design a circuit, which generates the following sequence of numbers:

$$001 \rightarrow 100 \rightarrow 010 \rightarrow 101 \rightarrow 110 \rightarrow 111 \rightarrow 011 \rightarrow 001$$

Assume that the circuit never generates 000. This circuit can be used to generate pseudo-random numbers.

Memories

Ex. 29 — Compare the power, area and time of a SRAM, DRAM, and latch.

Ex. 30 — Propose a design for the column mux/demux circuit.

Ex. 31 — What is the role of the *match* line in a CAM array?

Ex. 32 — What is the role of the *refresh logic* in a DRAM array?

Ex. 33 — Describe the design of a ROM and PROM cell.

Ex. 34 — Design a single PLA array to compute al the following Boolean functions:
   a)$A.B + B.C + C.A$
   b)$A.\overline{B}.\overline{C} + \overline{A}.B.C$
   c)$\overline{A + B}$

Design Problems

Ex. 35 — Design the following circuits using a circuit simulator such as Spice and verify their operation:
   a)NOT gate
   b)NAND gate
   c)D flip-flop
   d)SRAM cell

Ex. 36 — Prepare a report on novel memory technologies such as phase change memory, Ferro-electric RAM, and magneto-resistive RAM.

7
Computer Arithmetic

In Chapter 6, we described the basic circuits for logical operations and storage elements. In this chapter, we will use this knowledge to design hardware algorithms for arithmetic operations. This chapter also requires the knowledge of binary 2's complement numbers and floating point numbers that we gained in Chapter 2. The plan for this chapter is as follows.

In the first part, we describe algorithms for integer arithmetic. Initially, we describe the basic algorithms for adding two binary numbers. It turns out that there are many ways of doing these basic operations, and each method has its own set of pros and cons. Note that the problem of binary subtraction is conceptually the same as binary addition in the 2's complement system. Consequently, we do not need to treat it separately. Subsequently, we shall see that the problem of adding n numbers is intimately related to the problem of multiplication, and it is a fast operation in hardware. Sadly, very efficient methods do not exist for integer division. Nevertheless, we shall consider two popular algorithms for dividing positive binary numbers.

After integer arithmetic, we shall look at methods for floating point (numbers with a decimal point) arithmetic. Most of the algorithms for integer arithmetic can be ported to the realm of floating point numbers with minor modifications. As compared to integer division, floating point division can be done very efficiently.

7.1 Addition

7.1.1 Addition of Two 1-bit Numbers

Let us look at the problem of adding two 1-bit numbers, a and b. Both a and b can take two values – 0 or 1. Hence, there are four possible combinations of a and b. Their sum in binary can be either 00, 01, or 10. Their sum will be 10, when both a and b are 1. We should make an important observation here. The sum of two 1 bit numbers might potentially be two bits long. Let us call the LSB of the result as the *sum*, and the MSB as the *carry*. We can relate this concept to standard primary school addition of two 1 digit decimal numbers. If we are adding 8 and 9, then the result is 17. We say that the sum is 7, and the carry is 1. Similarly, if we add 3 and 4, then the result is 7. We say that the sum is 7, and the carry is 0.

We can extend the concept of sum and carry to adding three 1 bit numbers also. If we are adding three 1 bit numbers then the range of the result is between 00 and 11 in binary. In this case also, we call the LSB as the *sum*, and the MSB as the *carry*.

Definition 52

sum *The sum is the LSB of the result of adding two or three 1 bit numbers.*

carry *The carry is the MSB of the result of adding two or three 1 bit numbers.*

For an adder that can add two 1 bit numbers, there will be two output bits – a sum s and a carry c. An adder that adds two bits is known as a *half adder*. The truth table of a half adder is shown in Table 7.1.

Definition 53
A half adder *adds two bits to produce a sum and a carry.*

---

a	b	s	c
0	0	0	0
0	1	1	0
1	0	1	0
1	1	0	1

Table 7.1: Truth table of a half adder

From the truth table, we can conclude that $s = a \oplus b = \overline{a}.b + a.\overline{b}$, where $\oplus$ stands for exclusive or, '.' stands for boolean AND, and '+' stands for boolean OR. Secondly, $c = a.b$. The circuit diagram of a half adder is shown in Figure 7.1. As we can see, a half adder is a very simple structure and we have constructed it using just six gates in Figure 7.1.

7.1.2 Addition of Three 1-bit Numbers

The aim is to be ultimately able to add 32-bit numbers. To add the two least significant bits, we can use a half adder. However, for adding the second bit pair, we cannot use a half adder because there might be an output carry from the first half adder. In this case, we need to add three 1-bit numbers. Hence, we need to implement a *full adder* that can add 3 bits. One of these bits is a carry out of another adder and we call it the *input carry*. We represent the input carry as c_{in}, and the two other input bits as a and b.

Definition 54 *An adder than can add 3 bits is known as a full adder.*

Table 7.2 shows the truth table for the full adder. We have three inputs – a, b, and c_{in}. There are two output bits – the sum (s), and the carry out (c_{out}).

From the truth table, we can deduce the following relationships:

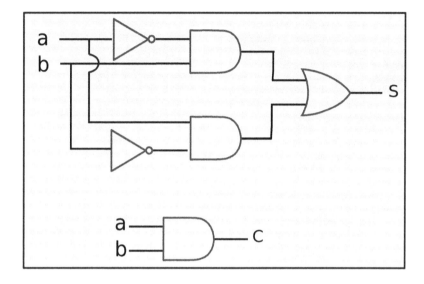

Figure 7.1: A half adder

a	b	c_{in}	s	c_{out}
0	0	0	0	0
0	1	0	1	0
1	0	0	1	0
1	1	0	0	1
0	0	1	1	0
0	1	1	0	1
1	0	1	0	1
1	1	1	1	1

Table 7.2: Truth table of a full adder

$$s = a \oplus b \oplus c_{in}$$
$$= (a.\overline{b} + \overline{a}.b) \oplus c_{in}$$
$$= (a.\overline{b} + \overline{a}.b).\overline{c_{in}} + \overline{(a.\overline{b} + \overline{a}.b)}.c_{in}$$
$$= a.\overline{b}.\overline{c_{in}} + \overline{a}.b.\overline{c_{in}} + \overline{(a.\overline{b})}.\overline{\overline{a}.b}.c_{in}$$
$$= a.\overline{b}.\overline{c_{in}} + \overline{a}.b.\overline{c_{in}} + (\overline{a} + b).(a + \overline{b}).c_{in}$$
$$= a.\overline{b}.\overline{c_{in}} + \overline{a}.b.\overline{c_{in}} + \overline{a}.\overline{b}.c_{in} + a.b.c_{in}$$
$$c_{out} = a.b + a.c_{in} + b.c_{in}$$

The circuit diagram of a full adder is shown in Figure 7.2. This is far more complicated than the circuit of a half adder. We have used 12 logic gates to build this circuit. Furthermore, some of these logic gates use three inputs. However, this degree of complexity is required because all our practical adders will use full adders as their basic element. We face the need of adding 3 bits in all of our arithmetic algorithms.

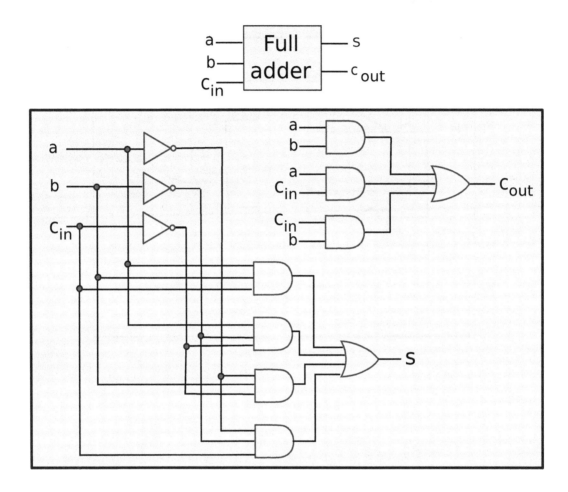

Figure 7.2: A full adder

7.1.3   Ripple Carry Adder

Let us now try to add two n bit numbers. Let us start with an example: $1011_2 + 0101_2$. The addition is shown in Figure 7.3. We have seen in Section 2.2.3 that binary numbers can be added the same way as decimal numbers. In the case of base 10 decimal numbers, we start at the unit's digit and proceed towards higher digits. In each step, a carry might be generated, which is then added to the immediately higher digits. In the case of binary numbers also we do the same. The only difference is that instead of base 10, we are using base 2.

For example, in Figure 7.3, we observe that when two binary bits are added a carry might be generated. The value of the carry is equal to 1. This carry needs to be added to the bits in the next position (more significant position). The computation is complete when we have finished the addition of the most significant bits. It is possible that a carry might propagate from one pair of bits to another pair of bits. This process of propagation of the carry from one bit pair to another is known as *rippling*.

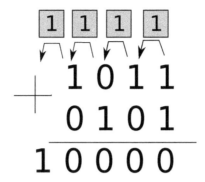

Figure 7.3: Addition of two binary numbers

Let us construct a simple adder to implement this procedure. Let us try to add two n bit binary numbers – A and B. We number the bits of A and B as $A_1 \ldots A_n$ and $B_1 \ldots B_n$ respectively. Let A_1 refer to A's LSB, and A_n refer to A's MSB. We can create an adder for adding A and B as follows. We use a half adder to add the LSBs. Then we use $n - 1$ full adders to add the rest of the corresponding bits of A and B and their input carry values. This n bit adder is known as a *ripple carry adder*. Its design is shown in Figure 7.4. We observe that we add two n bit numbers to produce a $n + 1$ bit result. The method of addition is exactly similar to the procedure we follow while adding two binary numbers manually. We start from the LSB and move towards the MSB. At every step we propagate the carry to the next pair of digits.

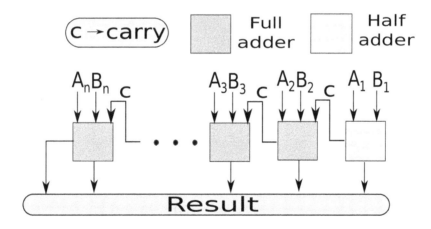

Figure 7.4: Addition of two binary numbers

Now, let us calculate the speed of this adder. Let us assume that it takes t_h units of time for a half adder to complete its operation, and t_f units of time for a full adder to complete its operation. If we assume that carries are propagated instantaneously across blocks, then the total time, $f(n)$, is equal to $t_h + (n - 1)t_f$. Here, n is equal to the number of bits being added.

However, as we shall see this is a rather cryptic basis of comparison, especially for large values of n. We do not wish to have a lot of constants in our timing model. Secondly, the values of these constants are heavily dependent on the specific technology used. It is thus hard to derive algorithmic insights. Hence, we introduce the notion of *asymptotic time complexity* that can significantly simplify the timing models, yet retain their basic characteristics. For example, in the case of a ripple carry adder, we can say that the complexity is almost equal to n multiplied by some constant. We can further abstract away the constant, and say that the time complexity is the order of n. Let us now formally define this notion.

Asymptotic Time Complexity

Let us consider two functions $f(n) = 2n^2 + 3$, and $g(n) = 10n$. Here, n is the size of the input, and $f(n)$, and $g(n)$ represent the number of time units it takes for a certain circuit to complete its operation. We plot the time values for different values of n in Figure 7.5. As we can see, $g(n)$ is greater than $f(n)$ for small values of n. However, for larger values of n, $f(n)$ is larger, and it continues to be so. This is because it contains a square term, and $g(n)$ does not. We can extend this argument to observe that even if $g(n)$ would have been defined to be $100n$, $f(n)$ would have ultimately exceeded it. The gist of the argument lies in the fact that $f(n)$ contains a quadratic term (n^2) and $g(n)$ only contains linear terms. For large n, we can conclude that $f(n)$ is slower than $g(n)$. Consequently, we need to define a new notion of time that precisely captures this fact. We call this new notion of time as the **asymptotic time complexity**. The name comes from the fact that we are interested in finding an envelope or asymptote to the time function such that the function is contained within this envelope for practically large values of n.

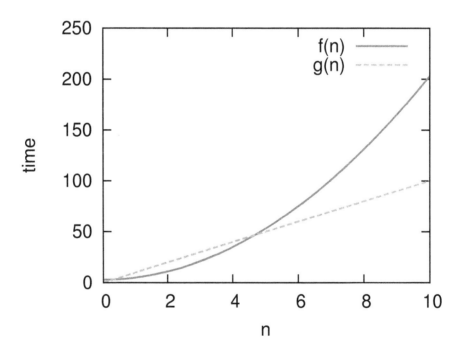

Figure 7.5: $f(n) = 2n^2 + 3$ and $g(n) = 10n$

For example, we can define the asymptotic time complexity of $f(n)$ to be n^2 and that of $g(n)$ to be n respectively. This notion of time is powerful enough to say that $f(n)$ is greater than $g(n)$ for values of n larger than some threshold. What if we consider: $f(n) = 2n^2 + 3$, and $f'(n) = 3n^2 + 10$. Needless to say, $f'(n) > f(n)$. However, we might not be interested in the difference. If we compare the asymptotic time complexity of $f(n)$ or $f'(n)$ with another function that has terms with different exponents (other than 2), then the results of the comparison will be the same. Consequently, for the sake of simplicity we can ignore the additive and multiplicative constants. We capture the definition of one form of asymptotic time in the big-O notation. It is precisely defined in Definition 55.

Definition 55
We say that: $f(n) = O(g(n))$
if $| f(n) | \leq c | g(n) |$ *for all* $n > n_0$. *Here, c is a positive constant.*

The big-O notation is actually a part of a set of asymptotic notations. For more details, the reader can refer to a standard text in computer algorithms [Cormen et al., 2009]. From our point of view, $g(n)$ gives a worst case time bound for $f(n)$ ignoring additive and multiplicative constants. We illustrate this fact with two examples: Examples 93 and 94. In this book, we will refer to asymptotic time complexity as *time complexity*.

Example 93
$f(n) = 3n^2 + 2n + 3$. *Find its asymptotic time complexity.*
Answer:

$$\begin{aligned}
f(n) &= 3n^2 + 2n + 3 \\
&\leq 3n^2 + 2n^2 + 3n^2 \quad (n > 0) \\
&\leq 8(n^2)
\end{aligned}$$

Hence, $f(n) = O(n^2)$.

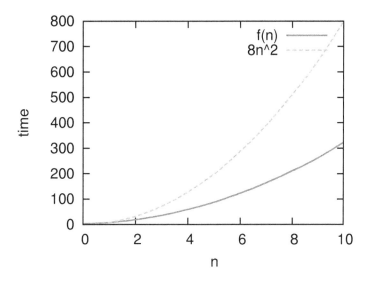

$8n^2$ *is a strict upper bound on $f(n)$ as shown in the figure.*

Example 94
$f(n) = 0.00001n^{100} + 10000n^{99} + 234344$. *Find its asymptotic time complexity.*
Answer: $f(n) = O(n^{100})$

Time Complexity of a Ripple Carry Adder

The worst case delay happens when the carry propagates from the least significant bit to the most significant bit. In this case, each full adder waits for the input carry, performs the addition, and then propagates the carry out to the next full adder. Since, there are n 1 bit adders, the total time taken is $O(n)$.

7.1.4 Carry Select Adder

A ripple carry adder is extremely slow for large values of n such as 32 or 64. Consequently, we desire faster implementations. We observe that in hardware we can potentially do a lot of tasks in parallel. Unlike purely sequential C or Java programs where one statement executes after the next, hundreds or even thousands of actions can be performed in parallel in hardware. Let us use this insight to design a faster adder that runs in $O(\sqrt{n})$ time.

Let us consider the problem of adding two numbers A and B represented as: $A_{32} \ldots A_1$ and $B_{32} \ldots B_1$ respectively. Let us start out by dividing the set of bits into blocks of let us say 4 bits. The blocks are shown in Figure 7.6. Each block contains a fragment of A and a fragment of B. We need to add the two fragments by considering the input carry to the block, and generate a set of sum bits and a carry out. This carry out is an input carry for the subsequent block.

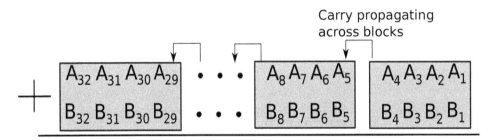

Figure 7.6: Dividing the numbers into blocks

In this case, a carry is propagated between blocks rather that between bit pairs. To add the pair of fragments within a block, we can use a simple ripple carry adder. For small values of n, ripple carry adders are not very inefficient. However, our basic problem of carry propagation has not been solved yet.

Let us now introduce the basic idea of the *carry select adder*. We divide the computation into two stages. In the first stage, we generate two results for each block. One result assumes that the input carry is 0, and the other result assumes that the input carry is 1. A result consists of 4 sum bits, and a carry out. We thus require two ripple carry adders per block. Note that each of these additions are independent of each other and thus can proceed in parallel.

Now, at the beginning of the second stage two sets of results for the nth block are ready. If we know the value of the input carry, C_{in} produced by the $(n-1)^{th}$ block, then we can quickly calculate the value of the output carry, C_{out}, by using a simple multiplexer. We do not need to perform any extra additions. The inputs to the multiplexer are the values of C_{out} generated by the two ripple carry adders that assume C_{in} to be 0 and 1 respectively. When the correct value of C_{in} is available, it can be used to choose between the two values of C_{out}. This process is much faster than adding the two blocks. Simultaneously, we can also choose the right set of sum bits. Then we need to propagate the output carry, C_{out}, to the $(n+1)^{th}$ block.

Let us now evaluate the time complexity of the carry select adder. Let us generalise the problem and assume the block size to be k. The first stage takes $O(k)$ time because we add each pair of fragments within a block using a regular ripple carry adder, and all the pairs of fragments are added in parallel. The second phase takes time $O(n/k)$. This is because we have have $\lceil n/k \rceil$ blocks and we assume that it takes 1 time unit for the input carry of a block to choose the right output carry in the multiplexer. The total time is thus: $O(k + n/k)$. Note that we are making some simplistic assumptions regarding the constants. However, our final answer will not change if we make our model more complicated.

Let us now try to minimise the time taken. This can be done as follows:

$$\frac{\partial (k + n/k)}{\partial k} = 0$$
$$\Rightarrow 1 - \frac{n}{k^2} = 0 \tag{7.1}$$
$$\Rightarrow k = \sqrt{n}$$

Thus, the optimal block size is equal to $\sqrt{n}$. The total time complexity is thus $O(\sqrt{n} + \sqrt{n})$, which is the same as $O(\sqrt{n})$.

7.1.5 Carry Lookahead Adder

We have improved the time complexity from $O(n)$ for a ripple carry adder to $O(\sqrt{n})$ for a carry select adder. The question is, "Can we do better?" In this section, we shall present the *carry lookahead adder* that can perform addition in $O(log(n))$ time. $O(log(n))$ has been proved as the theoretical lower bound for adding two n bit numbers. Note that the *log* operation in this book typically has a base equal to 2, unless explicitly mentioned otherwise. Secondly, since logarithms to different bases differ by constant multiplicative factors, the base is immaterial in the big-O notation.

Generate and Propagate Functions

Before introducing the adder, we need to introduce a little bit of theory and terminology. Let us again consider the addition of two numbers – A and B – represented as $A_{32} \ldots A_1$ and $B_{32} \ldots B_1$ respectively. Let us consider a bit pair – A_i and B_i. If it is equal to (0,0), then irrespective of the carry in, the carry out is 0. In this case, the carry is *absorbed*.

However, if the bit pair is equal to (0,1) or (1,0) then the value of the carry out is equal to the value of the carry in. If the carry in is 0, then the sum is 1, and the carry out is 0. If the carry in is 1, then the sum is 0, and the carry out is 1. In this case, the carry is *propagated*.

Lastly, if the bit pair is equal to (1,1), then the carry out is always equal to 1, irrespective of the carry in. In this case, a carry is *generated*.

We can thus define a *generate*(g_i) and *propagate*(p_i) function as follows:

$$g_i = A_i.B_i \tag{7.2}$$
$$p_i = A_i \oplus B_i \tag{7.3}$$

The generate function captures the fact that both the bits are 1. The propagate function captures the fact that only one of the bits is 1. We can now compute the carry out C_{out} in terms of the carry in C_{in}, g_i, and p_i. Note that by our case by case analysis, we can conclude that the carry out is equal to 1, only if a carry is either generated, or it is propagated. Thus, we have:

$$C_{out} = g_i + p_i.C_{in} \tag{7.4}$$

Example 95

$A_i = 0$, $B_i = 1$. *Let the input carry be* C_{in}. *Compute* g_i, p_i *and* C_{out}.

Answer:

$$g_i = A_i.B_i = 0.1 = 0$$
$$p_i = A_i \oplus B_i = 0 \oplus 1 = 1 \tag{7.5}$$
$$C_{out} = g_i + p_i.C_{in} = C_{in}$$

Let us now try to generalise the notion of generate and propagate functions to multiple bits. Let us consider a two bit system that has an input carry, and an output carry. Let the bit pairs be numbered 1 and 2, where 2 represents the most significant bit. Let C_{out}^i represent the output carry obtained after adding the ith bit pair. Likewise, C_{in}^i is the input carry for the ith bit pair. The output carry of the two bit system is thus equal to C_{out}^2. We have:

$$
\begin{aligned}
C_{out}^2 &= g_2 + p_2.C_{out}^1 \\
&= g_2 + p_2.(g_1 + p_1.C_{in}^1) \\
&= (g_2 + p_2.g_1) + p_2.p_1.C_{in}^1
\end{aligned} \tag{7.6}
$$

Similarly, for a 3 bit system, we have:

$$
\begin{aligned}
C_{out}^3 &= g_3 + p_3.C_{out}^2 \\
&= g_3 + p_3.((g_2 + p_2.g_1) + p_2.p_1.C_{in}^1) \\
&= (g_3 + p_3.g_2 + p_3.p_2.g_1) + p_3.p_2.p_1.C_{in}^1
\end{aligned} \tag{7.7}
$$

For a 4-bit system, we have:

$$
\begin{aligned}
C_{out}^4 &= g_4 + p_4.C_{out}^3 \\
&= g_4 + p_4.((g_3 + p_3.g_2 + p_3.p_2.g_1) + p_3.p_2.p_1.C_{in}^1) \\
&= (g_4 + p_4.g_3 + p_4.p_3.g_2 + p_4.p_3.p_2.g_1) + p_4.p_3.p_2.p_1.C_{in}^1
\end{aligned} \tag{7.8}
$$

Let us now try to derive a pattern, in these results (see Table 7.3).

We observe that for a system of n bits, it is possible to define a generate function (G_n) and a propagate function (P_n). If we are able to somehow precompute these functions, then we can generate C_{out} from C_{in} in a single step. However, as we can see from the example of the 4-bit system, the functions are fairly difficult to compute for large values of n. Let us now derive an interesting property of the generate and propagate functions.

Let us consider a sequence of n bits. Let us divide it into two parts $1 \ldots m$ and $(m + 1) \ldots n$. Let the generate and propagate functions for both the parts be $(G_{1,m}, P_{1,m})$ and $(G_{m+1,n}, P_{m+1,n})$ respectively. Furthermore, let the generate and propagate functions for the entire block be $G_{1,n}$ and $P_{1,n}$. We wish to find a relationship between the generate and propagate functions for the whole block with n bits and the functions for the sub blocks.

1 bit	$C_{out}^1 = \underbrace{g_1}_{G_1} + \underbrace{p_1}_{P_1}.C_{in}^1$
2 bit	$C_{out}^2 = \underbrace{(g_2 + p_2.g_1)}_{G_2} + \underbrace{p_2.p_1}_{P_2}.C_{in}^1$
3 bit	$C_{out}^3 = \underbrace{(g_3 + p_3.g_2 + p_3.p_2.g_1)}_{G_3} + \underbrace{p_3.p_2.p_1}_{P_3}.C_{in}^1)$
4 bit	$C_{out}^4 = \underbrace{(g_4 + p_4.g_3 + p_4.p_3.g_2 + p_4.p_3.p_2.g_1)}_{G_4} + \underbrace{p_4.p_3.p_2.p_1}_{P_4}.C_{in}^1)$
n bit	$C_{out}^n = G_n + P_n.C_{in}^1$

Table 7.3: Generate and propagate functions for multi bit systems

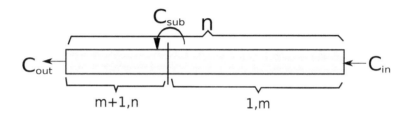

Figure 7.7: A block of n bits divided into two parts

Let the carry out and carry in of the n bit block be C_{out} and C_{in} respectively. Let the carry between the two sub-blocks be C_{sub}. See Figure 7.7. We have:

$$
\begin{aligned}
C_{out} &= G_{m+1,n} + P_{m+1,n}.C_{sub} \\
&= G_{m+1,n} + P_{m+1,n}.(G_{1,m} + P_{1,m}.C_{in}) \\
&= \underbrace{G_{m+1,n} + P_{m+1,n}.G_{1,m}}_{G_{1,n}} + \underbrace{P_{m+1,n}.P_{1,m}}_{P_{1,n}}.C_{in} \quad (7.9)\\
&= G_{1,n} + P_{1,n}.C_{in}
\end{aligned}
$$

Thus, for a block of n bits, we can easily compute $G_{1,n}$ and $P_{1,n}$ from the corresponding functions of its sub blocks. This is a very powerful property and is the basis of the carry lookahead adder.

Carry Lookahead Adder – Stage I

The carry lookahead adder's operation is divided into two stages. In the first stage, we compute the generate and propagate functions for different subsequences of bits. In the next stage, we use these functions to generate the result.

The diagram for the first stage is shown in Figure 7.8. Like the carry select adder, we divide bit pairs into blocks. In this diagram, we have considered a block size equal to 2. In the first level, we compute the generate and propagate functions for each block. We build a tree of (G,P) circuits(blocks) as follows. Each (G,P) block in level n takes as input the generate and propagate functions of two blocks in level $n-1$. Thus, at each level the number of (G,P) blocks decreases by a factor of 2. For example, the first (G,P) block in level 1 processes the bit pairs $(1, 2)$. Its parent processes the bit pairs $(1 \ldots 4)$, and so on. The ranges are shown in Figure 7.8. We create a tree of (G,P) blocks in this fashion.

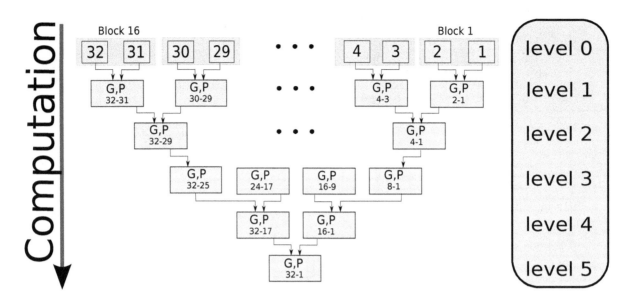

Figure 7.8: Carry Lookahead Adder – Stage I

For a n bit input, there are $O(log(n))$ levels. In each level, we are doing a constant amount of work since each (G,P) block is only processing the inputs from two other blocks. Hence, the time complexity of this stage is equal to $O(log(n))$.

Carry Lookahead Adder – Stage II

In this stage, we use the information generated in Stage I to compute the final sum bits, and the carry out. The block diagram for the second stage is shown in Figure 7.9.

Let us first focus at the rightmost (G,P) blocks in each level. The ranges for each of these blocks start at 1. They take the input carry, C_{in}^1, as input, and then calculate the output carry for the range of bit pairs that they represent as $C_{out} = G + P.C_{in}^1$. When we are adding two numbers, the input carry at the first bit is typically 0. However, some special instructions (ADC in ARM) can consider a non-zero value of C_{in}^1 also.

Each (G,P) block with a range $(r2, r1)$ $(r2 > r1)$, is connected to all (G,P) blocks that have a range of the form $(r3, r2 + 1)$. The output carry of the block is equal to the input carry of those blocks. To avoid excessive clutter in the diagram (Figure 7.9), we show the connections for only the (G,P) block with range (16-1) using solid lines. Each block is connected to the block to its left in the same level and to one (G,P) block in every lower level.

The arrangement of (G,P) blocks represents a tree like computation where the correct carry values propagate from different levels to the leaves. The leaves at level 0, contain a set of 2-bit ripple carry(RC) adders that compute the result bits by considering the correct value of the input carry. We show an example in Figure 7.9 of the correct carry in value propagating from the block with range (16-1) to the 2-bit adder representing the bits 31 and 32. The path is shown using dotted lines.

In a similar manner, carry values propagate to every single ripple carry adder at the zeroth level. The operation completes once all the result bits and the output carry have been computed.

The time complexity of this stage is also $O(log(n))$ because there are $O(log(n))$ levels in the diagram and there is a constant amount of work done per level. This work comprises of computing C_{out} and propagating it to (G,P) blocks at lower levels.

Hence, the total time complexity of the carry lookahead adder is $\boxed{O(log(n))}$.

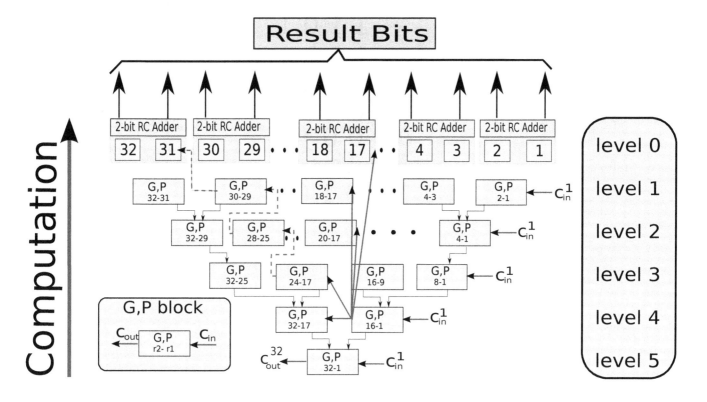

Figure 7.9: Carry Lookahead Adder – Stage II

Way Point 5
Time complexities of different adders:

- *Ripple Carry Adder: $O(n)$*

- *Carry Select Adder: $O(\sqrt{n})$*

- *Carry Lookahead Adder: $O(log(n))$*

7.2 Multiplication

7.2.1 Overview

Let us now consider the classic problem of binary multiplication. Similar to addition, let us first look at the most naive way of multiplying two decimal numbers. Let us try to multiply 13 times 9. In this case, 13 is known as the *multiplicand* and 9 is known as the *multiplier*, and 117 is the *product*.

Figure 7.10(a) shows the multiplication in the decimal number system, and Figure 7.10(b) shows the multiplication in binary. Note that multiplying two binary numbers can be done exactly the same way as decimal numbers. We need to consider each bit of the multiplier from the least significant position to the most significant position. If the bit is 1, then we write the value of the multiplicand below the line, otherwise

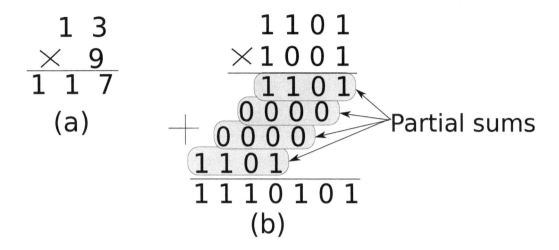

Figure 7.10: Multiplication in decimal and binary

we write 0. For each multiplier bit, we shift the multiplicand progressively one bit to the left. The reason for this is that each multiplier bit represents a higher power of two. We call each such value a *partial sum* (see Figure 7.10(b)). If the multiplier has m bits, then we need to add m partial sums to obtain the product. In this case the product is 117 in decimal and 1110101 in binary. The reader can verify that they actually represent the same number. Let us define another term called the *partial product* for ease of representation later. It is the sum of a contiguous sequence of partial sums.

Definition 56

Partial sum *It is equal to the value of the multiplicand left shifted by a certain number of bits, or it is equal to 0.*

Partial product *It is the sum of a set of partial sums.*

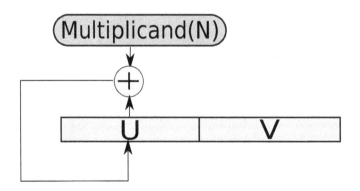

Figure 7.11: Iterative Multiplier

In this example, we have considered unsigned numbers. What about signed numbers? In Section 2.3.4, we proved that multiplying two 2's complement signed n bit binary numbers, and constraining the result to n bits without any concern for overflows, is not different from unsigned multiplication. We need to just multiply the 2's complement numbers without bothering about the sign. The result will be correct.

Let us now consider the issue of overflows in multiplication. If we are multiplying two signed 32-bit values, the product can be as large as $(2^{-31})^2 = 2^{-62}$. There will thus be an overflow if we try to save the result in 32 bits. We need to keep this in mind. If we desire precision, then it is best to allot 64 bits for storing the result of 32-bit multiplication. Let us now look at a naive approach for multiplying two 32-bit numbers by using an *iterative multiplier*.

7.2.2 Iterative Multiplier

In this section, we present the design of an iterative multiplier (see Figure 7.11) that multiplies two signed 32-bit numbers to produce a 64-bit result. We cannot treat the numbers as unsigned anymore and the algorithm thus gets slightly complicated. We use a 33-bit register U, and a 32-bit register V as shown in Figure 7.11. The multiplier is loaded into V at the beginning. The multiplicand is stored separately in register N. The size of the register N is equal to 33 bits, and we store the multiplicand in it by extending its sign by 1 position. The two registers U and V are treated as one large register for the purposes of shifting. If we perform a right shift on U and V, then the value shifted out of U, becomes the MSB of V. We have an adder that adds the multiplicand to the current value of U, and updates U. U is initialised to 0. Let us represent the multiplicand by N, the multiplier by M, and the product by P. We need to compute $P = MN$.

The algorithm used by the iterative multiplier is very similar to the multiplication algorithm that we learnt in elementary school. We need to consider each bit of the multiplier in turn and add a shifted version of the multiplicand to the partial product if the bit is 1. The algorithm is as follows:

Algorithm 1: Algorithm to multiply two 32-bit numbers and produce a 64-bit result

> **Data:** Multiplier in V, $U = 0$, Multiplicand in N
> **Result:** The lower 64 bits of UV contains the product

```
1  i ← 0
2  for i < 32 do
3  │   i ← i + 1
4  │   if LSB of V is 1 then
5  │   │   if i < 32 then
6  │   │   │   U ← U + N
7  │   │   end
8  │   │   else
9  │   │   │   U ← U − N
10 │   │   end
11 │   end
12 │   UV ← UV ≫ 1 (arithmetic right shift)
13 end
```

Let us now try to understand how this algorithm works. We iterate for 32 times to consider each bit of the multiplier. The multiplier is initially loaded into register V.

Now, if the LSB of V is 1 (Line 4), then we add the multiplicand N to U and save the result in U. This basically means that if a bit in the multiplier is equal to 1, then we need to add the multiplicand to the already accumulated partial product. The *partial product* is a running sum of the shifted values of the multiplicands. It is initialised to 0. In the iterative algorithm, the part of UV that does not contain the multiplier, contains the partial product. We then shift UV one step to the right (Line 12). The reason for this is as follows. In each step we actually need to shift the multiplicand 1 bit to the left and add it to the partial product. This is the same as not shifting the multiplicand but shifting the partial product 1 bit to the right assuming that we do not lose any bits. The relative displacement between the multiplicand and the partial product remains the same.

If in any iteration of the algorithm, we find the LSB of V to be 0, then nothing needs to be done. We do not need to add the value of the multiplicand to the partial product. We simply need to shift UV one position to the right using an arithmetic right shift operation.

Note that till the last step we assume that the multiplier is positive. If in the last step we see that the multiplier is not positive (MSB is 1), then we need to subtract the multiplicand from U (Line 9). This follows directly from Theorem 2.3.4.2. The theorem states that the value of the multiplier (M) in the 2's complement notation is equal to $(-M_n 2^{n-1} + \sum_{i=1}^{n-1} M_i 2^{i-1})$. Here M_i is the ith bit of the multiplier, M. In the first $n-1$ iterations, we effectively multiply the multiplicand with $\sum_{i=1}^{n-1} M_i 2^{i-1}$. In the last iteration, we take a look at the MSB of the multiplier, M_n. If it is 0, then we need not do anything. If it is 1, then we need to subtract $2^{n-1} \times N$ from the partial product. Since the partial product is shifted to the right by $n-1$ positions with respect to the multiplicand, the multiplicand is effectively shifted $n-1$ positions to the left with respect to the partial product. To subtract $2^{n-1} \times N$ to the partial product, we need to simply subtract N from register U, which is our last step.

Important Point 8

We assume that register U is 33 bits wide. We did this to avoid overflows while adding or subtracting N from U. Let us consider U and N again. $|N| \leq 2^{31}$ because N is essentially a 32-bit number. For our induction hypothesis, let us assume that $|U| \leq 2^{31}$ (true for the base case, $U = 0$). Thus $|U \pm N| \leq 2^{32}$. Hence, if we store both the numbers and their sum in 33-bit registers, we will never have overflows while adding or subtracting them. Note that we could have had overflows, if we would have used just 32 bits. Now, after the shift operation, the value in U is divided by 2. Since $U \pm N$ is assigned to U, and we have established that $|U \pm N| \leq 2^{32}$, we can prove that $|U| \leq 2^{31}$. Thus, our induction hypothesis holds, and we can thus conclude that during the operation of our algorithm, we shall never have an overflow. The absolute value of the product can at the most be $2^{31} \times 2^{31} = 2^{62}$. Hence, the product can fit in 64 bits(proved in Section 7.2.1), and we thus need to only consider the lower 64 bits of the UV register.

Examples

Example 96

Multiply 2×3 using an iterative multiplier. Assume a 4-bit binary 2's complement number system. Let 2 (0010_2) be the multiplicand and let 3 (0011_2) be the multiplier. For each iteration show the values of U and V just before the right shift on Line 12, and just after the right shift.
Answer:

| Multiplicand (N) | 0010 | 2 |
| Multiplier (M) | 0011 | 3 |

| | U | V |
| beginning: | 00000 | 0011 |

| 1 | before shift: | 00010 | 0011 |
| | after shift: | 00001 | 0001 |

| 2 | before shift: | 00011 | 0001 |
| | after shift: | 00001 | 1000 |

| 3 | before shift: | 00001 | 1000 |
| | after shift: | 00000 | 1100 |

| 4 | before shift: | 00000 | 1100 |
| | after shift: | 00000 | 0110 |

| Product(P) | 0110 | 6 |

Example 97

Multiply $3 \times (-2)$ using an iterative multiplier. Assume a 4-bit binary 2's complement number system. Let 3 (0011_2) be the multiplicand and let -2 (1110_2) be the multiplier. For each iteration show the values of U and V just before the right shift on Line 12, and just after the right shift.

Answer:

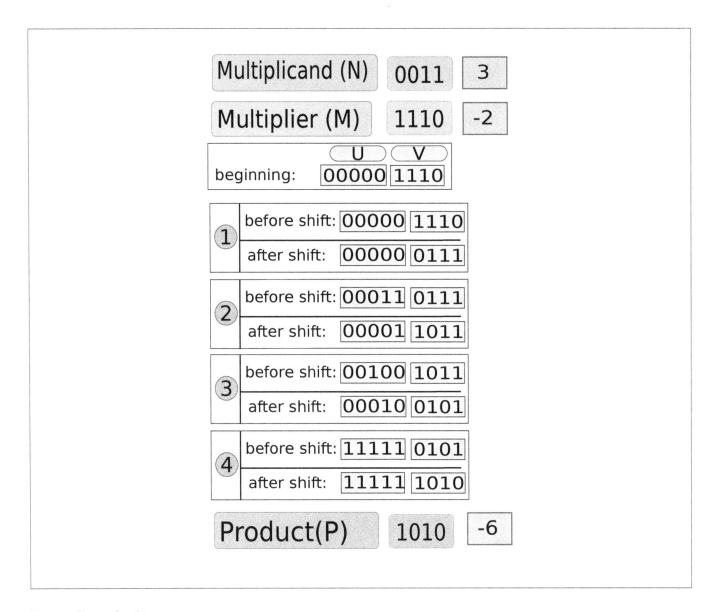

Time Complexity

If we are performing n bit multiplication, then there are n iterations of the loop, and each iteration performs one addition at the most. This takes $O(log(n))$ time. Hence, the total time required is $O(nlog(n))$.

7.2.3 Booth Multiplier

The iterative multiplier is a simple algorithm, yet it is slow. It is definitely not as fast as addition. Let us try to speed it up by making a simple alteration. This trick will not change the asymptotic time complexity of the algorithm. However, in practice the process of multiplication will become significantly faster. This algorithm is known as the *Booth* multiplication algorithm and has been used for designing fast multipliers in a lot of processors.

We observe that if a bit in the multiplier is 0, then nothing needs to be done other than a shift in the iterative multiplier. The complexity arises when a bit is 1. Let us assume that the multiplier contains a run of 1s. It is of the form - 0000111100. Let the run of 1s be from the ith to the jth position ($i \le j$). The value of the multiplier M is thus:

$$M = \sum_{k=i}^{k=j} 2^{k-1} = 2^j - 2^{i-1} \tag{7.10}$$

Now, the iterative multiplier will perform $j - i + 1$ additions. This is not required as we can see from Equation 7.10. We just need to do one subtraction when we are considering the ith bit, and do one addition when we are considering the $(j+1)^{th}$ bit. We can thus replace $j - i + 1$ additions with one addition and one subtraction. This insight allows us to reduce the number of additions if there are long runs of 1s in the 2's complement notation of the multiplier. If the multiplier is a small negative number, then it fits this pattern. It will have a long run of 1s especially in the most significant positions. Even otherwise, most of the numbers that we encounter will at least have some runs of 1s. The worst case arises, when we have a number of the form: 010101... . This is a very rare case.

If we consider our basic insight again, then we observe that we need to consider bit pairs consisting of the previous and the current multiplier bit. Depending on the bit pair we need to perform a certain action. Table 7.4 shows the actions that we need to perform.

(current value,previous value)	Action
0,0	-
1,0	subtract multiplicand from U
1,1	-
0,1	add multiplicand to U

Table 7.4: Actions in the Booth multiplier

If the current and previous bits are (0,0) respectively, then we do not need to do anything. We need to just shift UV and continue. Similarly, if the bits are (1,1), nothing needs to be done. However, if the current bit is 1, and the previous bit was 0, then a run of 1s is starting. We thus need to subtract the value of the multiplicand from U. Similarly, if the current bit is 0, and the previous bit was 1, then a run of 1s has just ended. In this case, we need to add the value of the multiplicand to U.

Algorithm 2: Booth's Algorithm to multiply two 32-bit numbers to produce a 64-bit result

Data: Multiplier in V, $U = 0$, Multiplicand in N
Result: The lower 64 bits of UV contain the result

1   $i \leftarrow 0$
2   $prevBit \leftarrow 0$
3   **for** $i < 32$ **do**
4     $i \leftarrow i + 1$
5     $currBit \leftarrow$ LSB of V
6   **if** $(currBit, prevBit) = (1,0)$ **then**
7       $U \leftarrow U - N$
8   **end**
9   **else if** $(currBit, prevBit) = (0,1)$ **then**
10      $U \leftarrow U + N$
11   **end**
12    $prevBit \leftarrow currBit$
13    $UV \leftarrow UV \gg 1$ (arithmetic right shift)
14 **end**

The Booth's algorithm is shown in Algorithm 2. Here, also, we assume that U is 33 bits wide, and V is 32 bits wide. We iterate for 32 times, and consider bit pairs (current bit, previous bit). For (0,0) and (1,1), we do not need to perform any action, else we need to perform an addition and subtraction.

Proof of Correctness*

Let us try to prove that the Booth's algorithm produces the same result as the iterative algorithm for a positive multiplier.

There are two cases. The multiplier (M) can either be positive or negative. Let us consider the case of the positive multiplier first. The MSB of a positive multiplier is 0. Now, let us divide the multiplier into several sequences of contiguous 0s and 1s. For example, if the number is of the form: 000110010111. The sequences are: 000, 11, 00, 1, 0, and 111. For a run of 0s, both the multipliers (Booth's and iterative) produce the same result result because they simply shift the UV register 1 step to the right.

For a sequence of continuous 1s, both the multipliers also produce the same result because the Booth multiplier replaces a sequence of additions with an addition and a subtraction according to Equation 7.10. The only special case arises for the MSB bit, when the iterative multiplier may subtract the multiplicand. In this case, the MSB is 0, and thus no special cases arise. Each run of continuous 0s and 1s in the multiplier is accounted for in the partial product correctly. Therefore, we can conclude that the final result of the Booth multiplier is the same as that of a regular iterative multiplier.

Let us now consider a negative multiplier M. Its MSB is 1. According to Theorem 2.3.4.2, $M = -2^{n-1} + \sum_{i=1}^{n-1} M_i 2^{i-1}$. Let $M' = \sum_{i=1}^{n-1} M_i 2^{i-1}$. Hence, for a negative multiplier (M):

$$M = M' - 2^{n-1} \tag{7.11}$$

M' is a positive number (MSB is 0). Note that till we consider the MSB of the multiplier, the Booth's algorithm does not know if the multiplier is equal to M or M'.

Now, let us split our argument into two cases. Let us consider the MSB bit (n^{th} bit), and the $(n-1)^{th}$ bit. This bit pair can either be 10, or 11.

Case 10: Let us divide the multiplier M into two parts as shown in Equation in Equation 7.11. The first part is a positive number M', and the second part is -2^{n-1}, where $M = M' - 2^{n-1}$. Since the two MSB bits of the binary representation of M are 10, we can conclude that the binary representation of M' contains 00 as its two MSB bits. Recall that the binary representation of M and M' contain the same set of $n-1$ least significant bits, and the MSB of M' is always 0.

Since the Booth multiplier was proven to work correctly for positive multipliers, we can conclude that the Booth multiplier correctly computes the partial product as $N \times M'$ in the first $(n-1)$ iterations. The proof of this fact is as follows. Till the end of $(n-1)$ iterations, we are not sure if the MSB is 0 or 1. Hence, we do not know if we are multiplying N with M or M'. The partial product will be the same in both the cases. If we were multiplying N with M', then no action will be taken in the last step because the two MSB bits of M' are 00. This means that in the second last step ($(n-1)$ iterations), the partial product contains NM'. We can similarly prove that the partial product computed by the iterative multiplier after $(n-1)$ iterations is equal to NM' because the MSB of M' is 0.

Hence, till this point, both the algorithms compute the same partial product, or alternatively have the same contents in the U and V registers. In the last step, both the algorithms find out that the MSB is 1. The iterative algorithm subtracts the multiplicand(N) from U, or alternatively subtracts $N \times 2^{n-1}$ from the partial product. The reason that we treat the multiplicand as shifted by $n-1$ places is because the partial product in the last iteration spans the entire U register and $n-1$ bits of the V register. Now, when we add or subtract the multiplicand(N) to U, effectively, we are adding N shifted by $n-1$ places to the left. Hence, the iterative multiplier correctly computes the product as $M'N - 2^{n-1}N = MN$ (see Equation 7.11). The Booth multiplier also does the same in this case. It sees a $0 \rightarrow 1$ transition. It subtracts N from U, which is exactly the same step as taken by the iterative multiplier. Thus, the operation of the Booth multiplier is correct in this case (same result as the iterative multiplier).

Case 11: Let us again consider the point at the beginning of the nth iteration. At this point of time, the partial product computed by the iterative algorithm is $M'N$, whereas the partial product computed by the Booth multiplier is different because the two MSB bits of M' are 0 and 1, respectively. Let us assume that we were originally multiplying N with M', then the MSB would have been 0, and this fact would have been discovered in the last iteration. The Booth's algorithm would have then added $2^{n-1}N$ to obtain the final result in the last step because of a $1 \rightarrow 0$ transition. Hence, after the $(n-1)^{th}$ iteration, the partial product of the Booth multiplier is equal to $M'N - 2^{n-1}N$. Note that till the last iteration, the Booth multiplier does not know whether the multiplier is M or M'.

Now, let us take a look at the last iteration. In this iteration both the algorithms find out that the MSB is 1. The iterative multiplier subtracts $2^{n-1}N$ from the partial product, and correctly computes the final product as $MN = M'N - 2^{n-1}N$. The Booth multiplier finds the current and previous bit to be 11, and thus does not take any action. Hence, its final product is equal to the partial product computed at the end of the $(n-1)^{th}$ iteration, which is equal to $M'N - 2^{n-1}N$. Therefore, in this case also the outputs of both the multipliers match.

We have thus proved that the Booth multiplier works for both positive and negative multipliers.

Important Point 9

Here, we use a 33-bit U register to avoid overflows. Let us show an example of an overflow, if we would have used a 32-bit U register. Assume that we are trying to multiply -2^{31} (multiplicand) with -1(multiplier). We will need to compute $0 - N$ in the first step. The value of U should be equal to 2^{31}; however, this number cannot be represented with 32 bits. Hence, we have an overflow. We do not have this issue when we use a 33-bit U register. Moreover, we can prove that with a 33-bit U register, the additions or subtractions in the algorithm will never lead to an overflow (similar to the proof for iterative multiplication).

Example 98

Multiply 2×3 using a Booth multiplier. Assume a 4-bit binary 2's complement number system. Let 3 (0011_2) be the multiplicand and let 2 (0010_2) be the multiplier. For each iteration show the values of U and V just before and after the right shift.
Answer:

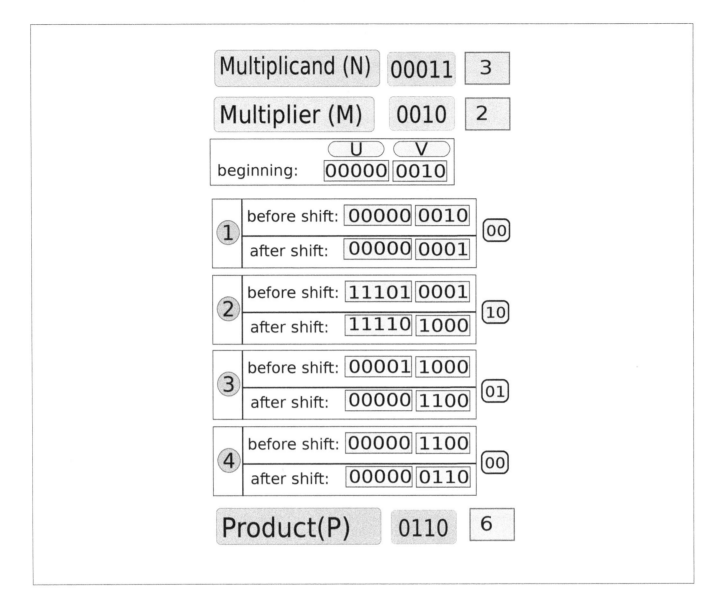

Example 99

Multiply $3 \times (-2)$ using a Booth multiplier. Assume a 4-bit binary 2's complement number system. Let 3 (0011_2) be the multiplicand and let -2 (1110_2) be the multiplier. For each iteration show the values of U and V just before and after the right shift.

Answer:

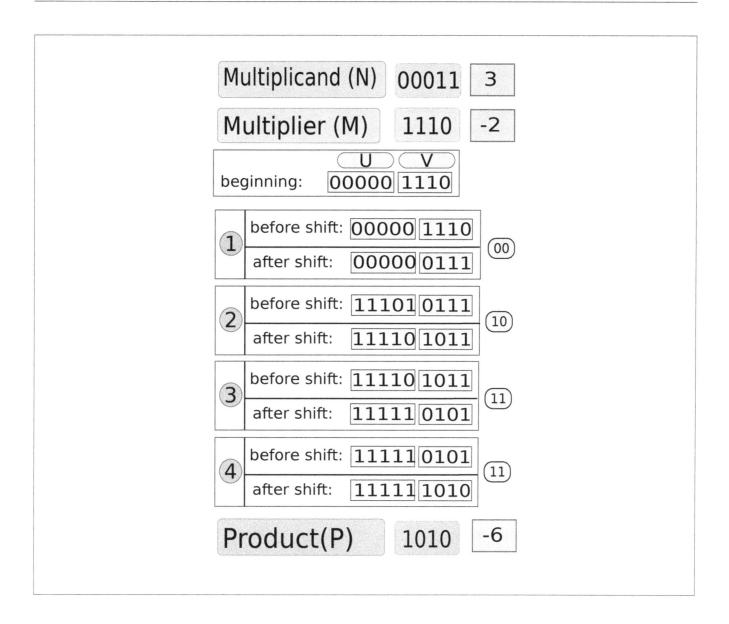

7.2.4   An $O(log(n)^2)$ Time Algorithm

Let us make our life slightly easier now. Let us multiply two n bit numbers, and save the product as also a n bit number. Let us ignore overflows, and concentrate only on performance. The issue of detecting overflows in a high performance multiplier is fairly complex, and is beyond the scope of this book. Using our results from Section 2.3.4, we use simple unsigned multiplication to compute the product of signed numbers. If there are no overflows then the result is correct.

Let us take a look at the problem of multiplication again. We basically consider each bit of the multiplier in turn, and multiply it with a shifted version of the multiplicand. We obtain n such *partial sums*. The product is the sum of the n partial sums. Generating each partial sum is independent of the other. This process can be performed in parallel in hardware. To generate the ith partial sum, we need to simply compute an AND operation between the ith bit of the multiplier and each bit of the multiplicand. This takes $O(1)$ time.

Now, we can add the n partial sums($P^1 \ldots P^n$) in parallel using a tree of adders as shown in Figure 7.12. There are $O(log(n))$ levels. In each level we are adding two $O(n)$ bit numbers; hence, each level takes

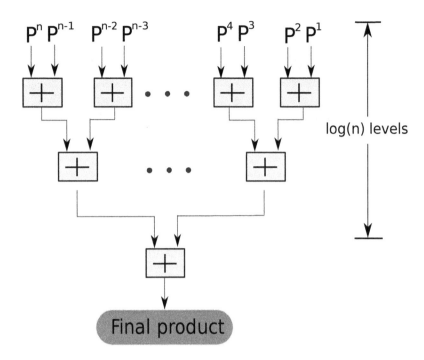

Figure 7.12: Tree of adders for adding partial sums

$O(log(n))$ time. The total time requirement is thus $O(log(n)^2)$. By exploiting the inherent parallelism, we have significantly improved the time from $O(nlog(n))$ to $O(log(n)^2)$. It turns out that we can do even better, and get an $O(log(n))$ time algorithm.

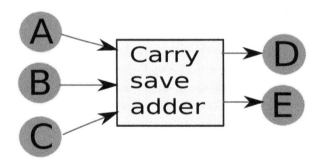

Figure 7.13: Carry Save Adder

7.2.5   Wallace Tree Multiplier

Before, we introduce the Wallace tree multiplier, let us introduce the carry save adder. A carry save adder adds three numbers, A, B, C, and produces two numbers D, and E such that: $A + B + C = D + E$(see Figure 7.13). We will extensively use carry save adders in constructing the Wallace tree multiplier that runs in $O(log(n))$ time.

Carry Save Adder

Let us consider the problem of adding three bits a, b, and c. The sum can range from 0 to 3. We can express all numbers between 0 to 3 in the form $2d + e$, where $(d, e) \in [0, 1]$. Using this relationship, we can express the sum of three numbers as the sum of two numbers as follows:

$$
\begin{aligned}
A + B + C &= \sum_{i=1}^{n} A_i 2^{i-1} + \sum_{i=1}^{n} B_i 2^{i-1} + \sum_{i=1}^{n} C_i 2^{i-1} \\
&= \sum_{i=1}^{n} (A_i + B_i + C_i) 2^{i-1} \\
&= \sum_{i=1}^{n} (2D_i + E_i) 2^{i-1} \\
&= \underbrace{\sum_{i=1}^{n} D_i 2^i}_{D} + \underbrace{\sum_{i=1}^{n} E_i 2^{i-1}}_{E} \\
&= D + E
\end{aligned}
\tag{7.12}
$$

Thus, we have $A + B + C = D + E$. The question is how to compute the bits D_i, and E_i such that $A_i + B_i + C_i = 2D_i + E_i$. This is very simple. We note that if we add A_i, B_i, and C_i, we get a two bit result, where s is the sum bit and c is the carry bit. The result of the addition can be written as $2 \times c + s$. We thus have two equations as follows:

$$
\begin{aligned}
A_i + B_i + C_i &= 2D_i + E_i \tag{7.13} \\
A_i + B_i + C_i &= 2c + s \tag{7.14}
\end{aligned}
$$

If we set D_i to the carry bit and E_i to the sum bit, then we are done! Now, E is equal to $\sum_{i=1}^{n} E_i 2^{i-1}$. We can thus obtain E by concatenating all the E_i bits. Similarly, D is equal to $\sum_{i=1}^{n} D_i 2^i$. D can be computed by concatenating all the D_i bits and shifting the number to the left by 1 position.

The hardware complexity of a carry save adder is not much. We need n full adders to compute all the sum and carry bits. Then, we need to route the wires appropriately to produce D and E. The asymptotic time complexity of a carry save adder is $O(1)$ (constant time).

Addition of n Numbers with Carry Save Adders

We can use carry save adders to add n partial sums (see Figure 7.14). In the first level, we can use a set of $n/3$ carry save adders to reduce the sum of n partial sums to a sum of $2n/3$ numbers in the second level. If we use $2n/9$ carry save adders in the second level, then we will have $4n/9$ numbers in the third level, and so on. In every level the set of numbers gets reduced by a factor of $2/3$. Thus, after $O(log_{3/2}(n))$ levels, there will only be two numbers left. Note that $O(log_{3/2}(n)$ is equivalent to $O(log(n))$. Since each stage takes $O(1)$ time because all the carry save adders are working in parallel, the total time taken up till now is $O(log(n))$.

In the last stage, when we have just two numbers left, we cannot use a carry save adder anymore. We can use a regular carry lookahead adder to add the two numbers. This will take $O(log(n))$ time. Hence, the total time taken by the Wallace tree multiplier is $O(log(n) + log(n)) = O(log(n))$. In terms of asymptotic time complexity, this is the fastest possible multiplier. It is possible to reduce the number of full adders by slightly modifying the design. This is known as the Dadda multiplier. The reader can refer to [Wikipedia,] for further information on this topic.

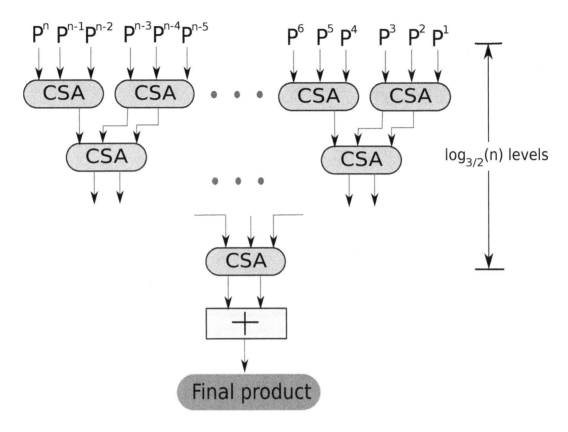

P^n P^{n-1} P^{n-2} P^{n-3} P^{n-4} P^{n-5} P^6 P^5 P^4 P^3 P^2 P^1

$\log_{3/2}(n)$ levels

Figure 7.14: Wallace Tree Multiplier

7.3 Division

7.3.1 Overview

Let us now look at integer division. Unfortunately, unlike addition, subtraction, and multiplication, division is a significantly slower process. Any division operation can be represented as follows:

$$N = DQ + R \tag{7.15}$$

Here, N is the dividend, D is the divisor, Q is the quotient, and R is the remainder. Division algorithms assume that the divisor and dividend are positive. The process of division needs to satisfy the following properties.

Property 1 $R < D$, and $R \geq 0$.

Property 2 Q is the largest positive integer that satisfies Equation 7.15.

If we wish to divide negative numbers, then we need to first convert them to positive numbers, perform the division, and then adjust the sign of the quotient and remainder. Some architectures try to ensure that the remainder is always positive. In this case, it is necessary to decrement the quotient by 1, and add the divisor to the remainder to make it positive.

Let us focus on the core problem, which is to divide two n bit positive numbers. The MSB is the sign bit, which is 0. Now, $DQ = \sum_{i=1}^{n} DQ_i 2^{i-1}$. We can thus write:

$$
\begin{aligned}
N &= DQ + R \\
&= DQ_{1\ldots n-1} + DQ_n 2^{n-1} + R \\
\underbrace{(N - DQ_n 2^{n-1})}_{N'} &= D \underbrace{Q_{1\ldots n-1}}_{Q'} + R \\
N' &= DQ' + R
\end{aligned}
\tag{7.16}
$$

We have thus reduced the original problem of division into a smaller problem. The original problem was to divide N by D. The reduced problem is to divide $N' = N - DQ_n 2^{n-1}$ by D. The remainder for both the problems is the same. The quotient, Q', for the reduced problem has the same least significant $n-1$ bits as the original quotient, Q. The nth bit of Q' is 0.

To create the reduced problem it is necessary to find Q_n. We can try out both the choices – 0 and 1. We first try 1. If $N - D2^{n-1} \geq 0$, then $Q_n = 1$ (Property 1 and 2). Otherwise, it is 0.

Once, we have created the reduced problem, we can proceed to further reduce the problem till we have computed all the quotient bits. Ultimately, the divided will be equal to the remainder, R, and we will be done. Let us now illustrate an algorithm that precisely follows the procedure that we have just outlined.

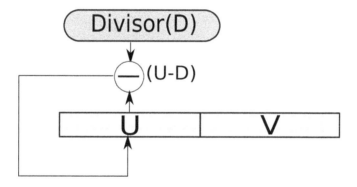

Figure 7.15: Iterative divider

7.3.2 Restoring Division

Let us consider a similar setup as the iterative multiplier to divide two positive 32-bit numbers. The divisor is stored in a 32-bit register called D. We have a 33 bit register U, and a 32-bit register V. If we left shift U and V, then the value shifted out of V, is shifted in to U. U is initialised to 0, and V is initialised to hold the dividend (see Figure 7.15). Note that the size of U is equal to 33 bits to avoid overflows (similar to the case of the iterative multiplier).

Algorithm 3: Restoring algorithm to divide two 32-bit numbers

Data: Divisor in D, Dividend in V, $U = 0$
Result: U contains the remainder (lower 32 bits), and V contains the quotient

```
1  i ← 0
2  for i < 32 do
3  │   i ← i + 1
   │   /* Left shift UV by 1 position */
4  │   UV ← UV << 1
5  │   U ← U - D
6  │   if U ≥ 0 then
7  │   │   q ← 1
8  │   end
9  │   else
10 │   │   U ← U + D
11 │   │   q ← 0
12 │   end
   │   /* Set the quotient bit */
13 │   LSB of V ← q
14 end
```

Algorithm 3 follows the discussion that we had in Section 7.3.1. We shall see that each iteration of the algorithm reduces the problem according to Equation 7.16. Let us prove its correctness.

Proof of Correctness*

To start out we iterate 32 times for each bit of the dividend (Lines 2 to 14). Let us consider the first iteration. At the beginning, the value in the combined register UV is equal to the value of the dividend N. The first step is to shift UV to the left by 1 position in Line 4. Since the dividend is originally loaded into register V, we are shifting the dividend to the left by 1 position. The next step is to subtract the divisor from register U in Line 5. If $U - D \geq 0$, then we set the MSB of the quotient to 1 (Line 7), otherwise we add D back to U in Line 10, and set the MSB of the quotient to 0.

We wish to use Equation 7.16 to reduce the problem in every iteration. Equation 7.16 states that the new dividend(N') is equal to:

$$N' = N - 2^{n-1}DQ_n \tag{7.17}$$

Q_n is the MSB of the quotient here. The divisor and remainder stay the same. The last $n - 1$ bits of the new quotient match those of the old quotient.

We wish to prove that the value of UV at the end of the first iteration is equal to $(2N')$(ignoring quotient bits) such that we can reduce the problem according to Equation 7.16. Let us consider the value stored in UV. Just after executing Line 4, it contains twice the dividend – $2N$ – because we shifted UV by 1 position to the left. Now, we are subtracting D from the upper n bits of UV. In effect, we are subtracting $2^n D$. Hence, after Line 5, UV contains $UV - 2^n D$. We have:

$$UV - 2^n D = 2N - 2^n D = 2 \times (N - 2^{n-1}D) \tag{7.18}$$

Subsequently, we test the sign of $U - D$ in Line 6. If $U - D$ is positive or zero, then it means that UV is greater than $2^n D$ because $V \geq 0$. If $U - D$ is negative, then let $U + \Delta = D$, where $\Delta \geq 1$. We have:

$$UV - 2^n D = 2^n U + V - 2^n D$$
$$= (U - D)2^n + V \qquad (7.19)$$
$$= V - \Delta \times 2^n$$

Now, $V < 2^n$. Hence, $V < \Delta \times 2^n$, and thus $UV - 2^n D$ is negative. We thus observe that the sign of $U - D$ is the same as the sign of $UV - 2^n D$, which is same as the sign of $(N - 2^{n-1}D)$.

$$sign(U - D) = sign(N - 2^{n-1}D) \qquad (7.20)$$

Now, for reducing the problem, if we observe that $U - D \geq 0$, then $N - 2^{n-1}D \geq 0$. Hence, we can set Q_n to 1, and set the new dividend to $N' = N - 2^{n-1}DQ_n$, and also conclude that at the end of the iteration UV contains $2N'$(Line 5 and 7). If $U - D < 0$, then we cannot set Q_n to 1. N' will become negative. Hence, the algorithm sets Q_n to 0 in Line 11 and adds D back to U. The value of UV is thus equal to $2N$. Since $Q_n = 0$, we have $N = N'$(Equation 7.17). In both the cases, the value of UV at the end of the iteration is $2N'$. We thus conclude that in the first iteration, the MSB of the quotient is computed correctly, and the value of UV ignoring the quotient bit is equal to $2N'$.

In the next iteration, we can use exactly the same procedure to prove that the value of UV(ignoring quotient bits) is equal to $4N''$. Ultimately, after 32 iterations, V will contain the entire quotient. The value of UV(ignoring quotient bits) at that point will be $2^n \times N^{32}$. Here N^i is the reduced dividend after the ith iteration. We have the following relation according to Equation 7.17:

$$N^{31} = DQ_1 + R$$
$$\Rightarrow \underbrace{N^{31} - DQ_1}_{N^{32}} = R \qquad (7.21)$$

Hence, U will contain the value of the remainder and V will contain the quotient.

Important Point 10

Let us now try to prove that the restoring algorithm does not suffer from overflows while performing a left shift, and adding or subtracting the divisor. Let us first prove that just before the shift operation in Line 4, $U < D$. Let us assume positive divisors $(D > 0)$ and non-negative dividends $(N \geq 0)$ for division. For the base case, $(U = 0)$, the proposition holds. Let us consider the nth iteration. Let the value of U before the shift operation be $\hat{U}$. From the induction hypothesis, we can conclude that $\hat{U} < D$, or alternatively, $\hat{U} \leq D - 1$ After the shift operation, we have $U \leq 2\hat{U} + 1$ because we are performing a left shift by 1 position, and shifting in the MSB of V. If $U < D$, then the induction hypothesis holds for the $(n+1)^{th}$ iteration. Otherwise, we subtract D from U. We have, $U = U - D \leq 2\hat{U} + 1 - D \leq 2(D-1) + 1 - D = D - 1$. Therefore, $U < D$. Thus, for the $(n+1)^{th}$ iteration, the induction hypothesis holds. Now that we have proved that $U < D$, let us prove that the largest value contained in register U is less than or equal to $2D - 1$.

After the shift operation, the largest value that U can contain is $(2(D-1)+1) = 2D - 1$. Henceforth, the value of U can only decrease. Since D is a 32-bit number, we require at the most 33 bits to store $(2D - 1)$. Consequently, having a 33-bit U register avoids overflows.

Time Complexity

There are n iterations of the *for* loop. Each iteration does one subtraction in Line 5 and maybe one addition in Line 10. The rest of the operations can be done in $O(1)$ time. Thus, per iteration it takes $O(log(n))$ time. Hence, the total time complexity is $O(nlog(n))$.

Example 100
Divide two 4-bit numbers: 7 (0111) / 3(0011) using restoring division. **Answer:**

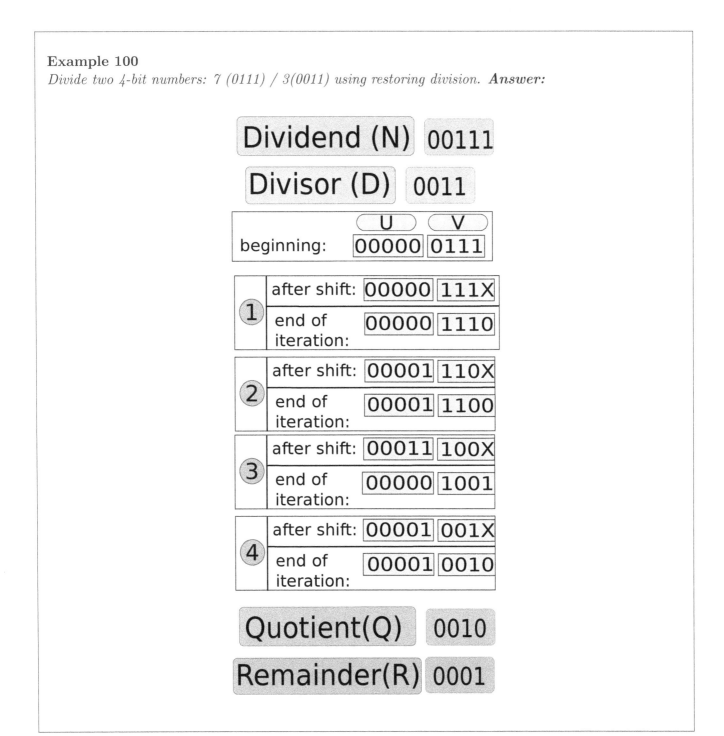

7.3.3   Non-Restoring Division

We observe that there can be a maximum of two add/subtract operations per iteration. It is possible to circumvent it by using another temporary register to store the result of the subtract operation $U - D$. We can move it to U only if $U - D \geq 0$. However, this also involves additional circuitry. The U register will get complicated and slower too.

The non-restoring algorithm does either one addition or one subtraction per iteration. Hence, it is more efficient even though the asymptotic time complexity is the same. The hardware setup (U and V registers, dividend (N), divisor (D)) is the same as that for the restoring algorithm.

Algorithm 4: Non-restoring algorithm to divide two 32-bit numbers

Data: Divisor in D, Dividend in V, $U = 0$
Result: U contains the remainder, and V contains the quotient

```
 1  i ← 0
 2  for i < 32 do
 3  |    i ← i + 1
    |    /* Left shift UV by 1 position */
 4  |    UV ← UV << 1
 5  |    if U ≥ 0 then
 6  |    |    U ← U − D
 7  |    end
 8  |    else
 9  |    |    U ← U + D
10  |    end
11  |    if U ≥ 0 then
12  |    |    q ← 1
13  |    end
14  |    else
15  |    |    q ← 0
16  |    end
    |    /* Set the quotient bit */
17  |    LSB of V ← q
18  end
19  if U < 0 then
20  |    U ← U + D
21  end
```

We see that the non-restoring algorithm is very similar to the restoring algorithm with some minor differences. The non-restoring algorithm shifts UV as the first step in an iteration. Then, if the value of U is negative, it adds D to U. Otherwise, it subtracts D from U. If the addition or subtraction has resulted in a value that is greater than or equal to zero, the non-restoring algorithm sets the appropriate quotient bit to 1, else it sets it to 0.

Finally, at the end V contains the entire quotient. If U is negative, then we need to add the divisor (D) to U. U will contain the remainder.

Proof of Correctness*

Like the restoring algorithm, let us assume that when we refer to the value of UV, we assume that all the quotient bits are equal to 0. As long as U remains positive or 0, the state of U and V is equal to that produced by the restoring algorithm. Let us assume that in the jth iteration, U becomes negative for the first time. Let us consider the value represented by the register UV just after it is shifted to the left by 1 position, and call it UV_j (j stands for the iteration number).

At the end of the jth iteration, $UV = UV_j - D'$, where $D' = D \times 2^n$. We shift D by n places to the left because we always add or subtract D from U, which is the upper half of UV. According to our assumption UV_j is negative. In this case the restoring algorithm would not have subtracted D', and it would have written 0 to the quotient. The non-restoring algorithm sets the quotient bit correctly since it finds UV to be negative (Line 15). Let us now move to the $(j+1)^{th}$ iteration.

$UV_{j+1} = 2UV_j - 2D'$. At the end of the $(j+1)^{th}$ iteration, $UV = 2UV_j - 2D' + D' = 2UV_j - D'$. If UV is not negative, then the non-restoring algorithm will save 1 in the quotient. Let us now see at this point what the restoring algorithm would have done (assuming UV is non-negative). In the $(j+1)^{th}$ iteration, the restoring algorithm would have started the iteration with $UV = UV_j$. It would have then performed a shift and subtracted D' to set $UV = 2UV_j - D'$, and written 1 to the quotient. We thus observe that at this point the state of the registers U and V matches exactly for both the algorithms.

However, if UV is negative then the restoring and non-restoring algorithms will have a different state. Nonetheless the quotient bits will be set correctly. $UV_{j+2} = 4UV_j - 2D'$. Since a negative number multiplied by 2 (left shifted by 1 position) is still negative, the non-restoring algorithm will add D' to U. Hence, the value of UV at the end of the $(j+2)^{th}$ iteration will be $4UV_j - D'$. If this is non-negative, then the restoring algorithm would also have exactly the same state at this point.

We can continue this argument to observe that the quotient bits are always set correctly and the state of U and V exactly matches that of the restoring algorithm when $UV \geq 0$ at the end of an iteration. Consequently, for dividing the same pair of numbers the states of the restoring and non-restoring algorithms will start as the same, then diverge and converge several times. If the last iteration leads to a non-negative UV then the algorithm is correct because the state exactly matches that produced by the restoring algorithm.

However, if the last iteration leaves us with UV as negative, then we observe that $UV = 2^{n-k}UV_k - D'$, where k is the iteration number at which the states had converged for the last time. If we add D' to UV, then the states of both the algorithms match, and thus the results are correct (achieved in Line 20).

Important Point 11

Let us now try to prove that the non-restoring algorithm does not suffer from overflows while performing a left shift, and adding or subtracting the divisor. Similar to the proof for the restoring algorithm, let us first prove that just before the shift operation, $|U| < D$. For the base case, ($U = 0$), the proposition holds. Let us consider the nth iteration, and let the value of U just before the shift operation be $\hat{U}$. Let us first assume that $\hat{U} \geq 0$. In this case, we can use the same logic as the restoring algorithm, and prove that $|U| < D$ at the beginning of the $(n+1)^{th}$ iteration. Let us now assume that $\hat{U} < 0$. From the induction hypothesis, $|\hat{U}| < D \Rightarrow \hat{U} \geq -(D-1)$. Now, if we shift $\hat{U}$ by 1 position, and shift in a 0 or 1, we compute $U \geq 2\hat{U}$ (for $\hat{U} < 0$, shifting in a 1 reduces the absolute value). After the shift operation, we add D to U. We thus have, $U = U + D \geq 2\hat{U} + D \geq 2 \times (1 - D) + D = 2 - D$. Thus, in this case also $|U| < D$, just before the shift, and after the shift we have $|U| \leq 2D - 1$. We thus need to allocate an extra bit to register U to correctly store all the possible intermediate values of U. Hence, the U register is 33 bits wide. We are thus guaranteed to not have overflows during the operation of the non-restoring algorithm.

Example 101
Divide two 4-bit numbers: 7 (0111) / 3(0011) using non-restoring division. **Answer:**

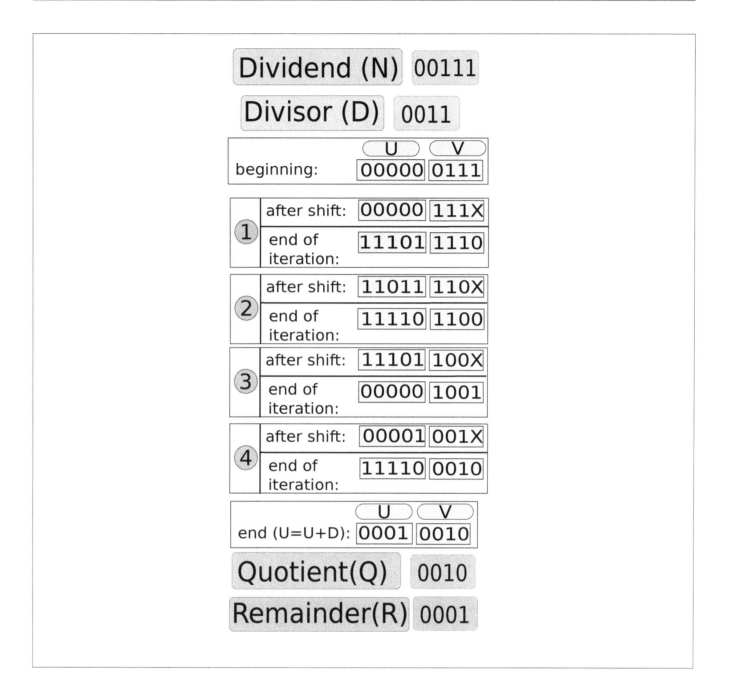

7.4   Floating Point Addition and Subtraction

The problems of floating point addition and subtraction are actually different faces of the same problem. $A - B$ can be interpreted in two ways. We can say that we are subtracting B from A, or we can say that we are adding $-B$ to A. Hence, instead of looking at subtraction separately, let us look at it as a special case of addition. We shall first look at the problem of adding two numbers with the same sign in Section 7.4.1, with opposite signs in Section 7.4.4 and then look at the generic problem of adding two numbers in Section 7.4.5.

Before going further, let us quickly recapitulate our knowledge of floating point numbers (see Table 7.5).

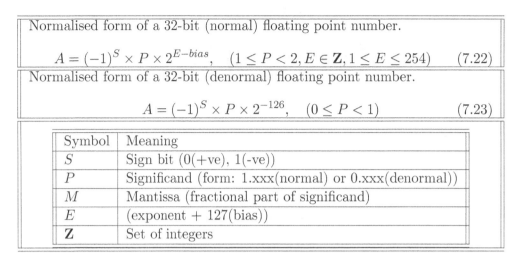

Normalised form of a 32-bit (normal) floating point number.

$$A = (-1)^S \times P \times 2^{E-bias}, \quad (1 \le P < 2, E \in \mathbf{Z}, 1 \le E \le 254) \qquad (7.22)$$

Normalised form of a 32-bit (denormal) floating point number.

$$A = (-1)^S \times P \times 2^{-126}, \quad (0 \le P < 1) \qquad (7.23)$$

Symbol	Meaning
S	Sign bit (0(+ve), 1(-ve))
P	Significand (form: 1.xxx(normal) or 0.xxx(denormal))
M	Mantissa (fractional part of significand)
E	(exponent + 127(bias))
$\mathbf{Z}$	Set of integers

Table 7.5: IEEE 754 format

7.4.1 Simple Addition with Same Signs

The problem is to add two floating point numbers A and B with the same sign. We want to compute a new floating point number $C = A + B$. In this case, the sign of the result is known in advance (sign of A or B). All of our subsequent discussion assumes the IEEE 32-bit format. However, the techniques that we develop can be extended to other formats, especially double-precision arithmetic.

First, the floating point unit needs to unpack different fields from the floating point representations of A and B. Let the E fields (exponent + bias) be E_A and E_B for A and B respectively. Let the E field of the result, C, be E_C. In hardware, let us use a register called E to save the exponent (in the bias notation). The final value of E needs to be equal to E_C.

Unpacking the significand is slightly more elaborate. We shall represent the significands as unsigned integers and ignore the decimal point. Moreover, we shall add a leading most significant bit that can act as the sign bit. It is initially 0. For example, if a floating point number is of the form: 1.0111×2^{10}, the significand is 1.0111, and we shall represent it as 010111. Note that we have added a leading 0 bit. Figure 7.16 shows an example of how the significand is unpacked, and placed in a register for a normal floating point number. In the 32-bit IEEE 754 format, there are 23 bits for the mantissa, and there is either a 0 or 1 before the decimal point. The significand thus requires 24 bits, and if we wish to add a leading sign bit(0), then we need 25 bits of storage. Let us save this number in a register, and call it W.

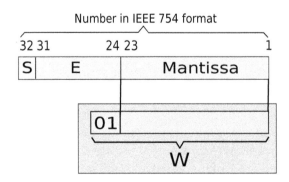

Figure 7.16: Expanding the significand and placing it in a register

Let us start out by observing that we cannot add A and B the way we have added integers, because the exponents might be different. The first task is to ensure that both the exponents are the same. Without no loss of generality, let us assume that $E_A \geq E_B$. This can be effected with a simple compare and swap in hardware. We can thus initialise the register E to E_A.

Let the significands of A and B be P_A and P_B respectively. Let us initially set W equal to the significand of $B(P_B)$ with a leading 0 bit as shown in Figure 7.16.

To make the exponent of A and B equal, we need to right shift W by $(E_A - E_B)$ positions. Now, we can proceed to add the significand of A termed as P_A to W.

$$W = W >> (E_A - E_B) \tag{7.24}$$
$$W = W + P_A \tag{7.25}$$

Let the significand represented by W be P_W. There is a possibility that P_W might be greater than or equal to 2. In this case, the significand of the result is not in normalised form. We will thus need to right shift W by 1 position and increment E by 1. This process is called *normalisation*. There is a possibility that incrementing E by 1 might make it equal to 255, which is not allowed. We can signal an overflow in this case. The final result can be obtained by constructing a floating point number out of the E, W, and the sign of the result (sign of either A or B).

Example 102
Add the numbers: $1.01_2 \times 2^3 + 1.11_2 \times 2^1$. Assume that the bias is 0.
Answer:

1. $A = 1.01 \times 2^3$ and $B = 1.11 \times 2^1$

2. $W = 01.11$ *(significand of B)*

3. $E = 3$

4. $W = 01.11 >> (3\text{-}1) = 00.0111$

5. $W + P_A = 00.0111 + 01.0100 = 01.1011$

6. *Result:* $C = 1.1011 \times 2^3$

Example 103
Add $1.01 \times 2^3 + 1.11 \times 2^2$. Assume that the bias is 0.
Answer:

1. $A = 1.01 \times 2^3$ and $B = 1.11 \times 2^2$

2. $W = 01.11$ *(significand of B)*

3. $E = 3$

4. $W = 01.11 >> (3\text{-}2) = 00.111$

5. $W + P_A = 00.111 + 01.010 = 10.001$

6. *Normalisation:* $W = 10.001 >> 1 = 1.0001$, $E = 4$

7. *Result:* $C = 1.0001 \times 2^4$

7.4.2 Rounding

In Example 103, let us assume that we were allowed only two mantissa bits. Then, there would have been a need to discard all the mantissa bits other than the two most significant ones. The result would have been 1.00. To incorporate the effect of the discarded bits, it might have been necessary to round the result. For example, let us consider decimal numbers. If we wish to round 9.99 to the nearest integer, then we should round it to 10. Similarly, if we wish to round 9.05 to the nearest integer, then we should round it to 9. Likewise, it is necessary to introduce rounding schemes while doing floating point operations such that the final result can properly reflect the value contained in the discarded bits.

Let us first introduce some terminology. Let us consider the sum of the significands after we have normalised the result. Let us divide the sum into two parts: $(\widehat{P} + R) \times 2^{-23} (R < 1)$. Here, $\widehat{P}$ is the significand of the temporary result in W multiplied by 2^{23}. It is an integer and it might need to be further rounded. R is a residue (beyond 23 bits) that will be discarded. It is less than 1. The aim is to modify $\widehat{P}$ appropriately to take into account the value of R. Now, there are two ways in which $\widehat{P}$ can be modified because of rounding. Either we can leave $\widehat{P}$ as it is, or we can increment $\widehat{P}$ by 1. Leaving $\widehat{P}$ as it is is also known as *truncation*. This is because we are truncating or discarding the residue.

The IEEE 754 format supports four rounding modes as shown in Table 7.6. An empty entry corresponds to truncating the result. We only show the conditions in which we need to increment $\widehat{P}$.

Rounding Mode	Condition for incrementing the significand	
	Sign of the result (+ve)	Sign of the result (-ve)
Truncation		
Round to $+\infty$	$R > 0$	
Round to $-\infty$		$R > 0$
Round to Nearest	$(R > 0.5) \| (R = 0.5 \wedge LSB(\widehat{P}) = 1)$	$(R > 0.5) \| (R = 0.5 \wedge LSB(\widehat{P}) = 1)$
$\widehat{P}$ (significand of the temporary result multiplied by 2^{23}), $\wedge$ (logical AND), R (residue)		

Table 7.6: IEEE 754 rounding modes

We give examples in decimal (base 10) in the next few subsections for the ease of understanding. Exactly the same operations can be performed on binary numbers. Our aim is to round $\widehat{P} + R$ to an integer. There are four possible ways of doing this in the IEEE 754 format.

Truncation

This is the simplest rounding mode. This rounding mode simply truncates the residue. For example, in truncation based rounding, if $\widehat{P} + R = 1.5$, then we will discard 0.5, and we are left with 1. Likewise, truncating -1.5 will give us -1. This is the easiest to implement in hardware, and is the least accurate out of the four methods.

Round to $+\infty$

In this rounding mode, we always round a number to the larger integer. For example, if $\widehat{P} + R = 1.2$, we round it to 2. If $\widehat{P} + R = -1.2$, we round it to -1. The idea here is to check the sign bit and the residue. If the number is positive, and the residue is non-zero, then we need to increment $\widehat{P}$, or alternatively the LSB of the significand. Otherwise, in all the other cases (either $R = 0$ or the number is negative), it is sufficient to truncate the residue.

Round to $-\infty$

This is the reverse of rounding to $+\infty$. In this case, we round 1.2 to 1, and -1.2 to -2.

Round to Nearest

This rounding mode is the most complicated, and is also the most common. Most processors use this rounding mode as the default. In this case, we try to minimise the error by rounding $\widehat{P}$ to the nearest possible value. If $R > 0.5$, then the nearest integer is $\widehat{P} + 1$. For example, we need to round 3.6 to 4, and -3.6 to -4. Similarly, if $R < 0.5$, then we need to truncate the residue. For example, we need to round 3.2 to 3, and -3.2 to -3.

The special case arises when $R = 0.5$. In this case, we would like to round $\widehat{P}$ to the nearest even integer. For example, we will round 3.5 to 4, and 4.5 to also 4. This is more of a convention than a profound mathematical concept. To translate this requirement in our terms, we need to take a look at the LSB of $\widehat{P}$. If it is 0, then $\widehat{P}$ is even, and we do not need to do anything more. However, if $LSB(\widehat{P}) = 1$, then $\widehat{P}$ is odd, and we need to increment it by 1.

7.4.3 Implementing Rounding

From our discussion on rounding, it is clear that we need to maintain some state regarding the discarded bits and $\widehat{P}$ such that we can make the proper rounding decision. In specific, we need four pieces of information – $LSB(\widehat{P})$, is $R = 0.5$, is $R > 0$, and is $R > 0.5$. The last three requirements can be captured with two bits – round and sticky.

The *round* bit is the MSB of the residue, R. The sticky bit is a logical OR of the rest of the bits of the residue. We can thus express the different conditions on the residue as shown in Table 7.7.

Condition on Residue	Implementation
$R > 0$	$r \vee s = 1$
$R = 0.5$	$r \wedge \overline{s} = 1$
$R > 0.5$	$r \wedge s = 1$
r (round bit), s(sticky bit)	

Table 7.7: Evaluating properties of the residue using round and sticky bits

Implementing rounding is thus as simple as maintaining the round bit, and sticky bit, and then using Table 7.6 to round the result. Maintaining the round and sticky bits requires us to simply update them on every single action of the algorithm. We can initialise these bits to 0. They need to be updated when B is shifted to the right. Then, they need to be further updated when we normalise the result. Now, it is possible that after rounding, the result is not in normalised form. For example, if $\widehat{P}$ contains all 1s, then incrementing it will produce 1 followed by 23 0s, which is not in the normalised form.

Renormalisation after Rounding

In case, the process of rounding brings the result to a state that is not in the normalised form, then we need to re-normalise the result. Note that in this case, we need to increment the exponent by 1, and set the mantissa to all 0s. Incrementing the exponent can make it invalid (if $E = 255$). We need to explicitly check for this case.

7.4.4   Addition of Numbers with Opposite Signs

Now let us look at the problem of adding two floating point numbers, A and B, to produce C. They have opposite signs. Again let us make the assumption that $E_A \geq E_B$.

The first step is to load the register W with the significand of $B(P_B)$ along with a leading 0. Since the signs are different, in effect we are subtracting the significand of B (shifted by some places) from the significand of A. Hence, we can take the 2's complement of W that contains P_B with a leading 0 bit, and then shift it to the right by $E_A - E_B$ places. This value is written back to the register W. Note that the shift needs to be an arithmetic right shift here such that the value is preserved. Secondly, the order of operations (shift and 2's complement) is not important.

We can now add the significand of A (P_A) to W. If the resulting value is negative, then we need to take its 2's complement, and set the sign of the result accordingly.

Next, we need to normalise the result. It is possible that $P_W < 1$. In this case, we need to shift W to the left till $1 \leq P_W < 2$. Most implementations of the floating point standard, use an extra bit called the *guard bit*. along with the round and sticky bits. They set the MSB of the residue to the guard bit, the next bit to the round bit, and the OR of the rest of the bits to the sticky bits. During the process of shifting a number left, they shift in the guard bit first, and then shift in 0s. At the end of the algorithm, it is necessary to set the round bit equal to the guard bit, and OR the sticky bit with the round bit such that our original semantics is maintained. This added complexity is to optimise for the case of a left shift by 1 position. If we did not have the guard bit, then we needed to shift the round bit into W, and we would thus lose the round bit forever.

Once W is normalised and the exponent(E) is updated, we need to round the result as per Table 7.6. This process might lead to another round of normalisation.

7.4.5   Generic Algorithm for Adding Floating Point Numbers

Note that we have not considered special values such as 0 in our analysis. The flowchart in Figure 7.17 shows the algorithm for adding two floating point numbers. This algorithm considers 0 values also.

7.5   Multiplication of Floating Point Numbers

The algorithm for multiplying floating point numbers is of exactly the same form as the algorithm for generic addition without a few steps. Let us again try to multiply $A \times B$ to obtain the product C. Again, let us assume without loss of generality that $E_A \geq E_B$.

The flowchart for multiplication is shown in Figure 7.18. We do not have to align the exponents in the case of multiplication. We initialise the algorithm as follows. We load the significand of B into register W. In this case, the width of W is equal to double the size of the operands such that the product can be accommodated. The E register is initialised to $E_A + E_B - bias$. This is because in the case of multiplication, the exponents are added together. We subtract the bias to avoid double counting. Computing the sign of the result is trivial.

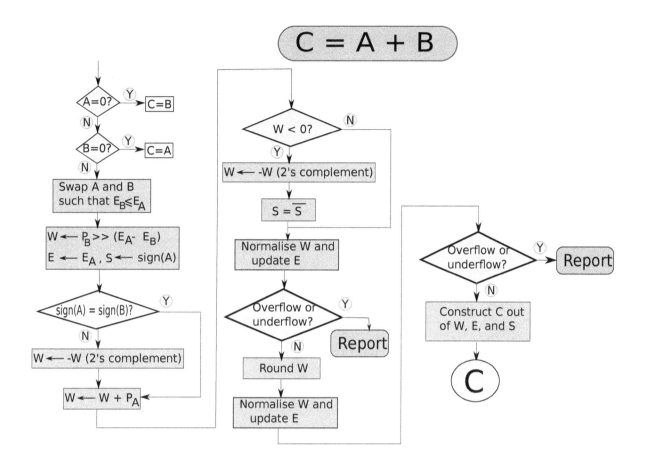

Figure 7.17: Flowchart for adding two floating point values

After initialisation, we multiply the significand of A with W and save the product in W. The product contains 46 bits after the floating point. We might need to discard some of the bits to ensure that the final mantissa is 23 bits long. Hence, it might be necessary to normalise the result by shifting it to the right (normal numbers), or shifting it to the left (denormal numbers).

As with the case of addition, we can then proceed to round the result to contain 23 bits in the mantissa, and renormalise if necessary. Since there are a constant number of add operations, the time complexity is equal to the sum of the time complexity of normal multiplication and addition. Both of them are $O(log(n))$ operations. The total time taken is thus $O(log(n))$.

7.6 Division of Floating Point Numbers

7.6.1 Simple Division

The major difference between integer and floating point division is that floating point division does not have a remainder. It only has a quotient. Let us try to divide A by B to obtain C.

We initialise the algorithm by setting the W register to contain the significand(P_A) of A. The E register is initialised as $E_A - E_B + bias$. This is done because in division, we subtract the exponents. Hence, in their biased representation we need to subtract E_B from E_A, and we need to add the value of the bias back. Computing the sign of the result is also trivial in this case.

We start out by dividing P_A by P_B. The rest of the steps are the same as that of multiplication (see

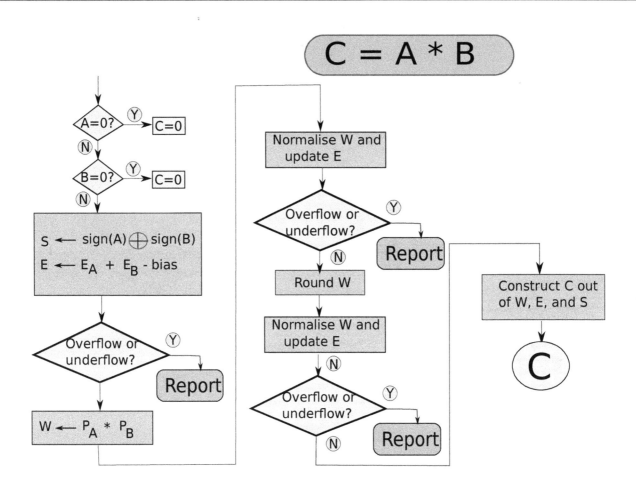

Figure 7.18: Flowchart for multiplying two floating point values

Section 7.5). We normalise the result, round it, and then renormalise if necessary.

The time complexity of this operation is the same as the time complexity of the restoring or non-restoring algorithms. It is equal to $O(nlog(n))$. It turns out that for the case of floating point division, we can do much better.

7.6.2 Goldschmidt Division

Let us try to simplify the process of division by dividing it into two stages. In the first stage, we compute the reciprocal of the divisor $(1/B)$. In the next stage, we multiply the obtained reciprocal with the dividend A. The product is equal to A/B. Floating point multiplication is an $O(log(n))$ time operation. Hence, let us focus on trying to compute the reciprocal of B.

Let us also ignore exponents in our discussion because, we just need to flip the sign of the exponent in the reciprocal. Let us only focus on the significand, P_B, and to keep matters simple, let us further assume that B is a normal floating point number. Thus, $1 \le P_B < 2$. We can represent $P_B = 1 + X(X < 1)$. We have:

$$\frac{1}{P_B} = \frac{1}{1+X} \quad (P_B = 1 + X, X < 1)$$
$$= \frac{1}{1+1-X'} \quad (X' = 1 - X, X' < 1)$$
$$= \frac{1}{2-X'} \qquad\qquad (7.26)$$
$$= \frac{1}{2} \times \frac{1}{1 - X'/2}$$
$$= \frac{1}{2} \times \frac{1}{1-Y} \quad (Y = X'/2, Y < 1/2)$$

Let us thus focus on evaluating $1/(1-Y)$. We have:

$$\frac{1}{1-Y} = \frac{1+Y}{1-Y^2}$$
$$= \frac{(1+Y)(1+Y^2)}{1-Y^4}$$
$$= \ldots \qquad\qquad (7.27)$$
$$= \frac{(1+Y)(1+Y^2)\ldots(1+Y^{16})}{1-Y^{32}}$$
$$\approx (1+Y)(1+Y^2)\ldots(1+Y^{16})$$

We need not proceed anymore. The reason for this is as follows. Since $Y < 1/2$, Y^n is less than $1/2^n$. The smallest mantissa that we can represent in the IEEE 32-bit floating point notation is $1/2^{23}$. Hence, there is no point in having terms that have an exponent greater than 23. Given the approximate nature of floating point mathematics, the product $(1+Y)(1+Y^2)\ldots(1+Y^{16})$ is as close to the real value of $1/(1-Y)$ as we can get.

Let us now consider the value $-(1+Y)(1+Y^2)\ldots(1+Y^{16})$. It has 5 add operations that can be done in parallel. To obtain $Y\ldots Y^{16}$, we can repeatedly multiply each term with itself. For example, to get Y^8, we can multiply Y^4 with Y^4 and so on. Thus, generating the powers of Y takes 4 multiply operations. Lastly, we need to multiply the terms in brackets $- (1+Y)$, $(1+Y^2)$,$(1+Y^4)$,$(1+Y^8)$, and $(1+Y^{16})$. This will required 4 multiplications. We thus require a total of 8 multiplications and 5 additions.

Let us now compute the time complexity. For an n-bit floating point number, let us assume that a fixed fraction of bits represent the mantissa. Thus, the number of bits required to represent the mantissa is $O(n)$. Consequently, the number of terms of the form $(1 + Y^{2k})$ that we need to consider is $O(log(n))$. The total number of additions, and multiplications for finding the reciprocal is also $O(log(n))$. Since each addition or multiplication takes $O(log(n))$ time, the time complexity of finding the reciprocal of B is equal to $O(log(n)^2)$. Since the rest of the operations such as adjusting the exponents and multiplying the reciprocal with A take $O(log(n))$ time, the total complexity is equal to $O(log(n)^2)$.

We observe that floating point division is asymptotically much faster than normal integer division. This is primarily because floating point mathematics is approximate, whereas integer mathematics is exact.

7.6.3 Division Using the Newton-Raphson Method

We detail another algorithm that also takes $O(log(n)^2)$ time. We assume that we are trying to divide A by B. Let us only consider normal numbers. Akin to Goldschmidt division, the key point of the algorithm is to find the reciprocal of the significand of B. Adjusting the exponents, computing the sign bit, and multiplying the reciprocal with A are fast operations ($O(log(n))$).

For readability, let us designate P_B as b ($1 \le b < 2$). We wish to compute $1/b$. Let us create a function: $f(x) = 1/x - b$. $f(x) = 0$ when $x = 1/b$. The problem of computing the reciprocal of b is thus the same as computing the root of f(x). Let us use the Newton Raphson method [Kreyszig, 2000].

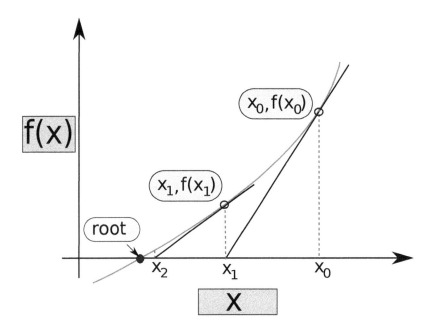

Figure 7.19: The Newton-Raphson method

The gist of this method is shown in Figure 7.19. We start with an arbitrary value of x such as x_0. We then locate the point on $f(x)$ that has x_0 as its x co-ordinate and then draw a tangent to $f(x)$ at $(x_0, f(x_0))$. Let the tangent intersect the x axis at x_1. We again follow the same procedure, and draw another tangent at $(x_1, f(x_1))$. This tangent will intersect the x axis at x_2. We continue this process. As we can observe in the figure, we gradually get closer to the root of f(x). We can terminate after a finite number of steps with an arbitrarily small error. Let us analyse this procedure mathematically.

The derivative of $f(x)$ at x_0 is $df(x)/dx = -1/x_0^2$. Let the equation of the tangent be $y = mx + c$. The slope is equal to $-1/x_0^2$. The equation is thus: $y = -x/x_0^2 + c$. Now, we know that at x_0, the value of y is $1/x_0 - b$. We thus have:

$$
\begin{aligned}
\frac{1}{x_0} - b &= -\frac{x_0}{x_0^2} + c \\
\Rightarrow \frac{1}{x_0} - b &= -\frac{1}{x_0} + c \\
\Rightarrow c &= \frac{2}{x_0} - b
\end{aligned}
\tag{7.28}
$$

The equation of the tangent is $y = -x/x_0^2 + 2/x_0 - b$. This line intersects the x axis when $y = 0$, and $x = x_1$. We thus have:

$$0 = -\frac{x_1}{x_0^2} + \frac{2}{x_0} - b$$
$$\Rightarrow x_1 = 2x_0 - bx_0^2 \tag{7.29}$$

Let us now define an error function of the form: $\mathcal{E}(x) = bx - 1$. Note that $\mathcal{E}(x)$ is 0, when x is equal to $1/b$. Let us compute the error: $\mathcal{E}(x_0)$ and $\mathcal{E}(x_1)$.

$$\mathcal{E}(x_0) = bx_0 - 1 \tag{7.30}$$

$$\begin{aligned}
\mathcal{E}(x_1) &= bx_1 - 1 \\
&= b\left(2x_0 - bx_0^2\right) - 1 \\
&= 2bx_0 - b^2 x_0^2 - 1 \\
&= -(bx_0 - 1)^2 \\
&= -\mathcal{E}(x_0)^2 \\
\mid \mathcal{E}(x_1) \mid &= \mid \mathcal{E}(x_0) \mid^2
\end{aligned} \tag{7.31}$$

Thus, the error gets squared every iteration, and if the starting value of the error is less than 1, then it will ultimately get arbitrarily close to 0. If we can place bounds on the error, then we can compute the number of iterations required.

We start out by observing that $1 \leq b < 2$ since we only consider normal floating point numbers. Let x_0 be $1/2$. The range of $bx_0 - 1$ is thus $[-1/2, 0]$. We can thus bound the error($\mathcal{E}(x_0)$) as $-1/2 \leq \mathcal{E}(x_0) < 0$. Therefore, we can say that $\mid \mathcal{E}(x_0) \mid \leq 1/2$. Let us now take a look at the maximum value of the error as a function of the iteration in Table 7.8.

Iteration	$\max(\mathcal{E}(x))$
0	$\frac{1}{2}$
1	$\frac{1}{2^2}$
2	$\frac{1}{2^4}$
3	$\frac{1}{2^8}$
4	$\frac{1}{2^{16}}$
5	$\frac{1}{2^{32}}$

Table 7.8: Maximum error vs iteration count

Since we only have 23 mantissa bits, we need not go beyond the fifth iteration. Thus, in this case also, the number of iterations is small, and bounded by a small constant. In every step we have a multiply and subtract operation. These are $O(log(n))$ time operations.

Let us compute the time complexity for n bit floating point numbers. Here, also we assume that a fixed fraction of bits are used to represent the mantissa. Like the case of Goldschmidt division, we need $O(log(n))$ iterations, and each iteration takes $O(log(n))$ time. Thus, the total complexity is $O(log(n)^2)$.

7.7 Summary and Further Reading

7.7.1 Summary

Summary 7

1. *Adding two 1 bit numbers (a and b) produces a sum bit(s) and a carry bit(c)*

    (a) $s = a \oplus b$

    (b) $c = a.b$

    (c) *We can add them using a circuit called a* half adder.

2. *Adding three 1 bit numbers (a, b, and c_{in}) also produces a sum bit(s) and a carry bit(c_{out})*

    (a) $s = a \oplus b \oplus c_{in}$

    (b) $c_{out} = a.b + a.c_{in} + b.c_{in}$

    (c) *We can add them using a circuit called a* full adder.

    (d)

3. *We can create a n bit adder known as a* ripple carry adder *by chaining together $n-1$ full adders, and a half adder.*

4. *We typically use the notion of asymptotic time complexity to express the time taken by an arithmetic unit such as an adder.*

    (a) $f(n) = O(g(n))$ *if* $|f(n)| \le c|g(n)|$ *for all* $n > n_0$, *where c is a positive constant.*

    (b) *For example, if the time taken by an adder is given by* $f(n) = 2n^3 + 1000n^2 + n$, *we can say that* $f(n) = O(n^3)$

5. *We discussed the following types of adders along with their time complexities:*

    (a) *Ripple carry adder –* $O(n)$

    (b) *Carry select adder –* $O(\sqrt{n})$

    (c) *Carry lookahead adder –* $O(log(n))$

6. *Multiplication can be done iteratively in* $O(n\,log(n))$ *time using an iterative multiplier. The algorithm is similar to the one we learned in elementary school.*

7. *We can speed it up by using a Booth multiplier that takes advantage of a continuous run of 1s in the multiplier.*

8. *The Wallace tree multiplier runs in* $O(log(n))$ *time. It uses a tree of* carry save adders *that express a sum of three numbers, as a sum of two numbers.*

9. *We introduced two algorithms for division:*

    (a) *Restoring algorithm*

    (b) *Non-restoring algorithm*

10. *Floating point addition and subtraction need not be considered separately. We can have one algorithm that takes care of the generic case.*

11. *Floating point addition requires us to perform the following steps:*

    (a) *Align the significand of the smaller number with the significand of the larger number.*

    (b) *If the signs are different then take a 2's complement of the smaller significand.*

    (c) *Add the significands.*

    (d) *Compute the sign bit of the result.*

    (e) *Normalise and round the result using one of four rounding modes.*

    (f) *Renormalise the result again if required.*

12. *We can follow the same steps for floating point multiplication and division. The only difference is that in this case the exponents get added or subtracted respectively.*

13. *Floating point division is fundamentally a faster operation than integer division because of the approximate nature of floating point mathematics. The basic operation is to compute the reciprocal of the denominator. It can be done in two ways:*

    (a) *Use the Newton-Raphson method to find the root of the equation $f(x) = 1/x - b$. The solution is the reciprocal of b.*

    (b) *Repeatedly multiply the numerator and denominator of a fraction derived from $1/b$ such that the denominator becomes 1 and the reciprocal is the numerator.*

7.7.2 Further Reading

For more details on the different algorithms for computer arithmetic, the reader can refer to classic texts such as the books by Israel Koren [Koren, 2001], Behrooz Parhami [Parhami, 2009], and Brent and Zimmermann [Brent and Zimmermann, 2010]. We have not covered the SRT division algorithm. It is used in a lot of modern processors. The reader can find good descriptions of this algorithm in the references. The reader is also advised to look at algorithms for multiplying large integers. The Karatsuba and Scönhage-Strassen algorithms are the most popular algorithms in this area. The area of approximate adders is gaining in prominence. These adders add two numbers by assuming certain properties such as a bound on the maximum number of positions a carry propagates. It is possible that they can occasionally make a mistake. Hence, they have additional circuitry to detect and correct errors. With high probability such adders can operate in $O(log(log(n)))$ time. Verma et. al. [Verma et al., 2008] describe one such scheme.

Exercises

Addition

Ex. 1 — Design a circuit to find the 1's complement of a number using half adders only.

Ex. 2 — Design a circuit to find the 2's complement of a number using half adders and logic gates.

Ex. 3 — Assume that the latency of a full adder is 2ns, and that of a half adder is 1ns. What is the latency of a 32-bit ripple carry adder?

* **Ex. 4** — Design a carry-select adder to add two n-bit numbers in $O(\sqrt{n})$ time, where the sizes of the blocks are $1, 2, ..., m$ respectively.

Ex. 5 — Explain the operation of a carry lookahead adder.

* **Ex. 6** — Suppose there is an architecture which supports numbers in base 3 instead of base 2. Design a Carry Lookahead Adder for this system. Assume that you have a simple full-adder which adds numbers in base 3.

* **Ex. 7** — Most of the time, a carry does not propagate till the end. In such cases, the correct output is available much before the worst case delay. Modify a ripple carry adder to consider such cases and set an output line to high as soon as the correct output is available.

* **Ex. 8** — Design a fast adder, which uses only the propagate function, and simple logic operations. It should NOT use the generate function. What is its time and space complexity?

Ex. 9 — Design a hardware structure to compute the sum of m, n bit numbers. Make it run as fast as possible. Show the design of the structure. Compute a tight bound on its asymptotic time complexity. [NOTE: Computing the time complexity is not as simple as it seems].

** **Ex. 10** — You are given a probabilistic adder, which adds two numbers and yields the output ensuring that each bit is correct with probability, a. In other words, a bit in the output may be wrong with probability, $(1 - a)$, and this event is independent of other bits being incorrect. How will you add two numbers using probabilistic adders ensuring that each output bit is correct with at least a probability of b, where $b > a$?

*** **Ex. 11** — How frequently does the carry propagate to the end for most numbers? Answer: Very infrequently. In most cases, the carry does not propagate beyond a couple of bits. Let us design an approximately correct adder. The insight is that a carry does not propagate by more than k positions most of the time. Formally, we have:
Assumption 1: While adding two numbers, the largest length of a chain of propagates is at most k.

Design an optimal adder in this case that has time complexity $O(\log k)$ assuming that Assumption 1 holds all the time. Now design a circuit to check if assumption 1 has ever been violated. Verma et. al. [Verma et al., 2008] proved that k is equal to $O(\log(n))$ with very high probability. Voila, we have an exactly correct adder, which runs most of the time in $O(\log(\log(n)))$ time.!!!

*** **Ex. 12** — Let us consider two n-bit binary numbers, A, and B. Further assume that the probability of a bit being equal to 1 is p in A, and q in B. Let us consider $(A + B)$ as one large chunk(block).

(a) What are the expected values of generate and propagate functions of this block as n tends to ∞?

(b) If $p = q = \frac{1}{2}$, what are the values of these functions?

(c) What can we infer from the answer to part (b) regarding the fundamental limits of binary addition?

Multiplication

Ex. 13 — Write a program in assembly language (any variant) to multiply two unsigned 32-bit numbers given in registers $r0$ and $r1$ and store the product in registers $r2$ (LSB) and $r3$ (MSB). Instead of using the multiply instruction, simulate the algorithm of the iterative multiplier.

Ex. 14 — Extend the solution to Exercise 13 for 32-bit signed integers.

* **Ex. 15** — Normally, in the Booth's algorithm, we consider the current bit, and the previous bit. Based on these two values, we decide whether we need to add or subtract a shifted version of the multiplicand. This is known as the radix-2 Booth's algorithm, because we are considering two bits at one time. There is a variation of Booth's algorithm, called radix-4 Booth's algorithm in which we consider 3 bits at a time. Is this algorithm faster than the original radix-2 Booth's algorithm? How will you implement this algorithm ?

* **Ex. 16** — Assume that in the sizes of the U and V registers are 32 bits in a 32-bit Booth multiplier. Is it possible to have an overflow? Answer the question with an example. [HINT: Can we have an overflow in the first iteration itself?]

* **Ex. 17** — Prove the correctness of the Booth multiplier in your own words.

Ex. 18 — Explain the design of the Wallace tree multiplier. What is its asymptotic time complexity?

** **Ex. 19** — Design a Wallace tree multiplier to multiply two signed 32-bit numbers, and save the result in a 32-bit register. How do we detect overflows in this case?

Division

Ex. 20 — Implementation of division using an assembly program.

   i) Write an assembly program for restoring division.

   ii) Write an assembly program for non-restoring division.

* **Ex. 21** — Design an $O(log(n)^k)$ time algorithm to find out if a number is divisible by 3. Try to minimise k.

* **Ex. 22** — Design an $O(log(n)^k)$ time algorithm to find out if a number is divisible by 5. Try to minimise k.

** **Ex. 23** — Design a fast algorithm to compute the remainder of the division of an unsigned number by a number of the form $(2^m + 1)$. What is its asymptotic time complexity?

** **Ex. 24** — Design a fast algorithm to compute the remainder of the division of an unsigned number by a number of the form $(2^m - 1)$. What is its asymptotic time complexity?

** **Ex. 25** — Design an $O(log(uv)^2)$ algorithm to find the greatest common divisor of two binary numbers u and v. [HINT: The gcd of two even numbers u and v is $2 * gcd(u/2, v/2)$]

Floating Point Arithmetic

Ex. 26 — Give the simplest possible algorithm to compare two 32-bit IEEE 754 floating point numbers. Do not consider $\pm\infty$, NAN, and (negative 0). Prove that your algorithm is correct. What is its time complexity ?

Ex. 27 — Design a circuit to compute $\lceil log_2(n) \rceil$. What is its asymptotic time complexity? Assume n is an integer. How can we use this circuit to convert n to a floating point number?

Ex. 28 — A and B, are saved in the computer as A' and B'. Neglecting any further truncation or roundoff errors, show that the relative error of the product is approximately the sum of the relative errors of the factors.

Ex. 29 — Explain floating point addition with a flowchart.

Ex. 30 — Explain floating point multiplication with a flowchart.

Ex. 31 — Can we use regular floating point division for dividing integers also? If not, then how can we modify the algorithm for performing integer division?

Ex. 32 — Describe in detail how the "round to nearest" rounding mode is implemented.

*** **Ex. 33** — We wish to compute the square root of a floating point number in hardware using the Newton-Raphson method. Outline the details of an algorithm, prove it, and compute its computational complexity. Follow the following sequence of steps.

    1.Find an appropriate objective function.

    2.Find the equation of the tangent, and the point at which it intersects the x-axis.

    3.Find an error function.

    4.Calculate an appropriate initial guess for x.

    5.Prove that the magnitude of the error is less than 1.

    6.Prove that the error decreases at least by a constant factor per iteration.

    7.Evaluate the asymptotic complexity of the algorithm.

Design Problems

Ex. 34 — Implement an adder and a multiplier in a hardware description language such as VHDL or Verilog.

Ex. 35 — Extend your design for implementing floating point addition and multiplication.

Ex. 36 — Read about the SRT division algorithm, comment on its computational complexity, and try to implement it in VHDL/Verilog.

8

Processor Design

Now, we are all set to design a basic processor for the *SimpleRisc* instruction set. We have assembled the arsenal to design a processor as well as making it efficient by our study of assembly languages, basic elements of a digital circuit (logical elements, registers, and memories), and computer arithmetic.

We shall start out by describing the basic elements of a processor in terms of fetching an instruction from memory, fetching its operands, executing the instruction, and writing the results back to memory or the register file. We shall see that along with the basic elements such as adders and multipliers, we need many more structures to efficiently route instructions between different units, and ensure fast execution. For modern processors, there are two primary design styles – hardwired, and microprogrammed. In the *hardwired* design style, we complicate a simple processor by adding more elaborate structures to process instructions. There is a net increase in complexity. In the microprogrammed design style, we have a very simple processor that controls a more complicated processor. The simple processor executes basic instructions known as microinstructions for each program instruction, and uses these microinstructions to control the operation of the complicated processor. Even though the hardwired design style is much more common today, the microprogrammed design style is still used in many embedded processors. Secondly, some aspects of microprogramming have crept into today's complex processors.

8.1 Design of a Basic Processor

Figure 8.1: Car Assembly Line

289

8.1.1 Overview

The design of a processor is very similar to that of a car assembly line (see Figure 8.1). A car assembly line first casts raw metal into the chassis of a car. Then the engine is built, and put on the chassis. Then it is time to connect the wheels, the dashboard, and the body of the car. The final operation is to paint the car, and test it for manufacturing defects. The assembly line represents a long chain of actions, where one station performs a certain operation, and passes on a half built car to the next station. Each station also uses a pool of raw materials to augment the half built car such as metal, paint, or accessories.

We can think of a processor on the same lines as a car assembly line. In the place of a car, we have an instruction. The instruction goes through various stages of processing. The same way that raw metal is transformed to a beautiful finished product in a car factory, a processor acts upon a sequence of bits to do complex arithmetic and logical computations.

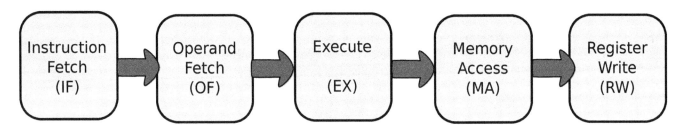

Figure 8.2: Five stages of instruction processing

We can broadly divide the operation of a processor into five stages as shown in Figure 8.2. The first step is to fetch the instruction from memory. The underlying organisation of the machine does not matter. The machine can be a Von Neumann machine (shared instruction and data memory), or a Harvard machine (dedicated instruction memory). The fetch stage has logical elements to compute the address of the next instruction. If the current instruction, is not a branch, then we need to add the size of the current instruction (4 bytes) to the address stored in the PC. However, if the current instruction is a branch, then the address of the next instruction depends on the outcome and target of the branch. This information is obtained from other units in the processor.

The next stage is to "decode" the instruction and fetch its operands from registers. *SimpleRisc* defines 21 instructions, and the processing required for different instruction types is very different. For example, load-store instructions use a dedicated memory unit, whereas arithmetic instructions do not. To decode an instruction, processors have dedicated logic circuits that generate signals based on fields in the instruction. These signals are then used by other modules to properly process the instruction. The *SimpleRisc* format is very simple. Hence, decoding the instruction is very easy. However, commercial processors such as Intel processors have very elaborate decode units. Decoding the x86 instruction set is very complicated. Irrespective of the complexity of decoding, the process of decoding typically contains the following steps – extracting the values of the operands, calculating the embedded immediate values and extending them to 32 or 64 bits, and generating additional information regarding the processing of the instruction. The process of generating more information regarding an instruction involves generating processor specific signals. For example, we can generate signals of the form "enable memory unit" for load/store instructions. For a store instruction, we can generate a signal to disable register write functionality.

In our *SimpleRisc* processor, we need to extract the immediate, and branch offset values embedded in the instruction. Subsequently, we need to read the values of the source registers. There is a dedicated structure in the processor called the register file that contains all the 16 *SimpleRisc* registers. For a read operation, it takes the number of the register as input, and produces the contents of the register as its output. In this step, we read the register file, and buffer the values of register operands in latches.

The next stage executes arithmetic and logical operations. It contains a arithmetic and logical unit(ALU) that is capable of performing all arithmetic and logical operations. The ALU is also required to compute the effective address of load-store operations. Typically this part of the processor computes the outcome of branches also.

Definition 57

The ALU (arithmetic logic unit) contains elements for performing arithmetic and logical computations on data values. The ALU typically contains an adder, multiplier, divider, and has units to compute logical bitwise operations.

The next stage contains the memory unit for processing load-store instructions. This unit interfaces with the memory system, and co-ordinates the process of loading and storing values from memory. We shall see in Chapter 10 that the memory system in a typical processor is fairly complex. Some of this complexity is implemented in this part of the processor. The last step in processing an instruction is to write the values computed by the ALU or loaded values obtained from the memory unit to the register file.

8.2 Units in a Processor

8.2.1 Instruction Fetch – Fetch Unit

We start out by fetching an instruction from main memory. Recall that a *SimpleRisc* instruction is encoded as a sequence of 32 bits or 4 bytes. Hence, to fetch an instruction we need the starting address of the instruction. Let us store the starting address of the instruction in a register called the *program counter (pc)*.

Important Point 12

Let us make an important distinction here between the terms PC and pc. PC is an acronym for "program counter". In comparison, pc is a register in our pipeline, and will only be used to refer to the register, and its contents. However, PC is a general concept and will be used in the place of the term, "program counter", for the sake of brevity.

Secondly, we need a mechanism to update the PC to point to the next instruction. If the instruction is not a branch then the PC needs to point to the next instruction, whose starting address is equal to the value of the old PC plus 4 (REASON: each instruction is 4 bytes long). If the instruction is a branch, and it is taken, then the new value of the PC needs to be equal to the address of the branch target. Otherwise, the address of the next instruction is equal to the default value (current PC + 4).

Figure 8.3 shows an implementation of the circuit for the fetch unit. There are two basic operations that need to be performed in a cycle – (1) computation of the next PC, and (2) fetching the instruction.

The PC of the next instruction can come from two sources in *SimpleRisc* as shown in Figure 8.3. We can either use an adder and increment the current PC by 4, or we can get the address from another unit that calculates the branch target(*branchPC*), and the fact that the branch is taken. We can use a multiplexer to choose between these two inputs. Once, the correct input is chosen, it needs to be saved in the *pc* register and sent to the memory system for fetching the instruction. We can either use a combined memory for both

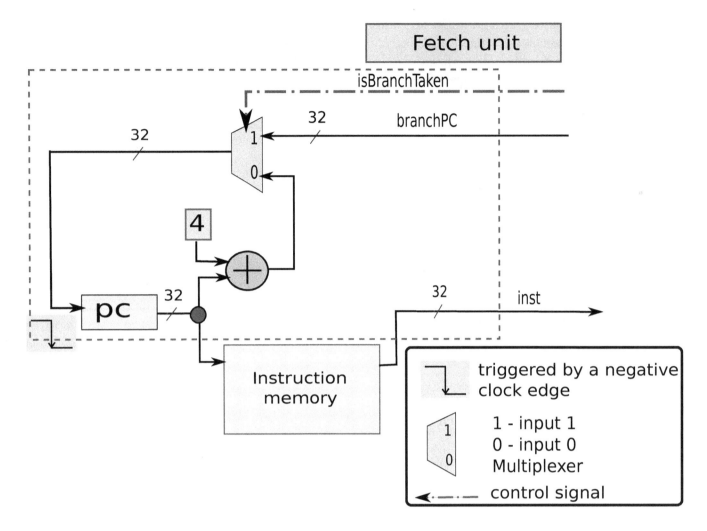

Figure 8.3: The Fetch Unit

instruction and data (Von Neumann Machine) or use a separate instruction memory (Harvard Machine). The latter option is more common. The instruction memory is typically implemented as an array of SRAM cells. The fetch unit provides the address in the SRAM array, and then uses the 32 bits stored at the specified starting address as the contents of the instruction.

Before proceeding to decode the instruction, let us make an important observation. Let us list down the external inputs of the fetch unit. They consist of the (1) branch target($branchPC$), (2) instruction contents, (3) and the signal to control the multiplexer ($isBranchTaken$). The branch target is typically provided by the decode unit, or the instruction execution unit. The instruction contents are obtained from the instruction memory. Let us now consider the case of the signal to control the multiplexer – $isBranchTaken$. The conditions for setting $isBranchTaken$ are shown in Table 8.1.

In our processor, a dedicated branch unit generates the $isBranchTaken$ signal. It first analyses the instruction. If the instruction is a non-branch instruction, or a $call/ret/b$ instruction, then the value of $isBranchTaken$ can be decided according to Table 8.1. However, if the instruction is a conditional branch instruction (beq/bgt), then it is necessary to analyse the flags register. Recall that the flags register contains the results of the last compare instruction (also see Section 3.3.2). We shall describe a detailed circuit for the branch unit in Section 8.2.4.

Instruction	Value of $isBranchTaken$
non-branch instruction	0
call	1
ret	1
b	1
beq	branch taken – 1 branch not taken – 0
bgt	branch taken – 1 branch not taken – 0

Table 8.1:   Conditions for setting the $isBranchTaken$ signal

Let us refer to this stage of instruction processing as the *IF* (instruction fetch) stage. Before, we proceed to other stages, let us slightly digress here, and discuss two important concepts – *data path*, and *control path*.

8.2.2   Data Path and Control Path

We need to make a fundamental observation here. There are two kinds of elements in a circuit. The first type of elements are registers, memories, arithmetic, and logic circuits to process data values. The second type of elements are control units that decide the direction of the flow of data. The *control unit* in a processor typically generates signals to control all the multiplexers. These are called *control signals* primarily because their role is to control the flow of information.

We can thus conceptually think of a processor as consisting of two distinct subsystems. The first is known as the *data path* that contains all the elements to store and process information. For example the data memory, instruction memory, register file, and the ALU (arithmetic logic unit), are a part of the data path. The memories and register file store information, whereas the ALU processes information. For example, it adds two numbers, and produces the sum as the result, or it can compute a logical function of two numbers.

In comparison, we have a control path that directs the proper flow of information by generating signals. We saw one example in Section 8.2.1, where the control path generated a signal to direct a multiplexer to choose between the branch target and the default next PC. The multiplexer in this case was controlled by a signal *isBranchTaken*.

We can think of the control path and data path as two distinct elements of a circuit much like the traffic network of a city. The roads and the traffic lights are similar to the data path, where instead of instructions, cars flow. The circuits to control traffic lights constitute the control path. The control path decides the time of the transitions of lights. In modern smart cities, the process of controlling all the traffic lights in a city is typically integrated. If it is possible to intelligently control traffic to route cars around traffic jams, and accident sites. Similarly, a processor's control unit is fairly intelligent. Its job is to execute instructions as quickly as possible. In this book, we shall study a basic version of a control unit. However, the control unit will get very complicated in an advanced course on computer architecture.

Definition 58

Data Path *The data path consists of all the elements in a processor that are dedicated to storing, retrieving, and processing data such as register files, memories, and ALUs.*

Control Path *The control path primarily contains the control unit, whose role is to generate appropriate signals to control the movement of instructions, and data in the data path.*

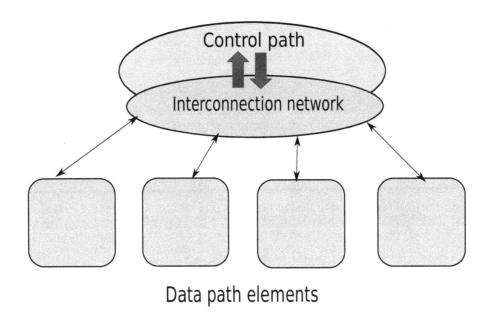

Figure 8.4: Relationship between the data path and control path

A conceptual diagram showing the relationship between the control path and the data path is shown in Figure 8.4. After this short digression, let us now move on to discuss the next stage of instruction processing.

8.2.3 Operand Fetch Unit

SimpleRisc Instruction Format

Let us quickly recapitulate our knowledge about the *SimpleRisc* instruction format. The list of *SimpleRisc* instructions is shown in Table 8.2 along with their opcodes, and instruction format.

SimpleRisc is a simple and regular instruction set. It has three classes of instruction formats as shown in Table 8.3. The instruction formats are *branch*, *register*, and *immediate*. The *add*, *sub*, *mul*, *div*, *mod*, *and*, *or*, *cmp*, *not*, *lsl*, *lsr*, *asr*, and *mov* instructions can have either the *register* or the *immediate* format. This is decided by the I bit (27th bit) in the instruction. The *cmp* instruction does not have a destination register. The *mov* and *not* instructions have only one source operand. For further details, the reader can refer to Table 8.2, or Section 3.3.

The Operand Fetch Unit

The operand fetch unit has two important functions – (1) calculate the values of the immediate operand and the branch target by unpacking the offset embedded in the instruction, and (2) read the source registers.

Inst.	Code	Format	Inst.	Code	Format
add	00000	add rd, rs1, (rs2/imm)	lsl	01010	lsl rd, rs1, (rs2/imm)
sub	00001	sub rd, rs1, (rs2/imm)	lsr	01011	lsr rd, rs1, (rs2/imm)
mul	00010	mul rd, rs1, (rs2/imm)	asr	01100	asr rd, rs1, (rs2/imm)
div	00011	div rd, rs1, (rs2/imm)	nop	01101	nop
mod	00100	mod rd, rs1, (rs2/imm)	ld	01110	ld rd, imm[rs1]
cmp	00101	cmp rs1, (rs2/imm)	st	01111	st rd, imm[rs1]
and	00110	and rd, rs1, (rs2/imm)	beq	10000	beq offset
or	00111	or rd, rs1, (rs2/imm)	bgt	10001	bgt offset
not	01000	not rd, (rs2/imm)	b	10010	b offset
mov	01001	mov rd, (rs2/imm)	call	10011	call offset
			ret	10100	ret

Table 8.2: List of instruction opcodes

Format	Definition				
branch	*op* (28-32)	*offset* (1-27)			
register	*op* (28-32)	*I* (27)	*rd* (23-26)	*rs1* (19-22)	*rs2* (15-18)
immediate	*op* (28-32)	*I* (27)	*rd* (23-26)	*rs1* (19-22)	*imm* (1-18)
op → opcode, *offset* → branch offset, *I* → immediate bit, *rd* → destination register					
rs1 → source register 1, *rs2* → source register 2, *imm* → immediate operand					

Table 8.3: Summary of instruction formats

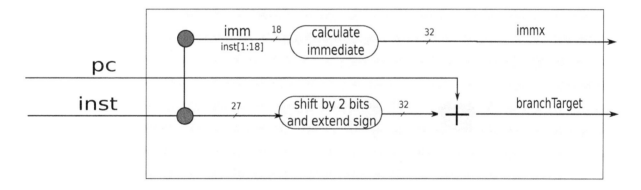

Figure 8.5: Calculation of the immediate operand and the branch target

Computation of the Immediate Operand and the Branch Target

Figure 8.5 shows the circuit for calculating the immediate operand, and the branch target. To calculate the immediate operand, we need to first extract the *imm* field (bits 1-18) from the instruction. Subsequently, we extract the lower 16 bits, and create a 32-bit constant in accordance with the modifiers (bit 17, and 18). When no modifier is specified, we extend the sign of the 16-bit number to make it a 32-bit number. For the *u* modifier, we fill the top 16 bits with 0s, and for the *h* modifier, we shift the 16-bit number, 16 positions to the left. The newly constructed 32-bit value is termed as *immx*.

In a similar manner, we can compute the signal, *branchTarget* (branch target for all types of branches excluding *ret*). We need to first extract the 27 bit offset (bits 1 to 27) from the instruction. Note that these 27 bits represent the offset in terms of memory words as described in Section 3.3.14. Thus, we need to shift the offset to the left by 2 bits to make it a 29 bit number, and then extend its sign to make it a 32-bit number. Since we use PC-relative addressing in *SimpleRisc* , to obtain the branch target we need to add the shifted offset to the PC. The branch target can either be derived from the instruction (*branchTarget* signal), as we have just described, or in the case of a *ret* instruction, the branch target is the contents of the *ra* register. In this case, the *ra* register comes from the register file. We choose between both the values in the next stage, and compute *branchPC*.

There is a need to make an important observation here. We are calculating *branchTarget* and *immx* for all instructions. However, any instruction in the *SimpleRisc* format will only require at the most one of these fields (*branchTarget* or *immx*). The other field will have junk values. Nevertheless, it does not hurt to pre-compute both the values in the interest of speed. It is necessary to ensure that the correct value is used in the later stages of processing.

Reading the Registers

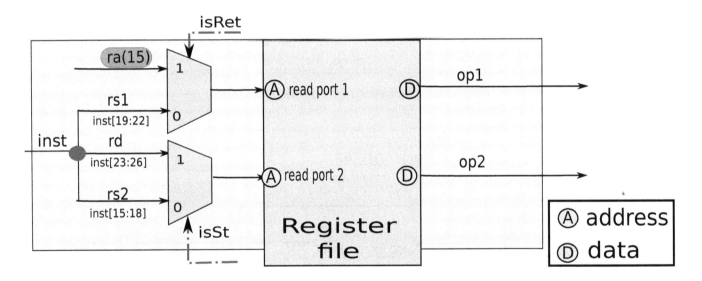

Figure 8.6: Reading the Source Registers

In parallel, we can read the values of the source registers as shown. Here, also we follow the same strategy. We read more than what we require. Critics might argue that this approach wastes power. However, there is a reason for doing so. Extra circuitry is required to decide if a given operand is actually required. This has an adverse impact in terms of area, and time. The operand fetch unit becomes slower. Hence, we prioritise the case of simplicity, and read all the operands that might be required.

The circuit for reading the values of source registers is shown in Figure 8.6. The register file has 16 registers, two read ports, and one write port (not shown in the figure). A *port* is a point of connection (an interface) in a hardware structure, and is used for the purpose of either entering inputs, or reading outputs. We can have a read port (exclusively for reading data), a write port (exclusively for writing data), and a read-write port (can be used for both reading and writing).

Definition 59

A port *is a point of connection in a hardware structure, and is used for the purpose of either entering inputs, or reading outputs. We can have a read port (exclusively for reading data), a write port (exclusively for writing data), and a read-write port (can be used for both reading and writing).*

For the first register operand, $op1$, we have two choices. For ALU, and memory instructions, we need to read the first source register, $rs1$ (bits 19 to 22). For the ret instruction, we need to read the value of the return address register, ra. To choose between the contents of the field, $rs1$, in the instruction and ra, we use a multiplexer. The multiplexer is controlled by a signal, $isRet$. If $isRet$ (is return) is equal to 1, then we choose ra, otherwise we choose $rs1$. This value is an input to the register file's first read port. We term the output of the first read port as $op1$ (operand 1).

We need to add a similar multiplexer for the second read port of the register file too. For all the instructions other than the store instruction, the second source register is specified by the $rs2$ (bits 15 to 18) field in the instruction. However, the store instruction is an exception. It contains a source register in rd (bits 23 to 26). Recall that we had to make this bitter choice at the cost of introducing a new instruction format. Since we have a very consistent instruction format (see Table 8.3) the process of decoding is very simple. To extract different fields of the instruction ($rs1$, $rs2$, opcode, and imm) we do not need additional logic elements. We need to save each bit of the instruction in a latch, and then route the wires appropriately.

Coming back to our original problem of choosing the second register operand, we observe that we need to choose the right source register – $rs2$ or rd. The corresponding multiplexer is controlled by the $isSt$ (is store) signal. We can quickly find out if the instruction is a store by using a set of logic gates to verify if the opcode is equal to 01111. The result of the comparison is used to set the $isSt$ signal. The corresponding output of the register file is termed as $op2$ (operand 2).

Lastly, it is necessary to send the opcode (5 bits), and the immediate bit (1 bit) to the control unit such that it can generate all the control signals. The complete circuit for the operand fetch unit is shown in Figure 8.7. $op1$, $op2$, $branchTarget$, and $immx$ are passed to the execute unit.

8.2.4 Execute Unit

Let us now look at executing an instruction. Let us start out by dividing instructions into two types – branch and non-branch. Branch instructions are handled by a dedicated branch unit that computes the outcome, and final target of the branch. Non branch instructions are handled by an ALU (arithmetic logic unit).

Branch Unit

The circuit for the branch unit is shown in Figure 8.8.

First, we use a multiplexer to choose between the value of the return address ($op1$), and the $branchTarget$ embedded in the instruction. The $isRet$ signal controls the multiplexer. If it is equal to 1, we choose $op1$; otherwise, we choose $branchTarget$. The output of the multiplexer, $branchPC$, is sent to the fetch unit.

Now, let us consider the circuit to compute the branch outcome. As an example, let us consider the case of the beq instruction. Recall that the *SimpleRisc* instruction set requires a *flags* register that contains the result of the last compare (cmp) instruction. It has two bits – E and GT. If the last compare instruction led to an equality, then the E bit is set, and if the first operand was greater than the second operand then the GT bit is set. For the beq instruction, the control unit sets the signal $isBeq$ to 1. We need to compute a logical AND of this signal and the value of the E bit in the *flags* register. If both are 1, then the branch is taken. Similarly, we need an AND gate to compute the outcome of the bgt instruction, as shown in Figure 8.8. The

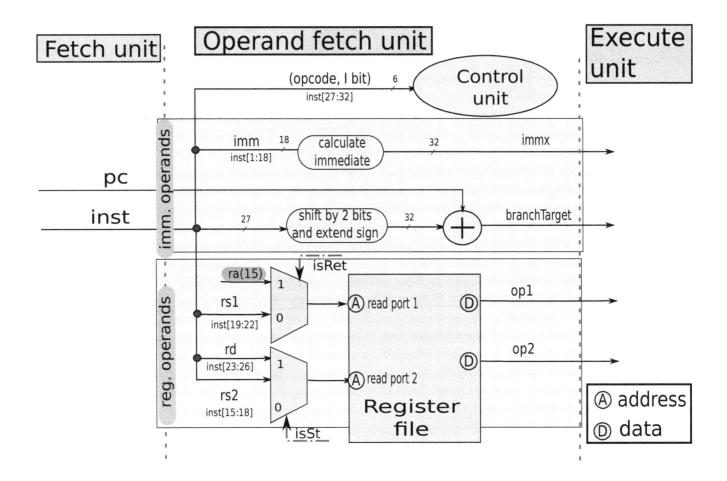

Figure 8.7:   Operand Fetch Stage

branch might also be unconditional (*call/ret/b*). In this case, the control unit sets the signal *isUBranch* to 1. If any of the above conditions is true, then the branch is taken. We subsequently use an OR gate that computes the outcome of the branch, and sets the *isBranchTaken* signal. This signal is used by the fetch unit to control the multiplexer that generates the next PC.

ALU

Figure 8.9 shows the part of the execution unit that contains the ALU. The first operand (A) of the ALU is always *op1* (obtained from the operand fetch unit). However, the second operand (B) can either be a register or the sign extended immediate. This is decided by the *isImmediate* signal generated by the control unit. The *isImmediate* signal is equal to the value of the immediate bit in the instruction. If it is 1, then the multiplexer in Figure 8.9 chooses *immx* as the operand. If it is 0, then *op2* is chosen as the operand. The ALU takes as input a set of signals known collectively as *aluSignals*. They are generated by the control unit, and specify the type of ALU operation. The result of the ALU is termed as *aluResult*.

Figure 8.10 shows the design of the ALU. The ALU contains a set of modules. Each module computes a separate arithmetic or logical function such as addition or division. Secondly, each module has a dedicated signal that enables or disables it. For example, there is no reason to enable the divider when we want to perform simple addition. There are several ways that we can enable or disable an unit. The simplest method is to use a transmission gate for every input bit. A transmission gate is shown in Figure 8.11. If the signal(S)

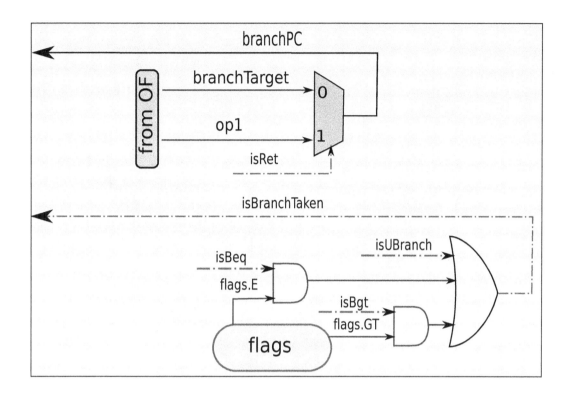

Figure 8.8: Branch Unit

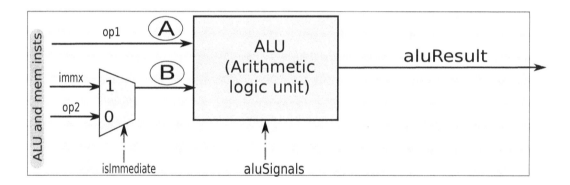

Figure 8.9: ALU

is turned on, then the output reflects the value of the input. Otherwise, it maintains its previous value. Thus, if the enabling signal is off, then the module does not see the new inputs. It thus does not dissipate any power, and is effectively disabled.

Let us consider each of the modules in the ALU one after another. The most commonly used module is the adder. It is used by *add*, *sub*, and *cmp* instructions, as well as by load and store instructions to compute the memory address. It takes A and B as inputs. Here, A and B are the values of the source operands. If the *isAdd* signal is turned on, then the adder adds the operands. Likewise, if the *isSub* signal is turned on, then the adder adds the 2's complement of B with A. In effect, it subtracts B from A. If the *isCmp* flag is turned on, then the adder unit subtracts B from A and sets the value of the *flags* register. If the

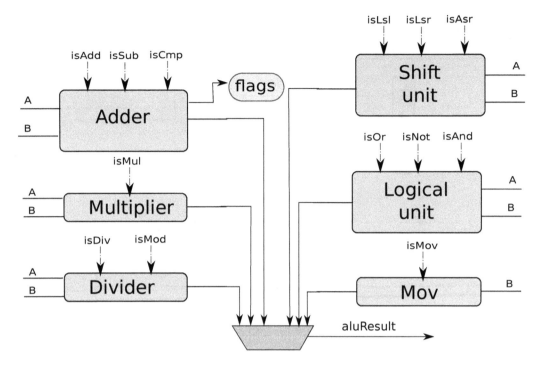

Figure 8.10: ALU

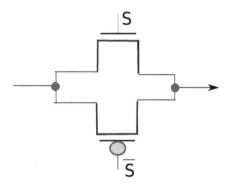

Figure 8.11: A transmission gate

output is 0, then it sets the E bit. If the output is positive, it sets the GT bit. If none of these signals ($isAdd/isSub/isCmp$) is true, then the adder is disabled.

The multiplier and divider function in a similar manner. The multiplier is enabled by the $isMul$ signal, and the divider is enabled by the $isDiv$ or $isMod$ signal. If the $isDiv$ signal is true, then the result is the quotient of the division, whereas, if the $isMod$ signal is true, the result is the remainder of the division.

The shift unit left shifts, or right shifts A, by B positions. It takes three signals – $isLsl$, $isLsr$, and $isAsr$. The logical unit consists of a set of AND, OR, and NOT gates. They are enabled by the signals $isOr$, $isAnd$, and $isNot$ respectively. The Mov unit is slightly special in the sense that it is the simplest. If the $isMov$ signal is true, then the output is equal to B. Otherwise, it is disabled.

To summarise, we show the full design of the execution unit (branch unit and ALU) in Figure 8.12. To set the output ($aluResult$), we need a multiplexer that can choose the right output out of all the modules in the ALU. We do not show this multiplexer in Figure 8.12. We leave the detailed design of the ALU circuit along with the transmission gates and output multiplexer as an exercise for the reader.

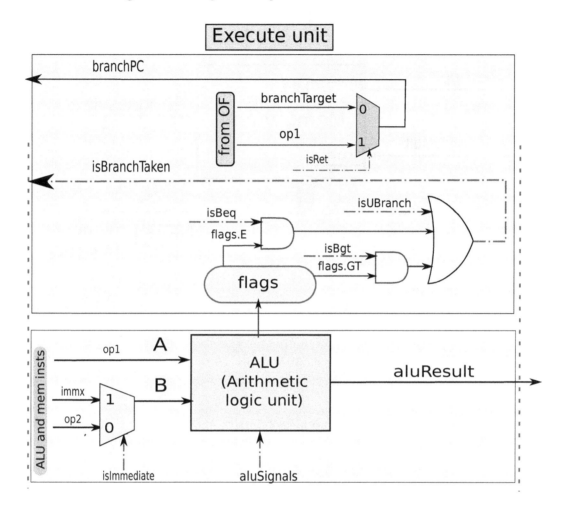

Figure 8.12: Execute Unit (Branch and ALU unit)

8.2.5 Memory Access Unit

Figure 8.13 shows the memory access unit. It has two inputs – data and address. The address is calculated by the ALU. It is equal to the result of the ALU (*aluResult*). Both the load and store instructions use this address. The address is saved in a register traditionally known as MAR (memory address register).

Let us now consider the case of a load instruction. In *SimpleRisc* , the format of the load instruction is *ld rd, imm[rs1]*. The memory address is equal to the immediate value plus the contents of register, *rs1*. This is the value of *aluResult*. The memory unit does not require any other inputs. It can proceed to fetch the value of the memory address from the data memory. The memory unit reads 4 bytes starting from the memory address. The result (*ldResult*) is now ready to be written to the destination register.

The format of the store instruction is : *st rd, imm[rs1]*. The address is computed using the ALU similar to the way the address is calculated for the load instruction. For the store instruction, *rd* is a source register. The contents of register *rd* (*reg[rd]*) are read by the operand fetch unit (see Section 8.2.3). This value is termed as *op2* in Figure 8.6. *op2* contains the contents of register *rd*, and represents the data of the store

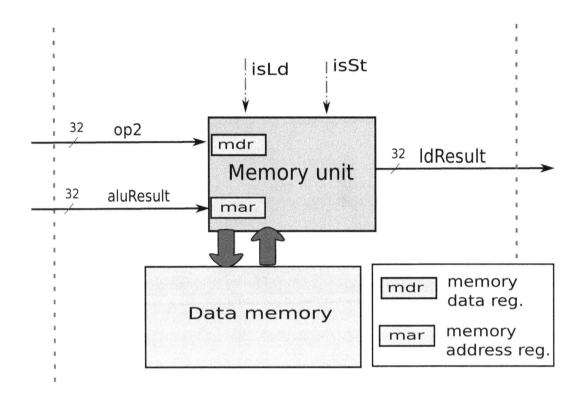

Figure 8.13: Memory Unit

instruction. The memory unit writes the value of *op2* to the *MDR* (memory data register) register. In parallel, it proceeds to write the data to data memory. The store instruction does not have an output.

Note that here also we follow the same naming scheme as we had followed for PC and *pc*. MAR is an acronym for (memory address register), whereas *mar* refers specifically to the *mar* register in the data path.

Now, the memory unit takes two control signals as inputs – *isLd*, and *isSt*. For obvious reasons, at most one of these signals can be true at any one time. If none of these signals is true, then the instruction is not a memory instruction, and the memory unit is disabled.

A subtle point needs to be discussed here. *MAR* and *MDR* are traditionally referred to as registers. However, they are not conventional edge triggered registers. They are used like temporary buffers that buffer the address and the store values till the memory request completes.

8.2.6 Register Writeback Unit

The last step of instruction processing is to write the computed values back to the register file. This value can be the output of a load or ALU instruction, or the return address written by the *call* instruction. This process is known as writeback, or register writeback. We refer to this unit as the *register writeback(RW) unit*. Its circuit diagram is shown in Figure 8.14.

We first need to choose the right source operand. We have three choices – *aluResult*, *ldResult*, or the return address. The return address is equal to the PC of the *call* instruction plus 4. We use a multiplexer to choose between the three input values. We use two control signals to control the multiplexer. The first control signal is *isLd* (is load), and the second control signal is *isCall*. We choose *aluResult*, when both the control signals are 0. We choose *ldResult*, when *isLd* = 1, and *isCall* = 0, and lastly, we choose $PC + 4$, when *isCall* is equal to 1. The output of the multiplexer, *result*, needs to be written to the register file.

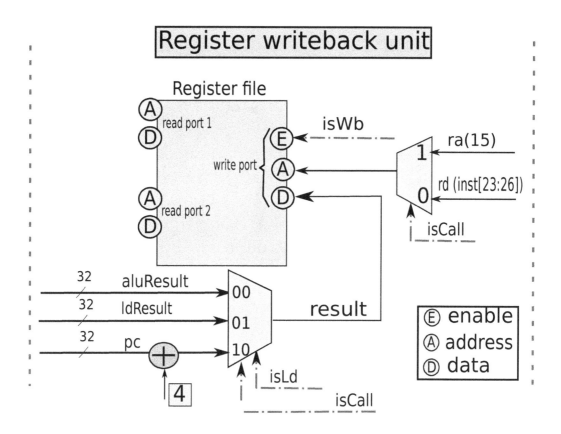

Figure 8.14: Register Writeback Unit

Note that we had shown a partial view of the register file when we discussed the operand fetch unit in Section 8.2.3. We showed only two read ports. However, the register file has also a write port that is used to write data. The write port has three inputs – address, data, and enable bit. The address is either the number of the destination register rd or the id of the return address register (15). The correct address needs to be chosen with a multiplexer. The destination register is specified by bits 23 to 26 of the instruction. The second multiplexer chooses the data that needs to be written. The output of this multiplexer is sent to the data pins of the write port. Lastly, we need an enable signal ($isWb$) that specifies if we need to write the value of a register. For example, the store, nop, and compare instructions do not need a register writeback. Hence, for these instructions, the value of $isWb$ is false. It is also false for branch (excluding $call$) instructions. $isWb$ is true for the rest of the ALU instructions, mov and ld instructions.

8.2.7 The Data Path

Let us now form the whole by joining all the parts. We have up till now divided a processor into five basic units: instruction fetch unit (IF), operand fetch unit (OF), execution unit (EX), memory access unit (MA), and register writeback unit (RW). It is time to combine all the parts and look at the unified picture. Figure 8.15 shows the result of all our hard work. We have omitted detailed circuits, and just focused on the flow of data and control signals.

Every clock cycle, the processor fetches an instruction from a new PC, fetches the operands, executes the instruction, and writes the results back to the data memory and register file. There are two memory elements in this circuit namely the data and instruction memory. They can possibly refer to the same physical memory structure, or refer to different structures. We shall have ample opportunities to discuss the different schemes

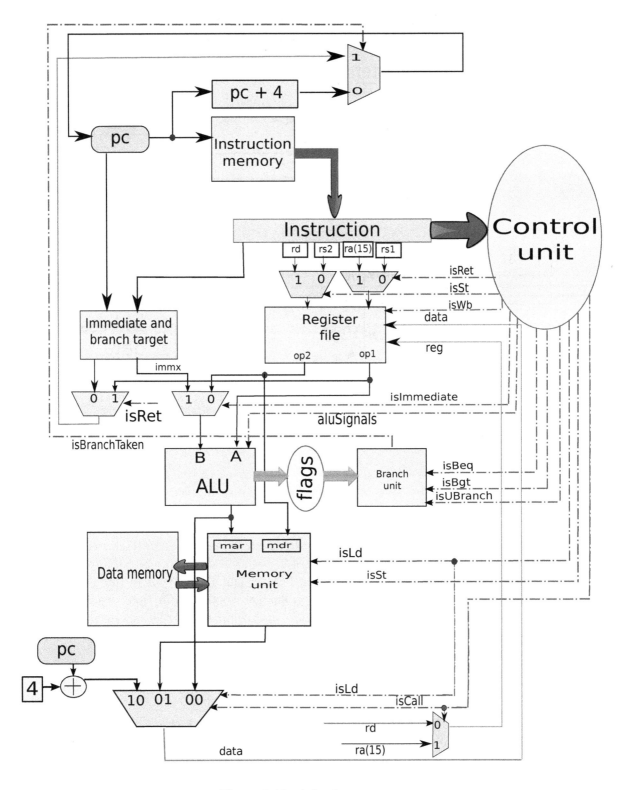

Figure 8.15: A basic processor

in Chapter 10.

The main state elements of the processor are the following registers: *pc*, and *flags* registers, and the register file. We can optionally add *mar* and *mdr* registers with the memory unit. Note that they are strictly not required in our simple version of the processor. However, they shall be required in advanced designs where a memory request can possibly take multiple cycles. We shall also require them in our microprogrammed processor. Hence, it is a good idea to keep them in our basic design.

Note that most of the sets of wires in the data path have a top-down orientation i.e., the source is above the destination in Figure 8.15. There are two notable exceptions. The source of these wires is below the destination in Figure 8.15. The first such exception is the set of wires that carry the branch target/outcome information from the execute unit to the fetch unit. The second exception is the set of wires that carry the data to be written from the register writeback unit to the register file.

We need to lastly note that the magic of a processor lies in the interplay of the data path and the control path. The control signals give a form to the data path. The unique values of the set of all the control signals determine the nature of instructions. It is possible to change the behavior of instructions, or in fact define new instructions by just changing the control unit. Let us take a deeper look at the control unit.

8.3   The Control Unit

Table 8.4 shows the list of control signals that need to be generated by the control unit along with their associated conditions. The only control signal that is not generated by the control unit is *isBranchTaken*. This is generated by the branch unit that is a part of the execute unit. However, the rest of the 22 signals need to be generated by the control unit. Recall that the inputs to the control unit are the opcode of the instruction, and the value of the *immediate* bit.

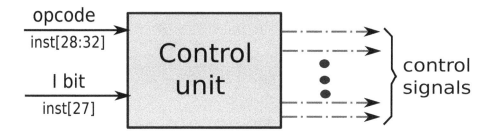

Figure 8.16: Abstraction of a hardwired control unit

The hardwired control unit for our simple processor can be thought of as a black box that takes 6 bits as input (5 opcode bits, and 1 immediate bit), and produces 22 control signals as its output. This is shown in Figure 8.16.

Internally, there are a set of logic gates that act on the input bits to produce each output bit. For example, to set the *isAdd* signal, we need to check if the opcode is equal to 00000. Let us number the five bits of the opcode as op_1, op_2, op_3, op_4 and op_5. Here op_1 is the LSB, and op_5 is the MSB. Let us refer to the immediate bit as I.

Table 8.5 shows the conditions for setting all the control signals. We leave the implementation of Table 8.5 using logic gates as an exercise to the reader. Note that it will take the maximum amount of time to compute the value of *isWb*. Nevertheless, this circuit is extremely simple as compared to a multiplier or a carry lookahead adder. Hence, the total execution time of the control unit is expected to be small as compared to the execute unit.

Serial No.	Signal	Condition
1	*isSt*	Instruction: *st*
2	*isLd*	Instruction: *ld*
3	*isBeq*	Instruction: *beq*
4	*isBgt*	Instruction: *bgt*
5	*isRet*	Instruction: *ret*
6	*isImmediate*	*I* bit set to 1
7	*isWb*	Instructions: *add, sub, mul, div, mod, and, or, not, mov, ld, lsl, lsr, asr, call*
8	*isUBranch*	Instructions: *b, call, ret*
9	*isCall*	Instructions: *call*
	aluSignals	
10	*isAdd*	Instructions: *add, ld, st*
11	*isSub*	Instruction: *sub*
12	*isCmp*	Instruction: *cmp*
13	*isMul*	Instruction: *mul*
14	*isDiv*	Instruction: *div*
15	*isMod*	Instruction: *mod*
16	*isLsl*	Instruction: *lsl*
17	*isLsr*	Instruction: *lsr*
18	*isAsr*	Instruction: *asr*
19	*isOr*	Instruction: *or*
20	*isAnd*	Instruction: *and*
21	*isNot*	Instruction: *not*
22	*isMov*	Instruction: *mov*

Table 8.4: List of control signals

The hardwired control unit is thus fast and efficient. This is the reason why most commercial processors today use a hardwired control unit. However, hardwired control units are not very flexible. For example, it is not possible to change the behavior of an instruction, or even introduce a new instruction, after the processor has been shipped. Sometimes we need to change the way an instruction is executed if there are bugs in functional units. For example, if the multiplier has a design defect, then it is theoretically possible to run the Booth's multiplication algorithm with the adder, and shift units. We will however, need a very elaborate control unit to dynamically reconfigure the way instructions are executed.

There are other more practical reasons for favoring a flexible control unit. Some instruction sets such as x86 have *rep* instructions that repeat an instruction a given number of times. They also have complicated string instructions that operate on large pieces of data. Supporting such instructions requires a very complicated data path. In principle, we can execute such instructions by having elaborate control units that in turn have simple processors to process these instructions. These sub processors can generate control signals for implementing complicated CISC instructions.

Serial No.	Signal	Condition
1	$isSt$	$\overline{op_5}.op_4.op_3.op_2.op_1$
2	$isLd$	$\overline{op_5}op_4.op_3.op_2.\overline{op_1}$
3	$isBeq$	$op_5.\overline{op_4}.\overline{op_3}.\overline{op_2}.\overline{op_1}$
4	$isBgt$	$op_5.\overline{op_4}.\overline{op_3}.\overline{op_2}.op_1$
5	$isRet$	$op_5.\overline{op_4}.op_3.\overline{op_2}.\overline{op_1}$
6	$isImmediate$	I
7	$isWb$	$\sim (op_5 + \overline{op_5}.op_3.op_1.(op_4 + \overline{op_2})) +$ $op_5.\overline{op_4}.\overline{op_3}.op_2.op_1$
8	$isUbranch$	$op_5.\overline{op_4}.(\overline{op_3}.op_2 + op_3.\overline{op_2}.\overline{op_1})$
9	$isCall$	$op_5.\overline{op_4}.\overline{op_3}.op_2.op_1$
	$aluSignals$	
10	$isAdd$	$\overline{op_5}.\overline{op_4}.\overline{op_3}.\overline{op_2}.\overline{op_1} + \overline{op_5}.op_4.op_3.op_2$
11	$isSub$	$\overline{op_5}.\overline{op_4}.\overline{op_3}.\overline{op_2}.op_1$
12	$isCmp$	$\overline{op_5}.\overline{op_4}.op_3.\overline{op_2}.op_1$
13	$isMul$	$\overline{op_5}.\overline{op_4}.\overline{op_3}.op_2.\overline{op_1}$
14	$isDiv$	$\overline{op_5}.\overline{op_4}.\overline{op_3}.op_2.op_1$
15	$isMod$	$\overline{op_5}.\overline{op_4}.op_3.\overline{op_2}.\overline{op_1}$
16	$isLsl$	$\overline{op_5}.op_4.\overline{op_3}.op_2.\overline{op_1}$
17	$isLsr$	$\overline{op_5}.op_4.\overline{op_3}.op_2.op_1$
18	$isAsr$	$\overline{op_5}.op_4.op_3.\overline{op_2}.\overline{op_1}$
19	$isOr$	$\overline{op_5}.\overline{op_4}.op_3.op_2.op_1$
20	$isAnd$	$\overline{op_5}.\overline{op_4}.op_3.op_2.\overline{op_1}$
21	$isNot$	$\overline{op_5}.op_4.\overline{op_3}.\overline{op_2}.\overline{op_1}$
22	$isMov$	$\overline{op_5}.op_4.\overline{op_3}.\overline{op_2}.op_1$

Table 8.5: Boolean conditions for setting all the control signals

Way Point 6

1. *We have successfully designed a hardwired processor that implements the entire SimpleRisc ISA.*

2. *Our processor is broadly divided into five stages: IF, OF, EX, MA, and RW.*

3. *The data path contains state elements (such as registers), arithmetic units, logical units, and multiplexers to choose the right set of inputs for each functional unit.*

4. *The multiplexers are controlled by control signals generated by the control unit.*

8.4   Microprogram-Based Processor

Let us now look at a different paradigm for designing processors. We have up till now looked at a processor with a hardwired control unit. We designed a data path with all the elements required to process, and execute an instruction. Where there was a choice between the input operands, we added a multiplexer that was controlled by a signal from the control unit. The control unit took the contents of the instruction as the input, and generated all the control signals. This design style is typically adopted by modern high performance processors. Note that efficiency comes at a cost. The cost is *flexibility*. It is fairly difficult for us to introduce new instructions. We need to possibly add more multiplexers, and generate many more control signals for each new instruction. Secondly, it is not possible to add new instructions to a processor after it has been shipped to the customer. Sometimes, we desire such flexibility.

It is possible to introduce this additional flexibility by introducing a translation table that translates instructions in the ISA to a set of simple microinstructions. Each microinstruction has access to all the latches, and internal state elements of a processor. By executing a group of microinstructions associated with an instruction, we can realise the functionality of that instruction. These microinstructions or *microcodes* are saved in a microcode table. It is typically possible to modify the contents of this table via software, and thus change the way hardware executes instructions. There are several reasons for wanting such kind of flexibility that allows us to add new instructions, or modify the behaviour of existing instructions. Some of the reasons are as follows:

Definition 60

We can have an alternate design style, where we break instructions in the ISA to a set of microinstructions (microcodes). For each instruction, a dedicated unit executes its associated set of microinstructions to implement its functionality. It is typically possible to dynamically change the set of microinstructions associated with an instruction. This helps us change the functionality of the instruction via software. Such kind of a processor is known as a microprogrammed *processor.*

---

1. Processors sometimes have bugs in the execution of certain instructions [Sarangi et al., 2006]. This is because of mistakes committed by designers in the design process, or due to manufacturing defects. One such famous example is the bug in division in the Intel® Pentium® processor. Intel had to recall all the Pentium processors that it had sold to customers [Pratt, 1995]. If it would have been possible to dynamically change the implementation of the division instruction, then it would not have been necessary to recall all the processors. Hence, we can conclude that some degree of reconfigurability of the processor can help us fix defects that might have been introduced in various stages of the design and manufacturing process.

2. Processors such as Intel Pentium 4, and later processors such as Intel® Core™ i3, and Intel® Core™ i7 implement some complex instructions by executing a set of microinstructions saved in memory. Complicated operations with strings of data, or instructions that lead to a series of repetitive computations are typically implemented using microcode. This means that the Intel processor internally replaces a complex instruction with a snippet of code containing simpler instructions. This makes it easier for the processor to implement complicated instructions. We do not need to unnecessarily make changes to the data path, add extra state, multiplexers, and control signals to implement complex instructions.

3. Nowadays processors are part of a chip with many other elements. This is known as a system-on-chip (SOC). For example, a chip in a cellphone might contain a processor, a video controller, an interface

to the camera, a sound and network controller. Processor vendors typically hardwire a set of simple instructions, and a lot of other instructions for interfacing with peripherals such as the video and audio controllers are written in microcode. Depending on the application domain and the set of peripheral components, the microcode can be customised.

4. Sometimes custom diagnostic routines are written using a set of dedicated microinstructions. These routines test different parts of the chip during its operation, report faults, and take corrective action. These built-in-self-test (BIST) routines are typically customisable, and are written in microcode. For example, if we desire high reliability, then we can modify the behaviour of instructions that perform reliability checks on the CPU to check all components. However, in the interest of time, these routines can be compressed to check fewer components.

We thus observe that there are some compelling reasons to be able to programatically alter the behaviour of instructions in a processor to achieve reliability, implement additional features, and improve portability. Hence, modern computing systems, especially, smaller devices such as phones, and tablets use chips that rely on microcode. Such microcode sequences are popularly referred to as *firmware*.

Definition 61

Modern computing systems, especially, smaller devices such as phones, modems, printers, and tablets use chips that rely on microcode. Such microcode sequences are popularly referred to as firmware.

Let us thus design a microprogram-based processor that provides us significantly more flexibility in tailoring the instruction set, even after the processor has been fabricated and sent to the customer. Before we proceed to design the data path and control path of a microprogrammed processor, we need to note that there is a fundamental tradeoff between a regular hardwired processor as presented in Section 8.2.7, and a microprogrammed processor. The tradeoff is efficiency versus flexibility. We cannot expect to have a very flexible processor that is fast and power efficient. Let us keep this important tenet in mind and proceed with the design.

8.5 Microprogrammed Data Path

Let us design the data path for a microprogrammed processor. Let us not design it from scratch. Let us rather modify the data path for the processor as shown in Section 8.2.7. Recall that it had some major units such as the fetch unit, register file, ALU, branch unit, and memory unit. These units were connected with wires, and whenever there was a possibility of multiple source operands, we added a multiplexer in the data path. The role of the control unit was to generate all the control signals for the multiplexers.

The issue is that the connections to the multiplexers are hardwired. It is not possible to establish arbitrary connections. For example, it is not possible to send the output of the memory unit to the input of the execute unit. Hence, we wish to have a design that is free of fixed interconnections between components. It should be theoretically possible for any unit to send data to any other unit.

The most flexible interconnect is a bus based structure. A *bus* is a set of common copper wires that connect all the units. It supports one writer, and multiple readers at any point of time. For example, unit A can write to the bus at a certain point of time, and all the other units can get the value that unit A writes. It is possible to send data from one unit to another unit, or from one unit to a set of other units if required. The control unit needs to ensure that at any point of time, only one unit writes to the bus, and the unit that needs to process the value that is being written, reads the value from the bus.

Definition 62 *A bus is a set of common wires that connect all the functional units in a processor. It supports one writer, and multiple readers at any point of time.*

Let us now proceed to design simplified versions of all the units that we introduced for our hardwired processor. These simplified versions can aptly be used in the data path of our microprogrammed processor.

8.5.1 Fetch Unit

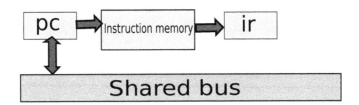

Figure 8.17: The fetch unit in a microprogrammed processor

Let us start out by explaining the design philosophy of the microprogrammed processor. We add registers with every unit. These registers store the input data for the specific unit, and a dedicated output register stores the results generated by the unit. Both these sets of registers are connected to the common bus. Unlike the hardwired processor, where there was a good amount of coupling across different units, units in a microprogrammed processor are fairly independent of each other. Their/ job is to perform a set of actions, and put the results back on to the bus. Each unit is like a function in a programming language. It has an interface comprising of a set of registers to read data in. It typically takes 1 cycle to compute its output, and then the unit writes the output value to an output register.

In concordance with this philosophy, we present the design of the fetch unit in Figure 8.17. It has two registers – *pc* (PC), and *ir* (instruction register). We shall use the acronym, IR, for the instruction register. *ir* contains the contents of the instruction. The *pc* register can read its value from the bus, and can also write its value to the bus. We have not connected *ir* to the bus because no other unit is typically interested in the exact contents of the instruction. Other units are only interested in different fields of the instruction. Hence, it is necessary to decode the instruction and break it into a set of different fields. This is done by the decode unit.

8.5.2 Decode Unit

This unit is similar in function to the operand fetch unit as described in Section 8.2.3. However, we do not include the register file in this unit. We treat it as a separate unit in the microprogrammed processor. Figure 8.18 shows the design of the operand fetch unit.

The job of the decode unit is to break down the contents of the instruction into multiple fields, and export them as registers. In specific, the following registers are made available to the bus, I (immediate bit), rd (destination register), $rs1$ (source register 1), $rs2$ (source register 2), $immx$ (after processing the modifiers), and *branchTarget* (branch target). To compute the branch target we calculate the offset from the current PC by extracting bits [1:27] from *ir*, and shifting it to the left by 2 places. This is added to the current value of the PC. Table 8.6 shows the range of bits extracted from *ir* for each output register.

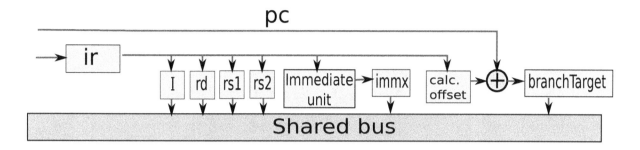

Figure 8.18: The decode unit in a microprogrammed processor

Register	Bits in ir
I	27
rd	23-26
$rs1$	19-22
$rs2$	15-18
$immx$	1-18 (process modifiers)
$branchTarget$	PC + ($ir[1:27] \ll 2$)

Table 8.6: List of bits in ir corresponding to each register in the decode unit

It is possible that a given program execution might not have values for all the registers. For example, an instruction in the *register* format will not have an embedded immediate value. Hence, in this case the *immx* register will have junk data. However, it does not hurt to extract all possible fields from the instruction, and store them in registers. We can use only those registers that contain valid data, and ignore those registers that are not relevant to the instruction. This ensures that our data path remains simple, and we do not need costly multiplexers in the decode unit.

8.5.3 Register File

We had combined the decode unit and the register file, into one unit called the operand fetch unit of the hardwired processor. However, we prefer to keep the register file separate in the microprogrammed processor. This is because in the hardwired processor it was accessed right after decoding the instruction. However, this might not be the case in the microprogrammed processor. It might need to be accessed possibly several times during the execution of an instruction.

The register file has two source registers – *regSrc*, and *regData*. The *regSrc* register contains the number of the register that needs to be accessed. In the case of a write operation, the *regData* register contains the value to be written. The *args* values are directly read from the bus. They contain the commands to the register file. We assume that there are dedicated wires in the shared bus to carry the arguments (*args*) values. They take different values, where each value corresponds to an unique operation of an unit. The value 00...0 is a distinguished value that corresponds to a *nop* (no operation).

The arguments to the register file, are very simple – *read*, *write*, and *nop*. If the args specify a *write* operation, then the value in *regData* is written to the register specified by the *regSrc* register. If a *read* operation is specified, then the register specified by *regSrc* is read and its value is stored in the register, *regVal* (register value).

To access the register file it is thus necessary to write the number of the register to the *regSrc* register,

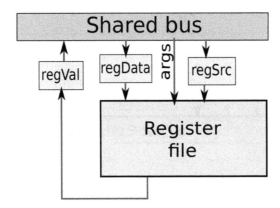

Figure 8.19: The register file in a microprogrammed processor

write the value to be written to the *regData* register if required, and finally specify the appropriate arguments. The assumption is that after 1 cycle the operation is complete. In the case of a read operation, the value is available in the *regVal* register.

8.5.4 ALU

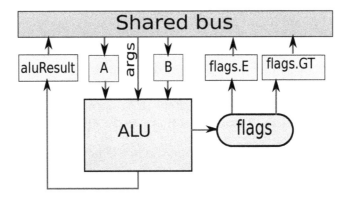

Figure 8.20: The ALU in a microprogrammed processor

The structure of the ALU is shown in Figure 8.20. It has two input registers, A and B. The ALU performs actions on the values contained in registers, A and B. The nature of the operation is specified by the *args* value. For example, if it specifies an add operation, then the ALU adds the values contained in registers, A and B. If it specifies a subtract operation, then the value in B is subtracted from the value contained in A. For the *cmp* instruction, the ALU updates the flags. Recall that in *SimpleRisc* we use two flags that specify the equality, and greater than conditions. They are saved in the registers *flags.E* and *flags.GT* respectively. The result of the ALU operation is then saved in the register *aluResult*. Here also, we assume that the ALU takes 1 cycle to execute after the args values are specified on the bus.

8.5.5 Memory Unit

The memory unit is shown in Figure 8.21. Like the hardwired processor, it has two source registers – *mar* and *mdr*. The memory address register(*mar*) buffers the memory address, and the memory data register

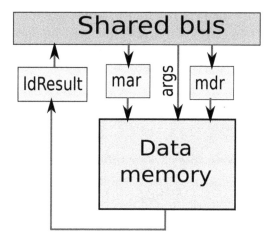

Figure 8.21: The memory unit in a microprogrammed processor

(mdr) buffers the value that needs to be stored. Here also, we require a set of arguments that specify the nature of the memory operation – load or store. Once, a load operation is done, the data is available in the $ldResult$ register.

8.5.6 Overview of the Data Path

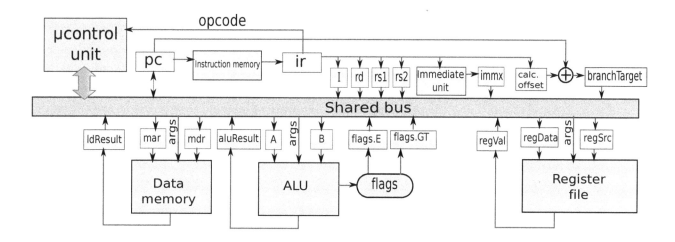

Figure 8.22: The data path in a microprogrammed processor

Let us now add all the individual units, and take a look at the entire data path as shown in Figure 8.22. Along with all the units that we just described, we have added an extra unit, which is the microprogrammed control unit (μcontrol unit). Its role is to execute a set of microinstructions corresponding to each program instruction, and orchestrate the flow of data values across the different units in the data path of the microprogrammed processor. It is mainly responsible for the execution of microinstructions, data transfers across the different units, and for transferring control to the correct program instruction by updating the PC. Note that we have also added an extra connection between the ir register and the μcontrol unit to transfer the opcode of the instruction. We require the μcontrol unit to load the appropriate set of microinstructions corresponding to the program instruction. By design, we do not wish to make the value of the opcode available to other units. This is because, we have a set of microinstructions for each opcode, and there is no reason why other units should require the value of the opcode.

Definition 63

The microcontrol unit, *also referred to as the μcontrol unit is a dedicated piece of hardware that is responsible for the execution of a set of microinstructions corresponding to each program instruction. Its role is to fetch the appropriate set of microinstructions from a dedicated* microprogram memory, *and execute them in sequence. A register called the* micro PC *(μpc) points to the currently executing microinstruction.*

We envision a microprogram memory that is a part of the μcontrol unit. It contains the set of microinstructions corresponding to each program instruction. It is thus necessary for the μcontrol unit to jump to the starting address of the set of microinstructions corresponding to each program instruction. We also need a microPC that points to the current microinstruction being executed.

Before discussing the design and implementation of the μcontrol unit, let us first look at programming, or rather microprogramming our new processor. We need to design a microassembly language that will help us write programs for it.

8.6   Microassembly Language

8.6.1   Machine Model

All the internal registers in Figure 8.22 are the set of registers that are visible to microassembly instructions. Ideally microassembly instructions are not supposed to be aware of regular architectural registers, and other aspects of architectural state. They are only supposed to be aware of internal registers that are not externally visible.

Table 8.7 shows the list of internal registers in our microprogrammed data path. Note that we have 1-bit registers, 4-bit registers, and 32-bit registers.

Microprogrammed instructions do not access memory. Hence, they do not need a view of memory.

8.6.2   Microinstructions

Let us look at the life cycle of a regular program instruction. The first step is to fetch the contents of the instruction from the instruction memory. Let us introduce a microinstruction to read the contents of the instruction from the instruction memory and place it in the IR (ir). Let us call it $mloadIR$. Note that we will add the prefix m (m for micro) to every microinstruction. This is to denote the fact that it is a microinstruction, and differentiate it from regular program instructions.

Microinstruction	Semantics
$mloadIR$	Loads the ir with the contents of the instruction

Once, we have loaded the instruction register, it automatically sends the contents to all the subunits in the decode unit, and they extract the appropriate bit fields, and save them in the decode registers – I, rd,

Serial No.	Register	Size (bits)	Function
1	pc	32	program counter
2	ir	32	instruction register
3	I	1	immediate bit in the instruction
4	rd	4	destination register id
5	$rs1$	4	id of the first source register
6	$rs2$	4	id of the second source register
7	$immx$	32	immediate embedded in the instruction (after processing modifiers)
8	$branchTarget$	32	branch target, computed as the sum of the PC and the offset embedded in the instruction
9	$regSrc$	4	contains the id of the register that needs to be accessed in the register file
10	$regData$	32	contains the data to be written into the register file
11	$regVal$	32	value read from the register file
12	A	32	first operand of the ALU
13	B	32	second operand of the ALU
14	$flags.E$	1	the equality flag
15	$flags.GT$	1	the greater than flag
16	$aluResult$	32	the ALU result
17	mar	32	memory address register
18	mdr	32	memory data register
19	$ldResult$	32	the value loaded from memory

Table 8.7: List of all the internal registers

$rs1$, $rs2$, $immx$, and $branchTarget$. We envision an $mdecode$ instruction in the 0-address format that makes the μcontrol unit wait for 1 cycle. In this cycle, all the decode registers get populated.

Microinstruction	Semantics
$mdecode$	Waits for 1 cycle. Meanwhile, all the decode registers get populated.

Note that these two steps ($mloadIR$ and $mdecode$) are common for all program instructions. After this, we need to load the microinstructions for the specific program instruction. This is achieved through a $mswitch$ instruction that instructs the μcontrol unit to jump to the appropriate location in the microinstruction memory, and begins executing microinstructions starting from that location.

Microinstruction	Semantics
mswitch	Load the set of microinstructions corresponding to the program instruction

Now, the processing of the instruction can start. The aim here is to use as few microinstructions as possible. We want to keep the microassembly interface very simple. Let us first introduce the *mmov* instruction that moves data from the source register to a destination register. Additionally, it can set the arguments of the unit corresponding to the destination register. We thus introduce a 2-address and 3-address format of the *mmov* instruction. The 3-address format contains the arguments (*args*) of the unit corresponding to the destination register, as shown below.

Microinstruction	Semantics
mmov r1, r2	$r1 \leftarrow r2$
mmov r1, r2, ⟨args⟩	$r1 \leftarrow r2$, send the value of *args* on the bus

We sometimes face the need to load constants into registers. Hence, we introduce the *mmovi* instruction that loads a constant into a register.

Microinstruction	Semantics
mmovi r1, ⟨imm⟩	$r1 \leftarrow imm$
mmovi r1, ⟨imm⟩, ⟨args⟩	$r1 \leftarrow imm$, send the value of *args* on the bus

We need an *madd* instruction because we need to increment the values of registers such as the *pc*. Instead of using the main ALU, we can have a small adder as a part of the μcontrol unit. We refer to this as the μadder. Here, there is a tradeoff to make. Do we need an add instruction that adds two registers, and saves it in another register? At the microinstruction level, this is seldom required. We definitely do not require this instruction to implement the *SimpleRisc* instruction set. Hence, we do not see a reason to include this microinstruction. If there is ever a need to have one such microinstruction, then we can always use the main ALU in the data path to perform the addition. We thus introduce a simple add instruction in the 2-address format. It adds an immediate value to a register. The semantics of this instruction is shown below.

Microinstruction	Semantics
madd r1, ⟨imm⟩	$r1 \leftarrow r1 + imm$
madd r1, ⟨imm⟩, ⟨args⟩	$r1 \leftarrow r1 + imm$, send the value of ⟨args⟩ on the bus

Here, the *madd* instruction adds *imm* to *r1*, and saves the result in *r1*. *imm* can be a positive or a negative number. We restrict it to a 12-bit number, because we do not need more bits in most cases. The range of the immediate is thus between -2048 and +2047.

Lastly, we need branch instructions. We need both conditional branches, and unconditional branches. We thus introduce two new microinstructions – *mb* (branch) and *mbeq* (branch if the arguments are equal). The *mb* microinstruction takes a single argument, which is the address of the target microinstruction (or its label while writing microassembly code). We use the PC-direct addressing mode here as compared to the PC-relative addressing mode because, we expect the total number of microinstructions to be small. Secondly, if we would have use a PC-relative addressing mode, then we would have required an extra adder in our data path to add the offset to the PC. The *SimpleRisc* instruction set allocates 5 bits for the opcode. This means that at the most we can have 32 instructions in our instruction set. Let us assume that in the worst case, an instruction translates to 20 microinstructions. We would thus need to store 640 microinstructions. We can thus allocate 10 bits for the specifying the address of the microinstruction and our μpc (micro-PC) can also be 10 bits wide. This means that at the most we can support a total of 1024 microinstructions. This is much more than what we actually require. However, it is not a bad idea to over design hardware because it cannot be changed later. Note that in the microinstruction memory, the address refers to the index of the microinstruction (not to the starting address of the first byte).

The *mbeq* instruction requires three operands. The first operand is a register, the second operand is an immediate, and the third operand is the address(label) of a microinstruction. If the value contained in the register is equal to the immediate operand, then the microPC jumps to the microinstruction specified by the third operand. Otherwise, the next microinstruction in sequence is executed.

Microinstruction	Semantics
$mb \langle addr \rangle$	execute the microinstruction at $\langle addr \rangle$(label) in the microprogram memory
$mbeq\ reg,\ imm,\ \langle addr \rangle$	If the value in the internal register reg is equal to imm, then the microPC needs to jump to $\langle add \rangle$(label)

Serial No.	Microinstruction	Semantics
1	$mloadIR$	$ir \leftarrow [pc]$
2	$mdecode$	populate all the decode registers
3	$mswitch$	jump to the μpc corresponding to the opcode
4	$mmov\ reg1,\ reg2,\ \langle args \rangle$	$reg1 \leftarrow reg2$, send the value of $args$ to the unit that owns $reg1$, $\langle args \rangle$ is optional
5	$mmovi\ reg1,\ imm,\ \langle args \rangle$	$reg1 \leftarrow imm$, $\langle args \rangle$ is optional
6	$madd\ reg1,\ imm,\ \langle args \rangle$	$reg1 \leftarrow reg1 + imm$, $\langle args \rangle$ is optional
7	$mbeq\ reg1,\ imm,\ \langle addr \rangle$	if $(reg1 = imm)$ $\mu pc \leftarrow addr(label)$
8	$mb\ \langle addr \rangle$	$\mu pc \leftarrow addr(label)$

Table 8.8: List of microinstructions

To summarise, Table 8.8 shows the 8 microinstructions that we have described in this section. We have a compact list of 8 microinstructions, and thus we can encode each microinstruction using just 3 bits.

8.6.3 Implementing Instructions in the Microassembly Language

Let us now try to implement program instructions in the microassembly language using the set of basic microinstructions enumerated in Table 8.8.

For all the instructions, they start with a common set of microinstructions as shown below. We refer to these 4 microinstructions as the *preamble*.

```
1 .begin:
2 mloadIR
3 mdecode
4 madd pc, 4
5 mswitch
```

Definition 64

A set of microinstructions that is common to all program instructions and is executed at the beginning before proceeding to implement the logic of the instruction, is known as the preamble, *or* microcode preamble.

Every instruction needs to pass through at least three of these steps. We need to fetch the contents of the PC and load them into the *ir* register. Then, we need to decode the instruction, and break it down into its constituent fields. For instructions, other than branches, we need to increment the value of the PC by 4. In our microcode we prefer to do this step for all the instructions. For taken branches, we need to later overwrite the PC with the branch target. Lastly, we need to execute the *mswitch* instruction to jump to the starting location of the set of microinstructions that are specific to the program instruction.

The label *.begin* points to the beginning of this routine. Note that after finishing the execution of an instruction, we need to jump to the *.begin* label such that we can start processing the next instruction in the program. Note that in our microassembly code we specify the label that we need to branch to. When the microassembly code is translated to actual machine level microinstructions, then each label is replaced by the address of the corresponding microinstruction.

8.6.4 3-Address Format ALU Instructions

Let us now look at implementing 3-address format ALU instructions. These instructions are: *add, sub, mul, div, mod, and, or, lsl, lsr*, and *asr*.

First, we need to read the value of the first operand stored in *rs1* from the register file, and send it to the ALU. The microcode snippet to achieve this is as follows:

```
1 mmov regSrc, rs1, <read>
2 mmov A, regVal
```

Note, that we are combining a functional unit operation, and a register transfer in the same cycle. This can be confusing at the beginning. Hence, the reader should read this example several times and ensure that she has a clear understanding. The reason that we fuse both the operations is because microcode registers are typically very small, and thus they can be accessed very quickly. Hence, it is not a good idea to use a complete cycle for transferring data between micro registers. It is a better idea to fuse a register transfer with a functional unit operation, such that we can ensure that we are roughly doing a similar amount of work every cycle.

Let us proceed. Subsequently, we need to check if the second operand is a register or an immediate. This can be achieved by comparing the *I* register with 1. If it is 1, then the second operand is an immediate, else it is a register. The following piece of code first checks this condition, and then performs data transfers accordingly.

```
1  mbeq I, 1, .imm
2  /* second operand is a register */
3  mmov regSrc, rs2, <read>
4  mmov B, regVal, <aluop>
5  mb .rw
6  /* second operand is an immediate */
7  .imm:
8  mmov B, immx, <aluop>
9  /* write the ALU result to the register file*/
10 .rw:
```

Here, we first check if the value stored in the I register is equal to 1, using the *mbeq* instruction. If it is not 1, then the second operand is a register, and we start executing the subsequent microinstruction. We move the contents of the register, $rs2$, to the *regSrc* register that contains the index of the register that we need to read from the register file. Then we move the value of the operand read from the register file (*regVal*) to the ALU (register B). Since the value in register A is already present, we can directly start the ALU operation. This is indicated to the ALU by sending an extra argument ($\langle aluop \rangle$) that encodes the ALU operation. $\langle aluop \rangle$ corresponds to one of the following operations: *add*, *sub*, *mul*, *div*, *mod*, *and*, *or*, *lsl*, *lsr*, and *asr*.

However, if the value of the I register is 1, then we need to branch to *.imm*. The value of the immediate embedded in the instruction is already available with appropriate sign extensions in the register *immx*. We need to simply transfer the value of *immx* to B (second ALU register), and the arguments ($\langle aluop \rangle$) to the ALU. Similar to the case with the second operand being a register, $\langle aluop \rangle$ encodes the ALU operation. Once, we are done, we need to start execution at the label, *.rw*.

The label *.rw* needs to point to code that writes the value of the computed result to the register file, and then proceeds to execute the next instruction. The code for these two operations is shown below.

```
1  .rw:
2        mmov regSrc, rd
3        mmov regData, aluResult, <write>
4        mb .begin
```

We write the result of the ALU into the register file, and then branch to the beginning, where we proceed to execute the next instruction. To summarise, here is the code for any 3-address format ALU instruction (other than the preamble).

```
1  /* transfer the first operand to the ALU */
2  mmov regSrc, rs1, <read>
3  mmov A, regVal
4
5  /* check the value of the immediate register */
6  mbeq I, 1, .imm
7  /* second operand is a register */
8  mmov regSrc, rs2, <read>
9  mmov B, regVal, <aluop>
10 mb .rw
```

```
11  /* second operand is an immediate */
12  .imm:
13  mmov B, immx, <aluop>
14
15  /* write the ALU result to the register file*/
16  .rw:
17  mmov regSrc, rd
18  mmov regData, aluResult, <write>
19  mb .begin
```

This code snippet has 10 microinstructions. Recall that we also need to execute 4 more microinstructions as a part of the preamble before this. They read the PC, decode the instruction, set the next PC, and jump to the beginning of the appropriate set of microinstructions. Executing 14 microinstructions for 1 program instruction is clearly a lot of effort. However, the reader must recall that we are not really after performance here. We wanted to design a very clean and flexible means of accessing different units.

8.6.5   2-Address Format ALU Instructions

The three ALU instructions in the 2-address format, are *not*, *mov*, and *cmp*. *not* and *mov* have a similar format. They do not use the first source operand, *rs1*. They operate on either *rs2*, or *immx*, and transfer the result to the register pointed by *rd*.

Let us look at the *mov* instruction first. We first check whether the second operand is an immediate, or not, by comparing the value in register *I* with 1. If it is equal to 1, then we jump to the label, *.imm*. Otherwise, we proceed to execute the subsequent instructions in Lines 4, and 5. In Line 4, we transfer *rs2* to *regSrc*, along with the ⟨*read*⟩ command. The operand is read and stored in *regVal*. In the next cycle, we transfer *regVal* to *regData* such that it can be written back to the register file. If the second operand was an immediate, then we execute the code in Line 9. We transfer the immediate (stored in *immx*) to the *regData* register. In either case, *regData* contains the value to be written to the register file. Then we transfer the id of the destination register (stored in *rd*) to *regSrc*, and simultaneously issue the write command in Line 13.

———————————————— *mov* instruction ————————————————
```
1   /* check the value of the immediate register */
2   mbeq I, 1, .imm
3   /* second operand is a register */
4   mmov regSrc, rs2, <read>
5   mmov regData, regVal
6   mb .rw
7   /* second operand is an immediate */
8   .imm:
9   mmov regData, immx
10
11  /* write to the register file*/
12  .rw:
13  mmov regSrc, rd, <write>
14
15  /* jump to the beginning */
16  mb .begin
```

Let us now write a similar routing for the *not* instruction. The only additional step is to transfer the value read from the register to the ALU, compute the logical negation, and then transfer the value back to the register file. A hallmark feature of our microassembly language is that we can transfer a value to a unit, and if all the other operands are in place, then we can also perform an operation in the unit in the same cycle. The implicit assumption here is that 1 clock cycle is enough to transfer the data between registers, and perform a computation. In line with this philosophy we transfer the value of *immx*, or *regVal* to register B of the ALU, and also perform a $\langle not \rangle$ operation in the same cycle (see Lines 5 and 9). Like the *mov* instruction, we transfer the ALU result to the *regData* register, and write it to the register file in Lines 13, and 14.

not instruction

```
1  /* check the value of the immediate register */
2  mbeq I, 1, .imm
3  /* second operand is a register */
4  mmov regSrc, rs2, <read>
5  mmov B, regVal, <not> /* ALU operation */
6  mb .rw
7  /* second operand is an immediate */
8  .imm:
9  mmov B, immx, <not> /* ALU operation */
10
11 /* write to the register file*/
12 .rw:
13 mmov regData, aluResult
14 mmov regSrc, rd, <write>
15
16 /* jump to the beginning */
17 mb .begin
```

Let us now look at the compare instruction that does not have a destination operand. It compares two operands, where one is a register operand, and the other can be either a register or an immediate. It saves the results automatically in the *flags.E* and *flags.GT* registers.

Let us now consider the microcode for the *cmp* instruction.

cmp instruction

```
1  /* transfer rs1 to register A */
2  mmov regSrc, rs1, <read>
3  mmov A, regVal
4
5  /* check the value of the immediate register */
6  mbeq I, 1, .imm
7  /* second operand is a register */
8  mmov regSrc, rs2, <read>
9  mmov B, regVal, <cmp> /* ALU operation */
10 mb .begin
11
12 /* second operand is an immediate */
13 .imm:
14 mmov B, immx, <cmp> /* ALU operation */
15 mb .begin
```

Here, we first transfer the value in register $rs1$ to the ALU (in register A). Then, we check if the second operand is an immediate. If it is an immediate, then we transfer the value of $immx$ to the ALU (in register B), and simultaneously issue a command to execute a compare in Line 14. However, if the second operand is a register, then we need to read it from the register file (Line 8), and then transfer it to the ALU (Line 9). The last step is to branch to the beginning ($mb\ .begin$).

8.6.6   The nop Instruction

Implementing the nop instruction is trivial. We just need to branch to the beginning as shown below.

```
1 mb .begin
```

8.6.7 ld and st instructions

Let us now look at the load instruction. We need to transfer the value of the first source register to the ALU. Then we transfer the value of the immediate to the second ALU register (B), and initiate the add operation to calculate the effective address. Once the effective address has been calculated, it is available in the $aluResult$ register. Subsequently, we move the contents of the $aluResult$ register to the memory address register (mar), and initiate a load operation. The result is available in the $ldResult$ register in the next cycle. We write the loaded value to the register specified by rd in the next two cycles.

———————————————— ld instruction ————————————————
```
1  /* transfer rs1 to register A */
2  mmov regSrc, rs1, <read>
3  mmov A, regVal
4
5  /* calculate the effective address */
6  mmov B, immx, <add> /* ALU operation */
7
8  /* perform the load */
9  mmov mar, aluResult, <load>
10
11 /* write the loaded value to the register file */
12 mmov regData, ldResult
13 mmov regSrc, rd, <write>
14
15 /* jump to the beginning */
16 mb .begin
```

The microcode for the store instruction is similar to that of the load instruction. We first calculate the effective memory address and store it in the mar register. Then we read the value of the rd register that contains the data to be stored (Line 10). We save this in the mdr register, and issue the store (Line 11).

———————————————— st instruction ————————————————
```
1  /* transfer rs1 to register A */
2  mmov regSrc, rs1, <read>
3  mmov A, regVal
4
5  /* calculate the effective address */
6  mmov B, immx, <add> /* ALU operation */
```

```
7
8  /* perform the store */
9  mmov mar, aluResult
10 mmov regSrc, rd, <read>
11 mmov mdr, regVal, <store>
12
13 /* jump to the beginning */
14 mb .begin
```

8.6.8   Branch Instructions

There are five branch instructions in *SimpleRisc* : *b*, *beq*, *bgt*, *call*, and *ret*.

Implementing the unconditional branch instruction is trivial.We simply need to transfer the value of the branch target to the PC.

──────────────── *b* instruction ────────────────
```
1 mmov pc, branchTarget
2 mb .begin
```

We can make a minor modification to this code to implement the *beq*, and *bgt* instructions. We need to check the value of the flags registers, and set the branchTarget to the PC only if the corresponding flags register contains a 1.

──────── *beq* instruction ────────
```
1 /* test the flags register */
2 mbeq  flags.E, 1, .branch
3 mb. begin
4
5 .branch:
6 mmov pc, branchTarget
7 mb .begin
```

──────── *bgt* instruction ────────
```
1 /* test the flags register */
2 mbeq  flags.GT, 1, .branch
3 mb. begin
4
5 .branch:
6 mmov pc, branchTarget
7 mb .begin
```

The last two instructions that we need to implement are the *call* and *ret* instructions. The *call* instruction is a combination of a simple branch, and a register write operation that adds the value of the next PC ($PC+4$) to the return address register (register 15). The microcode is as follows. Note that we do not increment the PC by 4 because it is already incremented in the preamble.

──────────────── *call* instruction ────────────────
```
1 /* save PC + 4 in the return address register */
2 mmov regData, pc
3 mmovi regSrc, 15, <write>
4
5 /* branch to the function */
6 mmov pc, branchTarget
7 mb .begin
```

We save the address of the next PC in the register file in lines 2 to 3. Then we move the *branchTarget* to the PC, and then proceed to execute the first instruction in the invoked function.

The *ret* instruction performs the reverse operation, and transfers the return address to the PC.

```
                                          ret instruction
1
2  /* save the contents of the return
3               address register in the PC */
4  mmovi regSrc, 15, <read>
5  mmov pc, regVal
6  mb .begin
```

We have thus implemented all our *SimpleRisc* instructions in microcode. A microcoded implementation is definitely slower that our hardwired datapath. However, we have gained a lot in terms of flexibility. We can implement some very complex instructions in hardware, and thus make the task of software developers significantly easier. We can also dynamically change the behaviour of instructions. For example, if we wish to store the return address on the stack rather than the return address register, we can do so easily (see Examples 104 and 105).

Example 104

Change the call instruction to store the return address on the stack. The preamble need not be shown (study carefully).

Answer:

```
                                   stack based call instruction
1
2  /* read and update the stack pointer */
3  mmovi regSrc, 14, <read> /* regSrc contains the id
4                    of the stack pointer */
5  madd regVal, -4 /* decrement the stack pointer */
6  mmov mar, regVal /* MAR contains the new stack pointer */
7
8  mmov regData, regVal, <write> /* update the stack pointer */
9
10 /* write the return address to the stack */
11 mmov mdr, pc, <store>
12
13 mb. begin
```

Example 105

Change the ret instruction to load the return address from the stack. The preamble need not be shown.

Answer:

```
                                   stack based call instruction
1  /* read the stack pointer */
2  mmovi regSrc, 14, <read>
3
4  /* set the memory address to the stack pointer */
5  mmov mar, regVal, <load>
```

```
 6
 7  mmov pc, ldResult /* set the PC */
 8
 9  /* update the stack pointer */
10  madd regVal, 4 /* sp = sp + 4 */
11  mmov regData, regVal, <write> /* update stack pointer */
12
13  /* jump to the beginning */
14  mb .begin
```

Example 106

Implement an instruction to compute the factorial of the number saved in register r2. You can destroy the contents of r2. Save the result in register r3. Assume that the number is greater than 1.

――――――――― stack based call instruction ―――――――――

```
 1
 2  /* code to set the inputs to the multiplier */
 3  mmovi B, 1
 4  mmovi regSrc, 2, <read>
 5  mmov  A, regVal
 6  /* at this point A = r2, B = 1 */
 7
 8  /* loop */
 9  .loop:
10  /* Now begin the multiplication */
11  mmov B, B, <multiply> /* aluResult = A * B */
12  mmov B, aluResult /* B = aluResult */
13
14  /* decrement and test */
15  madd A, -1 /* A = A - 1 */
16  mbeq A, 1, .out /* compare A with 1 */
17  mb .loop
18
19  .out:
20  mmov regData, aluResult
21  mmovi regSrc, 3, <write> /* all done */
22
23  mb .begin
```

Example 107

Implement an instruction to find if the value saved in register r2 is a cubic Armstrong Number. A cubic

Armstrong number is equal to the sum of the cubes of its decimal digits. For example, 153 is one such number. $153 = 1^3 + 5^3 + 3^3$. Save the Boolean result in r3. Assume two scratch registers: sr1 and sr2.

```
───────── stack based call instruction ─────────
1
2  /* Set the inputs of the ALU */
3  mmovi regSrc, 2, <read>
4  mmov  A, regVal
5  mmov  sr1, regVal
6  mmovi B, 10
7  mmovi sr2, 0 /* sum = 0 */
8
9  /* loop */
10 .loop:
11 /* test */
12 mbeq A, 0, .out
13
14 /* compute the mod and cube it */
15 mmov B, B, <mod> /* aluResult = A % B */
16 mmov B, aluResult /* B = aluResult */
17 mmov A, aluResult, <multiply> /* aluResult = (A%B)^2 */
18 mmov A, aluResult, <multiply> /* aluResult = (A%B)^3 */
19 mmov A, aluResult /* A =  (A%B)^3 */
20 mmov B, sr2, <add> /* add the running sum */
21 mmov sr2, aluResult /* sr2 has the new sum */
22
23 /* test */
24 mmov A, sr1 /* old value of A */
25 mmovi B, 10, <divide>
26 mmov A, aluResult /* A = A / 10 */
27 mmov sr1, A /* sr1 = A */
28
29 mb .loop
30
31 /* out of the loop */
32 .out:
33 mmov A, sr2 /* A contains the sum */
34 mmov B, regVal, <cmp> /* compare */
35 mmov regSrc, 3
36 mbeq flags.E, 1, .success
37
38 /* failure */
39 mmov regData, 0, <write>
40 mb .begin
41
42 .success:
43 mmov regData, 1, <write>
```

```
44  mb  .begin
```

Example 108

Implement an instruction to test if a number saved in register r2 is prime. Assume that the number is greater than 3. Save the result in r3.

```
                          _____ stack based call instruction _____
1
2  /* Read the register and set the ALU inputs */
3  mmovi regSrc, 2, <read>
4  mmov  A, regVal
5  mmovi B, 1
6
7  .loop:
8          /* test for divisibility */
9          madd B, 1, <mod> /* aluResult = A % (B+1), B = B + 1 */
10         mbeq aluResult, 0, .failure
11
12         /* test B */
13         mmov A, A, <cmp> /* compare A with B */
14         mbeq flags.E, 1, .success
15
16 mb .loop
17
18 .success:
19         mmovi regSrc, 3
20         mmovi regData, 1, <write>
21         mb .begin
22
23 .failure:
24         mmovi regSrc, 3
25         mmovi regData, 0, <write>
26         mb. begin
```

8.7 Shared Bus and Control Signals

Let us take a look again at the list of implemented microinstructions in Table 8.8. We observe that each microinstruction has at the most one register read operand, and one register write operand. We typically read from one internal register, and then use it as a part of a computation (addition or comparison), and then write the result to another internal register.

We thus propose the design of a shared bus that actually consists of two buses as shown in Figure 8.23. The first bus is known as the write bus that is connected to all the registers that might potentially write data to the bus. The output of the write bus, the embedded immediate (μimm) in the microinstruction, and the output of the μadder are sent to a multiplexer. Recall that the μadder adds the embedded immediate with the contents of a register. Now, this multiplexer chooses one value among the three, and then sends it on the read bus. We refer to this multiplexer as the *transfer multiplexer*. All the registers that might potentially read a value are connected to the read bus. The PC is connected to both the buses. The μadder has two inputs. One of them is the sign extended immediate that is a part of the microinstruction, and the other is the output of the write bus.

Simultaneously, we compare the value sent on the write bus with the embedded immediate (μimm). The result is contained in the *isMBranch* signal. The *isMBranch* signal is required for implementing the *mbeq* instruction.

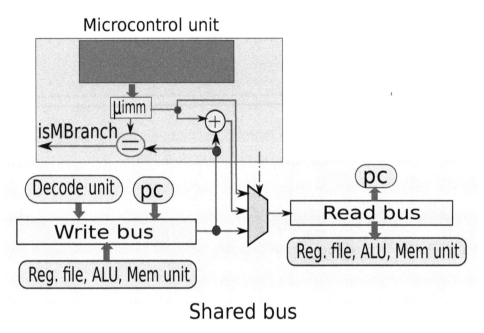

Figure 8.23: The design of the shared bus

To create a flexible data path, we need to add as many interconnections between units as possible. We thus decide to connect every register other than the decode, and flags registers to both the read and write buses. These registers are the input/output registers of the register file (*regSrc*, *regData*, and *regVal*), the ALU registers (*A*, *B*, *aluResult*), and the registers associated with the memory unit (*mar*, *mdr*, *ldResult*). To support branch instructions, it is also necessary to connect the PC to both the buses.

8.7.1 Control Signals

Each register that writes to the write bus needs a control signal. If it is asserted (equal to 1), then the value of the register appears on the write bus. Otherwise, the value of the register does not get reflected on the write bus. For example, the register, *aluResult*, contains the result of an ALU operation, and it is sometimes necessary to transfer its value to the write bus. The signal $aluResult_{out}$ controls the behaviour of the aluResult register. We associate similar signals with the subscript, $_{out}$ with all the registers that need to access the write bus.

Likewise, we associate a set of signals with the registers that are connected to the read bus. For example, the register *mar* is connected to the read bus. We associate the signal mar_{in} with it. If it is 1, then the value of the data on the read bus is transferred to *mar*. If $mar_{in} = 0$, the *mar* register is effectively disconnected from the read bus.

The PC has two signals associated with it: pc_{in} and pc_{out}. The μcontrol unit ensures that at one point of time only one register can write to the write bus. However, it is theoretically possible for multiple registers to read from the read bus concurrently.

8.7.2 Functional Unit Arguments

We augment the read bus to carry the arguments for the functional units (referred to as $\langle args \rangle$). These arguments specify the nature of the operation, which the functional unit needs to perform. For example, the two operations associated with the memory unit are $\langle load \rangle$, and $\langle store \rangle$, and the two operations associated with the register file are $\langle read \rangle$ and $\langle write \rangle$. Each ALU operation also has its separate code.

We propose to encode each operation in binary, and reserve the special value of 0 to indicate that no operation needs to be performed. Each functional unit needs to be connected to the read bus, and needs to process the value of the arguments. The $\langle args \rangle$ field can be split into two parts: $\langle unit\ id \rangle$, and $\langle opcode \rangle$. The $\langle unit\ id \rangle$ specifies the identifier for the functional unit. For example, we can assign 00 to the ALU, 01 to the register file, and 10 to the memory unit. The $\langle opcode \rangle$ contains the details of the operation to be performed. This is specific to the functional unit. We propose a 10-bit $\langle args \rangle$ bus that is a part of the read bus. We devote 3 bits to the $\langle unit\ id \rangle$, and 7 bits to the $\langle opcode \rangle$. Thus, for each unit we can support 128 different operations. Implementing the circuit to process the $\langle args \rangle$ is easy, and we leave it as an exercise to the reader.

8.8 The Microcontrol Unit

We now arrive at the last piece of our microprogrammed processor, which is the design of the μcontrol unit. It is a simple processor that executes microinstructions. It consists of a μfetch unit and a μpc. Every cycle we increment the μpc by 1 (addressed by the number of the instruction, not by bytes), or set it to the branch target. Then, we proceed to read the microinstruction from the microprogram memory, and process it. There are two main paradigms for designing an encoding of microinstructions, and executing them using a μcontrol unit. The first is known as *vertical microprogramming*. In principle, this paradigm is similar to executing regular program instructions using a hardwired processor. The second paradigm is known as *horizontal microprogramming*. This is more common, and is also a more efficient.

8.8.1 Vertical Microprogramming

In vertical microprogramming, we encode an instruction similar to encoding a regular RISC instruction in a hardwired processor.

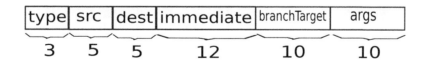

Figure 8.24: Encoding of a microinstruction (vertical microprogramming)

Figure 8.24 shows an encoding for our scheme. Here, we devote 3 bits for encoding the type of the microinstruction. We need 3 bits because we have a total of 8 microinstructions (see Table 8.8). Each microinstruction embeds the 5 bit id (because we have 19 registers visible to microprograms) of an internal source register, 5 bit id of an internal destination register, a 12-bit immediate, and a 10-bit branch target. At the end, we encode a 10-bit args value in the microinstruction. Each instruction thus requires 45 bits.

Now, to process a vertically encoded microinstruction, we need a dedicated μdecode unit that can generate all the control signals. These signals include all the enable signals for the internal registers, and the signals to select the right input in the transfer multiplexer. Additionally it needs to extract some fields from the microinstruction such as the immediate, branch target, and the *args* value, and subsequently extend their sign. We have already gone through a similar exercise for extracting the fields of an instruction, and generating control signals, when we discussed the operand fetch unit and control unit for our hardwired processors in Sections 8.2.3, and 8.3 respectively. The logic for generating the control signals, and extracting fields from the microinstruction is exactly the same. Hence, we leave the detailed design of these units as an exercise for the reader.

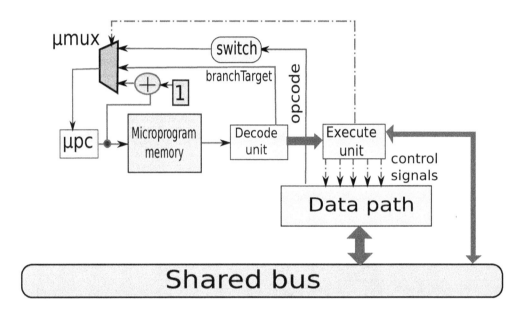

Figure 8.25: The μcontrol unit (vertical microprogramming)

The design of the vertical μcontrol unit is shown in Figure 8.25. We have a microPC (μpc), which saves the index of the currently executing microinstruction. Every cycle, we increment the μpc by 1. This is because each row of the microprogram memory saves 1 microinstruction. We assume that a row is wide enough to save the entire contents of the microinstructions. We do not have the requirement of saving data at the granularity of a fixed number of bytes here. After reading the microinstruction, we proceed to decode it. The process of decoding a microinstruction breaks it into a set of fields (instruction type, immediate, branch target, *args*, source, and destination registers). Subsequently, we generate all the control signals and dispatch the set of control signals to the execute unit. The execute unit sets all the control signals, and orchestrates an operation in the data path of the processor. The execute unit also sets the control signals of the transfer multiplexer. We need some additional support to process the *mswitch* instruction. We add a dedicated switch unit that takes inputs (the opcode) from the *ir* register, and computes the starting address for the microcode of the currently executing program instruction. It sends the address to the multiplexer, $\mu fetch$ (see Figure 8.25). The multiplexer chooses between three inputs – default microPC, branch target, and the address generated by the switch unit. It is controlled by the execute unit. The rules for choosing the input are shown in Table 8.9. In accordance with these rules, and the value of the *isMBranch* signal (generated by comparing μimm, and the contents of the shared bus), the execute unit generates the control signals for the $\mu fetch$ multiplexer.

Instruction	Output of the $\mu fetch$ multiplexer
$mloadIR$	next μpc
$mdecode$	next μpc
$mswitch$	output of the switch unit
$mmov$	next μpc
$mmovi$	next μpc
$madd$	next μpc
mb	branch target
$mbeq$	branch target if $isMBranch = 1$, else next μpc

Table 8.9: Rules for controlling the $\mu fetch$ multiplexer

8.8.2   Horizontal Microprogramming

We can further simplify the design of the μcontrol unit. We do not need three steps (fetch, decode, execute) to execute a microinstruction. The decode step is not required. We can embed all the control signals in the microinstruction itself. It is thus not required to have a dedicated signal generator to generate all the control signals. By doing so, we will increase the size of the encoding of an instruction. Since the number of microinstructions is small, and we do not have any significant constraints on the size of the encoding of a microinstruction, adding additional bits in the encoding is not an issue. This paradigm is known as *horizontal microprogramming*. The encoding of a microinstruction is shown in Figure 8.26.

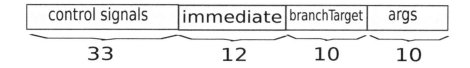

Figure 8.26: Encoding of a microinstruction (horizontal microprogramming)

We need the following fields – control signals (saved as a bit vector whose size is 33 bits), immediate (12 bits), branch target (10 bits), and args (10 bits). The reason we require 33 control signals is as follows. We have 19 registers (see Table 8.7) visible to microcode. Out of these register, the following 9 registers are exclusively connected to either the read bus or the write bus: ir, $flags.E$, $flags.GT$, I, rd, $rs1$, $rs2$, $branchTarget$, and $immx$. Hence, these registers require just one control signal. The rest of the registers have read-write functionality. Hence, these registers require two control signals. Thus, the total number of register enabling control signals are 29. We need 2 more signals each to control the transfer multiplexer, and the $\mu fetch$ multiplexer. We thus have a total of 33 control signals, and we require 65 bits to encode the instruction. Recall that with vertical microprogramming, we needed 45 bits.

Now, with additional storage we can completely eliminate the signal generator in the decode stage, and thus significantly simplify the μcontrol unit as shown in Figure 8.27

Here, we have eliminated the decode stage. All the signals are embedded in the instruction, and they are thus used to orchestrate a computation in the data path. The execute unit generates the $isMBranch$ signal (by comparing the μimm and the value on the read bus), which is used to choose between the next μpc, and the branch target using multiplexer, $M1$. Here, we slightly complicate the $\mu fetch$ multiplexer, and add a

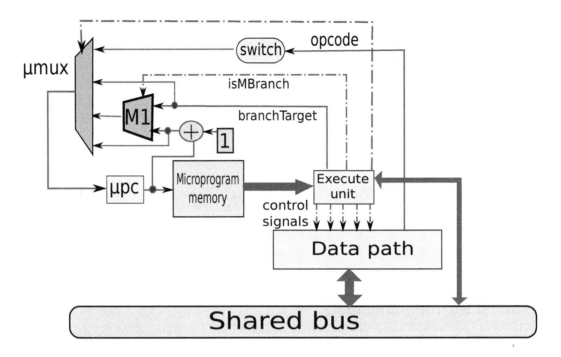

Figure 8.27: The μcontrol unit (horizontal microprogramming)

little bit of redundancy in the interest of simplicity. We make it a 4 input structure, and choose between the value from the switch unit, the branch target, the output of $M1$, and the next μpc. The 2-bit control signals for controlling the $\mu fetch$ multiplexer are embedded in the instruction in accordance with the rules given in Table 8.9. The rest of the operation of the circuit is the same as the circuit for vertical microprogramming as shown in Figure 8.25.

8.8.3 Tradeoffs between Horizontal and Vertical Microprogramming

The tradeoffs between horizontal and vertical microprogramming are the following:

1. Horizontal microprogramming requires more storage. However, this is not an issue in a microprogrammed processor. The additional storage is minimal.

2. Horizontal microprogramming eliminates the need for dedicated signal generation logic in the μcontrol unit.

3. To program a horizontally microprogrammed processor, it is necessary to expose the control signals to the programmer and the microassembler. This makes the microassembler very specific to a given processor. However, in vertical microprogramming, as long as the internal register set remains the same, we do not need different microassemblers.

To summarise, microprogramming is a very potent method to implement an instruction set. We can design very expressive instruction sets using this method. However, this is not a preferable approach for implementing all the instructions (especially the common ones) in a high performance processor.

8.9 Summary and Further Reading

8.9.1 Summary

Summary 8

1. We design a processor by dividing it into multiple stages, where the stages are mostly independent of each other. We divide our basic SimpleRisc processor into five stages: instruction fetch(IF), operand fetch(OF), execute (EX), memory access (MA), and register writeback (RW).

2. The roles of these stages are as follows:

   (a) The IF stage computes the next PC, and fetches the contents of the instruction, whose address is stored in the PC.

   (b) In the OF stage, we decode the instruction, and read its operands from the register file. Specifically, we compute the branch target, and expand the embedded immediate in the instruction according to the modifiers.

   (c) In the EX stage, we compute the branch outcome, branch target, and perform the ALU operations.

   (d) In the MA stage, we perform loads and stores.

   (e) Lastly, in the RW stage, we write back the values computed by ALU or load instructions, and the return address for a call instruction to the register file.

3. The data path consists of all the elements for storing, retrieving, and processing information such as the registers, memory elements, and the ALU. In contrast, the control path generates all the signals for controlling the movement of instructions and data.

4. We can use a hardwired control unit that generates all the signals for the control path.

5. For additional flexibility, and portability, we presented the design of a microprogrammed processor. This processor replaces every program instruction by a sequence of microinstructions.

6. We defined 8 microinstructions, and created a microprogrammed data path that connected all the units on a shared bus. Each unit in a microprogrammed data path exposes its input and output ports through registers. We use 19 registers in our design.

7. We subsequently showed implementations in microcode for all the instructions in the SimpleRisc ISA.

8. We designed a shared bus for such processors by interconnecting two physical buses (write bus, and read bus) with a multiplexer. The multiplexer (known as the transfer multiplexer) chooses between the output of the write bus, the output of the μadder, and the micro immediate.

9. We showed the design of a μcontrol unit for both vertical and horizontal microprogramming. Vertical microprogramming requires a decode stage for generating all the control signals. In comparison, horizontal microprogramming requires all the control signals to be embedded in the microinstruction.

8.9.2 Further Reading

Processor design is very heavily studied in courses on computer architecture. Readers should first start with Chapter 9 that discusses pipelining. Chapter 9 is a sequel to the current chapter. The reader can then take a look at the "Further Reading" section (Section 9.12.2) in Chapter 9. In general, for basic processor design, the reader can also consult other books on computer architecture [Mano, 2007, Stallings, 2010, Henessey and Patterson, 2010] to get a different perspective. The books by Morris Mano [Mano, 2007], and Carl Hamacher [Hamacher et al., 2001] consider different flavours of microprogramming, and define their own semantics. If the reader is interested in the history of microprogramming per se, then she can consult books dedicated to the design and history of microprogramming [Carter, 1995, Husson, 1970]. The PTLSim [Yourst, 2007] simulator translates x86 instructions into micro-instructions, and simulates these microinstructions on a data path similar to that of commercial processors. Readers can take a look at the code of this simulator, and appreciate the nuances of processing and executing microinstructions.

Exercises

Hardwired Processor Design

Ex. 1 — We have divided a *SimpleRisc* processor into 5 distinct units. List them, and describe their functions.

Ex. 2 — Explain the terms – *data path* and *control path*?

Ex. 3 — How does having a lesser number of instruction formats help in the process of decoding an instruction?

Ex. 4 — Draw the circuit for calculating the value of the 32-bit immediate, from the first 18 bits of the instruction. Take the modifiers into account.

Ex. 5 — Why is it necessary for the register file in our *SimpleRisc* processor to have 2 read ports, and 1 write port?

Ex. 6 — Why do we need 2 multiplexers in the OF stage of the processor? What are their functions?

Ex. 7 — Let us propose to compute the branch outcome and target in the OF stage. Describe the design of the OF stage with this functionality.

* Ex. 8 — For the ALU we use a multiplexer with a large number of inputs. How can we implement this multiplexer with transmission gates? (show a circuit diagram, and explain why your idea will work)

Ex. 9 — Draw a circuit for implementing the *cmp* instruction. It should show the circuit for subtraction, and the logic for updating the flags.

Ex. 10 — How do we implement the *call* instruction in our processor?

Ex. 11 — Draw the circuit diagram for computing the *isWb* signal.

Ex. 12 — Why do we use the *isAdd* control signal for the load, and store instructions also?

Microprogramming

Ex. 13 — Compare a hardwired control unit and a microprogrammed control unit.

Ex. 14 — Draw the block diagram of a microprogrammed processor.

Ex. 15 — Why do we need the *mswitch* instruction.

Ex. 16 — Describe the microcode implementation of the load and store instructions.

Ex. 17 — Write a program in microassembly to check if a number in register $r2$ is a perfect square. Save the Boolean result in register, r0.

Ex. 18 — Write a program in microassembly to check if the value in register $r2$ is a palindrome. A palindrome reads the same from both sides. For example, the 8 bit number, 11011011 is a palindrome. Save the Boolean result in register, r0.

* **Ex. 19** — Write a program in microassembly to check if the value in register $r2$ can be expressed as a sum of two cubes in two different ways. For example, 1729, is one such number. $1729 = 12^3 + 1^3 = 10^3 + 9^3$. Save the Boolean result in register, r0.

Ex. 20 — Outline the design of the shared bus, and microprogrammed data path. Explain the functionalities of each of its components.

Ex. 21 — Draw a detailed diagram of the μcontrol unit along with the transfer multiplexer in a vertically microprogrammed processor.

Ex. 22 — Draw a detailed diagram of the μcontrol unit along with the transfer multiplexer in a horizontally microprogrammed processor.

Ex. 23 — Compare the tradeoffs between horizontal and vertical microprogramming.

Design Problems

Ex. 24 — Implement the hardwired *SimpleRisc* processor using Logisim, which is an educational tool for designing and simulating digital circuits. It is freely available at `http://ozark.hendrix.edu/~burch/logisim`. Try to support all the instructions, and the modifiers.

Ex. 25 — Now, try to implement a horizontally microprogrammed processor using Logisim. This project has two parts.

   a)Write a microassembler that can translate microassembly instructions to their machine encodings. Use this microassembler to generate the microcode for all the instructions in the *SimpleRisc* ISA.

   b)Create a data path and control path in Logisim for a horizontally microprogrammed processor. This processor should be able to directly execute the code generated by the microassembler.

   c)Run regular *SimpleRisc* programs on this processor.

   d)Implement custom *SimpleRisc* instructions such as *multiply-add* ($a \leftarrow b * c + d$), or instructions to find the square of a number on this processor.

Ex. 26 — Implement the basic hardwired processor in a high-level description language such as VHDL. You can use the freely available open source tool GNU HDL (`http://gna.org/projects/ghdl/`) to implement and simulate your circuit.

Principles of Pipelining

9.1 A Pipelined Processor

Let us quickly review where, we are.

Way Point 7

1. *We have designed a processor with five main stages – IF, OF, EX, MA, and RW.*

2. *We have designed a detailed data path and control path for the hardwired implementation of our processor.*

3. *We introduced a microprogram based implementation of our processor in Section 8.4, and we designed a detailed data path and control path for it.*

Now, our aim is to make our processor fast and efficient. For this we focus on the hardwired implementation of our processor. We exclude microprogrammed processors from our discussion because we are explicitly looking for high performance, and flexibility/ reconfigurability are not important criteria for us in this section. Let us begin by pointing out some problems with the design of the hardwired processor as presented in Section 8.2.

9.1.1 The Notion of Pipelining

Issues with a Single-Cycle Processor

We assumed that our hardwired processor presented in Section 8.2 takes a single cycle to fetch, execute, and write the results of an instruction to either the register file or memory. At an electrical level, this is achieved by signals flowing from the fetch unit to ultimately the register writeback unit via other units. It takes time for electrical signals to propagate from one unit to the other.

For example, it takes some time to fetch an instruction from the instruction memory. Then it takes time to read values from the register file, and to compute the results with the ALU. Memory access, and writing the results back to the register file, are also fairly time taking operations. We need to wait for all of these individual sub-operations to complete, before we can begin processing the next instruction. In other words, this means that there is a significant amount of idleness in our circuit. When the operand fetch unit is doing its job, all other units are idle. Likewise, when the ALUs are active, all the other units are inactive. If we assume that each of the five stages (IF,OF,EX,MA,RW) takes the same amount of time, then at any instant, about 80% of our circuit is idle! This represents a waste in computational power, and idling resources is definitely not a good idea.

If we can find a method to keep all the units of a chip busy, then we can increase the rate at which we execute instructions.

9.1.2 Overview of Pipelining

Let us try to find an analogy to the problem of idleness in a simple single-cycle processor as we just discussed. Let us go back to our original example of the car factory. If we assume, that we start making a car, after the previous car has been completely manufactured, then we have a similar problem. When we are assembling the engine of a car, the paint shop is idle. Likewise, when we are painting a car, the engine shop is idle. Clearly, car factories cannot operate this way. They thus typically overlap the manufacturing stages of different cars. For example, when car A is in the paint shop, car B is in the engine shop. Subsequently, these cars move to the next stage of manufacturing and another new car enters the assembly line.

We can do something very similar here. When one instruction is in the EX stage, the next instruction can be in the OF stage, and the subsequent instruction can be in the IF stage. In fact, if we have 5 stages in our processor, where we simplistically assume that each stage roughly takes the same amount of time, we can assume that we have 5 instructions simultaneously being processed at the same time. Each instruction undergoes processing in a different unit of the processor. Similar to a car in an assembly line, an instruction moves from stage to stage in the processor. This strategy ensures that we do not have any idle units in our processor because all the different units in a processor are busy at any point in time.

In this scheme, the life cycle of an instruction is as follows. It enters the IF stage in cycle n, enters the OF stage in cycle $n+1$, EX stage in cycle $n+2$, MA stage in cycle $n+3$, and finally it finishes its execution in the RW stage in cycle $n+4$. This strategy is known as *pipelining*, and a processor that implements pipelining is known as a *pipelined* processor. The sequence of five stages (IF, OF, EX, MA, RW) conceptually laid out one after the other is known as the *pipeline* (similar to the car assembly line). Figure 9.1 shows the organisation of a pipelined data path.

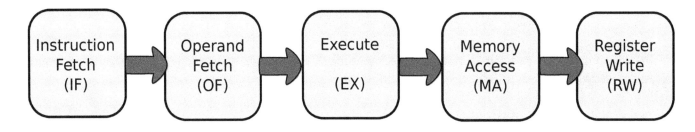

Figure 9.1: A pipelined data path

In Figure 9.1, we have divided the data path into five stages, where each stage processes a separate instruction. In the next cycle, each instruction passes on to the next stage as shown in the figure.

Definition 65

The notion of dividing a processor into a set of stages where the stages are ordered one after the other, and simultaneously process a set of instructions by assigning an instruction to each stage, is known as pipelining. The implicit assumption here is that it takes the same amount of time for each stage to complete its work. After this time quanta is over, each instruction moves to the subsequent stage.

The conceptual layout of stages where one stage is laid out after the other is known as a pipeline, and a processor that incorporates pipelining is known as a pipelined processor.

9.1.3 Performance Benefits

Let us quantify the expected benefit in terms of performance of a pipelined processor. We shall take a deeper look into performance issues in Section 9.9. Here, we shall look at this topic briefly. Let us assume that it takes τ nanoseconds for an instruction to travel from the IF to RW stage of the pipeline in the worst case. The minimum value of the clock cycle is thus limited to τ nanoseconds for the case of a single cycle pipeline. This is because in every clock cycle we need to ensure that an instruction executes completely. Alternatively, this mean that every τ nanoseconds, we finish the execution of an instruction.

Now, let us consider the case of a pipelined processor. Here, we have been assuming that the stages are balanced. This means that it takes the same amount of time to execute each stage. Most of the time, processor designers try to achieve this goal to the maximum extent that is possible. We can thus divide τ by 5, and conclude that it takes $\tau/5$ nanoseconds to execute each stage. We can thus set the cycle time to $\tau/5$. After the end of a cycle, the instructions in each stage of the pipeline proceed to the next stage. The instruction in the RW stage moves out of the pipeline and finished its execution. Simultaneously, a new instructions enters the IF stage. This is graphically shown in Figure 9.2.

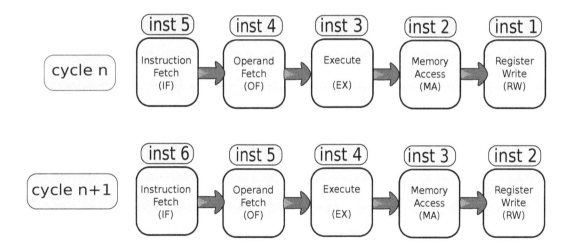

Figure 9.2: Instructions in the pipeline

In the nth cycle, we have five instructions (1-5) occupying the five stages of the pipeline. In the $(n+1)^{th}$ cycle each instruction progresses by 1 stage, and instruction 6 enters the pipeline. This pattern continues.

The noteworthy point is that we are finishing the execution of a new instruction, every $\tau/5$ nanoseconds. As compared to a single-cycle processor that finishes the execution of a new instruction every τ nanoseconds, the instruction throughput is 5 times higher for a pipelined processor. In a span of 1000 nanoseconds, a single cycle processor completes $1000/\tau$ instructions, whereas a pipelined processor completes $5000/\tau$ instructions, and is thus 5 times more efficient. Therefore, we observe a fivefold advantage with pipelining.

If we can obtain a fivefold advantage with a 5-stage pipeline, then by the same logic we should be able to obtain a 100-fold advantage with a 100-stage pipeline. In fact, we can keep on increasing the number of stages till a stage just contains one transistor. However, this is not the case, and there are fundamental limitations to the performance of a pipelined processor, as we shall show in the subsequent sections. It is not possible to arbitrarily increase the performance of a processor by increasing the number of pipeline stages. In fact, after a certain point, adding more stages is counterproductive.

9.2 Design of a Simple Pipeline

Let us now design a simple pipeline. Our main aim in this section is to split the data path of the single-cycle processor into five stages and ensure that five instructions can be processed concurrently (one instruction in each stage). We need to also ensure the seamless movement of instructions between the pipeline stages. Note that the problem of designing a pipeline in general is very complex, and we will explore some of the major nuances in the next few sections. For this section, let us not consider any dependences between instructions, or consider any correctness issues. We shall look at these issues in detail in Section 9.4. Let us reiterate that at the moment, we want to design a simple pipeline that needs to have the capability to process five instructions simultaneously, and ensure that they move to the subsequent stage every new cycle.

9.2.1 Splitting the Data Path

We have five distinct units in our data path, and all instructions traverse the units in the same order. These units are instruction fetch (IF), operand fetch (OF), execute (EX), memory access (MA), and the register write (RW) units. A layout of these five units in a pipelined fashion has already been shown in Figure 9.1. Let us now discuss the issue of splitting a data path in some more detail.

The reader needs to note that pipelining is a general concept, and any circuit can in principle be split into multiple parts and pipelined. There are however some rules that need to be followed. All the subparts of the circuit must preferably be distinct entities that have as few connections between them as possible. This is true in the case of our data path. All our units are distinct entities. The second is that all kinds of data must flow through the units in the same order, and lastly the work done by each unit should roughly be the same. This minimises the idleness in the circuit. In our case, we have tried to follow all these rules. The reader needs to note that the *div* and *mod* operations are exceptions to this rule. They are in general, significantly slower, than add or multiply operations. They thus increase the maximum delay of the EX stage, and the pipeline consequently becomes unbalanced. Hence, most simple pipelined processors either refrain from implementing these instructions, or have specialised logic to deal with them. We shall show one solution for this problem in Section 9.6 that proposes to stall a pipeline till a division operation completes. Let us nevertheless continue to assume that all our pipeline stages are balanced.

9.2.2 Timing

Now, we need to design a method that ensures that instructions seamlessly proceed to the subsequent pipeline stage. We need a global mechanism that ensures that all the instructions proceed to the next stages simultaneously. We already have this global mechanism built in, and is nothing else, but the *clock*. We can have a protocol that for example, ensures that at the falling edge of the clock, all the instructions proceed to the subsequent stages.

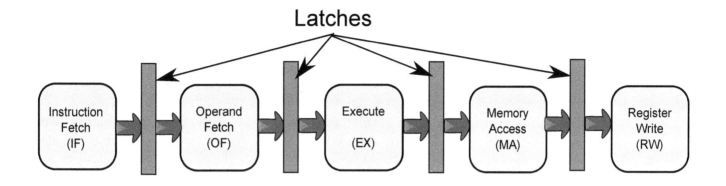

Figure 9.3: A pipelined data path with registers

Figure 9.3 shows a simple method to achieve this. We insert a register between two consecutive pipeline stages. Since we have five pipeline stages in our data path, we insert 4 registers. The four registers are named after their locations – IF-OF, OF-EX, EX-MA, and MA-RW. Each of these registers are called pipeline registers or pipeline latches. The reader needs to note that in this case, a *latch*, is actually referring to an edge triggered register. We shall use the terms interchangeably. All the pipeline registers are connected to a common clock, and read-write data at the same time.

Definition 66

A pipeline register, *or a* pipeline latch *is a register that is added between two consecutive pipeline stages. All the registers are connected to the common clock, and help in seamlessly transferring instructions between pipeline stages.*

Let us explain with an example. When an instruction enters the pipeline, it enters the IF unit. At the end of the first cycle, it gets saved in the IF-OF register. At the beginning of the second cycle, it enters the OF stage, and then again at the end of the second cycle, it gets latched into the OF-EX register. This pattern continues till the instruction leaves the pipeline. The pipeline registers essentially transfer their inputs to the outputs at the end of a cycle (negative edge of the clock). Then the logic of the pipeline stage processes the instruction, and at the end of the cycle, the instruction gets transferred to the register of the subsequent pipeline stage. In this manner, an instruction hops between stages till it reaches the end of the pipeline.

9.2.3 The Instruction Packet

Let us now proceed to design our data path with pipeline stages and registers in some more detail. Up till now we have been maintaining that the instruction needs to be transferred between registers. Let us elaborate on the term "instruction". We actually mean an *instruction packet* here, which contains all the details regarding the instruction, along with all of its intermediate results, and the control signals that it may require.

We need to create such an elaborate instruction packet because there are multiple instructions in the processor at the same time. We need to ensure that there is no overlap between the information required to process two different instructions. A clean way of designing this is to confine all the information required to process an instruction in a packet, and transfer the packet between pipeline registers every cycle. This mechanism also ensures that all the intermediate state required to process an instruction is removed after it leaves the pipeline.

What should an instruction packet contain? It needs to contain at the least, the PC and the contents of the instruction. It should also contain all the operands and control signals that are required by subsequent stages. The amount of information that needs to be stored in the instruction packet reduces as the instruction proceeds towards the last stage. For the sake of uniformity, we assume that all the pipeline registers have the same size, and are sized to hold the entire instruction packet. Some of the fields might not be used. However, this is a negligible overhead. Let us now proceed to design the data path of the pipeline. We shall use exactly the same design as we had used for the single-cycle processor. The only difference is that we add a register after each pipeline stage, other than the last stage, RW. Secondly, we add connections to transfer data in and out of the pipeline registers. Let us quickly take a look at each of the pipeline stages in our pipelined data path.

9.3 Pipeline Stages

9.3.1 IF Stage

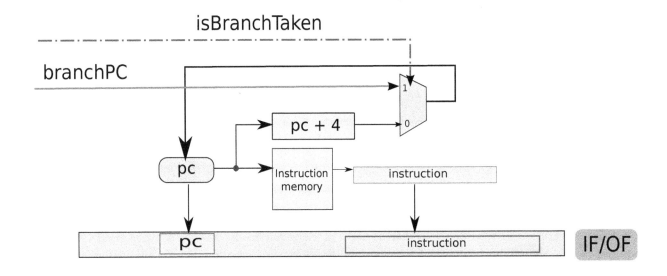

Figure 9.4: The IF stage in a pipelined processor

Figure 9.4 shows the IF stage augmented with a pipeline register. We save the value of the PC, and the contents of the instruction in the pipeline register. This is all the information that we need to carry forward to the subsequent stages of the pipeline. Other than this small change, we do not need to make any other change in this part of the data path.

9.3.2 OF Stage

Figure 9.5 shows the design of the operand fetch stage. The only extra additions are the connections to the two pipeline registers IF-OF, and OF-EX. The stage starts out by extracting the fields rd (bits 23-26), $rs1$ (bits 19-22), $rs2$ (bits 15-18), and the immediate (bits 1-18) from the instruction. These are sent to the register file, the immediate and branch units. Additionally, we send the contents of the instruction to the control unit that generates all the control signals. Three of the control signals namely *isRet*, *isImmediate*,

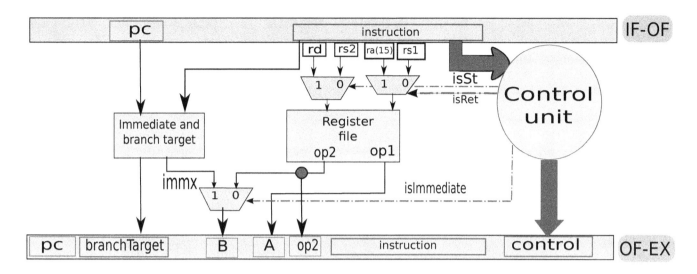

Figure 9.5: The OF stage in a pipelined processor

and *isSt* are used immediately. The rest of the control signals are for controlling multiplexers in subsequent stages of the pipeline. Hence, it is necessary for us to save them in the OF-EX pipeline register such that they can traverse the pipeline along with the instruction, and control the actions of different units accordingly. Therefore, we allocate some space within the instruction packet, and store all the control signals generated by the control unit (refer to the field *control* in Figure 9.5).

We need to carry all the intermediate results generated by the OF stage. In specific, the OF stage generates the *branchTarget*, both the inputs for the ALU (A, and B), and the value to be written to memory for a store instruction (*op2*). Thus, we allocate four fields in the instruction packet, and the OF-EX pipeline register to store this information as shown in Figure 9.5. Let us recall that the aim of designing the instruction packet was to have all the information required to process an instruction at one place. In accordance with this philosophy we have saved all the details of the instruction including its address, contents, intermediate results, and control signals in our pipeline registers.

9.3.3   EX Stage

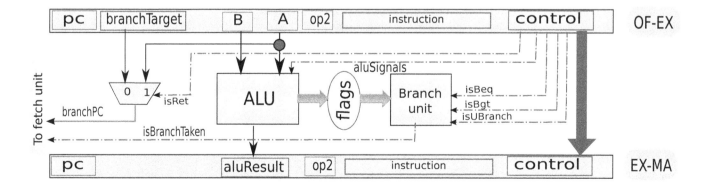

Figure 9.6: The EX stage in a pipelined processor

Let us now take a look at the EX stage in Figure 9.6. The ALU receives its inputs(A and B) from the OF-EX pipeline register. The results generated by this stage are the *aluResult* (result of the ALU operation), the final branch target, and the branch outcome. The branch outcome is 1, if the branch is taken, otherwise it is 0. The result of the ALU operation is added to the instruction packet, and saved in the EX-MA register. The EX-MA register also contains the rest of the fields of the instruction packet namely the PC, *instruction* (contents of the instruction), *control* signals, and the second operand read from the register file (*op2*).

For computing the final branch target, we need to choose between the branch target computed in the OF stage and the value of the return address register (possibly stored in A). The result of the choice is the final branch target(*branchPC*), and this is sent to the fetch unit. The branch unit computes the value of the signal, *isBranchTaken*. If it is 1, then the instruction is a branch, and it is taken. Otherwise, the fetch unit needs to use the default option of fetching the next PC.

9.3.4   MA Stage

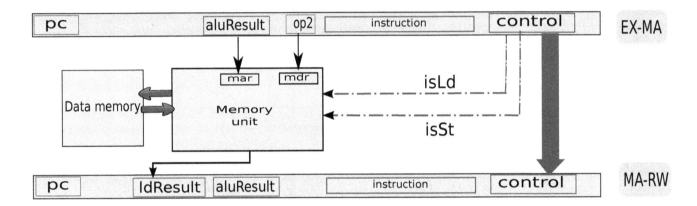

Figure 9.7: The MA stage in a pipelined processor

The MA stage is shown in Figure 9.7. The only operand that the load instruction uses is the result of the ALU, which contains the effective memory address. This is saved in the *aluResult* field of the EX-MA register. The data to be stored resides in the *rd* register. This value was read from the register file in the OF stage, and was stored in the *op2* field of the instruction packet. In this stage, the *op2* field is connected to the MDR (memory data register) register. The relevant control signals – *isLd* and *isSt* – are also a part of the instruction packet, and they are routed to the memory unit.

The only output of this stage is the result of the load instruction. This is saved in the *ldResult* field of the MA-RW register.

9.3.5   RW Stage

We need to lastly take a look at the RW stage in Figure 9.8. The inputs that it requires from the previous stages are the values of the ALU and load operations stored in the *aluResult* and *ldResult* fields respectively. These inputs along with the default next PC (current PC + 4) are connected to a multiplexer that chooses the value to be written back. The rest of the circuit is the same as that of the single-cycle processor. Note that there is no pipeline register at the end of the RW stage because it is the last stage in the pipeline.

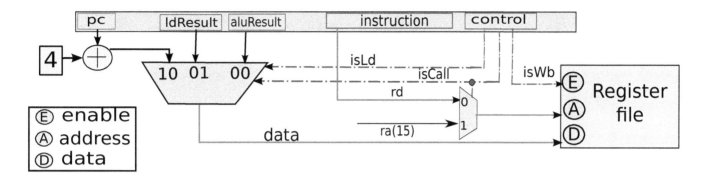

Figure 9.8: The RW stage in a pipelined processor

9.3.6 Putting it All Together

Let us now summarise our discussion regarding the simple pipeline by showing our data path with the pipeline registers in Figure 9.9. The figure is undoubtedly complex. However, the reader has seen all the parts of this figure before and thus should not have a significant amount of difficulty in putting the different parts together. Nonetheless, we should note that the design of our processor has already become fairly complex, and the size of our diagrams have already reached one page !!! We do not want to introduce more complicated diagrams. The reader should note that up till now our aim was to introduce the entire circuit. However, we shall now introduce some degree of abstraction such that we can introduce more complicated features into our processor. Henceforth, we shall broadly concentrate on the logic of the pipeline, and not talk about the implementation in detail. We shall leave the implementation of the exact circuit as an exercise for the reader.

Figure 9.10 shows an abstraction of our pipeline data path. This figure prominently contains block diagrams for the different units and shows the four pipeline registers. We shall use this diagram as the baseline for our discussion on advanced pipelines. Recall that the first register operand can either be the *rs*1 field of the instruction, or it can be the return address register in the case of a *ret* instruction. A multiplexer to choose between *ra* and *rs*1 is a part of our baseline pipeline design, and for the sake of simplicity, we do not show it in the diagram. We assume that it is a part of the register file unit. Similarly, the multiplexer to choose the second register operand (between *rd* and *rs*2) is also assumed to be a part of the register file unit, and is thus not shown in the diagram. We only show the multiplexer that chooses the second operand (register or immediate).

9.4 Pipeline Hazards

In our simple pipeline discussed in Section 9.2, we were not concerned with correctness issues in the pipeline. We were simply concerned with designing the pipeline, and having the capability to process five instructions at the same time. Now, we want to take a look at correctness issues. Let us start out by introducing the pipeline diagram, which will prove to be a very useful tool in our analyses.

9.4.1 The Pipeline Diagram

We typically use a pipeline diagram to study the behaviour of a pipeline. It shows the relationships between instructions, clock cycles, and the different stages of the pipeline. It can be used to study the nature of dependences across different instructions, and their execution in the pipeline.

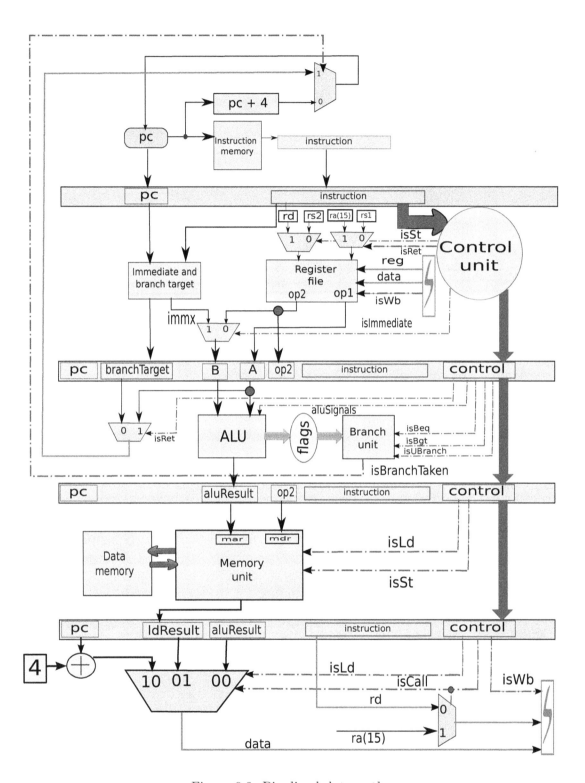

Figure 9.9: Pipelined data path

Figure 9.11 shows a pipeline diagram for three instructions as they proceed through the pipeline. Each row of the diagram corresponds to each pipeline stage. The columns correspond to clock cycles. In our

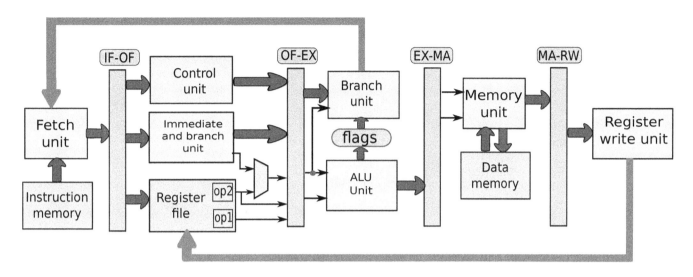

Figure 9.10: An abstraction of the pipelined data path

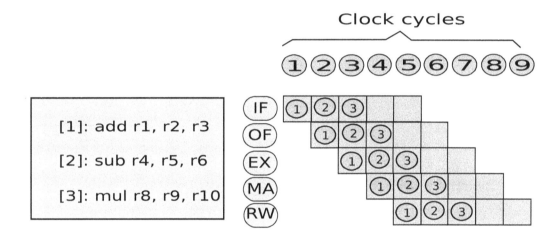

Figure 9.11: The Pipeline Diagram

sample code, we have three instructions that do not have any dependences between each other. We name these instructions – [1], [2], and [3] respectively. The earliest instruction, [1] enters the IF stage of the pipeline in the first cycle, and leaves the pipeline in the fifth cycle. Similarly, the second instruction, [2], enters the IF stage of the pipeline in the second cycle, and leaves the pipeline in the sixth cycle. Each of these instructions progresses to the subsequent stage of the pipeline in each cycle. The trace of each instruction in the pipeline diagram is a diagonal that is oriented towards the bottom-right. Note that this scenario will get fairly complicated after we consider dependences across instructions.

Here, are the rules to construct a pipeline diagram.

1. Construct a grid of cells, which has five rows, and N columns, where N is the total number of clock cycles that we wish to consider. Each of the five rows corresponds to a pipeline stage.

2. If an instruction ([k]) enters the pipeline in cycle m, then we add an entry corresponding to [k] in the

m^{th} column of the first row.

3. In the $(m+1)^{th}$ cycle, the instruction can either stay in the same stage (because the pipeline might be stalled, described later), or can move to the next row (OF stage). We add a corresponding entry in the grid cell.

4. In a similar manner, the instruction moves from the IF stage to the RW stage in sequence. It never moves backwards. However, it can stay in the same stage across consecutive cycles.

5. We cannot have two entries in a cell.

6. We finally remove the instruction from the pipeline diagram after it leaves the RW stage.

Example 109
Build a pipeline diagram for the following code snippet. Assume that the first instruction enters the pipeline in cycle 1.

```
[1]: add r1, r2, r3
[2]: sub r4, r2, r5
[3]: mul r5, r8, r9
```

Answer:

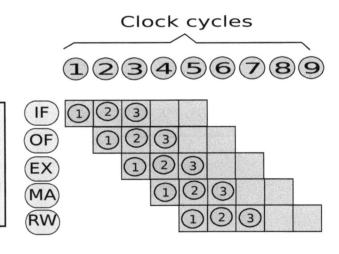

9.4.2 Data Hazards

Let us consider the following code snippet.

```
[1]: add r1, r2, r3
[2]: sub r3, r1, r4
```

Here, the *add* instruction is producing the value for register, $r1$, and the *sub* instruction is using it as a source operand. Let us now construct a pipeline diagram for just these instructions as shown in Figure 9.12.

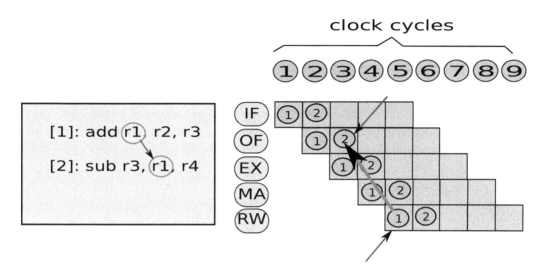

Figure 9.12: Pipeline diagram showing a RAW hazard

There is a problem. Instruction 1 writes the value of $r1$ in the fifth cycle, and instruction 2 needs to read its value in the third cycle. This is clearly not possible. We have added an arrow between the relevant pipeline stages of both the instructions to indicate that there is a dependency. Since the arrow is towards the left (backwards in time), we cannot execute this code sequence in a pipeline. This is known as a *data hazard*. A hazard is defined as the possibility of erroneous execution of an instruction in a pipeline. This specific case is classified as a *data hazard*, where it is possible that instruction 2 might get the wrong data unless adequate steps are taken.

Definition 67

A hazard is defined as the possibility of erroneous execution of an instruction in a pipeline. A data hazard represents the possibility of erroneous execution because of the unavailability of correct data.

This specific type of data hazard is known as a RAW (read after write) hazard. Here the subtract instruction is trying to read $r1$, which needs to be written by the add instruction. In this case, a read succeeds a write.

Note that this is not the only kind of data hazard. The two other types of data hazards are WAW (write after write), and WAR (write after read) hazards. These hazards are not an issue in our pipeline because we never change the order of instructions. A preceding instruction is always ahead of a succeeding instruction in the pipeline. This is an example of an *in-order pipeline*. In comparison, modern processors have out-of-order pipelines that execute instructions in different orders.

Definition 68

In an in-order *pipeline (such as ours), a preceding instruction is always ahead of a succeeding instruction in the pipeline. Modern processors use* out-of-order *pipelines that break this rule and it is possible for later instructions to execute before earlier instructions.*

Let us take a look at the following assembly code snippet.

```
[1]: add r1, r2, r3
[2]: sub r1, r4, r3
```

Here, instructions 1 and 2 are writing to register $r1$. In an in-order pipeline $r1$ will be written in the correct order, and thus there is no WAW hazard. However, in an out-of-order pipeline we run the risk of finishing instruction 2 before instruction 1, and thus $r1$ can end up with the wrong value. This is an example of a WAW hazard. The reader should note that modern processors ensure that $r1$ does not get the wrong value by using a technique known as *register renaming* (see Section 9.11.4).

Let us give an example of a potential WAR hazard.

```
[1]: add r1, r2, r3
[2]: add r2, r5, r6
```

Here, instruction 2 is trying to write to $r2$, and instruction 1 has $r2$ as a source operand. If instruction 2 executes first, then instruction 1 risks getting the wrong value of $r2$. In practice this does not happen in modern processors because of schemes such as register renaming. The reader needs to understand that a hazard is a theoretical risk of something wrong happening. It is not a real risk because adequate steps are taken to ensure that programs are not executed incorrectly.

In this book, we will mostly focus on RAW hazards, because WAW and WAR hazards are relevant only for modern out-of-order processors. Let us outline the nature of the solution. To avoid a RAW hazard it is necessary to ensure that the pipeline is aware of the fact that it contains a pair of instructions, where one instruction writes to a register, and another instruction that comes later in program order reads from the same register. It needs to ensure that the consumer instruction correctly receives the value of the operand (in this case, register) from the producer instruction. We shall look at solutions in both hardware and software.

9.4.3 Control Hazards

Let us now look at another type of hazards that arise when we have branch instructions in the pipeline. Let us consider the following code snippet.

```
[1]: beq .foo
[2]: mov r1, 4
[3]: add r2, r4, r3
...
...
.foo:
[100]: add r4, r1, r2
```

Let us show the pipeline diagram for the first three instructions in Figure 9.13.

Here, the outcome of the branch is decided in cycle 3, and is communicated to the fetch unit. The fetch unit starts fetching the correct instruction from cycle 4. Now, if the branch is taken, then instructions 2, and 3, should not be executed. Sadly, there is no way of knowing in cycles 2 and 3, about the outcome of the branch. Hence, these instructions will be fetched, and will be a part of the pipeline. If the branch is taken, then there is a possibility that instructions 2 and 3 might corrupt the state of the program, and consequently introduce an error. Instructions 2 and 3, are known as *instructions in the wrong path*. This scenario is known as a *control hazard*.

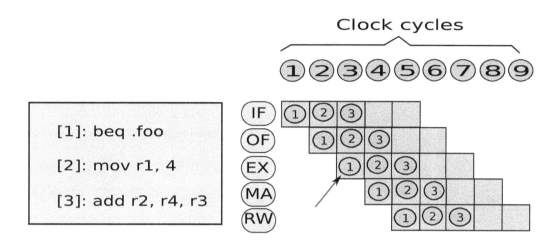

Figure 9.13: Pipeline diagram

Definition 69

Instructions that would have been executed if a branch would have had an outcome that is different from its real outcome, are said to be on the wrong path. *For example, instructions succeeding a branch instruction in the program, are in the wrong path, if the branch is taken.*

Definition 70

A control hazard *represents the possibility of erroneous execution in a pipeline because instructions in the* wrong path *of a branch can possibly get executed and save their results in memory, or in the register file.*

To avoid a control hazard, it is necessary to identify instructions in the wrong path, and ensure that their results do not get committed to the register file, and memory. There should be a way to nullify such instructions, or avoid them altogether.

9.4.4   Structural Hazards

Definition 71

A structural hazard *refers to the possibility of instructions not being able to execute because of resource constraints. For example, they can arise when multiple instructions try to access a functional unit in the same cycle, and due to capacity limitations, the unit cannot allow all the interested instructions to proceed. In this case, a few of the instructions in the conflict need to stall their execution.*

Structural hazards do not arise in the *SimpleRisc* pipeline. However, for the sake of completeness, we should still study them. They arise when different instructions try to access the same resource, and the resource cannot allow all of them to access it in the same cycle. Let us give an example. Let us suppose that we had an *add* instruction that could read one operand from memory. It could have the following form:

```
add  r1, r2, 10[r3]
```

Here, we have one register source operand, $r2$, and a memory source operand, $10[r3]$. Let us further assume that our pipeline reads the value of the memory operand in the OF stage. Let us now look at a potentially conflicting situation.

```
[1]: st r4, 20[r5]
[2]: sub r8, r9, r10
[3]: add r1, r2, 10[r3]
```

Note that there are no control and data hazards here. Let us nonetheless, consider a point in the pipeline diagram when the store instruction is in the MA stage. At this point instruction 2 is in the EX stage, and instruction 3 is in the OF stage. Note that in this cycle, both instructions 1 and 3 need to access the memory unit. However, if we assume that the memory unit can only service one request per cycle, then clearly there is a conflicting situation. One of the instructions needs to stall its execution. This situation is an example of a *structural hazard*.

We claim that in our *SimpleRisc* pipeline there are no structural hazards. In other words, we never have a situation in which multiple instructions across different pipeline stages wish to access the same unit, and that unit does not have the capacity to service all the requests. This statement can be proved by considering that the only units that are accessed by multiple stages are the fetch unit, and the register file. The fetch unit is accessed by an instruction in the IF stage, and by branch instructions in the EX stage. It is designed to handle both the requests. Likewise, the register file is accessed by instructions in the OF stage, and RW stage. Our register file has two read ports, and one write port. It can thus handle both the requests in the same cycle.

Let us thus focus on trying to eliminate RAW and control hazards.

9.5   Solutions in Software

9.5.1   RAW Hazards

Now, let us find a way of avoiding a RAW hazard. Let us look at our example again.

```
[1]: add r1, r2, r3
[2]: sub r3, r1, r4
```

Instruction 2 requires the value of $r1$ in the OF stage. However, at that point of time, instruction 1 is in the EX stage, and it would not have written back the value of $r1$ to the register file. Thus, instruction 2 cannot be allowed to proceed in the pipeline. Let us propose a naive software solution to this problem. A smart compiler can analyse the code sequence and realise that a RAW hazard exists. It can introduce *nop* instructions between these instructions to remove any RAW hazards. Let us consider the following code sequence

```
[1]: add r1, r2, r3
[2]: nop
```

```
[3]: nop
[4]: nop
[5]: sub r3, r1, r4
```

Here, when the *sub* instruction reaches the OF stage, the *add* instruction would have written its value and left the pipeline. Thus, the *sub* instruction will get the correct value. Note that adding *nop* instructions is a costly solution, because we are essentially wasting computational power. In this example, we have basically wasted 3 cycles by adding *nop* instructions. However, if we consider a longer sequence of code, then the compiler can possibly reorder the instructions such that we can minimise the number of *nop* instructions. The basic aim of any compiler intervention needs to be that there have to be a minimum of 3 instructions between a producer and consumer instruction. Let us consider Example 110.

Example 110

Reorder the following code snippet, and add a sufficient number of nop instructions to make it execute correctly on a SimpleRisc pipeline.

```
add r1, r2, r3
add r4, r1, 3
add r8, r5, r6
add r9, r8, r5
add r10, r11, r12
add r13, r10, 2
```

Answer:

```
add r1, r2, r3
add r8, r5, r6
add r10, r11, r12
nop
add r4, r1, 3
add r9, r8, r5
add r13, r10, 2
```

We need to appreciate two important points here. The first is the power of the *nop* instruction, and the next is the power of the compiler. The compiler is a vital tool in ensuring the correctness of the program, and also improving its performance. In this case, we want to reorder code in such a way that we introduce the minimum number of *nop* instructions.

9.5.2 Control Hazards

Let us now try to use the same set of techniques to solve the issue of control hazards. If we take a look at the pipeline diagram again, then we can conclude that there need to be a minimum of two instructions between the branch instruction and the instruction at the branch target. This is because, we get both the branch outcome, and the branch target at the end of the EX stage. At this point of time there are two more instructions in the pipeline. These instructions have been fetched when the branch instruction was in the OF, and EX stages respectively. They might potentially be on the wrong path. After the branch target, and outcome have been determined in the EX stage, we can proceed to fetch the correct instruction in the IF stage.

Now, let us consider these two instructions that were fetched, when we were not sure of the branch outcome. If the PC of the branch is equal to p_1, then their addresses are $p_1 + 4$, and $p_1 + 8$ respectively. They are not on the wrong path if the branch is not taken. However, if the branch is taken, then these instructions need to be discarded from the pipeline since they are on the wrong path. For doing this, let us look at a simple solution in software.

Let us consider a scheme where the hardware assumes that the two instructions immediately after a branch instruction are not on the wrong path. The positions of these two instructions are known as the *delay slots*. Trivially, we can ensure that the instructions in the delay slots do not introduce errors, by inserting two *nop* instructions after a branch. However, we will not gain any extra performance by doing this. We can instead find two instructions that execute before the branch instruction, and move them to the two delay slots immediately after the branch.

Note that we cannot arbitrarily move instructions to the delay slots. We cannot violate any data dependence constraints, and we need to also avoid RAW hazards. Secondly, we cannot move any compare instructions into the delay slots. If appropriate instructions are not available, then we can always fall back to the trivial solution and insert *nop* instructions. It is also possible that we may find just one instruction that we can reorder, then we just need to insert one *nop* instruction after the branch instruction. The method of delayed branches is a very potent method in reducing the number of *nop* instructions that need to be added to avoid control hazards.

The reader should convince herself that to support this simple software scheme, we do not need to make any changes in hardware. The pipelined data path shown in Figure 9.9 already supports this scheme. In our simple pipelined data path, the two instructions fetched after the branch have their PCs equal to $p_1 + 4$, and $p_1 + 8$ respectively (p_1 is the PC of the branch instruction). Since the compiler ensures that these instructions are always on the correct path irrespective of the outcome of the branch, we do not commit an error by fetching them. After the outcome of the branch has been determined, the next instruction that is fetched either has a PC equal to $p_1 + 12$ if the branch is not taken, or the PC is equal to the branch target if the branch is taken. Thus, in both the cases, the correct instruction is fetched after the outcome of the branch is determined, and we can conclude that our software solution executes programs correctly on the pipelined version of our processor.

To summarise, the crux of our software technique is the notion of the *delay slot*. We need two delay slots after a branch because we are not sure about the two subsequent instructions. They might be on the wrong path. However, using a smart compiler we can manage to move instructions that get executed irrespective of the outcome of the branch to the delay slots. We can thus avoid placing *nop* instructions in the delay slots, and consequently increase performance. Such a branch instruction is known as a *delayed branch* instruction.

Definition 72
A branch instruction is known as a delayed branch *if the processor assumes that all the succeeding instructions that are fetched before its outcome has been determined, are on the correct path. If the processor fetches n instructions between the time that a branch instruction has been fetched, and its outcome has been determined, then we say that we have n delay slots. The compiler needs to ensure that instructions on the correct path occupy the delay slots, and no additional control or RAW hazards are introduced. The compiler can also trivially introduce nop instructions in the delay slots.*

Now, let us consider a set of examples.

Example 111
Reorder the following piece of assembly code to correctly run on a pipelined SimpleRisc processor with delayed branches. Assume two delay slots per branch instruction.

```
add r1, r2, r3
add r4, r5, r6
b .foo
add r8, r9, r10
```

Answer:

```
b .foo
add r1, r2, r3
add r4, r5, r6
add r8, r9, r10
```

9.6 Pipeline with Interlocks

Up till now, we have only looked at software solutions for eliminating RAW and control hazards. However, compiler approaches, are not very generic. Programmers can always write assembly code manually, and try to run it on the processor. In this case, the likelihood of an error is high, because programmers might not have reordered their code properly to remove hazards. Secondly, there is an issue of portability. A piece of assembly code written for one pipeline, might not run on another pipeline that follows the same ISA. This is because it might have a different number of delay slots, or different number of stages. One of our main aims of introducing assembly programs gets defeated, if our assembly programs are not portable across different machines that use the same ISA.

Hence, let us try to design solutions at the hardware level. The hardware should ensure that irrespective of the assembly program, it is run correctly. The output should always match that produced by a single cycle processor. To design such kind of a processor, we need to ensure that an instruction never receives wrong data, and wrong path instructions are not executed. This can be done by ensuring that the following conditions hold.

- Condition: `Data-Lock` : We cannot allow an instruction to leave the OF stage unless it has received the correct data from the register file. This means that we need to effectively *stall* the IF and OF stages and let the rest of the stages execute till the instruction in the OF stage can safely read its operands. During this time, the instruction that passes from the OF to the EX stage needs to be a *nop* instruction.

- Condition: `Branch-Lock` : We never execute instructions on the wrong path. We either stall the processor till the outcome is known, or use techniques to ensure that instructions on the wrong path are not able to commit their changes to the memory, or registers.

Definition 73

In a purely hardware implementation of a pipeline, it is sometimes necessary to stop a new instruction from entering a pipeline stage, till a certain condition ceases to hold. The notion of stopping a pipeline stage from accepting and processing new data, is known as a pipeline stall, *or a* pipeline interlock. *Its primary purpose is to ensure the correctness of program execution.*

If we ensure that both the `Data-Lock` and `Branch-Lock` conditions hold, then our pipeline will execute instructions correctly. Note that both the conditions dictate that possibly some stages of the pipeline needs to be stalled for some time. These stalls are also known as *pipeline interlocks*. In other words, by keeping our pipeline idle for some time, we can avoid executing instructions that might potentially lead to an erroneous execution. Let us now quickly compare the pure software and hardware schemes in Table 9.1, and see what are the pros and cons of implementing the entire logic of the pipeline in hardware. Note that in the software solution we try to reorder code, and subsequently insert the minimum number of *nop* instructions to nullify the effect of hazards. In comparison, in the hardware solution, we dynamically stall parts of the pipeline to avoid executing instructions in the wrong path, or with wrong values of operands. Stalling the pipeline is tantamount to keeping some stages idle, and inserting *nop* instructions in other stages as we shall see later in this section.

Attribute	Software	Hardware (with interlocks)
Portability	Limited to a specific processor	Programs can be run on any processor irrespective of the nature of the pipeline
Branches	Possible to have no performance penalty, by using delay slots	Need to stall the pipeline for 2 cycles in our design
RAW hazards	Possible to eliminate them through code scheduling	Need to stall the pipeline
Performance	Highly dependent on the nature of the program	The basic version of a pipeline with interlocks is expected to be slower than the version that relies on software

Table 9.1: Comparison between software and hardware approaches for ensuring the correctness of a pipeline

We observe that the efficacy of the software solution is highly dependent on the nature of the program. It is possible to reorder the instructions in some programs to completely hide the deleterious effects of RAW hazards and branches. However, in some programs we might not find enough instructions that can be reordered. We would be thus compelled to insert a lot of *nop* instructions, and this would reduce our performance. In comparison, a pure hardware scheme, which obeys the `Data-Lock` and `Branch-Lock` conditions stalls the pipeline whenever it detects an instruction that might execute erroneously. It is a generic approach, which is slower than a pure software solution.

Now, it is possible to combine the hardware and software solutions to reorder code to make it "pipeline friendly" as much as possible, and then run it on a pipeline with interlocks. Note that in this approach, no guarantees of correctness are made by the compiler. It simply spaces producer and consumer instructions as far apart as possible, and takes advantage of delayed branches if they are supported. This reduces the number of times we need to stall the pipeline, and ensures the best of both worlds. Before proceeding to design a pipeline with interlocks, let us study the nature of interlocks with the help of pipeline diagrams.

9.6.1 A Conceptual Look at a Pipeline with Interlocks

Data Hazards

Let us now draw the pipeline diagram of a pipeline with interlocks. Let us consider the following code snippet.

```
[1]: add r1, r2, r3
[2]: sub r4, r1, r2
```

Here, instruction [1] writes to register $r1$ and instruction [2] reads from $r1$. Clearly, there is a RAW dependence. To ensure the **Data-Lock** condition, we need to ensure that instruction [2] leaves the OF stage only when it has read the value of $r1$ written by instruction [1]. This is possible only in cycle 6 (refer to the pipeline diagram in Figure 9.14). However, instruction [2] reaches the OF stage in cycle 3. If there would have been no hazard, then it would have ideally proceeded to the EX stage in cycle 4. Since we have an interlock, instruction [2] needs to stay in the OF stage in cycles 4,5 and 6 also. The question is, "what does the EX stage do when it is not processing a valid instruction in cycles 4, 5 and 6?" Similarly, the MA stage does not process any valid instruction in cycles 5, 6 and 7. We need to have a way to disable pipeline stages, such that we do not perform redundant work. The standard approach is to insert *nop* instructions into stages, if we want to effectively disable them.

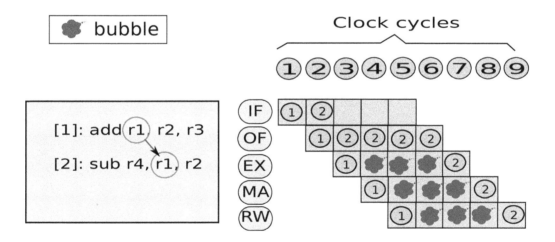

Figure 9.14: A pipeline diagram with bubbles

Let us refer to Figure 9.14 again. At the end of cycle 3, we know that we need to introduce an interlock. Hence, in cycle 4, instruction [2] remains in the OF stage, and we insert a *nop* instruction into the EX stage. This *nop* instructions moves to the MA stage in cycle 5, and RW stage in cycle 6. This *nop* instruction is called a *pipeline bubble*. A bubble is a *nop* instruction that is dynamically inserted by the interlock hardware. It moves through the pipeline stages akin to normal instructions. Similarly, in cycles 5 and 6 also, we need to insert a pipeline bubble. Finally, in cycle 7, instruction [2] is free to proceed to the EX, and subsequent stages. A bubble by definition does not do anything, and thus none of the control signals are turned on when a stage encounters a bubble. The other subtle point to note here is that we cannot read and write to the same register in the same cycle. We need to give preference to the write because it is an earlier instruction, and the read needs to stall for one cycle.

There are two ways to implement a bubble. The first is that we can have a separate bubble bit in the instruction packet. Whenever, the bit is 1, the instruction will be construed to be a bubble. The second is that we can change the opcode of the instruction to that of a *nop*, and replace all of its control signals by 0s. The latter approach is more invasive, but can eliminate redundant work in the circuit completely. In the former approach, the control signals will be on, and units that are activated by them, will remain operational. The hardware needs to ensure that a bubble is not able to make changes to registers or memory.

Definition 74
A pipeline bubble is a nop instruction that is inserted dynamically in a pipeline register by the interlock hardware. A bubble propagates through the pipeline in the same way as normal instructions.

We can thus conclude that it is possible to avoid data hazards, by dynamically inserting bubbles in the pipeline. Let us quickly take a look at the issue of slow instructions such as the *div* and *mod* instructions. It is highly likely that in most pipelines these instructions will take n ($n > 1$) cycles to execute in the EX stage. In each of the n cycles, the ALU completes a part of the processing of the *div* or *mod* instructions. Each such cycle is known as a *T State*. Typically, one stage has 1 T State; however, the EX stage for a slow instruction has many T states. Hence, to correctly implement slow instructions, we need to stall the IF and OF stages for $(n-1)$ cycles till the operations complete.

For the sake of simplicity, we shall not discuss this issue further. Instead, we shall move on with the simplistic assumption that all our pipeline stages are balanced, and take 1 cycle to complete their operation.

Control Hazards

Now, let us look at control hazards. Let us start out by considering the following code snippet.

```
[1]: beq .foo
[2]: add r1, r2, r3
[3]: sub r4, r5, r6
....
....
.foo:
[4]: add r8, r9, r10
```

Instead of using a delayed branch, we can insert bubbles in the pipeline if the branch is taken. Otherwise, we do not need to do anything. Let us assume that the branch is taken. The pipeline diagram for this case is shown in Figure 9.15.

In this case, the outcome of the branch condition of instruction [1] is decided in cycle 3. At this point, instructions [2] and [3] are already in the pipeline (in the IF and OF stages, respectively). Since the branch condition evaluates to *taken*, we need to cancel instructions [2] and [3], otherwise they will be executed erroneously. We thus, convert them to bubbles as shown in Figure 9.15. Instructions[2] and [3] are converted to bubbles in cycle 4. Secondly, we fetch from the correct branch target (.foo) in cycle 4, and thus instruction [4] enters the pipeline. Both of our bubbles proceed through all the pipeline stages, and finally leave the pipeline in cycles 6 and 7 respectively.

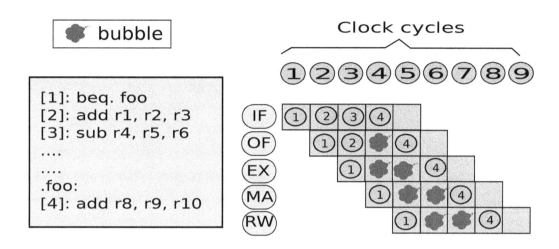

Figure 9.15: Pipeline diagram for a control hazard with bubbles

We can thus ensure both the conditions (`Data-Lock` and `Branch-Lock`) by dynamically introducing bubbles in the pipeline. Now, let us look at these approaches in some more detail.

9.6.2 Ensuring the `Data-Lock` Condition

To ensure the `Data-Lock` condition we need to ensure that there is no conflict between the instruction in the OF stage, and any instruction in the subsequent stages. A *conflict* is defined as a situation that can cause a RAW hazard. In other words, a conflict exists if an instruction in a subsequent stage writes to a register that is read by the instruction in the OF stage. There are thus two pieces of hardware that we require to implement the `Data-Lock` condition. The first is to check if a conflict exists, and the second is to ensure that the pipeline gets stalled.

Let us first look at the conflict detection hardware. The conflict detection hardware needs to compare the contents of the instruction in the OF stage with the contents of each of the instructions in the other three stages namely EX, MA, and RW. If there is a conflict with any of these instructions, we can declare a conflict. Let us thus focus on the logic of detecting a conflict. We leave the design of the exact circuit as an exercise for the reader. Let us outline the brief pseudo-code of a conflict detection circuit. Let the instruction in the OF stage be [A], and an instruction in a subsequent stage be [B]. The algorithm to detect a conflict is shown as Algorithm 5.

Algorithm 5: Algorithm to detect conflicts between instructions

Data: Instructions: [A] and [B]
Result: Conflict exists (**true**), no conflict (**false**)

1 if $[A].opcode \in (nop,b,beq,bgt,call)$ then
    /* Does not read from any register */
2 | return false
3 end
4 if $[B].opcode \in (nop, cmp, st, b, beq, bgt, ret)$ then
    /* Does not write to any register */
5 | return false
6 end
   /* Set the sources */
7 $src1 \leftarrow [A].rs1$
8 $src2 \leftarrow [A].rs2$
9 if $[A].opcode = st$ then
10 | $src2 \leftarrow [A].rd$
11 end
12 if $[A].opcode = ret$ then
13 | $src1 \leftarrow ra$
14 end
   /* Set the destination */
15 $dest \leftarrow [B].rd$
16 if $[B].opcode = call$ then
17 | $dest \leftarrow ra$
18 end
   /* Check if the first operand exists */
19 $hasSrc1 \leftarrow$ **true**
20 if $[A].opcode \in (not,mov)$ then
21 | $hasSrc1 \leftarrow$ **false**
22 end
   /* Check the second operand to see if it is a register */
23 $hasSrc2 \leftarrow$ **true**
24 if $[A].opcode \notin (st)$ then
25 | if $[A].I = 1$ then
26 | | $hasSrc2 \leftarrow$ **false**
27 | end
28 end
   /* Detect conflicts */
29 if $(hasSrc1 =$ **true**$)$ and $(src1 = dest)$ then
30 | return true
31 end
32 else if $(hasSrc2 =$ **true**$)$ and $(src2 = dest)$ then
33 | return true
34 end
35 return false

Implementing Algorithm 5 in hardware is straight forward. The reader can draw a simple circuit and implement this algorithm. All we need is a set of logic gates and multiplexers. Most hardware designers typically write the description of a circuit similar to Algorithm 5 in a hardware description language such as Verilog or VHDL, and rely on smart compilers to convert the description to an actual circuit. Hence, we shall refrain from showing detailed implementations of circuits henceforth, and just show the pseudo code.

We need three conflict detectors (OF ↔ EX, OF ↔ MA, OF ↔ RW). If there are no conflicts, then the instruction is free to proceed to the EX stage. However, if there is at least one conflict, we need to stall the IF and OF stages. Once an instruction passes the OF stage, it is guaranteed to have all of its source operands.

Stalling the Pipeline:

Let us now look at stalling the pipeline. We essentially need to ensure that till there is a conflict no new instruction enters the IF and OF stages. This can be trivially ensured by disabling the write functionality of the PC and the IF-OF pipeline register. They thus cannot accept new data on a clock edge, and thus will continue to hold their previous values.

Secondly, we also need to insert bubbles in the pipeline. For example, the instruction that passes from the OF to the EX stage needs to be an invalid instruction, or alternatively a bubble. This can be ensured by passing a *nop* instruction. Hence, the circuit for ensuring the Data-Lock condition is straight forward. We need a conflict detector that is connected to the PC, and the IF-OF register. Till there is a conflict, these two registers are disabled, and cannot accept new data. We force the instruction in the OF-EX register to contain a *nop*. The augmented circuit diagram of the pipeline is shown in Figure 9.16.

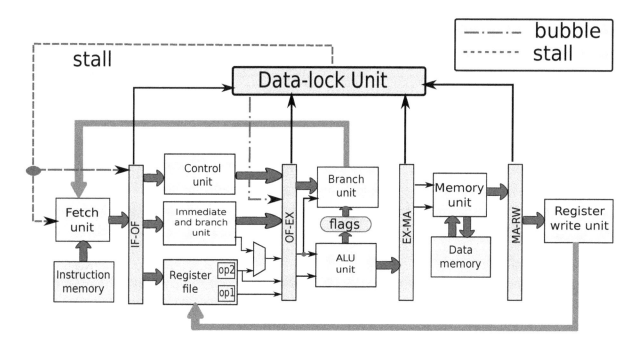

Figure 9.16: Data path of a pipeline with interlocks (implements the Data-Lock condition)

9.6.3 Ensuring the Branch-Lock condition

Let us now assume that we have a branch instruction in the pipeline (*b*, *beq*, *bgt*, *call*, *ret*). If we have delay slots, then our data path is the same as that shown in Figure 9.16. We do not need to do any changes, because the entire complexity of execution has been offloaded to software. However, exposing the pipeline to software has its pros and cons as discussed in Table 9.1. If we add more stages in the pipeline, then existing executables might cease to work. To avoid this let us design a pipeline that does not expose delay slots to software.

We have two design options here. The first is that we can assume that a branch is not taken till the outcome is decided. We can proceed to fetch the two instructions after a branch and process them. Once, the outcome of the branch is decided in the EX stage, we can take an appropriate action based on the outcome. If the branch is not taken, then the instructions fetched after the branch instruction, are on the correct path, and nothing more needs to be done. However, if the branch is taken, then it is necessary to cancel those two instructions, and replace them with pipeline bubbles (*nop* instructions).

The second option is to stall the pipeline till the outcome of the branch is decided, irrespective of the outcome. Clearly, the performance of this design is less than the first alternative that assumes that branches are not taken. For example, if a branch is not taken 30% of the time, then with the first design, we do useful work 30% of the time. However, with the second option, we never do any useful work in the 2 cycles after a branch instruction is fetched. Hence, let us go with the first design in the interest of performance. We cancel the two instructions after the branch only if the branch is taken. We call this approach *predict not taken*, because we are effectively predicting the branch to be *not taken*. Later on if this prediction is found to be wrong, then can cancel the instructions in the wrong path.

Important Point 13

If the PC of a branch instruction is equal to p, then we choose to fetch the instructions at $p + 4$, and $p + 8$ over the next two cycles. If the branch is not taken, then we resume execution. However, if the branch is taken, then we cancel these two instructions, and convert them to pipeline bubbles.

We do not need to make any significant changes to the data path. We need a small branch hazard unit that takes an input from the EX stage. If the branch is taken, then in the next cycle it converts the instructions in the IF-OF and OF-EX stages to pipeline bubbles. The augmented data path with the branch interlock unit is shown in Figure 9.17.

9.7 Pipeline with Forwarding

9.7.1 Basic Concepts

We have now implemented a pipeline with interlocks. Interlocks ensure that a pipeline executes correctly irrespective of the nature of dependences across instructions. For the `Data-Lock` condition we proposed to add interlocks in the pipeline that do not allow an instruction to leave the operand fetch stage until the correct values are available in the register file. However, we shall see in this section that we do not need to add interlocks always. In fact, in a lot of instances, the correct data is already present in pipeline registers, albeit not in the register file. We can design a method to properly pass data from the internal pipeline registers to the appropriate functional unit. Let us consider a small example by considering this *SimpleRisc* code snippet.

```
[1]: add r1, r2, r3
[2]: sub r4, r1, r2
```

Let us take a look at the pipeline diagram with just these two instructions in Figure 9.18. Figure 9.18(a) shows the pipeline diagram with interlocks. Figure 9.18(b) shows a pipeline diagram without interlocks and bubbles. Let us now try to argue that we do not need to insert a bubble between the instructions.

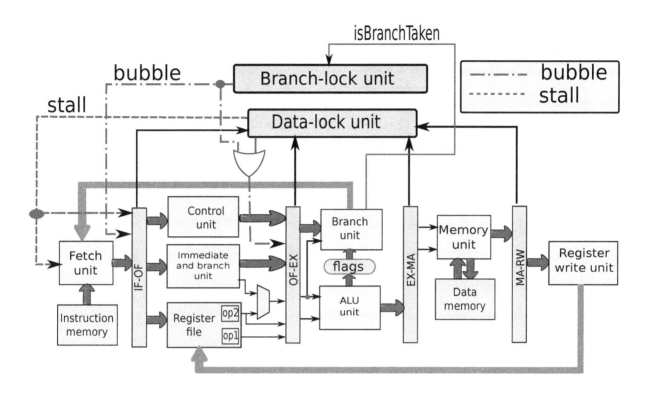

Figure 9.17: Data path of a pipeline with interlocks (implements both the Data-Lock and Branch-Lock conditions)

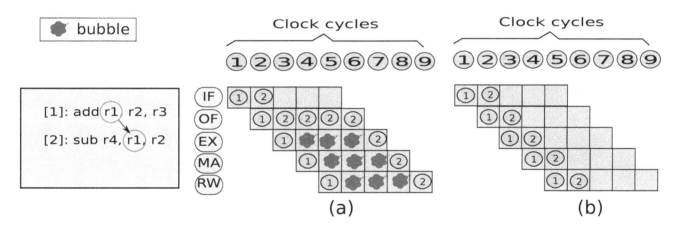

Figure 9.18: (a) Pipeline diagram with interlocks and bubbles (b) Pipeline diagram without bubbles

Let us take a deeper look at Figure 9.18(b). Instruction 1 produces its result at the end of the EX stage, or alternatively at the end of cycle 3, and writes to the register file in cycle 5. Instruction 2 needs the value of $r1$ in the register file at the beginning of cycle 3. This is clearly not possible, and thus we had proposed to add pipeline interlocks to resolve this issue. However, let us try an alternative solution instead. Let us allow the instructions to execute. Then in cycle 3, [2] will get the wrong value. We allow it to proceed to the EX stage in cycle 4. At this point of time, instruction [1] is in the MA stage, and its instruction packet contains the correct value of $r1$. This value of $r1$ was computed in the previous cycle, and is present in the *aluResult* field of the instruction packet. [1]'s instruction packet is in the EX-MA register in cycle 4. Now, if we add a connection between the *aluResult* field of the EX-MA register and an input of the ALU, then we can successfully transfer the correct value of $r1$ to the ALU. There will be no error in our computation, because the operands to the ALU are correct, and thus the result of the ALU operation will also be computed correctly. Figure 9.19 shows the result of our actions in the pipeline diagram. We add a line from the MA stage of instruction [1] to the EX stage of instruction [2]. Since the arrow does not go backwards in time, it is possible to **forward** the data (value of $r1$) from one stage to the other.

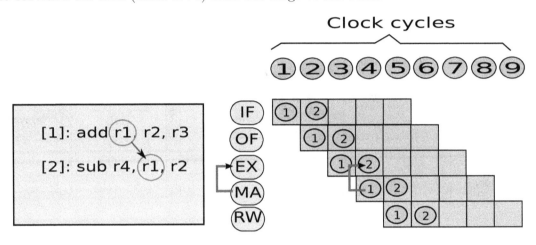

Figure 9.19: Example of forwarding in a pipeline

Definition 75

Forwarding *is a method to transfer values of operands between instructions in different pipeline stages through direct connections between the stages. We do not use the register file for transferring the values of operands across instructions. Forwarding allows us to avoid costly pipeline interlocks.*

We have just looked at an extremely powerful technique for avoiding stalls in pipelines. This technique is known as *forwarding*. Essentially, we allow the values of operands to flow between instructions by directly transferring them across stages. We do not use the register file to transfer values across instructions. The notion of forwarding has allowed us to execute instructions [1] and [2] back to back (in consecutive cycles). We do not need to add any stall cycles. Hence, it is not necessary to reorder code, or insert *nops*.

Before, we proceed to the implementation of forwarding, let us discuss forwarding conceptually using pipeline diagrams. To forward the value of $r1$ between instructions [1] and [2], we added a connection between the MA stage and the EX stage. We showed this connection in Figure 9.19 by drawing an arrow between the corresponding stages of instructions [1] and [2]. The direction of this arrow was vertically upwards. Since it did not go backwards in time, we concluded that it is possible to forward the value. Otherwise, it would not have been possible.

Let us now try to answer a general question. Can we forward values between all pairs of instructions. Note that these need not be consecutive instructions. Even if there is one instruction between an producer and a consumer ALU instruction, we still need to forward values. Let us now try to think of all possible forwarding paths between stages in a pipeline.

9.7.2 Forwarding Paths in a Pipeline

Let us discuss the basic tenets of forwarding that we shall broadly aim to follow.

1. We add a forwarding path between a later stage and an earlier stage.

2. We forward a value as late as possible in the pipeline. For example, if a given value is not required in a given stage, and it is possible to get the value in a later stage from the producer instruction, then we wait to get the forwarded value in the later stage.

Note that both of these basic tenets do not affect the correctness of programs. They simply allow us to eliminate redundant forwarding paths. Let us now systematically look at all the forwarding paths that we require in our pipeline.

RW → MA : Let us consider the MA stage. It needs a forwarding path from the RW stage. Let us consider the code snippet shown in Figure 9.20 Here, instruction [2] needs the value of $r1$ in the MA stage (cycle 5), and instruction [1] fetches the value of $r1$ from memory by the end of cycle 4. Thus, it can forward its value to instruction [2] in cycle 5.

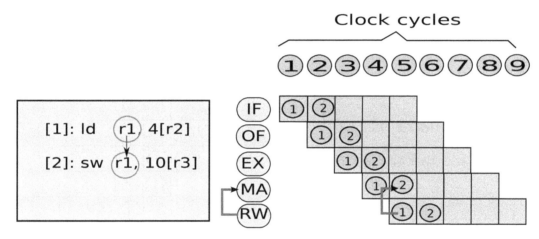

Figure 9.20: RW → MA forwarding

RW → EX : The code snippet shown in Figure 9.21 shows a load instruction that fetches the value of register $r1$ by the end of cycle 4, and a subsequent ALU instruction that requires the value of $r1$ in cycle 5. It is possible to forward the value because we are not going backwards in time.

MA → EX : The code snippet shown in Figure 9.22 shows an ALU instruction that computes the value of register $r1$ by the end of cycle 3, and a consecutive ALU instruction that requires the value of $r1$ in cycle 4. In this case also, it is possible to forward the data by adding an interconnection (forwarding path) between the MA and EX stages.

RW → OF : Typically the OF stage does not need forwarding paths because it does not have any functional units. Hence, it does not need to use a value immediately. We can thus forward the value later according to tenet 2. However, the only exception is forwarding from the RW stage. We cannot forward the value later because the instruction will not be there in the pipeline. Hence, it is necessary to add a forwarding path from the RW to the OF stage. An example of a code snippet that requires $RW \to OF$ forwarding is shown in Figure 9.23. Instruction [1] produces the value of $r1$ by reading its value from memory by the end of cycle

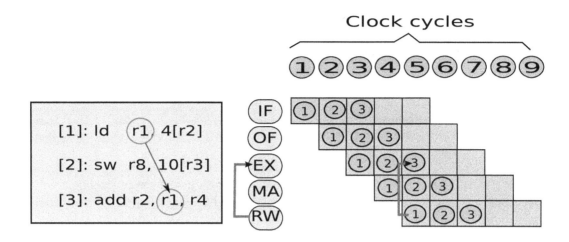

Figure 9.21: RW → EX forwarding

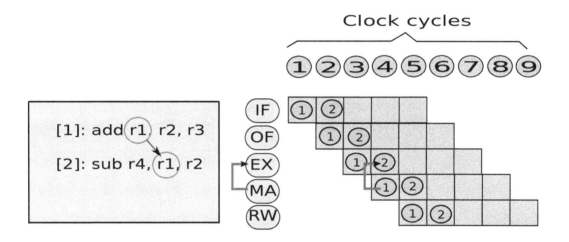

Figure 9.22: MA → EX forwarding

4. It then writes the value of $r1$ to the register file in cycle 5. Meanwhile, instruction [4] tries to read the value of $r1$ in the OF stage in cycle 5. Unfortunately, there is a conflict here. Hence, we propose to resolve the conflict by adding a forwarding path between the RW and OF stages. Thus, we prohibit instruction [4] from reading the register file for the value of $r1$. Instead, instruction [4] gets the value of $r1$ from instruction [1] using the $RW → OF$ forwarding path.

Important Point 14

Forwarding from the RW to the OF stage is a very tricky operation. This is because the instruction in the RW stage is writing to the register file, and the instruction in the OF stage is also reading from the register file. If the value of the register is the same in these two instructions, then it is typically not possible to perform both the operations (read and write) in the same cycle. This is because reading and

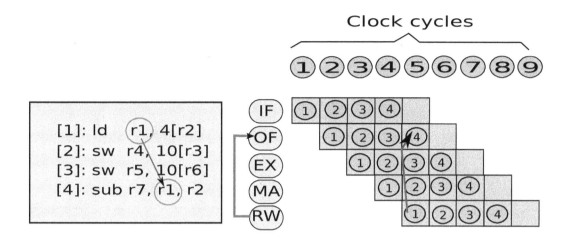

Figure 9.23: RW → OF forwarding

writing to the same SRAM cell can lead to incorrect operation of the circuit, and it is hard to ensure correctness. Consequently, it is a standard practice to allow the write from RW to go through, and cancel the register read operation issued by the instruction in the OF stage. Thus, this read operation does not go to the register file. Instead, the instruction in the OF stage gets the value of the register through the forwarding path. This strategy ensures that we do not have any remote chances of leaving data in an inconsistent state in the register file. The instruction in the OF stage also gets the right value of the operands.

It is not necessary to add the following forwarding paths: MA → OF, and EX → OF. This is because, we can use the following forwarding paths (RW → EX), and (MA → EX) instead. In accordance with tenet 2, we need to avoid redundant forwarding paths. Hence, we do not add the forwarding paths to the OF stage from the MA and EX stages. We do not add forwarding paths to the IF stage because at this stage, we have not decoded the instruction, and thus we do not know about its operands.

9.7.3 Data Hazards with Forwarding

Question 7
Has forwarding completely eliminated data hazards?

Let us now answer this question. Let us consider ALU instructions. They produce their result in the EX stage, and they are ready to forward in the MA stage. Any succeeding consumer instruction will need the value of an operand produced by the preceding ALU instruction at the earliest in its EX stage. At this point, we can effect a successful forwarding because the value of the operand is already available in the MA stage. Any subsequent instruction can always get the value using any of the available forwarding paths or from the register file if the producer instructions has left the pipeline. The reader should be convinced that if the producer instruction is an ALU instruction, then it is always possible to forward the result of the ALU operation to a consumer instruction. To prove this fact, the reader needs to consider all possible combinations of instructions, and find out if it is possible to forward the input operands to the consumer instruction.

The only other instruction that produces a register value explicitly is the load instruction. Recall that the store instruction does not write to any register. Let us look at the load instruction. The load instruction produces its value at the end of the MA stage. It is thus ready to forward its value in the RW stage. Let us now consider a code snippet and its pipeline diagram in Figure 9.24.

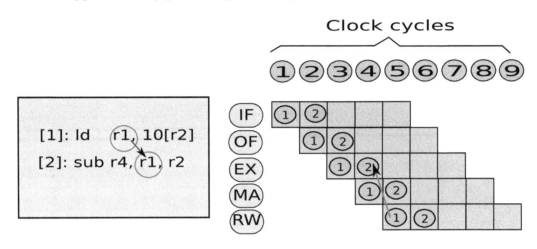

Figure 9.24: The load-use hazard

Instruction [1] is a load instruction that writes to register r1, and instruction [2] is an ALU instruction that uses register $r1$ as a source operand. The load instruction is ready to forward at the beginning of cycle 5. Sadly, the ALU instruction needs the value of $r1$ at the beginning of cycle 4. We thus need to draw an arrow in the pipeline diagram that flows backwards in time. Hence, we can conclude that in this case forwarding is not possible.

Definition 76

Load-Use Hazard A load-use *hazard is a situation where a load instruction supplies the loaded value to an immediately succeeding instruction that needs the value in its EX stage. A pipeline even with forwarding needs to insert a single stall cycle after the load instruction.*

This is the only case in which we need to introduce a stall cycle in our pipeline. This situation is known as a *load-use* hazard, where a load instruction supplies the loaded value to an immediately succeeding instruction that needs the value in its EX stage. The standard method of eliminating load-use hazards is by allowing the pipeline to insert a bubble, or by using the compiler to either reorder instructions or insert a *nop* instruction.

Thus, we can conclude that a pipeline with forwarding does need interlocks, albeit rarely. The only special condition is a load-use hazard.

Note that if there is a store instruction after a load instruction that stores the loaded value, then we do not need to insert a stall cycle. This is because the store instruction needs the value in its MA stage. At this point of time the load instruction is in the RW stage, and it is possible to forward the value.

9.7.4 Implementation of a Pipeline with Forwarding

Now, let us come to the most important part of our discussion. Let us design a pipeline with forwarding. We shall first design the data path, and then briefly look at the control path. To implement a data path that supports forwarding, we need to make minor changes to our pipeline stages. These changes will allow the functional units to use their default input values, as well as outputs of subsequent stages in the pipeline. The basic idea is to use a multiplexer before every input to a functional unit. The role of this multiplexer is to select the right input. Let us now look at each of the pipeline stages. Note that we do not need to make any changes to the IF stage because it does not send or receive any forwarded value.

OF Stage with Forwarding

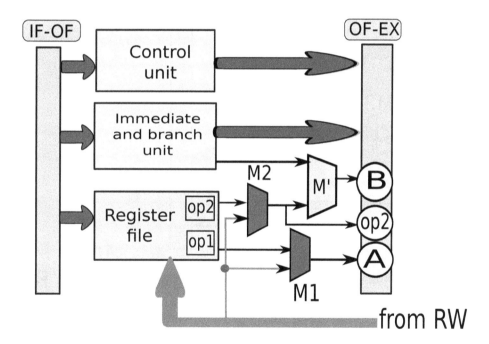

Figure 9.25: OF stage with forwarding

The OF stage with support for forwarding is shown in Figure 9.25. The multiplexers in our baseline pipeline without forwarding are coloured with a lighter colour. Whereas, the additional multiplexers added to enable forwarding are coloured with a darker colour. We shall use this convention for the rest of our discussion on forwarding. Let us focus on the two new multiplexers in the OF stage.

We only show those multiplexers that are relevant to our discussion on forwarding. We need to choose between the first operand read from the register file, and the value forwarded from the RW stage. We thus add a multiplexer($M1$) to help us choose between these two inputs. Likewise, we need to choose between the second operand read from the register file, and the value forwarded from the RW stage. To implement forwarding, we add a multiplexer ($M2$) to make a choice between the value fetched from the register file, and the value forwarded from the RW stage (see Figure 9.25). Multiplexer (M'), which is a part of our baseline design chooses between the second register operand and the immediate computed from the contents of the instruction. Recall that the three fields in the instruction packet that save the results of the OF stage are as follows. A saves the value of the first register operand, $op2$ saves the value of the second register operand (rd register in case of a store), and B saves the value of the second operand of the instruction (register or immediate). Recall that we had decided to read all the values that might possibly be required by any instruction in the interest of time. For example, the *not* instruction does not require the first register operand. Nevertheless, we still read it because we do not have enough time to take a decision about whether to read or not read the register operands.

EX Stage with Forwarding

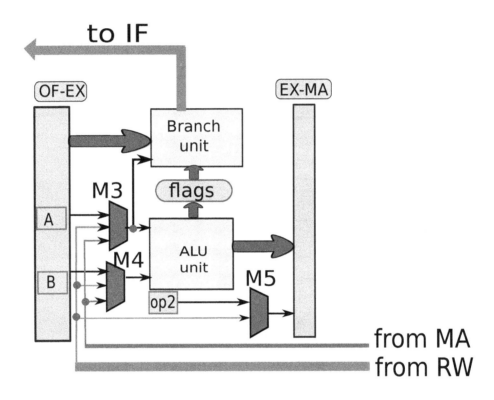

Figure 9.26: EX stage with forwarding

Figure 9.26 shows the modified EX stage. The three inputs that the EX stage gets from the OF stage are A (first ALU operand), B (second ALU operand), and $op2$ (second register operand). For A and B, we add two multiplexers, $M3$, and $M4$, to choose between the values computed in the OF stage, and the values forwarded from the MA and RW stages respectively. For the $op2$ field, which possibly contains the store value, we do not need $MA \rightarrow$ EX forwarding. This is because the store value is required in the MA stage, and thus we can use $RW \rightarrow MA$ forwarding. This observation allows us to reduce one forwarding path. Hence, multiplexer $M5$ has two inputs (default and the value forwarded from the RW stage).

MA Stage with Forwarding

Figure 9.27 shows the MA stage with additional support for forwarding. The memory address is computed in the EX stage, and saved in the *aluResult* field of the instruction packet. The memory unit directly uses this

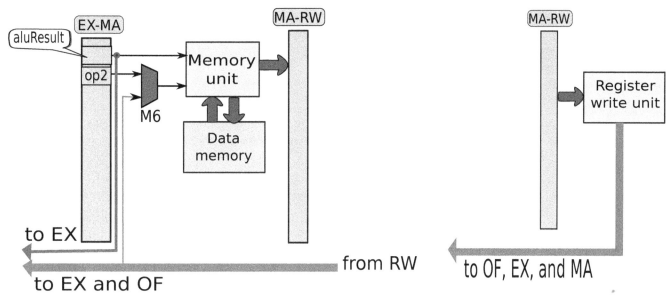

Figure 9.27: MA stage with forwarding

Figure 9.28: RW stage with forwarding

value for the address. However, in the case of a store, the value that needs to be stored (*op2*) can possibly be forwarded from the RW stage. We thus add multiplexer *M6*, which chooses between the *op2* field in the instruction packet and the value forwarded from the RW stage. The rest of the circuit remains the same.

RW Stage with Forwarding

Finally, Figure 9.28 shows the RW stage. Since this is the last stage, it does not use any forwarded value. However, it sends the value that it writes to the register file to the MA, EX, and OF stages, respectively.

Putting it All Together

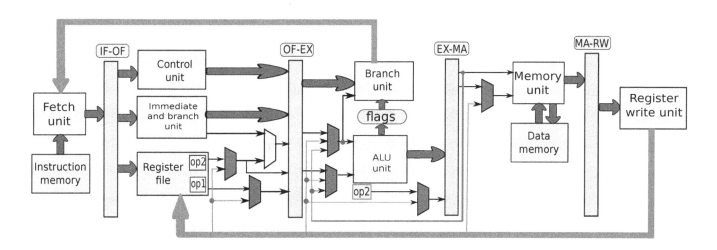

Figure 9.29: Pipelined data path with forwarding (abridged diagram)

Figure 9.29 puts all the pieces together and shows the pipeline with support for forwarding. To summarise, we need to add 6 multiplexers, and make some extra interconnections between units to pass the forwarded values. We envision a dedicated *forwarding unit* that computes the control signals for the multiplexers (not shown in the diagram). Other than these small changes, no other major change needs to be done to the data path.

We have been using an abridged diagram (similar to Figure 9.29) in our discussions on forwarding. The reader needs to note that the actual circuit has become fairly complicated now. Along with the augmentations to the data path, we need to also add a dedicated forwarding unit to generate the control signals for the multiplexers. A detailed picture of the pipeline is shown in Figure 9.30.

Let us now add the interlock logic to our pipeline. We need the interlock logic for both the `Data-Lock` and `Branch-Lock` conditions. Note that now we have successfully handled all RAW hazards other than the load-use hazard. In the case of a load-use hazard, we need to stall for only 1 cycle. This significantly simplifies our `Data-Lock` circuit. If there is a load instruction in the EX stage, then we need to check if there is a RAW data dependence between the load instruction, and the instruction in the OF stage. The only RAW hazard that we do not need to consider here is a load-store dependence, where the load writes to a register that contains the store value. We do not need need to stall because we can forward the value to be stored from the RW to the MA stage. For all other data dependences, we need to stall the pipeline by 1 cycle by introducing a bubble. This will take care of the load-use hazard. The circuit for ensuring the `Branch-Lock` condition remains the same. Here also, we need to inspect the instruction in the EX stage, and if it is a taken branch, we need to invalidate the instructions in the IF and OF stages. Lastly, the reader should note that interlocks always take precedence over forwarding.

9.7.5   Forwarding Conditions

After designing the data path for supporting forwarding, let us design the control path. The only extra addition to the control path is the *forwarding unit*. This unit computes the values of the signals to control the *forwarding* multiplexers. Let us now discuss the design of the forwarding unit.

The Forwarding Unit

As shown in Figure 9.31 the forwarding unit receives inputs from all the four pipeline registers. They provide the contents of the instructions resident in the OF, EX, MA, and RW stages respectively. Based on the contents of the instructions, the forwarding unit computes the values of the control signals.

Salient Points

Let us now consider the four forwarding paths in our architecture – $RW \rightarrow OF$, $RW \rightarrow EX$, $MA \rightarrow EX$, and $RW \rightarrow MA$. We note that the distance between the producer and consumer stages for these four paths are 3, 2, 1, and 1 respectively. Alternatively, we can say that instruction number i, can get its inputs from instructions $i-1$, $i-2$, and $i-3$. The reader needs to note that there are two forwarding paths between adjacent stages (distance equal to 1).

Forwarding Paths with Distance Equal to 1

These forwarding paths are $MA \rightarrow EX$, and $RW \rightarrow MA$. We actually need both these forwarding paths. The reason is as follows. The $MA \rightarrow EX$ path is required for forwarding results between consecutive ALU instructions. The $RW \rightarrow MA$ path is required when the value of the input is generated in the MA stage, and it is also required in the MA stage. The only instruction that generates a value in the MA stage is the load instruction, and the only instruction that requires register operands in the MA stage, is the store instruction. Thus, we need to use the $RW \rightarrow MA$ forwarding path between a load instruction, and an

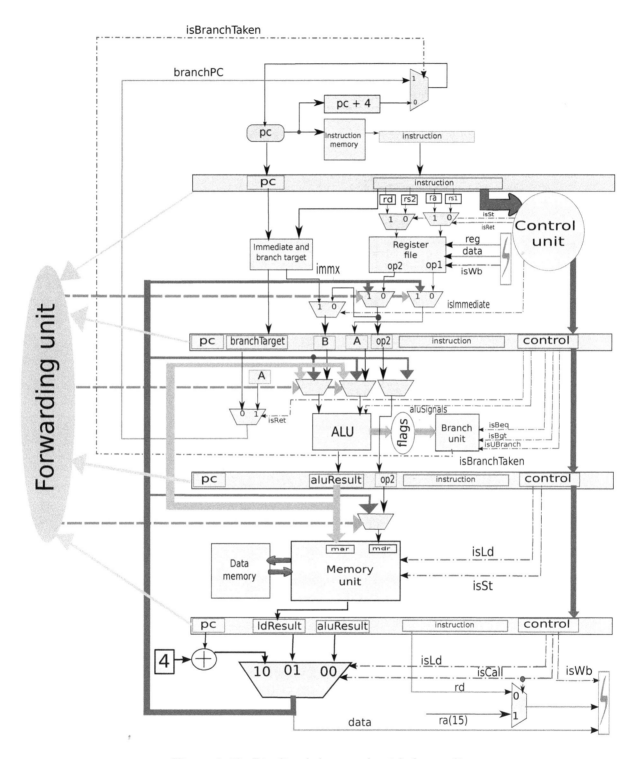

Figure 9.30: Pipelined data path with forwarding

immediately succeeding store instruction, when there is a register dependence. The following code snippet gives an example.

```
ld r1, 10[r2]
```

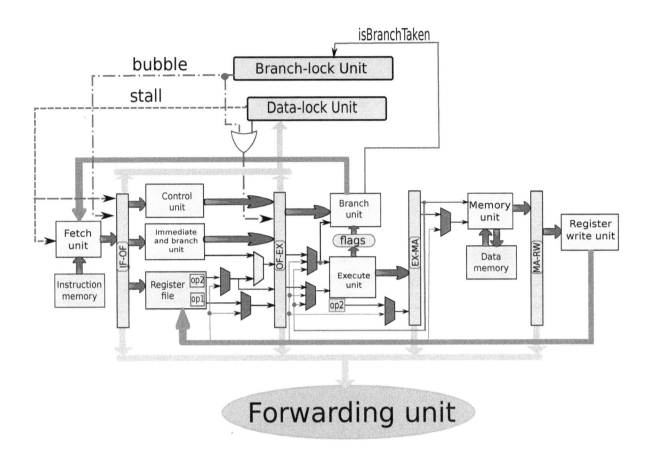

Figure 9.31: Pipelined processor with forwarding

```
st r1, 20[r4]
```

Note that sometimes we might have a choice of forwarding paths ($MA \rightarrow EX$, or $RW \rightarrow MA$). The following code snippet shows an example.

```
[1]: add r1, r2, r3
[2]: st r1, 20[r4]
```

Here, instruction [1] is ready to forward the value of $r1$ when it reaches the MA stage. However, instruction [2] requires the value of $r1$ when instruction [1] reaches the RW stage. We can thus use either forwarding path ($MA \rightarrow EX$, or $RW \rightarrow MA$). Let us choose to use $RW \rightarrow MA$ forwarding in this case (also see Section 9.7.4). This optimisation allows us to reduce a forwarding path between MA to EX for $op2$. This is also in accordance with tenet 2 mentioned in Section 9.7.2 that says that we should forward as late as possible.

Case of the *mov* Instruction

The other special case arises for the *mov* instruction. Since the EX stage does not produce its output value, we can theoretically use $RW \rightarrow MA$ forwarding for it. Ideally, if the consumer instruction in a load-use hazard, is a *mov* instruction, we should not have the necessity to stall the pipeline. However, for the purpose of simplicity, let us choose to treat a *mov* instruction as a regular ALU instruction, and choose to disregard any optimisations in this case.

Conflicts with Multiple Instructions

Let us look at our four forwarding paths: $RW \rightarrow OF$, $RW \rightarrow EX$, $MA \rightarrow EX$, and $RW \rightarrow MA$, again. We notice that the EX stage gets forwarded inputs from two stages – MA and RW. It is possible that the instruction in the EX stage has a conflict (RAW register dependence) with the instructions in both the MA and RW stages for the same input. In this case, we need to choose the input from the MA stage because it is an earlier instruction. Let us show an example.

```
[1]:add r1, r2, r3
[2]:sub r1, r4, r5
[3]:mul r8, r9, r1
```

In this case, when instruction [3] is in the EX stage, instruction [2] is in the MA stage, and instruction [1] is in the RW stage. The second source operand (value of register $r1$) needs to be forwarded. We need to get the value from the MA stage because instruction [2] will overwrite the value written by instruction [1]. We can design a simple circuit to give a higher priority to the MA stage than the RW stage while forwarding results to the EX stage. We leave this as an exercise for the interested reader.

Algorithms for Forwarding Conditions

We show the pseudo codes for the forwarding conditions. We need to first detect if a conflict exists for the first operand, which is typically the $rs1$ field of the instruction packet. In the case of a *ret* instruction, the first operand is the ra (return address) register. If a conflict exists, then we can potentially forward a value. For reasons of brevity, we do not show the code that disregards the case of forwarding if one of the instructions is a pipeline bubble.

Algorithm 6 shows the algorithm for detecting a conflict on the first operand. We first rule out the trivial cases in which instruction [A] does not read from any register, and [B] does not write to any register. Then, we set the first operand. It is equal to the $rs1$ field in the instruction packet. The only exception is the *ret* instruction whose first operand is the ra register. Similarly, the destination operand is always register rd, with the *call* instruction being the only exception. Its destination operand is the return address register, ra. Then we detect a conflict in Line 15, and we return true if a conflict (RAW dependence) exists, otherwise we return false. We can use the output of Algorithm 6 to set the input of the forwarding multiplexers for the first operand.

Algorithm 7 shows the pseudo code of the algorithm for detecting conflicts for the second operand. We first rule out the trivial cases, in which [A] does not read any register and [B] does not write to any register. Then, we need to see if the second operand of [A] is an immediate. In this case, forwarding is not required. The second operand is typically equal to the $rs2$ field of the instruction packet. However, in the case of a store instruction, it is equal to the rd field of the instruction packet. Similarly, we find the destination register of instruction [B], and take care of the special case of the *call* instruction. We finally detect a conflict in Line 20. Note that we do not consider the load-use hazard, or `Branch-Lock` conditions in the forwarding logic, because we always assume that interlocks have higher priority over forwarding. Secondly, whenever we do not have a forwarding path, the forwarding conditions do not apply. Finally, in the case of multiple conflicting instructions, the forwarding unit needs to ensure that the correct value is forwarded.

Special Case of Forwarding from the Call Instruction

Let us consider the following code snippet.

```
call .function
..
```

Algorithm 6: Conflict on the first operand (rs1/ra)

Data: Instructions: [A] and [B] (possible forwarding: [B] → [A])
Result: Conflict exists on rs1/ra (**true**), no conflict (**false**)

1 **if** *[A].opcode* ∈ *(nop,b,beq,bgt,call,not,mov)* **then**
          /* Does not read from the rs1 register */
2   **return false**
3 **end**
4 **if** *[B].opcode* ∈ *(nop, cmp, st, b, beq, bgt, ret)* **then**
          /* Does not write to any register */
5   **return false**
6 **end**
   /* Set the sources */
7 src1 ← *[A].rs1*
8 **if** *[A].opcode* = *ret* **then**
9   src1 ← *ra*
10 **end**
   /* Set the destination */
11 dest ← *[B].rd*
12 **if** *[B].opcode* = *call* **then**
13   dest ← *ra*
14 **end**
   /* Detect conflicts */
15 **if** *src1* = *dest* **then**
16   **return true**
17 **end**
18 **return false**

Algorithm 7: Conflict on the second operand (rs2/rd)

Data: Instructions: [A] and [B] (possible forwarding: [B] → [A])
Result: Conflict exists on second operand (rs2/rd) (**true**), no conflict (**false**)

1 **if** *[A].opcode* ∈ *(nop,b,beq,bgt,call)* **then**
       /* Does not read from any register */
2 | **return false**
3 **end**
4 **if** *[B].opcode* ∈ *(nop, cmp, st, b, beq, bgt, ret)* **then**
       /* Does not write to any register */
5 | **return false**
6 **end**
   /* Check the second operand to see if it is a register */
7 **if** *[A].opcode* ∉ *(st)* **then**
8 | **if** *[A].I = 1* **then**
9 | | **return false**
10 | **end**
11 **end**
   /* Set the sources */
12 src2 ← *[A].rs2*
13 **if** *[A].opcode = st* **then**
14 | src2 ← *[A].rd*
15 **end**
   /* Set the destination */
16 dest ← *[B].rd*
17 **if** *[B].opcode = call* **then**
18 | dest ← *ra*
19 **end**
   /* Detect conflicts */
20 **if** *src2 = dest* **then**
21 | **return true**
22 **end**
23 **return false**

```
...
.function:
ret
```

Here, we call a function and immediately return. In this case, the *call* instruction will still be in the pipeline, when the *ret* instruction enters the pipeline. Recall that the *call* instruction writes to register *ra* and the *ret* instruction reads from register *ra*. Moreover, the *call* instruction computes the value of *ra*, and writes it to the register file in the RW stage. We shall prove that this does not cause any correctness issues.

A *call* instruction is a taken branch. This means that when it enters the EX stage, the `Branch-Lock` circuitry will detect that it is a taken branch, and convert the instructions in the IF and OF stages to bubbles. Any instruction that requires the value of the *ra* register will at least be three stages behind the *call* instruction. This means that when the *call* instruction will reach the RW stage, the next valid instruction in the pipeline will be in the OF stage. If this is a *ret* instruction, or any other instruction that needs the value of the *ra* register, then it can simply get its value through the $RW \rightarrow OF$ forwarding path. Hence, the special case of forwarding from the call instruction is handled correctly.

9.8   Support for Interrupts/ Exceptions*

The process of building our pipelined processor is almost done. We just need to put the final piece together. We have up till now focused on building a fast pipeline that has interlocks for correctness and has forwarding for enhancing performance. We shall now discuss the interaction of our processor with external devices such as I/O devices and with specialised programs such as the operating system. The operating system is a master program that controls the behaviour of other programs, the processor, and I/O devices. The standard mechanism for supporting the operating system, and other I/O devices, is through a mechanism called an *interrupt*. We shall have ample opportunities to discuss interrupts in Chapter 12. In this section, we discuss the implementation of an interrupt from the point of view of a pipeline.

9.8.1   Interrupts

The main idea of an interrupt is as follows. Assume that we click a key on a keyboard. The keyboard records the ASCII code of the clicked key, and then sends a message to the processor with the code of the key that was clicked. This message is known as an *interrupt*. After the processor receives an interrupt, it stops the execution of the currently executing program and jumps to a dedicated program known as the *interrupt handler*. The interrupt handler reads the value sent by the I/O device (in this case, the keyboard), and sends it to the program that handles the display device (monitor/ laptop screen). This program shows the character typed. For example, if the user clicks the character, 'a', then monitor ultimately shows an 'a' on the screen through a sequence of steps.

Definition 77
An interrupt is a signal sent by an I/O device to the processor. An interrupt is typically used to draw the attention of the processor to new inputs, or changes in the status of an I/O device. For example, if we click a key on a keyboard, then a new interrupt is generated and sent to the processor. Upon receiving an interrupt, the processor stops the execution of the currently executing program, and jumps to an interrupt handler routine. *This routine* processes *the interrupt, by reading the values sent by the I/O device, and performing any other action if required.*

9.8.2 Exceptions

Interrupts are not the only kind of events sent to the processor. Sometimes some actions of the program can generate interrupts. For example, if a program accesses an illegal memory address, then it is necessary to take corrective action. The memory system typically sends an interrupt to the processor. The processor in turn invokes the interrupt handler routine, which in turn calls dedicated modules in the operating system. Note that in this book, we shall use the terms interrupt handler and exception handler interchangeably. These modules either take some kind of corrective action, or terminate the program. Such kind of interrupts that are generated as a result of actions of the executing program are called *exceptions*. Readers familiar with languages such as Java can relate to the concept of exceptions. For example, in Java if we access an illegal array index such as -1, an exception is generated, and the processor jumps to a pre-specified location to take corrective action.

Definition 78
An exception is a special event that is generated when the executing program typically performs an erroneous action, and it becomes necessary to take corrective action.

9.8.3 Precise Exceptions

Let us now discuss how we need to handle interrupts and exceptions. The processor needs to clearly stop what it is currently doing, and jump to the interrupt handling routine. After handling the interrupt, and performing the desired action, it needs to come back and start from exactly the same point in the program, at which it had stopped. Let us now define the notion of a *precise exception*. The term "precise exception" is also used in the case of interrupts. We can think of it as a generic term for all kinds of interrupts and exceptions.

Definition of Precise Exceptions

At any point of time, a program will typically have multiple instructions in the pipeline with different PCs. When the processor encounters an interrupt, it needs to branch to the starting location of the interrupt handler. To facilitate this process, it can have an interrupt handler table. This table typically stores a list of interrupt types, and the starting PCs of their interrupt handlers. The processor uses this table to branch to the appropriate interrupt handler. After finishing the processing of the interrupt handler, it needs to come back to exactly the same point in the original program. In other words, the original program should not be aware of the fact that another program such as the interrupt handler executed in the middle. This entire process needs to be orchestrated very carefully.

Let us elaborate. Assume that a program, P, is executing on the processor. Let us record all its dynamic instructions that leave the pipeline after successfully completing their execution, and number them $I_1, I_2, \ldots I_n$. A *dynamic instruction* is the instance of an instruction created by the processor. For example, if a loop has 5 instructions, and executes 100 times, then we have 500 dynamic instructions. Furthermore, an instruction *completes* its execution when it finishes its job and updates the state of the processor (registers or memory). A store instruction completes in the MA stage, and instructions with a destination register complete in the RW stage. All other instructions, are assumed to complete in the MA stage. The *nop* instruction is excluded from this discussion. Let I_k be the last instruction in P that completes its execution before the first instruction in the interrupt handler completes its execution. We wish to ensure that at the time that I_k leaves the pipeline, all the instructions in P before I_k have completed their execution and left the pipeline, and no instruction in P after I_k has completed or will complete its execution before the program resumes. Let the set of completed instructions at this point of time (when I_k leaves the pipeline) be $\mathcal{C}$. Formally, we have:

$$I_j \in \mathcal{C} \Leftrightarrow (j \le k) \qquad (9.1)$$

An interrupt or exception implemented in this manner is said to be *precise*.

Definition 79

An interrupt or exception is precise *if the following conditions are met:*

Condition 1: *Let I_k be the last dynamic instruction in the original program, P, that completes its execution before the first instruction in the interrupt handler completes its execution. Let I_k leave the pipeline at time, τ. At τ, all instructions I_j $(j < k)$ have also completed their execution.*

Condition 2: *No instruction after I_k in P completes its execution before all the instructions in the interrupt handler complete, and the program resumes execution.*

Condition 3: *After the interrupt handler finishes, we can seamlessly start executing all the instructions starting from I_k (if it has not completed successfully) or I_{k+1}.*

When the interrupt handler returns, it needs to start executing instruction, I_{k+1}. For some special types of interrupts/ exceptions it might be required to re-execute I_k. Secondly, the register state (values of all the registers) needs to be restored before the original program, P, starts executing again. We can thus ensure that a processor can seamlessly switch to an interrupt handler and back without violating the correctness of the program.

Marking Instructions

Let us now discuss how to implement precise exceptions. Let us look at the three conditions in Definition 79 in more detail.

When an interrupt arrives, we can at the most have 5 instructions in the pipeline. We can designate one of these instructions as the last instruction before the interrupt handler executes such that the three conditions outlined in Definition 79 are satisfied. Now, we cannot designate the instruction in the RW stage as the last instruction (I_k) because the instruction in the MA stage might be a store instruction. In the current cycle it will complete its execution, and thus condition 2 will get violated. However, we are free to designate instructions in any of the four other stages as the last instruction. Let us decide to mark the instruction in the MA stage as the last instruction.

Now, let us look at exceptions. Exceptions are typically caused by the erroneous execution of instructions. For example, in the IF stage we might fetch from an illegal address, try to perform an illegal arithmetic operation in the EX stage, or write to a non-existent address in the MA stage. In these situations it is necessary to take corrective action. The processor needs to invoke a dedicated exception handler. For example, a very common type of exception is a page fault as we shall discuss in Chapter 10. A page fault occurs when we try to read or write a memory address in a 4 KB block of memory for the first time. In this case, the operating system needs to read the 4 KB block from the hard disk and copy it to memory. The faulting instruction executes again, and it succeeds the second time. In this case, we need to re-execute the exception causing instruction I_k, and needless to say we need to implement a *precise* exception. To properly take core of exceptions, the first step is to mark an instruction, immediately after it causes an exception. For example, if we try to fetch from an uninitialised or illegal address we mark the instruction in the IF stage.

Making a Marked Instruction Proceed to the End of the Pipeline

Now, that we have marked instructions, we need to ensure two conditions. The first is that all the instructions before the *marked* instruction need to complete. The second is that all the instructions after the *marked* instruction should not be allowed to write to the register file, or the main memory. We should ideally not allow any writes to the *flags* register also. However, it is difficult to implement this functionality, because we are typically aware of interrupts at the end of the clock cycle. We shall devise an ingenious solution to handle updates to the *flags* register later.

For implementing a precise exception, we need to add an *exception* unit to our pipeline. Its role is to process interrupts and exceptions. Once an instruction is marked, it needs to let the exception unit know. Secondly, we envision a small circuit that sends a code identifying the exception/ interrupt to the exception unit. Subsequently, the exception unit needs to wait for the marked instruction to reach the end of the pipeline such that all the instructions before it complete their execution. Instructions fetched after the marked instruction need to be converted into bubbles. This needs to be done to ensure that instructions after a marked instruction do not complete. Once, the marked instruction reaches the end of the pipeline, the exception unit can load the PC with the starting address of the interrupt handler. The interrupt or exception handler can then begin execution. This mechanism ensures that asynchronous events such as interrupts and exceptions remain precise. Now, we have a mechanism to seamlessly transition to executing interrupt handlers. Sadly, we still do not have a mechanism to come back to exactly the same point in the original program, because we have not remembered the point at which we had left.

9.8.4 Saving and Restoring Program State

Let us define the term *program state* as the state of all the registers and memory elements associated with the program. In specific, the program state, comprises of the contents of the register file, PC, *flags* register, and main memory.

Definition 80
The term program state *is defined as the state of all the registers and memory elements associated with the program. In specific, the program state, comprises of the contents of the register file, PC, flags register, and main memory.*

We need to find effective means of saving and restoring the state of the executing program. Let us start by stating that we do not need a method to save and restore the state of main memory because the assumption is that the interrupt handler uses a different region of main memory. We shall discuss methods to enforce a separation of memory regions between programs in Chapter 10. Nonetheless, the bottom line is that there is no unintended overlap of the memory regions of the executing program and the interrupt handler. In the case of exceptions, the interrupt handler might access some parts of the memory space of the program such that it can add some data that the program requires. One such example of exceptions is a page fault. We will have ample opportunities to discuss page faults in Chapter 10.

Hence, we need to explicitly take care of the PC, the *flags* register, and the set of registers. The state of all of these entities is known as the *context* of a program. Hence, our problem is to successfully save and retrieve the context of a program upon an interrupt.

Definition 81

The context *of a program refers to the values of the PC, the flags register, and the values contained in all the registers.*

The *oldPC* Register

Let us add an NPC field for the next PC in the instruction packet. By default, it is equal to $PC + 4$. However, for branch instructions that are taken, the NPC field contains the branch target. We envision a small circuit in the EX stage that adds the branch target, or $PC + 4$ to the NPC field of the instruction packet. Recall that the instruction packet gets passed from one stage to the next in a pipeline. Once a marked instruction reaches the RW stage, the exception unit looks up a small internal table indexed by the interrupt/ exception code. For some types of interrupts such as I/O events, we need to return to the next PC ($PC + 4$ or the branch target). This value is stored in the NPC field of the MA-RW pipeline register. However, for some types of exceptions such as page faults, it is necessary to re-execute the faulting instruction once again. A page fault happens because a certain memory location is not loaded with its data. The interrupt handler (for a page fault) needs to load the data of the memory location by fetching values from the hard disk, and then re-execute the instruction. In this case, we need to return to the PC of the marked instruction. In either case, the exception unit transfers the correct return address to an internal *oldPC* register, and then starts fetching instructions for the interrupt handler.

Spilling General Purpose Registers

We need a mechanism to save and restore registers akin to spilling and restoring registers as in the case of function calls. However, there is an important difference in the case of interrupt handlers. Interrupt handlers have their own stacks that are resident in their private memory regions. To use the stack pointer of an interrupt handler, we need to load its value into *sp*. This step will overwrite the previous value, which is the value of the stack pointer of the program. Hence, to avoid losing the value of the stack pointer of the program, we add another register called *oldSP*. The interrupt handler first transfers the contents of *sp* to *oldSP*. Subsequently, it loads *sp* with the value of its stack pointer and then spills all the registers excluding *sp* to its stack. At the end of this sequence of steps, it transfers the contents of *oldSP* to the stack.

The *oldFlags* Register

The only part of the program state that we have not saved up till now is the *flags* register. Let us assume that the *flags* register is a 32-bit register. Its lower 2 bits contain the values, *flags.E* and *flags.GT* respectively. Moreover, let us add a *flags* field to the instruction packet. Instructions other than the *cmp* instruction write the contents of the *flags* register to the *flags* field in the instruction packet, in the EX stage. The *cmp* instruction writes the updated value of the *flags* register to the *flags* field in the EX stage and moves to the subsequent stages. When a marked instruction reaches the RW stage, the exception unit extracts the contents of the *flags* field in the instruction packet, and saves it in the *oldFlags* register. The *oldFlags* register is a special register that is visible to the ISA, and helps store the last value of the *flags* register that a valid instruction in the program had seen.

Smruti R. Sarangi
383

Saving and Restoring Program State

For saving the program state, the interrupt handler contains assembly routines to save the general purpose registers (excluding *sp*) and the *oldSP*, *oldFlags*, and *oldPC* registers. We save all of these values in the stack of the interrupt handler. Likewise, we can restore program state in almost the reverse order. We restore the value of *oldPC*, the *flags* register, the general purpose registers, and the stack pointer. As the last step, we need to transfer the contents of *oldPC* to PC such that we can resume executing the original program.

Privileged Instructions

We have added the following special registers namely *oldPC*, *oldSP*, *oldFlags* and *flags*. Note that we had the *flags* register before also. However, it was not accessible as a register. Next, we add a special category of instructions called *privileged instructions* that are only accessible to specialised programs such as operating systems, and interrupt handlers. The first privileged instruction that we introduce is *movz*. It transfers values between regular registers and the special registers (*oldPC*, *oldSP*, *oldFlags*, and *flags*).

The other privileged instruction that we introduce in this section is *retz*. It reads the value of *oldPC*, and transfers its contents to PC. In other words, we jump to the location contained in *oldPC*. We do not allow instructions to directly transfer the values of special registers to and from memory, because we have to create privileged versions of both load and store instructions. We wish to avoid creating two additional instructions.

Definition 82

A privileged instruction *is a special instruction that has access to the internals of the processor. It is typically meant to be used only by operating system programs such as the kernel (core of the operating system), device drivers (programs to interact with I/O devices), and interrupt handlers.*

To implement the *movz* instruction, we add a new instruction opcode. Recall that we introduced only 21 instructions in the *SimpleRisc* instruction set. We can afford to have 11 more instructions in the ISA. *movz* uses the same register format based encoding as the *mov* instruction. However, it sees a different view of registers. The registers visible to privileged instructions, and their identifiers are shown in Table 9.2.

Register	Encoding
r0	0000
oldPC	0001
oldSP	0010
flags	0011
oldFlags	0100
sp	1110

Table 9.2: View of registers for privileged instructions

Privileged instructions use a different register encoding. They can only see the four special registers, *r0*, and *sp*. We need to make a small modification to the OF and RW stages to implement the *movz* instruction. The first is that we need to have a circuit in the OF stage to quickly find out if the opcode of an instruction is *movz*. We can use a fast circuit similar to the one that we use to find out if an instruction is a store. Then, we can choose the right set of register inputs from either the normal register file, or from one of the privileged registers using multiplexers. Similarly, in the RW stage, we can choose to either write the value in the normal register file, or in one of the special registers, again, with the help of additional multiplexers. For the sake of brevity, we do not show the circuit. We leave implementing *movz* as an exercise for the reader. We can implement *retz* in a similar way as the *ret* instruction. The only difference is that instead of getting the return value from the *ra* register, we get it from the *oldPC* register. Note that we will also require forwarding and interlock logic that takes special registers into account. The pseudocode of the forwarding and interlock logic needs to be updated.

Let us summarise the discussion in terms of two new concepts that we have learnt. The first is the notion of *privileged instructions*. These instructions are typically used by interrupt handlers, and other modules of the operating systems. They have more visibility into the internals of the processor. Since they are very powerful, it is not a good idea to give programmers the ability to invoke them. They might corrupt system state, and introduce viruses. Hence, most systems typically disallow the usage of privileged instructions by normal programs. Most processors have a register that contains the *current privilege level* (CPL). It is typically 1 for user programs, and 0 for operating system programs such as interrupt handlers. There is a privilege level change, when we switch to processing an interrupt handler (1 to 0), and when we execute the *retz* instruction to return to a user program (0 to 1). Whenever, we execute a privileged instruction, the processor checks the CPL register, and if the program is not allowed to execute the instruction, then an exception is flagged. The operating system typically terminates the program, since it may be a virus.

Definition 83

Most processors have a register that contains the current privilege level *(CPL). It is typically 1 for user programs, and 0 for operating system programs such as interrupt handlers. We are allowed to execute privileged instructions, only when the CPL is equal to 0.*

The second important concept is the notion of different register views for different instructions, or different pieces of code. This concept is known as a *register window*, and was pioneered by the Sun Ultrasparc processors. The Sun processors used different register windows for different functions. This allowed the compiler to avoid costly register spills. Here, we use register windows to separate the set of registers that can be accessed by user programs and the interrupt handlers. The interrupt handlers can see all the special registers and two regular registers (*r0* and *sp*).

Definition 84

A register window is defined as the set of registers that a particular instruction or function can access. For example, in our case, privileged instructions can access only six registers, out of which four are special registers. In comparison regular instructions have a register window that contains all the 16 general purpose registers, but no special register.

9.8.5 *SimpleRisc* Assembly Code of an Interrupt Handler

Let us now quickly conclude our discussion by showing the assembly code of an interrupt handler. The code for saving the context is shown in Figure 9.32, and the code for restoring the context and returning to the

user program is shown in Figure 9.33. We assume that the stack pointer for the interrupt handler starts at
: 0x FF FF FF FC.

```
──────────────────── Saving the context ────────────────────
/* save the stack pointer */
movz oldSP, sp
mov sp, 0x FF FC

/* spill all the registers other than sp*/
st r0, -4[sp]
st r1, -8[sp]
st r2, -12[sp]
st r3, -16[sp]
st r4, -20[sp]
st r5, -24[sp]
st r6, -28[sp]
st r7, -32[sp]
st r8, -36[sp]
st r9, -40[sp]
st r10, -44[sp]
st r11, -48[sp]
st r12, -52[sp]
st r13, -56[sp]
st r15, -60[sp]

/* save the stack pointer */
movz r0, oldSP
st r0, -64[sp]

/* save the flags register */
movz r0, oldFlags
st r0, -68[sp]

/* save the oldPC */
movz r0, oldPC
st r0, -72[sp]

/* update the stack pointer */
sub sp, sp, 72

/* code of the interrupt handler */
....
....
....
```

Figure 9.32: *SimpleRisc* assembly code for saving the context

```
                                ─────── Restoring the context ───────
/* update the stack pointer */
add sp, sp, 72

/* restore the oldPC register */
ld r0, -72[sp]
movz oldPC, r0

/* restore the flags register */
ld r0, -68[sp]
movz flags, r0

/* restore all the registers other than sp*/
ld r0, -4[sp]
ld r1, -8[sp]
ld r2, -12[sp]
ld r3, -16[sp]
ld r4, -20[sp]
ld r5, -24[sp]
ld r6, -28[sp]
ld r7, -32[sp]
ld r8, -36[sp]
ld r9, -40[sp]
ld r10, -44[sp]
ld r11, -48[sp]
ld r12, -52[sp]
ld r13, -56[sp]
ld r15, -60[sp]

/* restore the stack pointer */
ld sp, -64[sp]

/* return to the program */
retz
```

Figure 9.33: *SimpleRisc* assembly code for restoring the context

9.8.6 Processor with Support for Exceptions

Figure 9.34 shows an abridged diagram of the data path with support for exceptions. We have added an exception unit that takes inputs from all the pipeline registers. Whenever, an instruction detects an exception, or an interrupt is detected, the exception unit is notified. The exception unit proceeds to *mark* an instruction as the last instruction. It waits till the marked instruction leaves the pipeline, and concurrently converts all the instructions fetched after the marked instruction to bubbles. Finally, when the marked instruction reaches the RW stage, the exception unit stores the PC, or NPC (next PC) value in the $oldPC$ register. It also saves the *flags* field in the instruction packet to the $oldFlags$ register. We add four registers namely $oldPC$, $oldSP$, $oldFlags$, and *flags*. The ALU immediately updates the *flags* register if it processes

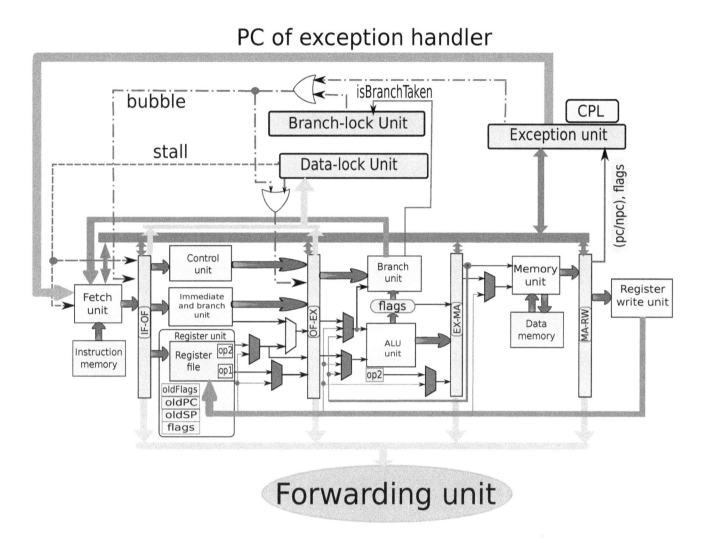

Figure 9.34: Pipelined data path with support for exceptions

a *cmp* instruction. The RW stage can also write to the *flags* register. These four registers are bundled with the regular register file. We call the new structure as the *register unit* (shown in Figure 9.34). We do not show the multiplexers to choose between the inputs from the register file, and the special registers. We assume that the multiplexers are embedded inside the register unit.

9.9   Performance Metrics

9.9.1   The Performance Equation

Let us now discuss the performance of our pipelined processor. We need to first define the meaning of "performance" in the context of processors. Most of the time, when we lookup the specifications of a laptop or smart phone, we are inundated with a lot of terms such as the clock frequency, RAM, and hard disk size. Sadly, none of these terms are directly indicative of the performance of a processor. The reason that the performance is never explicitly mentioned on the label of a computer, is because the term "performance" is rather vague. The term *performance of a processor* is always with respect to a given program or set of programs. This is because processors perform differently with respect to different programs.

Given a program, P, let us try to quantify the performance of a given processor. We say that processor A performs better than processor B, if it takes less time for P to execute P on A than on B. Thus, quantifying performance with respect to a given program is very simple. We measure the time it takes to run the program, and then compute its reciprocal. This number can be interpreted to be proportional to the performance of the processor with respect to the program.

Let us first compute the time(τ) it takes to run program P.

$$
\begin{aligned}
\tau &= \#seconds \\
&= \frac{\#seconds}{\#cycles} \times \frac{\#cycles}{\#instructions} \times (\#instructions) \\
&= \underbrace{\frac{\#seconds}{\#cycles}}_{1/f} \times \underbrace{\frac{\#cycles}{\#instructions}}_{CPI} \times (\#instructions) \\
&= \frac{CPI \times \#insts}{f}
\end{aligned}
\tag{9.2}
$$

The number of cycles per second is the processor's clock frequency (f). The average number of cycles per instruction is known as the *CPI*, and its inverse (number of instructions per cycle) is known as the *IPC*. The last term is the number of instructions (abbreviated to #insts). Note that this is the number of dynamic instructions, or, alternatively, the number of instructions that the processor actually executes. Note that it is NOT the number of instructions in the program's executable file.

Definition 85

Static Instruction *The binary or executable of a program contains a list of* instructions. *Each such instruction is a* static instruction.

Dynamic Instruction *A* dynamic instruction *is the instance of a static instruction, which is created by the processor when an instruction enters the pipeline.*

Definition 86

CPI *Cycles per instruction*

IPC *Instructions per cycle*

We can now define the performance P as a quantity that is inversely proportional to the time, τ. Equation 9.3 is known as the **Performance Equation**.

$$
P \propto \frac{IPC \times f}{\#insts}
\tag{9.3}
$$

We can thus quickly conclude that the performance of a processor with respect to a program is proportional to the IPC, and frequency, and inversely proportional to the number of instructions.

Let us now look at the performance of a single cycle processor. Its CPI is equal to 1 for all instructions. The performance is thus proportional to $f/\#insts$. This is a rather trivial result. It says that as we increase the frequency, a single cycle processor keeps getting faster proportionally. Likewise, if we are able to reduce the number of instructions in our program by a factor of X, then the performance also increases by a factor of X. Let us consider the performance of a pipelined processor. The analysis is more complicated, and the insights are very profound.

9.9.2 Performance of an Ideal Pipelined Processor

Let us look at the three terms in the performance equation (Equation 9.3), and consider them one by one. Let us first consider the number of instructions.

Number of Instructions

The number of instructions in a program is dependent on the intelligence of the compiler. A really smart compiler can reduce instructions by choosing the right set of instructions from the ISA, and by using smart code transformations. For example, programmers typically have some code, which can be categorised as *dead code*. This code has no effect on the final output. A smart compiler can remove all the dead code that it can find. Another source of additional instructions is the code to spill and restore registers. Compilers often perform *function inlining* for very small functions. This optimisation dynamically removes such functions and pastes their code in the code of the calling function. For small functions, this is a very useful optimisation since we are getting the rid of the code to spill and restore registers. There are many more compiler optimisations that help in reducing code size. The reader is referred to [Aho et al., 2006, Muchnick, 1997] for a detailed discussion on compiler design. For the rest of this section, we shall assume that the number of instructions is a constant. Let us exclusively focus on the hardware aspect.

Computing the Total Number of Cycles

Let us assume an ideal pipeline that does not need to insert any bubbles, or stalls. It will be able to complete one instruction every cycle, and thus will have a CPI of 1. Let us assume a program containing n instructions, and let the pipeline have k stages. Let us compute the total number of cycles it will take for all the n instructions to leave the pipeline.

Let the first instruction enter the pipeline in cycle 1. It leaves the pipeline in cycle k. Henceforth, one instruction will leave the pipeline every cycle. Thus, after $(n-1)$ cycles, all the instructions would have left the pipeline. The total number of cycles is therefore, $n + k - 1$. The CPI is equal to:

$$CPI = \frac{n + k - 1}{n} \tag{9.4}$$

Note that the CPI tends to 1, as n tends to ∞.

Relationship with the Frequency

Let the maximum amount of time that an instruction takes to finish its execution on a single cycle processor be t_{max}. This is also known as the total amount of *algorithmic work*. We are ignoring the delays of pipeline registers while computing t_{max}. Now, let us divide the data path into k pipeline stages. We need to add $k - 1$ pipeline registers. Let the delay of a pipeline register be l. If we assume that all the pipeline stages are balanced (do the same amount of work, and take the same amount of time), then the time that the slowest instruction will take to finish its work in a stage is equal to $\frac{t_{max}}{k}$. The total time per stage is equal to the circuit delay and the delay of a pipeline register.

$$t_{stage} = \frac{t_{max}}{k} + l \tag{9.5}$$

Now, the minimum clock cycle time has to be equal to the delay of a pipeline stage. This is because, the assumption while designing a pipeline is that each stage takes exactly one clock cycle. We thus have the minimum clock cycle time (t_{clk}), or the maximum frequency (f) equal to:

$$t_{clk} = \frac{1}{f} = \frac{t_{max}}{k} + l \tag{9.6}$$

Performance of a Pipeline

Let us now compute the performance of this pipeline, and make a simplistic assumption that performance is equal to (f / CPI) because the number of instructions is a constant(n).

$$
\begin{aligned}
P &= \frac{f}{CPI} \\
&= \frac{\frac{1}{\frac{t_{max}}{k}+l}}{\frac{n+k-1}{n}} \\
&= \frac{n}{(t_{max}/k + l) \times (n + k - 1)} \\
&= \frac{n}{((n-1)t_{max}/k + (t_{max} + ln - l) + lk}
\end{aligned}
\tag{9.7}
$$

Let us try to maximise performance by choosing the right value of k. We have:

$$
\begin{aligned}
&\frac{\partial\left((n-1)t_{max}/k + (t_{max} + ln - l) + lk\right)}{\partial k} = 0 \\
\Rightarrow &-\frac{(n-1)t_{max}}{k^2} + l = 0 \\
\Rightarrow &k = \sqrt{\frac{(n-1)t_{max}}{l}}
\end{aligned}
\tag{9.8}
$$

Equation 9.8 provides a theoretical estimate of the optimal number of pipeline stages as a function of the latch delay (l), the total algorithmic work (t_{max}), and the number of instructions (n). Let us gauge the trends predicted by this equation. The first is that as we increase the number of instructions, we can afford more pipeline stages. This is because the startup delay of k cycles, gets nullified when there are more instructions. Secondly, as we increase the amount of algorithmic work (t_{max}), we need a deeper pipeline. More are the number of pipeline stages, less is the amount of work we need to do per stage. We can thus have a higher frequency, and thus have a higher instruction throughput. Lastly, the optimal number of stages is inversely proportional to $\sqrt{l}$. As we increase the latch delay, we start wasting more time inserting and removing data from latches. Hence, it is necessary to adjust the number of pipeline stages with the latch delay. If the latches are very slow, we need to reduce the number of pipeline stages also such that we do not waste a lot of time in adding, and removing data from pipeline latches.

Sadly, an ideal pipeline does not exist in practice. This means that they do not have a CPI equal to $(n + k - 1)/n$. Almost all programs have dependences between instructions, and thus it becomes necessary to insert bubbles in the pipeline. Inserting bubbles increases the CPI from the ideal CPI computed in Equation 9.4. Equation 9.8 provides us with interesting insights. However, the reader needs to note that it is hypothetical. It predicts that the optimal number of stages approaches infinity, for very large programs. This is unfortunately not the case in practical scenarios.

9.9.3 Performance of a Non-Ideal Pipeline

Mathematical Characterisation

We need to incorporate the effect of stalls in the CPI equation. Let us assume that the number of instructions (n) is very very large. Let the ideal CPI be CPI_{ideal}. In our case, $CPI_{ideal} = 1$. We have:

$$CPI = CPI_{ideal} + stall\_rate \times stall\_penalty \qquad (9.9)$$

Example 112

Assume that the ideal CPI is 1. Assume that 10% of the instructions suffer a load-use hazard, and 20% of the instructions are taken branches. Find the CPI of the program.

Answer: *We need to insert 1 bubble for a load-use hazard, and 2 bubbles for a taken branch. Thus, the average number of bubbles that we need to insert per instruction is equal to: 0.1 * 1 + 0.2 * 2 = 0.5. Thus,*

$$CPI_{new} = CPI_{ideal} + 0.5 = 1 + 0.5 = 1.5$$

Example 113

Compare the performance of two programs, P_1 and P_2. Assume that the ideal CPI for both of them is 1. For P_1, 10% of the instructions have a load-use hazard, and 15% of its instructions are taken branches. For P_2, 20% of the instructions have a load-use hazard, and 5% of its instructions are taken branches.

Answer:

$$CPI_{P_1} = 1 + 0.1 * 1 + 0.15 * 2 = 1.4$$

$$CPI_{P_2} = 1 + 0.2 * 1 + 0.05 * 2 = 1.3$$

The CPI of P_2 is less than the CPI of P_1. Hence, P_2 is faster.

The final CPI is equal to the sum of the ideal CPI and number of mean stall cycles per instruction. The mean stall cycles per instruction is equal to the product of the average stall rate per instruction multiplied by the average number of bubbles that we need to insert per stall (*stall_penalty*). The *stall_rate* term is typically a function of the nature of dependences across instructions in a program. The *stall_penalty* term is also typically dependent on the design of the pipeline, and its forwarding paths. In our case, we need to stall for at most one cycle for RAW hazards, and for 2 cycles for taken branches. However, pipelines with more stages might have different behaviours. Let us now try to model this pipeline mathematically.

We assume that the *stall_rate* is only dependent on the program, and the *stall_penalty* is proportional to the number of stages in a pipeline. This assumption is again not completely correct. However, it is good enough for developing a coarse mathematical model. The reason, we assume that *stall_penalty* is proportional to the number of stages is because, we assume that we create deeper pipelines by essentially splitting the stages of our simple pipeline further. For example, we can pipeline the functional units. Let us assume that we divide each stage, into two sub-stages. Then, we need to stall for 2 cycles on a load-use hazard, and stall for 4 cycles for a taken branch.

Let us thus assume that CPI $= (n+k-1)/n + rck$, where r and c are constants, and k is the number of pipeline stages. r is equal to the average number of stalls per instruction (*stall_rate*). We assume that the *stall_penalty* $\propto k$, or alternatively, *stall_penalty* $= ck$, where c is the constant of proportionality.

We thus have:

$$
\begin{aligned}
P &= \frac{f}{CPI} \\
&= \frac{\frac{1}{t_{max}/k+l}}{(n+k-1)/n + rck} \\
&= \frac{n}{((n-1)t_{max}/k + (rcnt_{max} + t_{max} + ln - l) + lk(1+rcn)}
\end{aligned}
\tag{9.10}
$$

To maximise performance, we need to minimise the denominator. We get:

$$
\begin{aligned}
&\frac{\partial \left((n-1)t_{max}/k + (rcnt_{max} + t_{max} + ln - l) + lk(1+rcn)\right)}{\partial k} = 0 \\
&\Rightarrow -\frac{(n-1)t_{max}}{k^2} + l(1+rcn) = 0 \\
&\Rightarrow k = \sqrt{\frac{(n-1)t_{max}}{l(1+rcn)}} \approx \sqrt{\frac{t_{max}}{lrc}} \quad (as\ n \to \infty)
\end{aligned}
\tag{9.11}
$$

Equation 9.11 is more realistic than Equation 9.8. It is independent of the number of instructions. The implicit assumption is that the number of instructions tends to infinity, because in most programs, we execute billions of instructions. Akin to Equation 9.8, the optimal number of pipeline stages is proportional to $\sqrt{t_{max}}$, and inversely proportional to $\sqrt{l}$. Additionally, $k \propto 1/\sqrt{rc}$. This means that as the penalty for a stall increases, or the number of stall events per instruction increase, we need to use less pipeline stages.

Let us now find the performance for the optimal number of pipeline stages. In Equation 9.10, we assume that $n \to \infty$. Thus $(n+k-1)/n \to 1$. Hence, we have:

$$
\begin{aligned}
P_{ideal} &= \frac{1}{(t_{max}/k + l) \times (1+rck)} \\
&= \frac{1}{t_{max}/k + l + rct_{max} + lrck} \\
&= \frac{1}{t_{max} \times \sqrt{\left(\frac{lrc}{t_{max}}\right)} + l + rct_{max} + lrc \times \sqrt{\left(\frac{t_{max}}{lrc}\right)}} \\
&= \frac{1}{rct_{max} + 2\sqrt{lrct_{max}} + l} \\
&= \frac{1}{\left(\sqrt{rct_{max}} + \sqrt{l}\right)^2}
\end{aligned}
\tag{9.12}
$$

Implications of Equation 9.11 and Equation 9.12

Let us now study the different implications of the result regarding the optimal number of pipeline stages.

Implication 1

The crucial implication of these results is that for programs with a lot of dependences, we should use processors with a lesser number of pipeline stages. Inversely, for programs that have high IPC (less dependences across instructions), we should use processors that have deeper pipelines.

Implication 2

Let us compare two versions of our pipeline. One version uses interlocks for all dependences, and the other uses forwarding. For the pipeline with forwarding, the *stall_penalty* is much lower. Consequently, the value of the constant, c, is smaller in the case of the pipeline with forwarding turned on. This means that a pipeline with forwarding ideally requires more pipeline stages for optimal performance. As a general rule, we can conclude that as we increase the amount of forwarding in a pipeline, we should make it deeper.

Implication 3

The optimal number of pipeline stages is directly proportional to $\sqrt{(t_{max}/l)}$. If we have faster latches, we can support deeper pipelines. Secondly, with the progress of technology, t_{max}/l is not changing significantly [ITRS, 2011], because both logic gates, and latches are getting faster (roughly equally). Hence, the optimal number of pipeline stages for a processor has remained almost the same for at least the last 5 years.

Implication 4

As we increase l, r, c, and t_{max} the ideal performance goes down as per Equation 9.12. The latch delay can be a very sensitive parameter, especially, for processors that are designed to run workloads with few dependences. In this case, r, and c, will have relatively small values, and Equation 9.12 will be dominated by the value of the latch delay.

Example 114

Find the optimal number of pipeline stages for the following configuration. $t_{max}/l = 20$, $r = 0.2$, $c = 0.6$.

Answer: *We have:*

$$k = \sqrt{\frac{t_{max}}{lrc}} = \sqrt{20/(0.2 * 0.6)} = 12.9 \approx 13$$

Example 115

Consider two programs that have the following characteristics.

Program 1		Program 2	
Instruction Type	*Fraction*	*Instruction Type*	*Fraction*
loads	*0.4*	*loads*	*0.3*
branches	*0.2*	*branches*	*0.1*
ratio(taken branches)	*0.5*	*ratio(taken branches)*	*0.4*

The ideal CPI is 1 for both the programs. Let 50% of the load instructions suffer from a load-use hazard. Assume that the frequency of P_1 is 1, and the frequency of P_2 is 1.5. Here, the units of the frequency are not relevant. Compare the performance of P_1 and P_2.

Answer:

$$CPI_{new} = CPI_{ideal} + 0.5 \times (ratio(loads)) \times 1$$
$$+ ratio(branches) \times ratio(taken\ branches) \times 2 \tag{9.13}$$

We thus have:

$$CPI_{P_1} = 1 + 0.5 \times 0.4 + 0.2 \times 0.5 \times 2 = 1 + 0.2 + 0.2 = 1.4$$
$$CPI_{P_2} = 1 + 0.5 \times 0.3 + 0.1 \times 0.4 \times 2 = 1 + 0.15 + 0.08 = 1.23$$

The performance of P_1 can be expressed as $f/CPI = 1 / 1.4 = 0.71$ (arbitrary units). Similarly, the performance of P_2 is equal to $f/CPI = 1.5/1.23 = 1.22$ (arbitrary units). Hence, P_2 is faster than P_1. We shall often use the term, arbitrary units, a.u., when the choice of units is irrelevant.

9.9.4 Performance of a Suite of Programs

Most of the time, we do not measure the performance of a processor with respect to one program. We consider a set of known benchmark programs and measure the performance of our processor with respect to all the programs to get a consolidated figure. Most processor vendors typically summarise the performance of their processor with respect to the SPEC (`http://www.spec.org`) benchmarks. SPEC stands for "Standard Performance Evaluation Corporation". They distribute suites of benchmarks for measuring, summarising, and reporting the performance of processors, and software systems.

Computer architectures typically use the SPEC CPU benchmark suite to measure the performance of a processor. The SPEC CPU 2006 benchmarks have two types of programs – integer arithmetic benchmarks (SPECint), and floating point benchmarks (SPECfp). There are 12 SPECint benchmarks that are written in C/C++. The benchmarks contain parts of C compilers, gene sequencers, AI engines, discrete event simulators, and XML processors. On similar lines, the SPECfp suite contains 17 programs. These programs solve different problems in the domains of physics, chemistry, and biology.

Most processor vendors typically compute a SPEC score, which is representative of the performance of the processor. The recommended procedure is to take the ratio of the time taken by a benchmark on a reference processor, and the time taken by the benchmark on the given processor. The SPEC score is equal to the geometric mean of all the ratios. In computer architecture, when we report the mean relative performance (as in the case of SPEC scores), we typically use the geometric mean. For just reporting the average time of execution (absolute time), we can use the arithmetic mean.

Sometimes, instead of reporting SPEC scores, we report the average number of instructions that we execute per second, and in the case of scientific programs, the average number of floating point operations per second. These metrics give us an indication of the speed of a processor, or a system of processors. We typically use the following terms:

KIPS Kilo(10^3) instructions per second

MIPS Million(10^6) instructions per second

MFLOPS Million(10^6) floating point operations per second

GFLOPS Giga(10^9) floating point operations per second

TFLOPS Tera(10^{12}) floating point operations per second

PFLOPS Peta(10^{15}) floating point operations per second

9.9.5 Inter-Relationship between Performance, the Compiler, Architecture, and Technology

Let us now summarise our discussion by looking at the relationships between performance, compiler design, processor architecture, and manufacturing technology. Let us consider the performance equation again (see Equation 9.14) (let us assume arbitrary units for performance and replace the proportional sign by an equality).

$$P = \frac{f \times IPC}{\#insts} \tag{9.14}$$

If our final aim is to maximise performance, then we need to maximise the frequency (f), and the IPC. Simultaneously, we need to minimise the number of dynamic instructions ($\#insts$). There are three knobs that are under our control namely the processor architecture, manufacturing technology, and the compiler. Note that we loosely use the term "architecture" here. We wish to use the term "architecture" to refer to the actual organisation and design of the processor. However, in literature, it is common to use the term "architecture" to refer to both the ISA, and the design of a processor. Hence, we use the same terminology here. Let us look at each of our knobs in detail.

The Compiler

By using smart compiler technology we can reduce the number of dynamic instructions, and also reduce the number of stalls. This will improve the IPC. Let us consider two examples: Examples 116 and 117. Here, we remove one stall cycle by reordering the *add* and *ld* instructions. On similar lines, compilers typically analyse hundreds of instructions, and optimally reorder them to reduce stalls as much as possible.

Example 116
Reorder the following piece of code without violating the correctness of the program to reduce stalls.

```
add r1, r2, r3
ld  r4, 10[r5]
sub r1, r4, r2
```

Answer: *We have a load-use hazard here, between the ld and sub instructions. We can reorder the code as follows.*

```
ld  r4, 10[r5]
add r1, r2, r3
sub r1, r4, r2
```

Now, we do not have any load-use hazards, and the logic of the program remains the same.

Example 117
Reorder the following piece of code without violating the correctness of the program to reduce stalls. Assume delayed branches with 2 delay slots

```
add r1, r2, r3
ld  r4, 10[r5]
sub r1, r4, r2
add r8, r9, r10
b .foo
```

Answer:

```
add r1, r2, r3
ld  r4, 10[r5]
b .foo
sub r1, r4, r2
add r8, r9, r10
```

We eliminate the load-use hazard, and optimally used the delay slots.

The Architecture

We have designed an advanced architecture in this chapter by using pipelining. Note that pipelining by itself, does not increase performance. In fact because of stalls, pipelining reduces the IPC of a program as compared to a single cycle processor. The main benefit of pipelining is that it allows us to run the processor at a higher frequency. The minimum cycle time reduces from t_{max} for a single cycle pipeline to $t_{max}/k + l$ for a k-stage pipelined machine. Since we complete the execution of a new instruction every cycle unless there are stalls, we can execute a set of instructions much faster on a pipelined machine. The instruction execution throughput is much higher.

Important Point 15
The main benefit of pipelining is that it allows us to run the processor at a higher frequency. By running the processor at a higher frequency, we can ensure a higher instruction throughput (more instructions complete their execution per second). Pipelining by itself, reduces the IPC of a program as compared to a single cycle processor, and it also increases the time it takes to process any single instruction.

Techniques such as delayed branches, and forwarding help increase the IPC of a pipelined machine. We need to focus on increasing the performance of complex pipelines through a variety of techniques. The important point to note here is that architectural techniques affect both the frequency (via the number of pipeline stages), and the IPC (via the optimisations such as forwarding and delayed branches).

Manufacturing Technology

Manufacturing technology affects the speed of transistors, and in turn the speed of combinational logic blocks, and latches. Transistors are steadily getting smaller and faster. Consequently, the total algorithmic work

(t_{max}) and the latch delay (l), are also steadily reducing. Hence, it is possible to run processors at higher frequencies leading to improvements in performance (also see Equation 9.12). Manufacturing technology exclusively affects the frequency at which we can run a processor. It does not have any effect on the IPC, or the number of instructions.

We can thus summarise our discussion in Figure 9.35.

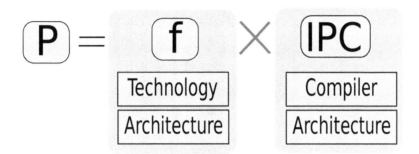

Figure 9.35: Relationship between performance, the compiler, architecture and technology

Note that the overall picture is not as simple as we describe in this section. We need to consider power and complexity issues also. Typically, implementing a pipeline beyond 20 stages is very difficult because of the increase in complexity. Secondly, most modern processors have severe power and temperature constraints. This problem is also known as the **power wall**. It is often not possible to ramp up the frequency, because we cannot afford the increase in power consumption. As a thumb rule, power increases as the cube of frequency. Hence, increasing the frequency by 10% increases the power consumption by more than 30%, which is prohibitively large. Designers are thus increasingly avoiding deeply pipelined designs that run at very high frequencies.

9.10 Power and Temperature Issues

9.10.1 Overview

Let us now briefly look at power and temperature issues. These issues have increasingly become more important over the last decade. High performance processor chips typically dissipate 60-120W of power during normal operation. If we have four chips in a server class computer, then we shall roughly dissipate 400W of power. As a general rule of thumb the rest of the components in a computer such as the main memory, hard disk, peripherals, and fans, also dissipate a similar amount of power. The total power consumption is roughly 800W. If we add additional overheads such as the non-ideal efficiency of the power supply, the display hardware, the power requirement goes up to about 1KW. Now, a typical server farm that has 100 servers will require 100 kW of power for running the computers. Additionally, it will require extra power for the cooling units such as air conditioners. Typically, to remove 1 W of heat, we require 0.5W of cooling power. Thus the total power dissipation of our server farm is about 150 kW. In comparison, a typical home has a rated power of 6-8 kW. This means that the power dissipated by one server farm is equivalent the power used by 20-25 homes, which is significant. Note that a server farm containing 100 machines is a relatively small setup, and in practice we have much larger server farms containing thousands of machines. They require megawatts of power, which is enough for the needs of a small town.

Let us now consider really small devices such as the processors in cell phones. Here, also power consumption is an important issue because of the limited amount of battery life. All of us would love devices that have very long battery lifes especially feature rich smart phones. Let us now consider even smaller devices such as small processors embedded inside the body for medical applications. We typically use small microchips in devices such as pacemakers. In such cases, we do not want to inconvenience the patient by forcing him or her to also carry heavy batteries, or recharge the batteries often. To prolong battery life, it is important to dissipate as little power as possible.

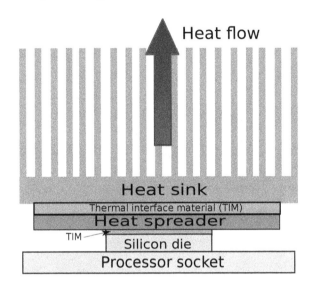

Figure 9.36: Diagram of a chip's package

Now, let us consider temperature, which is a very closely related concept. Let us take a look at the diagram of the typical package of a chip in Figure 9.36. We typically have a 200-400 mm^2 silicon die. The die refers to a rectangular block of silicon that contains the circuit of the chip. Since this small piece of silicon dissipates 60-100 W of power (equivalent to 6-10 CFL light bulbs), its temperature can rise to 200°C unless we take additional measures to cool the silicon die. We first add a 5cm × 5cm nickel plated copper plate on the silicon die. This is known as the *spreader*. The spreader helps in creating a homogeneous temperature profile on the die by spreading the heat, and thus eliminating hot spots. We need a spreader because all the parts of a chip do not dissipate the same amount of heat. The ALUs typically dissipate a lot of heat. However, the memory elements, are relatively cooler. Secondly, the heat dissipation depends on the nature of the program. For integer benchmarks, the floating point ALU is idle, and thus it will be much cooler. To ensure that heat properly flows from the silicon die to the spreader we typically add a thermally conducting gel known as the thermal interface material (TIM).

Most chips have a structure known as the *heat sink* on top of the spreader. It is a copper based structure that has an array of fins as shown in Figure 9.36. We add an array of fins to increase its surface area. This ensures that most of the heat generated by the processors can get dissipated to the surrounding air. In chips that are used in desktops, laptops, and servers, we have a fan mounted on the heat sink, or in the chassis of the computer that blows air over the heat sink. This ensures that hot air is dissipated away, and colder air from outside flows over the heat sink. The assembly of the spreader, heat sink, and fan help in dissipating most of the heat generated by the processor.

In spite of advanced cooling technology, processors still heat up to 60-100°C. While playing highly interactive computer games, or while running heavy number crunching applications like weather simulation, on-chip temperatures can go up to 120°C. Such temperatures are high enough to boil water, cook vegetables, and even warm a small room in winter. Instead of buying heaters, we can just run a computer!!! Note that temperature has a lot of deleterious effects. In particular, the reliability of on-chip copper wires, and transistors decreases exponentially with increasing temperature [Srinivasan et al., 2004]. Secondly, chips tend to age over time due to an effect known as NBTI (Negative Bias Temperature Instability). Ageing effectively slows down transistors. Hence, it becomes necessary to reduce the frequency of processors over time to ensure correct operation. Secondly, some power dissipation mechanisms such as leakage power are dependent on temperature. This means that as the temperature goes up the leakage component of the total power also goes up, and this further increases temperature.

Let us thus conclude that **it is very important** to reduce on chip power and temperature in the interest of lower electricity bills, reduced cooling costs, longer battery life, higher reliability, and slower ageing.

Let us now quickly review the main power dissipation mechanisms. We shall primarily focus on two mechanisms namely dynamic and leakage power. Leakage power is also known as static power.

9.10.2 Dynamic Power

Let us consider a chip's package as a closed black box. We have electrical energy flowing in, and heat coming out. Over a sufficiently long period of time, the amount of electrical energy flowing in to the chip is exactly equal to the amount of energy dissipated as heat according to the law of conservation of energy. Note that we disregard the energy spent in sending electrical signals along I/O links. In any case, this energy is negligible as compared to the power dissipation of the entire chip.

Any circuit consisting of transistors, and copper wires can be modelled as an equivalent circuit with resistors, capacitors, and inductors. Capacitors and inductors do not dissipate heat. However, resistors convert a part of the electrical energy that flows through them to heat. This is the only mechanism through which electrical energy can get converted to thermal energy in our equivalent circuit.

Let us now consider a small circuit that has a single resistor and a single capacitor as shown in Figure 9.37. The resistor represents the resistance of the wires in the circuit. The capacitor represents the equivalent capacitance of transistors in the circuit. We need to note that different parts of a circuit such as the gates of transistors have a certain potential at a given point in time. This means that the gate of a transistor is functioning as a capacitor, and hence storing charge. Similarly, the drain and source of a transistor have an equivalent drain and source capacitance. We typically do not consider equivalent inductance in a simplistic analysis, because most wires are typically short, and they do not function as inductors.

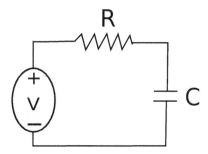

Figure 9.37: A circuit with a resistance and capacitance

If we analyse this simple circuit, then we can conclude that the total energy required to charge the capacitor is CV^2. $\frac{1}{2}CV^2$ is dissipated by the resistor while charging the capacitor, and the remaining energy is stored in the capacitor. Now, if the capacitor gets discharged, then the remaining $\frac{1}{2}CV^2$ gets dissipated via the resistor.

Now, let us generalise this result. In a large circuit with billions of transistors, we essentially have billions of subcircuits with resistive and capacitive elements. Each cycle, we can either have a transition in a bit

$(0 \rightarrow 1 \text{ or } 1 \rightarrow 0)$, or we might have no transitions at all. If there is a transition in the value of a bit, then either a capacitor gets charged or gets discharged. However, if there are no transitions, then there is no current flow, and thus there is no heat dissipation.

Let us assume that we have n subcircuits. Let, α_i be known as the *activity factor*. It is 1 if there is a transition, and 0 if there is no transition in subcircuit i. Let $E_1 \ldots E_n$ be the energy dissipated by all the n subcircuits. We thus have:

$$E_1 = \frac{1}{2}\alpha_1 C_1 V^2 \tag{9.15}$$

$$E_2 = \frac{1}{2}\alpha_2 C_2 V^2 \tag{9.16}$$

$$\ldots$$

$$E_n = \frac{1}{2}\alpha_n C_n V^2 \tag{9.17}$$

The total energy dissipated is equal to $\sum_{i=1}^{n} E_i$. Let us now group the small subcircuits into functional units, and assume that the capacitance values across all the subcircuits in a functional unit are roughly similar. Thus, for a given functional unit j, we can say that:

$$E_j \propto \alpha_j C_j V^2 \tag{9.18}$$

Here, C_j is a representative value of capacitance for the entire functional unit, and α_j is the activity factor for the entire functional unit. 0 represents no activity, and 1 represents 100% activity. $0 \leq \alpha_j \leq 1$. Note that we have also replaced the equality by a proportional sign because we are interested in the nature of power dissipation rather than the exact values.

We can thus express the total energy consumption of a circuit having n' functional units as:

$$E \propto \sum_{i=1}^{n'} \alpha_i C_i V^2 \tag{9.19}$$

This equation represents the energy consumed per cycle. Power is equal to energy divide by time. In this case the time is equal to the clock cycle time, or the reciprocal of the chip's frequency (f). Thus the total power ($\mathcal{P}$) is equal to:

$$\mathcal{P} \propto \sum_{i=1}^{n'} \alpha_i C_i V^2 f \tag{9.20}$$

The power dissipated is thus proportional to the frequency, and the square of the supply voltage. Note that this power dissipation represents the resistive loss due to the transitions in the inputs and outputs. Hence, it is known as the *dynamic power*, $\mathcal{P}_{dyn}$. Thus, we have:

$$\mathcal{P}_{dyn} \propto \sum_{i=1}^{n'} \alpha_i C_i V^2 f \tag{9.21}$$

Definition 87
Dynamic power *is the cumulative power dissipated due the transitions of inputs and outputs across all the transistors in a circuit.*

9.10.3   Leakage Power

Note that dynamic power is not the only power dissipation mechanism in processors. *Static* or *leakage* power is a major component of the power dissipation of high performance processors. It accounts for roughly 20-40% of the total processor power budget.

The main insight is as follows. We have up till now been assuming that a transistor does not allow any current to flow through it when it is in the off state. There is absolutely no current flow across the terminals of a capacitor, or between the gate and the source of an NMOS transistors. All of these assumptions are not strictly correct. No structure is a perfect insulator in practice. There is a small amount of current flow across its terminals, even in the *off* state. We can have many other sources of leakage power across other interfaces that are ideally not supposed to pass current. Such sources of current are together referred to as *leakage current*, and the associated power dissipation is known as the *leakage power*.

Definition 88

Leakage current *is the minimal amount of current that flows across two terminals of a circuit element that are ideally supposed to be completely electrically isolated from each other. For example, we do not expect any current flow between the drain and the source of an NMOS transistor in the* off *state. However, a small amount of current does flow, and this is known as the sub-threshold leakage current. When leakage current flows across a resistive element, it dissipates leakage power. Leakage power is* static *in nature and is dissipated all the time irrespective of the level of activity in a circuit.*

There are different mechanisms for leakage power dissipation such as sub-threshold leakage, and gate induced drain leakage. Researchers typically use the following equation from the BSIM3 model [Cheng and Hu, 1999] for leakage power (primarily captures sub-threshold leakage):

$$\mathcal{P}_{leak} = A \times \nu_T^2 \times e^{\frac{V_{GS}-V_{th}-V_{off}}{n \times \nu_T}} \left(1 - e^{\frac{-V_{DS}}{\nu_T}}\right) \qquad (9.22)$$

Variable	Definition (SI units)
A	Area dependent constant of proportionality
ν_T	Thermal voltage (kT/q)
k	Boltzmann's constant (1.38×10^{-23}) (SI units)
q	1.6×10^{-19}
T	Temperature (in Kelvins)
V_{GS}	Voltage between the gate and source
V_{th}	Threshold voltage. It is also dependent on temperature. $\frac{\partial V_{th}}{\partial T} = -2.5mV/K$
V_{off}	Offset voltage
n	Sub-threshold swing coefficient
V_{DS}	Voltage between the drain and source

Table 9.3: Definition of variables in Equation 9.22

Table 9.3 defines the variables used in Equation 9.22. Note that the leakage power is dependent on temperature via the variable $\nu_T = kT/q$. To show the temperature dependence, we can simplify Equation 9.22 to obtain Equation 9.23.

$$\mathcal{P}_{leak} \propto T^2 \times e^{A/T} \times \left(1 - e^{B/T}\right) \tag{9.23}$$

In Equation 9.23, A and B are constants, and can be derived from Equation 9.22. Around 10 years ago (as of 2002), when the transistor threshold voltages used to be higher (around 500 mV), leakage power was exponentially dependent on temperature. Hence, a small increase in temperature would translate to a large increase in leakage power. However, nowadays, the threshold voltages are between 100-150 mV. Consequently, the relationship between temperature and leakage has become approximately linear [Sarangi et al., 2014].

The important point to note here is that leakage power is dissipated all the time by all the transistors in a circuit. The amount of leakage current might be very small; but when we consider the cumulative effect of billions of transistors, the total amount of leakage power dissipation is sizeable, and can even become a large fraction of the dynamic power. Consequently, designers try to control temperature to keep leakage power under control.

Hence, the total power, $\mathcal{P}_{tot}$, is given by:

$$\mathcal{P}_{tot} = \mathcal{P}_{dyn} + \mathcal{P}_{leak} \tag{9.24}$$

9.10.4   Modeling Temperature*

Modeling the temperature on a chip is a fairly complex problem, and requires a fair amount of background in thermodynamics and heat transfer. Let us state a basic result here, and move on.

Let us divide the area of a silicon die into a grid. Let us number the grid points $1 \ldots m$. Let the power vector $\mathcal{P}_{tot}$ represent the total power dissipated by each grid point. Similarly, let the temperature of each grid point be represented by the vector T. Power and temperature are typically related by the following linear equation for a large number of grid points.

$$T - T_{amb} = \Delta T = A \times \mathcal{P}_{tot} \tag{9.25}$$

T_{amb} is known as the *ambient* temperature, and it is the temperature of the surrounding air. A is an $m \times m$ matrix, and is also known as the thermal resistance matrix. According to Equation 9.25 the change in temperature (ΔT), and the power consumption are linearly related to each other.

Note that $\mathcal{P}_{tot} = \mathcal{P}_{dyn} + \mathcal{P}_{leak}$, and $\mathcal{P}_{leak}$ is a function of temperature. Hence, Equations 9.24, and 9.25 form a feedback loop. We thus need to assume an initial value of temperature, compute the leakage power, estimate the new temperature, compute the leakage power, and keep iterating till the values converge.

9.10.5   The ED^2 Metric

Now, let us try to integrate performance, and energy into one model. The performance of a program is given by the performance equation (Equation 9.3). Let us simplistically assume that the time a program takes, or its delay (D) is inversely proportional to the frequency. Again, this is not strictly correct because the IPC is dependent on the frequency. We cannot appreciate the relationship between IPC and frequency right now, because we do not have adequate background. However, we shall touch this topic in Section 10.3, and see that there are components to the IPC that are frequency dependent such as the latency of main memory. In any case, let us move ahead with the approximation that $D \propto 1/f$.

Let us compare two processor designs for the same program. One design dissipates E_1 Joules for the execution of the entire program, and it takes D_1 units of time. The second design dissipates E_2 Joules, and takes D_2 units of time. How do we say, which design is better? It is possible that the second design is slightly faster but dissipates 3 times more energy per cycle. There has to be a common metric.

To derive a common metric, we need to either make the performance the same ($D_1 = D_2$), and then compare the energy, or make the energy the same ($E_1 = E_2$), and compare the performance. To ensure that $D_1 = D_2$ we need to either speed up one design or slowdown the other one. To achieve this, we can use a standard technique called dynamic voltage-frequency scaling (DVFS).

According to the DVFS technique, to scale up the frequency by a factor of κ_1, we scale the voltage by a factor of κ_2. Typically, we assume that $\kappa_1 = \kappa_2$. For example, to double the frequency, we double the voltage also. Note that with a higher frequency and consequent lower clock cycle time, we need to ensure that signals can rise and fall quickly. To ensure quicker signal transition, we increase the voltage such that it takes a lesser amount of time for a signal to rise and fall by ΔV volts. This fact can be proved by considering the basic capacitor charging and discharging equations. From our point of view, we need to appreciate the fact that the voltage and frequency need to be scaled together.

Definition 89

DVFS is a technique that is used to adjust the voltage and frequency of a processor at run time. If we scale the frequency by a factor of κ_1, then we need to scale the voltage by a factor of κ_2. In most cases, we assume that $\kappa_1 = \kappa_2$.

Now, let us try to equalise the execution time of designs 1 and 2, and compare the energy. We have made the following assumptions: $D \propto 1/f$, and $f \propto V$. Thus, $D \propto 1/V$. To make the delays equal we need to scale the delay of design 2 by D_1/D_2, or alternatively we need to scale its voltage and frequency by D_2/D_1. After equalising the delay, let the energy dissipation of design 2 be E_2'. Since $E \propto \alpha V^2$, we have:

$$
\begin{aligned}
E_2' &= E_2 \times \frac{V_1^2}{V_2^2} \\
&= E_2 \times \frac{f_1^2}{f_2^2} \\
&= E_2 \times \frac{D_2^2}{D_1^2}
\end{aligned}
\tag{9.26}
$$

Now, let us compare E_1 and E_2'.

$$
\begin{aligned}
&E_2' <=> E_1 \\
\Leftrightarrow &E_2 \times \frac{D_2^2}{D_1^2} <=> E_1 \\
\Leftrightarrow &E_2 D_2^2 <=> E_1 D_1^2
\end{aligned}
\tag{9.27}
$$

In this case, we observe that comparing E_2' and E_1 is tantamount to comparing $E_2 D_2^2$, and $E_1 D_1^2$. Since $E \propto V^2 (\propto 1/D^2)$, $ED^2 = \kappa$. Here, κ is a constant that arises out of the different constants of proportionality. It is thus a property that is independent of the voltage and frequency of the system. It is related to the activity factor, and the capacitance of the circuits, and is inherent to the design. Consequently, the ED^2 metric is used as an effective baseline metric to compare two designs.

Designers aim to reduce the ED^2 metric of a design as much as possible. This ensures that irrespective of the DVFS settings, a design with a lower value of ED^2 is a much better design than other designs that have a higher ED^2 metric. Note that a lot of performance enhancing schemes do not prove to be effective because they do not show any benefit with regards to the ED^2 metric. They do increase performance, but also disproportionately increase the energy dissipation. Likewise a lot of power reduction schemes are impractical because they increase the delay, and the ED^2 metric increases. Consequently, whenever we need to jointly optimise energy/power and performance we use the ED^2 metric to evaluate candidate designs.

9.11   Advanced Techniques*

Way Point 8

- *We designed a complete single cycle processor for the SimpleRisc instruction set in Section 8.1. This processor had a hardwired control unit.*

- *We designed a more flexible variant of our SimpleRisc processor using a micro-programmed control unit. This required a bus based data path along with a new set of microinstructions, and microassembly based code snippets for each program instruction.*

- *We observed that our processors could be significantly sped up by pipelining. However, a pipelined processor suffers from hazards that can be significantly eliminated by a combination of software techniques, pipeline interlocks, and forwarding.*

In this section, we shall take a brief look at advanced techniques for implementing processors. Note that this section is by no means self contained, and its primary purpose is to give the reader pointers for additional study. We shall cover a few of the broad paradigms for substantially increasing performance. These techniques are adopted by state of the art processors.

Modern processors typically execute multiple instructions in the same cycle using very deep pipelines (12-20 stages), and employ advanced techniques to eliminate hazards in the pipeline. Let us look at some of the common approaches.

9.11.1   Branch Prediction

Let us start with the IF stage, and see how we can make it better. If we have a taken branch in the pipeline then the IF stage in particular needs to stall for 2 cycles in our pipeline, and then needs to start fetching from the branch target. As we add more pipeline stages, the *branch penalty* increases from 2 cycles to more than 20 cycles. This makes branch instructions extremely expensive, and they are known to severely limit performance. Hence, it is necessary to avoid pipeline stalls even for taken branches.

What if, it is possible to predict the direction of branches, and also predict the branch target? In this case, the fetch unit can immediately start fetching from the predicted branch target. If the prediction is found to be wrong at a later point of time, then all the instructions after the mispredicted branch instruction need to be cancelled, and discarded from the pipeline. Such instructions are also known as *speculative* instructions.

Definition 90
Modern processors typically execute large sets of instructions on the basis of predictions. For example, they predict the direction of branches, and accordingly fetch instructions starting from the predicted

---

branch target. The prediction is verified later when the branch instruction is executed. If the prediction is found to be wrong, then all the instructions that were incorrectly fetched or executed are discarded from the pipeline. These instructions are known as speculative *instructions. Conversely, instructions that were fetched and executed correctly, or whose predictions have been verified are called* non-speculative *instructions.*

Note that it is extremely essential to prohibit speculative instructions from making changes to the register file or writing to the memory system. Thus, we need to wait for instructions to become non-speculative before we allow them to make permanent changes. Second, we also do not allow them to leave the pipeline before they become non-speculative. However, if there is a need to discard speculative instructions, then modern pipelines adopt a simpler mechanism. Instead of selectively converting speculative instructions into pipeline bubbles as we have done in our simple pipeline, modern processors typically remove all the instructions that were fetched after the mispredicted branch instruction. This is a simple mechanism that works very well in practice. It is known as a *pipeline flush*.

Definition 91
Modern processors typically adopt a simple approach of discarding all speculative instructions from a pipeline. They completely finish the execution of all instructions till the mispredicted instruction, and then clean up the entire pipeline, effectively removing all the instructions that were fetched after the mispredicted instruction. This mechanism is known as a pipeline flush.

Main Challenges

Let us now outline the main challenges in branch prediction.

1. We need to first find out in the fetch stage if an instruction is a branch, and if it is a branch, we need to find the address of the branch target.

2. Next, we need to predict the expected direction of the branch.

3. It is necessary to monitor the result of a predicted instruction. If there is a misprediction, then we need to perform a pipeline flush at a later point of time such that we can effectively remove all the speculative instructions.

Detecting a misprediction in the case of a branch is fairly straight forward. We add the prediction to the instruction packet, and verify the prediction with the actual outcome. If they are different, then we schedule a pipeline flush. The main challenge is to predict the target of a branch instruction, and its outcome.

Branch Target Buffer

Modern processors use a simple hardware structure called a *branch target buffer* (BTB). It is a simple memory array that saves the program counter of the last N branch instructions, and their targets (N typically varies from 128 to 8192). There is a high likelihood of finding a match, because programs typically exhibit some degree of *locality*. This means that they tend to execute the same piece of code repeatedly over a period of time such as loops. Hence, entries in the BTB tend to get repeatedly reused in a small window of time. If there is a match, then we can also automatically infer that the instruction is a branch.

2-bit Saturating Counter based Branch Predictor

It is much more difficult to effectively predict the direction of a branch. However, we can exploit a pattern here. Most branches in a program typically are found in loops, or in *if* statements where both the directions are not equally likely. In fact, one direction is far more likely that the other. For example, branches in loops are most of the time taken. Sometimes, we have *if* statements that are only evaluated if a certain exceptional condition is true. Most of the time, the branches associated with these *if* statements are not taken. Similarly, for most programs, designers have observed that almost all the branch instructions follow certain patterns. They either have a strong bias towards one direction, or can be predicted on the basis of past history, or can be predicted on the basis of the behaviour of other branches. There is of course no theoretical proof of this statement. This is just an observation made by processor designers, and they consequently design predictors to take advantage of such patterns in programs.

We shall discuss a simple 2-bit branch predictor in this book. Let us assume that we have a branch prediction table that assigns a 2-bit value to each branch in the table, as shown in Figure 9.38. If this value is 00, or 01, then we predict that the branch is not taken. If it is equal to 10, or 11, then we predict that the branch is taken. Moreover, every time the branch is taken, we increment the associated counter by 1, and every time, the branch is not taken we decrement the counter by 1. To avoid overflows, we do not increment 11 by 1 to produce 00, and we do not decrement 00 to produce 11. We follow the rules of saturating arithmetic that state that (in binary): $(11 + 1 = 11)$, and $(00 - 1 = 00)$. This 2-bit value is known as a 2-bit saturating counter. The state diagram for the 2-bit counter is shown in Figure 9.39.

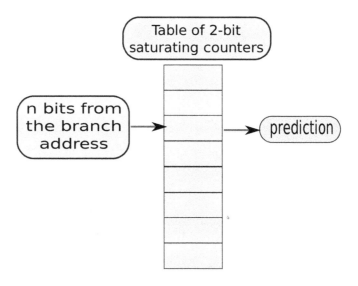

Figure 9.38: A branch prediction table

There are two basic operations for predicting a branch – prediction, and training. To *predict* a branch, we look up the value of its program counter in the branch prediction table. In specific, we use the last n bits of the address of the *pc* to access a 2^n entry branch predictor table. We read the value of the 2-bit saturating counter, and predict the branch on the basis of its value. When, we have the real outcome of the branch available, we *train* our predictor by incrementing or decrementing the value of our counter using saturating arithmetic (as per Table 9.39).

Let us now see why this predictor works. Let us consider a simple piece of C code, and its equivalent *SimpleRisc* code.

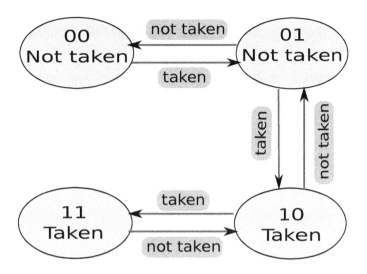

Figure 9.39: 2-bit saturating counter

-- C --

```c
void main(){
        foo();
        ...
        foo();
}

int foo() {
    int i, sum = 0
    for(i=0; i < 10; i++) {
        sum = sum + i;
    }
    return sum;
}
```

-- SimpleRisc --

```
1  .main:
2          call .foo
3          ...
4          call .foo
5
6  .foo:
7          mov r0, 0           /* sum = 0                  */
8          mov r1, 0           /* i = 0                    */
9  .loop:
10         add r0, r0, r1      /* sum = sum + i            */
11         add r1, r1, 1       /* i = i + 1                */
12         cmp r1, 10          /* compare i with 10        */
13         bgt .loop           /* if(r1 > 10) jump to .loop */
14         ret
```

Let us take a look at the branch in the loop statement (Line 13). For all the iterations other than the last one, the branch is taken. If we start our predictor in the state 10, then the first time, the branch is predicted correctly (taken). The counter gets incremented and becomes equal to 11. For each of the subsequent iterations, the branch is predicted correctly (taken). However, in the last iteration, it needs to be predicted as not taken. Here, there is a misprediction. The 2-bit counter thus gets decremented, and gets set to 10. Let us now consider the case when we invoke the function foo again. The value of the 2-bit counter is 10, and the branch (Line 13) is correctly predicted as taken.

We thus observe that our 2-bit counter scheme, adds a little bit of hysteresis (or past history) to the prediction scheme. If a branch has historically been taking one direction, then one anomaly, does not change the prediction. This pattern is very useful for loops, as we have seen in this simple example. The direction of the branch instruction in the last iteration of a loop is always different. However, the next time we enter a loop, the branch is predicted correctly, as we have seen in this example. Note that this is only one pattern. There are many more types of patterns that modern branch predictors exploit.

9.11.2 Multiple Issue In-Order Pipeline

In our simple pipeline, we executed only one instruction per cycle. However, this is not a strict necessity. We can design a processor such as the original Intel Pentium that had two parallel pipelines. This processor could execute two instructions simultaneously in one cycle. These pipeline have extra functional units such that instructions in both the pipelines can be executed without any significant structural hazards. This strategy increases the IPC. However, it also makes the processor more complex. Such a processor is said to contain a *multiple issue* in-order pipeline, because we can issue multiple instructions to the execution units in the same cycle. A processor, which can execute multiple instructions per cycle is also known as a *superscalar* processor.

Secondly, this processor is known as an in-order processor, because it executes instructions in program order. The *program order* is the order of execution of dynamic instances of instructions as they appear in the program. For example, a single cycle processor, or our pipelined processor, executes instructions in program order.

Definition 92

A processor that can execute multiple instructions per cycle is known as a superscalar processor.

Definition 93

An in-order processor executes instructions in program order. The program order *is defined as the order of dynamic instances of instructions that is the same as that is perceived if we execute each instruction of the program sequentially.*

Now, we need to look for dependences and potential hazards across both the pipelines. Secondly, the forwarding logic is also far more complex, because results can be forwarded from either pipeline. The original Pentium processor released by Intel had two pipelines namely the U pipe and the V pipe. The U pipe could execute any instruction, whereas the V pipe was limited to only simple instructions. Instructions were fetched as 2-instruction bundles. The earlier instruction in the bundle was sent to the U pipe, and the later instruction was sent to the V pipe. This strategy allowed the parallel execution of those instructions.

Let us try to conceptually design a simple processor on the lines of the original Pentium processor with two pipelines – U and V. We envisage a combined instruction and operand fetch unit that forms *2-instruction* bundles, and dispatches them to both the pipelines for execution simultaneously. However, if the instructions do not satisfy some constraints, then this unit forms a 1-instruction bundle, and sends it to the U pipeline. Whenever, we form such bundles, we can broadly adhere to some generic rules. We should avoid having two instructions that have a RAW dependence. In this case, the pipeline will stall.

Secondly, we need to be particularly careful about memory instructions because dependences across them cannot be discovered till the end of the EX stage. Let us assume that the first instruction in a bundle is a store instruction, and the second instruction is a load instruction, and they happen to access the same memory address. We need to detect this case, at the end of the EX stage, and forward the value from the store to the load. For the reverse case, when the first instruction is a load instruction, and the second is a store to the same address, we need to stall the store instruction till the load completes. If both the instructions in a bundle store to the same address, then the earlier instruction is redundant, and can be converted into a *nop*. We thus need to design a processor that adheres to these rules, and has a complex interlock and forwarding logic.

Let us show a simple example.

Example 118

Draw a pipeline diagram for the following SimpleRisc assembly code assuming a 2 issue in-order pipeline.

```
[1]: add r1, r2, r3
[2]: add r4, r5, r6
[3]: add r9, r8, r8
[4]: add r10, r9, r8
[5]: add r3, r1, r2
[6]: ld  r6, 10[r1]
[7]: st r6, 10[r1]
```

Answer: *Here, the pipeline diagram contains two entries for each stage, because two instructions can be in a stage at the same time. We start out by observing that we can execute instructions [1] and [2] in parallel. However, we cannot execute instructions [3] and [4] in parallel. This is because instruction [3] writes to r9, and instruction [4] has r9 as a source operand. We cannot execute both the instructions in the same cycle, because the value of r9 is produced in the EX stage, and is also required in the EX stage. We thus insert a bubble. We proceed to execute [4], and [5] in parallel. We can use forwarding to get the value of r9 in the case of instruction [4]. Lastly, we observe that we cannot execute instructions [6] and [7] in parallel. They access the same memory address. The load needs to complete before the store starts. We thus insert another bubble.*

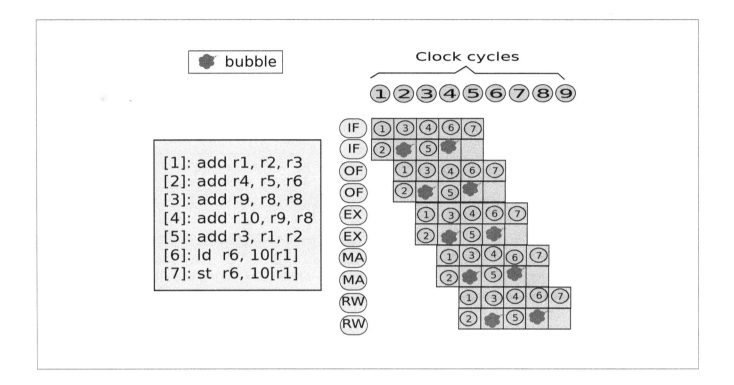

9.11.3 EPIC and VLIW Processors

Now, instead of preparing bundles in hardware, we can prepare them in software. The compiler has far more visibility into the code, and can perform extensive analyses to create multi-instruction bundles. The Itanium® processor designed by Intel and HP was a very iconic processor, which was based on similar principles.

Let us first start out by defining the terms – EPIC and VLIW.

Definition 94

VLIW → *Very Long Instruction Word: Compilers create bundles of instructions that do not have dependences between them. The hardware executes the instructions in each bundle in parallel. The complete onus of correctness is on the compiler.* EPIC → *Explicitly Parallel Instruction Computing: This paradigm extends VLIW computing. However, in this case the hardware ensures that the execution is correct regardless of the code generated by the compiler.*

EPIC/VLIW processors require very smart compilers to analyse programs and create bundles of instructions. For example, if a processor has 4 pipelines, then each bundle contains 4 instructions. The compilers create bundles such that there are no dependences across instructions in a bundle. The broader aim of designing EPIC/VLIW processors is to move all the complexity to software. Compilers arrange the bundles in a way such that we can minimise the amount of interlock, forwarding, and instruction handling logic required in the processor.

However, in hindsight, such processors failed to deliver on their promise because the hardware could not be made as simple as the designers had originally planned for. A high performance processor still needed a fair amount of complexity in hardware, and required some sophisticated architectural features. These features increased the complexity and power consumption of hardware.

9.11.4 Out-of-Order Pipelines

We have up till now been considering primarily in-order pipelines. These pipelines execute instructions in the order that they appear in the program. This is not strictly necessary. Let us consider the following code snippet.

```
[1]: add r1, r2, r3
[2]: add r4, r1, r1
[3]: add r5, r4, r2
[4]: mul r6, r5, r2
[5]: div r8, r9, r10
[6]: sub r11, r12, r13
```

Here, we are constrained to execute instructions 1 to 4 in sequence because of data dependences. However, we can execute instructions, 5 and 6 in parallel, because they are not dependent on instructions 1-4. We will not be sacrificing on correctness if we execute instructions 5 and 6 *out-of-order*. For example, if we can issue two instructions in one cycle, then we can issue (1,5) together, then (2,6), and finally, instructions 3, and 4. In this case, we can execute the sequence of 6 instructions in 4 cycles by executing 2 instructions for the first two cycles. Recall that such a processor that can potentially execute multiple instructions per cycle is known as a superscalar processor (see Definition 92).

Definition 95

A processor that can execute instructions in an order that is not consistent with their program order *is known as an* out-of-order *(OOO) processor.*

An out-of-order(OOO) processor fetches instructions in-order. After the fetch stage, it proceeds to decode the instructions. Most real world instructions require more than one cycle for decoding. These instructions are simultaneously added to a queue called the reorder buffer (ROB) in program order. After decoding the instruction, we need to perform a step called *register renaming*. The broad idea is as follows. Since we are executing instructions out of order, we can have WAR and WAW hazards. Let us consider the following code snippet.

```
[1]: add r1, r2, r3
[2]: sub r4, r1, r2
[3]: add r1, r5, r6
[4]: add r9, r1, r7
```

If we execute instructions [3] and [4] before instruction [1], then we have a potential WAW hazard. This is because instruction [1] might overwrite the value of $r1$ written by instruction [3]. This will lead to an incorrect execution. Thus, we try to rename the registers such that these hazards can be removed. Most modern processors define a set of architectural registers, which are the same as the registers exposed to software (assembly programs). Additionally, they have a set of physical registers that are only visible internally. The renaming stage converts architectural register names to physical register names. This is done to remove WAR and WAW hazards. The only hazards that remain at this stage are RAW hazards, which indicate a genuine data dependency. The code snippet will thus look as follows after renaming. Let us assume that the physical registers range from $p1 \ldots p128$.

```
[1]: add p1, p2, p3    /* p1 contains r1 */
[2]: sub p4, p1, p2
[3]: add p100, p5, p6 /* r1 is now begin saved in p100 */
[4]: add p9, p100, p7
```

We have removed the WAW hazard by mapping r1 in instruction 3, to $p100$. The only dependences that exist are RAW dependences between instructions $[1] \to [2]$, and $[3] \to [4]$. The instructions after renaming enter an instruction window. Note that up till now instructions have been proceeding in-order.

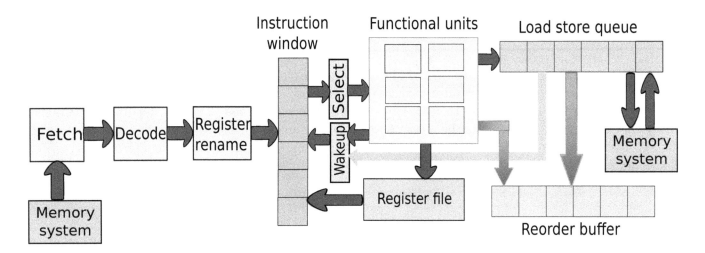

Figure 9.40: An out-of-order pipeline

The instruction window or instruction queue typically contains 64-128 entries (refer to Figure 9.40). For each instruction, it monitors its source operands. Whenever all the source operands of an instruction are ready, the instruction is ready to be *issued* to its corresponding functional unit. It is not necessary for instructions to access the physical register file all the time. They can also get values from forwarding paths. After the instructions finish their execution, they broadcast the value of their result to the waiting instructions in the instruction window. Instructions waiting for the result, mark their corresponding source operand as ready. This process is known as *instruction wakeup*. Now, it is possible that multiple instructions are ready in the same cycle. To avoid structural hazards, an *instruction select* unit chooses a set of instructions for execution.

We need another structure for load and store instructions known as the *load-store* queue. It saves the list of loads and stores in program order. It allows loads to get their values through an internal forwarding mechanism if there is an earlier store to the same address.

After an instruction finishes its execution, we mark its entry in the reorder buffer. Instructions leave the reorder buffer in program order. If an instruction does not finish quickly for some reason, then all the instructions after it in the reorder buffer need to stall. Recall that instruction entries in the reorder buffer are ordered in program order. Instructions need to leave the reorder buffer in program order such that we can ensure precise exceptions.

To summarise, the main advantage of an out-of-order processor(OOO) is that it can execute instructions that do not have any RAW dependences between them, in parallel. Most programs typically have such sets of instructions at most points of time. This property is known as instruction level parallelism (abbreviated as *ILP*). Modern OOO processors are designed to exploit as much of ILP as possible.

Definition 96

Typically, most programs have multiple instructions in a pipeline that can be executed in parallel. This is because they do not have any RAW dependences between them. Modern superscalar processors exploit this fact to increase their IPC by executing multiple instructions in the same cycle. This property of a program is known as instruction level parallelism (abbreviated as ILP).

9.12 Summary and Further Reading

9.12.1 Summary

Summary 9

1. *We observe that large parts of our basic SimpleRisc processor are idle while processing an instruction. For example, the IF stage is idle, when the instruction is in the MA stage.*

2. *We thus propose the notion of "pipelining". Here, we execute 5 instructions simultaneously (1 in each stage). At the negative edge of the clock, all the instructions proceed to the next stages simultaneously, the instruction in the RW stage completes its execution, and a new instruction enters the IF stage.*

3. *To design a pipeline we split the data path into five parts (1 stage per part), and add pipeline registers between subsequent stages. A pipeline register stores the instruction packet (instruction contents, control signals, source operands and intermediate results).*

4. *Each pipeline stage reads operands for its functional units from its corresponding pipeline register at the beginning of a clock cycle. It processes them, and writes the results to the pipeline register between the given stage and its adjacent stage, before the end of the clock cycle.*

5. *We can have RAW hazards, and control hazards in our pipeline because we cannot ascertain data dependences and branch outcomes before fetching subsequent instructions.*

6. *We can avoid RAW, and control hazards using pure software solutions. We can introduce nop instructions between producer and consumer instructions, and after branch instructions. Alternatively, we can reorder instructions to minimise the addition of nop instructions, and use delayed branching.*

7. *In the absence of software solutions, we can use pipeline interlocks to avoid hazards by stalling and cancelling instructions.*

8. *An efficient method of minimising stall cycles is forwarding.*

(a) *If a later stage contains the value of an operand, then we can forward the value from the producer stage to the consumer stage. We can thus bypass the register file.*

(b) *This allows us to avoid hazards because a consumer instruction can quickly get its operands from other pipeline stages.*

(c) *To detect dependences, and implement forwarding we propose a dedicated forwarding unit. Furthermore, it is necessary to augment, every functional unit with multiplexers to choose between the default inputs, and forwarded inputs. Forwarding eliminates all the data hazards, other than the load-use hazard.*

9. *Modern processors have interrupts and exceptions that require us to save the state of a program, and branch to an interrupt handler. We need to implement precise exceptions such that we can return to the exact same point at which we had stopped the execution of our original program.*

10. *Performance of a processor with respect to a program is defined to be proportional to the inverse of the time required to execute the program.*

11. *The performance equation is as follows:*

$$P \propto \frac{IPC \times f}{\#insts}$$

IPC (instructions per cycle), f(frequency), #insts (number of dynamic instructions)

12. *The performance of a processor is dependent on the manufacturing technology, architecture, and compiler optimisations. In specific, a pipelined processor has higher performance as compared to a single cycle processor, because it allows us to increase the frequency roughly as many times as the number of stages. There is a consequent loss in IPC, and wastage of time due to the latch delay. Hence, it is necessary to choose an optimal pipelining strategy.*

13. *The clock frequency is limited by power and temperature constraints.*

(a) *There are two power dissipation mechanisms in modern processors namely dynamic power and leakage power. Dynamic power is dissipated due to the switching activity in circuits. It is proportional to $\alpha CV^2 f$, where α is the activity factor, C is the lumped circuit capacitance, V is the supply voltage, and f is the frequency.*

(b) *Leakage power or static power is dissipated due to the flow of current through the terminals of a transistor, when it is in the off state. Leakage power is a superlinear function of the current temperature.*

(c) *Power and temperature for different points on a chip are typically related by a set of linear equations.*

(d) *Dynamic voltage-frequency scaling is a technique to dynamically modify the voltage and frequency of a processor. We typically assume that the frequency is proportional to voltage.*

(e) *We use the ED^2 metric to simultaneously compare the power and performance of competing processor designs.*

14. *Some advanced techniques for speeding up a processor are branch prediction, superscalar execution, EPIC/VLIW processors, and out-of-order pipelines.*

9.12.2 Further Reading

The design of high performance pipelines is a prime focus of computer architecture researchers. Researchers mostly look at optimising performance of pipelines and simultaneously reducing power consumption. The reader can start out with textbooks on advanced computer architecture [Hennessy and Patterson, 2012, Hwang, 2003, Baer, 2010, Sima et al., 1997, Culler et al., 1998]. After getting a basic understanding of the techniques underlying advanced processors such as out-of-order and superscalar execution, the reader should be able to graduate to reading research papers. The first step in this journey should be the book titled, "Readings in Computer Architecture" [Hill et al., 1999]. This book comprises of a set of foundational research papers in different areas of computer architecture. Subsequently, the reader can move on to reading research papers for getting a deeper understanding of state of the art techniques in processor design.

The reader may start with some of the basic papers in the design of out-of-order processors [Brown et al., 2001, Smith and Sohi, 1995, Hwu and Patt, 1987]. After getting a basic understanding, she can move on to read papers that propose important optimisations such as [Brown et al., 2001, Petric et al., 2005, Akkary et al., 2003]. For a thorough understanding of branch prediction schemes and fetch optimisation, the reader should definitely look at the work of Yeh and Patt [Yeh and Patt, 1991, Yeh and Patt, 1992, Yeh and Patt, 1993], and the patent on Pentium 4 trace caches [Krick et al., 2000].

Simultaneously, the reader can also look at papers describing the complete architecture of processors such as the Intel Pentium 4 [Boggs et al., 2004], Intel ATOM [Halfhill, 2008], Intel Sandybridge [Gwennap, 2010], AMD Opteron [Keltcher et al., 2003], and IBM Power 7 [Ware et al., 2010]. Finally, readers can find descriptions of state of the art processors in the periodical, "Microprocessor Report", along with emerging trends in the processor industry.

Exercises

Pipeline Stages

Ex. 1 — Show the design of the IF, OF, EX, MA, and RW pipeline stages. Explain their functionality in detail.

Ex. 2 — Why do we need to store the $op2$ field in the instruction packet? Where is it used?

Ex. 3 — Why is it necessary to have the *control* field in the instruction packet?

Ex. 4 — Why do we require latches in a pipeline? Why are edge sensitive latches preferred?

Ex. 5 — Why is it necessary to split the work in a data path evenly across the pipeline stages?

* **Ex. 6** — We know that in an edge sensitive latch, the input signal has to be stable for t_{hold} units of time after the negative edge. Let us consider a pipeline stage between latches L_1 and L_2. Suppose the output of L_1 is ready immediately after the negative edge, and almost instantaneously reaches the input of L_2. In this case, we violate the hold time constraint at L_2. How can this situation be avoided?

Pipeline Design

Ex. 7 — Enumerate the rules for constructing a pipeline diagram.

Ex. 8 — Describe the different types of hazards in a pipeline.

Ex. 9 — In the *SimpleRisc* pipeline, why don't we have structural hazards?

Ex. 10 — Why does a branch have two delay slots in the *SimpleRisc* pipeline?

Ex. 11 — What are the `Data-Lock` and `Branch-Lock` conditions?

Ex. 12 — Write pseudo-code for detecting and handling the `Branch-Lock` condition? (without delayed branches)

Ex. 13 — What is delayed branching?

* Ex. 14 — Let us consider two designs: D_1 and D_2. D_1 uses a software-based approach for hazards, and assumes delayed branching. D_2 uses interlocks, and assumes that a branch is not taken till the outcome is decided. Intuitively, which design is faster?

Ex. 15 — Assume that 20% of the dynamic instructions executed on a computer are branch instructions. We use delayed branching with one delay slot. Estimate the CPI, if the compiler is able to fill 85% of the delay slots. Assume that the base CPI is 1.5. In the base case, we do not use any delay slot. Instead, we stall the pipeline for the total number of delay slots.

Ex. 16 — Describe the role of the forwarding multiplexers in each stage of the pipeline.

Ex. 17 — Why do we not require a forwarding path from MA to EX for the *op2* field?

Ex. 18 — Answer the following questions.

   i) What are the six possible forwarding paths in our *SimpleRisc* processor?

   ii) Which four forwarding paths, are required, and why? (Give examples to support your answer).

Ex. 19 — Assume that we have an instruction immediately after a call instruction that reads ra. We claim that this instruction will get the correct value of ra in a pipeline with forwarding. Is this true? Prove your answer.

Ex. 20 — Reorder the following code snippet to minimise the execution time for the following configurations:

   1. We use software techniques, and have 2 delay slots.

   2. We use interlocks, and predict not taken.

   3. We use forwarding, and predict not taken.

```
add r1, r2, r3
sub r4, r1, r1
mul r8, r9, r10
cmp r8, r9
beq .foo
```

Ex. 21 — Reorder the following code snippet to minimise execution time for the following configurations:

   1. We use software techniques, and have 2 delay slots.

   2. We use interlocks, and predict not taken.

   3. We use forwarding, and predict not taken.

```
add r4, r3, r3
st  r3, 10[r4]
ld  r2, 10[r4]
mul r8, r9, r10
div r8, r9, r10
add r4, r2, r6
```

Ex. 22 — Answer the following:

```
add r1, r2, r3
sub r4, r1, r6
ld  r5, 10[r4]
add r6, r5, r5
sub r8, r8, r9
mul r10, r10, r11
cmp r8, r10
beq .label
add r5, r6, r8
st  r3, 20[r5]
ld  r6, 20[r5]
ld  r7, 20[r6]
lsl r7, r7, r10
```

i) Assuming a traditional *SimpleRisc* pipeline, how many cycles will this code take to execute in a pipeline with just interlocks? Assume that time starts when the first instruction reaches the RW stage. This means that if we had just one instruction, then it would have taken exactly 1 cycle to execute (Not 5). Moreover, assume that the branch is not taken. [Assumptions: No forwarding, No delayed branches, No reordering]

ii) Now, compute the number of cycles with forwarding (no delayed branches, no reordering).

iii) Compute the minimum number of cycles when we have forwarding, and we allow instruction reordering. We do not have delayed branches, and in the reordered code, the branch instruction cannot be one of the last three instructions.

iv) Compute the minimum number of cycles when we have forwarding, allow instruction reordering, and have delayed branches. Here, again, we are not allowed to have the branch instruction as one of the last three instructions in the reordered code.

** **Ex. 23** — We have assumed up till now that each memory access requires one cycle. Now, let us assume that each memory access takes two cycles. How will you modify the data path and the control path of the *SimpleRisc* processor in this case.

** **Ex. 24** — Assume you have a pipeline that contains a value predictor for memory. If there is a miss in the L2 cache, then we try to predict the value and supply it to the processor. Later this value is compared with the value obtained from memory. If the value matches, then we are fine, else we need to initiate a process of recovery in the processor and discard all the wrong computation. Design a scheme to do this effectively.

Performance and Power Modelling

Ex. 25 — If we increase the average CPI (Cycles per Instruction) by 5%, decrease the instruction count by 20% and double the clock rate, what is the expected speedup, if any, and why?

Ex. 26 — What should be the ideal number of pipeline stages (x) for a processor with $CPI = (1 + 0.2x)$ and clock cycle time $t_{clk} = (1 + 50/x)$?

Ex. 27 — What is the relationship between dependences in a program, and the optimal number of pipeline stages it requires?

Ex. 28 — Is a 4 GHz machine faster than a 2 GHz machine? Justify your answer.

Ex. 29 — How do the manufacturing technology, compiler, and architecture determine the performance of a processor?

Ex. 30 — Define dynamic power and leakage power.

* **Ex. 31** — We claim that if we increase the frequency, the leakage power increases. Justify this statement.

Ex. 32 — What is the justification of the ED^2 metric?

* **Ex. 33** — How do power and temperature considerations limit the number of pipeline stages? Explain your answer in detail. Consider all the relationships between power, temperature, activity, IPC, and frequency that we have introduced in this chapter.

* **Ex. 34** — Define the term DVFS.

** **Ex. 35** — Assume that we wish to estimate the temperature at different points of a processor. We know the dynamic power of different components, and the leakage power as a function of temperature. Furthermore, we divide the surface of the die into a grid as explained in Section 9.10.4. How do we use this information to arrive at a steady state value of temperature for all the grid points?

Interrupts and Exceptions

Ex. 36 — What are precise exceptions? How does hardware ensure that every exception is a precise exception?

Ex. 37 — Why do we need the *movz* and *retz* instructions?

Ex. 38 — List the additional registers that we add to a pipeline to support interrupts and exceptions.

Ex. 39 — What is the role of the CPL register? How do we set and reset it?

Ex. 40 — How do we locate the correct interrupt handler? What is the structure and role of an interrupt handler?

Ex. 41 — Why do we need the registers *oldPC*, and *oldSP*?

Ex. 42 — Why do we need to add a *flags* field to the instruction packet? How do we use the *oldFlags* register?

* **Ex. 43** — Consider a hypothetical situation where a write back to a register may generate an exception (register-fault exception). Propose a mechanism to handle this exception *precisely*.

* **Ex. 44** — Define the concept of register windows. How can we use register windows to speedup the implementation of functions?

Advanced Topics

Ex. 45 — Can you intuitively say why most of the branches in programs are predictable.

Ex. 46 — Is the following code sequence amenable to branch prediction. Why or why not?

```
int status=flip_random_unbiased_coin();
if (status==Head)
        print(\head");
else
        print(\tail");
```

Ex. 47 — We need to design a 2-issue inorder pipeline that accepts a bundle of two instructions every cycle. These bundles are created by the compiler.

(a) Given the different instruction types, design an algorithm that tells the compiler the different constraints in designing a bundle. For example, you might decide that you don't want to have two instructions in a bundle if they are of certain types, or have certain operands.

(b) To implement a two issue pipeline, what kind of additional functionality will you need in the MEM stage?

Ex. 48 — Describe the main insight behind out-of-order pipelines? What are their major structures?

Design Problems

Ex. 49 — Implement a basic pipelined processor with interlocks using Logisim (refer to the design problems in Chapter 8).

Ex. 50 — Implement a basic pipelined processor in a hardware description language such as Verilog or VHDL. Try to add forwarding paths and interrupt processing logic.

Ex. 51 — Learn the language SystemC. It is used to model hardware at a high level. Implement the *SimpleRisc* pipeline in SystemC.

Part III

Organisation: System Design

10

The Memory System

Up till now, we have considered the memory system to be one large array of bytes. This abstraction was good enough for designing an instruction set, studying assembly language, and even for designing a basic processor with a complicated pipeline. However, from a practical standpoint, this abstraction will need to be further refined to design a fast memory system. In our basic *SimpleRisc* pipeline presented in Chapter 8 and 9, we have assumed that it takes 1 cycle to access both data and instruction memory. We shall see in this chapter, that this is not always true. In fact, we need to make significant optimisations in the memory system to come close to the ideal latency of 1 cycle. We need to introduce the notion of a "cache" and a hierarchical memory system to solve the dual problems of having large memory capacity, and low latency.

Secondly, up till now we have been assuming that only one program runs on our system. However, most processors typically run multiple programs on a time shared basis. For example, if there are two programs, A and B, a modern desktop or laptop typically runs program A for a couple of milliseconds, executes B for a few milliseconds, and subsequently switches back and forth. In fact as your author is writing this book, there are a host of other programs running on his system such as a web browser, an audio player, and a calendar application. In general, a user does not perceive any interruptions, because the time scale at which the interruptions happen is much lower than what the human brain can perceive. For example, a typical video displays a new picture 30 times every second, or alternatively one new picture every 33 milliseconds. The human brain creates the illusion of a smoothly moving object by piecing the pictures together. If the processor finishes the job of processing the next picture in a video sequence, before 33 milliseconds, then it can execute a part of another program. The human brain will not be able to tell the difference. The point here is that without our knowledge, the processor in co-operation with the operating system switches between multiple programs many many times a second. The *operating system* is itself a specialised program that helps the processor manage itself, and other programs. Windows and Linux are examples of popular operating systems.

We shall see that we require special support in the memory system to support multiple programs. If we do not have this support, then multiple programs can overwrite each other's data, which is not desired behavior. Secondly, we have been living with the assumption that we have practically an infinite amount of memory. This is also not true. The amount of memory that we have is finite, and it can get exhausted by large memory intensive programs. Hence, we should have a mechanism to still run such large programs. We shall introduce the concept of virtual memory to solve both of these issues – running multiple programs, and handling large memory intensive programs.

To summarise, we observe that we need to design a memory system that is fast, and is flexible enough to support multiple programs with very large memory requirements.

10.1 Overview

10.1.1 Need for a Fast Memory System

Let us now look at the technological requirements for building a fast memory system. We have seen in Chapter 6 that we can design memory elements with four kinds of basic circuits – latches, SRAM cells, CAM cells and DRAM cells. There is a tradeoff here. Latches and SRAM cells are much faster than DRAM or CAM cells. However, as compared to a DRAM cell, a latch, CAM or SRAM cell is an order of magnitude larger in terms of area, and also consumes much more power. We observe that a latch is designed to read in and read out data at a negative clock edge. It is a fast circuit that can store and retrieve data in a fraction of a clock cycle. On the other hand, an SRAM cell is typically designed to be used as a part of a large array of SRAM cells along with a decoder and sense amplifiers. With this additional overhead, an SRAM cell is typically slower than a typical edge triggered latch. In comparison, CAM cells are best for memories that are content associative, and DRAM cells are best for memories that have very large capacities.

Now, our *SimpleRisc* pipeline assumes that memory accesses take 1 cycle. To satisfy this requirement, we need to build our entire memory from latches, or small arrays of SRAM cells. Table 10.1 shows the size of a typical latch, SRAM cell, and DRAM cell as of 2012.

Cell type	Area	Typical latency (array of cells)
Master Slave D flip flop	0.8 μm^2	fraction of a cycle
SRAM cell	0.08 μm^2	1-5 cycles
DRAM Cell	0.005 μm^2	50-200 cycles

Table 10.1: Sizes of a Latch, SRAM cell, and DRAM cell

We observe that a typical latch (master slave D flip flop) is 10 times larger than an SRAM cell, which in turn is around 16 times larger than a DRAM cell. This means that given a certain amount of silicon, we can save 160 times more data if we use DRAM cells. However, DRAM memory is also 200 times slower (if we consider a representative array of DRAM cells). Clearly, there is a tradeoff between capacity, and speed. The sad part is that we actually need both.

Let us consider the issue of capacity first. Due to several constraints in technology and manufacturability, as of 2012, it is not possible to manufacture chips with an area more than 400-$500 mm^2$ [ITRS, 2011]. Consequently, the total amount of memory that we can have on chip is limited. It is definitely possible to supplement the amount of available memory with additional chips exclusively containing memory cells. Keep in mind that off-chip memory is slow, and it takes tens of cycles for the processor to access such memory modules. To achieve our goal of having a 1-cycle memory access, we need to use the relatively faster on-chip memory most of the time. Here, also our options are limited. We cannot afford to have a memory system consisting exclusively of latches. For a large number of programs, we will not be able to fit all our data in memory. For example, modern programs typically require hundreds of megabytes of memory. Moreover, some large scientific programs require gigabytes of memory. Second, it is difficult to integrate large DRAM arrays along with a processor on the same chip due to technological constraints. Hence, designers are compelled to use large SRAM arrays for on-chip memories. As shown in Table 10.1 SRAM cells(arrays) are much larger than DRAM cells(arrays), and thus have much less capacity.

There is a conflicting requirement of latency. Let us assume that we decide to maximise storage, and make our memory entirely consisting of DRAM cells. Let us assume a 100 cycle latency for accessing DRAM. If we assume that a third of our instructions are memory instructions, then the effective CPI of a perfect 5 stage *SimpleRisc* pipeline is calculated to be $1 + 1/3 \times (100 - 1) = 34$. The point to note is that our CPI increases by 34X, which is completely unacceptable.

Hence, we need to make an equitable tradeoff between latency and storage. We want to store as much of data as possible, but not at the cost of a very low IPC. Unfortunately, there is no way out of this situation, if we assume that our memory accesses are completely random. If there is some pattern in memory accesses, then we can possibly do something better such that we can get the best of both worlds – high storage capacity, and low latency.

10.1.2   Memory Access Patterns

Before considering the technical topic of patterns in memory accesses, let us consider a simple practical problem that your author is facing at this point of time. He unfortunately, has a lot of books on his desk that are not organised. Not only are these books cluttering up his desk, it is also hard to search for a book when required. Hence, he needs to organise his books better and also keep his desk clean. He observes that he does not require all the books all the time. For example, he needs books on computer architecture very frequently; however, he rarely reads his books on distributed systems. Hence, it makes sense for him to move his books on distributed systems to the shelf beside his desk. Unfortunately, it is a small shelf, and there are still a lot of books on his desk. He observes that he can further classify the books in the small shelf. He has some books on philosophy that he never reads. These can be moved to the large cabinet in the corner of the room. This will create more space in the shelf, and also help him clean up his desk. What is the fundamental insight here? It is that your author does not read all his books with the same frequency. There are some books that he reads very frequently; hence, they need to be on his desk. Then there is another class of books that he reads infrequently; hence, they need to be in the small shelf beside his desk. Lastly, he has a large number of books that he reads extremely infrequently. He can safely keep them in the large cabinet. **Pattern 1:He reads a small set of books very frequently, and the rest of the books rather infrequently.** Hence, if he keeps the frequently accessed set of books on computer architecture on his desk, and the large infrequent set of books in the shelf and the cabinet, he has solved his problems.

Well, not quite. This was true for last semester, when he was teaching the computer architecture course. However, in the current semester, he is teaching a course on distributed systems. Hence, he does not refer to his architecture books anymore. It thus makes sense for him to bring his distributed systems books to his desk. However, there is a problem. What happens to his architecture books that are already there on his desk. Well, the simple answer is that they need to be moved to the shelf and they will occupy the slots vacated by the distributed systems books. In the interest of time, it makes sense for your author to bring a set of distributed systems books on to his desk, because in very high likelihood, he will need to refer to numerous books in that area. It does not make sense to fetch just one book on distributed systems. Hence, as a general rule we can conclude that if we require a certain book, then most likely we will require other books in the same subject. **Pattern 2:If your author requires a certain book, then most likely he will require other books in the same subject area in the near future.**

We can think of patterns 1 and 2, as general laws that are applicable to everybody. Instead of books, if we consider TV channels, then also both the patterns apply. We do not watch all TV channels equally frequently. Secondly, if a user has tuned in to a news channel, then most likely she will browse through other news channels in the near future. In fact this is how retail stores work. They typically keep spices and seasonings close to vegetables. This is because it is highly likely that a user who has just bought vegetables will want to buy spices also. However, they keep bathroom supplies and electronics far away.

Pattern 1 is called *temporal locality*. This means that users will tend to reuse the same item in a given time interval. Pattern 2 is called *spatial locality*. It means that if a user has used a certain item, then she will tend to use similar items in the near future.

Definition 97

Temporal Locality *It is a concept that states that if a resource is accessed at some point of time, then most likely it will be accessed again in a short time interval.*

Spatial Locality *It is a concept that states that if a resource is accessed at some point of time, then most likely similar resources will be accessed in the near future.*

The question that we need to ask is – "Is there temporal and spatial locality in memory accesses?". If there is some degree of temporal and spatial locality, then we can possibly do some critical optimisations that will help us solve the twin problems of large memory requirement, and low latency. In computer architecture, we typically rely on such properties such as temporal and spatial locality to solve our problems.

10.1.3 Temporal and Spatial Locality of Instruction Accesses

The standard approach for tackling this problem, is to measure and characterise locality in a representative set of programs such as the SPEC benchmarks(see Section 9.9.4). Let us first start out by dividing memory accesses into two broad types – instruction and data. Instruction accesses are much easier to analyse informally. Hence, let us look at it first.

Let us consider a typical program. It has assignment statements, decision statements (if,else), and loops. Most of the code in large programs is part of loops or some pieces of common code. There is a standard rule of thumb in computer architecture, which states that 90% of the code runs for 10% of time, and 10% of the code runs for 90% of the time. Let us consider a word processor. The code to process the user's input, and show the result on the screen runs much more frequently than the code for showing the help screen. Similarly, for scientific applications, most of the time is spent in a few loops in the program. In fact for most common applications, we find this pattern. Hence, computer architects have concluded that temporal locality for instruction accesses holds for an overwhelming majority of programs.

Let us now consider spatial locality for instruction accesses. If there are no branch statements, then the next program counter is the current program counter plus 4 bytes for an ISA such as *SimpleRisc* . We consider two accesses to be "similar", if their memory addresses are close to each other. Clearly, we have spatial locality here. A majority of the instructions in programs are non-branches; hence, spatial locality holds. Moreover, a nice pattern in branches in most programs is that the branch target is actually not very far away. If we consider a simple *if-then* statement or *for* loop then the distance of the branch target is equal to the length of the loop or the *if* part of the statement. In most programs this is typically 10 to 100 instructions long, definitely not thousands of instructions long. Hence, architects have concluded that instruction memory accesses exhibit a good amount of spatial locality also.

The situation for data accesses is slightly more complicated; however, not very different. For data accesses also we tend to reuse the same data, and access similar data items. Let us look at this in more detail.

10.1.4 Characterising Temporal Locality

Let us describe a method called the method of stack distances to characterise temporal locality in programs.

Stack Distance

We maintain a stack of accessed data addresses For each memory instruction (load/store), we search for the corresponding address in the stack. The position at which the entry is found (if found) is termed the "stack distance". Here, the distance is measured from the top of the stack. The top of the stack has distance equal to zero, whereas the 100th entry has a stack distance equal to 99. Whenever, we detect an entry in the stack we remove it, and push it to the top of the stack.

If the memory address is not found, then we make a new entry and push it to the top of the stack. Typically, the depth of the stack is bounded. It has length, L. If the number of entries in the stack exceeds L because of the addition of a new entry, then we need to remove the entry at the bottom of the stack. Secondly, while adding a new entry, the stack distance is not defined. Note that since we consider bounded stacks, there is no way of differentiating between a new entry, and an entry that was there in the stack, but had to be removed because it was at the bottom of the stack. Hence, in this case we take the stack distance to be equal to L (bound on the depth of the stack).

Note that the notion of stack distance gives us an indication of temporal locality. If the accesses have high temporal locality, then the mean stack distance is expected to be lower. Conversely, if memory accesses have low temporal locality, then the mean stack distance will be high. We can thus use the distribution of stack distances as a measure of the amount of temporal locality in a program.

Experiment to Measure Stack Distance

We perform a simple experiment with the SPEC2006 benchmark, Perlbench, which runs different Perl programs [1]. We maintain counters to keep track of the stack distance. The first million memory accesses serve as a warm-up period. During this time the stack is maintained, but the counters are not incremented. For the next million memory accesses, the stack is maintained, and the counters are also incremented. Figure 10.1 shows a histogram of the stack distance. The size of the stack is limited to 1000 entries. It is sufficient to capture an overwhelming majority of memory accesses.

We observe that most of the accesses have a very low stack distance. A stack distance between 0-9 is the most common value. Approximately 27% of all the accesses are in this bin. In fact, more than two thirds of the memory accesses have a stack distance less than 100. Beyond 100, the distribution tapers off, yet remains fairly steady. The distribution of stack distances is typically said to follow a heavy tailed distribution. This means that the distribution is heavily skewed towards smaller stack distances; however, large stack distances are not uncommon. The tail of the distribution continues to be non-zero for large stack distances. We observe a similar behavior here.

Trivia 3 *Researchers have tried to approximate the stack distance using the log-normal distribution.*

$$f(x) = \frac{1}{x\sigma\sqrt{2\pi}}e^{-\frac{(ln(x)-\mu)^2}{2\sigma^2}}$$

10.1.5 Characterising Spatial Locality

Address Distance

Akin to stack distance, we define the term *address distance*. The ith address distance is the difference in the memory address of the ith memory access, and the closest address in the set of the last K memory

---

[1] Dataset size 'ref', input 'split-mail'

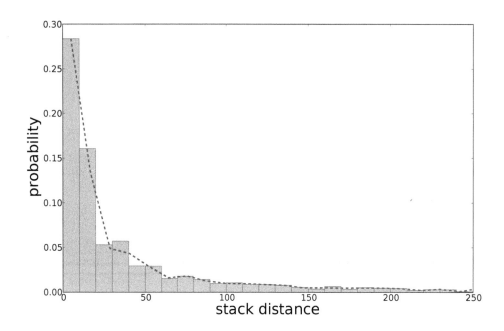

Figure 10.1: Stack distance distribution

accesses. Here, a memory access can be either a load or a store. There is an intuitive reason for defining address distance in this manner. Programs typically access different regions of main memory in the same time interval. For example, an operation on arrays, accesses an array item, then accesses some constants, performs an operation, saves the result, and then moves on the next array entry using a *for* loop. There is clearly spatial locality here, in the sense that consecutive iterations of a *for* loop access proximate addresses in an array. However, to quantify it, we need to search for the closest access (in terms of memory addresses) over the last K accesses. Here, K is the number of memory accesses in each iteration of the enclosing loop. We can readily observe that in this case that the address distance turns out to be a small value, and is indicative of high spatial locality. However, K needs to be well chosen. It should not be too small, nor too large. We have empirically found $K = 10$ to be an appropriate value for a large set of programs.

To summarise, we can conclude that if the average address distance is small, then it means that we have high spatial locality in the program. The program tends to access nearby memory addresses with high likelihood in the same time interval. Conversely, if the address distances are high, then the accesses are far apart from each other, and the program does not exhibit spatial locality.

Experiment to Characterise Address Distance

Here, we repeat the same experiment as described in Section 10.1.4 with the SPEC2006 benchmark, Perl-bench. We profile the address distance distribution for the first 1 million accesses. Figure 10.2 shows the address distance distribution.

Here also, more than a quarter of the accesses have an address distance between -5 and +5, and more than two thirds of the accesses have an address distance between -25 and +25. Beyond ±50, the address distance distribution tapers off. Empirically, this distribution also has a heavy tailed nature.

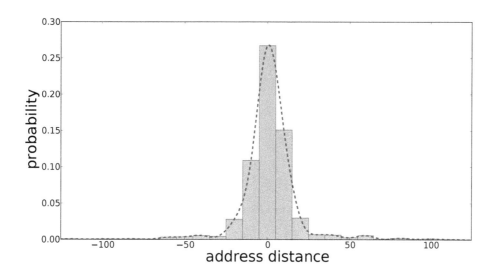

Figure 10.2: Address distance distribution

10.1.6   Utilising Spatial and Temporal Locality

Section 10.1.4 and 10.1.5 showed the stack and address distance distributions for a sample program. Similar experiments have been performed for thousands of programs that users use in their daily lives. These programs include computer games, word processors, databases, spreadsheet applications, weather simulation programs, financial applications, and software applications that run on mobile computers. Almost all of them exhibit a very high degree of temporal and spatial locality. In other words, temporal and spatial locality, are basic human traits. Whatever we do, including fetching books, or writing programs, these properties tend to hold. Note that these are just mere empirical observations. It is always possible to write a program that does not exhibit any form of temporal and spatial locality. Additionally, it is always possible to find regions of code in commercial programs that do not exhibit these properties. However, these examples are exceptions. They are not the norm. We need to design computer systems for the norm, and not for the exceptions. This is how we can boost performance for a large majority of programs that users are expected to run.

From now on, let us take temporal and spatial locality for granted, and see what can be done to boost the performance of the memory system, without compromising on storage capacity. Let us look at temporal locality first.

10.1.7   Exploiting Temporal Locality – Hierarchical Memory System

Let us reconsider the way in which we tried to exploit temporal locality for our simple example with books. If your author decides to look at a new topic, then he brings the set of books associated with that topic to his desk. The books that were already there on his desk, are moved to the shelf, and to create space in the shelf, some books are shifted to the cabinet. This behavior is completely consistent with the notion of stack distance as shown in Figure 10.1.

We can do the same with memory systems also. Akin to a desk, shelf, and cabinet, let us define a storage

location for memory values. Let us call it a *cache*. Each entry in the cache conceptually contains two fields
– memory address, and value. Like your author's office, let us define a hierarchy of caches as shown in
Figure 10.3.

Definition 98
A cache *contains a set of values for different memory locations.*

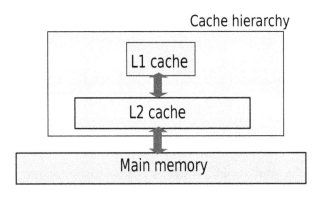

Figure 10.3: Memory hierarchy

Definition 99 *The* main memory*(physical memory) is a large DRAM array that contains values for all
the memory locations used by the processor.*

   The L1 cache corresponds to the desk, the L2 cache corresponds to the shelf, and the main memory
corresponds to the cabinet. The L1 cache is typically a small SRAM array (8-64 KB). The L2 cache is a
larger SRAM array (128 KB - 4 MB). Some processors such as the Intel Sandybridge processor have another
level of caches called the L3 cache (4MB+). Below the L2/L3 cache, there is a large DRAM array containing
all the memory locations. This is known as the *main memory* or *physical memory*. Note that in the example
with books, a book could either exclusively belong to the shelf or the cabinet. However, in the case of memory
values, we need not follow this rule. In fact, we shall see later that it is easier to maintain a subset of values
of the L2 cache in the L1 cache, and so on. This is known as a system with inclusive caches. We thus have
– $values(L1) \subset values(L2) \subset values(main\ memory)$ – for an inclusive cache hierarchy. Alternatively, we
can have exclusive caches, where a higher level cache does not necessarily contain a subset of values in the
lower level cache. Inclusive caches are by far used universally in all processors. This is because of the ease
of design, simplicity, and some subtle correctness issues that we shall discuss in Chapter 11. There are some
research level proposals that advocate exclusive caches. However, their utility for general purpose processors
has not been established as of 2012.

Definition 100 *A memory system in which the set of memory values contained in the cache at the nth level is a subset of all the values contained in the cache at the $(n+1)^{th}$ level, is known as an* inclusive *cache hierarchy. A memory system that does not follow strict inclusion is referred to as an* exclusive *cache hierarchy.*

Let us now consider the cache hierarchy as shown in Figure 10.3. Since the L1 cache is small, it is faster to access. The access time is typically 1-2 cycles. The L2 cache is larger and typically takes 5-15 cycles to access. The main memory is much slower because of its large size and use of DRAM cells. The access times are typically very high and are between 100-300 cycles. The memory access protocol is similar to the way your author accesses his books.

The memory access protocol is as follows. Whenever, there is a memory access (load or store), the processor first checks in the L1 cache. Note that each entry in the cache conceptually contains both the memory address and value. If the data item is present in the L1 cache, we declare a **cache hit**, otherwise we declare a **cache miss**. If there is a cache hit, and the memory request is a read, then we need to just return the value to the processor. If the memory request is a write, then the processor writes the new value to the cache entry. It can then propagate the changes to the lower levels, or resume processing. We shall look at these the different methods of performing a cache write in detail, when we discuss different write policies in Section 10.2.3. However, if there is a cache miss, then further processing is required.

Definition 101

Cache hit *Whenever a memory location is present in a cache, the event is known as a* cache hit.

Cache miss *Whenever a memory location is not present in a cache, the event is known as a* cache miss.

In the event of an L1 cache miss, the processor needs to access the L2 cache and search for the data item. If an item is found (cache hit), then the protocol is the same as the L1 cache. Since, we consider inclusive caches in this book, it is necessary to fetch the data item to the L1 cache. If there is an L2 miss, then we need to access the lower level. The lower level can be another L3 cache, or can be the main memory. At the lowest level, i.e., the main memory, we are guaranteed to not have a miss, because we assume that the main memory contains an entry for all the memory locations.

Performance Benefit of a Hierarchical Memory System

Instead of having a single flat memory system, processors use a hierarchical memory system to maximise performance. A hierarchical memory system is meant to provide the illusion of a large memory with an ideal single cycle latency.

Example 119 *Find the average memory access latency for the following configurations.*

Configuration 1		
Level	Miss Rate(%)	Latency
L1	10	1
L2	10	10
Main Memory	0	100
Configuration 2		
Main Memory	0	100

Answer: *Let us consider the first configuration. Here, 90% of the accesses hit in the L1 cache. Hence, their memory access time is 1 cycle. Note that even the accesses that miss in the L1 cache still incur the 1 cycle delay, because we do not know if an access will hit or miss in the cache. Subsequently, 90% of the accesses that go to the L2 cache hit in the cache. They incur a 10-cycle delay. Finally, the remaining accesses (1%) hit in the main memory, and incur an additional delay. The average memory access time(T) is thus:*

$$T = 1 + 0.1 * (10 + 0.1 * 100) = 1 + 1 + 1 = 3$$

Thus, the average memory latency of a hierarchical memory system such as configuration 1 is 3 cycles.

Configuration 2 is a flat hierarchy, which uses the main memory for all its accesses. The average memory access time is 100 cycles.

There is thus a speedup of 100/3 = 33.3 times using a hierarchical memory system.

Let us consider an example (see Example 119). It shows that the performance gain using a hierarchical memory system is 33.33 times that of a flat memory system with a single level hierarchy. The performance improvement is a function of the hit rates of different caches and their latencies. Moreover, the hit rate of a cache is dependent on the stack distance profile of the program, and the cache management policies. Likewise the cache access latency is dependent on the cache manufacturing technology, design of the cache, and the cache management schemes. We need to mention that optimising cache accesses has been a very important topic in computer architecture research for the past two decades. Researchers have published thousands of papers in this area. We shall only cover some basic mechanisms in this book. The interested reader can take a look at Section 10.5.2 for appropriate references.

10.1.8 Exploiting Spatial Locality – Cache Blocks

Let us now consider spatial locality. We observe in Figure 10.2 that a majority of accesses have an address distance within ±25 bytes. Recall that the address distance is defined as the difference in memory addresses between the current address and the closest address among the last K addresses. The address distance distribution suggests that if we group a set of memory locations into one block, and fetch it at one go from the lower level, then we can increase the number of cache hits because there is a high degree of spatial locality in accesses. This approach is similar to the way we decided to fetch all the architecture books at the same time from the shelf in Section 10.1.2.

Consequently, almost all processors create blocks of contiguous addresses, and the cache treats each block as an atomic unit. The entire block is fetched at once from the lower level, and also an entire block is evicted from the cache if required. A cache block is also known as a *cache line*. A typical cache block or a line is 32-128 bytes long. For ease of addressing, its size needs to be a strict power of 2.

Definition 102
A cache block or a line is a contiguous set of memory locations. It is treated as an atomic unit of data in a cache.

Thus, we need to slightly redefine the notion of a cache entry. Instead of having an entry for each memory address, we have a separate entry for each cache line. Note that in this book, we shall use the terms cache line and block synonymously. Also note that it is not necessary to have the same cache line size in the L1 cache and the L2 cache. They can be different. However, for maintaining the property of inclusiveness of caches, and minimising additional memory accesses, it is typically necessary to use an equal or larger block size in the L2 cache as compared to the L1 cache.

Way Point 9
Here is what we have learnt up till now.

1. *Temporal and spatial locality are properties inherent to most human actions. They apply equally well to reading books and writing computer programs.*

2. *Temporal locality can be quantified by the* stack *distance, and spatial locality can be quantified by the* address *distance.*

3. *We need to design memory systems to take advantage of temporal and spatial locality.*

4. *To take advantage of temporal locality, we use a hierarchical memory system consisting of a set of caches. The L1 cache is typically a small and fast structure that is meant to satisfy most of the memory accesses quickly. The lower level of the caches store larger amounts of data, are accessed infrequently, and have larger access times.*

5. *To take advantage of spatial locality, we group sets of contiguous memory locations into blocks (also known as lines). A block is treated as an atomic unit of data in a cache.*

Given that we have studied the requirements of a cache qualitatively, we shall proceed to discuss the design of caches.

10.2 Caches

10.2.1 Overview of a Basic Cache

Let us consider a cache as a black box as shown in Figure 10.4. In the case of a load operation, the input is the memory address, and the output is the value of the memory location if there is a cache hit. We envision the cache having a status line that indicates if the request suffered a hit or miss. If the operation is a store, then the cache takes two inputs – memory address, and value. The cache stores the value in the entry corresponding to the memory location if there is a cache hit. Otherwise, it indicates that there is a cache miss.

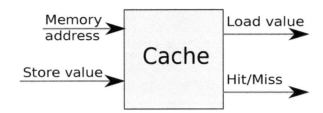

Figure 10.4: A cache as a black box

Let us now look at methods to practically implement this black box. We shall use an SRAM array as the building block (see Section 6.4). The reader might wish to revisit that section to recapitulate her knowledge on memory structures.

To motivate a design, let us consider an example. Let us consider a 32-bit machine with a block size of 64 bytes. In this machine, we thus have 2^{26} blocks. Let the size of the L1 cache be 8 KB. It contains 2^7 or 128 blocks. We can thus visualise the L1 cache at any point of time as a very small subset of the entire memory address space. It contains at the most 128 out of 2^{26} blocks. To find out if a given block is there in the L1 cache, we need to see if any of the 128 entries contains it.

We assume that our L1 cache, is a part of a memory hierarchy. The memory hierarchy as a whole supports two basic requests – *read* and *write*. However, we shall see that at the level of a cache, we require many basic operations to implement these two high level operations.

Basic Cache Operations

Akin to a memory address, let us define a block address as the 26 MSB bits of the memory address. The first problem is to find if a block with the given block address is present in the cache. We need to perform a *lookup operation* that returns a pointer to the block if it is present in the cache. If the block is present in the cache then we can declare a cache hit and service the request. For a cache hit, we need two basic operations to service the request namely *data read*, and *data write*. They read or write the contents of the block, and require the pointer to the block as an argument.

If there is a cache miss, then we need to fetch the block from the lower levels of the memory hierarchy and insert it in the cache. The procedure of fetching a block from the lower levels of the memory hierarchy, and inserting it into a cache, is known as a *fill* operation. The *fill* operation is a complex operation, and uses many atomic sub-operations. We need to first send a load request to the lower level cache to fetch the block, and then we need to insert in into the L1 cache.

The process of insertion is also a complex process. We need to first check, if we have space to insert a new block in a given set of blocks. If we have sufficient space in a set, then we can populate one of the entries using an *insert* operation. However, if all the locations at which we want to insert a block in the cache are already busy, then we need to evict an already existing block from the cache. We thus need to invoke a *replace* operation to find the cache block that needs to be evicted. Once, we have found an appropriate candidate block for replacement, we need to evict it from the cache using an *evict* operation.

Thus, to summarise the discussion up till now, we can conclude that we broadly need these basic operations to implement a cache – *lookup*, *data read*, *data write*, *insert*, *replace*, and *evict*. The *fill* operation is just a sequence of *lookup*, *insert*, and *replace* operations at different levels of the memory hierarchy. Likewise, the *read* operation is either primarily a *lookup* operation, or the combination of a *lookup* and *fill* operation.

10.2.2 Cache Lookup and Cache Design

As outlined in Section 10.2.1, we wish to design a 8 KB cache with a block size of 64 bytes for a 32-bit system. To do an efficient cache lookup, we need to find an efficient way to find out if the 26 bit block address exists among the 128 entries in the cache. There are thus two problems here. The first problem is to quickly locate a given entry, and the second is to perform a read/write operation. Instead of using a single SRAM array to solve both the problems, it is a better idea to split it into two arrays as shown in Figure 10.5.

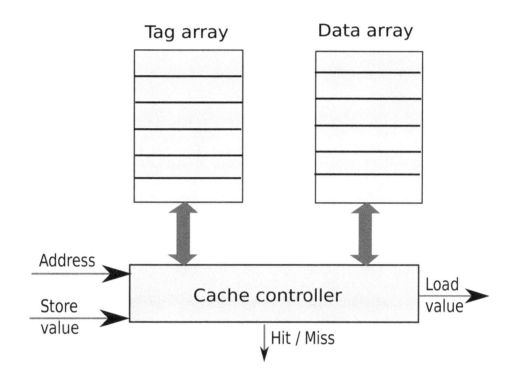

Figure 10.5: Structure of a cache

In a typical design, a cache entry is saved in two SRAM based arrays. One SRAM array known as the *tag array*, contains information pertaining to the block address, and the other SRAM array known as the *data array* contains the data for the block. The tag array contains a *tag* that uniquely identifies a block. The tag is typically a part of the block address, and depends on the type of the cache. Along with the tag and data arrays, there is a dedicated cache controller that executes the cache access algorithm.

Fully Associative(FA) Cache

Let us first consider a very simple way of locating a block. We can check each of the 128 entries in the cache possibly simultaneously to see if the block address is equal to the block address in the cache entry. This cache is known as a fully associative cache or a content addressable cache. The phrase "fully associative" means that a given block can be *associated* with any entry in the cache.

Each cache entry in a fully associative(FA) cache thus needs to contain two fields – *tag* and *data*. In this case, we can set the tag to be equal to the block address. Since the block address is unique to each block, it fits the definition of a *tag*. *Block data* refers to the contents of the block (64 bytes in this case). The block address requires 26 bits, and the block data requires 64 bytes, in our running example. The search operation needs to span the entire cache, and once an entry is located, we need to either read out the data, or write a

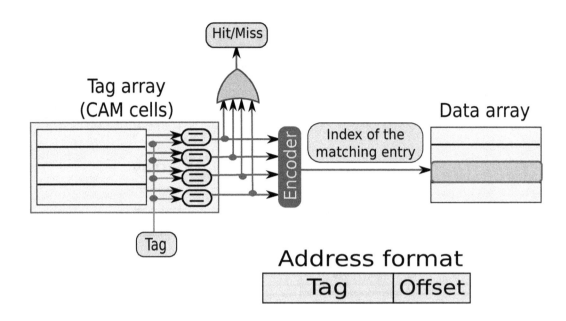

Figure 10.6: A fully associative cache

new value.

Let us first take a look at the tag array. Each tag in this case is equal to the 26 bit block address. After a memory request reaches a cache, the first step is to compute the tag by extracting the 26 most significant bits. Then, we need to match the extracted tag with each entry in the tag array using a set of comparators. If there is no match, then we can declare a cache miss and do further processing. However, if there is a cache hit, then we need to use the number of the entry that matches the tag to access the data entry. For example, in our 8 KB cache that contains 128 entries, it is possible that the 53rd entry in the tag array matches the tag. In this case, the cache controller needs to fetch the 53rd entry from the data array in the case of a read access, or write to the 53rd entry in the case of a write access..

There are two ways to implement the tag array in a fully associative cache. Either we can design it as a normal SRAM array in which the cache controller iterates through each entry, and compares it with the given tag. Or, we can use a CAM array (see Section 6.4.2) that has comparators in every row. They can compare the value of the tag with the data stored in the row and produce an output (1 or 0) depending on the result of the comparison. A CAM array typically uses an encoder to compute the number of the row that matches the result. A CAM implementation of the tag array of a fully associative cache is more common, primarily because sequentially iterating through the array is very time consuming.

Figure 10.6 illustrates this concept. We enable each row of the CAM array by setting the corresponding word line to 1. Subsequently, the embedded comparators in the CAM cells compare the contents of each row with the tag, and generate an output. We use an OR gate to determine if any of the outputs is equal to 1. If any of the outputs is 1, then we have a cache hit, otherwise, we have a cache miss. Each of these output wires are also connected to an encoder that generates the index of the row that has a match. We use this index to access the data array and read the data for the block. In the case of a write, we write to the block, instead of reading it.

A fully associative cache is very useful for small structures (typically 2-32) entries. However, it is not possible to use CAM arrays for larger structures. The area and power overheads of comparison, and encoding are very high. It is also not possible to sequentially iterate through every entry of an SRAM implementation of the tag array. This is very time consuming. Hence, we need to find a better way for locating data in larger structures.

Direct Mapped(DM) Cache

We saw that in a fully associative cache, we can store any block at any location in the cache. This scheme is very flexible; however, it cannot be used when the cache has a large number of entries primarily because of prohibitive area and power overheads. Instead of allowing a block to be stored anywhere in the cache, let us assign only one fixed location for a given block. This can be done as follows.

In our running example, we have a 8 KB cache with 128 entries. Let us restrict the placement of 64 byte blocks in the cache. For each block, let us assign a unique location in the tag array at which the tag corresponding to its address can be stored. We can generate such a unique location as follows. Let us consider the address of a block A, and the number of entries in our cache (128), and compute $A\%128$. The $\%$ operator computes the remainder of the division of A by 128. Since A is a binary value, and 128 is a power of 2, computing the remainder is very easy. We need to just extract the 7 LSB bits out of the 26-bit block address. These 7 bits can then be used to access the tag array. We can then compare the value of the tag saved in the tag array with the tag computed from the block address to determine if we have a hit or a miss.

Instead of saving the block address in the tag array as we did for a fully associative cache, we can slightly optimise its design. We observe that 7 out of the 26 bits in the block address are used to access the tag in the tag array. This means that all the blocks that can possibly be mapped to a given entry in the tag array will have their last 7 bits common. Hence, these 7 bits need not explicitly be saved as a part of the tag. We need to only save the remaining 19 bits of the block address that can vary across blocks. Thus a tag in a direct mapped implementation of our cache needs to contain 19 bits only.

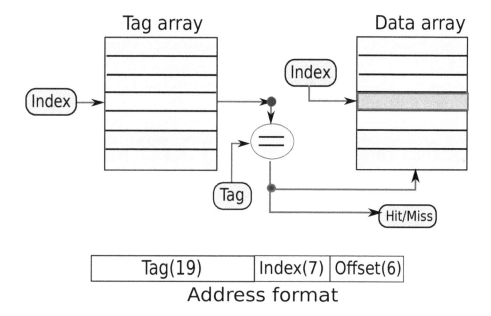

Figure 10.7: A direct mapped cache

Figure 10.7 describes this concept graphically. We divide a 32-bit address into three parts. The most significant 19 bits comprise the tag, the next 7 bits are referred to as the *index* (index in the tag array), and the remaining 6 bits point to the offset of the byte in the block. The rest of the access protocol is conceptually similar to that of a fully associative cache. In this case, we use the index to access the corresponding location in the tag array. We read the contents and compare it with the computed tag. If they are equal, then we declare a cache hit, otherwise, we declare a cache miss. Subsequently, in the case of a cache hit, we use the index to access the data array. In this case, we use the cache hit/miss result, to enable/disable the data array.

Way Point 10

Up till now we have taken a look at the fully associative and direct mapped caches.

- *The fully associative cache is a very flexible structure since a block can be saved in any entry in the cache. However, it has higher latency and power consumption. Since a given block can potentially be allocated in more entries of the cache, it has a higher hit rate than the direct mapped cache.*

- *The direct mapped cache on the other hand is a faster and less power consuming structure. Here, a block can reside in only one entry in the cache. Thus, the expected hit rate of this cache is less than that of a fully associative cache.*

We thus observe that there is a tradeoff between power, latency, and hit rate between the fully associative and direct mapped caches.

Set Associative Cache

A fully associative cache is more power consuming because we need to search for a block in all the entries of the cache. In comparison, a direct mapped cache is faster and power efficient because we need to check just one entry. However, it clearly has a lower hit rate, and that is not acceptable either. Hence, let us try to combine both the paradigms.

Let us design a cache in which a block can potentially reside in any one of a set of multiple entries in a cache. Let us associate a *set* of entries in the cache with a block address. Like a fully associative cache, we will have to check all the entries in the set before declaring a hit or a miss. This approach combines the advantages of both the fully associative and direct mapped schemes. If a set contains 4 or 8 entries, then we do not have to use an expensive CAM structure, nor, do we have to sequentially iterate through all the entries. We can simply read out all the entries of the set from the tag array in parallel and compare all of them with the tag part of the block address in parallel. If there is a match, then we can read the corresponding entry from the data array. Since multiple blocks can be associated with a set, we call this design a *set associative* cache. The number of blocks in a set is known as the associativity of the cache. Secondly, each entry in a set is known as a *way*.

Definition 103

Associativity *The number of blocks contained in a set is defined as the* associativity *of the cache.*

Way *Each entry in a set is known as also known as a* way.

Let us now describe a simple method to group cache entries into sets for our simple example, in which we considered a 32-bit memory system with an 8-KB cache and 64-byte blocks. As shown in Figure 10.8,

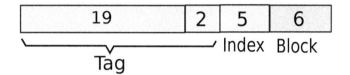

Figure 10.8: Division of a block address into sets

we first remove the lowest 6 bits from the 32-bit address because these specify the address of a byte within a block. The remaining 26 bits specify the block address. Our 8-KB cache has a total of 128 entries. If we want to create sets containing 4 entries each, then we need to divide all the cache entries into sets of 4 entries. There will be $32(2^5)$ such sets.

In a direct mapped cache, we devoted the lowest 7 bits out of the 26 bit block address to specify the index of the entry in the cache. We can now split these 7 bits into two parts as shown in Figure 10.8. One part contains 5 bits and indicates the address of the set, and the second part containing 2 bits is ignored. The group of 5 bits indicating the address of the set is known as the *set index*.

After computing the set index, i, we need to access all the elements belonging to the set in the tag array. We can arrange the tag array as follows. If the number of blocks in a set is S, then we can group all the entries belonging to a set contiguously. For the ith set, we need to access the elements iS, $(iS + 1)$ ... $(iS + S - 1)$ in the tag array.

For each entry in the tag array, we need to compare the tag saved in the entry to the *tag part* of the block address. If there is a match, then we can declare a hit. The notion of a tag in a set associative cache is rather tricky. As shown in Figure 10.8, it consists of the bits that are not a part of the index. In the case of our running example, it is the (21=26-5) MSB bits of the block address. The logic for deciding the number of tag bits is as follows.

Each set is specified by a 5-bit set index. These 5 bits are common to all the blocks that can be potentially mapped to the given set. We need to use the rest of the bits (26-5=21) to distinguish between the different blocks that are mapped to the same set. Thus, a tag in a set associative cache has a size between that of a direct mapped cache (19) and a fully associative cache (26).

Figure 10.9 shows the design of a set associative cache. We first compute the set index from the address of the block. For our running example, we use bits 7-11. Subsequently, we use the set index to generate the indices of its corresponding four entries in the tag array using the *tag array index generator*. Then, we access all the four entries in the tag array in parallel, and read their values. It is not necessary to use a CAM array here. We can use a single multi-port (multiple input, output) SRAM array. Next, we compare each element with the tag, and generate an output (0 or 1). If any of the outputs is equal to 1 (determined by an OR gate), then we have a cache hit. Otherwise, we have a cache miss. We use an encoder to find the index of the tag in the set that matched. Since, we are assuming a 4 way associative cache, the output of the encoder is between 00 to 11. Subsequently, we use a multiplexer to choose the index of the matching entry in the tag array. This index, can now be used to access the data array. The corresponding entry in the data array contains the data for the block. We can either read it or write to it.

We can perform a small optimisation here, for read operations. Note that in the case of a read operation, the access to the data array and tag array can proceed in parallel. If a set has 4 ways, then while we are computing a tag match, we can read the 4 data blocks corresponding to the 4 ways of the set. Subsequently, in the case of a cache hit, and after we have computed the matching entry in the tag array, we can choose the right data block using a multiplexer. In this case, we are effectively overlapping some or all of the time required to read the blocks from the data array with the tag computation, tag array access, and match

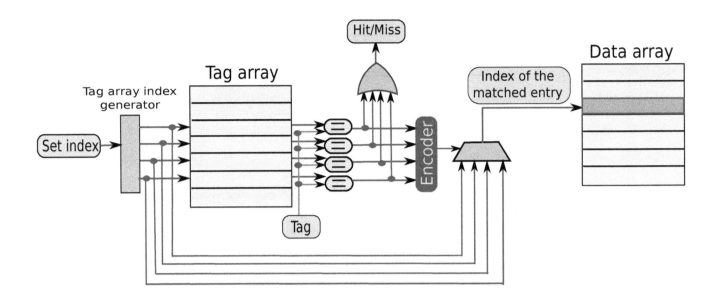

Figure 10.9: A set associative cache

operations. We leave the resulting circuit as an exercise to the reader.

To conclude, we note that the set associative cache is by far the most common design for caches. It has acceptable power consumption values and latencies for even very large caches. The associativity of a set associative cache is typically 2, 4 or 8. A set with an associativity of K is also known as a $K - way$ associative cache.

Important Point 16 *We need to answer a profound question while designing a set associative cache. What should be the relative ordering of the set index bits and the ignored bits? Should the ignored bits be towards the left (MSB) of the index bits, or towards the right (LSB) of the index bits? In Figure 10.8, we have chosen the former option. What is the logic behind this?*

Answer: *If we have the ignored bits to the left(MSB) of the index bits, then contiguous blocks map to different sets. However, for the reverse case in which the ignored bits are to the right(LSB) of the index bits, contiguous blocks map to the same set. Let us call the former scheme **NON-CONT**, and the latter scheme **CONT**. We have chosen NON-CONT in our design.*

Let us consider two arrays, A, and B. Let the sizes of A and B be significantly smaller than the size of the cache. Moreover, let some of their constituent blocks map to the same group of sets. The figure below shows a conceptual map of the regions of the cache that store both the arrays for the CONT and NON-CONT schemes. We observe that even though, we have sufficient space in the cache, it is not possible to save both the arrays in the cache concurrently using the CONT scheme. Their memory footprints overlap in a region of the cache, and it is not possible to save data for both the programs simultaneously in the cache. However, the NON-CONT scheme tries to uniformly distribute the blocks across all the sets. Thus, it is possible to save both the arrays in the cache at the same time.

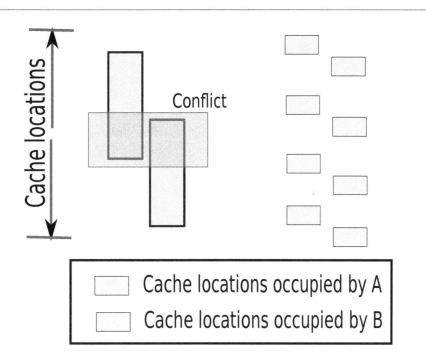

This is a frequently occurring pattern in programs. The CONT scheme reserves an entire area of the cache and thus it is not possible to accommodate other data structures that map to conflicting sets. However, if we distribute the data in the cache, then we can accommodate many more data structures and reduce conflicts.

Example 120

A cache has the following parameters in a 32-bit system.

Parameter	Value
Size	N
Associativity	K
Block Size	B

What is the size of the tag?

Answer:

- *The number of bits required to specify a byte within a block is $log(B)$.*

- *The number of blocks is equal to N/B, and the number of sets is equal to $N/(BK)$.*

- *Thus, the number of set index bits is equal to: $log(N) - log(B) - log(K)$.*

- *The remaining number of bits are tag bits. It is equal to: $32 - (log(N) - log(B) - log(K) + log(B))$ $= 32 - log(N) + log(K)$.*

10.2.3 *Data read* and *data write* Operations

The *data read* Operation

Once, we have established that a given block is present in a cache, we use the *basic* read operation to get the value of the memory location from the data array. We establish the presence of a block in a cache if the *lookup* operation returns a cache hit. If there is a miss in the cache, then the cache controller needs to raise a read request to the lower level cache, and fetch the block. The *data read* operation can start as soon as data is available.

The first step is to read out the block in the data array that corresponds to the matched tag entry. Then, we need to choose the appropriate set of bytes out of all the bytes in the block. We can use a set of multiplexers to achieve this. The exact details of the circuit are left to the reader as an exercise.

Secondly, as described in Section 10.2.2, it is not strictly necessary to start the *data read* operation after the *lookup* operation. We can have a significant overlap between the operations. For example, we can read the tag array and data array in parallel. We can subsequently select the right set of values using multiplexers after the matching tag has been computed.

The *data write* Operation

Before, we can write a value, **we need to ensure that the entire block is already present in the cache**. This is a very important concept. Note that we cannot make an argument that since we are creating new data, we do not need the previous value of the block. The reason is as follows. We typically write 4 bytes or at the most 8 bytes for a single memory access. However, a block is at least 32 or 64 bytes long. A *block* is an atomic unit in our cache. Hence, we cannot have different parts of it at different places. For example, we cannot save 4 bytes of a block in the L1 cache, and the rest of the bytes in the L2 cache. Secondly, for doing so, we need to maintain additional state that keeps track of the bytes that have been updated with writes. Hence, in the interest of simplicity, even if we wish to write just 1 byte, we need to populate the cache with the entire block.

After that we need to write the new values in the data array by enabling the appropriate set of word lines and bit lines. We can design a simple circuit to achieve this using a set of demultiplexers. The details are left to the reader.

There are two methods of performing a data write – write-back and write-through. Write-through is a relatively simpler scheme. In this approach, whenever we write a value into the data array, we also send a write operation to the lower level cache. This approach increases the amount of cache traffic. However, it is simpler to implement the cache because we do not have to keep track of the blocks that have been modified after they were brought into the cache. We can thus seamlessly evict a line from the cache if required. Here cache evictions and replacements are simple, at the cost of writes. We shall also see in Chapter 11 that it is easy to implement caches for mutiprocessors if the L1 caches follow a write-through protocol.

In the write-back scheme, we explicitly keep track of blocks that have been modified using write operations. We can maintain this information by using an additional bit in the tag array. This bit is typically known as the *modified* bit. Whenever, we get a block from the lower level of the memory hierarchy, the modified bit is 0. However, when we do a *data write* and update the data array, we set the modified bit in the tag array to 1. Evicting a line requires us to do extra processing that we shall describe in Section 10.2.6. For a write-back protocol, writes are cheap, and evict operations are more expensive. The tradeoff here is the reverse of that in write-through caches.

The structure of an entry in the tag array with the additional modified bit is shown in Figure 10.10.

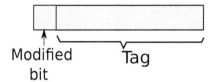

Figure 10.10: An entry in the tag array with the modified bit

10.2.4 The *insert* Operation

In this section, we shall discuss the protocol to insert a block in a cache. This operation is invoked when a block arrives from a lower level. We need to first take a look at all the ways of the set that a given block is mapped to, and see if there are any empty entries. If there are empty entries then we can choose one of the entries arbitrarily, and populate it with the contents of the given block. If we do not find any empty entries, we need to invoke the *replace* and *evict* operations to choose and remove an already existing block from the set.

We need to maintain some extra status information to figure out if a given entry is empty or non-empty. In computer architecture parlance, these states are also known as *invalid* and *valid* respectively. We need to store just 1 extra bit in the tag array to indicate the status of a block. It is known as the *valid* bit. We shall use the tag array for saving additional information regarding an entry, because it is smaller and typically faster than the data array.

The structure of an entry in the tag array with the addition of the valid bit is shown in Figure 10.11.

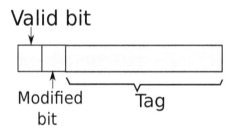

Figure 10.11: An entry in the tag array with the modified, and valid bits

The cache controller needs to check the valid bits of each of the tags while searching for invalid entries. Note that all the entries of a cache are invalid initially. If an invalid entry is found, then the corresponding entry in the data array can be populated with the contents of the block. The entry subsequently becomes valid. However, if there is no invalid entry, then we need to replace one entry with the given block that needs to be inserted into the cache.

10.2.5 The *replace* Operation

The task is here to find an entry in the set that can be replaced by a new entry. We do not wish to replace an element that is accessed very frequently. This will increase the number of cache misses. We ideally want to replace an element that has the least probability of being accessed in the future. However, it is difficult to predict future events. Hence, we need to make reasonable guesses based on past behavior. We can have different policies for the replacement of blocks in a cache. These are known as *replacement schemes* or *replacement policies*.

Definition 104

A cache replacement scheme *or* replacement policy *is a method to replace an entry in the set by a new entry.*

Random Replacement Policy

The most trivial replacement policy is known as the *random* replacement policy. Here, we pick a block at random and replace it. This scheme is very simple to implement. However, it is not very optimal in terms of performance, because it does not take into account the behaviour of the program and the nature of the memory access pattern. This scheme ends up often replacing very frequently accessed blocks.

FIFO Replacement Policy

The next scheme is slightly more complicated, and is known as the *FIFO (first in first out)* replacement policy. Here, the assumption is that the block that was brought into the cache at the earliest point of time, is the least likely to be accessed in the future. To implement the FIFO replacement policy, we need to add a counter to the tag array. Whenever, we bring in a block, we assign it a counter value equal to 0. We increment the counter values for the rest of the blocks. The larger is the counter, the earlier the block was brought into the cache.

Now to find a candidate for replacement, we need to find an entry with the largest value of the counter. This must be the earliest block. Unfortunately, the FIFO scheme does not strictly align with our principles of temporal locality. It penalises blocks that are present in the cache for a long time. However, they may also be very frequently accessed blocks, and should not be evicted in the first place.

Let us now consider the practical aspects of implementing a FIFO replacement policy. The maximum size of the counter needs to be equal to the number of elements in a set, i.e., the associativity of the cache. For example, if the associativity of a cache is 8, we need to have a 3 bit counter. The entry that needs to be replaced should have the largest counter value.

Note that in this case, the process of bringing in a new value into the cache is rather expensive. We need to increment the counters of all the elements in the set except one. However, cache misses, are more infrequent as compared to cache hits. Hence, the overhead is not significant in practice, and this scheme can be implemented without large performance overheads.

LRU Replacement Policy

The LRU (least recently used) replacement policy is known to be as one of the most efficient schemes. The LRU scheme follows directly from the definition of stack distance. We ideally want to replace a block that has the lowest chance of being accessed in the future. According to the notion of stack distance, the probability of being accessed in the future is related to the probability of accesses in the recent past. If a processor has been accessing a block frequently in the last window of n (n is not a very large number) accesses, then there is a high probability that the block will be accessed in the immediate future. However, if the last time that a block was accessed is long back in the past, then the chances are unlikely that it will be accessed soon.

In the LRU replacement policy, we maintain the time that a block was last accessed. We choose the block that was last accessed at the earliest point of time as a candidate for replacement. In a hypothetical implementation of a LRU replacement policy, we maintain a timestamp for every block. Any time that a block is accessed, its timestamp is updated to match the current time. For finding an appropriate candidate for replacement, we need to find the entry with the smallest timestamp in a set.

Let us now consider the implementation of an LRU scheme. The biggest issue is that we need to do additional work for every read and write access to the cache. There will be a significant performance impact because typically 1 in 3 instructions are memory accesses. Secondly, we need to dedicate bits to save a timestamp that is sufficiently large. Otherwise, we need to frequently reset the timestamps of every block in a set. This process will induce a further slowdown, and additional complexity in the cache controller. Implementing an LRU scheme that is as close to an ideal LRU implementation as possible, and that does not have significant overheads, is thus a difficult task.

Hence, let us try to design LRU schemes that use small timestamps (typically 1-3 bits), and approximately follow the LRU policy. Such kind of schemes are called pseudo-LRU schemes. Let us outline a simple method for implementing a basic pseudo-LRU scheme. Note that we can have many such approaches, and the reader is invited to try different approaches and test them on a cache simulator such as Dinero [Edler and Hill, 1999], or sim-cache [Austin et al., 2002]. Instead of trying to explicitly mark the least recently used element, let us try to mark the more recently used elements. The elements that are not marked will automatically get classified as the least recently used elements.

Let us start out by associating a counter with each block in the tag array. Whenever, a block is accessed (read/write), we increment the counter. However, once the counter reaches the maximum value, we stop incrementing it further. For example, if we use a 2-bit counter, then we stop incrementing the counter beyond 3. Now, we need to do something more. Otherwise, the counter associated with every block will ultimately reach 3 and stay there. To solve this problem, we can periodically decrement the counters of every block in a set by 1, or we can even reset them to 0. Subsequently, some of the counters will start increasing again. This procedure will ensure that for most of the time, we can identify the least recently used blocks by taking a look at the value of counters. The block associated with the lowest value of the counter is one of the least recently used blocks, and most likely "the most least recently used block". Note that this approach does involve some amount of activity per access. However, incrementing a small counter has little additional overhead. Secondly, it is not in the critical path in terms of timing. It can be done in parallel or sometime later also. Finding a candidate for replacement involves looking at all the counters in a set, and finding the block with the lowest value of the counter. After we replace the block with a new block, most processors typically set the counter of the new block to the largest possible value. This indicates to the cache controller, that the new block should have the least priority with respect to being a candidate for replacement.

10.2.6   The *evict* Operation

Lastly, let us take a look at the *evict* operation. If the cache follows a write-through policy, then nothing much needs to be done. The block can simply be discarded. However, if the cache follows a write-back policy, then we need to take a look at the modified bit. If the data is not modified, then it can be seamlessly evicted. However, if the data has been modified, then it needs to written back to the lower level cache.

10.2.7   Putting all the Pieces Together

Cache Read Operation

The sequence of steps in a cache read operation is shown in Figure 10.12. We start with a *lookup* operation. As mentioned in Section 10.2.2, we can have a partial overlap between the *lookup* and *data read* operations. If there is a cache hit, then the cache returns the value to the processor, or the higher level cache (whichever might be the case). However, if there is a cache miss, then we need to cancel the *data read* operation, and send a request to the lower level cache. The lower level cache will perform the same sequence of accesses,

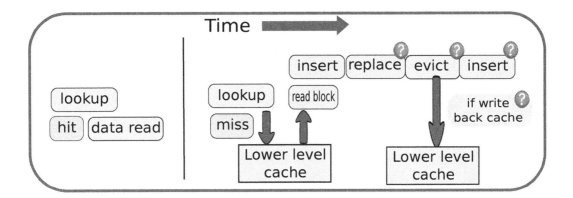

Figure 10.12: The *read* operation

and return the entire cache block (not just 4 bytes). The cache controller can then extract the requested data from the block, and send it to the processor. Simultaneously, the cache controller invokes the *insert* operation to insert the block into the cache. If there is an *invalid* entry in the set, then we can replace it with the given block. However, if all the ways in a set are valid, it is necessary to invoke the *replace* operation to find a candidate for replacement. The figure appends a question mark with this operation, because this operation is not invoked all the time (only when all the ways of a set contain valid data). Then, we need to *evict* the block, and possibly write it to the lower level cache if the line is modified, and we are using a write-back cache. The cache controller then invokes the *insert* operation. This time it is guaranteed to be successful.

Cache Write Operation (write-back Cache)

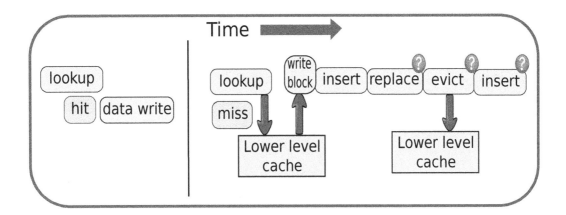

Figure 10.13: The *write* operation (write-back Cache)

Figure 10.13 shows the sequence of operations for a cache write operation for a write-back cache. The sequence of operations are roughly similar to that of a cache read. If there is a cache hit, then we invoke a *data write* operation, and set the modified bit to 1. Otherwise, we issue a read request for the block to the lower level cache. After the block arrives, most cache controllers typically store it in a small temporary buffer.

At this point, we write the 4 bytes (that we are interested in) to the buffer, and return. In some processors, the cache controller might wait till all the sub-operations complete. After writing into the temporary buffer (*write block* operation in Figure 10.13), we invoke the *insert* operation for writing the contents (modified) of the block. If this operation is not successful (because all the ways are valid), then we follow the same sequence of steps as the *read operation* (*replace*, *evict*, and *insert*).

Cache Write Operation (write-through Cache)

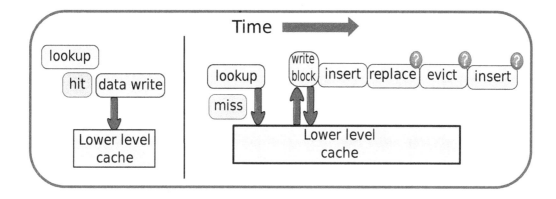

Figure 10.14:   The *write* operation (write-through Cache)

Figure 10.14 shows the sequence of operations for a write-through cache. The first point of difference is that we write the block to the lower level, even if the request hits in the cache. The second point of difference is that after we write the value into the temporary buffer (after a miss), we write back the new contents of the block to the lower level cache also. The rest of the steps are similar to the sequence of steps that we followed for the write-back cache.

10.3   The Memory System

We now have a fair understanding of the working of a cache, and all its constituent operations. A memory system is built using a hierarchy of caches as mentioned in Section 10.1.7. The memory system as a whole supports two basic operations: *read*, and *write*, or alternatively, *load* and *store*.

We have two caches at the highest level – The data cache (also referred to as the L1 cache), and the instruction cache (also referred to as the I Cache). Almost all the time both of them contain different sets of memory locations. The protocol for accessing the I Cache and L1 cache is the same. Hence, to avoid repetition let us just focus on the L1 cache from now on. The reader needs to just remember that accesses to the instruction cache follow the same sequence of steps.

The processor starts by accessing the L1 cache. If there is a L1 hit, then it typically receives the value within 1-2 cycles. Otherwise, the request needs to go to the L2 cache, or possibly even lower levels such as the main memory. In this case, the request can take tens or hundreds of cycles. In this section, we shall look at the system of caches in totality, and treat them as one single black box referred to as the *memory system*.

If we consider inclusive caches, which is the convention in most commercial systems, the total size of the memory system is equal to the size of the main memory. For example, if a system has 1 GB of main memory, then the size of the memory system is equal to 1 GB. It is possible that internally, the memory system might have a hierarchy of caches for improving performance. However, they do not add to the total storage

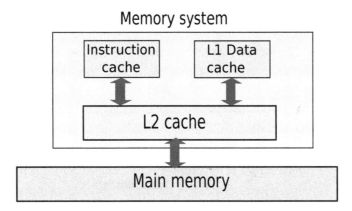

Figure 10.15: The memory system

capacity, because they only contain subsets of the data contained in main memory. Moreover, the memory access logic of the processor also views the entire memory system as a single unit, conceptually modelled as a large array of bytes. This is also known as the physical memory system, or the *physical address space*.

Definition 105
The physical address space comprises of the set of all memory locations contained in the caches, and main memory.

10.3.1 Mathematical Model of the Memory System

Performance

The memory system can be thought of as a black box that just services read and write requests. The time a request takes is variable. It depends on the level of the memory system at which the request hits. The pipeline is attached to the memory system in the memory access (MA) stage, and issues requests to it. If the reply does not come within a single cycle, then additional pipeline bubbles need to be introduced in our 5 stage *SimpleRisc* in-order pipeline.

Let the average memory access time be $AMAT$ (measured in cycles), and the fraction of load/store instructions be f_{mem}. Then the CPI can be expressed as:

$$CPI = CPI_{ideal} + stall\_rate * stall\_cycles$$
$$= CPI_{ideal} + f_{mem} \times (AMAT - 1) \tag{10.1}$$

CPI_{ideal} is the CPI assuming a perfect memory system having a 1 cycle latency for all accesses. Note that in our 5 stage in-order pipeline the ideal instruction throughput is 1 instruction per cycle, and the memory stage is allotted 1 cycle. In practice, if a memory access takes n cycles, then we have $n - 1$ stall cycles, and they need to be accounted for by Equation 10.1. In this equation, we implicitly assume that every memory access suffers a stall for $AMAT - 1$ cycles. In practice this is not the case since most of the instructions will hit in the L1 cache, and the L1 cache typically has a 1 cycle latency. Hence, accesses that hit in the L1 cache will not stall. However, long stall cycles will be introduced by accesses that miss in the L1 and L2 caches.

Nonetheless, Equation 10.1 still holds because we are only interested in the average CPI for a large number of instructions. We can derive this equation by considering a large number of instructions, summing up all the memory stall cycles, and computing the average number of cycles per instruction.

Average Memory Access Time

In Equation 10.1, CPI_{ideal} is determined by the nature of the program and the nature of the other stages (other than MA) of the pipeline. f_{mem} is also an inherent property of the program running on the processor. We need a formula to compute $AMAT$. We can compute it in a way similar to Equation 10.1.

Assuming, a memory system with an L1 and L2 cache, we have:

$$\begin{aligned} AMAT &= L1_{hit\,time} + L1_{miss\,rate} \times L1_{miss\,penalty} \\ &= L1_{hit\,time} + L1_{miss\,rate} \times (L2_{hit\,time} + L2_{miss\,rate} \times L2_{miss\,penalty}) \end{aligned} \tag{10.2}$$

All the memory accesses need to access the L1 cache irrespective of a hit or a miss. Hence, they need to incur a delay equal to $L1_{hit\,time}$. A fraction of accesses, $L1_{miss\,rate}$, will miss in the L1 cache, and move to the L2 cache. Here also, irrespective of a hit or a miss, we need to incur a delay of $L2_{hit\,time}$ cycles. If a fraction of accesses ($L2_{miss\,rate}$) miss in the L2 cache, then they need to proceed to main memory. We have assumed that all the accesses hit in the main memory. Hence, the $L2_{miss\,penalty}$ is equal to the main memory access time.

Now, if we assume that we have a n level memory system where the first level is the L1 cache, and the last level is the main memory, then we can use a similar equation.

$$\begin{aligned} AMAT &= L1_{hit\,time} + L1_{miss\,rate} \times L1_{miss\,penalty} \\ L1_{miss\,penalty} &= L2_{hit\,time} + L2_{miss\,rate} \times L2_{miss\,penalty} \\ L2_{miss\,penalty} &= L3_{hit\,time} + L3_{miss\,rate} \times L3_{miss\,penalty} \\ \ldots &= \ldots \\ L(n-1)_{miss\,penalty} &= Ln_{hit\,time} \end{aligned} \tag{10.3}$$

We need to note that the miss rate used in these equations for a certain level i is equal to the number of accesses that miss at that level divided by the total number of accesses to that level. This is known as the *local miss rate*. In comparison, we can define a *global miss rate* for level i, which is equal to the number of misses at level i divided by the total number of memory accesses.

Definition 106

local miss rate *It is equal to the number of misses in a cache at level i divided by the total number of accesses at level i.*

global miss rate *It is equal to the number of misses in a cache at level i divided by the total number of memory accesses.*

Let us take a deeper look at Equation 10.1. We observe that we can increase the performance of a system by either reducing the miss rate, the miss penalty or by decreasing the hit time. Let us first look at the miss rate.

10.3.2   Cache Misses

Classification of Cache Misses

Let us first try to categorise the different kinds of misses in a cache.

The first category of misses are known as *compulsory* misses or cold misses. These misses happen, when data is loaded into a cache for the first time. Since the data values are not there in the cache, a miss is bound to happen. The second category of cache misses are known as *capacity* misses. We have a capacity miss, when the amount of memory required by a program is more than the size of the cache. For example, let us assume that a program repeatedly accesses all the elements of an array. The size of the array is equal to 1 MB, and the size of the L2 cache is 512 KB. In this case, there will be capacity misses in the L2 cache, because it is too small to hold all the data. The set of blocks that a program accesses in a typical interval of time is known as its *working set*. We can thus alternatively say that conflict misses happen when the size of the cache is smaller than the working set of the program. Note that the definition of the working set is slightly imprecise because the length of the interval is considered rather subjectively. However, the connotation of the time interval is that it is a small interval compared to the total time of execution of the program. Nevertheless, it is large enough to ensure that the behaviour of the system achieves a steady state. The last category of misses are known as *conflict* misses. These misses occur in direct mapped and set associative caches. Let us consider a 4 way set associative cache. If there are 5 blocks that map to the same set in the working set of a program, then we are bound to have cache misses. This is because the number of blocks accessed is larger than the maximum number of entries that can be part of a set. These misses are known as conflict misses.

Definition 107

The memory locations accessed by a program in a short interval of time comprise the working set of the program at that point of time.

The categorisation of misses into these three categories – compulsory, capacity, and conflict – is also known as the three 'C's.

Reduction of the Miss Rate

To sustain a high IPC, it is necessary to reduce the cache miss rate. We need to adopt different strategies to reduce the different kinds of cache misses.

Let us start out with compulsory misses. We need a method to predict the blocks that will be accessed in the future, and fetch the blocks in advance. Typically schemes that leverage spatial locality serve as effective predictors. Hence, increasing the block size should prove beneficial in reducing the number of compulsory misses. However, increasing the block size beyond a certain limit can have negative consequences also. It reduces the number of blocks that can be saved in a cache, and secondly the additional benefit might be marginal. Lastly, it will take more time to read and transfer bigger blocks from the lower levels of the memory system. Hence, designers avoid very large block sizes. Any value between 32-128 bytes is reasonable.

Modern processors typically have sophisticated predictors that try to predict the addresses of blocks that might be accessed in the future based on the current access pattern. They subsequently fetch the predicted blocks from the lower levels of the memory hierarchy in an attempt to reduce the miss rate. For example, if we are sequentially accessing the elements of a large array, then it is possible to predict the future accesses based on the access pattern. Sometimes we access elements in an array, where the indices differ by a fixed value. For example, we might have an algorithm that accesses every fourth element in an array. In this case also, it is possible to analyse the pattern and predict future accesses because the addresses of consecutive accesses differ by the same value. Such kind of a unit is known as a *hardware prefetcher*. It is present in most modern processors, and uses sophisticated algorithms to "prefetch" blocks and consequently reduce the miss rate. Note that the hardware prefetcher should not be very aggressive. Otherwise, it will tend to displace more useful data from the cache than it brings in.

Definition 108
A hardware prefetcher is a dedicated hardware unit that predicts the memory accesses in the near future, and fetches them from the lower levels of the memory system.

Let us now consider capacity misses. The only effective solution is to increase the size of the cache. Unfortunately, the cache design that we have presented in this book requires the size of the cache to be equal to a power of two (in bytes). It is possible to violate this rule by using some advanced techniques. However, by and large most of the caches in commercial processors have a size that is a power of two. Hence, increasing the size of a cache is tantamount to at least doubling its size. Doubling the size of a cache requires twice the area, slows it down, and increases the power consumption. Here again, prefetching can help if used intelligently and judiciously.

The classical solution to reduce the number of conflict misses is to increase the associativity of a cache. However, increasing the associativity of a cache increases the latency and power consumption of the cache also. Consequently, it is necessary for designers to carefully balance the additional hit rate of a set associative cache, with the additional latency. Sometimes, it is the case that there are conflict misses in a few sets in the cache. In this case, we can have a small fully associative cache known as the *victim cache* along with the main cache. Any block that is displaced from the main cache, can be written to the victim cache. The cache controller needs to first check the main cache, and if there is a miss, then it needs to check the victim cache, before proceeding to the lower level. A victim cache at level i can thus filter out some of the requests that go to level $(i + 1)$.

Note that along with hardware techniques, it is possible to write programs in a "cache friendly" way. These methods can maximise temporal and spatial locality. It is also possible for the compiler to optimise the code for a given memory system. Secondly, the compiler can insert prefetching code such that blocks can be prefetched into the cache before they are actually used. Discussion of such techniques are beyond the scope of this book.

Let us now quickly mention two rules of thumb. Note that these rules are found to approximately hold empirically, and are by no means fully theoretically justified. The first is known as the *Square Root Rule* [Hartstein et al., 2006]. It says that the miss rate is proportional to the square root of the cache size.

$$miss\,rate \propto \frac{1}{\sqrt{cache\,size}} \qquad \text{[Square Root Rule]} \qquad (10.4)$$

Hartstein et. al. [Hartstein et al., 2006] try to find a theoretical justification for this rule, and explain the basis of this rule by using results from probability theory. From their experimental results, they arrive at a generic version of this rule that says that the exponent of the cache size in the Square Root Rule varies from -0.3 to -0.7.

The other rule is known as the "Associativity Rule". It states that the effect of doubling associativity is almost the same as doubling the cache size with the original associativity. For example, the miss rate of a 64 KB 4-way associative cache is almost the same as that of a 128 KB 2-way associative cache.

We would further like to caution the reader that the Associativity Rule and the Square Root Rule are just thumb rules, and do not hold exactly. They can be used as mere conceptual aids. We can always construct examples that violate these rules.

10.3.3 Reduction of Hit Time and Miss Penalty

Hit Time

The average memory access time can also be reduced by reducing the hit time and the miss penalty. To reduce the hit time, we need to use small and simple caches. However, by doing so, we increase the miss rate also.

Miss Penalty

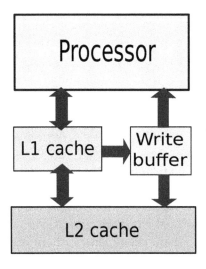

Figure 10.16: Write buffer

Let us now discuss ways to reduce the miss penalty. Note that the miss penalty at level i, is equal to the memory latency of the memory system starting at level $(i + 1)$. The traditional methods for reducing hit time, and miss rate can always be used to reduce the miss penalty at a given level. However, we are looking at methods that are exclusively targeted towards reducing the miss penalty. Let us first look at write misses in the L1 cache. In this case the entire block has to be brought into the cache from the L2 cache. This takes time (> 10 cycles), and secondly unless the write has completed, the pipeline cannot resume. Hence, processor designers use a small set associative cache known as a *write buffer* as shown in Figure 10.16. The processor can write the value to the write buffer, and then resume, or alternatively, it can write to the write buffer only if there is a miss in the L1 cache (as we have assumed). Any subsequent read needs to check the write buffer along with accessing the L1 cache. This structure is typically very small and fast (4-8 entries). Once, the data arrives in the L1 cache, the corresponding entry can be removed from the write buffer. Note that if a free entry is not available in the write buffer, then the pipeline needs to stall. Secondly, before the write miss has been serviced from the lower levels of the cache, it is possible that there might be another write to the same address. This can be seamlessly handled by writing to the allocated entry for the given address in the write buffer.

Let us now take a look at read misses. Let us start out by observing that the processor is typically interested in only up to 4 bytes per memory access. The pipeline can resume if it is provided those crucial 4 bytes. However, the memory system needs to fill the entire block before the operation can complete. The size of a block is typically between 32-128 bytes. It is thus possible to introduce an optimisation here, if the memory system is aware of the exact set of bytes that the processor requires. In this case, the memory system can first fetch the memory word (4 bytes) that is required. Subsequently, or in parallel it can fetch the rest of the block. This optimisation is known as *critical word first*. Then, this data can be quickly sent to the pipeline such that it can resume its operation. This optimisation is known as *early restart*. Implementing both of these optimisations increases the complexity of the memory system. However, *critical word first* and *early restart* are fairly effective in reducing the miss penalty.

10.3.4   Summary of Memory System Optimisation Techniques

Technique	Application	Disadvantages
large block size	compulsory misses	reduces the number of blocks in the cache
prefetching	compulsory misses, capacity misses	extra complexity and the risk of displacing useful data from the cache
large cache size	capacity misses	high latency, high power, more area
increased associativity	conflict misses	high latency, high power
victim cache	conflict misses	extra complexity
compiler based techniques	all types of misses	not very generic
small and simple cache	hit time	high miss rate
write buffer	miss penalty	extra complexity
critical word first	miss penalty	extra complexity and state
early restart	miss penalty	extra complexity

Table 10.2: Summary of different memory system optimisation techniques

Table 10.2 shows a summary of the different techniques that we have introduced to optimise the memory system. Note that every technique has some negative side effects. If a technique improves the memory system in one aspect, then it is detrimental in some other aspect. For example, by increasing the cache size we reduce the number of capacity misses. However, we also increase the area, latency, and power.

To summarise, we can conclude that it is necessary to design the memory system very carefully. The requirements of the target workload have to be carefully balanced with the constraints placed by the designers, and the limits of manufacturing technology. We need to maximise performance, and at the same time be mindful of power, area, and complexity constraints.

10.4 Virtual Memory

Up till now, we have considered only one program in our system. We have designed our entire system using this assumption. However, this assumption is not correct. For example, at the moment there are 232 programs running on your author's workstation. The reader can easily find out the number of programs running on her system by opening the Task Manger on Windows, or by entering the command "ps -ef" on a Linux or a Macintosh system. It is possible for one processor to run multiple programs by switching between different programs very quickly. For example, while a user is playing a game, her processor might be fetching her new email. The reason she does not feel any interruption, is because the time scale at which the processor switches back and forth between programs (typically several milliseconds) is much smaller than what humans can perceive.

Secondly, we have assumed up till now that all the data that a program needs is resident in main memory. However, this assumption is also not correct. Back in the old days, the size of main memory used to be several megabytes, whereas, users could run very large programs that needed hundreds of megabytes of data. Even now, it is possible to work with data that is much larger than the amount of main memory. Readers can easily verify this statement, by writing a C program that creates data structures that are larger than the amount of physical memory contained in their machine. In most systems, this C program will compile and run successfully.

We shall see in this section that by making a small change in the memory system, we can satisfy both of these requirements.

10.4.1 Process – A Running Instance of a Program

Up till now, we have assumed the existence of only one program in the system. We assumed that it was in complete control of the memory system, and the processor pipeline. However, this is not the case in practice.

Let us first start out by accurately defining the notion of a *process* and differentiating it from a *program*. Up till now we have been loosely using the term – *program* – and sometimes using it in place of a *process*. A program is an array of bytes and is saved as a file in the file system. The file is typically known as a *binary* or as an *executable*. The executable contains some meta data about the program such that its name and type, the constants used by the program, and the set of instructions. In comparison, a process is a running instance of a program. If we run one program several times, we create multiple processes. A process has access to the processor, peripheral devices, and the memory system. There is a dedicated area in the memory system that contains the data and code of the process. The program counter of the processor points to a given location in the code region of the process in memory when the process is executing. Memory values required by the process are obtained from its data region in the memory system. The *operating system* starts and ends a process, and manages it throughout its lifetime.

Definition 109

A process is a running instance of a program.

Operating System

Most of our readers must have heard of the term *operating system*. Most people mostly view an operating system such as Windows, Linux, or Mac OS X from the point of view of its user interface. However, this is a minor aspect of the operating system. It does many more things invisibly. Let us look at some of its important functionalities.

The operating system consists of a set of dedicated programs that manage the machine, peripheral devices, and all the processes running on the machine. Furthermore, the operating system facilitates efficient transfer of information between the hardware and software components of a computer system. The core component of an operating system is known as the *kernel*. Its main role is to manage the execution of processes, and manage memory. We shall look at the memory management aspect in Section 10.4.5. Let us now look at the process management aspect.

To run a program, a user needs to compile the program, and then either double click the program, or write the name of the program in the command line, and click the "enter" button. Once, this is done, the control passes to the operating system kernel. A component of the kernel known as the *loader* reads the content of the program, and copies it to a region in the memory system. Notably, it copies all the instructions in the *text* section, allocates space for all the data, and initialises memory with all the constants that a program will require during its execution. Subsequently, it initialises the values of registers, copies command line arguments to the stack, possibly initialises the stack pointer, and jumps to the entry point of the program. The user program can then begin to execute, in the context of a running process. Every process has a unique number associated with it. It is known as the *pid* (process id). After completion, it is the kernel's job to tear down the process, and reclaim all of its memory.

The other important aspect of process management is *scheduling*. A dedicated component of the *kernel* manages all the processes, including the kernel itself, which is a special process. It typically runs each process for a certain amount of time, and then switches to another process. As a user, we typically do not perceive this because every second, the kernel switches between processes hundreds of times. The time interval is too small for us to detect. However, behind the scenes, the kernel is busy at work. For example, it might be running a game for sometime, running a program to fetch data from the network for some time, and then running some of its own tasks for sometime. The kernel also manages aspects of the file system, inter-process communication, and security. The discussion of such topics is beyond the scope of this book. The reader is referred to textbooks on operating systems such as the book by Tanenbaum [Tanenbaum, 2007] or Silbserchatz and Galvin [Silberschatz et al., 2008].

The other important components in an operating system are device drivers, and system utilities. *Device drivers* are dedicated programs that communicate with dedicated devices and ensure the seamless flow of information between them and user processes. For example, a printer and scanner have dedicated device drivers that make it possible to print and scan documents, respectively. Network interfaces have dedicated device drivers that allow us to exchange messages over the internet. Lastly, system utilities provide generic services to all the processes such as file management, device management (Control Panel in Windows), and security.

Definition 110

Operating System *The operating system consists of a set of dedicated programs that manage the machine, peripheral devices, and the processes running on it. It facilitates the transfer of information between the hardware and software components of a computer system.*

Kernel *The kernel is a program that is the core of the operating system. It has complete control over the rest of the processes in the operating system, the user processes, the processor, and all external devices. It mainly performs the task of managing multiple processes, devices, and filesystems.*

Process Management *The two important components in the kernel to perform process management are the* loader, *and the* scheduler. *The loader creates a process out of a program by transferring*

> *its contents to memory, and setting up the appropriate execution environment. The scheduler schedules the execution of multiple processes including that of the kernel itself.*
>
> **Device Drivers** *These dedicated programs help the kernel and user processes communicate with devices.*
>
> **System Utilities** *These are generic services provided by the operating system such as the print queue manager and file manager. They can be used by all the processes in the system.*

Virtual 'View' of Memory

Since multiple processes are live at the same point of time. It is necessary to partition the memory between processes. If this is not done, then it is possible that processes might end up modifying each others' values. At the same time, we do not want the programmer or the compiler to be aware of the existence of multiple processes. This introduces unwanted complexity. Secondly, if a given program is compiled with a certain memory map, it might not run on another machine that has a process with an overlapping memory map. Even worse, it will not be possible to run two copies of the same program. Hence, it is essential that each program sees a virtual view of memory, in which it assumes that it owns the entire memory system.

As we can observe, there are two conflicting requirements. The memory system, and the operating system want different processes to access different memory addresses, whereas, the programmer and the compiler do not want to be aware of this requirement. Additionally, the programmer wishes to layout her memory map according to her wish. It turns out that there is a method to make both the programmer and the operating system happy.

We need to define a *virtual* and a *physical* view of of memory. In the physical view of memory, different processes operate in non-overlapping regions of the memory space. However, in the virtual view, every process accesses any address that it wishes to access, and the virtual views of different processes can overlap. The solution is obtained through a method called *paging* that we shall explain in Section 10.4.3. However, before proceeding to the solution, let us discuss the virtual view of memory that a process typically sees. The virtual view of memory, is also referred to as *virtual memory*. It is defined as a hypothetical memory system, in which a process assumes that it owns the entire memory space, and there is no interference from any other process.

> **Definition 111**
> *The virtual memory system is defined as a hypothetical memory system, in which a process assumes that it owns the entire memory space, and there is no interference from any other process. The size of the memory is as large as the total addressable memory of the system. For example, in a 32-bit system, the size of virtual memory is 2^{32} bytes (4 GB). The set of all memory locations in virtual memory is known as the virtual address space.*

In the virtual memory space, the operating system lays out the code and data in different regions. This arrangement of code, data, constants, and other information pertaining to a process is known as the *memory map*.

> **Definition 112**
> *The memory map of a process refers to the way an operating system lays out the code and data in memory.*

Memory Map of a Process

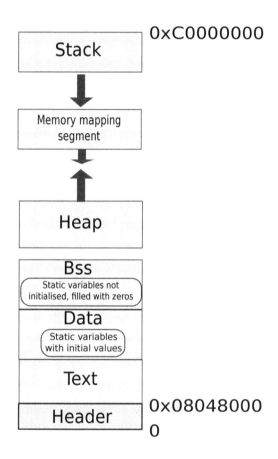

Figure 10.17: Memory map of a process in the Linux operating system (32 bits)

Figure 10.17 shows a simplified view of the memory map of a process in the 32-bit Linux operating system. Let us start from the bottom (lowest address). The first section contains the header. It starts out with details about the process, its format, and the target machine. Subsequently, the header contains the details of each section in the memory map. For example, it contains the details of the text section that contains the code of the program including its size, starting address, and additional attributes. The text section starts after the header. The operating system sets the program counter to the start of the text section while loading a program. All the instructions in a program are typically contained within the text section. The text section is followed by two more sections that are meant to contain static and global variables. Optionally some operating systems, also have an additional area to contain read only data such as constants.

The text section is typically followed by the *data* section. It contains all the static/global variables that have been initialised by the programmer. Let us consider a declaration of the form (in C or C++):

```
static int val = 5;
```

Here the 4 bytes corresponding to the variable – *val* – are saved in the data section. The data section is followed by the *bss* section. The *bss* section saves static and global variables that have not been explicitly initialised by the programmer. Most operating systems, fill the memory area corresponding to the *bss* section with zeros. This needs to be done in the interest of security. Let us assume that program A runs and writes its values in the *bss* section. Subsequently, program B runs. Before, writing to a variable in the *bss* section, B can always try to read its value. In this case, it will get the value written by program A. However, this is not desirable behavior. Program A might have saved some sensitive data in the bss section such as a password or a credit card number. Program B can thus gain access to this sensitive data without program A's knowledge, and possibly misuse the data. Hence, it is necessary to fill up the *bss* section with zeros such that such kind of security lapses do not happen.

The *bss* section is followed by a memory area known as the *heap*. The *heap* area is used to save dynamically allocated variables in a program. C programs typically allocate new data with the *malloc* call. Java and C++ use the *new* operator. Let us look at some examples.

```
int *intarray = (int *)malloc(10 * sizeof(int));        [C]
int *intarray = new int[10];                            [C++]
int[] intarray = new int[10];                           [Java]
```

Note that in these languages, dynamically allocating arrays is very useful because their sizes are not known at compile time. The other advantage of having data in the heap is that they survive across function calls. The data in the stack remains valid for only the duration of the function call. After that it gets deleted. However, data in the heap stays for the entire life of the program. It can be used by all the functions in the program, and pointers to different data structures in the heap can be shared across functions. Note that the heap grows upward (towards higher addresses). Secondly, managing the memory in a heap is a fairly difficult task. This is because dynamically, regions of the heap are allocated with malloc/new calls and freed with the free/delete calls in high level languages. Once an allocated memory region is freed, a hole gets created in the memory map. It is possible to allocate some other data structure in the hole if its size is less than the size of the hole. In this case, another smaller hole gets created in the memory map. Over time as more and more data structures are allocated and de-allocated, the number of holes tend to increase. This is known as *fragmentation*. Hence, it is necessary to have an efficient memory manager that can reduce the number of holes in the heap. A view of the heap with holes, and allocated memory is shown in Figure 10.18.

The next segment is reserved for storing data corresponding to memory mapped files, and dynamically linked libraries. Most of the time, operating systems transfer the contents of a file (such as a music, text, or video file) to a memory region, and treat the contents of the file as a regular array. This memory region is referred to as a *memory mapped file*. Secondly, programs might occasionally read the contents of other programs (referred to as libraries) dynamically, and transfer the contents of their text sections to their memory map. Such libraries are known as *dynamically linked libraries*, or *dll*s. The contents of such memory mapped structures are stored in a dedicated section in the process's memory map.

The next section is the *stack*, which starts from the top of the memory map and grows downwards (towards smaller addresses) as discussed in Section 3.3.10. The stack continuously grows and shrinks depending on the behavior of the program. Note that Figure 10.17 is not drawn to scale. If we consider a 32-bit memory system, then the total amount of virtual memory is 4 GB. However, the total amount of memory that a program might use is typically limited to hundreds of megabytes. Hence, there is a massive empty region in the map between the start of the *heap* and *stack* sections.

Note that the operating system needs to run very frequently. It needs to service device requests, and perform process management. As we shall see in Section 10.4.3 changing the virtual view of memory from

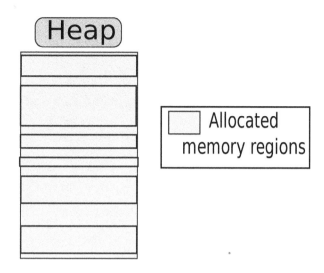

Figure 10.18: The memory map of a heap

process to process is slightly expensive. Hence, most operating systems partition the virtual memory between a user process and the kernel. For example, Linux gives the lower 3GB to a user process, and keeps the upper 1 GB for the kernel. Similarly, Windows keeps the upper 2GB for the kernel, and the lower 2 GB for user processes. Hence, it is not necessary to change the view of memory as the processor transitions from the user process to the kernel. Secondly, this small modification does not greatly impair the performance of a program because 2GB or 3GB is much more than the typical memory footprint of a program. Moreover, this trick does not also conflict with our notion of virtual memory. A program just needs to assume that it has a reduced memory space (reduced from 4GB to 3GB in the case of Linux). Refer to Figure 10.19.

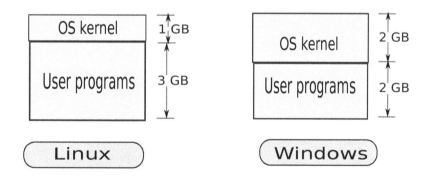

Figure 10.19: The memory map – user and kernel

10.4.2 The "Overlap" and "Size" Problems

Let us summarise all our discussion up till now. We basically want to solve two problems.

Overlap Problem Programmers and compilers write a program assuming that they own the entire memory space and they can write to any location at will. Unfortunately, the same assumption is made by all processes that are simultaneously active. Unless steps are taken, they may end up inadvertently writing to each other's memory space and corrupting each other's data. In fact, given that they use the same memory map, the chances of this happening in a naive system are extremely high. The hardware somehow needs to ensure that different processes are isolated from each other. This is the *overlap problem*.

Size Problem Occasionally we need to run processes that require more memory than the available physical memory. It is desirable if some space in other storage media such as the hard disk can be repurposed for storing the memory footprint of a process. This is known as the *size problem*.

Any implementation of virtual memory needs to effectively solve the size and overlap problems.

10.4.3 Implementation of Virtual Memory with Paging

To balance the requirements of the processor, operating system, compiler, and programmer we need to design a translation system that can translate the address generated by a process into an address that the memory system can use. By using a translator, we can satisfy the requirements of the programmer/compiler, who need virtual memory, and the processor/memory system, who need physical memory. A translation system is similar to what a translator in real life would do. For example, if we have a Russian delegation visiting Dubai, then we need a translator who can translate Russian to Arabic. Both the sides can then speak their own language, and thus be happy. A conceptual diagram of the translation system is shown in Figure 10.20.

Figure 10.20: Address translation system

Let us now try to design this address translation system. Let us first succinctly list the requirements that a program and compiler place on the nature of virtual memory.

1. Any address in the range of valid addresses should be accessible. For example, in a Linux based machine, a process's virtual memory size is limited to 3 GB. Hence, it should be possible to access any address in this range.

2. The virtual memory should be perceived as one contiguous memory space where the entire space is available to the program.

3. Unless explicitly desired by the program, there should be no interference from any other program.

Here are the requirements from the side of the memory system.

1. Different programs should access non-overlapping sets of addresses.

2. A program cannot be allotted a large continuous chunk of memory addresses. This will cause a high degree of wastage in space due to fragmentation.

3. If the total amount of physical memory is less than the size of the virtual memory, then there should be additional storage space available to support programs that require more space than the total amount of physical memory.

Let us now try to satisfy these requirements by designing a translation system that takes an address as specified in the program, and translates it to a real address that can be presented to the memory system. The address specified in the program is known as the *virtual address*, and the address sent to the memory system is known as the *physical* address.

Definition 113

Virtual Address *An address specified by the program in the virtual address space.*

Physical Address *An address presented to the memory system after address translation.*

We can trivially achieve a translation system by uniquely mapping every virtual address to a physical address at the level of every byte or memory word (4 bytes). In this case, the program perceives one contiguous memory space. Secondly, we need to only map those virtual addresses that are actually used by the program. If a program actually requires 3 MB of space, then we end up using only 3 MB of physical memory. Whenever, the process requires a new set of bytes that have not been already mapped, a smart memory management unit can allocate new space in physical memory. Lastly, note that it is necessary for every memory access to pass through this translation system.

Even though our basic translation system satisfies all our requirements, it is not efficient. We need to maintain a large table that maps every byte in the virtual address space to a byte in the physical address space. This mapping table between the virtual and physical addresses will be very large and slow. It is also not a very power efficient scheme. Secondly, our scheme does not take advantage of spatial and temporal locality. Hence, let us try to make our basic system more efficient.

Pages and Frames

Definition 114

Page *It is a block of memory in the virtual address space.*

Frame *It is a block of memory in the physical address space. A page and frame have the same size.*

Page Table *It is a mapping table that maps the address of each page to an address of a frame. Each process has its own page table.*

Instead of translating addresses at the granularity of bytes, let us translate addresses at the granularity of larger blocks. This will reduce the amount of state that we need to maintain, and also take advantage of spatial locality. Let us define a block of memory in the virtual address space and call it a *page*. Similarly, let us define a block of the same size in the physical address space and call it a *frame*. The size of a page or a frame is typically 4 KB. Secondly, note that the virtual address space is unique to each process; whereas, the physical address space is the same for all processes. For each process, we need to maintain a mapping table that maps each page to a frame. This is known as the *page table*. A page table can either be implemented in hardware or in software. A hardware implementation of the page table has dedicated structures to store the mapping between virtual and physical addresses. The lookup logic is also in hardware. In the case of a software implementation, the mappings are stored in a dedicated region of the physical address space. In most processors that use software page tables, the lookup logic is also in hardware. They typically do not use custom routines in software to lookup page tables because this approach is slow and complicated. Since the lookup logic of page tables is primarily in hardware, the design of page tables needs to be relatively simple. The page tables that we describe in the next few sections are oblivious to how they are implemented (software or hardware).

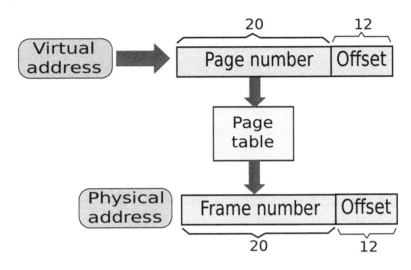

Figure 10.21: Translation of a virtual to a physical address

Let us consider a 32-bit memory address. We can now split it into two parts. If we consider a 4 KB page, then the lower 12 bits specify the address of a byte in a page (reason: $2^{12} = 4096 = 4KB$). This is known as the *offset*. The upper 20 bits specify the *page number* (see Figure 10.21). Likewise, we can split a physical address into two parts – frame number and offset. The process of translation as shown in Figure 10.21, first replaces the 20 bit page number with an equivalent 20 bit frame number. Then it appends the 12 bit offset to the physical frame number.

A Single Level Page Table

Figure 10.22 shows a basic page table that contains 2^{20} ($\approx 1,000,000$) rows. Each row is indexed by the page number, and it contains the corresponding 20 bit (2.5 byte) frame number. The total size of the table is thus 2.5 MB. If we have 200 processes in the system at any point of time, then we need to waste 500 MB of precious memory for just saving page tables! If our total main memory is 2 GB, then we are spending 25% of it in saving page tables, which appears to be a big waste of space. Secondly, it is possible that in some systems, we might not even have 500 MB of main memory available. In this case, we cannot support 200 live processes at the same time. We need to look for better solutions.

Let us now look for insights that might help us reduce the amount of storage. We start out by noticing that large parts of the virtual address space of a process are actually empty. In a 32-bit system, the size of the virtual address space is 4 GB. However, large programs do not use more than 100 MB. There is a massive empty region between the stack and the heap sections in the memory map, and thus it is not necessary to allocate space for mapping this region. Ideally, the number of entries in the page table should be equal to the number of pages actually used by a process rather than the theoretically maximum number of pages a process can use. If a process uses only 400 KB of memory space, then ideally its page table should just

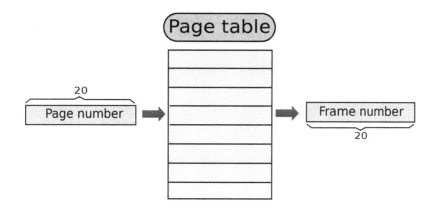

Figure 10.22: A single level page table

contain 100 entries. Let us design a two level page table to realise this goal.

Two Level Page Table

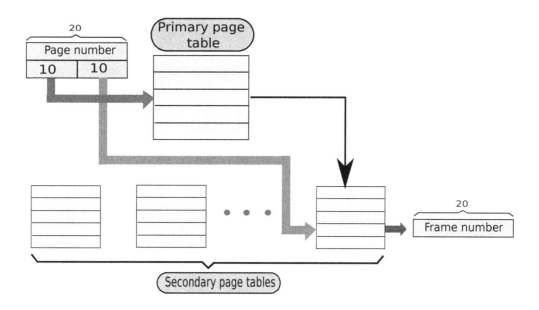

Figure 10.23: A two level page table

Let us further split a page number into two equal parts. Let us split the 20 bits into two parts containing 10 bits each as shown in Figure 10.23. Let us use the upper 10 bits to access a top level page table known as the *primary page table*. Each entry in the top level page table points to a secondary page table. Subsequently, each secondary page table is indexed by the lower 10 bits of the page number. An entry in the secondary page table contains the frame number. If no addresses map to a given entry in the primary page table, then it does not point to a secondary page table, and thus there is no need to allocate space for it. In a typical program, most of the entries in the primary page table are expected to be empty. Let us now calculate the size of this structure.

The primary page table contains 1024 entries, where each entry is 10 bits long. The total size is 1.25 KB (10 bits = 1.25 bytes). Let the number of secondary page tables be N. Each secondary page tables contains 1024 entries, where each entry is 20 bits long. Therefore, the size of each secondary page table is 2.5 KB, and the total storage requirement is $(1.25 + 2.5 \times N)$ KB. Because of spatial locality in a program, N is not expected to be a large number. Let us consider a program that has a memory footprint of 10 MB. It contains roughly 2500 pages. Each secondary page table can map at the most 1024 pages (4 MB of data). It is highly likely that this program might map to only 3 secondary page tables. Two page tables will contain the mappings for the *text*, *data*, and *heap* sections, and one page table will contain the mappings for the *stack* section. In this case, the total storage requirement for the page tables will be equal to 8.75 KB, which is very reasonable. Even, if we require double the number of secondary page tables because of lower spatial locality in the memory map, then also the total storage requirement is equal to 16.25 KB. This is an order of magnitude better than a single level page table that required 2.5 MB of storage per process. Hence, two level page tables are used in most commercial systems.

Inverted Page Table

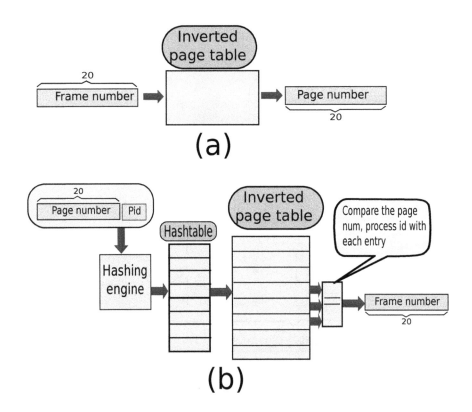

Figure 10.24: Inverted page table

Some processors such as the Intel Itanium, and PowerPC 603, use a different design for a page table. Instead of addressing the page table using the page number, they address it using the frame number. In this case, there is one page table for the entire system. Since one frame is typically uniquely mapped to a page in a process, each entry in this *inverted page table* contains the process id, and page number. Figure 10.24(a) shows the structure of an inverted page table. The main advantage of an inverted page table is that we do not need to keep a separate page table for each process. We can save space if there are a lot of processes, and the size of physical memory is small.

The main difficulty in inverted page tables is in performing a lookup for a virtual address. Scanning all the entries is a very slow process, and is thus not practical. Hence, we need to have a hashing function that maps the (process id, page number) pair to an index in a hash table. This index in the hash table needs to point to an entry in the inverted page table. Since multiple virtual addresses can point to the same entry in the hash table, it is necessary to verify that the (process id, page number) matches that stored in the entry in the inverted page table. Readers can refer to [Cormen et al., 2009] for a detailed explanation of the theory and operation of hash tables.

We show one scheme for using an inverted page table in Figure 10.24(b). After computing a hash of the page number, and process id pair, we access a hashtable indexed by the contents of the hash. The contents of the hashtable entry point to a frame, f, that might possibly map to the given page. However, we need to verify, since it is possible that the hash function maps multiple pages to the same frame. Subsequently, we access the inverted page table, and access the entry, f. An entry of the inverted page table, contains the page number, process id pair that is mapped to the given entry (or given frame). If we find that the contents do not match, then we keep searching for the page number, process id pair in the subsequent K entries. This method is called linear probing (see [Cormen et al., 2009]), where we keep searching in the target data structure till we get a match. If we do not get a match within K entries, then we may conclude that the page is not mapped. We need to then create a mapping, by evicting an entry (similar to caches), and writing it to a dedicated region in main memory that buffers all the entries that are evicted from the inverted page table. We need to always guarantee that the entry pointed to by the hash table, and the actual entry that contains the mapping, do not differ by more than K entries. If we do not find any free slots, then we need to evict an entry.

An astute reader might argue that we can directly use the output of the hashing engine to access the inverted page table. Typically, we add accessing a hashtable as an intermediate step, because it allows us to have better control over the set of frames that are actually used. Using this process, it is possible to disallow mappings for certain frames. These frames can be used for other purposes. Lastly, we need to note that the overhead of maintaining, and updating hash tables outweighs the gains in having a system wide page table. Hence, an inverted page table is typically not used in commercial systems.

Translation Lookaside Buffer (TLB)

For every single memory access it is necessary to lookup the page table for translating the virtual address. The page table itself is stored in physical memory. Hence, we need to do a separate memory access to read the corresponding entry of the page table. This approach doubles the number of memory accesses, and is thus very inefficient. However, we can minimise the number of extra memory accesses by maintaining a small cache of mappings in the processor. We typically use a structure known as the Translation Lookaside Buffer (TLB) that is a small fully associative cache. A TLB contains 32-64 entries. Each entry is indexed by the page number, and contains the corresponding frame number.

Once a memory address is calculated in the EX stage of the pipeline. It is sent to the TLB. The TLB is a very fast structure, and typically its access time is a fraction of a cycle. If there is a TLB hit, then the physical address is ready by the time we reach the memory access (MA) stage. The MA stage of the pipeline can then issue the read/write request to the memory system using the physical address obtained from the TLB. However, if there is a TLB miss, then the pipeline needs to stall, and the page table needs to be accessed. This is a slow process and takes tens of cycles. Fortunately, the hit rate of a TLB is very high ($\approx 99\%$) in most programs because of two reasons. First, programs have a high degree of temporal locality. Second, a 64 entry TLB covers 256 KB of the virtual address space (assuming a 4 KB page). The working set of most programs fits within this limit for small windows of time.

10.4.4   Swap Space

We have solved the first problem, i.e., ensuring that processes do not overwrite each other's data. Now, we need to solve the second problem, which is to ensure that our system can run even when the memory footprint of a program is more than the amount of physical memory. For example, we might need to run a program with a memory footprint of 3 GB on a machine with only 512 MB of main memory. Even on regular desktop machines it is possible that the combined memory footprint of all the processes is more than the size of main memory.

To support this requirement, we first need to find a location to save all the data that does not fit in main memory. Most processors typically have peripheral devices connected to the processor such as the hard disk, or USB flash drives that have a large amount of storage capacity. We shall study about storage devices in detail in Chapter 12. In this section, we only need to appreciate the following aspects of such connected storage devices.

1. Connected storage devices are very slow as compared to main memory. The access time to main memory is about 100-300 ns; whereas, the access time to a hard disk is of the order of milliseconds.

2. Storage devices typically have several orders of magnitude more storage than main memory. A hard disk contains about 500 GB of storage in a system with 4 GB of main memory.

3. They are conceptually treated as a large array of bytes similar to the way we treat the memory system. However, an address in the memory system is unrelated to the address in a hard disk. The storage device is **not a part of the memory system**.

4. It is not necessary to have a storage device physically close to the processor. It can be accessible over the network, and be in another part of the world.

A storage device can define an area known as the *swap space* that has space to contain all the frames that cannot be saved in main memory. Furthermore, this storage region need not be a superset of the main memory. If it is an extension of main memory, then we can define a larger physical memory. For example, if we have 2 GB of main memory, and 3 GB of swap space, then the total amount of physical memory can be 5 GB. In this case, if we need to displace a frame from main memory, then we need to allocate a location for it in swap space. Alternatively, the swap space can be inclusive. In the above example, we will effectively have 3 GB of physical memory, and the main memory acts like a cache for the swap space. In either case, the role of the swap space is to increase the amount of available physical memory.

Now, the obvious question that arises is, "How does the memory system know if a frame is present in main memory or the swap space? " We can augment each entry in the page table with an extra bit. If this bit is 1, then the frame is in main memory, else it is in the swap space. Note that this system can be made more complicated also. Instead of one swap space, we can have multiple swap spaces, and use multiple bits in a page table entry to indicate the corresponding swap space.

10.4.5   Memory Management Unit (MMU)

Up till now we have not discussed how page tables are actually managed and stored. Let us consider the typical life cycle of a process. When a process begins, the kernel allocates a primary page table in main memory, and clears off the TLB. It can then insert the mappings for the *text*, and *data*, sections. Secondly, the kernel can optionally allocate some space and insert some mappings for the *heap*, and *stack* sections. As long as there is a TLB hit, there is no problem. Once, there is a TLB miss, it is necessary to access the page tables, and secondly, the pipeline needs to stall. The job of accessing the page tables is typically handled by a dedicated unit known as the MMU (memory management unit). It can either be a hardware structure, or a software structure. If it is a hardware structure, then we have dedicated logic in the processor. Otherwise, it is necessary to invoke the MMU process by suspending the current process.

In either case, the operation of the MMU is the same. It needs to first locate the starting address of the primary page table. Note that this address cannot be a virtual address. Otherwise, we will need a page table for a page table. It is typically a physical address that does need additional translation. This starting address is either kept in a dedicated processor register (CR3 in x86), or in a designated location in physical memory. The MMU then needs to access the appropriate entry in the primary page table, and get the address of the secondary page table. The address of the secondary page table is another physical address. If a secondary page table exists, then the MMU accesses the relevant entry in the secondary page table, and gets the frame number. Subsequently, it evicts an entry from the TLB, and adds the new mapping. It can follow a LRU replacement scheme as described in Section 10.2.5. Note that it is necessary to have all the page tables in the main memory. They cannot be in the swap space.

Page Fault

There are several things that can go wrong in this process. If a page is being accessed for the first time, it is possible that it might not have a secondary page table, or its corresponding entry in the secondary page table might be empty. In this case, it is necessary to first find a free frame in main memory, create a secondary page table if required, and then insert the mapping in the secondary page table. To find a free frame in memory the MMU must maintain information about each frame. This information can be kept in the form of a bit vector, where each bit corresponds to a frame in main memory. If it is free, then the bit is 0, else if it is mapped, the bit is 1. If a free frame is available, then it can be used to map the new page. Otherwise, we need to forcibly free a frame by writing its data to the swap space. The method of finding a frame to evict from main memory is known as the *page replacement policy*. Subsequently, we need to change the page table entry of the page that was previously mapped to this frame. It needs to now say that the page is available in swap space. Once a frame has been freed, it can be mapped to another page.

Alternatively, it is also possible that the entry in the page table indicates that the frame is there in swap space. In this case, it is necessary to bring the frame into main memory. We first need to find a free frame, or if necessary evict a frame from main memory. Then, we need to create an appropriate page table mapping.

Definition 115
Whenever a page is not found in main memory, the event is known as a page fault.

Whenever a page is not found in main memory, we term the event as a *page fault*. It is subsequently necessary to create appropriate mappings in the page table and fetch the data from the swap space. Fetching an entire page from the swap space is a rather slow operation, and takes millions of cycles. Hence, it is very important for the MMU to manage pages efficiently. In specific, the page fault rate is very sensitive to the page replacement policy. Similar to cache block replacement policies, we can have different kinds of page replacement policies such as FIFO (first in first out), and LRU (least recently used). For more information on page replacement policies, the reader is referred to a textbook on operating systems [Silberschatz et al., 2008, Tanenbaum, 2007].

Figure 10.25 summarises the major steps in the process of address translation.

10.4.6 Advanced Features of the Paging System

It turns out that we can do several interesting things with the page table mechanism. Let us look at a few examples.

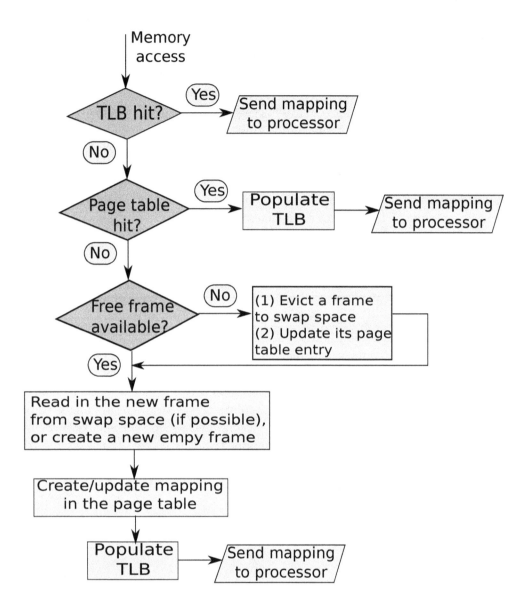

Figure 10.25: The process of address translation

Shared Memory

Let us assume that two processes want to share some memory between each other such that they can exchange data between them. Then each process needs to let the kernel know about this. The kernel can then map two pages in both the virtual address spaces to the same frame. Now, each process can write to a page in its own virtual address space, and magically, the data will get reflected in the virtual address space of the other process. It is sometimes necessary for several processes to communicate among each other, and the shared memory mechanism is one of the fastest methods.

Protection

Computer viruses typically change the code of a running process such that they can execute their own code. This is typically achieved by a giving a specific sequence of erroneous inputs to the program. If appropriate checks are not in place, then the values of specific variables within the program get overwritten. Some variables can get changed to pointers to the *text* section, and it is possible to exploit this mechanism to change instructions in the *text* section. It is possible to solve this problem by marking all the pages in *text* section as read-only. It will thus not be possible to modify their contents in run time.

Segmentation

We have been assuming that a programmer is free to layout the memory map according to her wish. She might for example decide to start the stack at a very high address such as $0xFFFFFFF8$. However, this code might not run on a machine that uses 16-bit addresses even if the memory footprint of the program is very small. Secondly, it is possible that a certain system might have reserved some parts of the virtual memory and made them unavailable to the process. For example, operating systems typically reserve the upper 1 or 2 GB for the kernel. To solve these problems, we need to create another virtual layer on top of virtual memory.

In a segmented memory (used in x86 systems), there are specific segment registers for the *text*, *data*, and *stack* sections. Each virtual address is specified as an offset to the specific segment register. By default instructions use the code segment register, and data uses the data segment register. The memory access (MA) stage of the pipeline adds the offset to the value stored in the segment register to generate the virtual address. Subsequently, the MMU uses this virtual address to generate the physical address.

10.5 Summary and Further Reading

10.5.1 Summary

Summary 10

1. A program perceives the memory system to be one large array of bytes. In practice, we need to design a memory system that preserves this abstraction, and is also fast and power efficient.

2. A physical memory system needs to be built out of SRAM and DRAM cells. An SRAM array is faster than a DRAM array. However, it takes much more area and consumes much more power. Building a memory with just DRAM cells will be too slow, and building a memory with just SRAM cells will be consume too much power.

3. We can use the properties of temporal and spatial locality to design more efficient memory systems. Temporal locality refers to the fact that there is a high likelihood of the same data item being accessed again in the near future. Spatial locality means that there is a high likelihood of adjacent memory locations being accessed in the near future.

4. To utilise temporal locality, we build a hierarchical memory system of caches. A cache is a memory structure that contains a subset of all the memory locations.

    (a) The cache at the highest level is known as the L1 cache. It is small and fast.

(b) *The L2 cache is at the next level. It is larger and slower.*

(c) *Some recent processors also have a third level of cache known as the L3 cache.*

(d) *The last level in the memory system is known as the* main memory. *It is a large DRAM array of cells, and contains an entry for all the memory locations in the system.*

(e) *Caches are typically inclusive. This means that a cache at a level i contains a subset of memory locations present at level $(i + 1)$.*

5. *To utilise spatial locality we group adjacent memory locations at the granularity of 32-128 byte blocks.*

6. *A cache contains a tag array and a data array. The tag array contains some of the bits of the address of the block, and the data array contains the contents of the block.*

7. *The basic operations needed to implement a cache are –* lookup, data read, data write, insert, replace, *and* evict.

(a) *There are three ways to store data in a cache – direct mapped, set associative, and fully associative.*

(b) *It is necessary to evict a block in a set if all the ways are non-empty.*

(c) *There are two major write policies – write-through (every write is immediately sent to the lower level), and write-back (writes are sent to the lower level, only upon an eviction)*

(d) *Some of the prominent replacement policies are – Random, FIFO, and LRU.*

8. *The average memory access time is given by:*

$$AMAT = L1_{hit\,time} + L1_{miss\,rate} \times L1_{miss\,penalty}$$
$$= L1_{hit\,time} + L1_{miss\,rate} \times (L2_{hit\,time} + L2_{miss\,rate} \times L2_{miss\,penalty})$$

9. *There are three types of cache misses – compulsory, capacity, and conflict.*

10. *Some of the methods and structures to optimise the memory system are: hardware prefetching, increased associativity/block size, victim cache, compiler techniques, write buffers, early restart and critical word first.*

11. *We need virtual memory to ensure that:*

(a) *Multiple programs do not overwrite each other's data unintentionally, or maliciously.*

(b) *The memory footprint of a program can be larger than the amount of available main memory.*

12. *To implement virtual memory, we divide a memory address into two parts – virtual page number, and an offset within a page. The virtual page number gets mapped to a physical frame number. The mapping is stored in a structure called a page table.*

13. *If a page is not found in main memory, then the event is known as a* page fault. *Servicing a page fault takes millions of cycles. Hence, it is necessary to avoid page faults by using sophisticated page replacement algorithms.*

14. *Some of the advanced features of the virtual memory system include shared memory, protection, and segmented addressing.*

10.5.2 Further Reading

The reader can refer to advanced text books on computer architecture by Henessey and Patterson [Hennessy and Patterson, 2012], Kai Hwang [Hwang, 2003], and Jean Loup Baer [Baer, 2010] for a discussion on advanced memory systems. Specifically, the books discuss advanced techniques for prefetching, miss rate reduction, miss penalty reduction, and compiler directed approaches. The reader can also refer to the book on memory systems by Bruce Jacob [Jacob, 2009]. This book gives a comprehensive survey of most of the major techniques employed in designing state of the art memory systems till 2009. The book by Balasubramaniam, Jouppi, and Muralimanohar on cache hierarchies also discusses some of the more advanced topics on the management of caches [Balasubramonian et al., 2011]. Managing the MMU is mostly studied in courses on operating systems [Tanenbaum, 2007, Silberschatz et al., 2008]. Research in DRAM memories [Mitra, 1999], and systems using advanced memory technologies is a hot topic of current research. A lot of research work is now focusing on phase change memories that do not require costly refresh cycles like DRAM. Readers can refer to the book by Qureshi, Gurumurthi, and Rajendran [Qureshi et al., 2011] for a thorough explanation of memory systems using phase change memories.

Exercises

Overview

Ex. 1 — Define temporal locality, and spatial locality.

Ex. 2 — Experimentally verify that the log-normal distribution is a heavy tailed distribution. What is the implication of a heavy tailed distribution in the context of the stack distance and temporal locality?

Ex. 3 — Define the term, *address distance*. Why do we find the nearest match in the last K accesses?

Ex. 4 — How do we take advantage of temporal locality in the memory system?

Ex. 5 — How do we take advantage of spatial locality in the memory system?

Caches and the Memory System

Ex. 6 — Consider a fully associative cache following the LRU replacement scheme and consisting of only 8 words. Consider the following sequence of memory accesses (the numbers denote the word address):
20, 21, 22, 23, 24, 25, 26, 27, 28, 29, 22, 30, 21, 23, 31

Assume that we begin when the cache is empty. What are the contents of the cache after the end of the sequence of memory accesses.

Ex. 7 — Answer Exercise 6 assuming a FIFO replacement scheme.

Ex. 8 — Consider a two-level cache using a write back policy. The L1 cache can store 2 words, and the L2 cache can store 4 words. Assume the caches to be fully associative (block size = 1 word); they follow the LRU replacement scheme. Consider the following sequence of memory accesses. The format of a write access is *write <address> <value>*, and the format for a read access is *read <address>* .

```
write 20 200
write 21 300
write 22 400
write 23 500
write 20 201
write 21 301
read 22
read 23
write 22 401
write 23 501
```

What are the contents of the caches at the end of the sequence of memory accesses? What are the contents of the caches, if we assume a write through policy ?

Ex. 9 — What is the total size (in bytes) of a direct mapped cache with the following configuration in a 32 bit system? It has a 10 bit index, and a block size of 64 bytes. Each block has 1 valid bit and 1 dirty bit.

Ex. 10 — Which sorting algorithm will have a better cache performance – bubble sort or selection sort? Explain your answer.

Ex. 11 — You have a cache with the following parameters:

- size : n bytes

- associativity : k

- block size : b bytes

Assuming a 32-bit address space, answer the following:

(a) What is the size of the tag in bits?

(b) What is the size of the set index in bits?

* Ex. 12 — Consider a direct mapped cache with 16 cache lines, indexed 0 to 15, where each cache line contains 32 integers (block size : 128 bytes).
Consider a two-dimensional, 32×32 array of integers a. This array is laid out in memory such that $a[0,0]$ is next to $a[0,1]$, and so on. Assume the cache is initially empty, and $a[0,0]$ maps to the first word of cache line 0.
Consider the following *column-first* traversal:

```
int sum = 0;
for (int i = 0; i < 32; i++) {
    for( int j=0; j < 32; j++) {
        sum += a[i,j];
    }
}
```

and the following *row-first* traversal:

```
int sum = 0;
for (int i = 0; i < 32; i++) {
    for( int j=0; j < 32; j++) {
```

```
        sum += a[j,i];
    }
}
```

Compare the number of cache misses produced by the two traversals, assuming the oldest cache line is evicted first. Assume that i, j, and *sum* are stored in registers, and that no part of array a is saved in registers. It is always stored in the cache.

Ex. 13 — A processor has a baseline IPC of 1.5, an L1 miss rate of 5%, and an L2 miss rate of 50%. The hit time of the L1 cache is 1 cycle (part of the baseline IPC computation), the L2 hit time is 10 cycles, and the L2 miss penalty is 100 cycles. Compute the final IPC. Assume that all the miss rates are local miss rates.

Ex. 14 — Consider the designs shown below

Design	Base CPI	L1 local miss rate (%)	L2 local miss rate (%)	L1 hit time (cycles)	L2 hit time (cycles)	L2 miss penalty (cycles)
$\mathcal{D}_1$	1	5	20	1	10	200
$\mathcal{D}_2$	1.5	10	25	1	20	150
$\mathcal{D}_3$	2	15	20	1	5	300

The base CPI assumes that all the instructions hit in the L1 cache. Furthermore, assume that a third of the instructions are memory instructions.
Write the formula for the average memory access time. What is the CPI of $\mathcal{D}_1$, $\mathcal{D}_2$ and $\mathcal{D}_3$?

* **Ex. 15** — Assume a cache that has n levels. For each level, the hit time is x cycles, and the local miss rate is y per cycle.

(a) What is the recursive formula for the average memory access time?

(b) What is the average memory access time as n tends to ∞?

** **Ex. 16** — Assume that you are given a machine with an unknown configuration. You need to find out a host of cache parameters by measuring the time it takes to execute different programs. These programs will be tailor made in such a way that they will reveal something about the underlying system. For answering the set of questions, you need to broadly describe the approach. Assume that the cache follows the LRU scheme for replacement.

(a) How will you estimate the size of the L1 cache?

(b) How will you estimate the L1 block size?

(c) How will you estimate the L1 cache associativity?

Virtual Memory

Ex. 17 — In a 32-bit machine with a 4 KB page size, how many entries are there in a single level page table? What is the size of each entry in the page table in bits?

Ex. 18 — Consider a 32-bit machine with a 4 KB page size, and a two level page table. If we address the primary page table with 12 bits of the page address, then how many entries are there in each secondary page table?

Ex. 19 — In a two level page table, should we index the primary page table with the most significant bits of the page address, or the least significant bits? Explain your answer.

Ex. 20 — We have a producer-consumer interaction between processes A and B. A writes data that B reads in a shared space. However, B should never be allowed to write anything into that shared space. How can we implement this using paging? How do we ensure that B will never be able to write into the shared space?

Ex. 21 — Assume a process A, forks a process B. Forking a process means that B inherits a copy of A's entire address space. However, after the fork call, the address spaces are separate. How can we implement this using our paging mechanism?

Ex. 22 — How is creating a new thread different from a fork() operation in terms of memory addressing?

Ex. 23 — Most of the time, the new process generated by a *fork* call does not attempt to change or modify the data inherited from the parent process. So is it really necessary to copy all the frames of the parent process to the child process? Can you propose an optimisation?

Ex. 24 — Explain the design of an inverted page table.

* **Ex. 25** — Calculate the expected value of the final CPI:
- Baseline CPI : 1
- Percentage of memory accesses: 30%
- TLB lookup time: 1 cycle (part of the baseline CPI)
- TLB miss rate: 20%
- Page table lookup time: 20 cycles (do not assume any page faults). Assume we can instantaneously insert entries into the TLB.
- L1 cache hit time: 1 cycle (Part of the baseline CPI)
- L1 local miss rate: 10%
- L2 cache hit time: 20 cycles
- L2 local miss rate: 50%
- L2 miss penalty: 100 cycles

** **Ex. 26** — Most of the time, programmers use libraries of functions in their programs. These libraries contain functions for standard mathematical operations, for supporting I/O operations, and for interacting with the operating system. The machine instructions of these functions are a part of the final executable. Occasionally, programmers prefer to use dynamically linked libraries (DLLs). DLLs contain the machine code of specific functions. However, they are invoked at run time, and their machine code is not a part of the program executable. Propose a method to implement a method to load and unload DLLs with the help of virtual memory.

Design Problems

Ex. 27 — You need to learn to use the CACTI tool (http://www.hpl.hp.com/research/cacti/) to estimate the area, latency, and power of different cache designs. Assume a 4-way associative 512 KB cache with 64 byte blocks. The baseline design has 1 read port, and 1 write port. You need to assume the baseline design, vary one parameter as mentioned below, and plot its relationship with the area, latency, or power consumption of a cache.

  a) Plot the area versus the number of read ports.

  b) Plot the energy per read access versus the number of read ports.

  c) Plot the cache latency versus the associativity.

  d) Vary the size of the cache from 256 KB to 4 MB (powers of 2), and plot its relationship with area, latency, and power.

Ex. 28 — Write a cache simulator that accepts memory read/write requests and simulates the execution of a hierarchical system of caches.

11

Multiprocessor Systems

Up till now, we have discussed the design and implementation of a processor in great detail including several methods to optimise its performance such as pipelining. We observed that by optimising the processor, and the memory system, it is possible to significantly increase the performance of a program. Now, the question is, "Is this enough?" Or, is it possible to do better?

A short answer to this question is "Maybe Not." For a long answer to this question, the reader needs to read through this entire chapter, and possibly take a look at the references. Let us start out by saying that processor performance has its limits. It is not possible to increase the speed of a processor indefinitely. Even with very complicated superscalar processors (see Chapter 9), and highly optimised memory systems, it is typically not possible to increase the IPC by more than 50%. Secondly, because of power and temperature considerations, it is very difficult to increase processor frequency beyond 3 GHz. The reader should note that processor frequencies have remained more of less the same over the last ten years (2002-2012). Consequently, CPU performance has also been increasing very slowly over the last ten years.

We illustrate these points in Figures 11.1, and 11.2. Figure 11.1 shows the peak frequency of processors released by multiple vendors such as Intel, AMD, Sun, Qualcomm, and Fujitsu from 2001 till 2010. We observe that the frequency has stayed more or less constant (mostly between 1 GHz to 2.5 GHz). The trends do not indicate a gradual increase in frequency. We expect that in the near future also, the frequency of processors will be limited to 3 GHz.

Figure 11.2 shows the average Spec Int 2006 score for the same set of processors from 2001 till 2010. We observe that CPU performance is slowly saturating over time, and it is getting increasingly difficult to increase performance.

Even though the performance of a single processor is not expected to significantly increase in the future, the future of computer architecture is not bleak. This is because processor manufacturing technology is steadily getting better, and this is leading to smaller and faster transistors. Till the late nineties processor designers were utilising the gains in transistor technology to increase the complexity of a processor by implementing more features. However, due to limitations in complexity, and power, designers resorted to using simpler processors after 2005. Instead of implementing more features in processors, vendors instead decided to put more than one processor on a single chip. This helps us run more than one program at the same time. Alternatively, sometimes it is possible to split a single program into multiple parts and run all the parts in parallel.

This paradigm of using multiple computing units running in parallel is known as *multiprocessing*. The

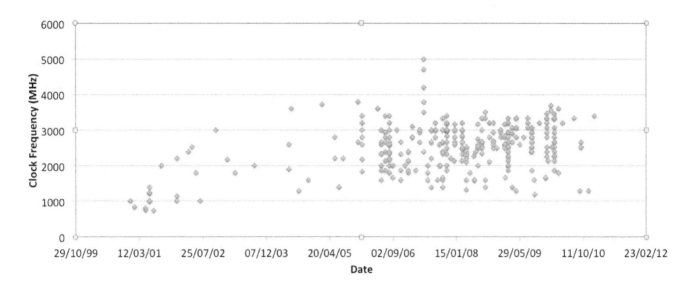

Figure 11.1: CPU frequencies (source [Danowitz et al., 2012])

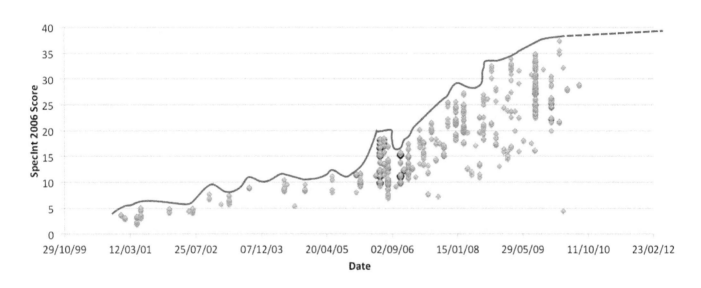

Figure 11.2: CPU performance (source [Danowitz et al., 2012])

term "multiprocessing" is a rather generic term. It can either refer to multiple processors in the same chip working in parallel, or it can refer to multiple processors across chips working in parallel. A multiprocessor is a piece of hardware that supports multiprocessing. When we have multiple processors within a chip, each processor is known as a *core*, and the chip is called a *multicore* processor.

Definition 116

The term multiprocessing *refers to multiple processors working in parallel. This is a generic definition, and it can refer to multiple processors in the same chip, or processors across different chips. A* multicore *processor is a specific type of multiprocessor that contains all of its constituent processors in the same chip. Each such processor is known as a core.*

We are now entering the era of multiprocessors, especially multicore systems. The number of cores per chip is increasing by roughly a factor of two every two years. New applications are being written to leverage this extra hardware. Most experts opine that the future of computing lies in multiprocessor systems.

Before proceeding to the design of different types of multiprocessors, let us quickly take a look at the background and history of multiprocessors.

11.1 Background

In the 60s and 70s large computers were primarily used by banks and financial institutions. They had a growing base of consumers, and consequently they needed computers that could perform more and more transactions per second. Typically just one processor proved to be insufficient in providing the computing throughput that was required. Hence, early computer designers decided to put multiple processors in a computer. The processors could share the computing load, and thus increase the computing throughput of the entire system.

One of the earliest multiprocessors was the Burroughs 5000, which had two processors – *A* and *B*. *A* was the main processor, and *B* was an auxiliary processor. When the load was high, processor *A* gave processor *B* some work to do. Almost all the other major vendors at that time also had multiprocessor offerings such as the IBM 370, PDP 11/74, VAX-11/782, and Univac 1108-II. These computers supported a second CPU chip. This was connected to the main processor. In all of these early machines, the second CPU was on a second chip that was physically connected to the first with wires or cables. They came in two flavors: symmetric and asymmetric. A *symmetric multiprocessor* consists of multiple processors, where each processor is of the same type, and has access to the services offered by the operating system, and peripherals; whereas, an *asymmetric multiprocessor* assigns different roles to different processors. There is typically a distinguished processor that controls the operating system, and the peripherals. The rest of the processors are slaves. They take work from the main processor, and return the results.

Definition 117

Symmetric Multiprocessing *This paradigm treats all the constituent processors in a multiprocessor system as the same. Each processor has equal access to the operating system, and the I/O peripherals. These are also known as SMP systems.*

Asymmetric Multiprocessing *This paradigm does not treat all the constituent processors in a multiprocessor system as the same. There is typically one* master *processor that has exclusive control of the operating system and I/O devices. It assigns work to the rest of the processors.*

In the early days, the second processor was connected to the main processor using a set of cables. It was typically housed in a different area of the main computer. Note that in those days, computers used to be the size of a room. With increased miniaturisation, gradually both the processors started coming closer. In the late eighties and early nineties, companies started putting multiple processors on the same motherboard. A motherboard is a printed circuit board that contains all the chips that a computer uses. The reader can take the lid off her laptop or desktop. The large green board with chips and metallic lines is the motherboard. By the late nineties, it was possible to have four or eight processors on a single motherboard. They were connected to each other using dedicated high speed buses.

Gradually, the era of multicore processors commenced. It was now possible to have multiple processors in the same chip. IBM was the first to announce a dual core (2 cores) multicore processor called the Power 4 in 2001. Intel and AMD followed with similar offerings in 2005. As of 2012, 8 core, and 10 core versions of multicore processors are available.

11.1.1 Moore's Law

Let us now take a deeper look at what happened between 1960 and 2012 in the world of processors. In the sixties, a computer was typically the size of a room, and today a computer fits in the pocket. A processor in a cell phone is around 1.6 million times faster than the IBM 360 machines in the early sixties. It is also several orders of magnitude more power efficient. The main driver for this continued evolution of computer technology is the miniaturisation of the transistor. Transistors used to have a channel length of several millimetres in the sixties, and now they are about 20-30 nanometers long. In 1971, a typical chip used to have 2000-3000 transistors. Nowadays, a chip has billions of transistors.

Over the last forty to fifty years, the number of transistors per chip has been roughly doubling every 1-2 years. In fact, the co-founder of Intel, Gordon Moore, had predicted this trend in 1965. The Moore's law (named in the honour of Gordon Moore) predicts that the number of transistors on a chip is expected to double every one to two years. Originally, Moore had predicted the period of doubling to be every year. However, over time, this period has become about 2 years. This was expected to happen because of the steady rate of advances in manufacturing technology, new materials, and fabrication techniques.

Historical Note 3

In 1965, Gordon Moore (co-founder of Intel) conjectured that the number of transistors on a chip will double roughly every one to two years. Initially, the number of transistors was doubling every year. Gradually, the rate slowed down to 18 months, and now it is about two years.

The Moore's law has approximately held true since it was proposed in the mid sixties. Nowadays, almost every two years, the dimensions of transistors shrink by a factor of $\sqrt{2}$. This ensures that the area of a transistor shrinks by a factor of 2, and thus it is possible to fit twice the number of transistors on a chip. Let us define the *feature size* as the size of the smallest structure that can be fabricated on a chip. Table 11.1 shows the feature sizes of Intel processors over the last 10 years. We observe that the feature size decreases by a factor of roughly $\sqrt{2}$ (1.41) every two years. This results in a doubling of the number of transistors.

11.1.2 Implications of the Moore's Law

Note that the Moore's law is an empirical law. However, because of the fact that it has predicted trends correctly for the last forty years, it is widely quoted in technical literature. It directly predicts a miniaturisation in the transistor size. A smaller transistor is more power efficient and faster. Designers were traditionally using these benefits to design bigger processors with extra transistors. They were using the additional transistor budget to add complexity to different units, increase cache sizes, increase the issue width, and the number of functional units. Secondly, the number of pipeline stages were also steadily increasing till about 2002, and there was an accompanying increase in the clock frequency also. However, after 2002 there was

Year	Feature Size
2001	130 nm
2003	90 nm
2005	65 nm
2007	45 nm
2009	32 nm
2011	22 nm

Table 11.1: Feature sizes between 2001 and 2012

a radical change in the world of computer architecture. Suddenly, power and temperature became major concerns. The processor power consumption figures started to exceed 100 W, and on chip temperatures started to exceed $100°C$. These constraints effectively put an end to the scaling in complexity, and clock frequencies of processors.

Instead, designers started to pack more cores per chip without changing its basic design. This ensured that the number of transistors per core remained constant, and according to Moore's law the number of cores doubled once every two years. This started the era of multicore processors, and processor vendors started doubling the number of cores on chip. As of 2012, we have processors that have 8-10 cores per chip. The number of cores per chip are expected to reach 32 or 64 in the next 5 to 10 years (by 2020). A large multiprocessor today has multiple cores per chip, and multiple chips per system. For example, your author is at the moment writing this book on a 32 core server. It has 4 chips, and each chip has 8 cores.

Along with regular multicore processors, there has been another important development. Instead of having 4 large cores per chip, there are architectures that have 64-256 very small cores on a chip such as graphics processors. These processors also follow the Moore's law, and are doubling their cores every 2 years. Such processors are increasingly being used in computer graphics, numerical and scientific computing. It is also possible to split the resources of a processor to make it support two program counters, and run two programs at the same time. These special kind of processors are known as multithreaded processors. It is not possible to cover the entire design space of multiprocessors in this book. This is the topic of a book on advanced architecture, and the reader can consult [Hwang, 2003, Hennessy and Patterson, 2012, Culler et al., 1998] for a detailed description of different kinds of multiprocessors.

In this chapter, we wish to make the reader aware of the broad trends in multiprocessor design. We shall first look at multiprocessing from the point of view of software. Once we establish the software requirements, we shall proceed to design hardware to support multiprocessing. We shall broadly consider multicore, multithreaded, and vector processors in this chapter.

11.2 Software for Multiprocessor Systems

11.2.1 Strong and Loosely Coupled Multiprocessing

Loosely Coupled Multiprocessing

There are two primary ways to harness the power of multiprocessors. The first method is to run multiple unrelated programs in parallel. For example, it is possible to run a text editor and a web browser at the same time. The text editor can run on processor 1, and the web browser can run on processor 2. Both of them can occasionally request for OS services, and connect to I/O devices. Users often use large multiprocessor systems containing more than 64-128 processors to run a set of jobs (processes) that are unrelated. For example, a user might want to conduct a weather simulation with 128 different sets of parameters. Then she can start 128 separate instances of the weather simulation software on 128 different processors on a large multiprocessor system. We thus have a speedup of 128 times as compared to a single processor system, which is significant. This paradigm is known as *loosely coupled multiprocessing*. Here, the dependences between programs is almost negligible. Note that using a multiprocessor in this manner, is not conceptually very different from using a cluster of computers that comprises of completely unrelated machines that communicate over a local area network. The only difference is that the latency between machines in a multiprocessor is lower than cluster computers. A loosely coupled multiprocessor such as a cluster of PCs is also known as a *multicomputer*.

Definition 118

A multicomputer *consists of a set of computers typically connected over the network. It is capable of running a set of programs in parallel, where the programs do not share their memory space with each other.*

Strongly Coupled Multiprocessing

However, the real benefit of a multiprocessor is accrued when there is a strong degree of overlap between different programs. This paradigm is known as *strongly coupled multiprocessing*. Here programs can share their memory space, file and network connections. This method of using multiprocessors harnesses their true power, and helps us speed up a large amount of existing software. The design and programming of strongly coupled multiprocessors is a very rich field, and is expected to grow significantly over the coming decade.

Definition 119

Loosely Coupled Multiprocessing *Running multiple unrelated programs in parallel on a multiprocessor is known as* loosely coupled multiprocessing.

Strongly Coupled Multiprocessing *Running a set of programs in parallel that share their memory space, data, code, file, and network connections is known as* strongly coupled multiprocessing.

In this book, we shall mainly look at strongly coupled multiprocessing, and primarily focus on systems that allow a set of programs to run co-operatively by sharing a large amount of data and code.

11.2.2   Shared Memory vs Message Passing

Let us now explain the methods of programming multiprocessors. For ease of explanation, let us draw an analogy here. Consider a group of workers in a factory. They co-operatively perform a task by communicating with each other orally. A supervisor often issues commands to the group of workers, and then they perform their work. If there is a problem, a worker indicates it by raising an alarm. Immediately, other workers rush to his assistance. In this small and simple setting, all the workers can hear each other, and see each other's actions. This proximity enables them to accomplish complex tasks.

We can alternatively consider another model, where workers cannot necessarily see or hear each other. In this case, they need to communicate with each other through a system of messages. Messages can be passed through letters, phone calls, or emails. In this setting, if a worker discovers a problem, he needs to send a message to his supervisor such that she can come and rectify the problem. Workers need to be typically aware of each other's identities, and explicitly send messages to all or a subset of them. It is not possible any more to shout loudly, and communicate with everybody at the same time. However, there are some advantages of this system. We can support many more workers because they do not have to be co-located. Secondly, since there are no constraints on the location of workers, they can be located at different parts of the world, and be doing very different things. This system is thus far more flexible, and scalable.

Inspired by these real life scenarios, computer architects have designed a set of protocols for multiprocessors following different paradigms. The first paradigm is known as *shared memory*, where all the individual programs see the same view of the memory system. If program A changes the value of x to 5, then program B immediately sees the change. The second setting is known as *message passing*. Here multiple programs communicate among each other by passing messages. The shared memory paradigm is more suitable for strongly coupled multiprocessors, and the message passing paradigm is more suitable for loosely coupled multiprocessors. Note that it is possible to implement message passing on a strongly coupled multiprocessor. Likewise, it is also possible to implement an abstraction of a shared memory on an otherwise loosely coupled multiprocessor. This is known as *distributed shared memory* [Keleher et al., 1994]. However, this is typically not the norm.

Shared Memory

Let us try to add n numbers in parallel using a multiprocessor. The code for it is shown in Example 121. We have written the code in C++ using the OpenMP language extension.

Example 121
Write a shared memory program to add a set of numbers in parallel.

Answer: *Let us assume that all the numbers are already stored in an array called numbers. The array numbers has SIZE entries. Assume that the number of parallel sub-programs that can be launched is equal to N.*

```
/* variable declaration */
int partialSums[N];
int numbers[SIZE];
int result = 0;

/* initialise arrays */
...

/* parallel section */
#pragma omp parallel {
    /* get my processor id */
    int myId = omp_get_thread_num();

    /* add my portion of numbers */
    int startIdx = myId * SIZE/N;
    int endIdx = startIdx + SIZE/N;
    for(int jdx = startIdx; jdx < endIdx; jdx++)
```

```
            partialSums[myId] += numbers[jdx];
}

/* sequential section */
for(int idx=0; idx < N; idx++)
    result += partialSums[idx];
```

It is easy to mistake the code for a regular sequential program, except for the directive *#pragma omp parallel*. This is the only extra semantic difference that we have added in our parallel program. It launches each iteration of this loop as a separate sub-program. Each such sub-program is known as a *thread*. A thread is defined as a sub-program that shares its address space with other threads. It communicates with them by modifying the values of memory locations in the shared memory space. Each thread has its own set of local variables that are not accessible to other threads.

The number of iterations, or the number of parallel threads that get launched is a system parameter that is set in advance. It is typically equal to the number of processors. In this case, it is equal to N. Thus, N copies of the parallel part of the code are launched in parallel. Each copy runs on a separate processor. Note that each of these copies of the program can access all the variables that have been declared before the invocation of the parallel section. For example, they can access *partialSums*, and the *numbers* arrays. Each processor invokes the function *omp_get_thread_num*, which returns the id of the thread. Each thread uses the thread id to find the range of the array that it needs to add. It adds all the entries in the relevant portion of the array, and saves the result in its corresponding entry in the *partialSums* array. Once all the threads have completed their job, the sequential section begins. This piece of sequential code can run on any processor. This decision is made dynamically at runtime by the operating system, or the parallel programming framework. To obtain the final result it is necessary to add all the partial sums in the sequential section.

Definition 120

A thread is a sub-program that shares its address space with other threads. It has a dedicated program counter, and a local stack that it can use to define its local variables. We refer to a thread as a software thread *to distinguish it from a hardware thread that we shall define later.*

A graphical representation of the computation is shown in Figure 11.3. A parent thread spawns a set of child threads. They do their own work, and finally *join* when they are done. The parent thread takes over, and aggregates the partial results.

There are several salient points to note here. The first is that each thread has its separate stack. A thread can use its stack to declare its local variables. Once it finishes, all the local variables in its stack are destroyed. To communicate data between the parent thread and the child threads, it is necessary to use variables that are accessible to both the threads. These variables need to be globally accessible by all the threads. The child threads can freely modify these variables, and even use them to communicate amongst each other also. They are additionally free to invoke the operating system, and write to external files and network devices. Once, all the threads have finished executing, they perform a *join* operation, and free their state. The parent thread takes over, and finishes the role of aggregating the results. Here, *join* is an example of a *synchronisation operation* between threads. There can be many other types of synchronisation

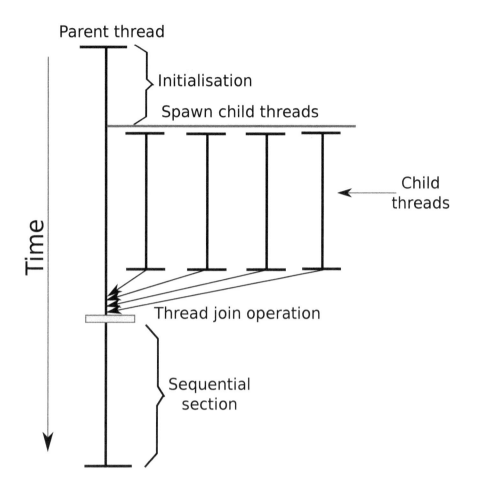

Figure 11.3: Graphical representation of the program to add numbers in parallel

operations between threads. The reader is referred to [Culler et al., 1998] for a detailed discussion on thread synchronisation. All that the reader needs to understand is that there are a set of complicated constructs that threads can use to perform very complex tasks co-operatively. Adding a set of numbers is a very simple example. Multithreaded programs can be used to perform other complicated tasks such as matrix algebra, and even solve differential equations in parallel.

Message Passing

Let us now briefly look at message passing. Note that message passing based loosely coupled systems are not the main focus area of this book. Hence, we shall just give the reader a flavor of message passing programs. Note that in this case, each program is a separate entity and does not share code, or data with other programs. It is a *process*, where a process is defined as a running instance of a program. Typically, it does not share its address space with any other process.

Definition 121

A process *represents the running instance of a program. Typically, it does not share its address space with any other process.*

Let us now quickly define our message passing semantics. We shall primarily use two functions, *send* and *receive* as shown in Table 11.2. The *send(pid, val)* function is used to send an integer (*val*) to the process whose id is equal to *pid*. The *receive(pid)* is used to receive an integer sent by a process whose id is equal to *pid*. If *pid* is equal to ANYSOURCE, then the receive function can return with the value sent by any process. Our semantics is on the lines of the popular parallel programming framework, MPI (Message Passing Interface) [Snir et al., 1995]. MPI calls have many more arguments, and their syntax is much more complicated than our simplistic framework. Let us now consider the same example of adding n numbers in parallel in Example 122.

Function	Semantics
send (pid, val)	Send the integer, *val*, to the process with an id equal to *pid*
receive (pid)	(1) Receive an integer from process pid (2) The function blocks till it gets the value (3) If the pid is equal to ANYSOURCE, then the *receive* function returns with the value sent by any process

Table 11.2: *send* and *receive* calls

Example 122

Write a message passing based program to add a set of numbers in parallel. Make appropriate assumptions.

Answer: *Let us assume that all the numbers are stored in the array, numbers, and this array is available with all the N processors. Let the number of elements in the numbers array be SIZE. For the sake of simplicity, let us assume that SIZE is divisible by N.*

```
/* start all the parallel processes */
SpawnAllParallelProcesses();

/* For each process execute the following code */
int myId = getMyProcessId();

/* compute the partial sums */
int startIdx = myId * SIZE/N;
int endIdx = startIdx + SIZE/N;
int partialSum = 0;
for(int jdx = startIdx; jdx < endIdx; jdx++)
            partialSum += numbers[jdx];

/* All the non-root nodes send their partial sums to the root */
if(myId != 0) {
        /* send the partial sum to the root */
        send (0, partialSum);
```

```
} else {
        /* for the root */
        int sum = partialSum;
        for (int pid = 1; pid < N; pid++) {
                sum += receive(ANYSOURCE);
        }

        /* shut down all the processes */
        shutDownAllProcesses();

        /* return the sum */
        return sum;
}
```

11.2.3 Amdahl's Law

We have now taken a look at examples for adding a set of n numbers in parallel using both the paradigms namely shared memory and message passing. We divided our program into two parts – a sequential part and a parallel part (refer to Figure 11.3). In the parallel part of the execution, each thread completed the work assigned to it, and created a partial result. In the sequential part, the root or master or parent thread initialised all the variables and data structures, and spawned all the child threads. After all the child threads completed (or joined), the parent thread aggregated the results produced by all the child threads. This process of aggregating results is also known as *reduction*. The process of initialising variables, and reduction, are both sequential.

Let us now try to derive the speedup of a parallel program vis-a-vis its sequential counterpart. Let us consider a program that takes T_{seq} units of time to execute. Let f_{seq} be the fraction of time that it spends in its sequential part, and $1 - f_{seq}$ be the fraction of time that it spends in its parallel part. The sequential part is unaffected by parallelism; however, the parallel part gets equally divided among the processors. If we consider a system of P processors, then the parallel part is expected to be sped up by a factor of P. Thus, the time (T_{par}) that the parallel version of the program takes is equal to:

$$T_{par} = T_{seq} \times \left(f_{seq} + \frac{1 - f_{seq}}{P} \right) \tag{11.1}$$

Alternatively, the speedup (S) is given by:

$$S = \frac{T_{seq}}{T_{par}} = \frac{1}{f_{seq} + \frac{1 - f_{seq}}{P}} \tag{11.2}$$

Equation 11.2 is known as the Amdahl's Law. It is a theoretical estimate (or rather the upper bound in most cases) of the speedup that we expect with additional parallelism.

Figure 11.4 plots the speedups as predicted by Amdahl's Law for three values of f_{seq} (10%, 5%, and 2%). We observe that with an increasing number of processors the speedup gradually saturates and tends to the limiting value, $1/f_{seq}$. We observe diminishing returns as we increase the number of processors beyond a certain point. For example, for $f_{seq} = 5\%$, there is no appreciable difference in speedups between a system with 35 processors, and a system with 200 processors. We approach similar limits for all three values of f_{seq}.

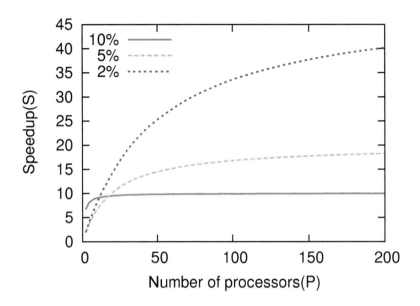

Figure 11.4: Speedup (S) vs number of processors (P)

The important point to note here is that increasing speedups by adding additional processors has its limits. We cannot expect to keep getting speedups indefinitely by adding more processors, because we are limited by the length of the sequential sections in programs.

To summarise, we can draw two inferences. The first is that to speedup a program it is necessary to have as much parallelism as possible. Hence, we need to have a very efficient parallel programming library, and parallel hardware. However, parallelism has its limits and it is not possible to increase the speedup appreciably beyond a certain limit. The speedup is limited by the length of the sequential section in the program. To reduce the sequential section, we need to adopt approaches both at the algorithmic level, and at the system level. We need to design our algorithms in such a way that the sequential section is as short as possible. For example, in Examples 121, and 122, we can also perform the initialisation in parallel (reduces the length of the sequential section). Secondly, we need a fast processor that can minimise the time it takes to execute the sequential section.

We looked at the latter requirement (designing fast processors) in Chapters 8, 9, and 10. Now, let us look at designing fast and power efficient hardware for the parallel section.

11.3   Design Space of Multiprocessors

Michael J. Flynn proposed the famous Flynn's classification of multiprocessors in 1966. He started out by observing that an ensemble of different processors might either share code, data, or both. There are four possible choices – SISD (single instruction single data), SIMD (single instruction multiple data), MISD (multiple instruction single data), and MIMD (multiple instruction multiple data).

Let us describe each of these types of multiprocessors in some more detail.

SISD This is a standard uniprocessor with a single pipeline as described in Chapter 8 and Chapter 9. A SISD processor can be thought of as a special case of the set of multiprocessors with just a single processor.

SIMD A SIMD processor can process multiple streams of data in a single instruction. For example, a SIMD instruction can add 4 sets of numbers with a single instruction. Modern processors incorporate SIMD instructions in their instruction set, and have special SIMD execution units also. Examples include x86 processors that contain the SSE set of SIMD instruction sets. Graphics processors, and vector processors are special examples of highly successful SIMD processors.

MISD MISD systems are very rare in practice. They are mostly used in systems that have very high reliability requirements. For example, large commercial aircraft typically have multiple processors running different versions of the same program. The final outcome is decided by voting. For example, a plane might have a MIPS processor, an ARM processor, and an x86 processor, each running different versions of the same program such as an autopilot system. Here, we have multiple instruction streams, yet a single source of data. A dedicated voting circuit computes a majority vote of the three outputs. For example, it is possible that because of a bug in the program or the processor, one of the systems can erroneously take a decision to turn left. However, both of the other systems might take the correct decision to turn right. In this case, the voting circuit will decide to turn right. Since MISD systems are hardly ever used in practice other than such specialised examples, we shall not discuss them any more in this book.

MIMD MIMD systems are by far the most prevalent multiprocessor systems today. They have multiple instruction streams and multiple data streams. Multicore processors, and large servers are all MIMD systems. Examples 121 and 122 pertained to MIMD systems. We need to carefully explain the meaning of multiple instruction streams. This means that instructions come from multiple sources. Each source has its unique location, and associated program counter. Two important branches of the MIMD paradigm have formed over the last few years.

The first is *SPMD* (single program multiple data), and the second is *MPMD* (multiple program multiple data). Most parallel programs are written in the SPMD style (Example 121 and 122). Here, multiple copies of the same program run on different cores, or separate processors. However, each individual processing unit has a separate program counter, and thus perceives a different instruction stream. Sometimes SPMD programs are written in such a way that they perform different actions depending on their thread ids. We saw a method in Example 121 on how to achieve this using OpenMP functions. The advantage of SPMD is that we do not have to write different programs for different processors. Parts of the same program can run on all the processors, though their behaviour might be different.

A contrasting paradigm is MPMD. Here, the programs running on different processors are actually different. They are more useful for specialised processors that have heterogeneous processing units. There is typically a single master program that assigns work to slave programs. The slave programs complete the quanta of work assigned to them, and then return the results to the master program. The nature of work of both the programs is actually very different, and it is often not possible to seamlessly combine them into one program.

From the above description, it is clear that the systems that we need to focus on are SIMD and MIMD. MISD systems are very rarely used, and thus will not be discussed anymore. Let us first discuss MIMD multiprocessing. Note that we shall only describe the SPMD variant of MIMD multiprocessing because it is the most common approach.

11.4 MIMD Multiprocessors

Let us now take a deeper look at strongly-coupled shared memory based MIMD machines. We shall first take a look at them from the point of view of software. After we have worked out a broad specification of these machines from the point of view of software, we can proceed to give a brief overview of the design of the hardware. Note that the design of parallel MIMD machines can take an entire book to describe. For additional information, or for added clarity, the reader can refer to the following references [Culler et al., 1998, Sorin et al., 2011].

Let us call the software interface of a shared memory MIMD machine as the "logical point of view", and refer to the actual physical design of the multiprocessor as the "physical point of view". When we describe the logical point of view, we are primarily interested in how the multiprocessor behaves with respect to software. What guarantees does the hardware make regarding its behaviour, and what can software expect? This includes correctness, performance, and even resilience to failures. The physical point of view is concerned with the actual design of the multiprocessor. This includes the physical design of the processors, the memory system, and the interconnection network. Note that the physical point of view has to conform to the logical point of view. The reader will recall that we are taking a similar approach here as we did for uniprocessors. We first explained the software view (architecture) by looking at assembly code. Then we provided an implementation for the assembly code by describing a pipelined processor (organisation). We shall follow a similar approach here.

11.4.1   Logical Point of View

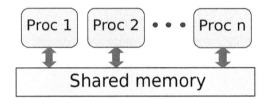

Figure 11.5: Logical view of a multiprocessor system

Figure 11.5 shows a logical view of a shared memory MIMD multiprocessor. Each processor is connected to the memory system that saves both code and data. The program counter of each processor points to the location of the instruction that it is executing. This is in the code section of memory. This section is typically read only, and thus is not affected by the fact that we have multiprocessors.

The main challenge in implementing a shared memory multiprocessor is in correctly handling data accesses. Figure 11.5 shows a scheme in which each computing processor is connected to the memory, and it is treated as a black box. If we are considering a system of processes with different virtual address spaces, then there is no problem. Each processor can work on its private copy of data. Since the memory footprints are effectively disjoint, we can easily run a set of parallel processes in this system. However, the main complexity arises when we are looking at shared memory programs that have multiple threads, and there is data sharing across threads. Note that we can also share memory across processes by mapping different virtual pages to the same physical frame as described in Section 10.4.6. We shall threat this scenario as a special case of parallel multi-threaded software.

A set of parallel threads typically share their virtual and physical address spaces. However, threads do have private data also, which is saved in their stacks. There are two methods to implement disjoint stacks. The first is that all the threads can have identical virtual address spaces, and different stack pointers can start at different points in the virtual address space. We need to further ensure that the size of the stack of a thread is not large enough to overlap with the stack of another thread. Another approach is to map the stack portion of the virtual address space of different threads to different memory frames. Thus, each thread can have different entries in its page table for the stack portion, yet have common entries for the rest of the sections of the virtual address space such as code, read-only data, constants, and heap variables.

In any case, the main problems of complexity of parallel software are not because of code that is read-only, or local variables that are not shared across threads. The main problem is due to data values that are potentially shared across multiple threads. This is what gives the power to parallel programs, and also makes them very complex. In the example that we showed for adding a set of numbers in parallel, we can clearly see the advantage that we obtain by sharing values and results of computation through shared memory.

However, sharing values across threads is not that simple. It is actually a rather profound topic, and advanced texts on computer architecture devote several chapters to this topic. We shall briefly look at two important topics in this area namely coherence, and memory consistency. *Coherence* is also known as cache coherence, when we refer to it in the context of caches. However, the reader needs to be aware that coherence is just not limited to caches, it is a generic term.

11.4.2 Coherence

The term *coherence* in the memory system refers to the way multiple threads access the same location. We shall see that many different behaviours are possible, when multiple threads access the same memory location. Some of the behaviours are intuitively wrong, yet possible. Before looking at coherence, we need to note that inside the memory system, we have many different entities such as caches, write buffers, and different kinds of temporary buffers. Processors typically write values to temporary buffers, and resume their operation. It is the job of the memory system to transfer the data from these buffers to a location in the cache subsystem. It is thus possible that internally, a given memory address might be associated with many different physical locations at a given point of time. Secondly, the process of transferring data from the processor to the correct location in the memory system (typically a cache block) is not instantaneous. It sometimes takes more than tens of cycles for the memory read or write request to reach its location. Sometimes these memory request messages can wait even longer, if there is a lot of memory traffic. Messages can also get reordered with other messages that were sent after them.

However, for the moment, let us assume that the memory looks like a large array of bytes to all the processors; although, internally it is a complicated network of different components that strive to provide a simple logical abstraction for read/write operations. The internal complexity of a multiprocessor memory system leads to several interesting behaviours for programs that access the same set of shared variables. Let us consider a set of examples.

In each of these examples, all shared values are initialised to 0. All the local variables start with t such as $t1$, $t2$, and $t3$. Let us say that thread 1 writes to a variable x that is shared across threads. Immediately later, thread 2 tries to read its value.

```
Thread 1:          Thread 2:
x = 1              t1 = x
```

Is thread 2 guaranteed to read 1? Or, can it get the previous value 0? What if thread 2, reads the value of x, 2 ns later, or even 10 ns later? What is the time that it takes for a write in one thread to propagate to the other threads? This depends on the implementation of the memory system. If a memory system has fast buses, and fast caches, then a write can propagate very quickly to other threads. However, if the buses and caches are slow then it can take some time for other threads to see a write to a shared variable.

Now, let us further complicate the example. Let us assume that thread 1 writes to x twice.

Example 123

$$
\begin{array}{ll}
\textit{Thread 1:} & \textit{Thread 2:} \\
x = 1 & t1 = x \\
x = 2 & t2 = x
\end{array}
$$

Let us now look at the set of possible outcomes. (t1,t2)=(1,2) is possible. (t1,t2) = (0,1) is also possible. This is possible when t1 was written before thread 1 started, and t2 was written after the first statement of thread 1 completed. Likewise we can systematically enumerate the set of all possible outcomes, which are: (0,0), (0,1), (0,2), (1,1), (1,2), (2,2). The reader is requested to write a simple program using a parallel multithreaded framework such as OpenMP or *pthreads* and look at the set of possible outcomes. The interesting question is whether the outcome (2,1) is possible? This might be possible if somehow the first write to x got delayed in the memory system, and the second write overtook it. The question is whether we should allow such behaviour.

The answer is NO. If we were to allow such behaviour, then implementing a multiprocessor memory system would undoubtedly become simpler. However, it will become very difficult to write and reason about parallel programs. Hence, most multiprocessor systems disallow such behaviour.

Let us now look at the issue of accesses to the same memory location by multiple threads slightly more formally. Let us define the term, *coherence*, as he behaviour of memory accesses to the same memory address such as x in our examples. We ideally want our memory system to be coherent. This basically means that it should observe a set of rules while dealing with different accesses to the same memory address such that it is easier to write programs.

Definition 122
The behaviour of memory accesses to the same memory address is known as coherence.

Typically, coherence has two axioms. These are as follows:

1. **Completion** A write must ultimately complete.

2. **Order** All the writes to the same memory address need to be seen by all the threads in the same order.

Both of these axioms are fairly sublime in nature. The completion axiom says that no write is ever lost in the memory system. For example, it is not possible that we write a value of 10 to variable x, and the write request gets dropped by the memory system. It needs to reach the memory location corresponding to x, and then it needs to update its value. It might get overwritten later by another write request. However, the bottom line is that the write request needs to update the memory location at some point of time in the future.

The order axiom says that all the writes to a memory location are perceived to be in the same order by all the threads. This means that it is not possible to read (2,1) in Example 123. Let us now explain the reasons for this. Thread 1 is aware that 2 was written after 1 to the memory location x. By the second axiom of coherence, all other threads need to perceive the same order of writes to x. Their view of x cannot be different from that of thread 1. Hence, they cannot read 2 after 1. If we think about it, the axioms of coherence make intuitive sense. They basically mean that all writes eventually complete, as is true for uniprocessor systems. Secondly, all the processors see the same view of a single memory location. If its value changes from 0 to 1 to 2, then all the processors see the same order of changes (0-1-2). No processor sees the updates in a different order. This further means that irrespective of how a memory system is implemented internally, externally each memory location is seen as a globally accessible single location.

11.4.3   Memory Consistency

Overview

Coherence was all about accesses to the same memory location. What about access to different memory locations? Let us explain with a series of examples.

Example 124

Thread 1:	*Thread 2:*
x = 1	t1 = y
y = 1	t2 = x

Let us look at the permissible values of $t1$, and $t2$ from an intuitive standpoint. We can always read (t1,t2)=(0,0). This can happen when thread 2 is scheduled before thread 1. We can also read $(t1,t2)=(1,1)$. This will happen when thread 2 is scheduled after thread 1 finishes. Likewise it is possible to read $(t1,t2)=(0,1)$. Figure 11.6 shows how we can get all the three outcomes.

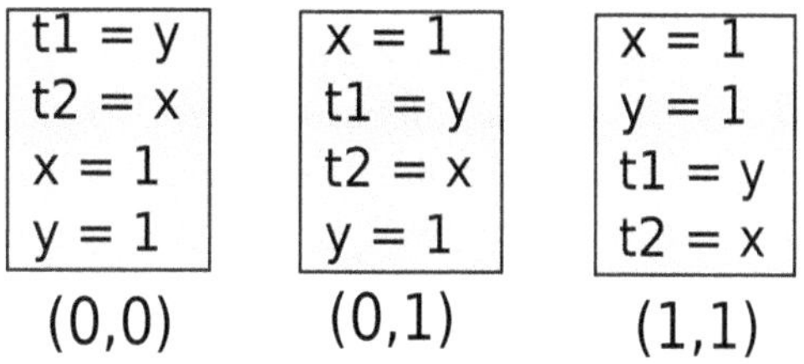

t1 = y	x = 1	x = 1
t2 = x	t1 = y	y = 1
x = 1	t2 = x	t1 = y
y = 1	y = 1	t2 = x
(0,0)	(0,1)	(1,1)

Figure 11.6:   Graphical representation of all the possible outcomes

The interesting question is whether (t1,t2)=(1,0) is allowed? This will happen when the write to x is somehow delayed by the memory system, whereas the write to y completes quickly. In this case $t1$ will get the updated value of y, and $t2$ will get the old value of x. The question is whether such kind of behaviour should be allowed. Clearly if such kind of behaviour is allowed it will become hard to reason about software, and the correctness of parallel algorithms. It will also become hard to program. However, if we allow such behaviour then our hardware design becomes simpler because we do not have to provide strong guarantees to software.

There is clearly no right or wrong answer? It all depends on how we want to program software, and what hardware designers want to build for software writers. But, still there is something very profound about this example, and the special case of (t1,t2) equal to (1,0). To find out why, let us take a look again at Figure 11.6. In this figure, we have been able to reason about three outcomes by creating an interleaving between the instructions of the two threads. In each of these interleavings, the order of instructions in the same thread is the same as the way it is specified in the program. This is known as *program order*.

Definition 123

An order of instructions (possibly belonging to multiple threads) that is consistent with the control-flow semantics of each constituent thread is said to be in program order. The control-flow semantics of a thread is defined as the set of rules that determine which instructions can execute after a given instruction. For example, the set of instructions executed by a single cycle processor is always in program order.

Observation: It is clear that we cannot generate the outcome (t1,t2)=(1,0) by interleaving threads in program order.

It would be nice if we can somehow exclude the output (1,0) from the set of possible outputs. It will allow us to write parallel software, where we can predict the possible outcomes very easily. A model of the memory system that determines the set of possible outcomes for parallel programs is known as a *memory model*.

Definition 124

The model of a memory system that determines the set of likely outcomes for parallel programs is known as a memory model.

Sequential Consistency

We can have different kinds of memory models corresponding to different kinds of processors. One of the most important memory models is known as *sequential consistency*(SC). Sequential consistency states that only those outcomes are allowed that can be generated by an interleaving of threads in program order. This means that all the outcomes shown in Figure 11.6 are allowed because they are generated by interleaving thread 1 and 2 in all possible ways, without violating their program order. However, the outcome (t1,t2)=(1,0) is not allowed because it violates program order. Hence, it is not allowed in a sequentially consistent memory model. Note that once we interleave multiple threads in program order, it is the same as saying that we have one processor that executes an instruction of one thread in one cycle and possibly another instruction from some other thread in the next cycle. Hence, a uniprocessor processing multiple threads produces a SC execution. In fact, if we think about the name of the model, the word "sequential" comes from the notion that the execution is equivalent to a uniprocessor *sequentially* executing the instructions of all the threads in some order.

Definition 125

A memory model is sequentially consistent if the outcome of the execution of a set of parallel threads is equivalent to that of a single processor executing instructions from all the threads in some order. Alternatively, we can define sequential consistency as a memory model whose set of possible outcomes are those that can be generated by interleaving a set of threads in program order.

Sequential consistency is a very important concept and is widely studied in the fields of computer architecture, and distributed systems. It reduces a parallel system to a serial system with one processor by equating the execution on a parallel system with the execution on a sequential system. An important point to note is that SC does not mean that the outcome of the execution of a set of parallel programs is the same all the time. This depends on the way that the threads are interleaved, and the time of arrival of the threads. All that it says that certain outcomes are not allowed.

Weak Consistency (WC)*

The implementation of SC comes at a cost. It makes software simple, but it makes hardware very slow. To support SC it is often necessary to wait for a read or write to complete, before the next read or write can be sent to the memory system. A write request W *completes* when all subsequent reads by any processor will get the value that W has written, or the value written by a later write to the same location. A read request completes, after it reads the data, and the write request that originally wrote the data completes.

These requirements/restrictions become a bottleneck in high performance systems. Hence, the computer architecture community has moved to *weak memory models* that violate SC. A weak memory model will allow the outcome (t1,t2)=(1,0) in the following multithreaded code snippet.

```
Thread 1:                        Thread 2:
x = 1                            t1 = y
y = 1                            t2 = x
```

Definition 126
A weakly consistent (WC) memory model does not obey SC. It typically allows arbitrary memory orderings.

There are different kinds of weak memory models. Let us look at a generic variant, and call it *weak consistency* (WC). Let us now try to find out why WC allows the (1,0) outcome. Assume that thread 1 is running on core 1, and thread 2 is running on core 2. Moreover, assume that the memory location corresponding to x is near core 2, and the memory location corresponding to y is near core 1. Also assume that it takes tens of cycles to send a request from the vicinity of core 1 to core 2, and the delay is variable. Let us first investigate the behaviour of the pipeline of core 1. From the point of view of the pipeline of core 1, once a memory write request is handed over to the memory system, the memory write instruction is deemed to have finished. The instruction moves on to the RW stage. Hence, in this case, the processor will hand over the write to x to the memory system in the nth cycle, and subsequently pass on the write to y in the $(n+1)^{th}$ cycle. The write to y will reach the memory location of y quickly, while the write to x will take a long time.

In the meanwhile, core 2 will try to read the value of y. Assume that the read request arrives at the memory location of y just after the write request (to y) reaches it. Thus, we will get the new value of y, which is equal to 1. Subsequently, core 2 will issue a read to x. It is possible that the read to x reaches the memory location of x just before the write to x reaches it. In this case, it will fetch the old value of x, which is 0. Thus, the outcome (1,0) is possible in a weak memory model.

Now, to avoid this situation, we could have waited for the write to x to complete fully, before issuing the write request to y. It is true that in this case, this would have been the right thing to do. However, in general when we are writing to shared memory locations, other threads are not reading them at exactly the same point of time. We have no way of distinguishing both the situations at run time since processors do not share their memory access patterns between each other. Hence, in the interest of performance, it is not worthwhile to delay every memory request till the previous memory requests complete. High performance implementations thus prefer memory models that allow memory accesses from the same thread to be reordered by the memory system. We shall investigate ways of avoiding the (1,0) outcome in the next subsection.

Let us summarise our discussion that we have had on weak memory models by defining the assumptions that most processors make. Most processors assume that a memory request completes instantaneously at some point of time after it leaves the pipeline. Furthermore, all the threads assume that a memory request completes instantaneously at exactly the same point of time. This property of a memory request is known as *atomicity*. Secondly, we need to note that the order of completion of memory requests might differ from their program order. When the order of completion is the same as the program order of each thread, the memory model obeys SC. If the completion order is different from the program order, then the memory model is a variant of WC.

Definition 127

A memory request is said to be atomic *or observe* atomicity, *when it is perceived to execute instantaneously by all threads at some point of time after it is issued.*

Important Point 17

To be precise, for every memory request, there are three events of interest namely start, finish, *and* completion. *Let us consider a write request. The request* starts *when the instruction sends the request to the L1 cache in the MA stage. The request* finishes, *when the instruction moves to the RW stage. In modern processors, there is no guarantee that the write would have reached the target memory location when the memory request* finishes. *The point of time at which the write request reaches the memory location, and the write is visible to all the processors, is known as the time of* completion. *In simple processors, the time of completion of a request, is in between the start and finish times. However, in high performance processors, this is not the case. This concept is shown in the following illustration.*

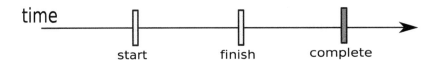

What about a read request? Most readers will naively assume that the completion time of a read is between the start and finish times, because it needs to return with the value of the memory location. This is however not strictly true. A read might return the value of a write that has not completed. In a memory model that requires write atomicity (illusion of writes completing instantaneously), a read completes, only when the corresponding write request completes. All the memory consistency models that assume write atomicity are defined using properties of the memory access completion order.

Trivia 4

Here, is an incident from your author's life. He had 200 US dollars in his bank account. He had gotten a cheque for 300$ from his friend. He went to his bank's nearest ATM, and deposited the cheque. Three days later, he decided to pay his rent (400$). He wrote a cheque to his landlord, and sent it to his postal address. A day later, he got an angry phone call from his landlord informing him that his cheque had bounced. How was this possible?

Your author then enquired. It had so happened that because of a snow storm, his bank was not able to send people to collect cheques from the ATM. Hence, when his landlord deposited the cheque, the bank account did not have sufficient money.

This example is related with the problem of memory consistency. Your author leaving his house to drop the cheque in the ATM is the start *time. He finished* the job when he dropped the cheque in the *ATM's drop box. However, the* completion time *was 5 days later, when the amount was actually credited to his account. Concurrently, another thread (his landlord) deposited his cheque, and it bounced. This is an example of* weak consistency *in real life.*

There is an important point to note here. In a weak memory model, the ordering between independent memory operations in the same thread is not respected. For example, when we wrote to x, and then to y, thread 2 perceived them to be in the reverse order. However, the ordering of operations of dependent memory instructions belonging to the same thread is always respected. For example, if we set the value of a variable x to 1, and later read it in the same thread. We will either get 1 or the value written by a later write to x. All the other threads will perceive the memory requests to be in the same order. There is NEVER any memory order violation between between dependent memory accesses by the same thread (refer to Figure 11.7).

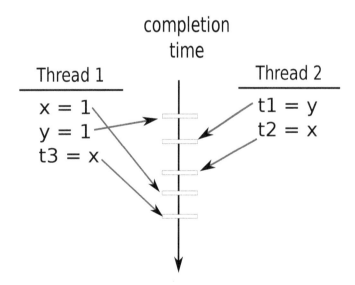

Figure 11.7: Actual completion time of memory requests in a multithreaded program

Examples

Let us now illustrate the difficulty with using a weak memory model that does not obey any ordering rules. Let us write our program to add numbers in parallel assuming a sequentially consistent system. Note that here we do not use OpenMP because OpenMP does a lot behind the scenes to ensure that programs run correctly in machines with weak memory models. Let us define a *parallel* construct that runs a block of code in parallel, and a getThreadId() function that returns the identifier of the thread. The range of the thread ids is from 0 to $N - 1$. The code for the parallel add function is shown in Example 125. We assume that before the parallel section begins, all the arrays are initialised to 0. In the parallel section, each thread adds its portion of numbers, and writes the result to its corresponding entry in the array, *partialSums*. Once, it is done, it sets its entry in the *finished* array to 1.

Let us now consider the thread that needs to aggregate the results. It needs to wait for all the threads to finish the job of computing the partial sums. It does this by waiting till all the entries of the *finished* array are equal to 1. Once, it establishes that all the entries in the *finished* array are equal to 1, it proceeds to add all the partial sums to get the final result. The reader can readily verify that if we assume a sequentially consistent system then this piece of code executes correctly. She needs to note that we compute the result, only when we read all the entries in the array *finished* to be 1. An entry in the *finished* array is equal to 1, if the partial sum is computed, and written to the *partialSums* array. Since we add the elements of the *partialSums* array to compute the final result, we can conclude that it is calculated correctly. Note that this is not a formal proof (left as an exercise for the reader).

Example 125

Write a shared memory program to add a set of numbers in parallel on a sequentially consistent machine.
Answer: *Let us assume that all the numbers are already stored in an array called numbers. The array numbers has SIZE entries. The number of parallel threads is given by N.*

```
/* variable declaration */
int partialSums[N];
int finished[N];
int numbers[SIZE];
int result = 0;
int doneInit = 0;

/* initialise all the elements in  partialSums and finished to 0 */
...
doneInit = 1;

/* parallel section */
parallel {
      /* wait till initialisation */
      while (!doneInit()){};

      /* compute the partial sum */
      int myId =          getThreadId();
      int startIdx = myId * SIZE/N;
      int endIdx = startIdx + SIZE/N;
      for(int jdx = startIdx; jdx < endIdx; jdx++)
```

```
                        partialSums[myId] += numbers[jdx];

        /* set an entry in the finished array */
        finished[myId] = 1;
}

/* wait till all the threads are done */
do {
        flag = 1;
        for (int i=0; i < N; i++){
                if(finished[i] == 0){
                        flag = 0;
                        break;
                }
        }
} while (flag == 0);

/* compute the final result */
for(int idx=0; idx < N; idx++)
        result += partialSums[idx];
```

Now, let us consider a weak memory model. We implicitly assumed in our example with sequential consistency that when the last thread reads $finished[i]$ to be 1, $partialSums[i]$ contains the value of the partial sum. However, this assumption does not hold if we assume a weak memory model because the memory system might reorder the writes to $finished[i]$ and $partialSums[i]$. It is thus possible that the write to the $finished$ array happens before the write to the $partialSums$ array in a system with a weak memory model. In this case, the fact that $finished[i]$ is equal to 1 does not guarantee that $partialSums[i]$ contains the updated value. This distinction is precisely what makes sequential consistency extremely programmer friendly.

Important Point 18

In a weak memory model, the memory accesses issued by the same thread are always perceived to be in program order by that thread. However, the order of memory accesses can be perceived differently by other threads.

Let us come back to the problem of ensuring that our example to add numbers in parallel runs correctly. We observe that the only way out of our quagmire is to have a mechanism to ensure that the write to $partialSums[i]$ is completed before another threads reads $finished[i]$ to be 1. We can use a generic instruction known as a *fence*. This instruction ensures that all the reads and writes issued before the fence complete before any read or write after the fence begins. Trivially, we can convert a weak memory model to a sequentially consistent one by inserting a fence after every instruction. However, this can induce a large overhead. It is best to introduce a minimal number of fence instructions as and when required. Let us look at our example for adding a set of numbers in parallel for weak memory models by adding fence instructions.

Example 126
Write a shared memory program to add a set of numbers in parallel on a machine with a weak memory model.
Answer: *Let us assume that all the numbers are already stored in an array called numbers. The array numbers has SIZE entries. The number of parallel threads is given by N.*

```
/* variable declaration */
int partialSums[N];
int finished[N];
int numbers[SIZE];
int result = 0;

/* initialise all the elements in  partialSums and finished to 0 */
...

/* fence */
/* ensures that the parallel section can read the initialised arrays */
fence();

/* All the data is present in all the arrays at this point */
/* parallel section */
parallel {
        /* get the current thread id */
        int myId =          getThreadId();

        /* compute the partial sum */
        int startIdx = myId * SIZE/N;
        int endIdx = startIdx + SIZE/N;
        for(int jdx = startIdx; jdx < endIdx; jdx++)
                partialSums[myId] += numbers[jdx];

        /* fence */
        /* ensures that finished[i] is written after
           partialSums[i] */
        fence();

        /* set the value of done */
        finished[myId] = 1;
}

/* wait till all the threads are done */
do {
        flag = 1;
        for (int i=0; i < N; i++){
                if(finished[i] == 0){
                        flag = 0;
```

```
                              break;
                    }
            }
    } while (flag == 0) ;

    /* sequential section */
    for(int idx=0; idx < N; idx++)
            result += partialSums[idx];
```

Example 126 shows the code for a weak memory model. The code is more or less the same as it was for the sequentially consistent memory model. The only difference is that we have added two additional fence instructions. We assume a function called $fence()$ that internally invokes a fence instruction. We first call $fence()$ before invoking all the parallel threads. This ensures that all the writes for initialising data structures have completed. After that we start the parallel threads. The parallel threads finish the process of computing and writing the partial sum, and then we invoke the fence operation again. This ensures that before $finished[myId]$ is set to 1, all the partial sums have been computed and written to their respective locations in memory. Secondly, if the the last thread reads $finished[i]$ to be 1, then we can say for sure that the value of $partialSums[i]$ is up to date and correct. Hence, this program executes correctly, in spite of a weak memory model.

We thus observe that weak memory models do not sacrifice on correctness if the programmer is aware of them, and inserts fences at the right places. Nonetheless, it is necessary for programmers to be aware of weak memory models, and they need to also understand that a lot of subtle bugs in parallel programs occur because programmers do not take the underlying memory model into account. Weak memory models are currently used by most processors because they allow us to build high performance memory systems. In comparison, sequential consistency is very restrictive, and other than the MIPS R10000 [Yeager, 1996] no other major vendor offers machines with sequential consistency. All our current x86 and ARM based machines use different versions of weak memory models.

11.4.4 Physical View of Memory

Overview

We have looked at two important aspects of the logical view of a memory system for multiprocessors namely coherence, and consistency. We need to implement a memory system that respects both of these properties. In this section, we shall study the design space of multiprocessor memory systems, and provide an overview of the design alternatives. We shall observe that there are two ways of designing a cache for a multiprocessor memory system. The first design is called a *shared cache*, where a single cache is shared among multiple processors. The second design uses a set of *private caches*, where each processor or set of processors typically have a private cache. All the private caches co-operate to provide the illusion of a shared cache. This is known as *cache coherence*.

We shall study the design of shared caches in Section 11.4.5, and private caches in Section 11.4.6. Subsequently, we shall briefly look at ensuring memory consistency in Section 11.4.7. We shall conclude that an efficient implementation of a given consistency model such as sequential, or weak consistency is difficult, and is a subject of study in an advanced computer architecture course. In this book, we propose a simple solution to this problem, and request the reader to look at research papers for more information. The casual reader can skip most of this section without any loss in continuity. Subsequently, we shall summarise the main results, observations, and insights; it is suitable for all our readers.

Design of a Multiprocessor Memory System – Shared and Private Caches

Let us start out by considering the first level cache. We can give every processor its individual instruction cache. Instructions represent read only data, and typically do not change during the execution of the program. Since sharing is not an issue here, each processor can benefit from its small private instruction cache. The main problem is with the data caches. There are two possible ways to design a data cache. We can either have a shared cache, or a private cache. A shared cache is a single cache that is accessible to all the processors. A *private cache* is accessible to either only one processor, or a set of processors. It is possible to have a hierarchy of shared caches, or a hierarchy of private caches as shown in Figure 11.8. We can even have combinations of shared and private caches in the same system.

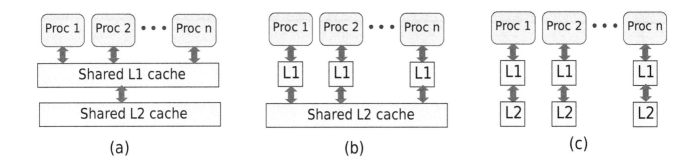

Figure 11.8: Examples of systems with shared and private caches

Let us now evaluate the tradeoffs between a shared and private cache. A shared cache is accessible to all the processors, and contains a single entry for a cached memory location. The communication protocol is simple, and is like any regular cache access. The additional complexity arises mainly from the fact that we need to properly schedule the requests coming from different individual processors. However, at the cost of simplicity, a shared cache has its share of problems. To service requests coming from all the processors, a shared cache needs to have a lot of read and write ports for handling requests simultaneously. Unfortunately, the size of a cache increases approximately as a square of the number of ports [Tarjan et al., 2006]. Additionally, the shared cache needs to accommodate the working sets of all the currently running threads. Hence, shared caches tend to become very large and slow. Because of physical constraints, it becomes difficult to place a shared cache close to all the processors. In comparison, private caches are typically much smaller, service requests for fewer cores, and have a lower number of read/write ports. Hence, they can be placed close to their associated processors. A private cache is thus much faster because it can be placed closer to a processor and is also much smaller in size.

To solve the problems with shared caches, designers often use private caches, especially in the higher levels of the memory hierarchy. A private cache can only be accessed by either one processor, or a small set of processors. They are small, fast, and consume a lesser amount of power. The major problem with private caches is that they need to provide the illusion of a shared cache to the programmer. For example, let us consider a system with two processors, and a private data cache associated with each processor. If one processor writes to a memory address, x, the other processor needs to be aware of the write. However, if it only accesses its private cache, then it will never be aware of a write to address x. This means that a write to address x is lost, and thus the system is not coherent. Hence, there is a need to tie the private caches of all the processors such that they look like one unified shared cache, and observe the rules of coherence. Coherence in the context of caches, is popularly known as *cache coherence*. Maintaining cache coherence represents an additional source of complexity for private caches, and limits the scalability of this approach. It works well for small private caches. However, for larger private caches, the overhead of maintaining coherence becomes prohibitive. For large lower level caches, the shared cache is more appropriate. Secondly, there is typically some data replication across multiple private caches. This wastes space.

Definition 128
Coherence in the context of a set of private caches is known as cache coherence.

By implementing a cache coherence protocol, it is possible to convert a set of disjoint private caches to appear as a shared cache to software. Let us now outline the major tradeoffs between shared and private caches in Table 11.3.

Attribute	Private Cache	Shared Cache
Area	low	high
Speed	fast	slow
Proximity to the processor	near	far
Scalability in size	low	high
Data replication	yes	no
Complexity	high (needs cache coherence)	low

Table 11.3: Comparison of shared and private caches

From the table it is clear that the first level cache should ideally be private because we desire low latency and high throughput. However, the lower levels need to be larger in size, and service a significantly lesser number of requests, and thus they should comprise of shared caches. Let us now describe the design of coherent private caches, and large shared caches. To keep matters simple we shall only consider a single level private cache, and not consider hierarchical private caches. They introduce additional complexity, and are best covered in an advanced textbook on computer architecture.

Let us discuss the design of shared caches first because they are simpler. Before proceeding further, let us review where we stand.

Way Point 11

1. *We defined a set of correctness requirements for caches in Section 11.4.1. They were termed as coherence and consistency.*

2. *In a nutshell, both the concepts place constraints on reordering memory requests in the memory system. The order and semantics of requests to the same memory location is referred to as coherence, and the semantics of requests to different memory locations by the same thread is referred to as consistency.*

3. *For ensuring that a memory system is consistent with a certain model of memory, we need to ensure that the hardware follows a set of rules with regards to reordering memory requests issued by the same program. This can be ensured by having additional circuitry that stalls all the memory requests, till a set of memory requests issued in the past complete. Secondly, programmer support is also required for making guarantees about the correctness of a program.*

4. *There are two approaches for designing caches – shared or private. A shared cache has a single physical location for each memory location. Consequently, maintaining coherence is trivial. However, it is not a scalable solution because of high contention, and high latency.*

5. *Consequently, designers often use private caches at least for the L1 level. In this case, we need to explicitly ensure cache coherence.*

11.4.5   Shared Caches

In the simplest embodiment of a shared cache, we can implement it as a regular cache in a uniprocessor. However, this will prove to be a very bad approach in practice. The reason for this is that in a uniprocessor, only one thread accesses the cache; however, in a multiprocessor multiple threads might access the cache, and thus we need to provide more bandwidth. If all the threads need to access the same data and tag array, then either requests have to stall or we have to increase the number of ports in the arrays. This will have very negative consequences in terms of area and power. Lastly, cache sizes (especially L2 and L3) are roughly doubling as per Moore's law. As of 2012, on-chip caches can be as large as 4-8 MB. If we have a single tag array for the entire cache, then it will be very large and slow. Let us define the term *last level cache* (LLC) as the on chip cache that has the lowest position in the memory hierarchy (with main memory being the lowest). For example, if a multicore processor has an on-chip L3 cache that is connected to main memory, then the LLC is the L3 cache. We shall use the term LLC frequently from now onwards.

To create a multi-megabyte LLC that can simultaneously support multiple threads, we need to split it into multiple subcaches. Let us assume that we have a 4 MB LLC. In a typical design, this will be split into 8-16 smaller subcaches. Thus each subcache will be 256-512 KB in size, which is an acceptable size. Each such subcache is a cache in its own right, and is known as a *cache bank*. Hence, we have in effect split a large cache into a set of cache banks. A cache bank can either be direct mapped, or can be set associative.

There are two steps in accessing a multibank cache. We first calculate the bank address, and then perform a regular cache access at the bank. Let us explain with an example. Let us consider a 16-bank, 4 MB cache. Each bank thus contains 256 KB of data. Now 4 MB $= 2^{22}$ bytes. We can thus dedicate bits 19-22 for choosing the bank address. Note that bank selection is independent of associativity in this case. After choosing a bank, we can split the remaining 28 bits between the offset within the block, set index, and tag.

There are two advantages of dividing a cache into multiple banks. The first is that we decrease the amount of contention at each bank. If we have 4 threads, and 16 banks, then the probability that 2 threads access the same bank is low. Secondly, since each bank is a smaller cache, it is more power efficient, and faster. We have thus achieved our twin aims of supporting multiple threads, and designing a fast cache. We shall look at the problem of placing processors, and cache banks in a multicore processor in Section 11.6.

11.4.6   Coherent Private Caches

Overview of a snoopy Protocol

The aim here is to make a set of private caches behave as if it is one large shared cache. From the point of view of software we should not be able to figure out whether a cache is private or shared. A conceptual diagram of the system is shown in Figure 11.9. It shows a set of processors along with their associated caches. The set of caches form a *cache group*. The entire cache group needs to appear as one cache.

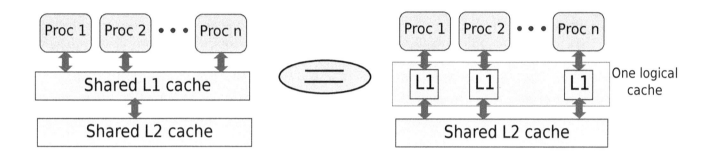

Figure 11.9: A system with many processors and their private caches

These caches are connected via an interconnection network, which can range from a simple shared bus type topology to more complex topologies. We shall look at the design of different interconnection networks in Section 11.6. In this section, let us assume that all the caches are connected to a shared bus. A shared bus allows a single writer and multiple readers at any point of time. If one cache writes a message to the bus, then all the other caches can read it. The topology is shown in Figure 11.10. Note that the bus gives exclusive access to only one cache at any point of time for writing a message. Consequently, all the caches perceive the same order of messages. A protocol that implements cache coherence with caches connected on a shared bus is known as a *snoopy protocol*.

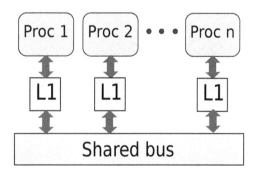

Figure 11.10: Caches connected with a shared bus

Let us now consider the operation of the snoopy protocol from the point of view of the two axioms of coherence – writes always complete (completion axiom), and writes to the same block are seen in the same order by all processors (order axiom). If cache i, wishes to perform a write operation on a block, then this write needs to be ultimately visible to all the other caches. We need to do this to satisfy the completion axiom, because we are not allowed to lose a write request. Secondly, different writes to the same block need to arrive at all the caches that might contain the block in the same order (order axiom). This ensures that for any given block, all the caches perceive the same order of updates. The shared bus automatically satisfies this requirement (the order axiom).

We present the design of two snoopy protocols – write-update and write-invalidate.

Write-Update Protocol

Let us now design a protocol, were a private cache keeps a copy of a write request, and broadcasts the write request to all the caches. This strategy ensures that a write is never lost, and the write messages to the same block are perceived in the same order by all the caches. This strategy requires us to broadcast, whenever we want to write. This is a large additional overhead; however, this strategy will work. Now, we need to incorporate reads into our protocol. A read to a location, x, can first check the private cache to see if a copy of it is already available. If a valid copy is available, then the value can be forwarded to the requesting processor. However, if there is a cache miss, then it is possible that it might be present with another sister cache in the cache group, or it might need to be fetched from the lower level. We need to first check if the value is present with a sister cache. We follow the same process here. The cache broadcasts a read request to all the caches. If any of the caches, has the value, then it replies, and sends the value to the requesting cache. The requesting cache inserts the value, and forwards it to the processor. However, if it does not get any reply from any other cache, then it initiates a read to the lower level.

This protocol is known as the write-update protocol. Each cache block needs to maintain three states, M, S, and I. M refers to the modified state. It means that the cache has modified the block. S(shared) means that the cache has not modified the block, and I(invalid) denotes the fact that the block does not contain valid data.

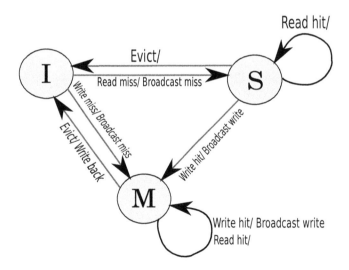

Figure 11.11: State transition diagram in the write-update protocol

Figure 11.11 shows a finite state machine (FSM) for each cache block. This FSM is executed by the cache controller. The format for state transitions is *event / action*. If the cache controller is sent an *event*, then it takes a corresponding *action*, which may include a state transition. Note that in some cases, the action field is blank. This means that in those cases, no action is taken. Note that the state of a cache block is a part of its entry in the tag array. If a block is not present in the cache, then its state is assumed to be invalid (I). Lastly, it is important to mention that Figure 11.11 shows the transitions for events generated by the processor. It does not show the actions for events sent over the bus by other caches in the cache group. Now, let us discuss the protocol in detail.

All blocks, initially are in the I state. If there is a read miss then it moves to the S state. We additionally need to broadcast the read miss to all the caches in the cache group, and either get the value from a sister cache, or from the lower level. Note that we give first preference to a sister cache, because it might have modified the block without writing it back to the lower level. Similarly, if there is a write miss in the I state, then we need to read the block from another sister cache if it is available, and move to the M state. If no other sister cache has the block, then we need to read the block from the lower level of the memory hierarchy.

If there is a read hit in the S state, then we can seamlessly pass the data to the processor. However, if we need to write to the block in the S state, we need to broadcast the write to all the other caches such that they get the updated value. Once, the cache gets a copy of its write request from the bus, it can write the value to the block, and change its state to M. To evict a block in the S state, we need to just evict it from the cache. It is not necessary to write back its value because the block has not been modified.

Now, let us consider the M state. If we need to read a block in the M state, then we can read it from the cache, and send the value to the processor. There is no need to send any message. However, if we wish to write to it, then it is necessary to send a write request on the bus. Once, the cache sees its own write request arrive on the shared bus, it can write its value to the memory location in its private cache. To evict a block in the M state, we need to write it back to the lower level in the memory hierarchy, because it has been modified.

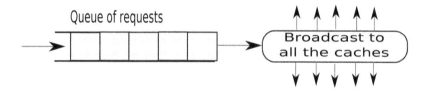

Figure 11.12: The bus arbiter

Every bus has a dedicated structure called an *arbiter* that receives requests to use the bus from different caches. It allots the bus to the caches in FIFO order. A schematic of the bus arbiter is shown in Figure 11.12. It is a very simple structure. It contains a queue of requests to transmit on the bus. Each cycle it picks a request from the queue, and gives permission to the corresponding cache to transmit a message on the bus.

Let us now consider a sister cache. Whenever it gets a *miss* message from the bus, it checks its cache to find if it has the block. If there is a cache hit, then it sends the block on the bus, or directly to the requesting cache. If it receives the notification of a write by another cache, then it updates the contents of the block if it is present in its cache.

Directory Protocol

Note that in the snoopy protocol we always broadcast a write, a read miss, or a write miss. This is strictly not required. We need to send a message to only those caches that contain a copy of the block. The *directory protocol* uses a dedicated structure called a directory to maintain this information. For each block address, the directory maintains a list of *sharers*. A sharer is the id of a cache that might contain the block. The list of sharers is in general a superset of caches that might contain the given block. We can maintain the list of sharers as a bit vector (1 bit per sharer). If a bit is 1, then a cache contains a copy, otherwise it does not.

The write-update protocol with a directory gets modified as follows. Instead of broadcasting data on the bus, a cache sends all of its messages to the directory. For a read or write miss, the directory fetches the block from a sister cache if it has a copy. It then forwards the block to the requesting cache. Similarly, for a write, the directory sends the write message to only those caches that might have a copy of the block. The list of sharers needs to be updated when a cache inserts or evicts a block. Lastly, to maintain coherence the directory needs to ensure that all the caches get messages in the same order, and no message is ever lost. The directory protocol minimises the number of messages that need to be sent, and is thus more scalable.

Definition 129

snoopy Protocol *In a snoopy protocol, all the caches are connected to a shared bus. A cache broadcasts each message to the rest of the caches.*

Directory Protocol *In a directory protocol, we reduce the number of messages by adding a dedicated structure known as a* directory. *The directory maintains the list of caches that might potentially contain a copy of the block. It sends messages for a given block address to only the caches in the list.*

Question 8
Why is it necessary to wait for the broadcast from the bus to perform a write?
Answer: *Let us assume this is not the case, and processor 1, wishes to write 1 to x, and processor 2 wishes to write 2 to x. They will then first write 1 and 2 to their copies of x respectively, and then broadcast the write. Thus, the writes to x will be seen in different orders by both the processors. This violates the order axiom. However, if they wait for a copy of their write request to arrive from the bus, then they write to x in the same order. The bus effectively resolves the conflict between processor 1 and 2, and orders one request after the other.*

Write-Invalidate Protocol

We need to note that broadcasting a write request for every single write is an unnecessary overhead. It is possible that most of the blocks might not be shared in the first place. Hence, there is no need to send an extra message on every write. Let us try to reduce the number of messages in the write update protocol by proposing the *write-invalidate protocol*. Here again, we can either use the snoopy protocol, or the directory protocol. Let us show an example with the snoopy protocol.

Let us maintain three states for each block – M, S, and I. Let us however, change the meaning of our states. The invalid state (I) retains the same meaning. It means that the entry is effectively not present in the cache. The shared state (S) means that a cache can read the block, but it cannot write to it. It is possible to have multiple copies of the same block in different caches in the shared state. Since the shared state assumes that the block is read-only, having multiple copies of the block does not affect cache coherence. The M (modified) state signifies the fact that the cache can write to the block. If a block is in the M state, then all the other caches in the cache group need to have the block in the I state. No other cache is allowed to have a valid copy of the block in the S or M states. This is where the write-invalidate protocol differs from the write-update protocol. It allows either only one writer at a time, or multiple readers at a time. It never allows a reader and a writer to co-exist at the same time. By restricting the number of caches that have write access to a block at any point of time, we can reduce the number of messages.

The basic insight is as follows. The write-update protocol did not have to send any messages on a read hit. It sent extra messages on a write hit, which we want to eliminate. It needed to send extra messages because multiple caches could read or write a block concurrently. For the write-invalidate protocol, we have eliminated this behaviour. If a block is in the M state, then no other cache contains a valid copy of the block.

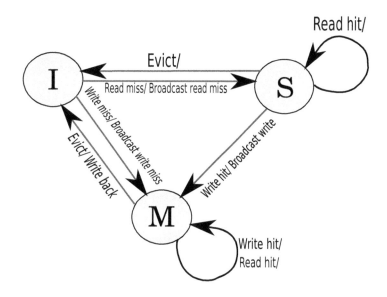

Figure 11.13: State transition diagram of a block due to actions of the processor

Figure 11.13 shows the state transition diagram because of actions of the processor. The state transition diagram is mostly the same as the state transition diagram of the write-update protocol. Let us look at the differences. The first is that we define three types of messages that are put on the bus namely *write*, *write miss*, and *read miss*. When we transition from the I to the S state, we place a read miss on the bus. If a sister cache does not reply with the data, the cache controller reads the block from the lower level. The semantics of the S state remains the same. To write to a block in the S state, we need to transition to the M state, after writing a *write* message on the bus. Now, when a block is in the M state, we are assured of the fact that no other cache contains a valid copy. Hence, we can freely read and write a block in the M state. It is not necessary to send any messages on the bus. If the processor decides to evict a block in the M state, then it needs to write its data to the lower level.

Figure 11.14 shows the state transitions due to messages received on the bus. In the S state, if we get a *read miss*, then it means that another cache wants read access to the block. Any of the caches that contains the block sends it the contents of the block. This process can be orchestrated as follows. All the caches that have a copy of the block try to get access to the bus. The first cache that gets access to the bus sends a copy of the block to the requesting cache. The rest of the caches immediately get to know that the contents of the block have been transferred. They subsequently stop trying. If we get a *write* or *write miss* message in the S state, then the block transitions to the I state.

Let us now consider the M state. If some other cache sends a *write miss* message then the cache

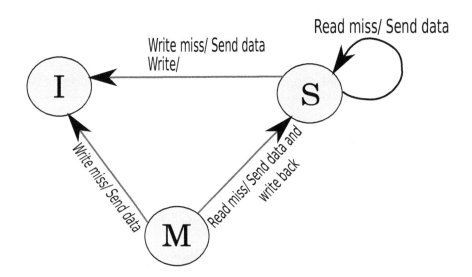

Figure 11.14:   State transition diagram of a block due to messages on the bus

controller of the cache that contains the block, sends the contents of the block to it, and transitions to the I state. However, if it gets a *read miss*, then it needs to perform a sequence of steps. We assume that we can seamlessly evict a block in the S state. Hence, it is necessary to write the data to the lower level before moving to the S state. Subsequently, the cache that originally has the block also sends the contents of the block to the requesting cache, and transitions the state of the block to the S state.

Write-Invalidate Protocol with a Directory

Implementing the write-invalidate protocol with a directory is fairly trivial. The state transition diagrams remain almost the same. Instead of broadcasting a message, we send it to the directory. The directory sends the message to the sharers of the block.

The life cycle of a block is as follows. Whenever, a block is brought in from the lower level, a directory entry is initialised. At this point it has only one sharer, which is the cache that brought it from the lower level. Now, if there are read misses to the block, then the directory keeps adding sharers. However, if there is a write miss, or a processor decides to write to the block, then it sends a *write* or *write miss* message to the directory. The directory cleans the sharers list, and keeps only one sharer, which is the processor that is performing the write access. When a block is evicted, its cache informs the directory, and the directory deletes a sharer. When the set of sharers becomes empty, the directory entry can be removed.

It is possible to make improvements to the write-invalidate and update protocols by adding an additional state known as the exclusive (E) state. The E state can be the initial state for every cache block fetched from the lower level of the memory hierarchy. This state stores the fact that a block exclusively belongs to a cache. However, the cache has read-only access to it, and does not have write access to it. For an E to M transition, we do not have to send a *write miss* or *write* message on the bus, because the block is owned exclusively by one cache. We can seamlessly evict data from the E state if required. Implementing the MESI protocol is left as an exercise for the reader.

11.4.7   Implementing a Memory Consistency Model*

A typical memory consistency model specifies the types of re-orderings that are allowed between memory operations issued by the same thread. For example, in sequential consistency all read/write accesses are completed in program order, and all other threads also perceive the memory accesses of any thread in its program order. Let us give a simple solution to the problem of implementing sequential consistency first.

Overview of an Implementation of Sequential Consistency*

Let us build a memory system that is coherent, and provides certain guarantees. Let us assume that all the write operations are associated with a time of *completion*, and appear to execute instantaneously at the time of *completion*. It is not possible for any read operation to get the value of a write before it completes. After a write *completes*, all the read operations to the same address either get the value written by the write operation or a newer write operation. Since we assume a coherent memory, all the write operations to the same memory address are seen in the same order by all the processors. Secondly, each read operation returns the value written by the latest completed write to that address. Let us now consider the case in which processor 1 issues a write to address x, and at the same time processor 2 issues a read request to the same address, x. In this case, we have a concurrent read and write. The behaviour is not defined. The read can either get the value set by the concurrent write operation, or it can get the previous value. However, if the read operation gets the value set by the concurrent write operation, then all subsequent reads issued by any processor, need to get that value or a newer value. We can say that a read operation *completes*, once it has finished reading the value of the memory location, and the write that generated its data also completes.

Now, let us design a multiprocessor where each processor issues a memory request after all the previous memory requests that it had issued have completed. This means that after issuing a memory request (read/write), a processor waits for it to complete before issuing the next memory request. We claim that a multiprocessor with such processors is sequentially consistent. Let us now outline a brief informal proof.

Let us first introduce a theoretical tool called an *access graph*.

Access Graph*

Figure 11.15 shows the execution of two threads and their associated sequence of memory accesses. For each read or write access, we create a circle or node in the access graph (see Figure 11.15(c)). In this case, we add an arrow (or edge) between two nodes if one access follows the other in program order, or if there is a read-write dependence across two accesses from different threads. For example, if we set x to 5 in thread 1, and the read operation in thread 2, reads this value of x, there is a dependence between this read and write of x, and thus we add an arrow in the access graph. The arrow signifies that the destination request must complete after the source request.

Let us now define a *happens-before* relationship between nodes a and b, if there is a path from a to b in the access graph.

Definition 130

Let us define a happens-before *relationship between nodes a and b, if there is a path from a to b in the access graph. A happens-before relationship signifies that b must complete its execution after a completes.*

The access graph is a general tool and is used to reason about concurrent systems. It consists of a set of nodes, where each node is a dynamic instance of an instruction (most often a memory instruction). There

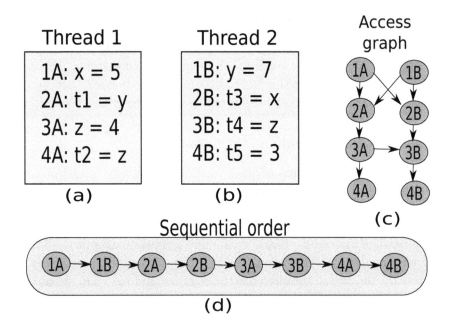

Figure 11.15: Graphical representation of memory accesses

are edges between nodes. An edge of the from $A \to B$ means that B needs to complete its execution after A. In our simple example in Figure 11.15 we have added two kinds of edges namely *program order* edges, and *causality* edges. Program order edges indicate the order of completion of memory requests in the same thread. In our system, where we wait for an instruction to complete, before executing the next instruction, there are edges between consecutive instructions of the same thread.

Causality edges are between load and store instructions across threads. For example, if a given instruction writes a value, and another instruction reads it in another thread, we add an edge from the store to the load.

To prove sequential consistency, we need to add additional edges to the access graph as follows (see [Arvind and Maessen, 2006]). Let us first assume that we have an *oracle*(a hypothetical entity that knows everything) with us. Now, since we assume coherent memory, all the stores to the same memory location are sequentially ordered. Furthermore, there is an order between loads and stores to the same memory location. For example, if we set x to 1, then set x to 3, then read $t1 = x$, and then set x to 5, there is a store-store-load-store order for the location, x. The oracle knows about such orderings between loads and stores for each memory location. Let us assume that the oracle adds the corresponding happens-before edges to our access graph. In this case the edge between the store and the load is a causality edge, and the store-store, and load-store edges are examples of *coherence edges*.

Next, let us describe how to use an access graph for proving properties of systems. First, we need to construct an access graph of a program for a given memory consistency model, $\mathcal{M}$, based on a given run of the program. We add coherence, and causality edges based on the memory access behaviour. Second, we add program order edges between instructions in the same thread based on the consistency model. For SC, we add edges between consecutive instructions, and for WC, we add edges between dependent instructions, and between regular instructions, and fences. It is very important to understand that the access graph is a theoretical tool, and it is most often not a practical tool. We shall reason about the properties of an access graph without actually building one for a given program, or system.

Now, if the access graph does not contain cycles, then we can arrange the nodes in a sequential order. Let us prove this fact. In the access graph, if there is a path from a to b, then let a be known as b's ancestor. We can generate a sequential order by following an iterative process. We first find a node, which does not have an ancestor. There has to be such a node because some operation must have been the first to complete (otherwise there is a cycle). We remove it from our access graph, and proceed to find another node that does not have any ancestors. We add each such node in our sequential order as shown in Figure 11.15(d). In each step the number of nodes in the access graph decreases by 1, till we are finally left with just one node, which becomes the last node in our sequential order. Now, let us consider the case when we do not find any node in the access graph that does not have an ancestor. This is only possible if there is a cycle in the access graph, and thus it is not possible.

Arranging the nodes in a sequential order is equivalent to proving that the access graph obeys the memory model that it is designed for. The fact that we can list the nodes in a sequential order without violating any happens-before relationships, means that the execution is equivalent to a uniprocessor executing each node in the sequential order one after the other. This is precisely the definition of a consistency model. Any consistency model consists of the ordering constraints between memory instructions, along with assumptions of coherence. The definition further implies that it should be possible for a uniprocessor to execute instructions in a sequential order without violating any of the happens-before relationships. This is precisely what we have achieved by converting the access graph to an equivalent sequential list of nodes. Now, the fact that program order, causality, and coherence edges are enough to specify a consistency model is more profound. For a detailed discussion, the reader is referred to the paper by Arvind and Maessen [Arvind and Maessen, 2006].

Hence, if an access graph (for memory model, $\mathcal{M}$) does not contain cycles, we can conclude that a given execution follows $\mathcal{M}$. If we can prove that all the possible access graphs that can be generated by a system are acyclic, then we can conclude that the entire system follows $\mathcal{M}$.

Proof of Sequential Consistency*

Let us thus prove that all possible access graphs (assuming SC) that can be generated by our simple system that waits for memory requests to complete before issuing subsequent memory requests are acyclic. Let us consider any access graph, G. We have to prove that it is possible to write all the memory accesses in G in a sequential order such that if node b is placed after node a, then there is no path from b to a in G. In other words, our sequential order respects the order of accesses as shown in the access graph.

Let us assume that the access graph has a cycle, and it contains a set of nodes, $\mathcal{S}$, belonging to the same thread, t_1. Let a be the earliest node in program order in $\mathcal{S}$, and b be the latest node in program order in $\mathcal{S}$. Clearly, a *happens before* b because we execute memory instructions in program order, and we wait for a request to complete before starting the next request in the same thread. For a cycle to form due to a causality edge, b needs to write to a value that is read by another memory read request (node), c, belonging to another thread. Alternatively, there can be a coherence edge between b and a node c belonging to another thread. Now, for a cycle to exist, c needs to *happen before* a. Let us assume that there are a chain of nodes between c and a and the last node in the chain of nodes is d. By definition, $d \notin t_1$. This means that either d writes to a memory location, and node a reads from it, or there is a coherence edge from d to a. Because there is a path from node b to node a (through c and d), it must be the case that the request associated with node b happens before the request of node a. This is not possible since we cannot execute the memory request associated with node b till node a's request completes. Thus, we have a contradiction, and a cycle is not possible in the access graph. Hence, the execution is in SC.

Now, let us clarify the notion of an *oracle*. The reader needs to understand that the problem here is not to generate a sequential order, it is to rather prove that a sequential order exists. Since we are solving the latter problem, we can always presume that a hypothetical entity adds additional edges to our access graph. The resulting sequential order respects program orders for each thread, causality and coherence-based happens-before relationships. It is thus a valid ordering.

Consequently, we can conclude that it is always possible to find a sequential order for threads in our system. Therefore, our multiprocessor is in SC. Now that we have proved that our system is sequentially consistent, let us describe a method to implement a multiprocessor with the assumptions that we have made. We can implement a system as shown in Figure 11.16.

Design of a Simple (yet impractical) Sequentially Consistent Machine*

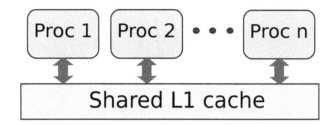

Figure 11.16: A simple sequentially consistent system

Figure 11.16 shows a design that has a large shared L1 cache across all the processors of a multiprocessor. There is only one copy of each memory location that can support only one read or write access at any single time. This ensures coherence. Secondly, a write completes, when it changes the value of its memory location in the L1 cache. Likewise, a read completes when it reads the value of the memory address in the L1 cache. We need to modify the simple in-order RISC pipeline described in Chapter 9 such that an instructions leaves the memory access (MA) stage only after it **completes** its read/write access. If there is a cache miss, then the instruction waits till the block comes to the L1 cache, and the access completes. This simple system ensures that memory requests from the same thread complete in program order, and is thus sequentially consistent.

Note that the system described in Figure 11.16 makes some unrealistic assumptions and is thus impractical. If we have 16 processors, and if the frequency of memory instructions is 1 in 3, then every cycle, 5-6 instructions will need to access the L1 cache. Hence, the L1 cache requires at least 6 read/write ports, which will make the structure too large and too slow. Additionally, the L1 cache needs to be large enough to contain the working sets of all the threads, which further makes the case for a very large and slow L1 cache. Consequently, a multiprocessor system with such a cache will be very slow in practice. Hence, modern processors opt for more high performance implementations with more complicated memory systems that have a lot of smaller caches. These caches co-operate among each other to provide the illusion of a larger cache (see Section 11.4.6).

It is fairly difficult to prove that a complex system follows sequential consistency(SC). Hence, designers opt to design systems with weak memory models. In this case, we need to prove that a *fence* instruction works correctly. If we take all the subtle corner cases that are possible with complicated designs, this also turns out to be a fairly challenging problem. Interested readers can take a look at pointers mentioned at the end of this chapter for research work in this area.

Implementing a Weak Consistency Model*

Let us consider the access graph for a weakly consistent system. We do not have edges to signify program order for nodes in the same thread. Instead, for nodes in the same thread, we have edges between regular read/write nodes and *fence* operations. We need to add causality and coherence edges to the access graph as we did for the case of SC.

An implementation of a weakly consistent machine needs to ensure that this access graph does not have cycles. We can prove that the following implementation does not introduce cycles to the access graph.

Let us ensure that a *fence* instruction starts after all the previous instructions in program order complete for a given thread. The *fence* instruction is a dummy instruction that simply needs to reach the end of the pipeline. It is used for timing purposes only. We stall the *fence* instruction in the MA stage till all the previous instructions complete. This strategy also ensures that no subsequent instruction reaches the MA stage. Once, all the previous instructions complete, the *fence* instruction proceeds to the RW stage, and subsequent instructions can issue requests to memory.

Summary of the Discussion on Implementing a Memory Consistency Model

Let us summarise the previous section on implementing memory consistency models for readers who decided to skip it. Implementing a memory consistency model such as sequential or weak consistency is possible by modifying the pipeline of a processor, and ensuring that the memory system sends an acknowledgement to the processor once it is done processing a memory request. Many subtle corner cases, are possible in high performance implementations and ensuring that they implement a given consistency model is fairly complicated.

11.4.8   Multithreaded Processors

Let us now look at a different method for designing multiprocessors. Up till now we have maintained that we need to have physically separate pipelines for creating multiprocessors. We have looked at designs that assign a separate program counter to each pipeline. However, let us look at a different approach that runs a set of threads on the same pipeline. This approach is known as multithreading. Instead of running separate threads on separate pipelines, we run them on the same pipeline. Let us illustrate this concept by discussing the simplest variant of multi-threading known as *coarse-grained multithreading*.

Definition 131

Multithreading is a design paradigm that proposes to run multiple threads on the same pipeline. A processor that implements multithreading is known as a multithreaded *processor.*

Coarse-Grained Multithreading

Let us assume that we wish to run four threads on a single pipeline. Recall that multiple threads belonging to the same process have their separate program counters, stacks, registers; yet, they have a common view of memory. All these four threads have their separate instruction streams, and it is necessary to provide an illusion that these four threads are running separately. Software should be oblivious of the fact that threads are running on a multithreaded processor. It should perceive that each thread has its dedicated CPU. Along with the traditional guarantees of coherence and consistency, we now need to provide an additional guarantee, which is that software should be oblivious to multithreading.

Let us consider a simple scheme, as shown in Figure 11.17.

Here, we run thread 1 for n cycles, then we switch to thread 2 and run it for n cycles, then we switch to thread 3, and so on. After executing thread 4 for n cycles, we start executing thread 1 again. To execute a thread we need to load its state or context. Recall that we had a similar discussion with respect to loading and unloading the state of a program in Section 9.8. We had observed that the context of the program comprises of the *flags* register, the program counter, and the set of registers. We had observed that it is not

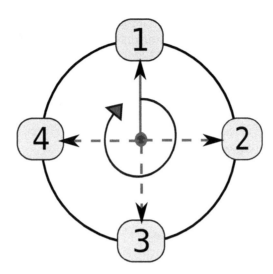

Figure 11.17: Conceptual view of coarse grain multithreading

necessary to keep track of main memory because the memory regions of different processes do not overlap, and in the case of multiple threads, we explicitly want all the threads to share the same memory space.

Instead of explicitly loading and unloading the context of a thread, we can adopt a simpler approach. We can save the context of a thread in the pipeline. For example, if we wish to support coarse-grained multithreading then we can have four separate *flags* registers, four program counters, and four separate register files (one per each thread). Additionally, we can have a dedicated register that contains the id of the currently running thread. For example, if we are running thread 2, then we use the context of thread 2, and if we are running thread 3, we use the context of thread 3. In this manner it is not possible for multiple threads to overwrite each other's state.

Let us now look at some subtle issues. It is possible that we can have instructions belonging to multiple threads at the same point of time in the pipeline. This can happen when we are switching from one thread to the next. Let us add a thread id field to the instruction packet, and further ensure that the forwarding and interlock logic takes the id of the thread into account. We never forward values across threads. In this manner it is possible to execute four separate threads on a pipeline with a negligible overhead of switching between threads. We do not need to engage the exception handler to save and restore the context of threads, or invoke the operating system to schedule the execution of threads.

Let us now look at coarse-grained multithreading in entirety. We execute n threads in quick succession, and in round robin order. Furthermore, we have a mechanism to quickly switch between threads, and threads do not corrupt each other's state. However, we still do not execute four threads simultaneously. Then, what is the advantage of this scheme?

Let us consider the case of memory intensive threads that have a lot of irregular accesses to memory. They will thus frequently have misses in the L2 cache, and their pipelines need to be stalled for 100-300 cycles till the values come back from memory. Out-of-order pipelines can hide some of this latency by executing some other instructions that are not dependent on the memory value. Nonetheless, it will also stall for a long time. However, at this point, if we can switch to another thread, then it might have some useful work to do. If that thread suffers from misses in the L2 cache also, then we can switch to another thread and finish some of its work. In this way, we can maximise the throughput of the entire system as a whole. We can envision two possible schemes. We can either switch periodically every n cycles, or switch to another thread upon an event such as an L2 cache miss. Secondly, we need not switch to a thread if it is waiting on a high latency event such as an L2 cache miss. We need to switch to a thread that has a pool of ready-to-execute instructions. It is possible to design a large number of heuristics for optimising the performance of a coarse-grained multithreaded machine.

Important Point 19

Let us differentiate between software threads *and* hardware threads. *A software thread is a subprogram that shares a part of its address space with other software threads. The threads can communicate with each other to co-operatively to achieve a common objective. In comparison, a hardware thread is defined as the instance of a software thread or a single threaded program running on a pipeline along with its execution state. A multithreaded processor supports multiple hardware threads on the same processor by splitting its resources across the threads. A software thread might physically be mapped to a separate processor, or to a hardware thread. It is agnostic to the entity that is used to execute it. The important point to be noted here is that a software thread is a programming language concept, whereas a hardware thread is physically associated with resources in a pipeline. We shall use the word "thread" for both software and hardware threads. The correct usage needs to be inferred from the context.*

Fine-Grained Multithreading

Fine-grained multithreading is a special case of coarse-grained multithreading where the switching interval, n, is a very small value. It is typically 1 or 2 cycles. This means that we quickly switch between threads. We can leverage grained multithreading to execute threads that are memory intensive. However, fine-grained multithreading is also useful for executing a set of threads that for example have long arithmetic operations such as division. In a typical processor, division operations and other specialised operations such as trigonometric or transcendental operations are slow (3-10 cycles). During this period when the original thread is waiting for the operation to finish, we can switch to another thread and execute some of its instructions in the pipeline stages that are otherwise unused. We can thus leverage the ability to switch between threads very quickly for reducing the idle time in scientific programs that have a lot of mathematical operations.

We can thus visualise fine-grained multithreading to be a more flexible form of coarse-grained multithreading where we can quickly switch between threads and utilise idle stages to perform useful work. Note that this concept is not as simple as it sounds. The devil is in the details. We need elaborate support for multithreading in all the structures in a regular in-order or out-of-order pipeline. We need to manage the context of each thread very carefully, and ensure that we do not omit instructions, and errors are not introduced. A thorough discussion on the implementation of multithreading is beyond the scope of this book.

The reader needs to appreciate that the logic for switching between threads is non-trivial. Most of the time the logic to switch between threads is a combination of time based criteria (number of cycles), and event based criteria (high latency event such as L2 cache miss or page fault). The heuristics have to be finely adjusted to ensure that the multithreaded processor performs well for a host of benchmarks.

Simultaneous Multithreading

For a single issue pipeline, if we can ensure that every stage is kept busy by using sophisticated logic for switching between threads, then we can achieve high efficiency. Recall that any stage in a single issue pipeline can process only one instruction per cycle. In comparison, a multiple issue pipeline can process multiple instructions per cycle. We had looked at multiple issue pipelines (both in-order and out-of-order) in

Section 9.11. Moreover, we had defined the number of issue slots to be equal to the number of instructions that can be processed by the pipeline every cycle. For example, a 3 issue processor, can at the most fetch, decode, and finally execute 3 instructions per cycle.

For implementing multithreading in multiple issue pipelines, we need to consider the nature of dependences between instructions in a thread also. It is possible that fine and coarse-grained schemes do not perform well because a thread cannot issue instructions to the functional units for all the issue slots. Such threads are said to have low instruction level parallelism. If we use a 4 issue pipeline, and the maximum IPC for each of our threads is 1 because of dependences in the program, then 3 of our issue slots will remain idle in each cycle. Thus the overall IPC of our system of 4 threads will be 1, and the benefits of multithreading will be limited.

Hence, it is necessary to utilise additional issue slots such that we can increase the IPC of the system as a whole. A naive approach is to dedicate one issue slot to each thread. Secondly, to avoid structural hazards, we can have four ALUs and allot one ALU to each thread. However, this is a suboptimal utilisation of the pipeline because a thread might not have an instruction to issue every cycle. It is best to have a more flexible scheme, where we dynamically partition the issue slots among the threads. This scheme is known as simultaneous multithreading (popularly known as SMT). For example, in a given cycle we might find 2 instructions from thread 2, and 1 instruction each from threads 3, and 4. This situation might reverse in the next cycle. Let us graphically illustrate this concept in Figure 11.18, and simultaneously also compare the SMT approach with fine and coarse-grained multithreading.

The columns in Figure 11.18 represent the issue slots for a multiple issue machine, and the rows represent the cycles. Instructions belonging to different threads have different colours. Figure 11.18(a) shows the execution of instructions in a coarse-grained machine, where each thread executes for two consecutive cycles. We observe that a lot of issue slots are empty because we do not find sufficient number of instructions that can execute. Fine-grained multithreading (shown in Figure 11.18(b)) also has the same problem. However, in an SMT processor, we are typically able to keep most of the issue slots busy, because we always find instructions from the set of available threads that are ready to execute. If one thread is stalled for some reason, other threads compensate by executing more instructions. In practice, all the threads do not have low ILP[1] phases simultaneously. Hence, the SMT approach has proven to be a very versatile and effective method for leveraging the power of multiple issue processors. Since the Pentium 4 (released in the late nineties), most of the Intel processors support different variants of simultaneous multithreading. In Intel's terminology SMT is known as hyperthreading . The latest (as of 2012) IBM Power 7 processor has 8 cores, where each core is a 4-way SMT (can run 4 threads per each core).

Note that the problem of selecting the right set of instructions to issue is very crucial to the performance of an SMT processor. Secondly, the memory bandwidth requirement of an n-way SMT processor is higher than that of an equivalent uniprocessor. The fetch logic is also far more complicated, because now we need to fetch from four separate program counters in the same cycle. Lastly, the issues of maintaining coherence, and consistency further complicate the picture. The reader can refer to the research papers mentioned in the "Further Reading" section at the end of this chapter.

11.5 SIMD Multiprocessors

Let us now discuss SIMD multiprocessors. SIMD processors are typically used for scientific applications, high intensity gaming, and graphics. They do not have a significant amount of general purpose utility. However, for a limited class of applications, SIMD processors tend to outperform their MIMD counterparts.

SIMD processors have a rich history. In the good old days we had processors arranged as arrays. Data typically entered through the first row, and first column of processors. Each processor acted on input

---

[1]ILP (instruction level parallelism, defined as the number of instructions that are ready to execute in parallel each cycle)

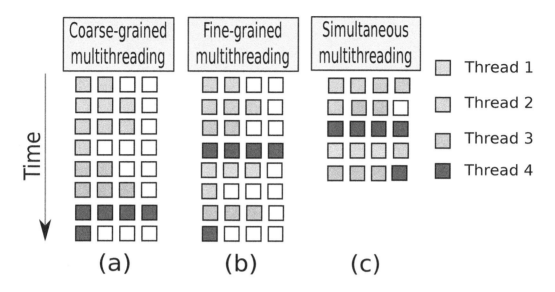

Figure 11.18: Instruction execution in multithreaded processors

messages, generated an output message, and sent the message to its neighbours. Such processors were known as *systolic arrays*. Systolic arrays were used for matrix multiplication, and other linear algebra operations. Subsequently, several vendors notably, Cray, incorporated SIMD instructions in their processors to design faster and more power efficient supercomputers. Nowadays, most of these early efforts have subsided. However, some aspects of classical SIMD computers where a single instruction operates on several streams of data, have crept into the design of modern processors.

We shall discuss an important development in the area of modern processor design, which is the incorporation of SIMD functional units, and instructions, in high-performance processors.

11.5.1   SIMD – Vector Processors

Background

Let us consider the problem of adding two n element arrays. In a single threaded implementation, we need to load the operands from memory, add the operands, and store the result in memory. Consequently, for computing each element of the destination array, we require two load instructions, one add instruction, and one store instruction. Traditional processors try to attain speedups by exploiting the fact that we can compute $(c[i] = a[i] + b[i])$, in parallel with $(c[j] = a[j] + b[j])$ because these two operations do not have any dependences between them. Hence, it is possible to increase IPC by executing many such operations in parallel.

Let us now consider superscalar processors. If they can issue 4 instructions per cycle, then their IPC can at the most be 4 times that of a single cycle processor. In practice, the peak speedup over a single cycle processor that we can achieve with such inherently parallel array processing operations is around 3 to 3.5 times for a 4 issue processor. Secondly, this method of increasing IPC by having wide issue widths is not scalable. We do not have 8 or 10 issue processors in practice because the logic of the pipeline gets very complicated, and the area/power overheads become prohibitive.

Hence, designers decided to have special support for vector operations that operate on large vectors (arrays) of data. Such processors were known as *vector processors*. The main idea here is to process an entire array of data at once. Normal processors use regular *scalar* data types such as integers and floating point numbers; whereas, vector processors use vector data types, which are essentially arrays of scalar data types.

Definition 132

A vector processor *considers a vector of primitive data types (integer or floating point numbers) as its basic unit of information. It can load, store, and perform arithmetic operations on entire vectors at once. Such instructions that operate on vectors of data, are known as* vector instructions.

One of the most iconic products that predominantly used vector processors was the Cray 1 Supercomputer. Such supercomputers were primarily used for scientific applications that mainly consisted of linear algebra operations. Such operations work on vectors of data and matrices, and are thus well suited to be run on vector processors. Sadly, beyond the realm of high intensity scientific computing, vector processors did not find a general purpose market till the late nineties.

In the late nineties, personal computers started to be used for research, and for running scientific applications. Secondly, instead of designing custom processors for supercomputers, designers started to use regular commodity processors for building supercomputers. Since then, the trend continued till the evolution of graphics processors. Most supercomputers between 1995 and 2010, consisted of thousands of commodity processors. Another important reason to have vector instructions in a regular processor was to support high intensity gaming. Gaming requires a massive amount of graphics processing. For example, modern games render complex scenes with multiple characters, and thousands of visual effects. Most of these visual effects such as illumination, shadows, animation, depth, and colour processing, are at its core basic linear algebra operations on matrices containing points or pixels. Due to these factors regular processors started to incorporate a limited amount of vector support. Specifically, the Intel processors provided the MMX, SSE 1-4 vector instruction sets, AMD processors provided the 3DNow! vector extensions, and ARM processors provide the ARM® Neon™ vector ISA. There are a lot of commonalities between these ISAs, and hence let us not focus on any specific ISA. Let us instead the discuss the broad principles behind the design and operation of vector processors.

11.5.2 Software Interface

Let us first consider the model of the machine. We need a set of vector registers. For example, the x86 SSE (Streaming SIMD Extensions) instruction set defines sixteen 128-bit registers (XMM0 ... XMM15). Each such register can contain four integers, or four floating point values. Alternatively, it can also contain eight 2-byte short integers, or sixteen 1-byte characters. On the same lines, every vector ISA defines additional vector registers that are wider than normal registers. Typically, each register can contain multiple floating point values. Hence, in our *SimpleRisc* ISA, let us define eight 128-bit vector registers: $vr0 \ldots vr7$.

Now, we need instructions to load, store, and operate on vector registers. For loading, vector registers, there are two options. We can either load values from contiguous memory locations, or from non-contiguous memory locations. The former case is more specific, and is typically suitable for array based applications, where all the array elements are anyway stored in contiguous memory locations. Most vector extensions to ISAs support this variant of the load instruction because of its simplicity, and regularity. Let us try to design such a vector load instruction *v.ld* for our *SimpleRisc* ISA. Let us consider the semantics shown in Table 11.4. Here, the *v.ld* instruction reads in the contents of the memory locations ([r1+12], [r1+16], [r1+20], [r1+ 24]) into the vector register $vr1$. In the table below note that $\langle vreg \rangle$ is a vector register.

Now, let us consider the case of matrices. Let us consider a 10,000 element matrix, $A[100][100]$, and assume that data is stored in row major order (see Section 3.2.2). Assume that we want to operate on two

Example	Semantics	Explanation
v.ld vr1, 12[r1]	v.ld ⟨vreg⟩, ⟨mem⟩	vr1 ← ([r1+12], [r1+16], [r1+20], [r1+ 24])

Table 11.4: Semantics of the contiguous variant of the vector load instruction

columns of the matrix. In this case, we have a problem because the elements in a column are not saved in contiguous locations. Hence, a vector load instruction that relies on the assumption that the input operands are saved in contiguous memory locations, will cease to work. We need to have dedicated support to fetch all the data for the locations in a column and save them in a vector register. Such kind of an operation, is known as a *scatter-gather* operation. This is because, the input operands are essentially *scattered* in main memory. We need to *gather*, and put them in one place, which is the vector register. Let us consider a scatter-gather variant of the vector load instruction, and call it *v.sg.ld*. Instead of making assumptions about the locations of the array elements, the processor reads another vector register that contains the addresses of the elements (semantics shown in Table 11.5). In this case, a dedicated vector load unit reads the memory addresses stored in *vr2*, fetches the corresponding values from memory, and writes them in sequence to the vector register, *vr1*.

Example	Semantics	Explanation
v.sg.ld vr1, vr2	v.sg.ld ⟨vreg⟩, ⟨vreg⟩	vr1 ← ([vr2[0]], [vr2[1]], [vr2[2]], [vr2[3]])

Table 11.5: Semantics of the non-contiguous variant of the vector load instruction

Once, we have data loaded in vector registers, we can operate on two such registers directly. For example, if we consider 128-bit vector registers, $vr1$, and $vr2$. Then, the assembly statement *v.add vr3, vr1, vr2*, adds each pair of corresponding 4-byte floating point numbers stored in the input vector registers ($vr1$ and $vr2$), and stores the results in the relevant positions in the output vector register ($vr3$). Note that we use the vector add instruction (*v.add*) here. We show an example of a vector add instruction in Figure 11.19.

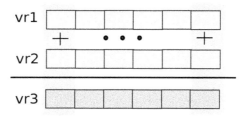

Figure 11.19: Example of a vector addition

Vector ISAs define similar operations for vector multiplication, division, and logical operations. Note that it is not necessary for a vector instruction to always have two input operands, which are vectors. We can multiply, a vector with a scalar, or we can have an instruction that operates on just one vector operand. For example, the SSE instruction set has dedicated instructions for computing trigonometric functions such as *sin*, and *cos*, for a set of floating point numbers packed in a vector register. If a vector instruction can simultaneously perform operations on n operands, then we say that we have n data lanes, and the vector instruction simultaneously performs an operation on all the n data lanes.

Definition 133

If a vector instruction can simultaneously perform operations on n operands, then we say that we have n data lanes, and the vector instruction simultaneously performs an operation on all the n data lanes.

The last step is to store the vector register in memory. Here again, there are two options. We can either store to contiguous memory locations, which is simpler, or save to non-contiguous locations. We can design two variants of the vector store instruction (contiguous and non-contiguous) on the lines of the two variants of vector load instructions (*v.ld* and *v.sg.ld*). Sometimes it is necessary to introduce instructions that transfer data between scalar and vector registers. We shall not describe such instructions for the sake of brevity. We leave designing such instructions as an exercise for the reader.

11.5.3 A Practical Example using SSE Instructions

Let us now consider a practical example using the x86 based SSE instruction set. We shall not use actual assembly instructions. We shall instead use functions provided by the *gcc* compiler that act as wrappers for the assembly instructions. These functions are called *gcc intrinsics*.

Let us now solve the problem of adding two arrays of floating point numbers. In this case, we wish to compute $c[i] = a[i] + b[i]$, for all values of i.

The SSE instruction set contains 128-bit registers. Each register can be used to store four 32-bit floating point numbers. Hence, if we have an array of N numbers, we need to have $\lceil N/4 \rceil$ iterations, because we can add at the most 4 pairs of numbers in each cycle. In each iteration, we need to load vector registers, add them, and store the result in memory. This process of breaking up a vector computation into a sequence of loop iterations based on the sizes of vector registers is known as *strip mining*.

Definition 134

The process of breaking up a vector computation into a sequence of loop iterations based on the sizes of vector registers is known as strip mining. *For example, if a vector register can hold 16 integers, and we wish to operate on 1024 integer vectors, then we need a loop with 64 iterations.*

Example 127

Write a function in C/C++ to add the elements in the arrays a and b pairwise, and save the results in the array, c, using the SSE extensions to the x86 ISA. Assume that the number of entries in a and b are the same, and are a multiple of 4.

Answer:

```
                              ____ vector addition ____
1  void sseAdd (const float a[], const float b[], float c[],  int N)
2  {
3        /* strip mining */
4        int numIters = N / 4;
5
6        /* iteration */
```

```
 7      for (int i = 0; i < numIters; i++) {
 8              /* load the values */
 9              __m128 val1 = _mm_load_ps (a);
10              __m128 val2 = _mm_load_ps (b);
11
12              /* perform the vector addition */
13              __m128 res = _mm_add_ps(val1, val2);
14
15              /* store the result */
16              _mm_store_ps(c, res);
17
18              /* increment the pointers */
19              a += 4 ; b += 4; c+= 4;
20      }
21 }
```

Let us consider the C code snippet in Example 127. We first calculate the number of iterations in Line 4. In each iteration, we consider a block of 4 array elements. In Line 9, we load a set of four floating point numbers into the 128-bit vector variable, $val1$. $val1$ is mapped to a vector register by the compiler. We use the function $\_mm\_load\_ps$ to load a set of 4 contiguous floating point values from memory. For example, the function $\_mm\_load\_ps(a)$ loads four floating point values in the locations, a, $a + 4$, $a + 8$, and $a + 12$ into a vector register. Similarly, we load the second vector register, $val2$, with four floating point values starting from the memory address, b. In Line 13, we perform the vector addition, and save the result in a 128-bit vector register associated with the variable res. We use the intrinsic function, $\_mm\_add\_ps$, for this purpose. In Line 16, we store the variable, res, in the memory locations namely c, $c + 4$, $c + 8$, and $c + 12$.

Before proceeding to the next iteration, we need to update the pointers a, b, and c. Since we process 4 contiguous array elements every cycle, we update each of the pointer by 4 (4 array elements) in Line 19.

We can quickly conclude that vector instructions facilitate bulk computations such as bulk loads/stores and adding a set of numbers pairwise, in one go. We compared the performance of this function, with a version of the function that does not use vector instructions on a quad core Intel Core i7 machine. The code with SSE instructions ran 2-3 times faster for million element arrays. If we would have had wider SSE registers, then we could have gained more speedups. The latest AVX vector ISA on x86 processors supports 256 and 512-bit vector registers. Interested readers can implement the function shown in Example 127 using the AVX vector ISA, and compare the performance.

11.5.4 Predicated Instructions

We have up till now considered vector load, store, and ALU operations. What about branches? Typically, branches have a different connotation in the context of vector processors. For example, let us consider a processor with vector registers that are wide enough to hold 32 integers, and we have a program which requires us to pair-wise add only 18 integers, and then store them in memory. In this case, we cannot store the entire vector register to memory because we risk overwriting valid data.

Let us consider another example. Assume that we want to apply the function $inc10(x)$ on all elements of an array. In this case, we wish to add 10 to the input operand, x, if it is less than 10. Such patterns are very common in programs that run on vector processors, and thus we need additional support in vector ISAs to support them.

```
function inc10(x):
if (x < 10)
        x = x + 10;
```

Let us add a new variant of a regular instruction, and call it a *predicated instruction* (similar to conditional instructions in ARM). For example, we can create *predicated* variants of regular load, store, and ALU instructions. A predicated instruction executes if a certain condition is true, otherwise it does not execute at all. If the condition is false, a predicated instruction is equivalent to a *nop*.

Definition 135

A predicated instruction is a variant of a normal load, store, or ALU instruction. It executes normally, if a certain condition is true. However, if the associated condition is false, then it gets converted to a nop. For example, the addeq instruction in the ARM ISA, executes like a normal add instruction if the last comparison has resulted in an equality. However, if this is not the case, then the add instruction does not execute at all.

Let us now add support for predication in the *SimpleRisc* ISA. Let us first create a vector form of the *cmp* instruction, and call it *v.cmp*. It compares two vectors pair-wise, and saves the results of the comparison in the *v.flags* register, which is a vector form of the *flags* register. Each component of the *v.flags* register contains an E and GT field, similar to the *flags* register in a regular processor.

```
v.cmp vr1, vr2
```

This example compares $vr1$, and $vr2$, and saves the results in the *v.flags* register. We can have an alternate form of this instruction that compares a vector with a scalar.

```
v.cmp vr1, 10
```

Now, let us define the predicated form of the vector add instruction. This instruction adds the ith elements of two vectors, and updates the ith element of the destination vector register, if the $v.flags[i]$ (i^{th} element of $v.flags$) register satisfies certain properties. Otherwise, it does not update the ith element of the destination register. Let the generic form of the predicated vector add instruction be: *v.p.add*. Here, p is the predicate condition. Table 11.6 lists the different values that p can take.

Predicate Condition	Meaning
lt	less than
gt	greater than
le	less than or equal
ge	greater than or equal
eq	equal
ne	not equal

Table 11.6: List of conditions for predicated vector instructions in *SimpleRisc*

Now, let us consider the following code snippet.

```
v.lt.add vr3, vr1, vr2
```

Here, the value of the vector register $vr3$ is the sum of the vectors represented by $vr1$ and $vr2$. The predication condition is less than (lt). This means that if both the E and GT flags are false for element i in the $v.flags$ register, then only we perform the addition for the ith element, and set its value in the $vr3$ register. The elements in the $vr3$ register that are not set by the add instruction maintain their previous value. Thus, the code to implement the function $inc10(x)$ is as follows. We assume that $vr1$ contains the values of the input array.

```
v.cmp vr1, 10
v.lt.add vr1, vr1, 10
```

Likewise, we can define predicated versions of the load/store instructions, and other ALU instructions.

11.5.5 Design of a Vector Processor

Let us now briefly consider the design of vector processors. We need to add a vector pipeline similar to the scalar pipeline. In specific, the OF stage reads the vector register file for vector operands, and the scalar register file for scalar operands. Subsequently, it buffers the values of operands in the pipeline registers. The EX stage sends scalar operands to the scalar ALU, and sends vector operands to the vector ALU. Similarly, we need to augment the MA stage with vector load and store units. For most processors, the size of a cache block is an integral multiple of the size of a vector register. Consequently, vector load and store units that operate on contiguous data do not need to access multiple cache blocks. Hence, a vector load and store access is almost as fast as a scalar load and store access because the atomic unit of storage in a cache is a *block*. In both cases (scalar and vector), we read the value of a block and choose the relevant bytes using the column muxes. We need to change the structure of the L1 cache to read in more data at a time. Lastly, the writeback stage writes back scalar data to the scalar register file and vector data to the vector register file.

In a pipelined implementation of a vector processor, the interlock and forwarding logic is complicated. We need to take into account the conflicts between scalar instructions, between vector instructions, and between a scalar and vector instruction. The forwarding logic needs to forward values between different functional unit types, and thus ensure correct execution. Note that vector instructions need not always be as fast as their scalar counterparts. Especially, scatter-gather based vector load store instructions are slower. Since modern out-of-order pipelines already have dedicated support for processing variable latency instructions, vector instructions can seamlessly plug into this framework.

11.6 Interconnection Networks

11.6.1 Overview

Let us now consider the problem of interconnecting different processing and memory elements. Typically multicore processors use a checkerboard design. Here, we divide the set of processors into *tiles*. A *tile* typically consists of a set of 2-4 processors. A tile has its private caches (L1 and possibly L2). It also contains a part of the shared last level cache (L2 or L3). The part of the shared last level cache that is a part of a given tile is known as a *slice* . Typically, a slice consists of 2-4 banks (see Section 11.4.5). Additionally, a tile, or a group of tiles might share a memory controller in modern processors. The role of the *memory controller* is to co-ordinate the transfer of data between the on-chip caches, and the main memory. Figure 11.20 shows a representative layout of a 32 core multiprocessor. The cores have a darker colour as compared to the cache banks. We use a tile size of 2 (2 processors and 2 cache banks), and assume that the shared L2 cache has 32 cache banks evenly distributed across the tiles. Moreover, each tile has a dedicated memory controller, and a structure called a *router*.

A router is a specialised unit, and is defined in Definition 136.

Definition 136

1. *A router sends messages originating from processors or caches in its tile to other tiles through the on chip network.*

2. *The routers are interconnected with each other via an on-chip network.*

3. *A message travels from the source router to the destination router (of a remote tile) via a series of routers. Each router on the way forwards the message to another router, which is closer to the destination.*

4. *Finally the router associated with the destination tile forwards the message to a processor or cache in the remote tile.*

5. *Adjacent routers are connected via a link. A link is a set of passive copper wires that are used to transmit messages (more details in Chapter 12).*

6. *A router typically has many incoming links, and many outgoing links. One set of incoming and outgoing links connect it to processors and caches in its tile. Each link has a unique identifier.*

7. *A router has a fairly complicated structure, and typically consists of a 3 to 5-stage pipeline. Most designs typically dedicate pipeline stages to buffering a message, computing the id of the outgoing link, arbitrating for the link, and sending the message over the outgoing link.*

8. *The arrangement of routers and links is referred to as the* on chip network, *or* network on chip. *It is abbreviated as the* NOC.

9. *Let us refer to each router connected to the NOC as a* node. *Nodes communicate with each other by sending* messages.

During the course of the execution of a program, it sends billions of messages over the NOC. The NOC carries coherence messages, LLC (last level cache) request/response messages, and messages between caches, and memory controllers. The operating system also uses the NOC to send messages to cores for loading and unloading threads. Due to the high volume of messages, large parts of the NOC often experience a sizeable amount of congestion. Hence, it is essential to design NOCs that reduce congestion to the maximum extent possible, are easy to design and manufacture, and ensure that messages quickly reach their destination. Let us define two important properties of an NOC namely bisection bandwidth and diameter.

11.6.2 Bisection Bandwidth and Network Diameter

Bisection Bandwidth

Let us consider a network topology where the vertices are the nodes, and the edges between the vertices are the links. Suppose there is a link failure, or for some other reason such as congestion, a link is unavailable,

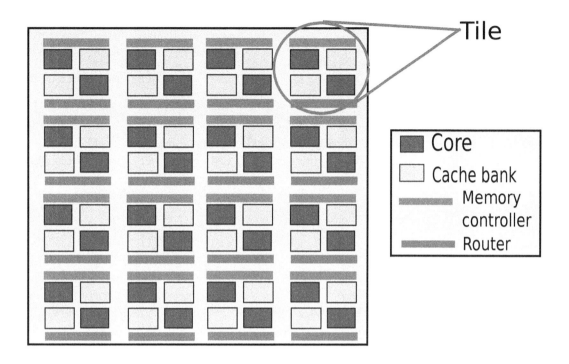

Figure 11.20: The layout of a multicore processor

then it should be possible to route messages through alternate paths. For example, let us consider a network arranged as a ring. If one link fails, then we can always send a message through the other side of the ring. If we were sending the message in a clockwise fashion, we can send it in an anti-clockwise fashion. However, if there are two link failures, it is possible that the network can get disconnected into two equal parts. We would thus like to maximise the number of link failures that are required to completely disconnect the network into sizeably large parts (possibly equal). Let us refer to the number of such failures as the *bisection bandwidth*. The bisection bandwidth is a measure of the reliability of the network. It is precisely defined as the minimum number of links that need to fail to partition the network into two equal parts.

There can be an alternative interpretation of the bisection bandwidth. Let us assume that nodes in one half of the network are trying to send messages to nodes in the other half of the network. Then the number of messages that can be simultaneously sent is at least equal to the bisection bandwidth. Thus, the bisection bandwidth is also a measure of the bandwidth of a network.

Definition 137
The bisection bandwidth *is defined as the minimum number of link failures that are required to partition a network into two equal parts.*

Network Diameter

We have discussed reliability, and bandwidth. Now, let us focus on latency. Let us consider pairs of nodes in the network. Let us subsequently consider the shortest path between each pair of nodes. Out of all of these shortest paths, let us consider the path that has the maximum length. The length of this path is an upper bound on the proximity of nodes in the network, and is known as the *diameter* of the network. Alternatively, we can interpret the diameter of a network as an estimate of the worst case latency between any pair of nodes.

Definition 138
Let us consider all pairs of nodes, and compute the shortest path between each pair. The length of the longest such path is known as the network diameter. *It is a measure of the worst case latency of the network.*

11.6.3 Network Topologies

Let us review some of the most common network topologies in this section. Some of these topologies are used in multicore processors. However, most of the complex topologies are used in loosely coupled multiprocessors that use regular Ethernet links to connect processors. For each topology, let us assume that it has N nodes. For computing the bisection bandwidth, we can further make the simplistic assumption that N is divisible by 2. Note that measures like the bisection bandwidth, and the diameter are approximate measures, and are merely indicative of broad trends. Hence, we have the leeway to make simplistic assumptions. Let us start out with considering simpler topologies that are suitable for multicores. We need to aim for a high bisection bandwidth, and low network diameter.

Chain and Ring

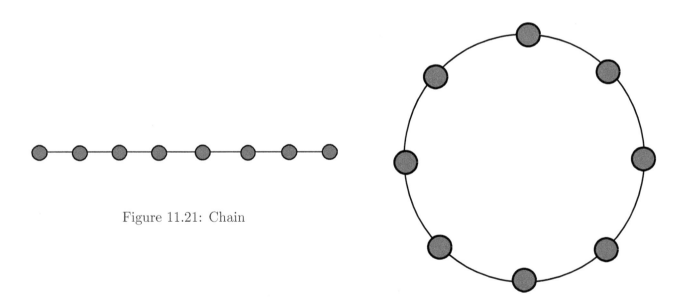

Figure 11.21: Chain

Figure 11.22: Ring

Figure 11.21 shows a chain of nodes. Its bisection bandwidth is 1, and the network diameter is $N-1$. This is our worst configuration. We can improve both the metrics by considering a ring of nodes (Figure 11.22). The bisection bandwidth is now 2, and the network diameter is $N/2$. Both of these topologies are fairly simple, and have been superseded by other topologies. Let us now consider a topology known as a *fat tree*, which is commonly used in cluster computers. A cluster computer refers to a loosely coupled multiprocessor that consists of multiple processors connected over the local area network.

Definition 139

A cluster computer refers to a loosely coupled computer that consists of multiple processors connected over the local area network.

Fat Tree

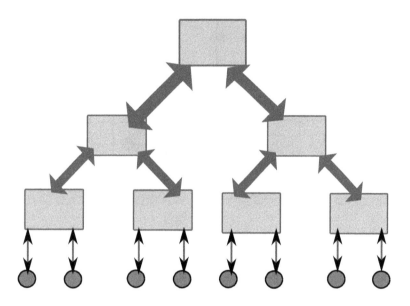

Figure 11.23: Fat Tree

Figure 11.23 shows a fat tree. In a fat tree, all the nodes are at the leaves, and all the internal nodes of the tree are routers dedicated to routing messages. Let us refer to these internal nodes as *switches*. A message from node a to node b first travels to the closest node that is a common ancestor of both a and b. Then it travels downwards towards b. Note that the density of messages is the highest near the root. Hence, to avoid contention, and bottlenecks, we gradually increase the number of links connecting a node and its children, as we move towards the root. This strategy reduces the message congestion at the root node.

In our example, two subtrees are connected to the root node. Each subtree has 4 nodes. At the most the root can receive 4 messages from each subtree. Secondly, at the most, it needs to send 4 messages to each subtree. Assuming a duplex link, the root needs to have 4 links connecting it to each of its children. Likewise, the next level of nodes need 2 links between them and each of their child nodes. The leaves need 1 link each. We can thus visualise the tree growing fatter, as we proceeds towards the root, and hence it is referred to as a *fat tree*.

The network diameter is equal to 2log(N). The bisection bandwidth is equal to the minimum number of links that connect the root node to each of its children. If we assume that the tree is designed to ensure that there is absolutely no contention for links at the root, then we need to connect the root with $N/2$ links to each subtree. Thus, the bisection bandwidth in this case is $N/2$. Note that we do not allot $N/2$ links between the root and its children in most practical scenarios. This is because the probability of all the nodes in a subree transmitting messages at the same time is low. Hence, in practice we reduce the number of links at each level.

Mesh and Torus

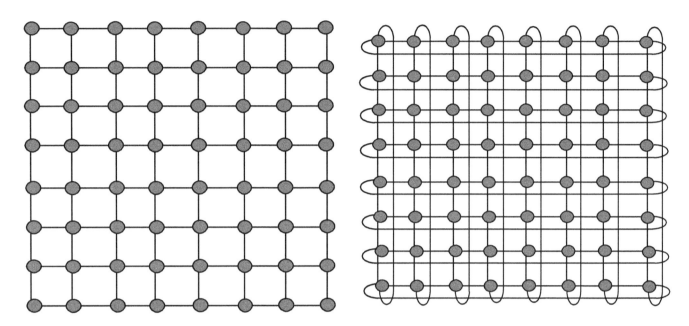

Figure 11.24: Mesh   Figure 11.25: Torus

Let us now look at topologies that are more suitable for multicores. One of the most common topologies is a mesh where all the nodes are connected in a matrix like fashion (see Figure 11.24). Nodes at the corner have two neighbours, nodes on the rim have three neighbours, and the rest of the nodes have four neighbours. Let us now compute the diameter and bisection bandwidth of a mesh. The longest path is between two corner nodes. The diameter is thus equal to ($2\sqrt{N}$ - 2). To divide the network into two equal halves we need to either split the mesh in the middle (horizontally or vertically). Since we have $\sqrt{N}$ nodes in a row, or column, the bisection bandwidth is equal to $\sqrt{N}$. The mesh is better than a chain and a ring in terms of these parameters.

Unfortunately, the mesh topology is asymmetric in nature. Nodes that are at the rim of the mesh are far away from each other. Consequently, we can augment a mesh with cross links between the extremities of each row and column. The resulting structure is known as a *torus*, and is shown in Figure 11.25. Let us now look at the properties of tori (plural of torus). In this case, nodes on opposite sides of the rim of the network, are only one hop apart. The longest path is thus between any of the corner nodes and a node at the center of the torus. The diameter is thus again equal to (ignoring small additive constants) $\sqrt{N}/2 + \sqrt{N}/2 = \sqrt{N}$. Recall that the length of each side of the torus is equal to $\sqrt{N}$.

Now, to divide the network into two equal parts let us split it horizontally. We need to thus snap $\sqrt{N}$ vertical links, and $\sqrt{N}$ cross links (links between the ends of each column). Hence, the bisection bandwidth is equal to $2\sqrt{N}$.

By adding $2\sqrt{N}$ cross links ($\sqrt{N}$ for rows, and $\sqrt{N}$ for columns), we have halved the diameter, and doubled the bisection bandwidth of a torus. However, this scheme still has some problems. Let us elaborate.

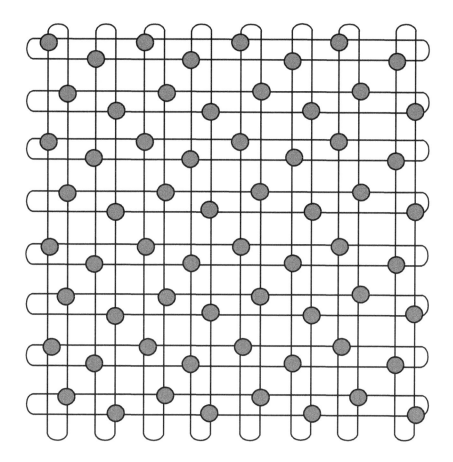

Figure 11.26: Folded Torus

While defining the diameter, we made an implicit assumption that the length of every link is almost the same, or alternatively the time a message takes to traverse a link is almost the same for all the links in the network. Hence, we defined the diameter in terms of the number of links that a message traverses. This assumption is not very unrealistic because in general the propagation time through a link is small as compared to the latencies of routers along the way. Nevertheless, there are limits to the latency of a link. If a link is very long, then our definition of the diameter needs to be revised. In the case of tori, we have such a situation. The cross links are physically $\sqrt{N}$ times longer than regular links between adjacent nodes. Hence, as compared to a mesh, we have not significantly reduced the diameter in practice because nodes at the ends of a row are still far apart.

We can fortunately solve this problem by using a slightly modified structure called a *folded torus* as shown in Figure 11.26. Here, the topology of each row and column is like a ring. One half of the ring consists of regular links that were originally a part of the mesh topology, and the other half comprises of the cross links that were added to convert a mesh into a torus. We alternately place nodes on the regular links and on the cross links. This strategy ensures that the distance between adjacent nodes in a folded torus is twice the distance between adjacent nodes in a regular torus. However, we avoid the long cross links ($\sqrt{N}$ hops long) between the two ends of a row or column.

The bisection bandwidth and the diameter of the network remain the same as that of the torus. In this case, there are several paths that can qualify as the longest path. However, the path between a corner to the center is not the longest. One of the longest paths is between opposite corners. The folded torus is typically the preferred configuration in multicore processors because it avoids long cross links.

Hypercube

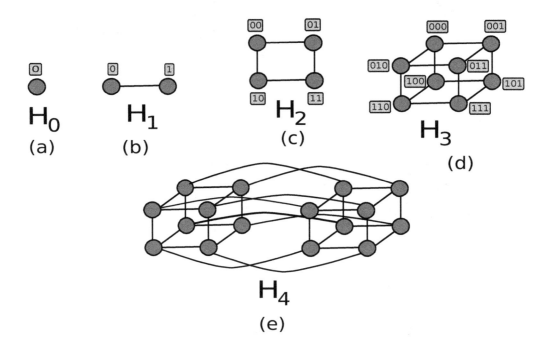

Figure 11.27: Hypercube

Let us now consider a network that has $O(log(N))$ diameter. These networks use a lot of links; hence, they are not suitable for multicores. However, they are used often in larger cluster computers. This network is known as a *hypercube*. A hypercube is actually a family of networks, where each network has an *order*. A hypercube of order k is referred to as H_k.

Figure 11.27(a) shows a hypercube of order 0 (H_0). It is a single point. To create a hypercube of order 1, we take two copies of a hypercube of order 0, and connect the corresponding points with lines. In this case, H_0 has a single point. Therefore, H_1 is a simple line segment (see Figure 11.27(b)). Now, let us follow the same procedure to create a hypercube of order 2. We place two copies of H_1 close to each other and connect corresponding points with lines. Hence, H_2 is a rectangle (see Figure 11.27(c)). Let us follow the same procedure to create a hypercube of order 3 in Figure 11.27(d). This network is equivalent to a normal cube (the "cube" in hypercube). Finally, Figure 11.27(e), shows the topology of H_4, where we connect the corresponding points of two cubes. We can proceed in a similar manner to create hypercubes of order k.

Let us now investigate the properties of a hypercube. The number of nodes in H_k is equal to twice the number of nodes in H_{k-1}. This is because, we form H_k by joining two copies of H_{k-1}. Since H_1 has 1 node, we can conclude that H_k has 2^k nodes. Let us propose a method to label the nodes of a hypercube as shown in Figure 11.27. We label the single node in H_0 as 0. When we join two copies of a hypercube of order, $k-1$, we maintain the same labelling of nodes for $(k-1)$ least significant digits. However, for nodes in one copy, we set the MSB as 1, and for nodes in the other copy, we set the MSB to be 0.

Let us consider, H_2 (Figure 11.27(c)). The nodes are labelled 00, 01, 10, and 11. We have created a similar 3-bit labelling for H_3 (Figure 11.27(d)). In our labelling scheme, a node is connected to all other nodes that have a label differing in only one bit. For example, the neighbours of the node 101, are 001, 111, and 100. A similar labelling for H_k requires $k = log(N)$) bits per node.

This insight will help us compute the diameter of a hypercube. Let us explain through an example. Consider the 8 node hypercube, H_3. Assume that we want a message to travel from node A (000) to node B (110). Let us scan the labels of both the nodes from the MSB to the LSB. The first bit (MSB) does not match. Hence, to make the first bit match, let us route the message to node A_1 (100). Let us now scan the next bit. Here, again there is a mismatch. Hence, let us route the message to node A_2 (110). Now, we take a look at the third bit (LSB), and find it to match. The message has thus reached its destination. We can follow the same approach for an N-bit hypercube. Since each node has a $log(N)$ bit label, and in each step we flip at most one bit in the label of the current node, we require a maximum of $log(N)$ routing steps. Thus the network diameter is $log(N)$.

Let us now compute the bisection bandwidth. We shall state the result without proof because the computation of the bisection bandwidth of a hypercube requires a thorough theoretical treatment of hypercubes. This is beyond the scope of this book. The bisection bandwidth of an N-node hypercube is equal to $N/2$.

Butterfly

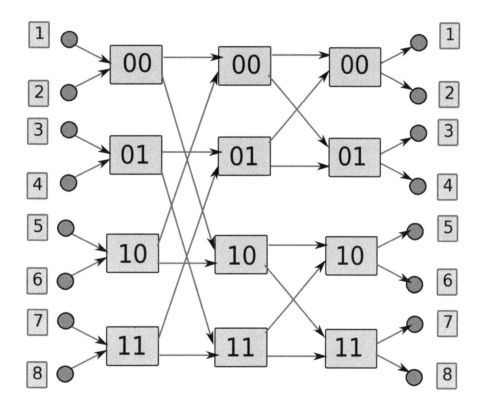

Figure 11.28: Butterfly

Let us now look at our last network called the *butterfly* that also has $O(log(N))$ diameter, yet, is suitable for multicores. Figure 11.28 shows a butterfly network for 8 nodes. Each node is represented by a circle. Along with the nodes, we have a set of switches or internal nodes (shown with rectangles) that route messages between nodes. The messages start at the left side, pass through the switches, and reach the right side of the diagram. Note that the nodes on the leftmost and rightmost sides of the figure are actually the same set of nodes. We did not want to add left to right cross links to avoid complicating the diagram; hence, we show the set of nodes in duplicate.

Let us start from the left side of the diagram. For N nodes (assuming N is a power of 2), we have $N/2$ switches in the first column. Two nodes are connected to each switch. In our example in Figure 11.28, we have labelled the nodes $1 \ldots 8$. Each node is connected to a switch. Once a message enters a switch, it gets routed to the correct switch in the rightmost column through the network of switches. For 8 nodes, we have 4 switches in each column. For each column, we have labelled them $00 \ldots 11$ in binary.

Let us consider an example. Assume that we want to send a message from node 4 to node 7. In this case, the message enters switch 01 in the first column. It needs to reach switch 11 in the third column. We start out by comparing the MSBs of the source switch, and the destination switch. If they are equal, then the message proceeds horizontally rightwards to a switch in the adjacent column and same row. However, if the MSBs are unequal (as is the case in our example), then we need to use the second output link to send it to a switch in a different row in the next column. The label of the new switch differs from the label of the original switch by just 1 bit, which is the MSB bit in this case. Similarly, to proceed from the second to the third column, we compare the second bit position (from the MSB). If they are equal, then the message proceeds horizontally, otherwise it is routed to a switch such that the first two bits match. In this case, the label of the switch that we choose in the second column is 11. The first two bits match the label of the switch in the third column. Hence, the message proceeds horizontally, and is finally routed to node 7.

We can extend this method for a butterfly consisting of k columns. In the first column, we compare the MSB. Similarly, in the ith column, we compare the ith bit (MSB is the 1st bit). Note that the first $k - i$ bits of the label of the switch that handles the message in the ith column are equal to the first $k - i$ bits of the destination switch. This strategy ensure that the message gets routed to ultimately the correct switch in the kth column.

Now, let us investigate the properties of the network. Let us assume that we have N nodes, where N is a power of 2. We require $log(N)$ columns, where each column contains $N/2$ switches. Thus, we require an additional $Nlog(N)/2$ switches. An astute reader would have already concluded that routing a message in a butterfly network is almost the same as routing in a message in a hypercube. In every step we increase the size of the matching prefix between the labels of the source and destination switches by 1. We thus require $log(N) + 1$ steps (1 additional step for sending the message to the destination node from the last switch) for sending a message between a pair of nodes. We can thus approximate the diameter of the network to $log(N)$.

Let us now compute the bisection bandwidth. Let us consider our example with 8 nodes first. Here, we can split the network horizontally. We thus need to snap 4 links, and hence the bisection bandwidth of the network shown in Figure 11.28 is 4. Let us now consider $N > 8$ nodes. In this case, also the best solution is to split the network horizontally. This is because if we draw an imaginary horizontal line between the $(N/4)^{th}$ and $(N/4 + 1)^{th}$ row of switches then it will only intersect the links between the first and second columns. The outgoing links of the rest of the columns will not intersect with our imaginary line. They will either be below it or above it. Since each switch in the first column has only one outgoing link that intersects the imaginary line, a total of $N/2$ links intersect the imaginary line. All of these links need to be disconnected to divide the network into two equal parts. Hence, the bisection bandwidth is equal to $N/2$.

Comparison of Topologies

Let us now compare the topologies with respect to four parameters – number of internal nodes (or switches), number of links, diameter, and bisection bandwidth in Table 11.7. In all the cases, we assume that the networks have N nodes that can send and receive messages, and N is a power of 2.

Topology	# Switches	# Links	Diameter	Bisection Bandwidth
Chain	0	N-1	N-1	1
Ring	0	N	$N/2$	2
Fat Tree	N - 1	2N-2	2 log(N)	N/2†
Mesh	0	$2N - 2\sqrt{N}$	$2\sqrt{N} - 2$	$\sqrt{N}$
Torus	0	2N	$\sqrt{N}$	$2\sqrt{N}$
Folded Torus	0	2N	$\sqrt{N}$	$2\sqrt{N}$
Hypercube	0	$Nlog(N)/2$	$log(N)$	$N/2$
Butterfly	$Nlog(N)/2$	$N + Nlog(N)$	$log(N) + 1$	$N/2$
† Assume that the capacity of each link is equal to the number of leaves in its subtree				

Table 11.7: Comparison of topologies

11.7   Summary and Further Reading

11.7.1   Summary

Summary 11

1. *Processor frequency and performance is beginning to saturate.*

2. *Concomitantly, the number of transistors per chip is roughly doubling very two years as per the original predictions of Gordon Moore. This empirical law is known as the* **Moore's Law**.

3. *The additional transistors are not being utilised to make a processor larger, or more complicated. They are instead being used to add more processors on chip. Each such processor is known as a* core, *and a chip with multiple cores is known as a* multicore *processor.*

4. *We can have multiprocessor systems where the processors are connected over the network. In this case the processors do not share any resources between them, and such multiprocessors are known as* loosely coupled multiprocessors. *In comparison, multicore processors, and most small sized server processors that have multiple processors on the same motherboard, share resources such as the I/O devices, and the main memory. Programs running on multiple processors in these systems might also share a part of their virtual address space. These systems are thus referred to as* strongly coupled multiprocessors.

5. *Multiprocessor systems can be used to run multiple sequential programs simultaneously, or can be used to run parallel programs. A parallel program contains many sub-programs that run concurrently. The sub-programs co-operate among themselves to achieve a bigger task. When sub-programs share their virtual memory space, they are known as* threads.

6. *Parallel programs running on strongly coupled multiprocessors typically communicate values between themselves by writing to a shared memory space. In comparison, programs running on loosely coupled multiprocessors communicate by passing messages between each other.*

7. *Most parallel programs have a sequential section, and a parallel section. The parallel section can be divided into smaller units and distributed among the processors of a multiprocessor system. If we have N processors, then we ideally expect the parallel section to be sped up by a factor of N. An equation describing this relationship is known as the Amdahl's Law. The speedup, S is given by:*

$$S = \frac{T_{seq}}{T_{par}} = \frac{1}{f_{seq} + \frac{1-f_{seq}}{P}}$$

8. *The Flynn's taxonomy classifies computing systems into four types : SISD (single instruction, single data), SIMD (single instruction, multiple data), MISD (multiple instruction, single data), and MIMD (multiple instruction, multiple data).*

9. *The memory system in modern shared memory MIMD processors is in reality very complex. Coherence and consistency are two important aspects of the behaviour of the memory system.*

10. *Coherence refers to the rules that need to be followed for accessing the same memory location. Coherence dictates that a write is never lost, and all writes to the same location are seen in the same order by all the processors.*

11. *Consistency refers to the behaviour of the memory system with respect to different memory locations. If memory accesses from the same thread get reordered by the memory system (as is the case with modern processors), many counter intuitive behaviours as possible. Hence, most of the time we reason in terms of the* sequentially consistent memory model *that prohibits reordering of messages to the memory system from the same thread. In practice, multiprocessors follow a weak consistency model that allows arbitrary reorderings. We can still write correct programs because such models define synchronisation instructions (example: f ence) that try to enforce an ordering between memory accesses when required.*

12. *We can either have a large shared cache, or multiple private caches (one for each core or set of cores). Shared caches can be made more performance and power efficient by dividing it into a set of subcaches known as banks. For a set of private caches to logically function as one large shared cache, we need to* implement *cache coherence.*

    (a) *The snoopy cache coherence protocol connects all the processors to a shared bus.*

    (b) *The MSI write-update protocol works by broadcasting every write to all the cores.*

    (c) *The MSI write-invalidate protocol guarantees coherence by ensuring that only one cache can write to a block at any single point of time.*

13. *To further improve performance, we can implement a multithreaded processor that shares a pipeline across many threads. We can either quickly switch between threads (fine and coarse-grained multithreading), or execute instructions from multiple threads in the same cycle using a multi-issue processor (simultaneous multithreading).*

14. *SIMD processors follow a different approach. They operate on arrays of data at once.* Vector processors *have a SIMD instruction set. Even though, they are obsolete now, most modern processors have vector instructions in their ISA.*

    (a) *Vector arithmetic/logical instructions fetch their operands from the vector register file, and operate on large vectors of data at once.*

(b) Vector load-store operations can either assume that data is stored in contiguous memory regions, or assume that data is scattered *in memory.*

(c) Instructions on a branch path are implemented as predicated instructions in vector ISAs.

15. *Processors and memory elements are connected through an interconnection network. The basic properties of an interconnection network are the diameter (worst case end to end delay), and the bisection bandwidth (number of links that need to be snapped to partition the network equally). We discussed several topologies: chain, ring, fat tree, mesh, torus, folded torus, hypercube, and butterfly.*

11.7.2 Further Reading

The reader should start by reading the relevant sections in advanced textbooks on computer architecture [Culler et al., 1998, Hwang, 2003, Baer, 2010, Jacob, 2009]. For parallel programming, the reader can start with Michael Quinn's book on parallel programming with OpenMP and MPI [Quinn, 2003]. The formal MPI specifications are available at http://www.mpi-forum.org. For an advanced study of cache coherence the reader can start with the survey on coherence protocols by Stenstrom [Stenstrom, 1990], and then look at one of the earliest practical implementations [Borrill, 1987]. The most popular reference for memory consistency models is a tutorial by Adve and Gharachorloo [Adve and Gharachorloo, 1996], and a paper published by the same authors [Gharachorloo et al., 1992]. For a different perspective on memory consistency models in terms of ordering, and atomicity, readers can refer to [Arvind and Maessen, 2006]. [Guiady et al., 1999] looks at memory models from the point of view of performance. [Peterson et al., 1991] and [russell, 1978] describe two fully functional SIMD machines. For interconnection networks the reader can refer to [Jerger and Peh, 2009].

Exercises

Overview of Multiprocessor Systems

Ex. 1 — Differentiate between *strongly coupled*, and *loosely coupled* multiprocessors.

Ex. 2 — Differentiate between *shared memory*, and *message passing* based multiprocessors.

Ex. 3 — Why is the evolution of multicore processors a direct consequence of Moore's Law?

Ex. 4 — The fraction of the potentially parallel section in a program is 0.6. What is the maximum speedup that we can achieve over a single core processor, if we run the program on a quad-core processor?

Ex. 5 — You need to run a program, 60% of which is strictly sequential, while the rest 40% can be fully parallelised over a maximum of 4 cores. You have 2 machines:

(a) A single core machine running at 3.2 GHz

(b) A 4-core machine running at 2.4 GHz

Which machine is better if you have to minimise the total time taken to run the program? Assume that the two machines have the same IPC per thread and only differ in the clock frequency and the number of cores.

* Ex. 6 — Consider a program, which has a sequential and a parallel portion. The sequential portion is 40% and the parallel portion is 60%. Using Amdahl's law, we can compute the speedup with n processors, as $S(n)$. However, increasing the number of cores increases the cost of the entire system. Hence, we define a utility function, $g(n)$, of the form:

$$g(n) = e^{-n/3}(2n^2 + 7n + 6)$$

The buyer wishes to maximise $S(n) \times g(n)$. What is the optimal number of processors, n?

Ex. 7 — Define the terms: SISD, SIMD, MISD, and MIMD. Give an example of each type of machine.

Ex. 8 — What are the two classes of MIMD machines introduced in this book?

Coherence and Consistency

Ex. 9 — What are the axioms of cache coherence?

Ex. 10 — Define sequential and weak consistency.

Ex. 11 — Is the outcome (t1,t2) = (2,1) allowed in a system with coherent memory?

Thread 1:	Thread 2:
`x = 1;` `x = 2;`	`t1 = x;` `t2 = x;`

Ex. 12 — Assume that all the global variables are initialised to 0, and all variables local to a thread start with 't'. What are the possible values of $t1$ for a sequentially consistent system, and a weakly consistent system? (source [Adve and Gharachorloo, 1996])

Thread 1:	Thread 2:
`x = 1;` `y = 1;`	`while(y == 0){}` `t1 = x;`

Ex. 13 — Is the outcome (t1,t2) = (1,1) possible in a sequentially consistent system?

Thread 1:	Thread 1:

`x = 1;`
`if(y == 0)`
`    t1 = 1;`
	`y = 1;`
	`if(x == 0)`
	`    t2 = 1;`

Ex. 14 — Is the outcome $t1 \neq t2$ possible in a sequentially consistent system? (source [Adve and Gharachorloo, 1996])

Thread 1:	Thread 2:	Thread 3:	Thread 4:

`z = 1;`
`x = 1;`
	`z = 2;`
	`y = 1;`
		`while (x != 1) {}`
		`while (y != 1) {}`
		`t1 = z;`
			`while (x != 1) {}`
			`while (y != 1) {}`
			`t2 = z;`

* Ex. 15 — Is the outcome (t1 = 0) allowed in a system with coherent memory and atomic writes? Consider both sequential and weak consistency?

Thread 1:

```
x = 1;
```

Thread 2:

```
while(x != 1) {}
y = 1;
```

Thread 3:

```
while (y != 1) {}
t1 = x;
```

* Ex. 16 — Consider the following code snippet for implementing a *critical section*. A critical section is a region of code that can only be executed by one thread at any single point of time. Assume that we have two threads with ids 0 and 1 respectively. The function *getTid*() returns the id of the current thread.

```
void enterCriticalSection() {
        tid = getTid();
        otherTid = 1 - tid;
        interested[tid] = true;
        flag = tid;

        while ( (flag == tid) && (interested[otherTid] == 1) ) {}
}

void leaveCriticalSection{
        tid = getTid();
        interested[tid] = false;
}
```

Is it possible for two threads to be in the critical section at the same point of time?

Ex. 17 — In the snoopy protocol, why do we write back data to the main memory upon a M to S transition?

Ex. 18 — Assume that two nodes desire to transition from the S state to the M state at exactly the same point of time. How will the snoopy protocol ensure that only one of these nodes enters the M state, and finishes its write operation? What happens to the other node?

Ex. 19 — The snoopy protocol clearly has an issue with scalability. If we have 64 cores with a private cache per core, then it will take a long time to broadcast a message to all the caches. Can you propose solutions to circumvent this problem?

Ex. 20 — Let us assume a cache coherent multiprocessor system. The L1 cache is private and the coherent L2 cache is shared across the processors. Let us assume that the system issues a lot of I/O requests. Most of the I/O requests perform DMA (Direct Memory Access) from main memory. It is possible that the I/O requests might overwrite some data that is already present in the caches. In this case we need to extend the cache coherence protocol that also takes I/O accesses into account. Propose one such protocol.

Ex. 21 — Let us define a new state in the traditional MSI states based snoopy protocol. The new E state refers to the "exclusive" state, in which a processor is sure that no other cache contains the block in a valid state. Secondly, in the E state, the processor hasn't modified the block yet. What is the advantage of having the E state? How are evictions handled in the E state?

Ex. 22 — Show the state transition diagrams for a MSI protocol with a directory. You need to show the following:

   1.Structure of the directory

2.State transition diagram for events received from the host processor.

3.State transition diagram for events received from the directory.

4.State transition diagram for an entry in the directory (if required).

Ex. 23 — Assume that we have a system with private L1 and L2 caches. The L1 layer is not coherent. However, the L2 layer maintains cache coherence. How do we modify our MSI snoopy protocol to support cache coherence for the entire system?

Ex. 24 — In the snoopy write-invalidate protocol, when should a processor actually perform the write operation? Should it perform the write as soon as possible, or should it wait for the write-invalidate message to reach all the caches? Explain your answer.

* Ex. 25 — Assume that a processor wants to perform an atomic exchange operation between two memory locations a and b. a and b cannot be allocated to registers. How will you modify the MSI coherence protocol to support this operation? Before proceeding with the answer think about what are the things that can go wrong. An exchange is essentially equivalent to the following sequence of operations: (1) temp = a; (2) a = b; (3) b = temp. If a read arrives between operations (2) and (3) it might get the wrong value of b. We need to prevent this situation.

** Ex. 26 — Assume that we want to implement an instruction called $MCAS$. The $MCAS$ instruction takes k (known and bounded) memory locations as arguments, a set of k old values, and a set of k new values. Its pseudo-code is shown below. We assume here that mem is a hypothetical array representing the entire memory space.

```
/* multiple compare and set */
boolean MCAS(int memLocs[], int oldValues[], int newValues[]){
        /* compare */
        for(i=0; i < k; i++) {
                if(mem[memLocs[i]] != oldValues[i]) {
                        return false;
                }
        }

        /* set */
        for(i=0; i < k; i++) {
                mem[memLocs[i]] = newValues[i];
        }

        return true;
}
```

The challenge is to implement this instruction such that it appears to execute instantaneously. Let us look at some subtle cases. Assume that we want to write (4,5,6) to three memory locations if their previous contents are (1,2,3). It is possible that after writing 4, and 5, there is a small delay. During this time another thread reads the three memory locations, and concludes that their values are 4,5, and 3 respectively. This result is incorrect because it violates our assumption that $MCAS$ executes instantaneously. We should either read (1,2,3) or (4,5,6).

Now, let us look at the case of reading the three memory locations. Let us say that their initial values are 1,2, and 0. Our $MCAS$ instruction reads the first two locations and since they are equal to the old values, proceeds to the third location. Before reading it, a store operation from another thread changes the values of the three locations as follows. $(1,2,0) \rightarrow (5,2,0) \rightarrow (5,2,3)$. Subsequently, the $MCAS$ instruction takes a look at the third memory location and finds it to be 3. Note that the three memory locations were never equal to $(1,2,3)$. We thus arrive at a wrong conclusion.

How should we fix these problems? We want to implement a $MCAS$ instruction purely in hardware, which provides an illusion of instantaneous execution. It should be free of deadlocks, and should complete in a finite amount of time. How can we extend our coherence protocols to implement it?

*** **Ex. 27** — Assume a processor that has a sequentially consistent(SC) memory. We implement SC by making each thread wait for a memory request to complete before issuing the next request. Now, assume that we modify the architecture by allowing a processor to read a value that the immediately preceding instruction has written without waiting for it to complete. Prove that the memory system still follows SC.

*** **Ex. 28** — Assume a processor with a weak consistency model. Let us run a "properly labelled" program on it. A *properly labelled*(PL) program does not allow conflicting accesses (read-write, write-read, or write-write) to a shared variable at the same time. For example, the following code sequence is not properly labelled because it allows x to be modified concurrently.

Thread 1:   Thread 2:

```
x = 0                                            x = 1
```

In reality, the coherence protocol orders one write access before the other. Nevertheless, both the threads **try** to modify x concurrently at the programmer's level. This is precisely the behaviour that we wish to avoid.

In a PL program, two threads do not **try** to modify x at the same time. This is achieved by having two magic instructions known as *lock* and *unlock*. Only one thread can lock a memory location at any point of time. If another thread tries to lock the location before it is unlocked, then it stalls till the lock is free. If multiple threads are waiting on the same lock, only one of them is given the lock after an *unlock* instruction. Secondly, both the *lock* and *unlock* instructions have a built in $fence$ operation, and all the *lock* and *unlock* instructions execute in program order. The PL version of our program is as follows:

Thread 1:   Thread 2:

```
lock(x)                                          lock(x)
x = 0                                            x = 1
unlock(x)                                        unlock(x)
```

We can thus think of a lock-unlock block as a sequential block that can only be executed by one thread at a given time. Moreover, assume that a lock-unlock block can only have one memory instruction inside it. Now, prove that all PL programs running on a weakly consistent machine have a sequentially consistent execution. In other words we can interleave the memory accesses of all the threads such that they appear to be executed by a single cycle processor that switches among the threads. [HINT: Construct access graphs for your system, and prove that they are acyclic.]

Multithreading

Ex. 29 — What is the difference between a fine grained and coarse grained multithreaded machine?

Ex. 30 — Describe a simultaneous multithreaded (SMT) processor in detail.

Ex. 31 — Describes the steps that we need to take to ensure that a SMT processor executes correctly.

Ex. 32 — Assume a mix of workloads in a 4-way SMT processor. 2 threads are computationally intensive,

1 thread is I/O intensive, and the last thread sleeps for a long time. Design an efficient instruction selection scheme.

Interconnection Networks

Ex. 33 — What is the bisection bandwidth and diameter of a 2D $n \times n$ mesh?

Ex. 34 — What is the bisection bandwidth and diameter of a 3D $n \times n \times n$ mesh?

Ex. 35 — What is the diameter of a ring containing n nodes? Give a precise answer that holds for even and odd n.

Ex. 36 — What is the bisection bandwidth and diameter of a hypercube of order n.

Ex. 37 — What is the bisection bandwidth and diameter of a $n \times n \times n$, 3D torus?

Ex. 38 — What is the bisection bandwidth and diameter of a clique of n nodes (n is even)? In a clique, all pairs of nodes are connected.

** Ex. 39 — Assume we have a $n \times n$ mesh. There are n^2 routers, and each processor is connected to one router. Note that at any point of time, a router can only store 1 message. It will discard a message only if the message gets stored in another router. In our previous example, router (i, j) will keep the message until it has been delivered and stored at a neighbouring router such as $(i + 1, j)$. Now, an interesting deadlock situation can develop. Let us assume the following scenario.

- •(1,1) wants to send a message to (1,2).
- •(1,2) wants to send a message to (2,2).
- •(2,2) wants to send a message to (2,1).
- •(2,1) wants to send a message to (1,1).

In this case all the four nodes have 1 message each. They are not able to forward the packet to the next node, because the next node already stores a packet, and is thus busy. Since there is a cyclic wait, we have a deadlock. Design a message routing protocol between a source and destination node that is provably deadlock free.

Vector Processors

Ex. 40 — What is the advantage of vector processors over scalar processors?

Ex. 41 — Why are vector load-store instructions easy to implement in systems that have caches with large block sizes?

Ex. 42 — How can we efficiently implement a scatter-gather based load-store unit?

Ex. 43 — What is a predicated instruction, and how does it help speed up a vector processor?

* Ex. 44 — Assume that we have a processor with a 32 entry vector register file. We wish to add two arrays that have 17 entries each. How can we implement this operation, with the *SimpleRisc* vector instructions introduced in the chapter? Feel free to introduce new vector instructions if required.

* Ex. 45 — Design a dedicated SIMD hardware unit to sort n integers in roughly n time steps by using the bubble sort algorithm. You have a linear array of n processors connected end to end. Each processor is capable of storing two integers, and has some logic inside it. Design the logic for each processor and explain the overall working of the system.

Design Problems

Ex. 46 — Write a program to sort a billion integers using OpenMP and MPI.

Ex. 47 — Implement a distributed shared memory system on a cluster of computers connected via an Ethernet LAN.

12

I/O and Storage Devices

We have now arrived at a very interesting point in our study of processors. We have learnt how to design a full processor and its accompanying memory system using basic transistors. This processor can execute the entire *SimpleRisc* instruction set, and can run very complicated programs ranging from chess games to weather simulations. However, there is a vital aspect missing in our design. There is no way for us to communicate with our computer. To render our computer usable, we need to have a method to write input data, and display the outputs.

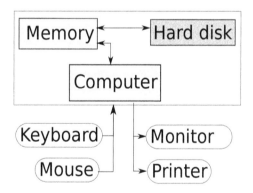

Figure 12.1: A typical computer system

We thus need an I/O (Input/Ouput) system in our computer. Let us look at the structure of a typical computer in Figure 12.1. The processor is the core of the computer. It is connected to a host of I/O devices for processing user inputs, and for displaying results. These I/O devices are known as *peripherals*. The most common user input devices are the keyboard and the mouse. Likewise, the most common display devices, are the monitor, and the printer. The computer can also communicate with a host of other devices such as cameras, scanners, mp3 players, camcorders, microphones, and speakers through a set of generic I/O ports. An I/O port consists of: (1) a set of metallic pins that help the processor to connect with external devices, and (2) a port controller that manages the connection with the peripheral device. The computer can also communicate with the outside world through a special peripheral device called a network card. The network card contains the circuits to communicate with other computers via wired or wireless connections.

> **Definition 140**
> *An I/O port consists of a set of metallic pins that are used to attach to connectors provided by external devices. Every port is associated with a port controller that co-ordinates the exchange of data on the communication link.*

We give a special preference to a particular class of devices in this chapter known as *storage* devices. Storage devices such as the hard disk, and flash drives help us permanently store data even when the system is powered off. We looked at them briefly in Chapter 10 while discussing swap space. In this chapter, we shall study them in more detail, and look at the methods of data storage, and retrieval. The reason we stress on storage devices in this chapter is because they are integral to computer architecture. The nature of peripherals across computers varies. For example, a given computer might have a microphone, whereas another computer might not have a monitor because it is accessed remotely over the network. However, invariably all computers from small handheld phones to large servers have some form of permanent storage. This storage is used to save files, system configuration data, and the swap space during the operation of a program. Hence, architects pay special attention to the design an optimisation of storage systems, and no book in computer architecture is complete without discussing this vital aspect of computer architecture.

12.1   I/O System – Overview

12.1.1   Overview

Let us now distance ourselves from the exact details of an I/O device. While designing a computer system, it is not possible for designers to consider all possible types of I/O devices. Even if they do, it is possible that a new class of devices might come up after the computer has been sold. For example, tablet PCs such as the Apple iPad were not there in 2005. Nonetheless, it is still possible to transfer data between an iPad and older PCs. This is possible because most designers provide standard interfaces in their computer system. For example, a typical desktop or laptop has a set of USB ports. Any device that is compliant with the USB specification can be connected to the USB port, and can then communicate with the host computer. Similarly, it is possible to attach almost any monitor or projector with any laptop computer. This is because laptops have a generic DVI port that can be connected to any monitor. Laptop companies obey their part of the DVI specification by implementing a DVI port that can seamlessly transfer data between the processor and the port. On similar lines, monitor companies obey their part of the DVI specification by ensuring that their monitors can seamlessly display all the data that is being sent on the DVI port. Thus, we need to ensure that our computer provides support for a finite set of interfaces with peripherals. It should then be possible to attach any peripheral at run time.

The reader should note that just because it is possible to attach a generic I/O device by implementing the specification of a port, it does not mean that the I/O device will work. For example, we can always connect a printer to the USB port. However, the printer might not be able to print a page. This is because, we need additional support at the software level to operate the printer. This support is built into the printer device drivers in the operating system that can efficiently transfer data from user programs to the printer.

Roles of Software and Hardware

We thus need to clearly differentiate between the roles of software and hardware. Let us first look at software. Most operating systems define a very simple user interface for accessing I/O devices. For example, the Linux operating system has two system calls, *read* and *write*, with the following specifications.

```
read(int file_descriptor, void *buffer, int num_bytes)
write(int file_descriptor, void *buffer, int num_bytes)
```

Linux treats all devices as files, and allots them a file descriptor. The file descriptor is the first argument, and it specifies the id of the device. For example, the speaker has a certain file descriptor, and a printer has a different file descriptor. The second argument points to an area in memory that contains the source or destination of the data, and the last argument represents the number of bytes that need to be transferred. From the point of view of an user, this is all that needs to be done. It is the job of the operating system's device drivers, and the hardware to co-ordinate the rest of the process. This approach has proved to be an extremely versatile method for accessing I/O devices.

Unfortunately, the operating system needs to do more work. For each I/O call it needs to locate the appropriate device driver and pass on the request. It is possible that multiple processes might be trying to access the same I/O device. In this case, the different requests need to be properly scheduled.

The job of the device driver is to interface with native hardware and perform the desired action. The device driver typically uses assembly instructions to communicate with the hardware device. It first assesses its status, and if it is free, then it asks the peripheral device to perform the desired action. The device driver initiates the process of transfer of data between the memory system and the peripheral device.

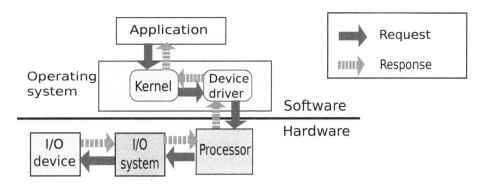

Figure 12.2: The I/O system (software and hardware)

Figure 12.2 encapsulates the discussion up till now. The upper part of the diagram shows the software modules (application, operating system, device driver), and the lower part of the diagram shows the hardware modules. The device driver uses I/O instructions to communicate with the processor, and the processor then routes the commands to the appropriate I/O device. When the I/O device has some data to send to the processor, it sends an interrupt, and then the interrupt service routine reads the data, and passes it on to the application.

We summarised the entire I/O process in just one paragraph. However, the reader should note that this is an extremely complicated process, and entire books are devoted to the study and design of device drivers. In this book, we shall limit our discussion to the hardware part of the I/O system, and take a cursory look at the software support that is required. The important points of difference between the software and hardware components of the I/O system are enumerated in Point 20.

Important Point 20
The role of software and hardware in the I/O system:

1. *The software component of the I/O system consists of the application, and the operating system. The application is typically provided a very simple interface to access I/O devices. The role of the operating system is to collate the I/O requests from different applications, appropriately schedule them, and pass them on to the corresponding device drivers.*

2. *The device drivers communicate with the hardware device through special assembly instructions. They co-ordinate the transfer of data, control, and status information between the processor and the I/O devices.*

3. *The role of the hardware (processor, and associated circuitry) is to just act as a messenger between the operating system, and the I/O devices, which are connected to dedicated I/O ports. For example, if we connect a digital camera to an USB port, then the processor is unaware of the details of the connected device. Its only role is to ensure seamless communication between the device driver of the camera, and the USB port that is connected to the camera.*

4. *It is possible for the I/O device to initiate communication with the processor by sending an interrupt. This interrupts the currently executing program, and invokes the interrupt service routine. The interrupt service routine passes on control to the corresponding device driver. The device driver then processes the interrupt, and takes appropriate action.*

Let us now discuss the architecture of the hardware component of the I/O system in detail.

12.1.2   Requirements of the I/O System

Device	Bus Technology	Bandwidth	Typical Values
Video display via graphics card	PCI Express (version 4)	High	1-10 GB/s
Hard disks	ATA/SCSI/SAS	Medium	150-600 MB/s
Network card (wired/wireless)	PCI Express	Medium	10-100 MB/s
USB devices	USB	Medium	60-625 MB/s
DVD audio/video	PCI	Medium	1-4 MB/s
Speaker/Microphone	AC'97/Intel High. Def. Audio	Low	100 KB/s to 3 MB/s
Keyboard/Mouse	USB/PCI	Very Low	10-100 B/s

Table 12.1: List of I/O devices along with bandwidth requirements (as of 2012)

Let us now try to design the architecture of the I/O system. Let us start out by listing out all the devices that we want to support, and their bandwidth requirements in Table 12.1. The component that requires the maximum amount of bandwidth is the display device (monitor, projector, TV). It is attached to a graphics card. The *graphics card* contains the graphics processor that processes image and video data.

Note that we shall use the term *card* often in the discussion of I/O devices. A card is a printed circuit board(PCB), which can be attached to the I/O system of a computer to implement a specific functionality. For example, a graphics card helps us process images and videos, a sound card helps us process high definition audio, and a network card helps us connect to the network. The picture of a network card is shown in Figure 12.3. We can see a set of chips interconnected on a printed circuit board. There are a set of ports that are used to connect external devices to the card.

Figure 12.3: Photograph of a network card This article uses material from the Wikipedia article "Network Interface Controller" [nic,], which is released under the Creative Commons Attribution-Share-Alike License 3.0 [ccl,]

Definition 141

A card *is a printed circuit board(PCB), which can be attached to the I/O system of a computer to implement a specific functionality.*

Along with the graphics card, the other high bandwidth device that needs to be connected to the CPU is the main memory. The main memory bandwidth is of the order of 10-20 GB/s. Hence, we need to design an I/O system that gives special treatment to the main memory and the graphics card.

The rest of the devices have a relatively lower bandwidth. The bandwidth requirement of the hard disk, USB devices, and the network card is limited to 500-600 MB/s. The keyboard, mouse, CD-DVD drives, and audio peripherals have an extremely minimal bandwidth requirement ($< 3 - 4$ MB/s).

12.1.3 Design of the I/O System

I/O Buses

Let us take a look at Table 12.1 again. We notice that there are different kinds of bus technologies such as USB, PCI Express, and SATA. Here, a bus is defined as a link between two or more than two elements in the I/O system. We use different kinds of buses for connecting different kinds of I/O devices. For example, we use the USB bus to connect USB devices such as pen drives, and cameras. We use SATA or SCSI buses to connect to the hard disk. We need to use so many different types of buses for several reasons. The first is that the bandwidth requirements of different I/O devices are very different. We need to use extremely high speed buses for graphics cards. Whereas, for the keyboard, and mouse, we can use a significantly simpler bus technology because the total bandwidth demand is minimal. The second reason is historical. Historically, hard disk vendors have used the SATA or IDE buses, whereas graphics card vendors have been using the AGP bus. After 2010, graphics card companies shifted to using the PCI Express bus. Hence, due to a combination of factors, I/O system designers need to support a large variety of buses.

Definition 142
A bus is a set of wires that is used to connect multiple devices in parallel. The devices can use the bus to transmit data and control signals between each other.

Now, let us look deeper into the structure of a bus. A bus is much more than a set of copper wires between two end points. It is actually a very complex structure and its specifications are typically hundreds of pages long. We need to be concerned about its electrical properties, error control, transmitter and receiver circuits, speed, power, and bandwidth. We shall have ample opportunity to discuss high speed buses in this chapter. Every node (source or destination) connected to a bus requires a *bus controller* to transmit and receive data. Although the design of a bus is fairly complicated, we can abstract it as a logical link that seamlessly and reliably transfers bytes from a single source to a set of destinations.

The Chipset and Motherboard

For designing the I/O system of a computer, we need to first provide external I/O ports that consist of a set of metallic pins or sockets. These I/O ports can be used to attach external devices. The reader can look at the side of her laptop or the back of her desktop to find the set of ports that are supported by her computer. Each port has a dedicated port controller that interfaces with the device, and then the port controller needs to send the data to the CPU using one of the buses listed in Table 12.1.

Here, the main design issue is that it is not possible to connect the CPU to each and every I/O port through an I/O bus. There are several reasons for this.

1. If we connect the CPU to each and every I/O port, then the CPU needs to have bus controllers for every single bus type. This will increase the complexity, area, and power utilisation of the CPU.

2. The number of output pins of a CPU is limited. If the CPU is connected to a host of I/O devices, then it requires a lot of extra pins to support all the I/O buses. Most CPUs typically do not have enough pins to support this functionality.

3. From a commercial viewpoint, it is a good idea to separate the design of the CPU from the design of the I/O system. It is best to keep both of them separate. This way, it is possible to use the CPU in a large variety of computers.

Hence, most processors are connected to only a single bus, or at most 2 to 3 buses. We need to use ancillary chips that connect the processor to a host of different I/O buses. They need to aggregate the traffic from I/O devices, and properly route data generated by the CPU to the correct I/O devices and vice versa. These extra chips comprise the *chipset* of a given processor. The chips of the chipset are interconnected with each other on a printed circuit board known as the *motherboard*.

Definition 143

Chipset *These are a set of chips that are required by the main CPU to connect to main memory, the I/O devices, and to perform system management functions.*

Motherboard *All the chips in the chipset are connected to each other on a printed circuit board, known as the* motherboard.

Architecture of the Motherboard

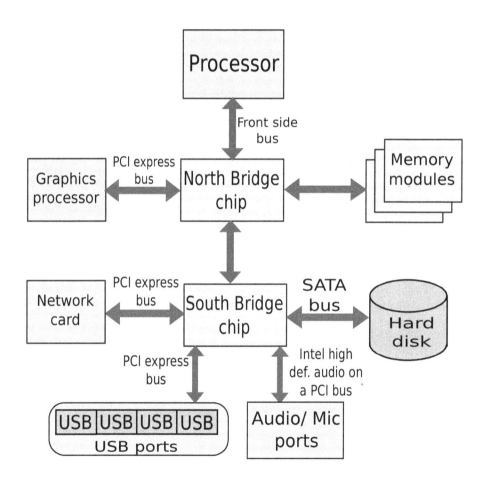

Figure 12.4: Architecture of the I/O system

Most processors typically have two important chips in their chipset – North Bridge and South Bridge – as shown in Figure 12.4. The CPU is connected to the North Bridge chip using the Front Side Bus (FSB). The North Bridge chip is connected to the DRAM memory modules, the graphics card, and the South Bridge chip. In comparison, the South Bridge chip is meant to handle much slower I/O devices. It is connected to all the USB devices including the keyboard and mouse, audio devices, network cards, and the hard disk.

For the sake of completeness, let us mention two other common types of buses in computer systems. The first type of bus is called a *back side bus*, which is used to connect the CPU to the L2 cache. In the early days, processors used off chip L2 caches. They communicated with them through the back side bus. Nowadays, the L2 cache has moved on chip, and consequently the back side bus has also moved on chip. It is typically clocked at the core frequency, and is a very fast bus. The second type of bus is known as a *backplane bus*. It is used in large computer or storage systems that typically have multiple motherboards, and peripheral devices such as hard disks. All these entities are connected in parallel to a single backplane bus. The backplane bus itself consists of multiple parallel copper wires with a set of connectors that can be used to attach devices.

Definition 144

Front side bus *A bus that connects the CPU to the memory controller, or the North Bridge chip in the case of Intel systems.*

Back side bus *A bus that connects the CPU to the L2 cache.*

Backplane bus *A system wide bus that is attached to multiple motherboards, storage, and peripheral devices.*

Both the North Bridge, and South Bridge chips need to have bus controllers for all the buses that they are attached with. Each bus controller co-ordinates the access to its associated bus. After successfully receiving a *packet* of data, it sends the packet to the destination (towards the CPU, or the I/O device). Since these chips interconnect various types of buses, and temporarily buffer data values if the destination bus is busy, they are known as *bridges* (bridge between buses).

The memory controller is a part of the North Bridge chip and implements read/write requests to main memory. In the last few years processor vendors have started to move the memory controller into the main CPU chip, and also make it more complicated. Most of the augmentations to the memory controller are focused on reducing main memory power, reducing the number of refresh cycles, and optimising performance. Starting from the Intel Sandybridge processor the graphics processor has also moved on chip. The reason for moving things into the CPU chip is because (1) we have extra transistor's available, and (2) on-chip communication is much faster than off-chip communication. A lot of embedded processors also integrate large parts of the South Bridge chip, and port controllers, along with the CPU in a single chip. This helps in reducing the size of the motherboard, and allows more efficient communication between the I/O controllers and the CPU. Such kind of systems are known as SOCs (System on Chip).

Definition 145
A system on a chip (SOC) typically packages all the relevant parts of a computing system into one single chip. This includes the main processor, and most of the chips in the I/O system.

12.1.4 Layers in the I/O System

Most complex architectures are typically divided into layers such as the architecture of the internet. One layer is mostly independent of the other layer. Hence, we can choose to implement it in any way we want, as long as it adheres to a standard interface. The I/O architecture of a modern computer is also fairly complicated, and it is necessary to divide its functionality into different layers.

We can broadly divide the functionality of the I/O system into four different layers. Note that our classification of the functionality of an I/O system into layers is broadly inspired from the 7 layer OSI model for classifying the functions of wide area networks into layers. We try to conform as much as possible to the OSI model such that readers can relate our notion of layers to concepts that they would study in a course on networking.

Physical Layer The physical layer of a bus primarily defines the electrical specifications of the bus. It is divided into two sublayers namely the *transmission sublayer* and the *synchronisation sublayer*. The transmission sublayer defines the specifications for transmitting a bit. For example, a bus can be active high (logical 1, if the voltage is high), and another bus can be active low (logical 1, if the voltage is zero). Today's high speed buses use high speed differential signalling. Here, we use two copper wires to transmit a single bit. A logical 0 or 1 is inferred by monitoring the sign of the difference of voltages between the two wires (similar to the concept of bit lines in SRAM cells). Modern buses extend this idea and encode a logical bit using a combination of electrical signals. The synchronisation sublayer specifies the timing of signals, and methods to recover the data sent on the bus by the receiver.

Data Link Layer The data link layer is primarily designed to process logical bits that are read by the physical layer. This layer groups sets of bits into frames, performs error checking, controls the access to the bus, and helps implement I/O transactions. In specific, it ensures that at any point of time, only one entity can transmit signals on the bus, and it implements special features to leverage common message patterns.

Network Layer This layer is primarily concerned with the successful transmission of a set of frames from the processor to an I/O device or vice versa through various chips in the chip set. We uniquely define the address of an I/O device, and consider approaches to embed the addresses of I/O devices in I/O instructions. Broadly we discuss two approaches – I/O port based addressing, and memory mapped addressing. In the latter case, we treat accesses to I/O devices, as regular accesses to designated memory locations.

Protocol Layer The top most layer referred to as the *protocol layer* is concerned with executing I/O requests end to end. This includes methods for high level communication between the processor, and the I/O devices in terms of the message semantics. For example, I/O devices can interrupt the processor, or the processor can explicitly request the status of each I/O device. Secondly, for transferring data between the processor and devices, we can either transfer data directly or delegate the responsibility of transferring data to dedicated chips in the chipset known as DMA controllers.

Figure 12.5 summaries the 4 layered I/O architecture of a typical processor.

12.2 Physical Layer – Transmission Sublayer

The physical layer is the lower most layer of the I/O system. This layer is concerned with the physical transmission of signals between the source and receiver. Let us divide the physical layer into two sublayers. Let us call the first sublayer as the *transmission sublayer* because it deals with the transmission of bits from the source to the destination. This layer is concerned with the electrical properties of the links (voltage, resistance, capacitance), and the methods of representing a logical bit (0 or 1) using electrical signals.

Let us refer to the second sublayer as the *synchronisation sublayer*. This sublayer is concerned with reading an entire *frame* of bits from the physical link. Here, a frame is defined as a group of bits demarcated

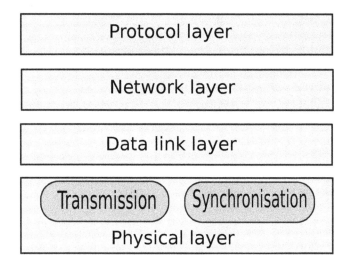

Figure 12.5: The 4 layers of the I/O system

by special markers. Since I/O channels are plagued with jitter (unpredictable signal propagation time), it is necessary to properly synchronise the arrival of data at the receiver, and read each frame correctly.

In this section, we shall discuss the transmission sublayer. We shall discuss the synchronisation sublayer in the next section.

Note that the reason that we create multiple sublayers, instead of creating multiple layers is because sublayers need not be independent of each other. However, in general layers should be independent of each other. It should be theoretically possible to use any physical layer, with any other data link layer protocol. They should ideally be completely oblivious of each other. In this case, the transmission and synchronisation sublayers have strong linkages, and thus it is not possible to separate them into separate layers.

Figure 12.6: A generic view of an I/O link

Figure 12.6 shows the generic view of an I/O link. The source (transmitter) sends a sequence of bits to the destination (receiver). At the time of transmission, the data is always synchronised with respect to the clock of the source. This means that if the source runs at 1 GHz, then it sends bits at the rate of 1 GHz. Note that the frequency of the source is not necessarily equal to the frequency of the processor, or I/O element that is sending the data. The transmission circuitry, is typically a separate submodule, which has a clock that is derived from the clock of the module that it is a part of. For example, the transmission circuitry of a processor might be transmitting data at 500 MHz, whereas the processor might be running at 4 GHz. In any case, we assume that the transmitter transmits data at its internal clock rate. This clock rate is also known as the *frequency of the bus, or bus frequency* , and this frequency is in general lower than the clock frequency of the processors, or other chips in the chipset. The receiver can run at the same frequency, or can use a faster frequency. Unless explicitly stated, we do not assume that the source and destination have the same frequency. Lastly, note that we shall use the terms *sender*, *source*, and *transmitter* interchangeably. Likewise, we shall use the terms *destination*, and *receiver* interchangeably.

12.2.1 Single Ended Signalling

Let us consider a naive approach, where we send a sequence of 1s and 0s, by sending a sequence of pulses from the source to the destination. This method of signalling is known as *single ended signalling*, and it is the simplest approach.

In specific, we can associate a high voltage pulse with a 1, and a low voltage pulse with a 0. This convention is known as *active high*. Alternatively, we can associate a low voltage pulse with a logical 1, and a high voltage pulse with a logical 0. Conversely, this convention is known as *active low*. Both of these conventions are shown in Figure 12.7.

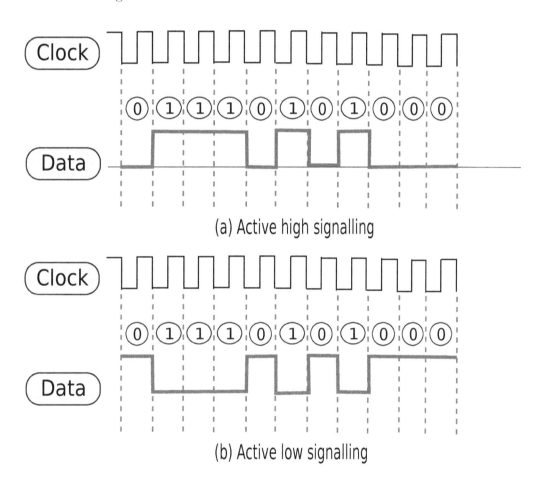

Figure 12.7: Active High and Active Low Signalling Methods

Sadly, both of these methods are extremely slow and outdated. Recall from our discussion of SRAM cells in Section 6.4.1 that a fast I/O bus needs to reduce the voltage difference between a logical 0, and 1 to as low a value as possible. This is because the voltage difference is detected after it has charged the detector that has an internal capacitance. The higher the voltage required, the longer it takes to charge the capacitors. If the voltage difference is 1 Volt, then it will take a long time to detect a transition from 0 to 1. This will limit the speed of the bus. However, if the voltage difference is 30 mV, then we can detect the transition in voltage much sooner, and we can thus increase the speed of the bus.

Hence, modern bus technologies try to minimise the voltage difference between a logical 0 and 1 to as low a value as possible. Note that we cannot arbitrarily reduce the voltage difference between a logical 0 and 1, in the quest for increasing bus speed. For example, we cannot make the required voltage difference 0.001 mV. This is because there is a certain amount of electrical noise in the system that is introduced due to several factors. Readers might have noticed that if a cell phone starts ringing when the speakers of a car or computer are on, then there is some amount of noise in the speakers also. If we take a cell phone close to a microwave oven while it is running, then there is a decrease in the sound quality of the cell phone. This happens because of electromagnetic interference. Likewise there can be electromagnetic interference in processors also, and voltage spikes can be introduced. Let us assume that the maximum amplitude of such voltage spikes is 20 mV. Then the voltage difference between a 0 and 1, needs to be more than 20 mV. Otherwise, a voltage spike due to interference can flip the value of a signal leading to an error. Let us take a brief look at one of the most common technologies for on-chip signalling namely LVDS.

12.2.2   Low Voltage Differential Signalling (LVDS)

LVDS uses two wires to transmit a single signal. The difference between the voltages of these wires is monitored. The value transferred is inferred from the sign of the voltage difference.

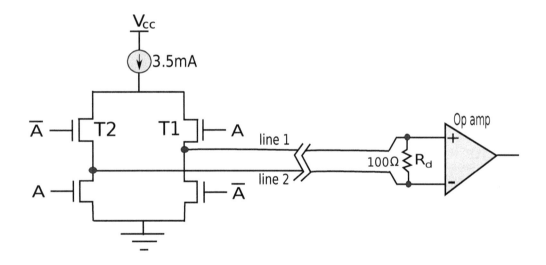

Figure 12.8: LVDS Circuit

The basic LVDS circuit is shown in Figure 12.8. There is a fixed current source of 3.5 mA. Depending on the value of the input A, the current flows to the destination through either line 1 or line 2. For example, if A is 1, then the current flows through line 1 since transistor $T1$ starts conducting, whereas T_2 is off. In this case, the current reaches the destination, passes through the resistor R_d, and then flows back through line 2. Typically the voltage of both the lines when no current is flowing is maintained at 1.2 V. When current flows through them, there is a voltage swing. The voltage swing is equal to 3.5 mA times R_d. R_d is typically 100 Ohms. Hence, the total differential voltage swing is 350 mV. The role of the detector is to sense the sign of the voltage difference. If it is positive, it can declare a logical 1. Otherwise, it can declare a logical 0. Because of the low swing voltage (350 mV), LVDS is a very fast physical layer protocol.

12.2.3   Transmission of Multiple Bits

Let us now consider the problem of transmitting multiple bits in sequence. Most I/O channels are not busy all the time. They are busy only when data is being transmitted, and thus their duty cycle (percentage of time that a device is in operation) tends to be highly variable, and most of the time it is not very high. However, detectors are on almost all the time and they keep sensing the voltage of the bus. This can have implications on both power consumption and correctness. *Power* is an issue because the detectors keep sensing either a logical 1 or 0 every cycle, and it thus becomes necessary for the higher level layers to process the data. To avoid this, most systems typically have an additional line that indicates if the data bits are valid or invalid. This line is traditionally known as the *strobe*. The sender can indicate the period of the validity of data to the receiver by setting the value of the strobe. Again, it becomes necessary to synchronise the data lines and the strobe. This is getting increasingly difficult for high speed I/O buses, because it is possible that signals on the data lines, and the strobe can suffer from different amounts of delay. Hence, there is a possibility that both the lines might move out of synchronisation. It is thus a better idea to define three types of signals – zero, one, and *idle*. *Zero* and *one* refer to the transmission of a logical 0 and 1 on the bus. However, the *idle* state refers to the fact that no signal is being transmitted. This mode of signalling is also known as *ternary signalling* because we are using three states.

Definition 146
Ternary *signalling refers to a convention that uses three states for the transmission of signals – one (logical one), zero (logical zero), and* idle *(no signal).*

We can easily implement ternary signalling with LVDS. Let us refer to the wires in LVDS, as A and B respectively. Let V_A be the voltage of line A. Likewise, let us define the term, V_B. If $\mid V_A - V_B \mid < \tau$, where τ is the detection threshold, then we infer that the lines are idle, and we are not transmitting anything. However, if $V_A - V_B > \tau$, we conclude that we are transmitting a logical 1. Similarly, if $V_B - V_A > \tau$, we conclude that we are transmitting a logical 0. We thus do not need to make any changes to our basic LVDS protocol.

Let us now describe a set of techniques that are optimised for transmitting multiple bits in the physical layer. We present examples that use ternary signalling. Some of the protocols can also be used with simple binary signalling (zero and one state) also.

12.2.4   Return to Zero (RZ) Protocols

In this protocol we transmit a pulse (positive or negative), and then pause for a while in a bit period. Here, we define the *bit period* as the time it takes to transmit a bit. Most I/O protocols assume that the bit period is independent of the value of the bit (0 or 1) that is being transmitted. Typically, a 1-bit period is equal to the length of one I/O clock cycle. The I/O clock is a dedicated clock that is used by the elements of the I/O system. We shall interchangeably use the terms *clock cycle*, and *bit period*, where we do not wish to emphasise a difference between the terms.

Definition 147

bit period *The time it takes to transfer a single bit over a link.*

I/O clock   *We assume that there is a dedicated I/O clock in our system that is typically synchronised with the processor clock. The I/O clock is slower than the processor clock, and is used by elements of the I/O subsystem.*

In the RZ protocol, if we wish to transmit a logical 1, then we send a positive voltage pulse on the link for a fraction of a bit period. Subsequently, we stop transmitting the pulse, and ensure that the voltage on the link returns to the *idle* state. Similarly, while transmitting a logical 0, we send a negative voltage pulse along the lines for a fraction of a cycle. Subsequently, we wait till the line returns to the *idle* state. This can be done by allowing the capacitors to discharge, or by applying a reverse voltage to bring the lines to the *idle* state. In any case, the key point here is that while we are transmitting, we transmit the actual value for some part of the bit period, and then we allow the lines to fall back to the default state, which in our discussion we have assumed to be the *idle* state. We shall see that returning to the *idle* state helps the receiver circuitry synchronise with the clock of the sender, and thus read the data correctly. The implicit assumption here is that the sender sends out one bit every cycle (sender cycle). Note that the clock period of the sender and the receiver may be different. We shall take a look at such timing issues in Section 12.4.

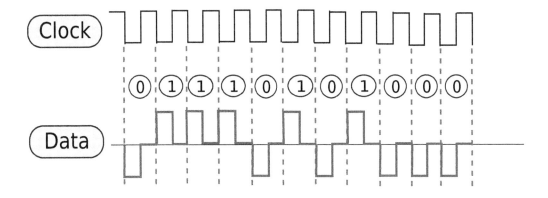

Figure 12.9: Return to zero (RZ) protocol (example)

Figure 12.9 shows an example of the RZ protocol with ternary signalling. If we were to use binary signalling, then we can have an alternative scheme as follows. We could transmit a short pulse in a cycle for a logical 1, and not transmit anything for a logical 0. Here, the main issue is to figure out if a logical 0 is being sent or not by taking a look at the length of the pause after transmitting a logical 1. This requires complicated circuitry at the end of the receiver.

Nevertheless, a major criticism of the RZ (return to zero) approaches is that it wastes bandwidth. We need to introduce a short pause (period of idleness) after transmitting a logical 0 or 1. It turns out that we can design protocols that do not have this limitation.

12.2.5   Manchester Encoding

Before proceeding to discuss Manchester encoding, let us differentiate between a *physical bit*, and a *logical bit*. Up till now we have assumed that they mean the same thing. However, this will cease to be true from now onwards. A physical bit such as a physical one or zero, is representative of the voltage across a link.

For example, in an active high signalling method, a high voltage indicates that we are transmitting the bit, 1, and a low voltage (physical bit 0) indicates that we are transmitting the 0 bit. However, this ceases to be the case now because we assume that a logical bit (logical 0 or 1) is a function of the values of physical bits. For example, we can infer a logical 0, if the current and the previous physical bit are equal to 10. Likewise, we can have a different rule for inferring a logical 1. It is the job of the receiver to translate physical signals (or rather physical bits), into logical bits, and pass them to the higher layers of the I/O system. The next layer (data link layer discussed in Section 12.4) accepts logical bits from the physical layer. It is oblivious to the nature of the signalling, and the connotations of physical bits transmitted on the link.

Let us now discuss one such mechanism known as Manchester encoding. Here, we encode logical bits as a transition of physical bits. Figure 12.10 shows an example. A $0 \rightarrow 1$ transition of physical bits encodes a logical 1, and conversely a $1 \rightarrow 0$ transition of physical bits encodes a logical 0.

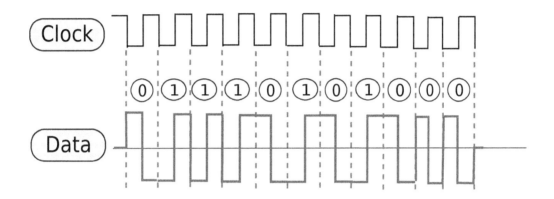

Figure 12.10: Manchester code (example)

A Manchester code always has a transition to encode data. Most of the time at the middle of a bit period, we have a transition. If there is no transition, we can conclude that no signal is being transmitted and the link is idle. One advantage of Manchester encoding is that it is easy to decode the information that is sent on the link. We just need to detect the nature of the transition. Secondly, we do not need external strobe signals to synchronise the data. The data is said to be *self clocked*. This means that we can extract the clock of the sender from the data, and ensure that the receiver reads in data at the same speed at which it is sent by the sender.

Definition 148
A self clocked signal allows the receiver to extract the clock of the sender by examining the transition of the physical bits in the signal. If there are periodic transitions in the signal, then the period of these transitions is equal to the clock period of the sender, and thus the receiver can read in data at the speed at which it is sent.

Manchester encoding is used in the IEEE 802.3 communication protocol that forms the basis of today's Ethernet protocol for local area networks. Critics argue that since every logical bit is associated with a transition, we unnecessarily end up dissipating a lot of power. Every single transition requires us to charge/discharge a set of capacitors associated with the link, the drivers, and associated circuitry. The associated resistive loss is dissipated as heat. Let us thus try to reduce the number of transitions.

12.2.6   Non Return to Zero (NRZ) Protocol

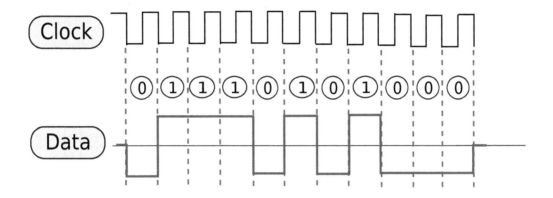

Figure 12.11: Non return to zero protocol (example)

Here, we take advantage of a run of 1s and 0s. For a transmitting a logical 1, we set the voltage of the link equal to high. Similarly, for transmitting a logical 0, we set the voltage of the link to low. Let us now consider a run of two 1 bits. For the second bit, we do not induce any transitions in the link, and we maintain the voltage of the link as high. Similarly, if we have a run of n 0s. Then for the last $(n-1)$ 0s we maintain the low voltage of the link, and thus we do not have transitions. Figure 12.11 shows an example. We observe that we have minimised the number of transitions by completely avoiding voltage transitions when the value of the logical bit that needs to be transmitted remains the same. This protocol is fast because we are not wasting any time (such as the RZ protocols), and is power efficient because we eliminate transitions for a run of the same bit (unlike RZ and Manchester codes).

However, the added speed and power efficiency comes at the cost of complexity. Let us assume that we want to transmit a string of hundred 1s. In this case, we will have a transition only for the first and last bit. Since the receiver does not have the clock of the sender, it has no way of knowing the length of a bit period. Even if the sender and receiver share the same clock, due to delays induced in the link, the receiver might conclude that we have a run of 99 or 101 bits with a non-zero probability. Hence, we have to send additional synchronisation information such that the receiver can properly read all the data that is being sent on the link.

12.2.7   Non Return to Zero (NRZI) Inverted Protocol

This is a variant of the NRZ protocol. Here, we have a transition from 0 to 1, or 1 to 0, when we wish to encode a logical 1. For logical 0s, there are no transitions. Figure 12.12 shows an example.

12.3   Physical Layer – Synchronisation Sublayer

The transmission sublayer ensures that a sequence of pulses is successfully sent from the transmitter to either one receiver, or to a set of receivers. However, this is not enough. The receiver needs to read the signal at

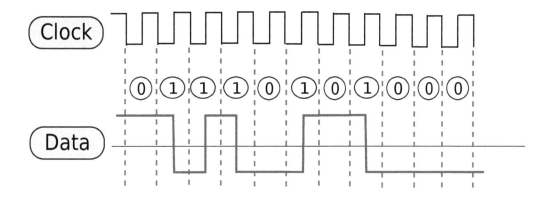

Figure 12.12: Non return to zero inverted protocol (example)

the right time, and needs to assume the correct bit period. If it reads the signal too early or too late, then it risks getting the wrong value of the signal. Secondly, if it assumes the wrong values of the bit period, then the NRZ protocol might not work. Hence, there is a need to maintain a notion of time between the source and destination. The destination needs to know exactly when to transfer the value into a latch. Let us consider solutions for a single source and destination. Extending the methods to a set of destinations is left as an exercise to the reader.

To summarise, the synchronisation sublayer receives a sequence of logical bits from the transmission sublayer without any timing guarantees. It needs to figure out the values of the bit periods, and read in an entire *frame* (a fixed size chunk) of data sent by the sender, and send it to the data link layer. Note that the actual job of finding out the frame boundaries, and putting sets of bits in a frame is done by data link layer.

12.3.1 Synchronous Buses

Simple Synchronous Bus

Let us first consider the case of a synchronous system where the sender and the receiver share the same clock, and it takes a fraction of a cycle to transfer the data from the sender to the receiver. Moreover, let us assume that the sender is transmitting all the time. Let us call this system a *simple synchronous bus*.

In this case, the task of synchronising between the sender and receiver is fairly easy. We know that data is sent at the negative edge of a clock, and in less than a cycle it reaches the receiver. The most important issue that we need to avoid is *metastability* (see Section 6.3.8). A flip flop enters a metastable state when the data makes a transition within a small window of time around the negative edge of the clock. In specific, we want the data to be stable for an interval known as the *setup time* before the clock edge, and the data needs to be stable for another interval known as the *hold time* after the clock edge. The interval comprising of the setup and hold intervals, is known as the keep-out region of the clock as defined in Section 6.3.8 and [Dally and Poulton, 1998].

In this case, we assume that the data reaches the receiver in less than $t_{clk} - t_{setup}$ units of time. Thus, there are no metastability issues, and we can read the data into a flip-flop at the receiver. Since digital circuits typically process data in larger chunks (bytes or words), we use a serial in – parallel out register at the receiver. We serially read in n bits, and read out an n-bit chunk in one go. Since the sender and the receiver clocks are the same, there is no rate mismatch. The circuit for the receiver is shown in Figure 12.13.

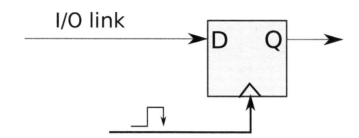

Figure 12.13: The receiver of a simple synchronous bus

Mesochronous Bus

In a *mesochronous system*, the phase difference between the signal and the clock is a constant. The phase difference can be induced in the signal because of the propagation delay in the link, and because there might be a phase difference in the clocks of the sender and the receiver. In this case, it is possible that we might have a metastability issue because the data might arrive in the crucial keep-out region of the receiver clock.

Hence, we need to add a delay element that can delay the signal by a fixed amount of time such that there are no transitions in the keep-out region of the receiver clock. The rest of the circuit remains the same as that used for the simple synchronous bus. The design of the circuit is shown in Figure 12.14.

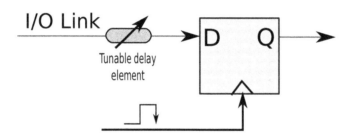

Figure 12.14: The receiver of a mesochronous bus

A delay element can be constructed by using a delay locked loop (DLL). DLLs can have different designs and some of them can be fairly complex. A simple DLL consists of a chain of inverters. Note that we need to have an even number of inverters to ensure that the output is equal to the input. To create a tunable delay element, we can tap the signals after every pair of inverters. These signals are logically equivalent to the input, but have a progressive phase delay due to the propagation delay of the inverters. We can then choose the signal with a specific amount of phase delay by using a multiplexer.

Plesiochronous Bus*

Let us now consider a more realistic scenario. In this case the clocks of the sender and receiver might not exactly be the same. We might have a small amount of clock drift. We can assume that over a period of tens or hundreds of cycles it is minimal. However, we can have a couple cycles of drift over millions of cycles. Secondly, let us assume that the sender does not transmit data all the time. There are idle periods in the bus. Such kind of buses are found in server computers where we have multiple motherboards that theoretically run at the same frequency, but do not share a common clock. There is some amount of clock drift (around 200 ppm [Dally and Poulton, 1998]) between the processors when we consider timescales of the order of millions of cycles.

Let us now make some simplistic assumptions. Typically a given frame of data contains 100s or possibly 1000s of bits. We need not worry about clock drift when we are transmitting a few bits (< 100). However, for more bits (> 100), we need to periodically resynchronise the clocks such that we do not miss data. Secondly, ensuring that there are no transitions in the keep-out region of the receiver's clock is a non-trivial problem.

To solve this problem, we use an additional signal known as the *strobe* that is synchronised with the sender's clock. We toggle a strobe pulse at the beginning of the transmission of a frame (or possibly a few cycles before sending the first data bit). We then periodically toggle the strobe pulse once every n cycles. In this case, the receiver uses a tunable delay element. It tunes its delay based on the interval between the time at which it receives the strobe pulse, and the clock transition. After sending the strobe pulse for a few cycles, we start transmitting data. Since the clocks can drift, we need to readjust or retune the delay element. Hence, it is necessary to periodically send strobe pulses to the receiver. We show a timing diagram for the data and the strobe in Figure 12.15.

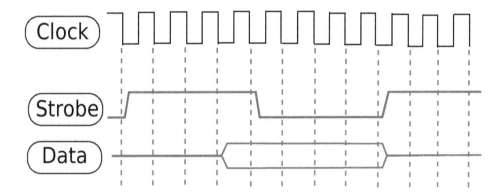

Figure 12.15: The timing diagram of a plesiochronous bus

Similar to the case of the mesochronous bus, every n cycles the receiver can read out all the n bits in parallel using a serial in – parallel out register. The circuit for the receiver is shown in Figure 12.16. We have a delay calculator circuit that takes the strobe and the receiver clock ($rclk$) as input. Based on the phase delay, it tunes the delay element such that data from the source arrives at the middle of the receiver's clock cycle. This needs to be done because of the following reason. Since the sender and receiver clock periods are not exactly the same, there can be an issue of rate mismatch. It is possible that we might get two valid data bits in one receiver clock cycle, or get no bits at all. This will happen, when a bit arrives towards the beginning or end of a clock cycle. Hence, we want to ensure that bits arrive at the middle of a clock cycle. Additionally, there are also metastability avoidance issues.

Sadly, the phase can gradually change and bits might start arriving at the receiver at the beginning of a clock cycle. It can then become possible to receive two bits in the same cycle. In this case, dedicated circuitry needs to predict this event, and a priori send a message to the sender to pause sending bits. Meanwhile, the delay element should be retuned to ensure that bits arrive at the middle of a cycle.

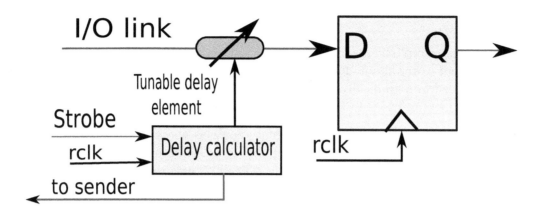

Figure 12.16: The receiver of a plesiochronous bus

12.3.2 Source Synchronous Bus*

Sadly, even plesiochronous buses are hard to manufacture. We often have large and unpredictable delays while transmitting signals, and even ensuring tight clock synchronisation is difficult. For example, the AMD hypertransport [Consortium et al., 2006] protocol that is used to provide a fast I/O path between different processors on the same motherboard does not assume synchronised or plesiosynchronised clocks. Secondly, the protocol assumes an additional jitter (unpredictability in the signal propagation time) of up to 1 cycle.

In such cases, we need to use a more complicated strobe signal. In a source synchronous bus, we typically send the sender clock as the strobe signal. The main insight is that if delays are introduced in the signal propagation time, then the signal and the strobe will be equally affected. This is a very realistic assumption, and thus most high performance I/O buses use source synchronous buses as of 2013. The circuit for a source synchronous bus is again not very complicated. We clock in data to the serial in – parallel out register using the clock of the sender (sent as the strobe). It is referred to as $xclk$. We read the data out using the clock of the receiver as shown in Figure 12.17. As a rule whenever a signal travels across clock boundaries we need a tunable delay element to keep transitions out of the keep-out region. We thus have a delay calculator circuit that computes the parameters of the delay element depending upon the phase difference between the sender clock received as a strobe ($xclk$), and the receiver clock ($rclk$).

Note that it is possible to have multiple parallel data links such that a set of bits can be sent simultaneously. All the data lines can share the strobe that carries the synchronising clock signal.

12.3.3 Asynchronous Buses

Clock Detection and Recovery*

Now, let us consider the most general class of buses known as *asynchronous buses*. Here, we do not make any guarantees regarding the synchronisation of the clocks of the sender and the receiver. Nor, do we send the clock of the sender along with the signal. It is the job of the receiver, to extract the clock of the sender from the signal, and read the data in correctly. Let us take a look at the circuit for reading in the data as shown in Figure 12.18.

For the sake of explanation, let us assume that we use the NRZ method of encoding bits. Extending the design to other kinds of encodings is fairly easy, and we leave it as an exercise for the reader. The logical bit stream passed on by the transmission sublayer is sent to the first D flip-flop, and simultaneously to the clock detector and recovery circuit. These circuits examine the transitions in the I/O signal and try to guess the

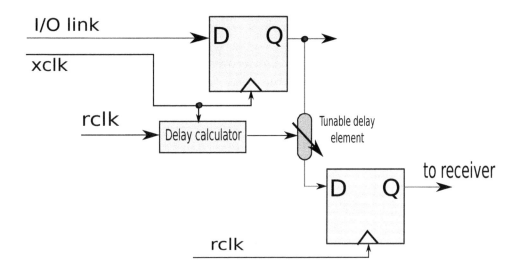

Figure 12.17: The receiver of a source synchronous bus

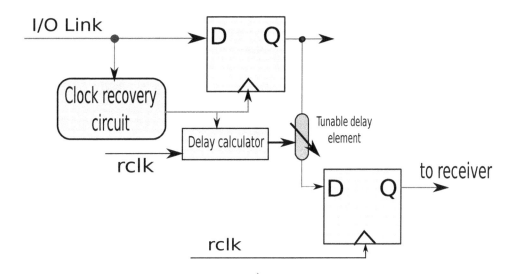

Figure 12.18: The receiver circuit in an asynchronous bus

clock of the sender. Specifically, the clock recovery circuit contains a PLL (phase locked loop). A *PLL* is an oscillator that generates a clock signal, and tries to adjust its phase and frequency such that it is as close as possible to the sequence of transitions in the input signal. Note that this is a rather involved operation.

In the case of the RZ or Manchester encodings, we have periodic transitions. Hence, it is easier to synchronise the PLL circuits at the receiver. However, for the NRZ encoding, we do not have periodic transitions. Hence, it is possible that the PLL circuits at the receiver might fall out of synchrony. A lot of protocols that use the NRZ encoding (notably the USB protocol) insert periodic transitions or dummy bits in the signal to resynchronise the PLLs at the receiver. Secondly, the PLL in the clock recovery circuit also needs to deal with the issue of long periods of inactivity in the bus. During this time, it can fall out of synchronisation. There are advanced schemes to ensure that we can correctly recover the clock from an asynchronous signal. These topics are taught in advanced courses in communication, and digital systems. We shall only take a cursory look in this chapter, and assume that the clock recovery circuit does its job correctly.

We connect the output of the clock detection and recovery circuit to the clock input of the first D flip-flop. We thus clock in data according to the sender's clock. To avoid metastability issues we introduce delay elements between the two D flip-flops. The second D flip-flop is in the receiver's clock domain. This part of the circuit is similar to that of source synchronous buses.

Note that in the case of ternary signalling, it is easy to find out when a bus is active (when we see a physical 0 or 1 on the bus). However, in the case of binary signalling, we do not know when the bus is active, because in principle we have a 0 or 1 bit being transmitted all the time. Hence, it is necessary to use an additional strobe signal to indicate the availability of data. Let us now look at protocols that use a strobe signal to indicate the availability of data on the bus. The strobe signals can also be optionally used by ternary buses to indicate the beginning and end of an I/O request. In any case, the reader needs to note that both the methods that we present using strobe signals are rather basic, and have been superseded by more advanced methods.

Asynchronous Communication with Strobe Signals

Let us assume that the source wishes to send data to the destination. It first places data on the bus, and after a small delay sets (sets to 1) the strobe as shown in the timing diagram in Figure 12.19. This is done to ensure that the data is stable on the bus before the receiver perceives the strobe to be set. The receiver immediately starts to read data values. Till the strobe is on, the receiver continues to read data, places it in a register, and transfers chunks of data to higher layers. When the source decides to stop sending data, it resets (sets to 0) the strobe. Note that timing is important here. We typically reset the strobe just before we cease sending data. This needs to be done because we want the receiver to treat the contents of the bus after the strobe is reset as the last bit. In general, we want the data signal to hold its value for some time after we have read it (for metastability constraints).

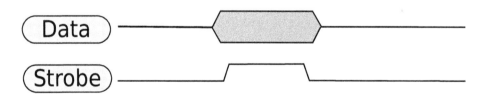

Figure 12.19: Timing diagram of a strobe based asynchronous communication system

Asynchronous Communication with Handshaking (4 Phase)

Note that in simple asynchronous communication with strobe signals the source has no way of knowing if the receiver has read the data. We thus introduce a handshaking protocol where the source is explicitly made aware of the fact that the receiver has read all its data. The associated timing diagram is shown in Figure 12.20.

At the outset, the sender places data on the bus, and then sets the strobe. The receiver begins to read data off the bus, as soon as it observes the strobe to be set. After it has read the data, it sets the *ack* line to

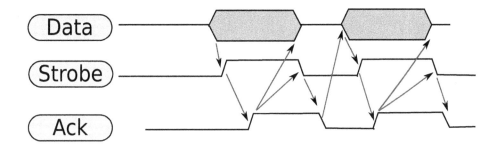

Figure 12.20: Timing diagram of a strobe based asynchronous communication system with handshaking

1. After the transmitter observes the *ack* line set to 1, it can be sure of the fact that the receiver has read the data. Hence, the transmitter resets the strobe, and stops sending data. When the receiver observes that the strobe has been reset, it resets the *ack* line. Subsequently, the transmitter is ready to transmit again using the same sequence of steps.

This sequence of steps ensures that the transmitter is aware of the fact that the receiver has read the data. Note that this diagram makes sense when the receiver can ascertain that it has read all the data that the transmitter wished to transmit. Consequently, designers mostly use this protocol for transmitting single bits. In this case, after the receiver has read the bit, it can assert the *ack* line. Secondly, this approach is also more relevant for the RZ and Manchester coding approaches because the transmitter needs to return to the default state before transmitting a new bit. After it receives the acknowledgement, the transmitter can begin the process of returning to the default state, as shown in Figure 12.19.

To transmit multiple bits in parallel, we need to have a strobe for each data line. We can however, have a common acknowledgement line. We need to set the *ack* signal when all the receivers have read their bits, and we need to reset the *ack* line, when all the strobe lines have been reset. Lastly, let us note that there are four separate events in this protocol (as shown in the diagram). Hence, this protocol is known as a 4-phase handshake protocol.

Asynchronous Communication with Handshaking (2 Phase)

If we are using the NRZ protocols, then we do not need to return to the default state. We can immediately start transmitting the next bit after receiving the acknowledgement. However, in this case, we need to slightly change the semantics of the strobe and acknowledgement signals. Figure 12.21 shows the timing diagram.

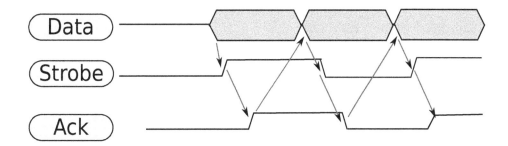

Figure 12.21: Timing diagram of a strobe based asynchronous communication system with 2-phase handshaking

In this case, after placing the data on the bus, the transmitter toggles the value of the strobe. Subsequently, after reading the data, the receiver toggles the value of the *ack* line. After the transmitter detects that the *ack* line has been toggled, it starts transmitting the next bit. After a short duration, it toggles the value of the strobe to indicate the presence of data. Again, after reading the bit, the receiver toggles the *ack* line, and the protocol thus continues. Note that in this case, instead of setting and resetting the *ack* and strobe lines, we toggle them instead. This reduces the number of events that we need to track on the bus. However, this requires us to keep some additional state at the side of the sender and the receiver. This a negligible overhead. Our 4-phase protocol thus gets significantly simplified. The NRZ protocols are more amenable to this approach because they have continuous data transmission, without any intervening *pause* periods.

Definition 149

Simple Synchronous Bus *A simple synchronous bus that assumes that the transmitter and the receiver share the same clock, and there is no skew (deviation) between the clocks.*

Mesochronous Bus *Here, the transmitter and receiver have the same clock frequency, but there can be a phase delay between the clocks.*

Plesiochronous Bus *In a plesiochronous bus, there is a small amount of mismatch between the frequencies of the clocks of the transmitter and receiver.*

Source Synchronous Bus *In a source synchronous bus, there is no relationship between the clocks of the transmitter and receiver. Consequently, we send the clock of the transmitter to the receiver along with the message, such that it can use it to sample the bits in the message.*

Asynchronous Bus *An asynchronous bus does not assume any relationship between the clocks of the transmitter and receiver. It typically has sophisticated circuitry to recover the clock of the transmitter by analysing the voltage transitions in the message.*

12.4 Data Link Layer

Now, we are ready to discuss the data link layer. The data link layer gets sequences of logical bits from the physical layer. If the width of the serial in – parallel out register is n bits, then we are guaranteed to get n bits at one go. The job of the data link layer is to break the data into frames, and buffer frames for transmission on other outgoing links. Secondly, it performs rudimentary error checking and correction. It is possible that due to electromagnetic interference, errors might be induced in the signal. For example, a logical 1 might flip to a logical 0, and vice versa. It is possible to correct such single bit errors in the data link layer. If there are a lot of errors, and it is not possible to correct the errors, then at this stage, the receiver can send a message to the transmitter requesting for a retransmission. After error checking the frame is ready to be forwarded on another link if required.

It is possible that multiple senders might be trying to access a bus at the same time. In this case, we need to arbitrate between the requests, and ensure that only one sender can send data at any single point of time. This process is known as *arbitration*, and is also typically performed in the data link layer. Lastly, the arbitration logic needs to have special support for handling requests that are part of a transaction. For example, the bus to the memory units might contain a load request as a part of a memory transaction. In response, the memory unit sends a response message containing the contents of the memory locations. We need a little bit of additional support at the level of the bus controller to support such message patterns.

To summarise the data link layer breaks data received from the physical layer into frames, performs error checking, manages the bus by allowing a single transmitter at a single time, and optimises communication for common message patterns.

12.4.1 Framing and Buffering

The processing in the data link layer begins by reading sets of bits from the physical layer. We can either have one serial link, or multiple serial links that transmit bits simultaneously. A set of multiple serial links is known as a *parallel link*. In both cases, we read in data, save them in serial in – parallel out shift registers, and send chunks of bits to the data link layer. The role of the data link layer is to create frames of bits from the values that it gets from the physical layer. A *frame* might be one byte for links that transfer data from the keyboard and mouse, and might be as high as 128 bytes for links that transfer data between the processor and the main memory, or the main memory and the graphics card. In any case, the data link layer for each bus controller is aware of the frame size. The main problem is to demarcate the boundaries of a frame.

Demarcation by Inserting Long Pauses Between two consecutive frames, the bus controller can insert long pauses. By examining, the duration of these pauses, the receiver can infer frame boundaries. However, because of jitter in the I/O channel, the duration of these pauses can change, and new pauses can be introduced. This is not a very reliable method and it also wastes valuable bandwidth.

Bit Count We can fix the number of bits in a frame a priori. We can simply count the number of bits that are sent, and declare a frame to be over once the required number of bits have reached the receiver. However, the main issue is that sometimes pulses can get deleted because of signal distortion, and it is very easy to go out of synchronisation.

Bit/Byte Stuffing This is the most flexible approach and is used in most commercial implementations of I/O buses. Here, we use a pre-specified sequence of bits to designate the start and end of a frame. For example, we can use the pattern 0xDEADBEEF to indicate the start of a frame, and 0x12345678 to indicate the end of a frame. The probability that any 32-bit sequence in the frame will match the special sequences at the start and end is very small. The probability is equal to 2^{-32}, or $2.5e - 10$. Sadly, the probability is still non zero. Hence, we can adopt a simple solution to solve this problem. If the sequence, 0xDEADBEEF appears in the content of the frame, then we add 32 more dummy bits and repeat this pattern. For example, the bit pattern 0xDEADBEEF gets replaced with 0xDEADBEEFDEADBEEF. The link layer of the receiver can find out that the pattern repeats an even number of times. Half of the bits in the pattern are a part of the frame, and the rest are dummy bits. The receiver can then proceed to remove the dummy bits. This method is flexible because it can be made very resilient to jitter and reliability problems. These sequences are also known as *commas*.

Once, the data link layer creates a frame, it sends it to the error checking module, and also buffers it.

12.4.2 Error Detection and Correction

Errors can get introduced in signal transmission for a variety of reasons. We can have external electromagnetic interference due to other electronic gadgets operating nearby. Readers would have noticed a loss in the voice quality of a mobile phone after they switch on an electronic gadget such as a microwave oven. This happens because electromagnetic waves get coupled to the copper wires of the I/O channel and introduce current pulses. We can also have additional interference from nearby wires (known as *crosstalk*), and changes in the transmission delay of a wire due to temperature. Cumulatively, interference can induce jitter (introduce variabilities in the propagation time of the signal), and introduce distortion (change the shape of the pulses). We can thus wrongly interpret a 0 as a 1, and vice versa. It is thus necessary to add redundant information, such that the correct value can be recovered.

The reader needs to note that the probability of an error is very low in practice. It is typically less than 1 in every million transfers for interconnects on motherboards. However, this is not a very small number either. If we have a million I/O operations per second, which is plausible, then we will typically have 1 error per second. This is actually a very high error rate. Hence, we need to add extra information to bits such that we can detect and recover from errors. This approach is known as forward error correction. In comparison, in backward error correction, we detect an error, discard the message, and request the sender to retransmit. Let us now discuss the prevalent error detection and recovery schemes.

Definition 150

Forward Error Correction *In this method, we add additional bits to a frame. These additional bits contain enough information to detect and recover from single or double bit errors if required.*

Backward Error Correction *In this method also, we add additional bits to a frame, and these bits help us detect single or double bit errors. However, they do not allow us to correct errors. We can discard the message, and ask the transmitter for a retransmission.*

Single Error Detection

Since single bit errors are fairly improbable, it is extremely unlikely that we shall have two errors in the same frame. Let us thus focus on detecting a single error, and also assume that only one bit flips its state due to an error.

Let us simplify our problem. Let us assume that a frame contains 8 bits, and we wish to detect if there is a single bit error. Let us number the bits in the frame as $D_1, D_2, \ldots, D_8$ respectively. Let us now add an additional bit known as the *parity bit*. The parity bit, P is equal to:

$$P = D_1 \oplus D_2 \oplus \ldots \oplus D_8 \tag{12.1}$$

Here, the $\oplus$ operation is the XOR operator. In simple terms, the parity bit represents the XOR of all the data bits ($D_1 \ldots D_8$). For every 8 bits, we send an additional bit, which is the parity bit. Thus, we convert a 8-bit message to an equivalent 9 bit message. In this case, we are effectively adding a 12.5% overhead in terms of available bandwidth, at the price of higher reliability. Figure 12.22 shows the structure of a frame or message using our 8-bit parity scheme. Note that we can support larger frame sizes also by associating a separate parity bit with each sequence of 8 data bits.

When the receiver receives the message, it computes the parity by computing the XOR of the 8 data bits. If this value matches the parity bit, then we can conclude that there is no error. However, if the parity bit in the message does not match the value of the computed parity bit, then we can conclude that there is a single bit error. The error can be in any of the data bits in the message, or can even be in the parity bit. In this case, we have no way of knowing. All that we can detect is that there is a single bit error. Let us now try to correct the error also.

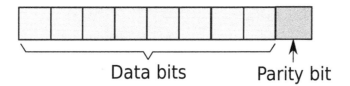

Figure 12.22: An 8-bit message with a parity bit

Single Error Correction

To correct a single bit error, we need to know the index of the bit that has been flipped if there is an error. Let us now count the set of possible outcomes. For an n-bit block, we need to know the index of the bit that has an error. We can have n possible indices in this case. We also need to account for the case, in which we do not have an error. Thus for a single error correction (SEC) circuit there are a total of $n + 1$ possible outcomes (n outcomes with errors, and one outcome with no error). Thus, from a theoretical point of view, we need $\lceil log(n + 1) \rceil$ additional bits. For example, for an 8-bit frame, we need $\lceil log(8 + 1) \rceil = 4$ bits. Let us design a (8,4) code that has four additional bits for every 8-bit data word.

Let us start out by extending the parity scheme. Let us assume that each of the four additional bits are parity bits. However, they are not the parity functions of the entire set of data bits. Instead, each bit is the parity of a subset of data bits. Let us name the four parity bits P_1, P_2, P_3, and P_4. Moreover, let us arrange the 8 data bits, and the 4 parity bits as shown in Figure 12.23.

Figure 12.23: Arrangement of data and parity bits

We keep the parity bits, P_1, P_2, P_3, and P_4 in positions 1, 2, 4 and 8 respectively. We arrange the data bits, $D_1 \ldots D_8$, in positions 3, 5, 6, 7, 9, 10, 11, and 12 respectively. The next step is to assign a set of data bits to each parity bit. Let us represent the position of each data bit in binary. In this case, we need 4 binary bits because the largest number that we need to represent is 12. Now, let us associate the first parity bit, P_1, with all the data bits whose positions (represented in binary) have 1 as their LSB. In this case, the data bits with 1 as their LSB are D_1 (3), D_2 (5), D_4 (7), D_5 (9), and D_7 (11). We thus compute the parity bit P_1 as:

$$P_1 = D_1 \oplus D_2 \oplus D_4 \oplus D_5 \oplus D_7 \tag{12.2}$$

Similarly, we associate the second parity bit, P_2, with all the data bits that have a 1 in their 2nd position (assumption is that the LSB is in the first position). We use similar definitions for the 3rd, and 4th parity bits.

Table 12.2 shows the association between data and parity bits. An "X" indicates that a given parity bit is a function of the data bit. Based, on this table, we arrive at the following equations for computing the parity bits.

Parity Bits	Data Bits							
	D_1	D_2	D_3	D_4	D_5	D_6	D_7	D_8
	0011	0101	0110	0111	1001	1010	1011	1100
P_1	X	X		X	X		X	
P_2	X		X	X		X	X	
P_3		X	X	X				X
P_4					X	X	X	X

Table 12.2: Relationship between data and parity bits

$$P_1 = D_1 \oplus D_2 \oplus D_4 \oplus D_5 \oplus D_7 \tag{12.3}$$
$$P_2 = D_1 \oplus D_3 \oplus D_4 \oplus D_6 \oplus D_7 \tag{12.4}$$
$$P_3 = D_2 \oplus D_3 \oplus D_4 \oplus D_8 \tag{12.5}$$
$$P_4 = D_5 \oplus D_6 \oplus D_7 \oplus D_8 \tag{12.6}$$

The algorithm for message transmission is as follows. We compute the parity bits according to Equations 12.3 – 12.6. Then, we insert the parity bits in the positions 1, 2, 4, and 8 respectively, and form a message according to Figure 12.23 by adding the data bits. Once the data link layer of the receiver gets the message it first extracts the parity bits, and forms a number of the form $P = P_4 P_3 P_2 P_1$, that is composed of the four parity bits. For example, if $P_1 = 0$, $P_2 = 0$, $P_3 = 1$, and $P_4 = 1$, then $P = 1100$. Subsequently, the error detection circuit at the receiver computes a new set of parity bits (P_1', P_2', P_3', P_4') from the received data bits, and forms another number of the form $P' = P_4' P_3' P_2' P_1'$. Ideally P should be equal to P'. However, if there is an error in the data or parity bits, then this will not be the case. Let us compute $P \oplus P'$. This value is also known as the *syndrome*.

Let us now try to correlate the value of the syndrome with the position of the erroneous bit. Let us first assume that there is an error in a parity bit. In this case, the first four entries in Table 12.3 show the position of the erroneous bit in the message, and the value of the syndrome. The value of the syndrome is equal to the position of the erroneous bit in the message. This should come as no surprise to the reader, because we designed our message to explicitly ensure this. The parity bits are at positions 1, 2, 4, and 8 respectively. Consequently, if any parity bit has an error, its corresponding bit in the syndrome gets set to 1, and the rest of the bits remain 0. Consequently, the syndrome matches the position of the erroneous bit.

Bit	Position	Syndrome	Bit	Position	Syndrome
P_1	1	0001	D_3	6	0110
P_2	2	0010	D_4	7	0111
P_3	4	0100	D_5	9	1001
P_4	8	1000	D_6	10	1010
D_1	3	0011	D_7	11	1011
D_2	5	0101	D_8	12	1100

Table 12.3: Relationship between the position of an error and the syndrome

Let us now consider the case of single bit errors in data bits. Again from Table 12.3, we can conclude that the syndrome matches the position of the data bit. This is because once a data bit has an error, all its associated parity bits get flipped. For example, if D_5 has an error then the parity bits, P_1 and P_4, get flipped. Recall that the reason we associate P_1 and P_4 with D_5 is because D_5 is bit number 9 (1001), and the two 1s in the binary representation of 9 are in positions 1 and 4 respectively. Subsequently, when there is an error in D_5, the syndrome is equal to 1001, which is also the index of the bit in the message. Similarly, there is a unique syndrome for every data and parity bit (refer to Table 12.2).

Thus, we can conclude that if there is an error, then the syndrome points to the index of the erroneous bit (data or parity). Now, if there is no error, then the syndrome is equal to 0. We thus have a method to detect and correct a single error. This method of encoding messages with additional parity bits is known as the SEC (single error correction) code.

Single Error Correction, Double Error Detection (SECDED)

Let us now try to use the SEC code to additionally detect double errors (errors in two bits). Let us show a counterexample, and prove that our method based on syndromes will not work. Let us assume that there are errors in bits D_2, and D_3. The syndrome will be equal to 0111. However, if there is an error in D_4, the syndrome will also be equal to 0111. There is thus no way of knowing whether we have a single bit error (D_4), or a double bit error (D_2 and D_3).

Let us slightly augment our algorithm to detect double errors also. Let us add an additional parity bit, P_5, that computes the parity of all the data bits ($D_1 \ldots D_8$), and the four parity bits ($P_1 \ldots P_4$) used in the SEC code, and then let us add P_5 to the message. Let us save it in the 13th position in our message, and exclude it from the process of calculation of the syndrome. The new algorithm is as follows. We first calculate the syndrome using the same process as used for the SEC (single error correction) code. If the syndrome is 0, then there can be no error (single or double). The proof for the case of a single error can be readily verified by taking a look at Table 12.2. For a double error, let us assume that two parity bits have gotten flipped. In this case, the syndrome will have two 1s. Similarly, if two data bits have been flipped, then the syndrome will have at least one 1 bit, because no two data bits have identical columns in Table 12.2. Now, if a data and a parity bit have been flipped, then also the syndrome will be non-zero, because a data bit is associated with multiple parity bits. The correct parity bits will indicate that there is an error.

Hence, if the syndrome is non-zero, we suspect an error; otherwise, we assume that there are no errors. If there is an error, we take a look at the bit P_5 in the message, and also recompute it at the receiver. Let us designate the recomputed parity bit as P_5'. Now, if $P_5 = P_5'$, then we can conclude that there is a double bit error. Two single bit errors are essentially cancelling each other while computing the final parity. Conversely, if $P_5 \neq P_5'$, then it means that we have a single bit error. We can thus use this check to detect if we have errors in two bits or one bit. If we have a single bit error, then we can also correct it. However, for a double bit error, we can just detect it, and possible ask the source for retransmission. This code is popularly known as the SECDED code .

Hamming Codes

All of the codes described up till now are known as *Hamming codes*. This is because they implicitly rely on the *Hamming distance*. The Hamming distance is the number of corresponding bits that are different between two sequences of binary bits. For example, the Hamming distance between 0011 and 1010 is 2 (MSB and LSB are different).

Let us now consider a 4-bit parity code. If a message is 0001, then the parity bit is equal to 1, and the transmitted message with the parity bit in the MSB position is 10001. Let us refer to the transmitted message as the code word. Note that 00001 is not a valid code word, and the receiver will rely on this fact to adjudge if there is an error or not. In fact, there is no other valid code word within a Hamming distance of 1 of a valid code word. The reader needs to prove this fact. Likewise for a SEC code, the minimum Hamming distance between code words is 2, and for a SECDED code it is 3. Let us now consider a different class of codes that are also very popular.

Cyclic Redundancy Check (CRC) Codes

CRC codes are mostly used for detecting errors, even though they can be used to correct single bit errors in most cases. To motivate the use of CRC codes let us take a look at the patterns of errors in practical I/O systems. Typically in I/O channels, we have interference for a duration of time that is longer than a bit period. For example, if there is some external electro-magnetic interference, then it might last for several cycles, and it is possible that several bits might get flipped. This pattern of errors is known as a *burst error*. For example, a 32-bit CRC code can detect burst errors as long as 32 bits. It typically can detect most 2-bit errors, and all single bit errors.

The mathematics behind CRC codes is complicated, and interested readers are referred to texts on coding theory [Neubauer et al., 2007]. Let us show a small example in this section.

Let us assume, that we wish to compute a 4-bit CRC code, for an 8-bit message. Let the message be equal to 10110011_2 in binary. The first step is to pad the message by 4 bits, which is the length of the CRC code. Thus, the new message is equal to $10110011\ 0000$ (a space has been added for improving readability). The CRC code requires another 5 bit number, which is known as the *generator polynomial* or the *divisor*. In principle, we need to divide the number represented by the message with the number represented by the divisor. The remainder is the CRC code. However, this division is different from regular division. It is known as modulo-2 division. In this case, let us assume that the divisor is 11001_2. Note that for an n-bit CRC code, the length of the divisor is $n + 1$ bits.

Let us now show the algorithm. We start out by aligning the MSB of the divisor with the MSB of the message. If the MSB of the message is equal to 1, then we compute a XOR of the first $n + 1$ (5 in this case) bits, and the divisor, and replace the corresponding bits in the message with the result. Otherwise, if the MSB is 0, we do not do anything. In the next step, we shift the divisor one step to the right, treat the bit in the message aligned with the MSB of the divisor as the MSB of the message, and repeat the same process. We continue this sequence of steps till the LSB of the divisor is aligned with the LSB of the message. We show the sequence of steps in Example 128. At the end, the least significant n (4 bits) contain the CRC code. For sending a message, we append the CRC code with the message. The receiver recomputes the CRC code, and matches it with the code that is appended with the message.

Example 128
Show the steps for computing a 4-bit CRC code, where the message is equal to 10110011_2, and the divisor is equal to 11001_2.
Answer:

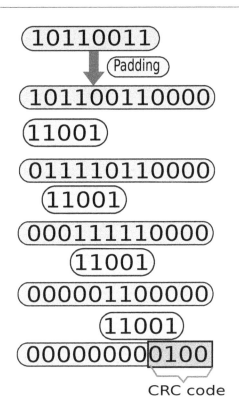

In this figure, we ignore the steps in which the MSB of the relevant part of the message is 0, because in these cases nothing needs to be done.

12.4.3 Arbitration

Let us now consider the problem of *bus arbitration*. The word "arbitration" literally means "resolution of disputes." Let us consider a *multidrop* bus, where we can potentially have multiple transmitters. Now, if multiple transmitters are interested in sending a value over the bus, we need to ensure that only one transmitter can send a value on the bus at any point of time. Thus, we need an arbitration policy to choose a device that can send data over the bus. If we have point-to-point buses, where we have one sender and one receiver, then arbitration is not required. If we have messages of different types waiting to be transmitted, then we need to schedule the transmission of messages on the link with respect to some optimality criteria.

Definition 151

We need to ensure that only one transmitter sends values on the bus at any point of time. Secondly, we need to ensure that there is fairness, and a transmitter does not need to wait for an indefinite amount of time for getting access to the bus. Furthermore, different devices connected to a bus, typically have different priorities. It is necessary to respect these priorities also. For example, the graphics card, should have more priority than the hard disk. If we delay the messages to the graphics card, the user will perceive jitter on her screen, and this will lead to a bad user experience. We thus need a bus allocation policy that is fair to all the transmitters, and is responsive to the needs of the computer system. This bus allocation policy is popularly known as the arbitration policy.

We envision a dedicated structure known as an *arbiter*, which performs the job of bus arbitration. All the devices are connected to the bus, and to the arbiter. They indicate their willingness to transmit data by sending a message to the arbiter. The arbiter chooses one of the devices. There are two topologies for connecting devices to an arbiter. We can either use a star like topology, or we can use a *daisy chain* topology. Let us discuss both the schemes in the subsequent sections.

Star Topology

In this centralised protocol, we have a single central entity called the *arbiter*. It is a dedicated piece of circuitry that accepts *bus request* requests from all the devices that are desirous of transmitting on the bus. It enforces priorities and fairness policies, and grants the right to individual devices to send data on the bus. Specifically, after a request finishes, the arbiter takes a look at all the current requests, and then asserts the *bus grant* signal for the device that is selected to send data. The selected device subsequently becomes the *bus master* and gets exclusive control of the bus. It can then configure the bus appropriately, and transmit data. An overview the system is shown in Figure 12.24.

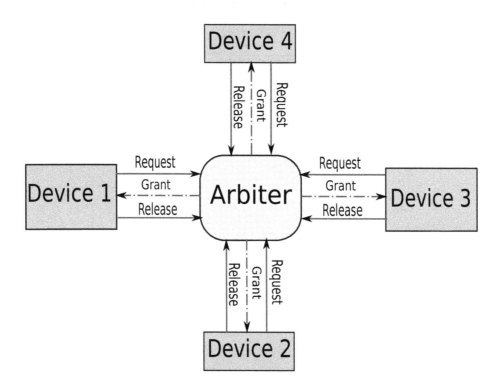

Figure 12.24: Centralised arbiter-based architecture

We can follow two kinds of approaches to find out when a current request has finished. The first approach is that every device connected to the bus transmits for a given number of cycles, n. In this case, after n cycles have elapsed, the *arbiter* can automatically presume that the bus is free, and it can schedule another request. However, this might not always be the case. We might have different speeds of transmission, and different message sizes. In this case, it is the responsibility of each transmitting device to let the arbiter know that it is done. We envision an additional signal *bus release*. Every device has a dedicated line to the arbiter that is used to send the *bus release* signal. Once it is done with the process of transmitting, it asserts this line (sets it equal to 1). Subsequently, the arbiter allocates the bus to another device. It typically follows standard policies such as round-robin or FIFO.

Daisy Chain Based Arbitration

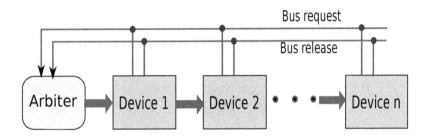

Figure 12.25: Daisy chain architecture

If we have multiple devices connected to a single bus, the arbiter needs to be aware of all of them, and their relative priorities. Moreover, as we increase the number of devices connected to the bus, we start having high contention at the arbiter, and it becomes slow. Hence, we wish to have a scheme, where we can easily enforce priorities, guarantee some degree of fairness, and not incur slowdowns in making bus allocation decisions as we increase the number of connected devices. The *daisy chain* bus was proposed with all of these requirements in mind.

Figure 12.25 shows the topology of a daisy chain based bus. The topology resembles a linear chain, with the arbiter at one end. Each device other than the last one has two connections. The protocol starts as follows. A device starts out by asserting its *bus request* lines. The *bus request* lines of all the devices are connected in a wired OR fashion. The *request* line that goes to the arbiter essentially computes a logical OR of all the bus request lines. Subsequently, the arbiter passes a token to the device connected to it if it has the token. Otherwise, we need to wait till the arbiter gets the release signal. Once a device gets the token, it becomes the *bus master*. It can transmit data on the bus if required. After transmitting messages, each device passes the token to the next device on the chain. This device also follows the same protocol. It transmits data if it needs to, otherwise, it just passes the token. Finally, the token reaches the end of the chain. The last device on the chain asserts the *bus release* signal, and destroys the token. The *release* signal is a logical OR of all the *bus release* signals. Once, the arbiter observes the *release* signal to be asserted, it creates a token. It re-inserts this token into the daisy chain after it sees the *request* line set to 1.

There are several subtle advantages to this scheme. The first is that we have an implicit notion of priority. The device that is connected to the arbiter has the highest priority. Gradually, as we move away form the arbiter the priority decreases. Secondly, the protocol has a degree of fairness because after a high priority device has relinquished the token, it cannot get it back again, until all the low priority devices have gotten the token. Thus, it is not possible for a device to wait indefinitely. Secondly, it is easy to plug in and remove devices to the bus. We never maintain any individual state of a device. All the communication to the arbiter is aggregated, and we only compute OR functions for the *bus request*, and *bus release* lines. The only state that a device has to maintain is the information regarding its relative position in the daisy chain, and the address of its immediate neighbour.

We can also have purely distributed schemes that avoid a centralised arbiter completely. In such schemes, all the nodes take decisions independently. However, such schemes are rarely used, and thus we shall refrain from discussing them.

12.4.4   Transaction-Oriented Buses

Up till now, we have been only focussing on unidirectional communication, where only one node can transmit to the other nodes at any single point of time. Let us now consider more realistic buses. In reality, most high performance I/O buses are not multidrop buses. Multidrop buses potentially allow multiple transmitters, albeit not at the same point of time. Modern I/O buses are instead point-to-point buses, which typically have two end points. Secondly, an I/O bus typically consists of two physical buses such that we can have bidirectional communication. For example, if we have an I/O bus connecting nodes A and B. Then it is possible for them to send messages to each other simultaneously.

Some early systems had a bus that connected the processor directly to the memory. In this case, the processor was designated as the *master*, because it could only initiate the transfer of a bus message. The memory was referred to as the *slave*, which could only respond to requests. Nowadays, the notion of a master and a slave has become diluted. However, the notion of concurrent bidirectional communication is still common. A bidirectional bus is known as a *duplex* bus or full duplex bus. In comparison, we can have a *half duplex bus*, which only allows one side to transmit at any point of time.

Definition 152

Full Duplex Bus *It is a bus that allows both of the nodes connected at its endpoints to transmit data at the same time.*

Half Duplex Bus *It only allows one of its endpoints to transmit at any point of time.*

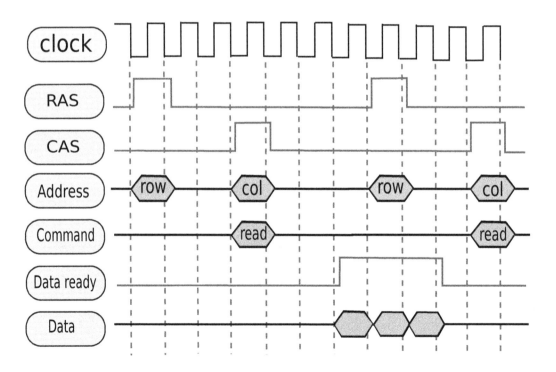

Figure 12.26: DRAM read timing

Let us look at a typical scenario of duplex communication between the memory controller chip, and the DRAM module in Figure 12.26. Figure 12.26 shows the sequence and timing of messages for a memory read operation. In practice, we have two buses. The first bus connects the memory controller to the DRAM module. It consists of address lines (lines to carry the memory address), and lines to carry dedicated control signals. The control signals indicate the timing of operations, and the nature of operation that needs to be performed on the DRAM arrays. The second bus connects the DRAM module to the memory controller. This contains data lines (lines to carry the data read from the DRAM), and timing lines (lines to convey timing information).

The protocol is as follows. The memory controller starts out by asserting the RAS (row address strobe) signal. The RAS signal activates the decoder that sets the values of the word lines. Simultaneously, the memory controller places the address of the row on the address lines. It has an estimate of the time (t_{row}) it takes for the DRAM module to buffer the row address. After t_{row} units of time, it asserts the CAS signal (column address strobe), and places the address of the columns in the DRAM array on the bus. It also enables the *read* signal indicating to the DRAM module that it needs to perform a read access. Subsequently, the DRAM module reads the contents of the memory locations and transfers it to its output buffers. It then asserts the *ready* signal, and places the data on the bus. However, at this point of time, the memory controller is not idle. It begins to place the row address of the next request on the bus. Note that the timing of a DRAM access is very intricate. Often the processing of consecutive messages is overlapped. For example, we can proceed to decode the row address of the $(n + 1)^{th}$ request, when the nth request is transferring its data. This reduces the DRAM latency. However, to support this functionality, we need a duplex bus, and a complex sequence of messages.

Let us note a salient feature of the basic DRAM access protocol that we showed in Figure 12.26. Here, the request and response are very strongly coupled with each other. The source (memory controller) is aware of the intricacies of the destination (DRAM module), and there is a strong interrelationship between the nature and timing of the messages sent by both the source and destination. Secondly, the I/O link between the memory controller and the DRAM module is locked for the duration of the request. We cannot service any intervening request between the original request and response. Such a sequence of messages is referred to as a *bus transaction*.

Definition 153

A bus transaction is defined as a sequence of messages on a duplex or multidrop bus by more than one node, where there is a strong relationship between the messages in terms of timing and semantics. It is in general not possible to send another unrelated sequence of messages in the middle, and then resume sending the original sequence of messages. The bus is locked for the entire duration.

There are pros and cons of transaction oriented buses. The first is complexity. They make a lot of assumptions regarding the timing of the receiver. Hence, the message transfer protocol becomes very specific to each type of receiver. This is detrimental to portability. It becomes very difficult to plug in a device that has different message semantics. Moreover, it is possible that the bus might get locked for a long duration, with idle periods. This wastes bandwidth. However, in some scenarios such as the example that we showed, transaction-oriented buses perform very well and are preferred over other types of buses.

12.4.5 Split Transaction Buses

Let us now look at *split transaction* buses that try to rectify the shortcomings of transaction oriented buses. Here, we do not assume a strict sequence of messages between different nodes. For example, for the DRAM and memory controller example, we break the message transfer into two smaller transactions. First, the memory controller sends the memory request to the DRAM. The DRAM module buffers the message, and proceeds with the memory access. Subsequently, it sends a separate message to the memory controller with the data from memory. The interval between both the message sequences can be arbitrarily large. Such a bus is known as a *split transaction* bus, which breaks a larger transaction into smaller and shorter individual message sequences.

The advantage here is simplicity and portability. All our transfers are essentially unidirectional. We send a message, and then we do not wait for its reply by locking the bus. The sender proceeds with other messages. Whenever, the receiver is ready with the response, it sends a separate message. Along with simplicity, this method also allows us to connect a variety of receivers to the bus. We just need to define a simple message semantics, and any receiver circuit that conforms with the semantics can be connected to the bus. We cannot use this bus to do complicated operations such as overlapping multiple requests, and responses, and fine grained timing control. For such requirements, we can always use a bus that supports transactions.

12.5   Network Layer

In Sections 12.2,12.3, and 12.4, we studied how to design a full duplex bus. In specific, we looked at signalling, signal encoding, timing, framing, error checking, and transaction related issues. Now, we have arrived at a point, where we can assume I/O buses that correctly transfer messages between end points, and ensure timely and correct delivery. Let us now look at the entire chipset, which is essentially a large network of I/O buses.

The problems that we intend to solve in this section, are related to I/O addressing. For example, if the processor wishes to send a message to an USB port, then it needs to have a way of uniquely addressing the USB port. Subsequently, the chipset needs to ensure that it properly routes the message to the appropriate I/O device. Similarly, if a device such as the keyboard, needs to send the ASCII code (see Section 2.5) of the key pressed to the processor, it needs to have a method of addressing the processor. We shall looking at routing messages in the chipset in this section.

12.5.1   I/O Port Addressing

Software Interface of an I/O Port

In Definition 140, we defined a hardware I/O port as a connection endpoint for an externally attached device. Let us now consider a *software port*, which we define to be an abstract entity that is visible to software as a single register, or a set of registers. For example, the USB port physically contains a set of metallic pins, and a port controller to run the USB protocol. However, the "software version of the USB port", is an addressable set of registers. If we wish to write to the USB device, then we write to the set of registers exposed by the USB port to software. The USB port controller implements the software abstraction, by physically writing the data sent by the processor to the connected I/O device. Likewise, for reading the value sent by an I/O device through the USB port, the processor issues a read instruction to the software interface of the USB port. The corresponding port controller forwards the output of the I/O device to the processor.

Let us graphically illustrate this concept in Figure 12.27. We have a physical hardware port that has a set of metallic pins, and associated electrical circuitry that implements the physical and data link layers. The port controller implements the network layer by fulfilling requests sent by the processor. It also exposes a set of 8 to 32-bit registers. These registers can be either read-only, write-only, or read-write. For example, the port for the display device such as the monitor contains write-only registers, because we do not get any inputs

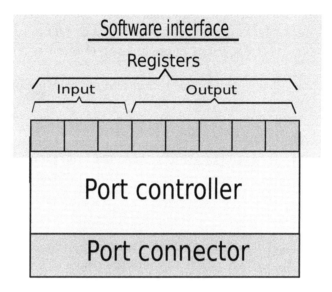

Figure 12.27: Software interface of an I/O port

from it. Similarly, the port controller of a mouse, contains read-only registers, and the port controller of a scanner contains read-write registers. This is because we typically send configuration data and commands to the scanner, and read the image of the document from the scanner.

For example, Intel processors define 64K (2^{16}) 8-bit I/O ports. It is possible to fuse 4 consecutive ports to have a 32-bit port. These ports are equivalent to registers that are accessible to assembly code. Secondly, a given physical port such as the Ethernet port or the USB port can have multiple such software ports assigned to them. For example, if we wish to write a large piece of data to the Ethernet in one go, then we might use hundreds of ports. Each port in the Intel processor is addressed using a 16-bit number that varies from 0 to 0xFFFF. Similarly, other architectures define a set of I/O ports that act as software interfaces for actual hardware ports.

Let us define the term *I/O address space* as the set of all the I/O port addresses that are accessible to the operating system and user programs. Each location in the I/O address space corresponds to an I/O port, which is the software interface to a physical I/O port controller.

Definition 154

The I/O address space *is defined as the set of all the I/O port addresses that are accessible to the operating system and user programs. Each location in the I/O address space corresponds to an I/O port, which is the software interface to a physical I/O port controller.*

ISA Support for I/O Ports

Most instruction set architectures have two instructions: *in* and *out*. The semantics of the instructions are as follows.

The *in* instruction transfers data from an I/O port to a register. Conversely, the *out* instruction transfers data from a register to an I/O port. This is a very generic and versatile mechanism for programming I/O

Instruction	Semantics
in r1, ⟨I/O port⟩	$r1 \leftarrow$ contents of ⟨I/O port⟩
out r1, ⟨I/O port⟩	contents of ⟨I/O port⟩ $\leftarrow r1$

Table 12.4: Semantics of the *in* and *out* instructions

devices. For example, if we want to print a page, then we can transfer the contents of the entire page to the I/O ports of the printer. Finally, we write the print command to the I/O port that accepts commands for the printer. Subsequently, the printer can start printing.

Routing Messages to I/O Ports

Let us now implement the *in* and *out* instructions. The first task is to ensure that a message reaches the appropriate port controller, and the second task is to route the response back to the processor in the case of an *out* instruction.

Let us again take a look at the architecture of the motherboard in Figure 12.4. The CPU is connected to the North Bridge chip via the front side bus. The DRAM memory modules, and the graphics card are also connected to the North Bridge chip. Additionally, the North Bridge chip is connected to the South Bridge chip that handles slower devices. The South Bridge chip is connected to the USB ports, the PCI Express Bus (and all the devices connected to it), the hard disk, the mouse, keyboard, speakers and the network card. Each of these devices has a set of associated I/O ports, and I/O port numbers.

Typically the motherboard designers have a scheme for allocating I/O ports. Let us try to construct one such scheme. Let us suppose that we have 64K 8-bit I/O ports like the Intel processors. The addresses of the I/O ports thus range from 0 to 0xFFFF. Let us first allocate I/O ports to high-bandwidth devices that are connected to the North Bridge chip. Let us give them port addresses in the range of 0 to 0x00FF. Let us partition the rest of the addresses for the devices connected to the South Bridge chip. Let us assume that the hard disk has a range of ports from 0x0100 to 0x0800. Let the USB ports have a range from 0x0801 to 0x0FFF. Let us assign the network card the following range: 0x1000 to 0x4000. Let us assign a few of the remaining ports to the rest of the devices, and keep a part of the range empty for any new devices that we might want to attach later.

Now, when the processor issues an I/O instruction (*in* or *out*), the processor recognises that it is an I/O instruction, sends the I/O port address, and the instruction type to the North Bridge chip through the FSB (front side bus). The North Bridge chip maintains a table of ranges for each I/O port type, and their locations. Once it sees the message from the processor, it accesses this table and finds out the relative location of the destination. If the destination is a device that is directly connected to it, then the North Bridge chip forwards the message to the destination. Otherwise, it forwards the request to the South Bridge chip. The South Bridge chip maintains a similar table of I/O port ranges, and device locations. After performing a lookup in this table, it forwards the received message to the appropriate device. These tables are called I/O routing tables. I/O routing tables are conceptually similar to network routing tables used by large networks and the internet.

For the reverse path, the response is typically sent to the processor. We assign a unique identifier to the processor, and the messages gets routed appropriately by the North Bridge and South Bridge chips. Sometimes it is necessary to route the message to the memory modules (see Section 12.6.3). We use a similar addressing scheme.

This scheme essentially maps the set of physical I/O ports to locations in the I/O address space, and the dedicated I/O instructions use the port addresses to communicate with them. This method of accessing and addressing I/O devices is commonly known as I/O mapped I/O.

> **Definition 155** *I/O mapped I/O is a scheme for addressing and accessing I/O devices by assigning each physical I/O port a unique address in the I/O space, and by using dedicated I/O instructions to transfer data to/from locations in the I/O address space.*

12.5.2 Memory Mapped Addressing

Let us now take a look at the *in* and *out* I/O instructions again. The executing program needs to be aware of the naming schemes for I/O ports. It is possible that different chipsets and motherboards use different addresses for the I/O ports. For example, one motherboard might assign the USB ports the I/O port address range, 0xFF80 to 0xFFC0, and another motherboard might assign the range, 0xFEA0 to 0xFFB0. Consequently, a program that runs on the first motherboard might not work on the second motherboard.

To solve this issue, we need to add an additional layer between the I/O ports and software. Let us propose a solution similar to virtual memory. In fact, virtualisation is a standard technique for solving various problems in computer architecture. Let us proceed to design a virtual layer between user programs and the I/O address space.

Let us assume that we have a dedicated device driver in the operating system that is specific to the chipset and motherboard. It needs to be aware of the semantics of the I/O ports, and their mappings to actual devices. Now, let us consider a program (user program or OS) that wishes to access the USB ports. At the outset, it is not aware about the I/O port addresses of the USB ports. Hence, it needs to first request the relevant module in the operating system to map a memory region in its virtual address space to the relevant portion of the I/O address space. For example, if the I/O ports for the USB devices are between 0xF000 to 0xFFFF, then this 4 KB region in the I/O address space can be mapped to a page in the program's virtual address space. We need to add a special bit in the TLB and page table entries to indicate that this page actually maps to I/O ports. Secondly, instead of storing the address of the physical frame, we need to store the I/O port addresses. It is the role of the motherboard driver that is a a part of the operating system to create this mapping. After the operating system has mapped the I/O address space to a process's virtual address space, the process can proceed with the I/O access. Note that before creating the mapping, we need to ensure that the program has sufficient privileges to access the I/O device.

After the mapping has been created, the program is free to access the I/O ports. Instead of using I/O instructions such as *in*, and *out*, it uses regular load and store instructions to write to locations in its virtual address space. After such instructions reach the memory access (MA) stage of the pipeline, the effective address is sent to the TLB for translation. If there is a TLB hit, then the pipeline also becomes aware of the fact that the virtual address maps to the I/O address space rather than the physical address space. Secondly, the TLB also translates the virtual address to an I/O port address. Note that at this stage it is not necessary to use the TLB, we can use another dedicated module to translate the address. In any case, the processor receives the equivalent I/O port address in the MA stage. Subsequently, it creates an I/O request and dispatches the request to the I/O port. This part of the processing is exactly similar to the case of I/O mapped I/O.

> **Definition 156** *Memory mapped I/O is a scheme for addressing and accessing I/O devices by assigning each address in the I/O address space to a unique address in the process's virtual address space. For accessing an I/O port, the process uses regular load and store instructions.*

This scheme is known as memory mapped I/O. Its main advantage is that it uses regular load and store instructions to access I/O devices instead of dedicated I/O instructions. Secondly, the programmer need not be aware of the actual addresses of the I/O ports in the I/O address space. Since dedicated modules in the operating system, and the memory system, set up a mapping between the I/O address space and the process's virtual address space, the program can be completely oblivious of the semantics of addressing the I/O ports.

12.6 Protocol Layer

Let us now discuss the last layer in the I/O system. The first three layers ensure that a message is correctly delivered from one device to another in the I/O system. Let us now look at the level of a complete I/O request such as printing an entire page, scanning an entire document, or reading a large block of data from the hard disk. Let us consider the example of printing a document.

Assume that the printer is connected to an USB port. The printer device driver starts out by instructing the processor to send the contents of the document to the buffers associated with the USB port. Let us assume that each such buffer is assigned a unique port address, and the entire document fits within the set of buffers. Moreover, let us assume that the device driver is aware that the buffers are empty. To send the contents of the document, the device driver can use a sequence of *out* instructions, or can use memory mapped I/O. After transferring the contents of the document, the last step is to write the PRINT command to a pre-specified I/O port. The USB controller manages all the I/O ports associated with it, and ensures that messages sent to these ports are sent to the attached printer. The printer starts the job of printing after receiving the PRINT command from the USB controller.

Let us now assume that the user clicks the print button for another document. Before sending the new document to the printer, the driver needs to ensure that the printer has finished printing the previous document. The assumption here is that we have a simple printer that can only handle one document at a time. There should thus be a method for the driver to know if the printer is free.

Before looking at different mechanisms for the printer to communicate with its driver, let us consider an analogy. Let us consider a scenario in which Sofia is waiting for a letter to be delivered to her. If the letter is being sent through one of Sofia's friends, then Sofia can keep calling her friend to find out when she will be back in town. Once she is back, Sofia can go to her house, and collect the letter. Alternatively, the sender can send the letter through a courier service. In this case, Sofia simply needs to wait for the courier delivery boy to come and deliver the letter. The former mechanism of receiving messages is known as *polling*, and the latter is known as *interrupts*. Let us now elaborate.

12.6.1 Polling

Let us assume that there is a dedicated register called the *status register* in the printer that maintains the status of the printer. Whenever there is a change in the status of the printer, it updates the value of the status register. Let us assume that the status register can contain two values namely 0 (*free*) and 1 (*busy*). When the printer is printing a document, the value of the status register is 1 (*busy*). Subsequently, when the printer completes printing the document, it sets the value of the status register to 0 (*free*).

Now, let us assume that the printer driver wishes to read the value of the *status* register of the printer. It sends a message to the printer asking it for the value of the *status* register. The first step in sending a message is to send a sequence of bytes to the relevant I/O ports of the USB port controller. The port controller in turn sends the bytes to the printer. If it uses a split transaction bus, then it waits for the response to arrive. Meanwhile, the printer interprets the message, and sends the value of the *status* register as the response, which the USB port controller forwards to the processor through the I/O system.

If the printer is free, then the device driver can proceed to print the next document. Otherwise, it needs to wait for the printer to finish. It can keep on requesting the printer for its status till it is free. This method of repeatedly querying a device for its state till its state has a certain value is called *polling*.

Definition 157

Polling *is a method for waiting till an I/O device reaches a given state. It is implemented by repeatedly querying the device for its state in a loop.*

Let us show a snippet of *SimpleRisc* code that implements polling in a hypothetical system. We assume that the message for getting the status of the printer is 0xDEADBEEF. We need to first send the message to the I/O port 0xFF00, and then subsequently read the response from the I/O port 0xFF04.

```
───────────────────── Assembly Code for Polling ─────────────────────
/* load DEADBEEF in r0 */
movh r0, 0xDEAD
addu r0, r0, 0xBEEF

/* polling loop */
.loop:
        out r0, 0xFF00
        in  r1, 0xFF04
        cmp r1, 1
        beq .loop /* keep looping till status = 1 */
```

12.6.2 Interrupts

There are several shortcomings of the polling based approach. It keeps the processor busy, wastes power, and increases I/O traffic. We can use interrupts instead. Here, the idea is to send a message to the printer to notify the processor when it becomes free. After the printer becomes free, or if it is already free, the printer sends an interrupt to the processor. The I/O system typically treats the interrupt as a regular message. It then delivers the interrupt to the processor, or a dedicated interrupt controller. These entities realise that an interrupt has come from the I/O system. Subsequently, the processor stops executing the current program as described in Section 9.8, and jumps to the interrupt handler.

Note that every interrupt needs to identify itself, or the device that has generated it. Every device that is on the motherboard typically has a unique code. This code is a part of the interrupt. In some cases, when we connect devices to generic ports such as the USB port, the interrupt code contains two parts. One part is the address of the port on the motherboard that is connected to the external device. The other part is an id that is assigned to the device by the I/O port on the motherboard. Such interrupts that contain a unique code are known as *vectored interrupts*.

In some systems such as x86 machines, the first stage of interrupt processing is done by a *programmable interrupt controller* (PIC). These interrupt controllers are called APICs (advanced programmable interrupt controllers) in x86 processors. The role of these interrupt controllers is to buffer interrupt messages, and send them to the processor according to a set of rules.

Let us take a look at the set of rules that PICs follow. Most processors disable interrupt processing during some critical stages of computation. For example, when an interrupt handler is saving the state of the original program, we cannot allow the processor to get interrupted. After the state is successfully saved, interrupt handlers might re-enable interrupts. In some systems, interrupts are completely disabled whenever an interrupt handler is running. A closely related concept is interrupt masking that selectively enables some interrupts, and disables some other interrupts. For example, we might allow high priority interrupts from the temperature controller during the processing of an interrupt handler, and choose to temporarily ignore low priority interrupts from the hard disk. The PIC typically has a vector that has one entry per interrupt type. It is known as the *interrupt mask vector*. For an interrupt, if the corresponding bit in the interrupt mask vector is 1, then the interrupt is enabled, otherwise it is disabled.

Lastly, PICs need to respect the priority of interrupts if we have multiple interrupts arriving in the same window of time. For example, interrupts from a device with real time constraints such as an attached high speed communication device have a high priority, whereas keyboard and mouse interrupts have lower priority. The PIC orders interrupts using heuristics that take into account their priority and time of arrival, and presents them to the processor in that order. Subsequently, the processor processes the interrupt according to the methods explained in Section 9.8.

Definition 158

Vectored Interrupt *An interrupt that contains the id of the device that generated it, or the I/O port address that is connected to the external device.*

Programmable Interrupt Controller(PIC) *A dedicated module called the programmable interrupt controller (PIC) buffers, filters, and manages the interrupts sent to a processor.*

Interrupt Masking *The user, or operating system can choose to selectively disable a set of interrupts at some critical phases of programs such as while running device drivers and interrupt handlers. This mechanism is known as interrupt masking. The interrupt mask vector in the PIC is typically a bit vector (one bit per each interrupt type). If a bit is set to 1, then the interrupt is enabled, otherwise it is disabled, and the interrupt will either be ignored, or buffered in the PIC and processed later.*

12.6.3 DMA

For accessing I/O devices, we can use both polling and interrupts. In any case, for each I/O instruction we transfer typically 4 bytes at a time. This means that if we need to transfer a 4KB block to an I/O device, we need to issue 1024 *out* instructions. Similarly, if we wish to read in 4 KB of data, we need to issue 1024 *in* instructions. Each I/O instruction typically takes more than ten cycles, because it reaches an I/O port after several levels of indirection. Secondly, the frequency of I/O buses is typically a third to a quarter of the processor frequency. Thus, I/O for large blocks of data is a fairly slow process, and it can keep the processor busy for a long time. Our objective is to keep sensitive code such as device drivers and interrupt handlers as short as possible.

Hence, let us try to devise a solution that can offload some of the work of the processor. Let us consider an analogy. Let us assume that a professor is teaching a class of more than 100 students. After an exam, she needs to grade more than 100 scripts. This will keep her busy for at least a week, and the process of grading scripts is a very tiring and time consuming process. Hence, she can offload the work of grading exam scripts to teaching assistants. This will ensure that the professor has free time, and she can focus on solving state of the art research problems. We can take cues from this example, and design a similar scheme for processors.

Let us envision a dedicated unit called a DMA (direct memory access) engine that can do some work on behalf of the processor. In specific, if the processor wishes to transfer a large amount of data in memory to an I/O device, or vice versa, then instead of issuing a large number of I/O instructions, the DMA engine can take over the responsibility. The procedure for using a DMA engine is as follows. At the outset, the device driver program, determines that there is a necessity to transfer a large amount of data between memory and an I/O device. Subsequently, it sends the details of the memory region (range of bytes), and the details of the I/O device (I/O port addresses) to the DMA engine. It further specifies, whether the data transfer is from memory to I/O or in the reverse direction. Subsequently, the device driver program suspends itself, and the processor is free to run other programs. Meanwhile, the DMA engine or the DMA controller begins the process of transferring data between the main memory and I/O devices. Depending on the direction of the transfer, it reads the data, temporarily buffers it, and sends it to the destination. Once the transfer is over, it sends an interrupt to the processor indicating that the transfer is over. Subsequently, the device driver of the I/O device is ready to resume operation and complete any remaining steps.

The DMA based approach is typically used by modern processors to transfer a large amount of data between main memory, and the hard disk, or the network card. The transfer of data is done in the background, and the processor is mostly oblivious of this process. Secondly, most operating systems have libraries to program the DMA engine to perform data transfers.

There are two subtle points that need to be discussed in the context of DMA engines. The first is that the DMA controller needs to occasionally become the bus master. In most designs, the DMA engine is typically a part of the North Bridge chip. The DMA engine needs to become the bus master of the bus to memory, and the bus to the South Bridge chip, when required. It can either transfer all the data in one go (also known as a *burst*), or it can wait for idle periods in the bus, and use these cycles to schedule its own transfers. The former approach is known as the *burst* mode, and the latter approach is known as the *cycle stealing mode*.

The second subtle point is that there might be correctness issues if we are not careful. For example, it is possible that we have a given location in the cache, and simultaneously, the DMA engine is writing to the location in main memory. In this case, the value in the cache will become stale, and sadly, the processor will have no way of knowing this fact. Hence, it is important to ensure that locations accessed by DMA controllers are not present in the cache. This is typically achieved through a dedicated piece of logic called a DMA *snoop circuit* that dynamically evicts locations present in the cache, if they are written to by the DMA engine.

12.7 Case Studies – I/O Protocols

In this section, we shall describe the operation of several state of the art I/O protocols. We shall provide a brief overview of each of these protocols in this book. For a detailed study, or wherever there is a doubt, the reader should take a look at their formal specifications posted on the web. The formal specifications are typically released by a consortium of companies that support the I/O protocol. Most of the material that we present is sourced from these specifications.

12.7.1 PCI Express®

Overview

Most motherboards require local buses that can be used to attach devices such as dedicated sound cards, network cards, and graphics cards to the North Bridge or South Bridge chips. In response to this requirement, a consortium of companies created the PCI (Peripheral Component Interconnect) bus specification in 1993. In 1996, Intel created the AGP (Accelerated Graphics Port) bus for connecting graphics cards. In the late nineties, many new bus types were being proposed for connecting a variety of hardware devices to the North Bridge and South Bridge chips. Designers quickly realised that having many different bus protocols hampers standardisation efforts, and compels device vendors to support multiple bus protocols. Hence, a consortium of companies started a standardisation effort, and created the PCI Express bus standard in 2004. This technology superseded most of the earlier technologies, and till date it is the most popular bus on the motherboard.

The basic idea of the PCI express bus is that it is a high speed point to point serial (single bit) interconnect. A point to point interconnect has only two end points. To connect multiple devices to the South Bridge chip, we create a tree of PCI express devices. The internal nodes of the tree are PCI express switches that can multiplex traffic from multiple devices. Secondly, as compared to older protocols, each PCI Express bus sends bits serially on a single bit line. Typically high speed buses avoid transmitting multiple bits in parallel using several copper wires, because different links experience different degrees of jitter and signal distortion. It becomes very hard to keep all the signals in the different wires in synchrony with each other. Hence, modern buses are mostly serial.

A single PCI Express bus is actually composed of many individual serial buses known as *lanes*. Each lane has its separate physical layer. A PCI Express packet is *striped* across the lanes. *Striping* means dividing a block of data (packet) into smaller blocks of data and distributing them across the lanes. For example, in a bus with 8 lanes, and a 8-bit packet, we can send each bit of the packet on a separate lane. The reader needs to note that sending multiple bits in parallel across different lanes is not the same as a parallel bus that has multiple wires to send data. This is because a parallel bus has one physical layer circuit for all the copper wires, whereas in this case, each lane has its separate synchronisation, and timing. The data link layer does the job of framing by aggregating the subparts of each packet collected from the different lanes.

Definition 159
The process of striping *refers to dividing a block of data into smaller blocks of data and distributing them across a set of entities.*

A *lane* consists of two LVDS based wires for full duplex signalling. One wire is used to send a message from the first end point to the second, and the second wire is to send a signal in the reverse direction. A set of lanes are grouped together to form an I/O link that is assumed to transfer a full packet (or frame) of data. The physical layer then transfers a packet to the data link layer that performs error correction, flow control, and implements transactions. The PCI Express protocol is a layered protocol, where the functionality of each layer is roughly similar to the I/O layers that we have defined. Instead of considering transactions to be a part of the data link layer, it has a separate transaction layer. We shall however use the terminology that we have defined in this chapter for explaining all the I/O protocols unless mentioned otherwise.

Summary

A summary of the specifications of the PCI Express protocol is shown in Table 12.5. We can have 1-32 lanes. Here, each lane is an asynchronous bus, which uses a sophisticated version of data encoding called the 8bit/10bit encoding. The 8bit/10bit encoding can be conceptually thought of as an extension of the NRZ protocol. It maps a sequence of 8 logical bits to a sequence of 10 physical bits. It ensures that we do not have more than five 1s or 0s consecutively such that we can efficiently recover the clock. Recall that the receiver recovers the sender's clock by analysing transitions in the data. Secondly, the encoding ensures that we have almost the same number of physical 1s and 0s in the transmitted signal. In the data link layer the

PCI Express (Peripheral Component Interconnect Express)	
Usage	As a motherboard bus
Specification	[pci,]
Topology	
Connection	Point to point with multiple *lanes*
Lane	A single bit full duplex channel with data striping
Number of Lanes	1 – 32
Physical Layer	
Signalling	LVDS based differential signalling
Encoding	8 bit/ 10 bit
Timing	Source synchronous
Data Link Layer	
Frame Size	1 byte
Error Correction	32-bit CRC
Transactions	Split transaction bus
Bandwidth	250 MB/s per lane
Network Layer	
Routing Nodes	Switches

Table 12.5: The PCI Express I/O Protocol

PCI Express protocol implements a split transaction bus with a 1-128 byte frame, and 32-bit CRC based error correction.

The PCI Express bus is normally used to connect generic I/O devices. Sometimes some slots are left unused such that users can later connect cards for their specific applications. For example, if a user is interested in working with specialised medical devices, then she can attach an I/O card that can connect with medical devices externally, and to the PCI Express bus internally. Such free PCI Express slots are known as *expansion slots*.

12.7.2 SATA

Overview

Let us now take a look at a bus, which was primarily developed for connecting storage devices such as hard disks, and optical drives. Since the mid eighties, designers, and storage vendors, began designing such buses. Several such buses developed over time such as the IDE (Integrated Drive Electronics) and PATA (Parallel Advanced Technology Attachment) buses. These buses were predominantly parallel buses, and their constituent communication links suffered from different amounts of jitter and distortion. Thus, these technologies got replaced by a serial standard known as SATA (Serial ATA), that is a point to point link like PCI Express.

The SATA protocol for accessing storage devices is now used in an overwhelming majority of laptop and desktop processors. It has become the de facto standard. The SATA protocol has three layers – physical, data link, and transport. We map the transport layer of the SATA protocol to our protocol layer. Each SATA link contains a pair of single-bit links that use LVDS signalling. Unlike PCI Express, it is not possible for an end point in the SATA protocol to read and write data at the same time. Only one of the actions can be performed at any point of time. It is thus a half duplex bus. It uses 8b/10b encoding, and it is an asynchronous bus. The data link layer does the job of framing. Let us now discuss the network layer. Since SATA is a point to point protocol, a set of SATA devices can be connected in a tree structure. Each internal node of the tree is know as a *multiplier*. It routes requests from the parent to one of its children, of from one of its children to its parent. Finally, the protocol layer acts on the frames and ensures that they are transmitted in the correct sequence, and implements SATA commands. In specific, it implements DMA requests, accesses the storage devices, buffers data, and sends it to the processor in a predefined order.

Summary

SATA (Serial ATA)	
Usage	Used to connect storage devices such as hard disks
Source	[sat,]
Topology	
Connection	Point to point, half duplex
Topology	Tree based, internal nodes known as *multipliers*
Physical Layer	
Signalling	LVDS based differential signalling
Number of parallel links	4
Encoding	8 bit/ 10 bit
Timing	Asynchronous (clock recovery + comma symbols)
Data Link Layer	
Frame Size	variable
Error Correction	CRC
Transactions	Split transaction bus, command driven
Bandwidth	150-600 MB/s
Network Layer	
Routing Nodes	Multipliers
Protocol Layer	
Each SATA node has dedicated support for processing commands, and their responses. Examples of commands can be DMA reads, or I/O transfers	

Table 12.6: The SATA Protocol

Table 12.6 shows the specification of the SATA protocol. We need to note that the SATA protocol has a very rich protocol layer. It defines a wide variety of commands for storage based devices. For example, it has dedicated commands to perform DMA accesses, perform direct hard disk accesses, encode and encrypt data, and control the internals of storage devices. The SATA bus is a split transaction bus, and the data link layer differentiates between commands and their responses. The protocol layer implements the semantics of all the commands.

12.7.3   SCSI and SAS

Overview of SCSI

Let us now discuss another I/O protocol also meant for peripheral devices known as the SCSI protocol (pronounced as "scuzzy"). SCSI was originally meant to be a competitor of PCI. However, over time the

SCSI protocol metamorphosed to a protocol for connecting storage devices.

The original SCSI bus was a multidrop parallel bus that could have 8 to 16 connections. The SCSI protocol differentiates between a *host* and a peripheral device. For example, the South Bridge chip is a host, whereas the controller of a CD drive is a peripheral. Any pair of nodes (host or peripheral) can communicate between each other. The original SCSI bus was synchronous and ran at a relatively low frequency as compared to today's high speed buses. SCSI has still survived till date and state of the art SCSI buses use a 80-160 MHz clock to transmit 16 bits in parallel. They thus have a theoretical maximum bandwidth of 320-640 MB/s. Note that serial buses can go up till 1 GHz, are more versatile, and can support larger bandwidths.

Given the fact that there are issues with multidrop parallel buses, designers started retargetting the SCSI protocol for point to point serial buses. Recall that PCI Express and SATA buses were also created for the same reason. Consequently, designers proposed a host of buses that extended the original SCSI protocols, but were essentially point to point serial buses. Two such important technologies are the SAS (Serially Attached SCSI), and FC (fibre channel) buses. FC buses are mainly used for very high end systems such as supercomputers. The SAS bus is more commonly used for enterprise and scientific applications.

Let us thus primarily focus on the SAS protocol, because it is the most popular variant of the SCSI protocol in use today. SAS is a serial point to point technology that is also compatible with previous versions of SATA based devices, and its specification is very close to the specification of SATA.

Overview of SAS

SAS was designed to be backward compatible with SATA. Hence, both the protocols are not very different in the physical and data link layers. However, there are still some differences. The biggest difference is that SAS allows full duplex transmission, whereas SATA allows only half duplex transmission. Secondly, SAS can in general support larger frame sizes, and it supports a larger cable length between the end points as compared to SATA (8m for SAS, as compared to 1m for SATA).

The network layer is different from SATA. Instead of using a multiplier (used in SATA), SAS uses a much more sophisticated structure known as an *expander* for connecting to multiple SAS targets. Traditionally, the bus master of a SAS bus is known as the *initiator*, and the other node is known as the *target*. There are two kinds of expanders – *edge expander*, and *fanout expander*. An *edge expander* can be used to connect up to 255 SAS devices, and a *fanout expander* can be used to connect up to 255 edge expanders. We can add a large number of devices in a tree based topology using a root node, and a set of expanders. Each device at boot up time is assigned a unique SCSI id. A device might further be subdivided into several logical partitions. For example, your author at this moment is working on a storage system that is split into two logical partitions. Each partition has a logical unit number (LUN). The routing algorithm is as follows. The initiator sends a command to either a device directly if there is a direct connection or to an expander. The expander has a detailed routing table that maintains the location of the device as a function of its SCSI id. It looks up this routing table and forwards the packet to either the device, or to an edge expander. This edge expander has another routing table, which it uses to forward the command to the appropriate SCSI device. The SCSI device then forwards the command to the corresponding LUN. For sending a message to another SCSI device, or to the processor, a request follows the reverse path.

Lastly, the protocol layer is very flexible for SAS buses. It supports three kinds of protocols. We can either use SATA commands, SCSI commands, or SMP (SAS Management Protocol) commands. SMP commands are specialised commands for configuring and maintaining the network of SAS devices. The SCSI command set is very extensive, and is designed to control a host of devices (mostly storage devices). Note that a device has to be compatible with the SCSI protocol layer before we can send SCSI commands to it. If a device does not understand a certain command, then there is a possibility that something catastrophic might happen. For example, if we wish to read a CD, and the CD driver does not understand the command, then it might eject the CD. Even worse, it is possible that it might never eject the CD because it does not understand the eject command. The same argument holds true for the case of SATA also. We need to have SATA compatible devices such as SATA compatible hard drives and SATA compatible optical drives, if we wish to use SATA commands. SAS buses are by design compatible with both SATA devices and SAS/SCSI devices because of the flexibility of the protocol layer. For the protocol layer, SAS initiators send SCSI commands to SAS/SCSI devices, and SATA commands to SATA devices.

Nearline SAS (NL-SAS) drives are essentially SATA drives, but have a SCSI interface that translates SCSI commands to SATA commands. NL-SAS drives can thus be seamlessly used on SAS buses. Since the SCSI command set is more expressive and more efficient, NL-SAS drives are 10-20% faster than pure SATA drives.

Let us now very briefly describe the SCSI command set in exactly 4 sentences. The initiator begins by sending a command to the target. Each command has a 1-byte header, and it has a variable length payload. The target then sends a reply with the execution status of the command. The SCSI specifications defines at least 60 different commands for device control, and transferring data. For additional information, the readers can look up the SCSI specification at [scs,].

12.7.4   USB

Overview

Let us now consider the USB protocol, which was primarily designed for connecting external devices to a laptop or desktop computer such as keyboards, mice, speakers, web cameras, and printers. In the mid nineties vendors realised that there are many kinds of I/O bus protocols and connectors. Consequently, motherboard designers, and device driver writers were finding it hard to support a large range of devices. There was thus a need for standardisation. Hence, a consortium of companies (DEC, IBM, Intel, Nortel, NEC, and Microsoft) conceived the USB protocol (Universal Serial Bus).

The main aim of the USB protocol was to define a standard interface for all kinds of devices. The designers started out by classifying devices into three types namely low speed (keyboards, mice), full speed (high definition audio), and high speed (scanners, and video cameras). Three versions of the USB protocol have been proposed till 2012 namely versions 1.0, 2.0, and 3.0. The basic USB protocol is more or less the same. The protocols are backward compatible. This means that a modern computer that has a USB 3.0 port supports USB 1.0 devices. Unlike the SAS or SATA protocols that are designed for a specific set of hardware, and can thus make a lot of assumptions regarding the behaviour of the target device, the USB protocol was designed to be very generic. Consequently, designers needed to provide extensive support for the operating system to discover the type of the device, its requirements, and configure it appropriately. Secondly, a lot of USB devices do not have their power source such as keyboards and mice. It is thus necessary to include a power line for running connected devices in the USB cable. The designers of the USB protocol kept all of these requirements in mind.

From the outset, the designers wanted USB to be a fast protocol that could support high speed devices such as high definition video in the future. They thus decided to use a point to point serial bus (similar to PCI Express, SATA, and SAS). Every laptop, desktop, and midsized server, has an array of USB ports on the front or back panels. Each USB port, is considered a *host* that can connect with a set of USB devices. Since we are using serial links, we can create a tree of USB devices similar to trees of PCI Express and SAS devices. Most of the time we connect only one device to a USB port. However, this is not the only configuration. We can alternatively connect a USB hub, which acts like an internal node of the tree. An *USB hub* is in principle similar to a SATA multiplier and SAS expander.

A USB hub is most of the time a passive device, and typically has four ports to connect to other devices and hubs *downstream*. The most common configuration for a hub consists of one upstream port (connection to the parent), and four downstream ports. We can in this manner create a tree of USB hubs, and connect multiple devices to a single USB host on the motherboard. The USB protocol supports 127 devices per host, and we can at the most connect 5 hubs serially. Hubs can either be powered by the host, or be self powered. If a hub is self powered it can connect more devices. This is because, the USB protocol has a limit on the amount of current that it can deliver to any single device. At the moment, it is limited to 500 mA, and power is allocated in blocks of 100 mA. Hence, a hub that is powered by the host can have at the most 4 ports because it can give each device 100 mA, and keep 100 mA for itself. Occasionally, a hub needs to become an active device. Whenever, a USB device is disconnected from a hub, the hub detects this event, and sends a message to the processor.

Layers of the USB Protocol

Physical Layer
Let us now discuss the protocol in some more detail, and start with the physical layer. The standard USB connector has 4 pins. The first pin is a power line that provides a fixed 5V DC voltage. It is typically referred to as V_{cc} of V_{bus}. We shall use V_{cc}. There are two pins namely D^+ and D^- for differential signalling. Their default voltage is set to 3.3V. The fourth pin is the ground pin (GND). The mini and micro USB connectors have an additional pin called ID that helps differentiate between a connection to the host, and to a device.

The USB protocol uses differential signalling. It uses a variant of the NRZI protocol. For encoding logical bits, it assumes that a logical 0 is represented by a transition in physical bits, whereas a logical 1 is represented by no transitions (reverse of the traditional NRZI protocol). A USB bus is an asynchronous bus that recovers the clock. To aid in clock recovery, the synchronisation sublayer introduces dummy transitions if there are no transitions in the data. For example, if we have a continuous run of 1s, then there will be no transitions in the transmitted signal. In this case, the USB protocol introduces a 0 bit after every run of six 1s. This strategy ensures that we have some guaranteed transitions in the signal, and the receiver can recover the clock of the transmitter without falling out of synchrony. The USB connectors only have one pair of wires for differential signalling. Hence, full duplex signalling is not possible. Instead, USB links use half duplex signalling.

Data Link Layer
For the data link layer, the USB protocol uses CRC based error checking, and variable frame lengths. It uses bit stuffing (dedicated frame begin and end symbols) to demarcate frame boundaries. Arbitration is a rather complex issue in USB hubs. This is because, we have many kinds of traffic and many kinds of devices. The USB protocol defines four kinds of traffic.

Control Control messages that are used to configure devices.

Interrupt A small amount of data that needs to be sent to a device urgently.

Bulk A large amount of data without any guarantees of latency and bandwidth. E.g., image data in scanners.

Isochronous A fixed rate data transfer with latency and bandwidth guarantees. E.g., audio/video in web cameras.

Along with the different kinds of traffic, we have different categories of USB devices namely low speed devices (192 KB/s), full speed devices (1.5 MB/s), and high speed devices (60 MB/s). The latest USB 3.0 protocol has also introduced super speed devices that require up to 384 MB/s. However, this category is still not very popular (as of 2012); hence, we shall refrain from discussing it.

Now, it is possible to have a high-speed and a low-speed device connected to the same hub. Let us assume that the high speed device is doing a bulk transfer, and the low speed device is sending an interrupt. In this case, we need to prioritise the access to the upstream link of the hub. Arbitration is difficult because we need to conform to the specifications of each class of traffic and each class of devices. We have a dilemma between performing the bulk transfer, and sending the interrupt. We would ideally like to strike a balance between conflicting requirements by having different heuristics for traffic prioritisation. A detailed explanation of the arbitration mechanisms can be found in the USB specification [usb,].

Let us now consider the issue of transactions. Let us assume that a high speed hub is connected to the host. The high speed hub is also connected to full and low speed devices downstream. In this case, if the host starts a transaction to a low speed device through the high speed hub, then it will have to wait to get the reply from the device. This is because the link between the high speed hub and the device is slow. There is no reason to lock up the bus between the host, and the hub in this case. We can instead implement a split transaction. The first part of the split transaction sends the command to the low speed device. The second part of the split transaction consists of a message from the low speed device to the host. In the interval between the split transactions, the host can communicate with other devices. A USB bus implements similar split transactions for many other kinds of scenarios (refer to the USB Specification [usb,]).

Network Layer

Let us now consider the network layer. Each USB device including the hubs is assigned a unique ID by the host. Since we can support up to 127 devices per host, we need a 7-bit device id. Secondly, each device has multiple I/O ports. Each such I/O port is known as an end point. We can either have data end points (interrupt, bulk, or isochronous), or control end points. Additionally, we can classify end points as IN or OUT. The IN end point represents an I/O port that can only send data to the processor, and the OUT end point accepts data from the processor. Every USB device can have at the most 16 IN end points, and 16 OUT end points. Any USB request clearly specifies the type of end point that it needs to access (IN or OUT). Given that the type of the end point is fixed by the request, we need only 4 bits to specify the address of the end point.

All USB devices have a default set of IN and OUT end points whose id is equal to 0. These end points are used for activating the device, and establishing communication with it. Subsequently, each device defines its custom set of end points. Simple devices such as a mouse or keyboard that typically send data to the processor define just one IN end point. However, more complicated devices such as web cameras define multiple end points. One end point is for the video feed, one end point is for the audio feed, and there can be multiple end points for exchanging control and status data.

The responsibility of routing messages to the correct USB device lies with the hubs. The hubs maintain routing tables that associate USB devices with local port ids. Once a message reaches the device, it routes it to the correct end point.

Protocol Layer

The USB protocol layer is fairly elaborate. It starts out by defining two kinds of connections between end points known as *pipes*. It defines a *stream pipe* to be a stream of data without any specific message structure. In comparison, *message pipes* are more structured and define a message sequence that the sender and receiver must both follow. A typical message in the *message pipe* consists of three kinds of packets. The communication starts with a *token* packet that contains the device id, id of the end point, nature of communication, and additional information regarding the connection. The hubs on the path route the token packet to the destination, and a connection is thus set up. Then depending upon the direction of the transfer (host to device or device to host), the host or the device sends a sequence of *data* packets. Finally, at the end of the sequence of data packets, the receiver of the packets sends a *handshake* packet to indicate the successful completion of the I/O request.

Summary

USB (Universal Serial Bus)	
Usage	Connecting peripheral devices such as keyboards, mice, web cameras, and pen drives
Source	[usb,]
Topology	
Connection	Point to point, serial
Width	Single bit, half duplex
Physical Layer	
Signalling	LVDS based differential signalling.
Encoding	NRZI (transition represents a logical 0)
Timing	Asynchronous (a 0 added after six continuous 1s for clock recovery)
Data Link Layer	
Frame Size	46 – 1058 bits
Error Correction	CRC
Transactions	Split transaction bus
Bandwidth	192 KB/s (low speed), 1.5 MB/s (full speed), 60 MB/s (high speed)
Network Layer	
Address	7-bit device id, 4-bit end point id
Routing	Using a tree of hubs
Hub	Has one upstream port, and up to 4 downstream ports
USB network	Can support a maximum of 127 devices
Protocol Layer	
Connections	Message pipe (structured), and stream pipe (unstructured)
Types of traffic	Control, Interrupt, Bulk, Isochronous

Table 12.7: The USB Protocol

Table 12.7 summarises our discussion on USB up till now. The reader can refer to the specifications of the USB protocol [usb,] for additional information.

12.7.5 FireWire Protocol

Overview

FireWire started out with being a high speed serial bus in Apple computers. However, nowadays it is being perceived as a competitor to USB. Even though it is not as popular as USB, it is still commonly used. Most laptops have FireWire ports. The FireWire ports are primarily used for connecting video cameras, and high speed optical drives. FireWire is now an IEEE standard (IEEE 1394), and its specifications are thus open and standardised. Let us take a brief look at the FireWire protocol.

Like all the buses that we have studied, FireWire is a high speed serial bus. For the same generation,

FireWire is typically faster than USB. For example, FireWire (S800) by default has a bandwidth of 100 MB/s, as compared to 60 MB/s for high speed USB devices. Secondly, the FireWire bus was designed to be a hybrid of a peripheral bus and a computer network. A single FireWire bus can support up to 63 devices. It is possible to construct a tree of devices by interconnecting multiple FireWire buses using FireWire bridges.

The most interesting thing about the FireWire protocol is that it does not presume a connection to a computer. Peripherals can communicate among themselves. For example, a printer can talk to a scanner without going through the computer. It implements a real network in the true sense. Consequently, whenever a FireWire network boots up, all the nodes co-operate and elect a leader. The leader node, or the root node is the root of a tree. Subsequently, the root node sends out messages, and each node is aware of its position in the tree.

The physical layer of the FireWire protocol consists of two LVDS links (one for transmitting data, and one for transmitting the strobe). The channel is thus half duplex. Note that latest versions of the Firewall protocol that have bandwidths greater than 100 MB/s also support full duplex transmission. They however, have a different connector that requires more pins. For encoding logical bits, most FireWire buses use a method of encoding known as *data strobe (DS) encoding*. The DS encoding has two lines. One line contains the data (NRZ encoding), and the other line contains the strobe. The strobe is equal to the data XORed with the clock. Let the data signal be D (sequence of 0s and 1s), the strobe signal be S, and the clock of the sender be C. We have:

$$
\begin{aligned}
S &= D \oplus C \\
\Rightarrow D \oplus S &= C
\end{aligned}
\tag{12.7}
$$

At the side of the receiver, it can recover the clock of the sender by computing $D \oplus S$ (XOR of the data and the strobe). Thus, we can think of the DS encoding as a variant of source synchronous transmission, where instead of sending the clock of the sender, we send the strobe.

The link layer of the FireWire protocol implements CRC based error checking, and split transactions. FireWire protocols have a unique way of performing arbitration. We divide time into 125 μs cycles. The root node broadcasts a start packet to all the nodes. Nodes that wish to transmit isochronous data (data at a constant bandwidth) send their requests along with bandwidth requirements to the root node. The root node typically uses FIFO scheduling. It gives one device permission to use the bus and transmit data for a portion of the 125 μs cycle. Once the request is over, it gives permission to the next isochronous request and so on. Note that in a given cycle, we can only allot 80% of the time for isochronous transmission. Once, all the requests are over, or we complete 80% of the cycle, all isochronous transactions stop. The root subsequently considers asynchronous requests (single message transfers).

Devices that wish to send asynchronous data send their requests to the root through internal nodes in the tree (other FireWire devices). If an internal node represented by a FireWire device wishes to send an asynchronous packet in the current cycle, it denies the request to all the requesters that are in its subtree. Once a request reaches the root node, it sends a packet back to the requester to grant it permission to transmit a packet. The receiver is supposed to acknowledge the receipt of the packet. After a packet transmission has finished, the root node schedules the next request. The aspect of denying requests made by downstream nodes is similar to the concept of a daisy chain (see Section 12.4.3).

For the network layer, each FireWire device also defines its internal set of I/O ports. All the devices export a large I/O space to the processor. Each I/O port contains a device address and a port address within the device. The tree of devices first routes a request to the right device, and then the device routes the request to the correct internal port. Typically, the entire FireWire I/O address space is mapped to memory, and most of the time we use memory mapped I/O for FireWire devices.

Summary

FireWire (IEEE 1394)	
Usage	Connection to video cameras and optical drives
Source	[fir,]
Topology	
Connection	Point to Point, serial, daisy chain based tree
Width	Single bit, half duplex (till FireWire 400, full duplex beyond that)
Physical Layer	
Signalling	LVDS based differential signalling.
Encoding	Data Strobe Encoding (FireWire 800 and above also support 8bit/10 bit encoding)
Timing	Source Synchronous (sends a data strobe rather than a clock)
Data Link Layer	
Frame Size	12.5 KB (FireWire 800 protocol)
Error Correction	CRC
Transactions	Split Transaction Bus
Arbitration	(1) Elect a leader, or root node. (2) Each 125 μs cycle, the root sends a start packet, and each device willing to transmit sends its requirements to the root. (3) The root allots 100 μs for isochronous traffic, and the rest for asynchronous traffic
Bandwidth	100 MB/s (FireWire 800)
Network Layer	
Address Space	The tree of FireWire devices export a large I/O address space.
Routing	Using a tree of bridges

Table 12.8: The FireWire Protocol

Table 12.8 summarises our discussion on the FireWire protocol.

12.8 Storage

Out of all the peripheral devices that are typically attached to a processor, storage devices have a special place. This is primarily because they are integral to the functioning of the computer system.

The storage devices maintain *persistent state*. Persistent state refers to all the data that is stored in the computer system even when it is powered off. Notably, the storage systems store the operating system, all the programs, and their associated data. This includes all our documents, songs, images, and videos. From the point of view of a computer architect, the storage system plays an active role in the boot process, saving files and data, and virtual memory. Let us discuss each of these roles one by one.

When a processor starts (process is known as booting), it needs to load the code of the operating system.

Typically, the code of the operating system is available at the beginning of the address space of the primary hard disk. The processor then loads the code of the operating system into main memory, and starts executing it. After the boot process, the operating system is available to users, who can use it to run programs, and access data. Programs are saved as regular files in the storage system, and data is also saved in files. Files are essentially blocks of data in the hard disk, or similar storage devices. These blocks of data need to be read into main memory such that they are accessible by the processor.

Lastly storage devices play a very important role in implementing virtual memory. They store the swap space (see Section 10.4.4). Recall that the swap space contains all the frames that cannot be contained in main memory. It effectively helps to extend the physical address space to match the size of the virtual address space. A part of the frames are stored in main memory, and the remaining frames are stored in the swap space. They are brought into (swapped in), when there is a page fault.

Almost all types of computers have attached storage devices. There, however can be some exceptions. Some machines especially, in a lab setting, might access a hard disk over the network. They typically use a network boot protocol to boot from a remote hard disk, and access all the files including the swap space over the network. Conceptually, they still have an attached storage device. It is just not physically attached to the motherboard. It is nonetheless, accessible over the network.

Now, let us take a look at the main storage technologies. Traditionally, magnetic storage has been the dominant technology. This storage technology records the values of bits in tiny areas of a large ferro-magnetic disk. Depending on the state of magnetisation, we can either infer a logical 0 or 1. Instead of magnetic disk technology, we can use optical technology such as CD/DVD/Blu-ray drives. A CD/DVD/Blu-ray disk contains a sequence of pits (aberrations on the surface) that encodes a sequence of binary values. The optical disk drive uses a laser to read the values stored on the disk. Most of the operations of a computer typically access the hard disk, whereas optical disks are mainly used to archive videos and music. However, it is not uncommon to boot from the optical drives.

A fast emerging alternative to magnetic disks, and optical drives is solid state drives. Unlike magnetic, and optical drives that have moving parts, solid state drives are made of semiconductors. The most common technology used in solid state drives is *flash*. A flash memory device uses charge stored in a semiconductor to signify a logical 0 or 1. They are much faster than traditional hard drives. However, they can store far less data, and as of 2012, are 5-6 times more expensive. Hence, high end servers opt for hybrid solutions. They have a fast SSD drive that acts as a cache for a much larger hard drive.

Let us now take a look at each of these technologies. Note that in this book, our aim is to give the reader an understanding of the basic storage technologies such that she can optimise the computer architecture. For a deeper understanding of storage technologies the reader can take a look at [Brewer and Gill, 2008, Micheloni et al., 2010].

12.8.1 Hard Disks

A hard disk is an integral part of most computer systems starting from laptops to servers. It is a storage device made of ferromagnetic material and mechanical components that can provide a large amount of storage capacity at low cost. Consequently, for the last three decades hard disks have been exclusively used to save persistent state in personal computers, servers, and enterprise class systems.

Surprisingly, the basic physics of data storage is very simple. We save 0s and 1s in a series of magnets. Let us quickly review the basic physics of data storage in hard disks.

Physics of Data Storage in Hard Disks

Let us consider a typical magnet. It has a *north pole*, and a *south pole*. Like poles repel each other, and opposite poles attract each other. Along with mechanical properties, magnets have electrical properties also.

For example, when the magnetic field passing through a coil of wire changes due to the relative motion between the magnet and the coil, an EMF (voltage) is induced across the two ends of the wire according to Faraday's law. Hard disks use Faraday's law as the basis of their operation.

The basic element of a hard disk is a small magnet. Magnets used in hard disks are typically made of iron oxides and exhibit permanent magnetism. This means that their magnetic properties hold all the time. They are called permanent magnets or Ferromagnets (because of iron oxides). In comparison, we can have electromagnets that consist of coils of current carrying wires wrapped around iron bars. Electromagnets lose their magnetism after the current is switched off.

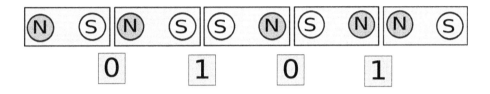

Figure 12.28: A sequence of tiny magnets on the surface of a hard disk

Now, let us consider a set of magnets in series as shown in Figure 12.28. There are two options for their relative orientation namely N-S (north–south), or S-N (south–north). Let us now move a small coil of wire over the arrangement of magnets. Whenever, it crosses the boundary of two magnets that have opposite orientations, there is a change in the magnetic field. Hence, as a direct consequence of Faraday's law, an EMF is induced across the two ends of the coil. However, when there is no change in the orientation of the magnetic field, the EMF induced across the ends of the coil is negligible. The transition in the orientation of the tiny magnets corresponds to a logical 1 bit, and no transition represents a logical 0 bit. Thus, the magnets in Figure 12.28 represent the bit pattern 0101. In principle, this is similar to the NRZI encoding for I/O channels.

Since we encode data in transitions, we need to save blocks of data. Consequently, hard disks save a block of data in a *sector*. A sector has traditionally between 512 bytes for hard disks. It is treated as an atomic block, and an entire sector is typically read or written in one go. The structure that contains the small coil, and passes over the magnets is known as the *read head*.

Let us now look at writing data to the hard disk. In this case, the task is to set the orientation of the magnets. We have another structure called the *write head* that contains a tiny electromagnet. An electromagnet can induce magnetisation of a permanent magnet if it passes over it. Secondly, the direction of magnetisation is dependent on the direction of the current. If we reverse the direction of the current, the direction of magnetisation changes.

For the sake of brevity, we shall refer to the combined assembly of the read head, and write head, as the *head*.

Structure of the Platter

A hard disk typically consists of a set of *platters*. A platter is a circular disk with a hole in the middle. A spindle is attached to the platter through the circular hole in the middle. The platter is divided into a set of concentric rings called tracks. A track is further divided into fixed length sectors as shown in Figure 12.29.

Definition 160
A hard disk consists of multiple platters. *A platter is a circular disk that is attached to a spindle. A*

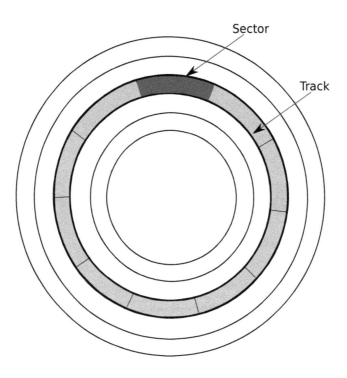

Figure 12.29: The structure of a platter

> *platter further consists of a set of concentric rings called* tracks, *and each track consists of a set of sectors. A sector typically contains a fixed number of bytes irrespective of the track.*

Now, let us outline the basic operation of a hard disk. The platters are attached to a spindle. During the operation of a hard disk, the spindle, and its attached platters are constantly in rotation. Let us for the sake of simplicity assume a single platter disk. Now, the first step is to position the head on the track that contains the desired data. Next, the head needs to wait at this position till the desired sector arrives under the head. Since the platter is rotating at a constant speed, we can calculate the amount of time that we need to wait based on the current position of the head. Once the desired sector, arrives under the head, we can proceed to read or write the data.

There is an important question that needs to be considered here. Do we have the same number of sectors per track, or do we have a different number of sectors per track? Note that there are technological limitations on the number of bits that can be saved per track. Hence, if we have the same number of sectors per track, then we are effectively wasting storage capacity in the tracks towards the periphery. This is because we are limited by the number of bits that we can store in the track that is closest to the center. Consequently, modern hard disks avoid this approach.

Let us try to store a variable number of sectors per track. Tracks towards the center contain fewer sectors, and tracks towards the periphery contain more sectors. This scheme also has its share of problems. Let us compare the innermost and outermost tracks, and let us assume that the innermost track contains N sectors, and the outermost track contains $2N$ sectors. If we assume that the number of rotations per minute is constant, then we need to read data twice as fast on the outermost track as compared to the innermost track. In fact for every track, the rate of data retrieval is different. This will complicate the electronic circuitry in the disk. We can explore another option, which is to rotate the disk at different speeds for each track, such that the rate of data transfer is constant. In this case, the electronic circuitry is simpler, but the sophistication required to run the spindle motor at a variety of different speeds is prohibitive. Hence, both the solutions are impractical.

How about, combining two impractical solutions to make it practical !!! We have been following similar approaches throughout this book. Let us divide the set of tracks into a set of zones. Each *zone* consists of a consecutive set of m tracks. If we have n tracks in the platter, then we have n/m zones. In each zone, the number of sectors per track is the same. The platter rotates with a constant angular velocity for all the tracks in a zone. In a zone, data is more densely packed for tracks that are closer to the center as compared to tracks towards the periphery of the platter. In other words, sectors have physically different sizes for tracks in a zone. This is not a problem since the disk drive assumes that it takes the same amount of time to pass over each sector in a zone, and rotation at a constant angular velocity ensures this.

Figure 12.30 shows a conceptual breakup of the platter into zones. Note that the number of sectors per track varies across zones. This method is known as *Zoned-Bit Recording*(ZBR). The two impractical designs that we refrained from considering, are special cases of ZBR. The first design assumes that we have one zone, and the second design assumes that each track belongs to a different zone.

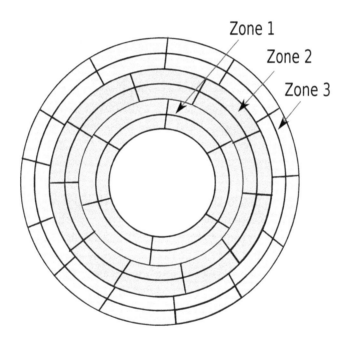

Figure 12.30: Zoned-Bit Recording

Let us now try to see why this scheme works. Since we have multiple zones, the storage space wasted is not as high as the design with just a single zone. Secondly, since the number of zones is typically not very large, the motor of the spindle does not need to readjust its speed frequently. In fact because of spatial locality, the chances of staying within the same zone are fairly high.

Structure of the Hard Disk

Let us now put all the parts together and take a look at the structure of the hard disk in Figure 12.31 and Figure 12.32. We have a set of platters connected to a single rotating spindle, and a set of disk arms (one for

Figure 12.31: The structure of a hard disk (source [har,])

each side of the platter) that contain a head at the end. Typically, all the arms move together, and all the heads are vertically aligned on the same *cylinder*. Here, a cylinder is defined as a set of tracks from multiple platters, which have the same radius. In most hard disks only one head is activated at a point of time. It performs a read or write access on a given sector. In the case of a read access, the data is transmitted back to the drive electronics for post processing (framing, error correction), and then sent on the bus to the processor through the bus interface.

Let us now consider some subtle points in the design of a hard disk (refer to Figure 12.32). It shows two platters connected to a spindle, and each platter has two recording surfaces. The spindle is connected to a motor (known as the spindle motor), which adjusts its speed depending on the zone that we wish to access. The set of all the arms move together, and are connected using a spindle to the *actuator*. The actuator is a small motor used for moving the arms clock wise or anti-clockwise. The role of the actuator is to position the head of an arm on a given track by rotating it clockwise or ant-clockwise a given number of degrees.

A typical disk drive in a desktop processor has a track density of about 10,000 tracks per inch. This means that the distance between tracks is 2.5 μm, and thus the actuator has to be incredibly accurate. Typically there are some markings on a sector indicating the number of the track. Consequently, the actuator typically needs to make slight adjustments to come to the exact point. This control mechanism is known as *servo control*. Both the actuator and the spindle motor are controlled by electronic circuits that are inside the chassis of the hard disk. Once the actuator has placed the head on the right track, it needs to wait for the desired sector to come under the head. A track has markings to indicate the number of the sector. The head keeps reading the markings after its positioned on a track. Based on these markings it can accurately predict when the desired sector will be underneath the head.

Along with the mechanical components, a hard disk has electronic components including small processors. They receive and transmit data on the bus, schedule requests on the hard disk, and perform error correction. The reader needs to appreciate the fact that we have just scratched the surface in this book. A hard disk is an incredible feat of human engineering. The hard disk can most of the time seamlessly tolerate errors, dynamically invalidate bad sectors (sectors with faults), and remap data to good sectors. The reader is

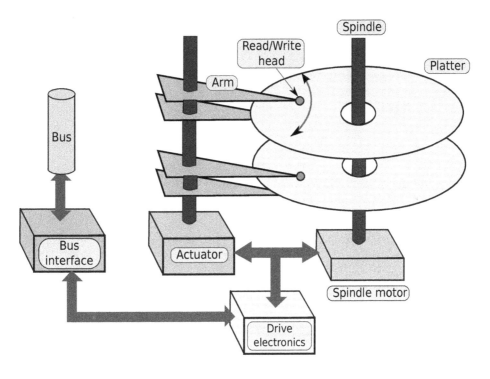

Figure 12.32: Internals of a hard disk

referred to [Jacob et al., 2007] for further study.

Mathematical Model of a Hard Disk Access

Let us now construct a quick mathematical model for the time a request takes to complete its access to the hard disk. We can divide the time taken into three parts. The first is the *seek time*, which is defined as the time required for the head to reach the right track. Subsequently, the head needs to wait for the desired sector to arrive under it. This time interval is known as the *rotational latency*. Lastly, the head needs to read the data, process it to remove errors and redundant information, and then transmit the data on the bus. This is known as the *transfer time*. Thus, we have the simple equation.

$$T_{disk\_access} = T_{seek} + T_{rot\_latency} + T_{transfer} \qquad (12.8)$$

Definition 161

Seek Time *The time required for the actuator to move the head to the right track.*

Rotational Latency *The time required for the desired sector to arrive under the head, after the head is correctly positioned on the right track.*

Transfer Time *The time required to transfer the data from the hard disk to the processor.*

Example 129
Assume that a hard disk has an average seek time of 12 ms, rotates at 600 rpm, and has a bandwidth of
10^6 *B/s. Find the average time to transfer 10,000 bytes of data (assuming that the data is in consecutive sectors).*

Answer: $T_{seek} = 12$ *ms*
Since the disk rotates at 600 rpm, it takes 100 ms per rotation. On an average, the rotational latency is half this amount because the offset between the current position of the head, and the desired offset is assumed to be uniformly distributed between $0°$ and $360°$. Thus, the rotational latency($T_{rot\_latency}$) is 50 ms. Now, the time it takes to transfer 10^4 contiguous bytes is 0.01s or 10 ms, because the bandwidth is 10^6 B/s.

Hence, the average time per disk access is 12 ms + 50 ms + 10 ms = 72 ms

---

12.8.2   RAID Arrays

Most enterprise systems have an array of hard disks because their storage, bandwidth, and reliability requirements are very high. Such arrays of hard disks are known as RAID arrays (Redundant Arrays of Inexpensive Disks). Let us review the design space of RAID based solutions in this section.

Definition 162
RAID (Redundant Array of Inexpensive Disks) is a class of technologies for deploying large arrays of disks. There are different RAID levels in the design space of RAID solutions. Each level makes separate bandwidth, capacity, and reliability guarantees.

RAID 0

Let us consider the simplest RAID solution known as RAID 0. Here, the aim is to increase bandwidth, and reliability is not a concern. It is typically used in personal computers optimised for high performance gaming.

The basic idea is known as *data striping*. Here, we distribute blocks of data across disks. A *block* is a contiguous sequence of data similar to cache blocks. Its size is typically 512 B; however, its size may vary depending on the RAID system. Let us consider a two disk system with RAID 0 as shown in Figure 12.33. We store all the odd numbered blocks (B1, B3, ...) in disk 1, and all the even numbered blocks (B2, B4, ...) in disk 2. If a processor has a page fault, then it can read blocks from both the disks in parallel, and thus in effect, the hard disk bandwidth is doubled. We can extend this idea and implement RAID 0, using N disks. The disk bandwidth can thus be theoretically increased N times.

RAID 1

Let us now add reliability to RAID 0. Note that the process of reading and writing bits in a hard disk is a mechanical process. It is possible that some bits might not be read or written correctly because there might be a slight amount of deviation from ideal operation in the actuator, or the spindle motor. Secondly, external electro-magnetic radiation, and cosmic particle strikes can flip bits in the hard disk and its associated electronic components. The latter type of errors are also known as *soft errors*. Consequently, each sector of

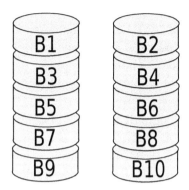

Figure 12.33: RAID 0

the disk typically has error detecting and correcting codes. Since an entire sector is read or written atomically, error checking and correction is a part of hard disk access. We typically care about more catastrophic failures such as the failure of an entire hard disk drive. This means that the there is break down in the actuator, spindle motor, or any other major component that prevents us from reading or writing to most of the hard disk. Let us consider disk failures from this angle. Secondly, let us also assume that disks follow the *fail stop* model of failure. This means that whenever there is a failure, the disks are not operational anymore, and the system is aware of it.

In RAID 1, we typically have a 2 disk system (see Figure 12.34), and we mirror data of one disk on the other. They are essentially duplicates of each other. We are definitely wasting half of our storage space here. In the case of reads, we can leverage this structure to theoretically double the disk bandwidth. Let us assume that we wish to read the blocks 1 and 3. In the case of RAID 0, we needed to serialise the accesses, because both the blocks map to the same disk. However, in this case, since each disk has a copy of all the data, we can read block 1 from disk 1, and read block 3 from disk 3 in parallel. Thus, the read bandwidth is potentially double that of a single disk. However, the write bandwidth is still the same as that of a single disk, because we need to write to both the disks. Note that here it is not necessary to read both the disks and compare the contents of a block in the interest of reliability. We assume that if a disk is operational, it contains correct data.

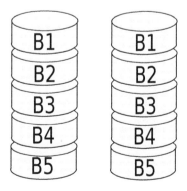

Figure 12.34: RAID 1

RAID 2

Let us now try to increase the efficiency of RAID 1. In this case, we consider a system of N disks. Instead of striping data at the block level, we stripe data at the bit level. We dedicate a disk for saving the parity bit. Let us consider a system with 5 disks as shown in Figure 12.35. We have 4 data disks, and 1 parity disk. We distribute contiguous sequences of 4 bits in a logical block across the 4 data disks. A *logical block* is defined as a block of contiguous data as seen by software. Software should be oblivious of the fact that we are using a RAID system instead of a single disk. All software programs perceive a storage system as an array of logical blocks. Now, the first bit of a logical block is saved in disk 1, the second bit is saved in disk 2, and finally the fourth bit is saved in disk 4. Disk 5, contains the parity of the first 4 bits. Each physical block in a RAID 2 disk thus contains a subset of bits of the logical blocks. For example, $B1$ contains bit numbers $1, 5, 9, \ldots$ of the first logical block saved in the RAID array. Similarly, $B2$ contains bit numbers $2, 6, 10, \ldots$. To read a logical block, the RAID controller assembles the physical blocks and creates a logical block. Similarly, to write a logical block, the RAID controller breaks it down into its constituent physical blocks, computes the parity bits, and writes to all the disks.

Reads are fast in RAID 2. This is because we can read all the 9 disks in parallel. Writes are also fast, because we can write parts of a block to different disks, in parallel. RAID 2 is currently not used because it does not allow parallel access to different logical blocks, introduces complexity because of bit level striping, and every I/O request requires access to all the disks. We would like to iterate again that the parity disk is not accessed on a read. The parity disk is accessed on a write because its contents need to be updated. Its main utility is to keep the system operational if there is a single disk failure. If a disk fails, then the contents of a block can be recovered by reading other blocks in the same row from the other disks, and by reading the parity disk.

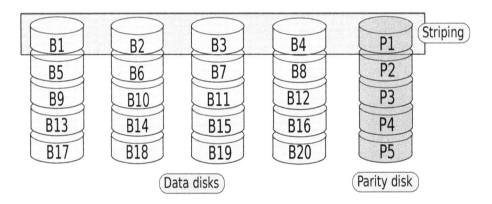

Figure 12.35: RAID 2

RAID 3

RAID 3 is almost the same as RAID 2. Instead of striping at the bit level, it stripes data at the byte level. It has the same pros and cons as RAID 2, and is thus seldom used.

RAID 4

RAID 4 is designed on the same lines as RAID 2 and 3. It stripes data at the block level. It has a dedicated parity disk that saves the parity of all the blocks on the same row. In this scheme, a read access for a single block is not as fast as RAID 2 and 3 because we cannot access different parts of a block in parallel. A write access is also slower for the same reason. However, we can read from multiple blocks at the same time if they do not map to the same disk. We cannot unfortunately do this for writes.

For a write access, we need to access two disks – the disk that contains the block, and the disk that contains the parity. An astute reader might try to argue that we need to access all the disks because we need to compute the parity of all the blocks in the same row. However, this is not true. Let us assume that there are m data disks, and the contents of the blocks in a row are $B_1 \ldots B_m$ respectively. Then the parity block, P, is equal to $B_1 \oplus B_2 \oplus \ldots \oplus B_m$. Now, let us assume that we change the first block from B_1 to B_1'. The new parity is given by $P' = B_1' \oplus B_2 \ldots \oplus B_m$. We thus have:

$$
\begin{aligned}
P' &= B_1' \oplus B_2 \ldots \oplus B_m \\
&= B_1 \oplus B_1 \oplus B_1' \oplus B_2 \ldots \oplus B_m \\
&= B_1 \oplus B_1' \oplus P
\end{aligned}
\tag{12.9}
$$

The results used in Equation 12.9 are: $B_1 \oplus B_1 = 0$ and $0 \oplus P' = P'$. Thus, to compute P', we need the values of B_1, and P. Hence, for performing a write to a block, we need two read accesses (for reading B_1 and P), and two write accesses (for writing B_1' and P') to the array of hard disks. Since all the parity blocks are saved in one disk, this becomes a point of contention, and the write performance becomes very slow. Hence, RAID 4 is also seldom used.

RAID 5

RAID 5 mitigates the shortcomings of RAID 4. It distributes the parity blocks across all the disks for different rows as shown in Figure 12.36. For example, the 5th disk stores the parity for the first row, and then the 1st disk stores the parity for the second row, and the pattern thus continues in a round robin fashion. This ensures that no disk becomes a point of contention, and the parity blocks are evenly distributed across all the disks.

Note that RAID 5 provides high bandwidth because it allows parallel access for reads, has relatively faster write speed, and is immune to one disk failure. Hence, it is heavily used in commercial systems.

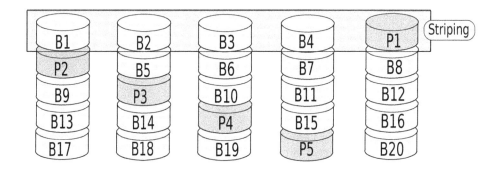

Figure 12.36: RAID 5

RAID 6

Sometimes, we might desire additional reliability. In this case, we can add a second parity block, and distribute both the parity blocks across all the disks. In this case, a write to the RAID array becomes slightly slower at the cost of higdher reliability. RAID 6 is mostly used in enterprises that desire highly reliable storage. It is important to note that the two parity blocks in RAID 6 are not a simple XOR of bits. The contents of the two parity blocks for each row differ from each other, and are complex functions of the data. The reader requires background in field theory to understand the operation of the error detection blocks in RAID 6.

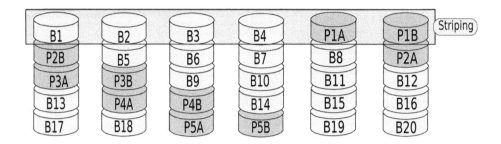

Figure 12.37: RAID 6

12.8.3 Optical Disks – CD, DVD, Blu-ray

We typically use optical disks such as CDs, DVDs, and Blu-ray disks to store videos, music, and software. As a matter of fact, optical disks have become the default distribution media for videos and music (other than the internet of course). Consequently, almost all desktops and laptops have a built-in CD or DVD drive. The reader needs to note that the physics of optical disks is very different from that of hard disks. We read the data stored in a hard disk by measuring the change in magnetic field due to the relative motion of tiny magnets embedded in the platters of the hard disk. In comparison, in an optical disk, we read data by using photo-detectors (light detectors) to measure the intensity of optical signals reflected off the surface of the disk.

The reader needs to note that CDs (compact disks), DVDs (Digital Video Disks, or Digital Versatile Disks), and Blu-ray disks, basically use the same technology. CDs represent first generation optical disks, DVDs represent second generation optical disks, and Blu-ray disks are representative of the third generation. Successive generations are typically faster and can provide more storage capacity. Let us now consider the physics of optical storage media.

Basic Physics of Optical Storage Media

An optical disk is shown in Figure 12.38. It is a circular disk, and is typically 12 cm in diameter. It has a hole in the center that is meant for attaching to a spindle (similar to hard disks). The hole is 1.5 cm in diameter, and the entire optical disk is 1.2 mm thick. An optical disk is made of multiple layers. We are primarily concerned with the reflective layer that reflects laser light to a set of detectors. We encode data bits by modifying the surface of the reflective layer. Let us elaborate.

The data is saved in a spiral pattern that starts from the innermost track, covers the entire surface of the disk, and ends at the outermost track. The width of the track, and the spacing between the tracks depends on the optical disk generation. Let us outline the basic mechanism that is used to encode data on the spiral path. The spiral path has two kinds of regions namely *lands* and *pits*. Lands reflect the optical signal, and thus represent the physical bit, 1. Lands are represented by a flat region in the reflective layer. In comparison, pits have lower reflectivity, and the reflected light is typically out of phase with the light

Figure 12.38: An optical disk (source [dis,])

reflected off the lands, and thus they represent the physical bit, 0. A *pit* is a depression on the surface of the reflective layer. The data on a CD is encoded using the NRZI encoding scheme (see Section 12.2.7). We infer a logical 1 when there is a pit to land, or land to pit transition. However, if there are no transitions, then we keep on inferring logical 0s.

Optical Disk Layers

An optical disk typically has four layers (refer to Figure 12.39).

Polycarbonate Layer The polycarbonate layer is a layer of polycarbonate plastic. Lands and pits are created at its top using an injection moulding process.

Reflective Layer The reflective layer consists a thin layer of aluminium or gold that reflects the laser light.

Lacquer Layer The lacquer based layer on top of the reflective layer protects the reflective layer from scratches, and other forms of accidental damage.

Surface Layer Most vendors typically add a plastic layer over the lacquer layer such that it is possible to add a label to the optical disk. For example, most optical disks typically have a poster of the movie on their top surface.

The optical disk reader sends a laser signal that passes through the polycarbonate layer and gets focused on the lands or pits. In CDs, the polycarbonate layer is typically very deep and it occupies most of the volume. In comparison the polycarbonate layer occupies roughly half the volume in DVDs. For third generation optical disks the reflective layer is very close to the bottom surface.

Optical Disk Reader

An optical disk reader is very similar to a hard disk drive (refer to Figure 12.40). The optical disk rotates on a spindle. The label of the optical disk is oriented towards the top. The actuator and head assembly are located at the bottom. Unlike a hard disk that uses a rotary actuator (rotating arm), an optical disk

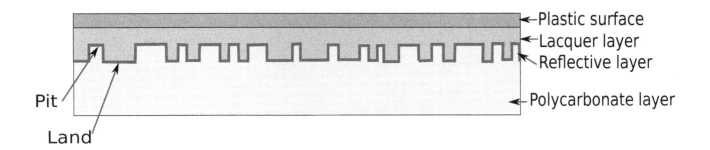

Figure 12.39: Optical disk layers

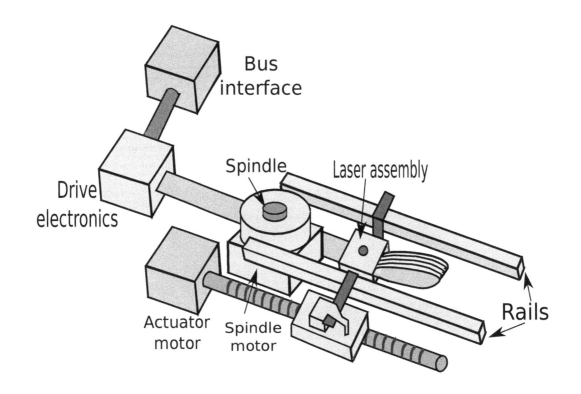

Figure 12.40: Optical disk reader

drive uses a linear actuator [Abramovitch, 2001] that slides radially in or out. Figure 12.40 shows a laser assembly that slides on a set of rails. The laser assembly is connected to an actuator via a system of gears and mechanical components. The actuator motor can very precisely rotate its spindle, and the system of gears translate rotational motion into linear motion of the laser assembly.

The head is a part of the laser assembly. The head typically contains a light source (laser) that is focused on the reflective layer through a system of lenses. The reflective layer then reflects the light, and a part of the reflected light gets captured by the optical disk head. The reflected light is converted to electrical signals within the head by photodetectors. The sequence of electrical signals are processed by dedicated circuitry in the drive, and converted to a sequence of logical bits. Similar to hard disks, optical drives perform error detection and correction.

One important point of difference from hard disks is that the optical disk rotates at constant linear velocity. This means that pits and lands traverse under the head at the same velocity irrespective of the track. In other words, the data transfer rate is the same irrespective of the position of the head. To support this feature, it is necessary to change the rotational speed of the spindle according to the position of the head. When the head is travelling towards the periphery of the disk, it is necessary to slow the disk down. The spindle motor has sophisticated support for acceleration and deceleration in optical drives. To simplify the logic, we can implement zoning here similar to the zoning in hard disk drives (see Section 12.8.1). However, in the case of optical drives, zoning is mostly used in high performance drives.

Advanced Features

Most audio, video, and software CDs/DVDs are written once by the original vendors, and are sold as read-only media. Users are not expected to overwrite the optical storage media. Such kind of optical disks use 4 layers as described in Figure 12.39. Optical disks are also used to archive data. Such disks are typically meant to be written once, and read multiple times (CD-R and DVD-R formats). To create such recordable media, the polycarbonate layer is coated with an organic dye that is sensitive to light. The organic dye layer is coated with the reflective metallic layer, the lacquer layer, and the surface layer. While writing the CD, a high powered write-laser focuses light on the dye and changes its reflectivity. *Lands* are regions of high reflectivity, and *pits* are regions of low reflectivity. Such write-once optical media were superseded by optical media (CDs or DVDs) that can be read and written many times. Here, the reflective layer is made of a silver-indium-antimony-tellurium alloy. When it is heated to 500°C, spots in the reflective layer lose their reflectivity because the structure of the alloy becomes amorphous. To make the spots reflective they are heated to 200°C such that the state of the alloy changes to the polycrystalline state. We can thus encode lands and pits in the reflective layer, erase them, and rewrite them as required.

Modern disks can additionally have an extra layer of lands and pits. The first layer is coated with a chemical that is partially transparent to light. For example, pits can be coated with fluorescent material. When irradiated with red light they glow and emit light of a certain wavelength. However, most of the red light passes to the second layer, and then interacts with the fluorescent material in the pits, which is different from the material in the first layer. By analysing the nature of reflected light, and by using sophisticated image filtering algorithms, it is possible to read the encoded data in both the layers. A simpler solution is to encode data on both sides of the optical disk. This is often as simple as taking two single side disks and pasting their surface layers together. To read such a disk, we need two laser assemblies.

Comparison of CDs, DVDs, and Blu-ray Disks

	CD	DVD	Blu-ray
Generation	1st	2nd	3rd
Capacity	700 MB	4.7 GB	25 GB
Uses	Audio	Video	High definition Video
Laser wavelength	780 nm	650 nm	405 nm
Raw 1X transfer rate	153 KB/s	1.39 MB/s	4.5 MB/s

Table 12.9: Comparison between CD, DVD, and Blu-ray disks

Refer to Table 12.9 for a comparison of CD, DVD, and Blu-ray disks.

12.8.4 Flash Memory

Hard disks, and optical drives are fairly bulky, and need to be handled carefully because they contain sensitive mechanical parts. An additional shortcoming of optical storage media is that they are very sensitive to scratches and other forms of minor accidental damage. Consequently, these devices are not ideally suited for portable and mobile applications. We need a storage device that does not consist of sensitive mechanical parts, can be carried in a pocket, can be attached to any computer, and is extremely durable. Flash drives such as USB pen drives satisfy all these requirements. A typical pen drive can fit in a wallet, can be attached to all kinds of devices, and is extremely robust and durable. It does not lose its data when it is disconnected from the computer. We have flash based storage devices in most portable devices, medical devices, industrial electronics, disk caches in high end servers, and small data storage devices. Flash memory is an example of an EEPROM (Electrically Erasable Programmable Read Only Memory) or EPROM (Erasable Programmable Read Only Memory). Note that traditionally EPROM based memories used ultraviolet light for erasing data. They have been superseded by flash based devices.

Let us look at flash based technology in this section. The basic element of storage is a floating gate transistor.

The Floating Gate Transistor

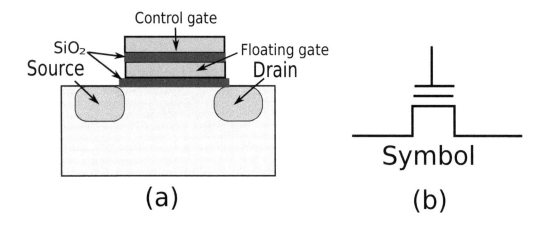

Figure 12.41: A floating gate transistor

Figure 12.41 shows a floating gate transistor. The figure shows a regular NMOS transistor with two gates instead of one. The gate on top is known as the control gate, and is equivalent to the gate in normal MOS transistors. The gate below the control gate is known as the floating gate. It is surrounded on all sides by an SiO_2 based electrical insulation layer. Hence, the floating gate is electrically isolated from the rest of the device. By some means if we are able to implant a certain amount of charge in the floating gate, then the floating gate will maintain its potential for a very long time. In practice, there is a negligible amount of current flow between the floating gate and the rest of the components in the floating gate transistor under normal conditions. Let us consider two scenarios. In the first scenario, the floating gate is not charged. In this case, the floating gate transistor acts as a regular NMOS transistor. However, if the floating gate has accumulated electrons containing negative charge, then we have a negative potential gradient between the channel and the control gate. Recall that to create a n-type channel in the transistor, it is necessary to apply a positive voltage to the gate, where this voltage is greater than the threshold voltage. In this case the threshold voltage is effectively higher because of the accumulation of electrons in the floating gate. In other words, to induce a channel in the substrate, we need to apply a larger positive voltage at the control gate.

Let the threshold voltage when the floating gate is not charged with electrons be V_T, and let the threshold voltage when the floating gate contains negative charge be V_T^+ ($V_T^+ > V_T$). If we apply a voltage that is in between V_T and V_T^+ to the control gate, then the NMOS transistor conducts current if no charge is stored in the floating gate (threshold voltage is V_T). If the threshold voltage of the transistor is equal to V_T^+, then the transistor remains in the *off* state. It thus does not conduct any current. We typically assume that the default state (no charge on the floating gate) corresponds to the 1 state. When the floating gate is charged with electrons, we assume that the transistor is in the 0 state. When we set the voltage at the control gate to a value between V_T and V_T^+, we enable the floating gate transistor.

Now, to write a value of 0 or *program* the transistor, we need to deposit electrons in the floating gate. This can be done by applying a strong positive voltage to the control gate, and a smaller positive voltage to the drain terminal. Since there is a positive potential difference between the drain and source, a channel gets established between the drain and source. The control gate has an even higher voltage, and thus the resulting electric field pulls electrons from the n-type channel and deposits some of them in the floating gate.

Similarly, to *erase* the stored 0 bit, we apply a strong negative voltage between the control gate and the source terminal. The resulting electric field pulls the electrons away from the floating gate into the substrate, and source terminal. At the end of this process, the floating gate loses all its negative charge, and the flash device comes back to its original state. It now stores a logical 1.

To summarise, programming a flash cell means writing a logical 0, and erasing it means writing a logical 1. There are two fundamental ways in which we can arrange such floating gate transistors to make a basic flash memory cell. These methods are known as NOR flash and NAND flash respectively.

NOR FLash

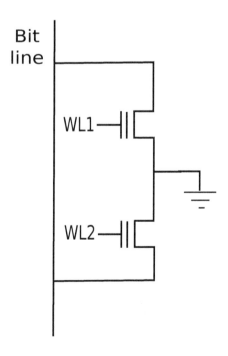

Figure 12.42: NOR Flash Cell

Figure 12.42 shows the topology of a two transistor NOR flash cell that saves 2 bits. Each floating gate

transistor is connected to a bit line on one side, and to the ground on the other side. Each of the control gates are connected to distinct word lines. After we enable a floating gate transistor it pulls the bit line low if it stores a logical 1, otherwise it does not have any effect because it is in the *off* state. Thus the voltage transition in the bit line is logically the reverse of the value stored in the transistor. The bit line is connected to a sense amplifier that senses its voltage, flips the bit, and reports it as the output. Similarly, for writing and erasing we need to set the word lines, bit lines, and source lines to appropriate voltages. The advantage of NOR flash is that it is very similar to a traditional DRAM cell. We can build an array of NOR flash cells similar to a DRAM array. The array based layout allows us to access each individual location in the array uniquely.

NAND Flash

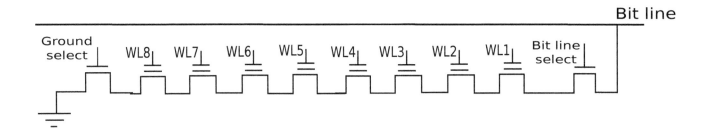

Figure 12.43: NAND Flash Cell

A NAND flash cell has a different topology. It consists of a set of NMOS floating gate transistors in series similar to series connections in CMOS NAND gates (refer to Figure 12.43). There are two dedicated transistors at both ends known as the *bit line select transistor*, and *ground select* transistor. A typical array of transistors connected in the NAND configuration contains 8 or 16 transistors. To read the value saved in a certain transistor in a NAND flash array, there are three steps. The first step is to enable the ground select, and bit line transistors. The second step is to turn on the rest of the floating gate transistors other than the one we wish to read by setting their word line voltages to V_T^+. Lastly, we read a specific transistor by setting its word line voltage to some value between V_T and V_T^+. If the cell is not programmed (contains a 1), it drives the bit line low, otherwise it does not change the voltage on the bit line. Sense amplifiers infer the value of the logical bit saved in the transistor. Such arrays of floating gate transistors known as NAND flash cells are connected in a configuration similar to NOR flash cells.

This scheme might look complicated at the outset; however, it has a lot of advantages. Consequently, most of the flash devices in use today use NAND flash memories instead of NOR flash memories. The bit storage density is much higher. A typical NAND flash cell uses a lesser number of wires than a NOR flash cell because all the floating gate transistors are directly connected to each other, and there is just one connection to the bit line and ground terminal. Hence, NAND flash memories have at least 40-60% higher density as compared to NOR flash cells. Let us thus only consider NAND flash memories from now on, and refrain from discussing NOR flash memories.

Blocks and Pages

The most important point to note here is that a (NAND) flash memory device is not a memory device, it is a storage device. Memory devices provide byte level access. In comparison, storage devices typically provide block level access, where one block can be hundreds of kilobytes long. Due to temporal and spatial locality in accesses to storage media, the working set of most programs is restricted to a few blocks. Secondly, to reduce the number of accesses to storage devices, most operating systems have in-memory storage caches such as hard disk caches. Most of the time, the operating system reads and writes to the in-memory caches. This reduces the I/O access time.

However, after certain events it is necessary to synchronise the cache with the underlying storage device. For example, after executing a *sync()* system call in Linux, the hard disk cache writes its updates to the hard disk. Depending on the semantics of the operating system, and file system, writes are sent to the underlying storage media after a variety of events. For example, when we right click on the icon for an USB drive in the "My Computer" screen on Windows and select the eject option, the operating system ensures that all the outstanding write requests are sent to the USB device. Most of the time users simply unplug an USB device. This practice can occasionally lead to data corruption, and unfortunately your author has committed this mistake several times. This is because, when we pull out an USB drive, some uncommitted changes are still present in the in-memory cache. Consequently, the USB pen drive contains stale and possibly half-written data.

Data in NAND flash devices is organised in the granularity of pages and blocks. A *page* of data typically contains 512 – 4096 bytes (in powers of 2). Most NAND flash devices can typically read or write data at the granularity of pages. Each page additionally has extra bits for error correction based on CRC codes. A set of pages are organised into a block. Blocks can contain 32 – 128 pages, and their total size ranges from 16 – 512 KB. Most NAND flash devices can erase data at the level of blocks. Let us now look at some of the salient points of NAND flash devices.

Program/Erase Cycles

Writing to a flash device essentially means writing a logical 0 bit since by default each floating gate transistor contains a logical 1. In general, after we have written data to a block, we cannot write data again to the same block without performing additional steps. For example, if we have written 0110 to a set of locations in a block, we cannot write 1001 to the same set of locations without erasing the original data. This is because, we cannot convert a 0 to a 1, without erasing data. Erasing is a slow operation, and consumes a lot of power. Hence, the designers of NAND flash memories decided to erase data at large granularities, i.e., at the granularity of a block. We can think of accesses to flash memory as consisting of a *program phase*, where data is written, and an *erase phase*, where the data stored in all the transistors of the block is erased. In other words, after the erase phase, each transistor in the block contains a logical 1. We can have an indefinite number of read accesses between the program phase, and the erase phase. A pair of program and erase operations is known as a program/erase cycle, or P/E cycle.

Unfortunately, flash devices can endure a finite number of P/E cycles. As of 2013, this number is between 100,000 to 1 million. This is because each P/E cycle damages the silicon dioxide layer surrounding the floating gate. There is a gradual breakdown of this layer, and ultimately after hundreds of thousands of P/E cycles it does not remain an electrical insulator anymore. It starts to conduct current, and thus a flash cell loses its ability to hold charge. This gradual damage to the insulator layer is known as *wear and tear*. To mitigate this problem, designers use a technique called *wear levelling*.

Wear Levelling

The main objective of *wear levelling* is to ensure that accesses are symmetrically distributed across blocks. If accesses are non-uniformly distributed, then the blocks that receive a large number of requests will wear out faster, and develop faults. Since data accesses follow both temporal and spatial locality we expect a small set of blocks to be accessed most often. This is precisely the behaviour that we wish to prevent. Let us further elaborate with an example. Consider a pen drive that contains songs. Most people typically do not listen to all the songs in a round robin fashion. Instead they most of the time listen to their favourite songs. This means that a few blocks that contain their favourite songs are accessed most often, and these blocks will ultimately develop faults. Hence, to maximise the lifetime of the flash device, we need to ensure that all the blocks are accessed with roughly the same frequency. This is the best case scenario, and is known as *wear levelling*.

The basic idea of wear levelling is that we define a logical address and a physical address for a flash device. A *physical address* corresponds to the address of a block within the flash device. The logical address is used by the processor and operating system to refer to data in the flash drive. We can think of the logical address as virtual memory, and the physical address as physical memory. Every flash device contains a circuit that maps logical addresses to physical addresses. Now, we need to ensure that accesses to blocks are uniformly distributed. Most flash devices have an access counter associated with each block. This counter is incremented once every P/E cycle. Once the access count for a block exceeds the access counts of other blocks by a predefined threshold, it is time to swap the contents of the frequently accessed block with another less frequently accessed block. Flash devices use a separate temporary block for implementing the swap. First the contents of block 1 are copied to it. Subsequently, block 1 is erased, and the contents of block 2 are copied to block 1. The last step is to erase block 2, and copy the contents of the temporary block to it. Optionally, at the end, we can erase the contents of the temporary block. By doing such periodic swaps, flash devices ensure that no single block wears out faster than others. The logical to physical block mapping needs to be updated to reflect the change.

Definition 163
A technique to ensure that no single block wears out faster than other blocks is known as wear levelling. *Most flash devices implement wear levelling by swapping the contents of a block that is frequently accessed with a block that is less frequently accessed.*

Read Disturbance

Another reliability issue in flash memories is known as *read disturbance*. If we read the contents of one page continuously, then the neighbouring transistors in each NAND cell start getting programmed. Recall that the control gate voltage of the neighbouring transistors needs to be greater than V_T^+ such that they can pass current. In this case, the voltage of the gate is not as high as the voltage that is required to program a transistor, and it also lasts for a shorter duration. Nonetheless, a few electrons do accumulate in the floating gate. After thousands of read accesses to just one transistor, the neighbouring transistors start accumulating negative charge in their floating gates, and ultimately get programmed to store a 0 bit.

To mitigate this problem, most designs have a read counter with each page or block. If the read counter exceeds a certain threshold, then the flash controller needs to move the contents of the block to another location. Before copying the data, the new block needs to be erased. Subsequently, we transfer the contents of the old block to the new block. In the new block, all the transistors that are not programmed start out with a negligible amount of negative charge in their floating gates. As the number of read accesses to the new block increases, transistors start getting programmed. Before we reach a threshold, we need to migrate the block again.

12.9 Summary and Further Reading

12.9.1 Summary

Summary 12

1. The I/O system connects the processor to the I/O devices. The processor and all the chips for processing I/O data (chipset), are attached to a printed circuit board known as the motherboard. The motherboard also contains ports (hardware connectors) for attaching I/O devices.

   (a) The most important chips in the chipset are known as the North Bridge and Soutbridge chips in Intel-based systems.

   (b) The North Bridge chip connects the processor to the graphics card, and main memory.

   (c) The South Bridge chip is connected to the North Bridge chip and a host of I/O and storage devices such as the keyboard, mouse, hard disk, and network card.

2. Most operating system define two basic I/O operations namely read and write. An I/O request typically passes from the application to the I/O device through the kernel, device driver, the processor, and elements of the I/O system.

3. We divide the functionality of the I/O system into 4 layers.

   (a) The physical layer defines the electrical specifications, signalling and timing protocols of a bus. It is further divided into two sublayers namely the transmission sublayer, and the synchronisation sublayer.

   (b) The data link layer gets a sequence of logical bits from the physical layer, and then performs the tasks of framing, buffering, and error correction. If multiple devices want to access the bus, then the process of scheduling the requests is known as arbitration. The data link layer implements arbitration, and also has support for I/O transactions (sequence of messages between sender and receiver), and split transactions (transactions divided into multiple mini transactions).

   (c) The network layer helps to route data from the processor to I/O devices and back.

   (d) The protocol layer is concerned with implementing an entire I/O request end-to-end.

4. Physical Layer:

   (a) Transmission Sublayer Protocols: active high, active low, return to zero (RZ), non return to zero (NRZ), non return to zero inverted (NRZI), and Manchester encoding.

   (b) Synchronisation Sublayer Protocols: synchronous (same clock for both ends), mesochronous (fixed phase delay), plesiochronous (slow drift in the clock), source synchronous (clock passed along with the data), and asynchronous (2 phase handshake, and 4 phase handshake).

5. Data Link Layer

   (a) Framing protocols: bit stuffing, pauses, bit count

   (b) Error Detection/ Correction: parity, SEC, SECDED, CRC

    (c) Arbitration: centralised, daisy chain (supports priority, and notion of tokens)

    (d) Transaction: single transaction (example, DRAM bus), split transaction (break a transaction into smaller transactions)

6. *Network Layer*

    (a) I/O Mapped I/O: Each I/O port is mapped to a set of registers that have unique addresses. The in and out instructions are used to read and write data to the ports respectively.

    (b) Memory Mapped I/O: Here, we map the I/O ports to the virtual address space.

7. *Protocol Layer:*

    (a) Polling: Keep querying the device for a change in its state.

    (b) Interrupts: The device sends a message to the processor, when its status changes.

    (c) DMA (Direct Memory Access): Instead of transferring data from an I/O device to main memory by issuing I/O instructions, the device driver instructs the DMA engine to transfer a chunk of data between I/O devices and main memory. The DMA engine interrupts the processor after it is done.

8. *Case Studies:*

Protocol	Usage	Salient Points
PCI Express	motherboard bus	high speed asynchronous bus, supports multiple lanes
SATA	storage devices	half duplex, asynchronous bus, supports low level commands on storage devices
SAS	storage devices	full duplex, asynchronous bus, backward compatible with SATA, extensive SCSI command set
USB	peripherals	single bit, half duplex, asynchronous bus. Extensive support for all kinds of traffic (bulk, interrupt, and isochronous).
FireWire	peripherals	full duplex, data strobe encoding. Peripherals organised as a computer network with a leader node.

9. *Storage Devices: Hard Disk*

    (a) In a hard disk we encode data by changing the relative orientations of tiny magnets on the surface of the platter.

    (b) We group a set of typically 512 bytes into a sector. On a platter, sectors are arranged in concentric circles known as tracks.

    (c) The head of a hard disk first needs to move to the right track (seek time), then wait for the correct sector to arrive under the head (rotational latency). Finally, we need to transfer the data to the processor after post processing (transfer latency).

10. *Storage Devices: Optical disc*

   (a) *The surface of an optical disc contains flat region (lands), and depressions (pits). The pits have lower reflectivity.*

   (b) *Optical discs rotate on a spindle similar to a platter in a hard disk. The optical head focuses a laser light on the surface of the disc, and then an array of photodetectors analyse the reflected light. A transition between a pit and a land (or vice versa) indicates a logical 1. Otherwise, we read a logical 0.*

   (c) *CDs (compact discs) are first generation optical discs, DVDs are second generation optical discs, and Blu-Ray discs are third generation optical discs.*

11. *Storage Devices: Flash Memory*

   (a) *Flash memory contains a floating gate transistor that has two gates – control and floating. If the floating gate has accumulated electrons then the transistor stores a logical 0 (else it stores a logical 1).*

   (b) *We program (set to 0) a floating gate transistor by applying a high positive voltage pulse to the control gate. Likewise, we erase the value when we apply a pulse with the opposite polarity.*

   (c) *Floating gate transistors can be connected in the NAND and NOR configurations. The NAND configuration has much higher density and is thus more commonly used.*

   (d) *While designing flash devices we need to perform wear levelling, and take the phenomenon of read disturbance into account.*

12.9.2 Further Reading

For the latest designs of motherboards, and chipsets, the most accurate and up to date source of information is the vendor's website. Most vendors such as Intel and AMD post the details and configurations of their motherboards and chipsets after they are released. However, they typically do not post a lot of details about the architecture of the chips. The reader can refer to research papers for the architectural details of the AMD Opteron North Bridge chip [Conway and Hughes, 2007], Intel Blackford North Bridge chip [Radhakrishnan et al., 2007], and AMD North Bridge chip [Owen and Steinman, 2008] for the Griffin processor family. The book by Dally and Poulton [Dally and Poulton, 1998] is one of the best sources for information on the physical layer, and is a source of a lot of information presented in this book. Other books on digital communication [Proakis and Salehi, 2007, Sklar, 2001] are also excellent resources for further reading. Error control codes are mostly taught in courses on coding and information theory. Hence, for a deeper understanding of error control codes, the reader is referred to [Ling and Xing, 2004, Cover and Thomas, 2013]. For a detailed description of the Intel's I/O architecture and I/O ports, we shall point the reader to Intel's software developer manuals at [int,]. The best sources for the I/O protocols are their official specifications – PCI Express [pci,], SATA [sat,], SCSI and SAS [scs,], USB [usb,], and FireWire [fir,]. The book on memory systems by Jacob, Ng, and Wang [Jacob et al., 2007] is one of the best resources for additional information on hard disks, and DRAM memories. They explain the structure of a hard disk, and its internals in great detail. The official standards for compact discs are documented in the rainbow books. Each book in this collection contains the specifications of a certain type of optical disc. One of the earliest and most influential books in this collection is the Red Book [red,] that contains the specifications for audio CDs. The latest DVD standards are available from `http://www.dvdforum.org`, and the latest Blu Ray standards are available at the official website of the Blu Ray Disc Association (`http://www.blu-raydisc.com/en`).

Exercises

Overview of the I/O System

Ex. 1 — What are the roles of the North Bridge and South Bridge chips?

Ex. 2 — What is the role of the chipset in a motherboard?

Ex. 3 — Describe the four layers in the I/O system.

Ex. 4 — Why is it a good idea to design a complex system as a sequence of layers?

Physical Layer

Ex. 5 — What is the advantage of LVDS signalling?

Ex. 6 — Draw the circuit diagram of a LVDS transmitter and receiver.

Ex. 7 — Assume that we are transmitting the bit sequence: 01101110001101. Show the voltage on the bus as a function of time for the following protocols: RZ, NRZ, Manchester, NRZI.

Ex. 8 — What is the advantage of the NRZI protocol over the NRZ protocol?

* **Ex. 9** — Draw the circuit diagram of the receiver of a plesiochronous bus.

* **Ex. 10** — What are the advantages of a source synchronous bus?

* **Ex. 11** — Why is it necessary to avoid transitions in the keep-out region?

Ex. 12 — Differentiate between a 2-phase handshake, and a 4-phase handshake?

* **Ex. 13** — Why do we set the strobe after the data is stable on the bus?

** **Ex. 14** — Design the circuit for a tunable delay element.

Data Link, Network, and Protocol Layer

Ex. 15 — What are the different methods for demarcating frames?

Ex. 16 — Consider a 8-5 SECDED code. Encode the message: 10011001.

** **Ex. 17** — Construct a code that can detect 3 bit errors.

** **Ex. 18** — Construct a fully distributed arbiter. It should not have any central node that schedules requests.

Ex. 19 — What is the advantage of split transaction buses?

Ex. 20 — How do we access I/O ports?

Ex. 21 — What is the benefit of memory mapped I/O?

Ex. 22 — What are the various methods of communication between an I/O device and the processor? Order them in the increasing order of processor utilisation.

Ex. 23 — Assume that for a single polling operation, a processor running at 1 MHz takes 200 cycles. A processor polls a printer 1000 times per minute. What percentage of time does the processor spend in polling?

Ex. 24 — When is polling more preferable than interrupts?

Ex. 25 — When are interrupts more preferable than polling?

Ex. 26 — Explain the operation of the DMA controller.

Hard Disks

Ex. 27 — What is the advantage of zoned recording?

Ex. 28 — Describe the operation of a hard disk.

Ex. 29 — We have a hard disk with the following parameters:

Seek Time	50 ms
Rotational Speed	600 RPM
Bandwidth	100 MB/s

(a) How long will it take to read 25 MB on an average if 25 MB can be read in one pass.

(b) Assume that we can only read 5 MB in one pass. Then, we need to wait for the platter to rotate by $360°$ such that the same sector comes under the head again. Now, we can read the next chunk of 5 MB. In this case, how long will it take to read the entire 25MB chunk?

* **Ex. 30** — Typically, in hard disks, all the heads do not read data in parallel. Why is this the case?

Ex. 31 — Let us assume that we need to read or write long sequences of data. What is the best way of arranging the sectors on a hard disk? Assume that we ideally do not want to change tracks, and all the tracks in a cylinder are aligned.

* **Ex. 32** — Now, let us change the assumptions in the previous exercise. Assume that it is faster to move to the next track on the same recording surface, than starting to read from another track in the same cylinder. With these assumptions, how should we arrange the sectors? [NOTE: The question is not as easy as it sounds.]

Ex. 33 — Explain the operation of RAID 0,1,2,3,4,5, and 6.

Ex. 34 — Consider 4 disks D0, D1, D2, D3 and a parity disk P using RAID 4. The following table shows the contents of the disks for a given sector address, S, which is the same across all the disks. Assume the size of a block to be 16 bits.

D0	D1	D2	D3
0xFF00	0x3421	0x32FF	0x98AB

Compute the value of the parity block? Now the contents of D0 are changed to 0xABD1. What is the new value of the parity block?

Ex. 35 — Assume that we want to read a block as fast as possible, and there are no parallel accesses. Which RAID technology should we choose?

Ex. 36 — What is the advantage of RAID 5 over RAID 4?

Optical and Flash Drives

Ex. 37 — What is the main difference between a CD and DVD?

Ex. 38 — How do we use the NRZI encoding in optical drives?

* **Ex. 39** — What is the advantage of running a drive at constant linear velocity over running it at constant angular velocity?

* **Ex. 40** — For an optical drive that runs at constant linear velocity, what is the relationship between the angular velocity, and the position of the head?

Ex. 41 — What are the basic differences between NAND and NOR flash?

Ex. 42 — Explain *wear levelling*, and *read disturbance*? How are these issues typically handled in modern flash drives?

Design Problems

Ex. 43 — Read more about the Hypertransport^{TM}, Intel Quickpath, Infiniband^{TM}, and Myrinet® protocols? Try to divide their functionality into layers as we have presented in this chapter.

Part IV

Appendix

Case Studies of Real Processors

Let us now look at the design of some real processors such that we can put all the concepts that we have learned up till now in a practical perspective. We shall study embedded (for smaller mobile devices), and server processors of three major processor companies namely ARM, AMD, and Intel. Let us start with a disclaimer. The aim of this section is not to compare and contrast the design of processors across the three companies, or even between different models of the same company. Every processor is designed optimally for a certain market segment with certain key business decisions in mind. Hence, our focus in this section would be to study the designs from a technical perspective, and appreciate the nuances of the design.

A.1 ARM® Processors

Let us now describe the design of ARM processors. The most important point to note about the ARM processors (popularly referred as *ARM cores*) is that ARM designs the processors, and then licenses the design to customers. Unlike other vendors such as Intel or IBM, ARM does not manufacture silicon chips. Instead, vendors such as Texas Instruments and Qualcomm buy the license to use the design of ARM cores, and add additional components. They then give a contract to semiconductor manufacturing companies, or use their own manufacturing facilities to manufacture an entire SOC(System on Chip) in silicon.

ARM has three processor lines for its latest (as of 2012) ARMv8 architecture. The first line of processors is known as the ARM® Cortex® -M series. These processors are mainly designed to be used as microcontrollers in embedded applications such as medical devices, automobiles, and industrial electronics. The main focus behind the design of such processors is power efficiency, and cost. In this section, we shall describe the ARM Cortex-M3 processor that has a three stage pipeline.

The second line of processors is known as the ARM® Cortex® -R series. These processors are designed for real time applications. The main focus here is reliability, high speed and real time response. They are not meant to be used by consumer electronics devices such as smart phones. The Cortex-R series processors do not have support for running operating systems that use virtual memory.

The ARM® Cortex® -A series processors are designed to run regular user applications on smart phones, tablets, and a host of high end embedded devices. These ARM cores typically have complex pipelines, support for vector operations, and can run complex operating systems that require hardware support for virtual memory. We shall study the Cortex-A8 and Cortex-A15 processors in this section.

A.1.1 ARM® Cortex® -M3

System Design

Let us begin with the ARM Cortex-M series processors that have been designed primarily for the embedded processor market. For such embedded processors, energy efficiency and cost are more important than raw performance. Consequently, ARM engineers designed a 3 issue pipeline devoid of very complicated features.

The Cortex-M3 supports a basic version of the ARMv7-M instruction set as described in Chapter 4. It is typically attached to other components using the ARM® AMBA® bus as shown in Figure A.1.

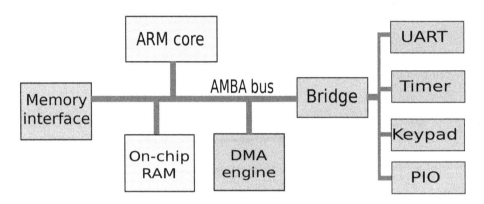

Figure A.1: The ARM Cortex-M3 connected to the AMBA bus along with other components , source [arm, b]. Reproduced with permission from ARM Limited. Copyright ©ARM Limited (or its affiliates)

AMBA (Advanced Microcontroller Bus Architecture) is a bus architecture designed by ARM. It is used to connect an ARM core with other components in SOC based systems. For example, most of the processors in smart phones and mobile devices use the AMBA bus to connect to high speed memory devices, DMA engines, and other external buses through bridge devices. One such external bus is the APB bus (Advanced Peripheral Bus) that is used to connect to peripherals such as the keyboard, UART controller (Universal Asynchronous Receiver/Transmitter Protocol), timer, and the PIO (parallel input output) interface.

Pipeline Design

Figure A.2 shows the pipeline of the ARM Cortex-M3. It has three stages namely fetch (F), decode (D), and execute (E). The fetch stage fetches the instruction from memory, and is the smallest stage of all the three stages.

The decode stage(D stage) has three different sub-units as shown in Figure A.2. The D stage has an instruction decode and register read unit, which is similar to the operand fetch unit in *SimpleRisc* . It decodes the instruction, and forms the instruction packet. Simultaneously, it reads the values of the operands that are embedded in the instruction, and also reads values from the register file. The AGU (address generation unit) extracts all the fields in the instruction, and schedules the execution of the load or store instruction in the next stage of the pipeline. It plays a special role while processing the *ldm* (load multiple) and *stm* (store multiple) instructions. Recall from our discussion in Section 4.3.2 that these instructions can read or write to multiple registers at the same time. The AGU creates multiple operations out of a single *ldm* or *stm* instruction in the pipeline. The *branch* unit is used for branch prediction. It predicts both the branch outcome, and the branch target.

The execute stage is fairly heavy in terms of functionality, and some instructions take 2 cycles to execute. Let us look at the regular ALU and branch instructions first. Recall from our discussion in Section 4.2.2

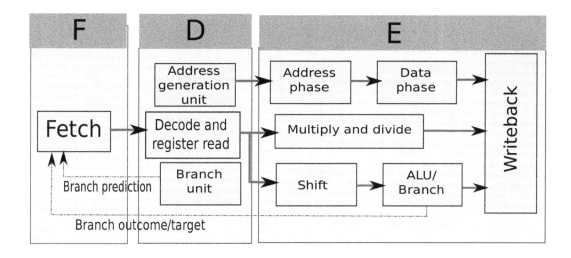

Figure A.2: The pipeline of the ARM Cortex-M3 , source [arm, b]. Reproduced with permission from ARM Limited. Copyright ©ARM Limited (or its affiliates).

that ARM instructions can have one shifter operand. Secondly, computing the value of the 32-bit immediate from its 12 bit encoding is essentially a shift (rotate is a type of shift) operation. Both of these operations are executed by the shift unit that has a hardware structure known as a *barrel shifter*. Once the operands are ready, they are passed to the ALU and branch unit that computes the branch outcome/target, and the ALU result.

ARM has two kinds of branches – direct and indirect. For direct branches, the offset of the branch target from the current PC is embedded in the instruction. For example, a branch to a label is an example of a direct branch. It is possible to compute the branch target of a direct branch in the decode stage. ARM also supports indirect branches, where the branch target is the result of an ALU or memory instruction. For example, the instruction *ldr pc, [r1, #10]* is an example of an indirect branch. Here, the value of the branch target is equal to the value loaded from memory by the load instruction. It is in general difficult to predict the target of indirect branches. In the Cortex-M3 processor, whenever there is a branch misprediction (either target or outcome), the two instructions fetched after the branch are cancelled. The processors starts fetching instructions from the correct branch target.

Along with the basic ALU, the Cortex-M3 has a multiply and divide unit that can perform both signed and unsigned, multiplication and division. The Cortex-M3 supports two instructions, *sdiv*, and *udiv* for signed and unsigned division respectively. Along with these instructions it has support for multiply, and multiply-accumulate operations as described in Section 4.2.1.

The load and store instructions typically take two cycles. They have an address generation phase, and a memory access phase. The load instructions takes 2 cycles to execute. Note that in the second cycle, it is not possible for other instructions to execute in the *E* stage. The pipeline is thus stalled for one cycle. This specific feature reduces the performance of the pipeline. ARM removed this restriction in its high performance processors. The store instruction also takes 2 cycles to execute. However, the second cycle that accesses memory does not stall the pipeline. The processor writes the value to a store buffer (similar to a write buffer as discussed in Section 10.3.3), and proceeds with its execution. It is further possible to issue back to back (consecutive cycles) store and load instructions, where the load reads the value written by the store. The pipeline does not need to stall for the load instruction because it reads the value written by the store from the store buffer.

A.1.2   ARM® Cortex® -A8

As compared to the Cortex-M3, which is an embedded processor, the Cortex-A8 was designed to be a full fledged processor that can run on sophisticated smart phones and tablet processors. Here, *A* stands for *application*, and ARM's intent was to use this processor to run regular applications on mobile devices. Secondly, these processors were designed to support virtual memory, and also contained dedicated floating point and SIMD units.

Overview of the Cortex-A8

The defining feature of the pipeline of the Cortex-A8 core is that it is a dual issue superscalar processor. However, it is not a full blown out-of-order processor. The issue logic is inorder. The Cortex-A8 has a 13-stage integer pipeline with sophisticated branch prediction logic. Since it uses a deep pipeline, it is possible to clock it at a higher frequency than other ARM processors that have shallower pipelines. The Cortex-A8 core is designed to be clocked between 500 MHz and 1GHz, which is a fairly fast clock speed in the embedded domain.

Along with the integer pipeline, the Cortex-A8 contains a dedicated floating point and SIMD unit. The floating point unit implements ARM's VFP (vector floating point) ISA extension, and the SIMD unit implements the ARM® NEON® instruction set. This unit is also pipelined and has 10 stages. Moreover, the ARM Cortex-A8 processor has a separate instruction and data cache, which can be optionally connected to a large shared L2 cache.

Design of the Pipeline

Figure A.3 shows the design of the pipeline of the ARM Cortex-A8 processor. The fetch unit is pipelined across two stages. Its primary purpose is to fetch an instruction, and update the PC. Additionally, it also has a built in instruction prefetcher, ITLB (instruction TLB), and branch predictor. The advanced features of the branch predictors of Cortex-A8 and Cortex A-15 are discussed in Section A.1.3. The instructions subsequently pass to the decode unit.

The decode unit is pipelined across 5 stages. The decode unit is more complicated in the Cortex-A8 processor than the Cortex-M3 because it has the additional responsibility of checking the dependences across instructions, and issuing two instructions together. The forwarding, stall, and interlock logic is thus much more complicated. Let us number the two instruction issue slots 0 and 1. If the decode stage finds two instructions that do not have any interdependences, then it fills both the issue slots with instructions, and sends them to the execution unit. Otherwise, the decode stage just fills one issue slot.

The execution unit is pipelined across 6 stages, and it contains 4 separate pipelines. It has two ALU pipelines that can be used by both the instructions. It has a multiply pipeline that can be used by the instruction issued in slot 0 only. Lastly, it has a load/store pipeline that can again be used by instructions issued in both the issue slots.

NEON and VFP instructions are sent to the NEON/VFP unit. It takes three cycles to decode and schedule the NEON/VFP instructions. Subsequently, the NEON/VFP unit fetches the operands from the NEON register file that contains thirty two 64-bit registers. NEON instructions can also view the register file as sixteen 128 bit registers. The NEON/VFP unit has six 6 stage pipelines for arithmetic operations, and it has one 6 stage pipeline for load/store operations. As discussed in Section 11.5.2, loading vector data is a very performance critical operation in SIMD processors. Hence, ARM has a dedicated load queue in the NEON unit for populating the NEON register file by loading data from the L1 cache. For storing data, the NEON unit writes data directly back to the L1 cache.

Each L1 cache (instruction/data) has a 64 byte block size, has an associativity of 4, and can either be 16 KB of 32 KB. Secondly, each L1 cache has two ports, and can provide 4 words per cycle for NEON and

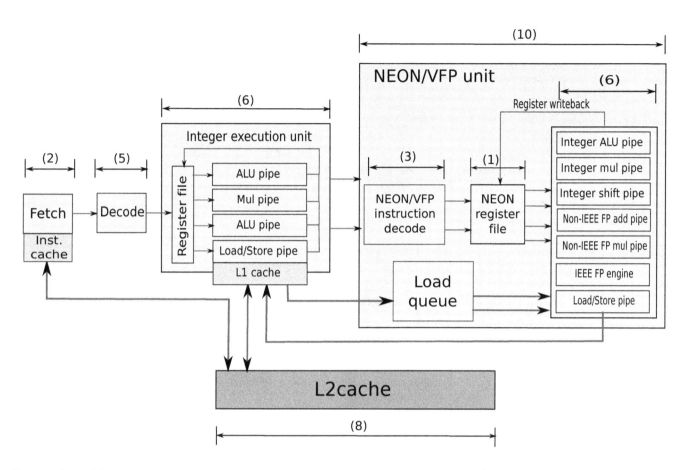

Figure A.3: The pipeline of the ARM Cortex-A8 processor , source [arm, a]. Reproduced with permission from ARM Limited. Copyright ©ARM Limited (or its affiliates).

floating point operations. The point to note here is that the NEON/VFP unit and the integer pipelines share the L1 data cache. The L1 caches are optionally connected to a large L2 cache. It has a block size of 64 bytes, is 8 way set associative, and can be as large as 1 MB. The L2 cache is split into multiple banks. We can lookup two tags at the same time, and the data array accesses proceed in parallel.

A.1.3   ARM® Cortex® -A15

The ARM Cortex-A15 is the latest ARM processor to be released as of early 2013. This processor is targeted towards high performance applications.

Overview

The Cortex-A15 processor is much more complicated, and much more powerful than the Cortex-M3 and Cortex-A8. Instead of using an inorder core, it uses a 3-issue superscalar out-of-order core. It also has a deeper pipeline. Specifically, it has a 15 stage integer pipeline, and a 17-25 stage floating point pipeline. The deeper pipeline allows it to run at a significantly higher frequency (1.5 – 2.5 GHz). Additionally, it fully integrates VFP and NEON units on the core instead of having them as separate execution units. Like server processors, it is designed to access a large amount of memory. It can support a 40 bit physical address, which means that it can address up to 1 TB of memory using the latest AMBA bus protocol that supports system level coherence. The Cortex-A15 is designed to run modern operating systems, and virtual machines. Virtual machines are special programs that can help run multiple operating systems concurrently on the same processor. They are used in server and cloud computing environments to support users with varying software requirements. The Cortex-A15 incorporates sophisticated power management techniques that dynamically shut off parts of the processor when they are not being used.

Another iconic feature of the Cortex-A15 processor is that it is a multicore processor. It organises 4 cores per cluster, and we can have multiple clusters per chip. The Snoop Control Unit provides coherency within a cluster. The AMBA4 specification defines the protocol for supporting cache and system level coherence across clusters. Additionally, the AMBA4 bus also supports synchronisation operations. The memory system is also faster and more reliable. The Cortex-A15's memory system uses SECDED (single error correct, double error detect) error control codes.

Design of the Pipeline

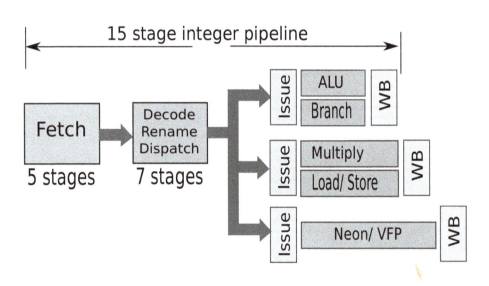

Figure A.4:   Overview of the ARM Cortex A-15 processor, source [arm, d]. Reproduced with permission from ARM Limited. Copyright ©ARM Limited (or its affiliates).

Figure A.4 shows an overview of the pipeline of a Cortex-A15 core. We have 5 fetch stages. Here, fetch is more complicated because, the Cortex-A15 has a sophisticated branch predictor that can handle many types of branch instructions. The decode, rename, and instruction dispatch units are pipelined across 7 stages. Recall from our discussion in Section 9.11.4 that the register rename unit, and instruction window are critical to the performance of out-of-order processors. Their role is to find sets of instructions that are ready to execute in a given cycle.

The Cortex-A15 has several execution pipelines. The integer ALU, and branch pipelines require 3 cycles each. However, the multiply, and load/store pipelines are longer. Unlike other ARM processors that treat the NEON/VFP units as a physically separate unit, the Cortex-A15 integrates it on the core. It is a part of the out-of-order pipeline. Let us now look at the pipeline in some more detail (refer to Figure A.5).

The Cortex-A15 core's (the same features are available in the branch predictor of the Cortex-A8 also) branch predictor contains a predictor for direct branches, a predictor for indirect branches, and a predictor to predict the return address. The indirect branch predictor tries to predict the branch target based on the PC of the branch instruction. It has a 256 entry buffer that is indexed by the history of a given branch,

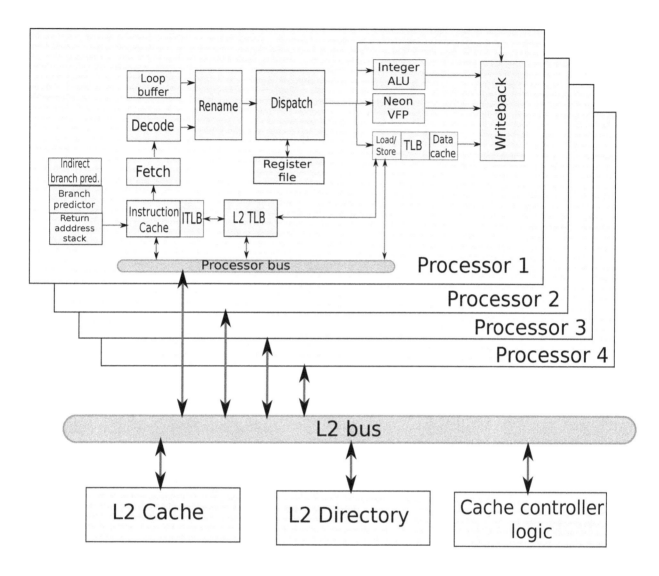

Figure A.5: The pipeline of the ARM Cortex A-15 processor , source [arm, c]. Reproduced with permission from ARM Limited. Copyright ©ARM Limited (or its affiliates).

and its PC. We do not actually need sophisticated branch prediction logic to predict the target of a return instruction. A simpler method is to record the return address whenever we call a function, and push it on a stack (referred to as the *return address stack*(RAS)). Since function calls exhibit last in-first out behaviour, we need to simply pop the RAS and get the value of the return address while returning from a function. Lastly, to support wider issue widths the fetch unit is designed to fetch 128 bits at once from the instruction cache.

The *loop buffer* (present in the Cortex-A8 also) is a very interesting addition to the decode stage. Let us assume that we are executing a set of instructions in a loop, which is most often the case. In any other processor, we need to fetch the instructions in a loop repeatedly, and decode them. This process wastes energy, and memory bandwidth. We can optimise this process by saving all the decoded instruction packets in a loop buffer such that we can bypass the fetch and decode units altogether while executing a loop. The register rename stage can thus get instructions from the decode unit or the loop buffer.

The core maintains a reorder buffer (ROB) (see Section 9.11.4) that contains the results of all the instructions. Recall that entries in the ROB are allocated in program order. The rename stage maps operands to entries in the ROB (referred to as the result queue in ARM's documentation). For example, if instruction 3 needs a value that is going to be produced by instruction 1, then the corresponding operand is mapped to the ROB entry of instruction 1. All the instructions subsequently enter the instruction window and wait for their source operands to be ready. Once they are ready, they are dispatched to the corresponding pipelines. The Cortex-A15 has 2 integer ALUs, 1 branch unit, 1 multiply unit, and 2 load/store units. The NEON/VFP unit can accept 2 instructions per cycle.

The load/store unit has a 4 stage pipeline. For ensuring precise exceptions stores are only issued to the memory system, when the instruction reaches the head of the ROB (there are no earlier instructions in the pipeline). Meanwhile, any load operation that has a store operation to the same address in the pipeline gets its value through a forwarding path. Both the L1 caches (instruction and data) are typically 32 KB each.

The Cortex-A15 processor supports a large L2 cache (up to 4 MB). It is a 16 way set associative cache with an aggressive prefetcher. The L1 caches, and the L2 cache are a part of the cache coherence protocol. The Cortex-A15 uses a directory based MESI protocol. The L2 cache contains a *snoop tag array* that maintains a copy of all the directories at the L1 level. If an I/O operation wishes to modify some line, then the L2 cache uses the snoop tag array to find if the line resides in any L1 cache. If any L1 cache contains a copy of the line, then this copy is invalidated. Likewise, if there is a DMA read operation, then the L2 controller fetches the line from the L1 cache that contains a copy of it. It is additionally possible to extend this protocol to support L3 caches, and a host of peripherals.

A.2   AMD® Processors

Let us now study the design of AMD processors. Recall that AMD processors implement the x86 instruction set, and AMD manufactures processors for mobile devices, netbooks, laptops, desktops, and servers. In this section, we shall look at two processors at both the ends of the design spectrum. The AMD Bobcat processor is meant for mobile devices, tablets, and netbooks. It implements a subset of the x86 instruction set, and the main objectives of its design are power efficiency, and an acceptable level of performance. The AMD Bulldozer processor is at the other end of the spectrum, and is meant for high end servers. It is optimised for performance and instruction throughput. It is also AMD's first multithreaded processor, which uses a novel type of core known as a *conjoined core* for implementing multithreading.

A.2.1   AMD Bobcat

Overview

The Bobcat processor (original paper [Burgess et al., 2011]) was designed to operate within a 10-15W power budget. Within this power budget, the designers of Bobcat were able to implement a large number of complex architectural features in the processor. For example, Bobcat uses a fairly elaborate 2 issue out-of-order pipeline. Bobcat's pipeline uses a sophisticated branch predictor, and is designed to fetch 2 instructions in the same cycle. It can subsequently decode them at that rate and convert them to complex micro-ops (Cops). A complex micro-op (Cop) in AMD's terminology is a CISC like instruction that can read and write to memory. The set of Cops are subsequently sent to the instruction queue, renaming engine, and scheduler.

The scheduler selects instructions out-of-order and dispatches them to the ALU, memory address generation units, and the load/store units. The load/store unit also sends requests to the memory system out-of-order in the interest of performance. Hence, we can readily conclude that Bobcat supports a weak memory model. Along with sophisticated micro-architectural features, the Bobcat processor also supports

SIMD instruction sets (up to SSE 4), methods to automatically save the processor state in memory, and 64-bit instructions. To ensure that the power consumption of the processor is within limits, Bobcat contains a large number of power saving optimisations. One such prominent mechanism is known as *clock gating*. Here, the clock signal is set to a logical 0 for units that are unused. This ensures that there are no signal transitions in the unused units, and consequently there is no dissipation of dynamic power. The Bobcat processor also uses pointers to data as much as possible, and tries to minimise copying data across different locations in the processor. Let us now look at the design of the pipeline in some more detail.

Design of the Pipeline

Figure A.6 shows a block diagram of the pipeline of the AMD Bobcat processor. A distinguishing feature of the Bobcat processor is the fairly sophisticated branch predictor. We need to first predict if an instruction is a branch or not. This is because, there is no way of finding this out quickly in the x86 ISA. If an instruction is predicted to be a branch, we need to compute its outcome (taken/not taken), and the target. AMD uses an advanced pattern matching based proprietary algorithm for branch prediction. After branch prediction, the fetch engine fetches 32 bytes from the I cache at once, and sends it to an instruction buffer.

The decoder considers 22 instruction bytes at a time, and tries to demarcate instruction boundaries. This is a slow and computationally intensive process because x86 instruction lengths can have a lot of variability. Larger processors typically cache this information such that decoding an instruction for the second time is easier. Since the decode throughput of Bobcat is only limited to 2 instructions, it does not have this feature. Now, most pairs of x86 instructions fit within 22 bytes, and thus the decoder can most of the time extract the contents of both the x86 instructions. The decoder typically converts each x86 instruction to 1-2 Cops. For some infrequently used instructions, it replaces the instruction with a microcode sequence.

Subsequently, the Cops are added to a 56 entry reorder buffer (ROB). Bobcat has two schedulers. The integer scheduler has 16 entries, and the floating point scheduler has 18 entries. The integer scheduler selects two instructions for execution every cycle. The integer pipeline has two ALUs, and two address generation units (1 for load, and 1 for store). The floating point pipeline can also execute two Cops per cycle with some restrictions.

The load-store unit in the processor forwards values from store to load instructions in the pipeline whenever possible. Bobcat has 32 KB (8 way associative) L1 D and I caches. They are connected to a 512 KB L2 cache (16 way set associative). The bus interface connects the L2 cache to the main memory, and system bus.

Let us now consider the timing of the pipeline. The Bobcat integer pipeline is divided into 16 stages. Because of the deep pipeline, it is possible to clock the core at frequencies between 1-2 GHz. The Bobcat pipeline has 6 fetch cycles, and 3 decode cycles. The last 3 fetch cycles are overlapped with the decode cycles. The renaming engine, and scheduler take 4 more cycles. For most integer instructions, we require 1 cycle to read the register file, 1 cycle to access the ALU, and 1 more cycle to write the results back to the register file. The floating point pipeline has 7 additional stages, and the load-store unit requires 3 additional stages for address generation, and data cache access.

A.2.2 AMD Bulldozer

As the name suggests, the Bulldozer core (original paper [Butler et al., 2011]) is at the other end of the spectrum, and is primarily meant for high end desktops, workstations, and servers. Along with being an aggressive out-of-order machine, it also has multithreading capabilities. The Bulldozer is actually a combination of a multicore, fine grained multithreaded processor and an SMT. The Bulldozer core is actually a "conjoined core", which consists of two smaller cores that share functional units.

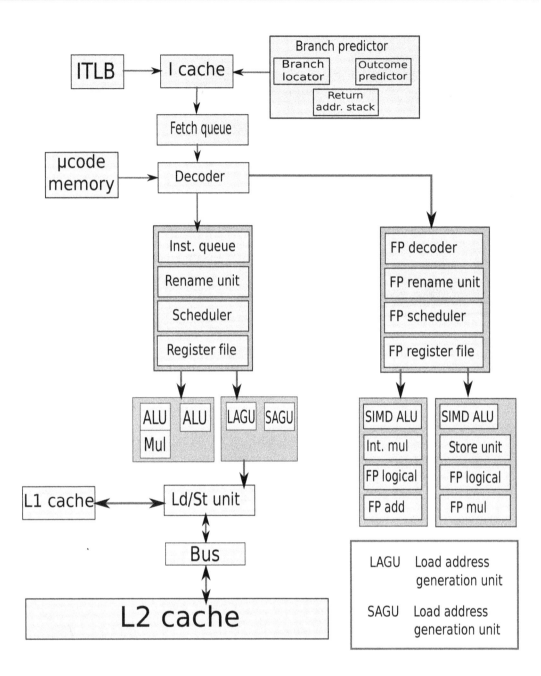

Figure A.6: The pipeline of the AMD Bobcat processor. ©[2011] IEEE. Adapted and reprinted, with permission. Source [Burgess et al., 2011]

Overview

Both the Bulldozer threads share the fetch engine (refer to Figure A.7), and decode logic. This part of the pipeline (known as the *front end*) switches between the two threads once every cycle, or few cycles. The integer, load-store, and branch instructions, are then dispatched to one of the two cores. Each core contains an instruction scheduler, register file, integer execution units, L1 caches, and a load-store unit. We can think of each core as a self sufficient core without instruction fetch and decode capabilities. Both the cores share the floating point unit that runs in SMT mode. It has its dedicated scheduler, and execution units. The

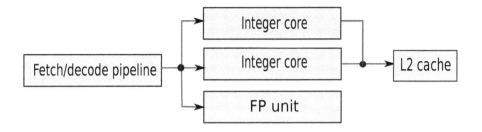

Figure A.7: Overview of the Bulldozer processor

Bulldozer processor is designed to run server as well as numerical workloads at 3-4 GHz. The maximum power dissipation is limited to 125-140W.

Detailed Design

Let us now consider a more detailed view of the processor in Figure A.8.

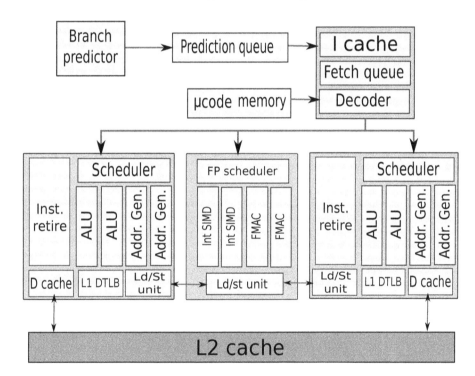

Figure A.8: Detailed view of the Bulldozer processor. ©[2011] IEEE. Adapted and reprinted, with permission. Source [Butler et al., 2011]

The Bulldozer processor has twice the fetch width of the Bobcat processor. It can fetch and decode up to 4 x86 instructions per cycle. Akin to Bobcat, the Bulldozer processor has sophisticated branch prediction logic that predicts whether an instruction is a branch, the branch outcome, and the branch target. It has a multilevel branch target buffer that saves the predicted branch targets of roughly 5500 branch instructions. The decode engine converts x86 instructions into Cops. One Cop in AMD is a CISC instruction albeit sometimes simpler than the original x86 instruction. Most x86 instructions get converted to just one Cop. However, some instructions get translated to more than one Cop, and it is sometimes necessary to use the microcode memory for instruction translation. An interesting aspect of the decode engine is that it can dynamically merge instructions to make a larger instruction. For example, it can merge a compare instruction, and a subsequent branch instruction, into one Cop. This is known as *macro-instruction fusion*.

Subsequently, the integer instructions are dispatched to the cores for execution. Each core has a rename engine, instruction scheduler (40 entries), a register file, and a 128 entry ROB. The core's execution unit consists of 4 separate pipelines. Two pipelines have ALUs, and two other pipelines are dedicated to memory address generation. The load-store unit co-ordinates access to memory, forwards data between stores to loads, and performs aggressive prefetching using stride prefetchers. Recall that stride prefetchers can automatically deduce array accesses, and fetch from array indices that are most likely to be accessed in the future.

Both the cores share a 64 KB instruction cache. However, each core has a 16 KB write-through L1 cache, where each load access takes 4 cycles. The L1 caches are connected to an L2 cache that comes in various sizes (ranging from 1-2 MB in the design presented in [Butler et al., 2011]). It is shared across the cores, and has a 18 cycle latency.

The floating point unit is shared between both the cores. It is more than a mere functional unit. We can think of it as an SMT processor that schedules and executes instructions for two threads simultaneously. It has its own instruction window, register file, rename, and wakeup-select (out of order scheduling) logic. Bulldozer's floating point unit has 4 pipelines that process SIMD instructions (both integer and floating point), and regular floating point instructions. The first two pipelines have 128 bit floating point ALUs called FMAC units. An FMAC (floating point multiply accumulate) unit can perform an operation of the form $(a \leftarrow a + b \times c)$, along with regular floating point operations. The last two pipelines have 128 bit integer SIMD units, and additionally the last pipeline is also used to store results to memory. Lastly, the floating point unit has a dedicated load-store unit to access the caches present in the cores.

A.3   Intel® Processors

Let us now discuss the design of Intel processors. As of writing this book (2012-13) Intel processors dominate the laptop and desktop markets. In this section, we shall present the design of two Intel processors that have very different designs. The first processor is the Intel® Atom™, which has been designed for mobile phones, tablets, and embedded computers. At the other end of the spectrum lies the Sandy Bridge multicore, which is a part of the Intel® Core™i7 line of processors. These processors are meant to be used by high end desktops and servers. Both of these processors have very different business requirements. This has translated to two very different designs

A.3.1   Intel® Atom™

Overview

The Intel Atom processor started out with a unique set of requirements (see [Halfhill, 2008]). The designers had to design a core that was extremely power efficient, had enough features to run commercial operating systems and web browsers, and was fully x86 compatible. A naive approach to reduce power would have been to implement a subset of the x86 ISA. This approach would have led to a simpler and more power efficient decoder. Since the decoding logic is known to be power hungry in x86 processors, reducing its complexity is one of the simplest methods to reduce power. However, full x86 compatibility precluded this option.

Hence, the designers were forced to consider novel designs that are extremely power efficient, and do not compromise on performance. Consequently, they decided to simplify the pipeline, and consider 2-issue inorder pipelines only. Recall from our discussion in Section 9.11.4 that out-of-order pipelines have complicated structures for finding the dependences between instructions, and for executing them out of order. Some of these structures are the instruction window, renaming logic, scheduler, and wakeup-select logic. These structures add to the complexity of the processor, and increase its power dissipation.

Secondly, most Intel processors typically translate CISC instructions into RISC like micro-ops. These micro-ops execute like normal RISC instructions in the pipeline. The process of instruction translation consumes a lot of power. Hence, the designers of the Intel Atom decided to discard instruction translation. The Atom pipeline processes CISC instructions directly. For some instructions that are very complicated, the Atom processor does use a microcode ROM to translate them into simpler CISC instructions. However, this is more of an exception that the norm.

(3)	(3)	(2)	(1)	(1)	(2)	(1)	(2)	(1)
Fetch	Decode	Schedule Dispatch	Operand fetch	AG	Cache access	Execute	Exceptions, Multiple thread handling	Commit
					Memory access			

Figure A.9: The pipeline of the Intel Atom processor. (AG → address generation) ©[2008] The Linley Group. Adapted and reprinted, with permission. (Originally published in the Microprocessor Report. source [Halfhill, 2008])

As compared to RISC processors, the fetch and decode stages are more complicated in CISC processors. This is because instructions have variable lengths, and demarcating instruction boundaries is a tedious process. Secondly, the process of decoding is also more complicated. Hence, Atom dedicates 6 stages out of its 16-stage pipeline to instruction fetch and decoding as shown in Figure A.9. The remaining stages perform the traditional functions of register file access, data cache access, and instruction execution. Along with the simpler pipeline, another hallmark feature of the Intel Atom processor is that it supports 2-way multithreading. Modern mobile devices typically run multitasking operating systems, and users run multiple programs at the same time. Multithreading can support this requirement, enable additional parallelism, and reduce idle time in processor pipelines. The last 3 stages in the pipeline are dedicated to handling exceptions, handling multithreading related events, and writing data back to register or memory. Like all modern processors, store instructions are not on the critical path. In general, processors that do not obey sequential consistency write their store values to a write buffer and proceed with executing subsequent instructions.

Detailed Design

Let us now describe the design in some more detail. Let us start with the fetch, and decode stages (see Figure A.10). In the fetch stage, the Atom processor predicts the direction and target of branches, and fetches a stream of bytes into the instruction prefetch buffers. The next task is to demarcate instructions in the fetched stream of bytes. Finding, the boundaries of x86 instructions is one of the most complicated tasks performed by this part of the pipeline. Consequently, the Atom processor has a 2 stage *pre-decode* step that adds 1 bit markers between instructions, after it decodes them for the first time. This step is performed by the ILD (instruction length decoder) unit It then saves the instructions in the I cache. Subsequently, pre-decoded instructions fetched from the I cache can bypass the pre-decoding step, and directly proceed to the decoding step because its length is already known. Saving these additional markers, reduces the effective size of the I cache. The size of the I cache is 36 KB; however, after adding the markers, it is effectively 32 KB. The decoder does not convert most CISC instructions into RISC like micro-ops. However, for some complicated x86 instructions, it is necessary to translate them into simpler micro-ops by accessing

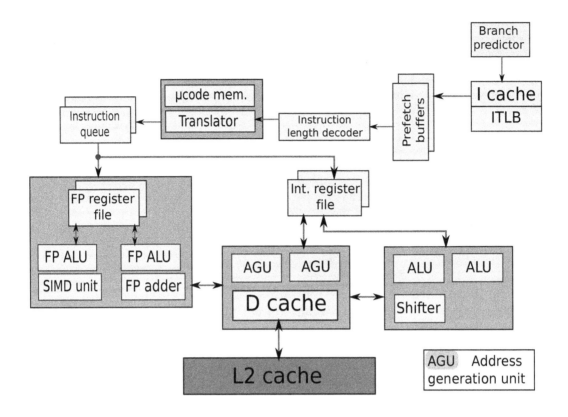

Figure A.10: A block diagram of the Intel Atom processor ©[2008] The Linley Group. Adapted and reprinted, with permission. (Originally published in the Microprocessor Report. source [Halfhill, 2008])

the microcode memory.

Subsequently, integer instructions are dispatched to the integer execution units, and the FP instructions are dispatched to the FP execution units. Atom has two integer ALUs, two FP ALUs, and two address generation units for memory operations. For supporting multithreading, it is necessary to have two copies of the instruction queue (1 per thread), and two copies of the integer and FP register files. Instead of creating a copy of a hardware structure like an instruction queue, Intel follows a different approach. For example, in the Atom processor, the 32 entry instruction queue is split into two parts (with 16 entries each). Each thread uses its part of the instruction queue.

Let us now discuss a general point about multithreading. Multithreading increases the utilisation of resources on a chip by decreasing the time that they remain idle. Thus, a multithreaded processor is ideally expected to have a higher power overhead (because of higher activity), and also have better instruction throughput. It is important to note that unless a processor is designed wisely, the throughput might not predictably increase. Multithreading increases the contention in shared resources such as the caches, the TLBs, and the instruction schedule/dispatch logic. Especially, the caches get partitioned between the threads, and we expect the miss rates to increase. Similar is the case for the TLBs also. On the other hand, the pipeline need not remain idle in the shadow of an L2 miss or in low ILP (instruction level parallelism) phases of a program. Hence, there are pros and cons of multithreading, and we have performance benefits only when the good effects (performance increasing effects) outweigh the bad effects (contention increasing effects).

A.3.2 Intel Sandy Bridge

Overview

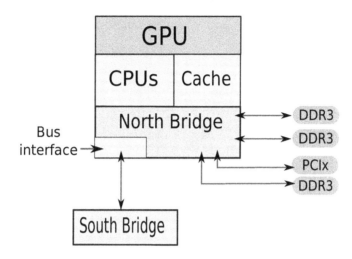

Figure A.11: Overview of the Sandy Bridge processor ©[2010] The Linley Group. Adapted and reprinted, with permission. (Originally published in the Microprocessor Report. Source [Gwennap, 2010])

Let us now discuss the design of a high performance Intel processor called the Sandy Bridge processor, which is a part of some of the latest (as of 2012) Intel Core i7 processors in the market. The main aims [Gwennap, 2010] while designing the Sandy Bridge processor was to support emerging multimedia workloads, numerically intensive applications, and multicore friendly parallel applications.

The most distinguishing features of the Sandy Bridge processor is that it contains an on-chip graphics processor. The graphics processor is loaded with specialised units for performing image rendering, video encoding/decoding, and custom image processing. The CPU and GPU communicate through a large shared on chip L3 cache. An overview of the Sandy Bridge processor is shown in Figure A.11.

Along with the addition of more components on chip, a lot of modifications to the CPU were also made. Sandy Bridge processor has full support for the new AVX instruction set, which is a 256 bit SIMD instruction set. For each SIMD unit, it is possible to perform 4 double precision operations or 8 single precision operations simultaneously. Since so many high performance features were being added it was necessary to add many power saving features also. Nowadays, techniques such as DVFS (dynamic voltage frequency scaling), clock gating (shutting off the clock) and power gating (shutting off the power for a set of functional units) for unused units are common. Additionally, the Sandy Bridge designers modified the design of the core to minimise copying values between units as much as possible (recall that a similar design decision was also taken by the designers of AMD Bobcat also), and also made basic changes to the design of some core structures such as the branch predictor and branch target buffer for power efficiency.

An important point to note here is that processors such as the Intel Sandy Bridge are designed to support multiple cores (4-8). Secondly, each core supports 2-way multithreading. Hence, we can run 16 threads on an 8 core machine. These threads can actively communicate between each other, the L3 cache banks, the GPU, and the on chip North Bridge controller. With so many communicating entities we need to design flexible on chip networks that facilitate high bandwidth and low latency communication. The designers of the Sandy Bridge have opted for a ring based interconnect over the traditional bus.

The Sandy Bridge processor was designed for a 32 nm [1] semiconductor process. Its successor is the Intel Ivy Bridge processor, which has the same design, but is designed for a 22 nm process.

Detailed Design

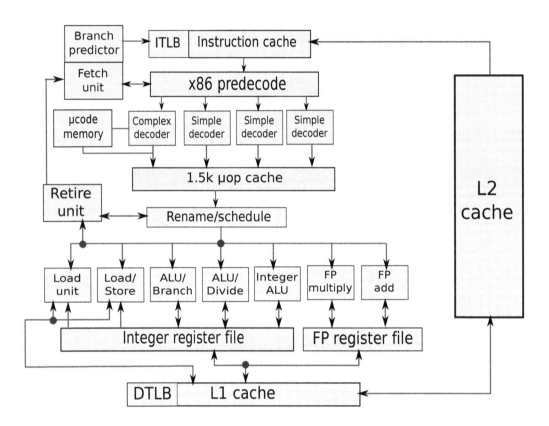

Figure A.12: Detailed view of the Sandy Bridge processor ©[2010] The Linley Group. Adapted and reprinted, with permission. (Originally published in the Microprocessor Report. Source [Gwennap, 2010])

Let us now consider the detailed design of a Sandy Bridge Core in Figure A.12 (also refer to [Gwennap, 2010]). The Sandy Bridge processor has a 32 KB instruction cache, that can provide 4 x86 instructions every cycle. The first step in decoding a stream of x86 instructions, is to demarcate their boundaries (known as predecoding). Once, 4 instructions are predecoded, they are sent to the decoders. Sandy Bridge has 4 decoders. Three of them are simple decoders, and one decoder is known as a complex decoder that uses the microprogram memory. All the decoders convert CISC instructions into RISC like micro-ops. Sandy Bridge has a L0 cache for micro-ops that can store roughly 1500 micro-ops. The L0 micro-op cache has performance benefits in terms of both performance and power. It reduces the branch misprediction latency if the instruction at the branch target is available in the L0 cache. Since most of the branches in programs are near branches, we expect to have a good hit rate at the L0 cache. Secondly, we can also save power. If an instruction's micro-ops are available in the L0 cache, then we do not need to fetch, predecode, and decode the instruction once again. We thus avoid these power hungry operations.

We need to point out an interesting design decision (see [Gwennap, 2010]) that was taken by the designers with respect to the branch predictor. This design decision is representative of many similar problems in

---

[1]The smallest possible structure that can be fabricated reliably has a dimension of 32 nm

computer architecture. One such problem is whether we should design a small structure with complicated entries, or should we design a large structure with simple entries? For example, should we have a 4-way associative 16 KB cache, or a 2-way associative 32 KB cache? In general, there is no definite answer to questions of this nature. They are highly dependent on the nature of the target workloads. For the Sandy Bridge processors, the designers had a choice. They could have either chosen a branch predictor with 2-bit saturating counters, or a predictor with more entries, and a 1 bit saturating counter. The power and performance tradeoffs of the latter design was found to be better. Hence, they chose to have 1 bit counters.

Subsequently, 4 micro-ops are sent to the rename and dispatch units that perform out-of-order scheduling. In earlier processors such as the Nehalem processor, temporary results of instructions that were in flight were saved in the ROB. Once the instructions finished, they were copied to the register file. This operation involves copying data, and is thus not efficient from the point of view of power. Hence, Sandy Bridge avoids this, and saves results directly in the physical register file similar to high performance RISC processors. When an instruction reaches the rename stage, we check the mappings in the rename table, and find the ids of the physical registers that contain, or are supposed to contain at a future point of time, the values of source operands. We subsequently either read the physical register file, or wait for their values to be generated. In your author's view, using physical register files is a better approach than using other approaches that save the results of unfinished instructions in the ROB, and later copy the results back to the register files. Using physical register files is fast, simple, and power efficient. By using this approach in the Sandy Bridge processor, the ROB got simplified, and it was possible to have 168 in-flight instructions at any point of time.

The Sandy Bridge processor has 3 integer ALUs, 1 load unit, and 1 load/store unit. The integer units read and write their operands from a 160 entry register file. For supporting floating point operations, it has one FP add unit, and 1 FP multiply unit. They support the AVX SIMD instruction set (256-bit operations on sets of single and double precision numbers). Moreover, to support 256 bit operations, Intel added new 256-bit vector registers (YMM registers) in the x86 AVX ISA.

To implement the AVX instruction set, it is necessary to support 256-bit transfers from the 32 KB data cache. The Sandy Bridge processor can perform two 128 bit loads, and one 128 bit store per cycle. In the case of loading a YMM (256 bit) register, both the 128 bit load operations are fused into one (256 bit) load operation. Sandy Bridge has a 256 KB L2 cache, and a large (1-8 MB) L3 cache that is divided into banks. The L3 banks, cores, GPU, and North Bridge controllers are connected using a unidirectional ring based interconnect. Note that the diameter of an unidirectional ring is $(N - 1)$ because we can send messages in only one direction. To overcome this restriction, each node is actually connected to two points on the ring. These points are diametrically opposite to each other. Hence, the effective diameter is close to $N/2$.

Let us conclude by describing a unique feature of the Sandy Bridge processor called *turbo mode*. The idea is as follows. Assume that a processor has a period of quiescence (less activity). In this case, the temperature of all the cores will remain relatively low. Now, assume that the user decides to perform a computationally intensive activity such as sharpen an image, and remove "red eyes." This requires numerically intensive computations that are also power intensive. Every processor has a rated thermal design power (TDP), which is the maximum amount of power a processor is allowed to dissipate. In the turbo mode, the processor is permitted to dissipate more power than the TDP for short durations of time (20-25s). This allows the processor to run all the units at a frequency higher than the nominal value. Once the temperature reaches a certain threshold, the turbo mode is automatically switched off, and the processor resumes normal operation. The main point to note is that dissipating a large amount of power for a short duration is not a problem. However, having very high temperatures for even a short duration is not allowed. This is because high temperature can permanently damage a chip. For example, if a wire melts, then the entire chip is destroyed. Since it takes several seconds for a processor to heat up, we can take advantage of this effect to have high frequency and high power phases to quickly complete sporadic jobs. Note that the turbo mode is not useful for long running jobs that take hours.

B

Graphics Processors

B.1 Overview

High intensity graphics is a hallmark of contemporary computer systems. Today's computers from smart phones to high end desktops use a variety of sophisticated visual effects to enhance user experience. Additionally, users use computers to play graphics intensive games, watch high definition videos, and for computer aided engineering design. All of these applications require a significant amount of graphics processing.

In the early days, graphics support in computers was very rudimentary. The programmer needed to specify the co-ordinates of every single shape that was drawn on the screen. For example, to draw a line the programmer needed to explicitly provide the co-ordinates of the line, and specify its colour. The range of colours was very limited, and there was almost no hardware for off loading graphics intensive tasks. Since each line or circle drawn on the screen required several assembly statements, the process of creating, and using computer graphics was very slow. Gradually, a need arose to have some support for graphics in hardware.

Let us discuss a little bit of background before delving into hardware accelerated graphics. A typical computer monitor contains a matrix of pixels. A pixel is a small point on the screen. For example a 1920×1080 monitor has 1920 pixels in each row, and 1080 pixels in each column. Each pixel has a colour at a certain point of time. Modern computer systems can set 16 million colours for each pixel. A picture on a computer screen is essentially an array of coloured pixels, and a video is essentially a sequence of pictures. In a video, we typically show 50-100 pictures every second (known as the *refresh rate*), where one picture is marginally different from the previous one. The human eye cannot figure out the fact that the pictures on the computer screen are changing in rapid succession. The brain creates an illusion of a continuous animation.

B.1.1 Graphics Applications

We can divide modern graphics applications into two types. The first type is automatic image synthesis. For example, let us consider a complex scene in a game, where a character is running with a machine gun in a moonlit night. In this case, the programmer is not manually setting the value of every pixel to a given colour. This process is too slow and time consuming. None of our interactive games would work, if this method was used. Instead, the programmer writes a program at the level of high level objects. For example, she can define a scene with a set of objects like roads, plants, and obstacles. She can define a character, and the artefacts that he carries such as a machine gun, a knife, and a cloak. The programmer writes a program

643

in terms of these objects. Additionally, she specifies a set of rules that define the interactions of such objects. For example, she might specify that if a character collides with a wall, then the character turns around and runs in the other direction. Along with defining objects, and the semantics of objects, it is essential to define the sources of light in a scene. In this case, the programmer needs to specify the intensity of light in a moonlit night. The illumination of the character and the background is then automatically calculated by dedicated graphics software and hardware.

Sadly, the graphics hardware does not understand the language of complex objects, and characters. Hence, most graphics toolkits have graphics libraries to break down complex structures into a set of basic shapes. Most shapes in computer graphics applications are broken down into a set of triangles. All operations such as object collision, movement, lighting, shadows, and illumination, are converted to basic operations on triangles. However, graphics libraries do not use the regular processor to process these triangles and ultimately create an array of pixels to be displayed on a computer screen. Once, the programmer's intent has been translated to operations on basic shapes, the graphics libraries send the code to *a dedicated graphics processor* that does the rest of the processing. The graphics processor generates a complex scene from data and rules supplied by the user. It operates on shapes specified by edges and vertices. Most of the time these shapes are triangles in 2D space, or tetrahedra in 3D space. The graphics processors also calculate the effect of lighting, object position, depth, and perspectives while generating the final image. Once, the graphics processor has generated the final image, it sends it to the display device. If we are playing a computer game, then this process needs to be done at least 50-100 times every second.

To summarise, we observe that since generating complex graphics scenes is difficult, and slow, programmers operate on a high-level description of objects. Subsequently, graphics libraries convert the programmer's directives into operations on basic shapes, and send the set of shapes, and rules for operating on them to the graphics processor. The graphics processor generates the final scene by operating on the basic shapes, and then converting them to an array of pixels.

The second important application of graphics processors is to display animated content such as videos. A high definition video has millions of pixels per scene. To reduce the storage requirements, most high definition videos are severely compressed (encoded). Hence, a computer needs to decode or decompress a video, compute the array of pixels 50-100 times per second, and display them on screen. This is a very compute intensive process, and can tie up the resources of a CPU. Hence, video decoding is also typically offloaded to the graphics processor that contains specialised units for handling videos.

Almost all modern computer systems contain a graphics processor, and it is referred to as the GPU (Graphics Processing Unit). A modern GPU contains more than 64-128 cores, and thus is designed for extensive parallel processing.

B.1.2   Graphics Pipeline

Let us now look at the pipeline of a typical graphics processor in Figure B.1.

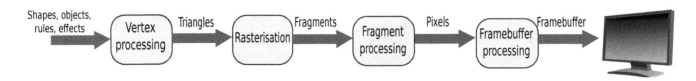

Figure B.1: A graphics pipeline [Blythe, 2008]

The first stage is called *vertex processing*. In this stage, the set of vertices, shapes, and triangles, are processed. The GPU performs complex operations such as object rotation, and translation. The programmer might specify that she wants a given object to move at a certain velocity towards another object. It is thus necessary to translate the position of a shape at a given rate. Such operations are also performed in this stage. The output of this stage is a set of simple triangles in a 2D plane.

The second stage is known as *rasterisation*. The process of rasterisation converts each of the triangles into a set of pixels, known as *fragments*. Moreover, it associates each pixel in a fragment with a set of parameters. These parameters are later used to interpolate the value of the colour. The third stage does *fragment processing*. This stage either colours the pixels of a fragment according to a fixed set of rules using the intermediate results computed in the previous stage, or, it maps a given texture to the fragment. For example, if a fragment represents the surface of a wooden table, then this stage maps the texture of wood to the colours of the pixels. This stage is also used to incorporate effects such as shadows and illumination.

Note that up till now we have computed the colours of the fragments for all the objects in a scene. However, it is possible that one object might be in front of another object, and thus a part of the second object might be hidden. The fourth stage aggregates all the fragments from the third stage, and performs an operation called *frame buffer* processing. The frame buffer is a large array that contains the colour values for each pixel. The graphics card passes the frame buffer to the display device 50-100 times per second. One of the operations performed in this stage is known as *depth buffering*. Here, it computes a 2D view of the 3D space at a certain angle by hiding parts of objects. Once the final scene is created, the graphics pipeline transfers the image to the frame buffer.

This is precisely the way complex games, or even standard operations such as minimising or maximising a window are rendered by a graphics processor. *Rendering* is defined as the process of generating a scene in pixels, by processing the high level description of a scene in terms of objects, rules, and visual effects. Discussing the exact details of rendering is beyond the scope of this book. The interested reader can refer to a book on computer graphics [Hughes et al., 2013]. The only point that the user should appreciate is that the process of rendering essentially involves a lot of linear algebra operations. Readers familiar with linear algebra will quickly appreciate the fact that object rotation or translation are all matrix operations. These operations process a large number of floating point values, and are inherently parallel.

B.1.3   Fusion of High Performance Computing and Graphics Computing

Towards the late nineties, there was a rapid growth in the field of computer graphics. There was a surge in computer gaming, desktop visual effects, and advanced engineering software that required sophisticated hardware accelerators for computer graphics. Hence, designers increasingly faced the need to create more vivid scenes, and more life like objects. Readers can compare the animation movies produced in the late eighties and today's Hollywood movies. Animated movies today have very life like characters with very detailed facial expressions. Thanks to graphics hardware, all of this is possible. To create such immersive experiences it became necessary to add a great degree of flexibility in graphics processors to incorporate different kinds of visual effects. Hence, graphics processor designers exposed a lot of internals of the processor to low level software and allowed the programmers to use the processor more flexibly. A set of programs called shaders were born in the early years of 2000. They allowed the programmer to create flexible fragment, and pixel processing routines.

By 2006, major GPU vendors had the realisation that the graphics pipeline can be used for general purpose computations also. For example, heavily numerical scientific code is conceptually similar to fragment, or pixel processing operations. Hence, if we allow regular user programs to access the graphics processor to perform their tasks then we can run a host of scientific programs on graphics processors. In response to this requirement, NVIDIA released the CUDA API that allowed C programmers to write code in C, and run it on a graphics processor. Hence, the term GPGPU (General Purpose GPU) was born.

> **Definition 164**
> *GPGPU stands for General Purpose Graphics Processing Unit. It is essentially a graphics processor that allows regular users to write and run their code on it. Users typically use dedicated languages, or extensions to standard languages for producing code that is compatible with GPGPUs.*

In this book we shall discuss the design of the NVIDIA® Tesla® GPU architecture. Specifically, we will discuss the design of the GeForce® 8800 GPU. The fastest parts of the GPU (the cores) typically operate at 1.5 GHz. Other parts operate at 600 MHz, or 750 MHz.

B.2   NVIDIA Tesla Architecture

Figure B.2 shows the Tesla architecture. Let us start explaining from the top of the figure. The host CPU sends sequences of commands and data to the graphics processor through a dedicated bus. The dedicated bus then transfers the set of commands and data to buffers on the GPU. Subsequently, the units of the GPU process the information. In Figure B.2 the work flows from top to bottom. Before we start discussing the details of the GPU, the reader needs to understand that the GPU is essentially a set of very simple inorder cores. Additionally, it has a large amount of extra hardware to co-ordinate the execution of complex tasks and allocate work to the set of cores. The GPU also supports a multilevel memory hierarchy, and has specialised units that exclusively perform a few graphics specific operations.

B.2.1   Work Distribution

Three kinds of work can be assigned to the GPU – vertex processing, pixel processing, and regular computing jobs. The GPU defines its own assembly code, which uses the PTX and SASS instruction sets. Each instruction in these instruction sets defines a basic operation on the GPU. It uses either register operands, or memory operands. Unlike CPUs the structure of the register file in a GPU is typically not exposed to software. The programmer is expected to use an unlimited number of virtual registers. The GPU or the device driver map them to real registers.

Now, for processing vertices, low level graphics software sends a sequence of assembly instructions to the GPU. The GPU has a hardware assembler that produces binary code, and sends it to a dedicated vertex processing unit that co-ordinates and distributes the work among the cores in the GPU. Alternatively, the CPU can send pixel processing operations to the GPU. The GPU does the process of rasterisation, fragment processing, and depth buffering. A dedicated unit in the GPU generates code snippets for these operations, and sends them to a pixel processing unit that distributes the work items among the set of GPU cores. The third unit is a compute work distributor that accepts regular computational tasks from the CPU such as adding two matrices, or computing a dot product of two vectors. The programmer specifies a set of subtasks. The role of the compute work distribution engine is to send these set of subtasks to cores in the GPU.

Beyond this stage, the GPU is more or less oblivious of the source of the instructions. Note that this piece of engineering is the key contribution behind making GPUs successful. Designers have successfully split the functionality of a GPU into two layers. The first layer is specific to the type of operation (graphics or general purpose). The role of each pipeline in this stage is to transform the specific sequence of operations into a generic set of actions such that irrespective of the nature of the high level operation, the same set of hardware units can be used. Let us now take a look at the second half of the GPGPU that contains the compute engines.

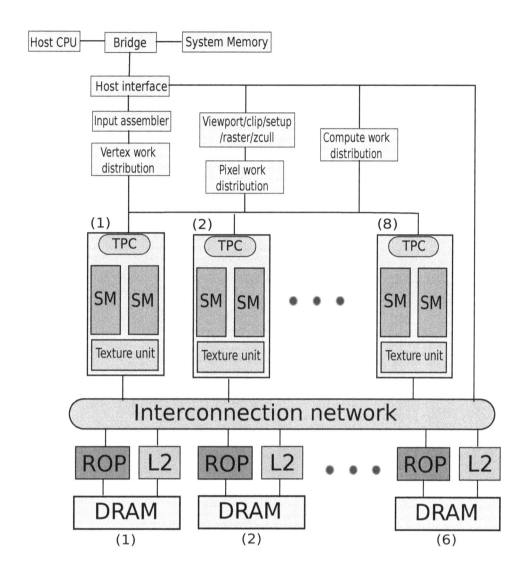

Figure B.2: NVIDIA Tesla Architecture ©[2008] IEEE. Reprinted, with permission. Source [Lindholm et al., 2008]

B.2.2   GPU Compute Engines

The GeForce 8800 GPU has 128 cores. The Cores are organised into 8 groups. Each group is known as a TPC (texture/ processor cluster). Each TPC contains two SMs (Streaming Multiprocessors). Moreover, each SM contains 8 cores known as streaming processors (SPs). Each SP is a simple inorder core that has an IEEE 754 compliant floating point ALU, branch and memory access units. Along with the set of simple cores, each SM contains some dedicated memory structures. These memory structures contain constants, texture data, and GPU instructions. All the SPs can execute a set of instructions in parallel, and are tightly synchronised with each other.

B.2.3   Interconnection Network, DRAM Modules, L2 Caches, and ROPs

The 8 TPCs are connected via an interconnection network to a set of caches, DRAM modules, and ROPs (raster operation processors). The SMs contain the first level caches. Upon a cache miss, the SP cores access the relevant L2 cache bank via the NOC. In the case of GPUs, the L2 cache is a shared cache split at the level of banks. Beneath the L2 caches, GPUs have a large external DRAM memory. The GeForce 8800 had 384 pins to connect to external DRAM modules. The set of pins are divided into 6 groups, where each group contains 64 pins. The physical memory space is also split into 6 parts, across the 6 groups. Rasterisation operations typically require some specialised processing routines. Unfortunately, these routines run inefficiently on TPCs. Hence, the GeForce 8800 chip has 6 ROPs. Each ROP processor can process at the most 4 pixels per cycle. It mostly interpolates the colour of pixels, and performs colour blending operations.

We are primarily interested in the design of the SMs. Hence, let us look at them in slightly greater detail.

B.3   Streaming Multiprocessors (SMs)

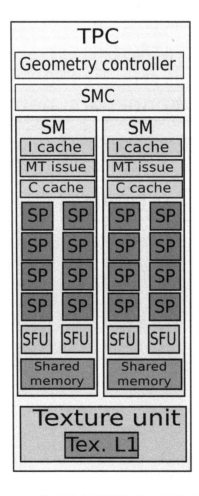

Figure B.3:   A texture/processor cluster ©[2008] IEEE. Reprinted, with permission. Source [Lindholm et al., 2008]

Figure B.3 shows the structure of a TPC with two SMs. The geometry controller orchestrates vertex and shape processing on the individual cores. It brings in vertex data from the memory hierarchy, directs the cores to process them, and then co-ordinates the process of storing the output in the memory hierarchy. Moreover, it also helps in forwarding the output to the next stage of processing. The SMC (SM controller) schedules the requests for external resources. For example, it is possible that multiple cores in an SM might want to write to the DRAM memory, or access the texture unit. In this case, the SMC arbitrates the requests. Let us now look at the structure of an SM.

Each SM has an I Cache (instruction cache), a C cache (constant cache), and a built in thread scheduler for multithreaded workloads (MT Issue Unit). The 8 SP cores can access the shared memory unit embedded in the SM for communication between themselves. An SP core has an IEEE 754 compliant floating point ALU. It can perform regular floating point operations such as add, subtract, and multiply. It also supports a special instruction called multiply-add, which is required very frequently in graphics computations. This instruction computes the value of the expression: $a * b + c$. Along with the FP ALU each SP has an integer ALU that can execute regular integer instructions, and logical instructions. Moreover, the SP core can execute memory instructions, and branch instructions. Similar to vector processors, SP cores implement predicated instructions. This means that they dedicate issue slots to instructions in the wrong path; though, they are replaced with *nop* instructions. The SPs are optimised for speed, and are the fastest units in the entire GPU. This is due to the fact that they implement a very simple RISC like instruction set, which consists mostly of basic instructions.

For computing more sophisticated mathematical functions such as transcendental functions or trigonometric functions there are two special function units (SFUs) in each SM. The SFUs also have specialised units for interpolating the value of colours inside a fragment. GPUs use this functionality for colouring the inside of each triangular fragment. Along with specialised units, the SFUs have regular integer/ floating point ALUs also that are used to run general purpose codes.

The two SMs in a TPC share a texture unit. The texture unit can simultaneously process four threads, and fill the triangles produced after rasterisation with the texture of the surface associated with the triangles. The texture information is stored in a small cache within the texture unit. Upon a cache miss, the texture unit can fetch data from the relevant L2 cache, or from main DRAM memory. Now that we have described the different parts of a GPU, let us discuss how to perform a computation on a GPU.

Each thread in an SM (mapped to an SP) can either access per thread local memory (saved on external DRAM), or shared memory (shared across all the threads in an SM, and saved on chip), or global DRAM memory. Programmers can explicitly direct the GPU to use a certain kind of memory.

B.4 Computation on a GPU

The graphics processing model is actually a combination of multi-threading, multi-programming, and SIMD execution. NVIDIA calls its model SIMT (Single Instruction, Multi-threaded). Let us look at NVIDIA's SIMT execution model.

The programmer starts out by writing code in the CUDA programming language. CUDA stands for Compute Unified Device Architecture. It is a custom extension to C/C++ that is compiled by NVIDIA's *nvcc* compiler to generate code in both the CPU's ISA (for the CPU), and in the PTX instruction set (for the GPU). A CUDA program contains a set of *kernels* that run on the GPU and a set of functions that run on the host CPU. The functions on the host CPU transfer data to and from the GPU, initialise the variables, and co-ordinate the execution of kernels on the GPU. A *kernel* is defined as a function that executes in parallel on the GPU. The graphics hardware creates multiple copies of each CUDA kernel, and each copy executes on a separate thread.

The GPU maps each such thread to an SP core. It is possible to seamlessly create and execute hundreds of threads for a single CUDA kernel. An astute reader might argue that if the code is the same for multiple

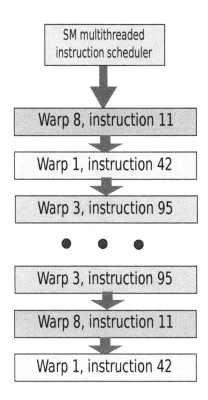

Figure B.4: Scheduling of warps ©[2008] IEEE. Reprinted, with permission. Source [Lindholm et al., 2008]

copies then what is the point of running multiple copies. Well, the answer is that the code is not exactly the same. The code implicitly takes the id of the thread as an input. For example, if we generate 100 threads for each CUDA kernel, then each thread has an unique id in the set $[0\ldots99]$. Based on the id of the thread, the code in the CUDA kernel performs appropriate processing. Recall that we had seen a very similar example, when we had written OpenMP programs (see Example 121). Now, it is possible that the threads of many separate applications might be running at the same time. The MT issue logic of each SM schedules the threads and co-ordinates their execution. An SM in this architecture can handle up to 768 threads.

If we are running multiple applications in parallel then the GPU as a whole will need to schedule thousands of threads. The scheduling overhead is prohibitive. Hence, to make the task of scheduling simpler, the GeForce 8800 GPU groups a set of 32 threads into a *warp*. Each SM can manage 24 warps. A warp is an atomic unit of threads, and either all the threads of a warp are scheduled, or no thread in the warp is scheduled. Moreover, all the threads in a warp belong to the same kernel, and start at exactly the same address. However, after they have started they can have different program counters.

Each SM maps the threads of a warp to SP cores. It executes the warp instruction by instruction. This is similar to classic SIMD execution, where we execute one instruction on multiple data streams, and then move to the next instruction. The SM executes an instruction for each thread in the warp, and after all the threads have completed the instruction, it executes the next instruction. If the kernel has a branch that is data or thread dependent, then the SM executes instructions for only those threads that have instructions in the correct branch path. The GeForce GPU uses predicated instructions. For the instructions on the wrong path, the predicated condition is false. Hence, these instructions are dynamically replaced with *nop* instructions. Once the branch paths (taken, and not taken) reconverge, all the threads in a warp become active again. The main difference from the SIMD model is that in a SIMD processor, the same thread handles multiple data streams in the same instruction. Whereas, in this case, the same instruction is executed in multiple threads, and each instruction operates on different data streams. After executing an instruction in a warp the MT issue unit might schedule the same warp, another warp from the same application, or a warp from another application. The GPU essentially implements fine grained multithreading at the level of warps. Figure B.4 shows an example.

For executing, a 32 thread warp, an SM typically uses 4 cycles. In the first cycle, it issues 8 threads to each of the 8 SP cores. In the second cycle, it issues 8 more threads to the SFUs. Since the two SFUs have 4 functional units each, they can process 8 instructions in parallel without any structural hazards. In the third cycle, 8 more threads, are sent to the SP cores, and finally in the fourth cycle, 8 threads are sent to the two SFU cores. This strategy of switching between using SFUs, and SP cores, ensures that both the units are kept busy. Since a warp is an atomic unit, it cannot be split across SMs, and each instruction of the warp must finish executing for all the active threads, before we can execute the next instruction in the warp. We can conceptually equate the concept of warps to a 32 lane wide SIMD machine. Multiple warps in the same application can execute independently. To synchronise between warps we need to use global memory, or sophisticated synchronisation primitives available in modern GPUs.

B.5 CUDA Programs

A CUDA program naturally maps to the structure of a GPU. We first write a kernel in CUDA that performs a set of operations depending on the thread id that it is assigned at runtime. A dynamic instance of a kernel is a *thread* (similar to a thread in the context of a CPU). We group a set of threads into a *block*, or a *CTA* (co-operative thread array). A block or a CTA corresponds to a warp. We can have 1–512 threads in a block, and each SM can buffer the state of at most 8 blocks at any point of time. Each thread in a block has a unique thread id. Similarly, blocks are grouped together in a *grid*. The grid contains all the threads for an application. Different blocks (or warps) may execute independently of each other, unless we explicitly enforce some form of synchronisation. In our simple example, we consider a block to be a linear array of threads, and a grid to be a linear array of blocks. Additionally, we can define a block to be a 2D or 3D array of threads, or a grid to be a 2D or 3D array of blocks.

Let us now look at a small CUDA program to add two n element arrays. Let us consider the CUDA program in parts. In the following code snippet, we initialise three arrays a, b, and c. We wish to add a and b element wise and save the results in c.

```
1   #define N 1024
2
3   void main() {
4           /* Declare three arrays a, b, and c */
5           int a[N], b[N], c[N];
6
7           /* Declare the corresponding arrays in the GPU */
8           int size = N * sizeof(int);
9           int *gpu_a, *gpu_b, *gpu_c;
10
11          /* allocate space for the arrays in the GPU */
12          cudaMalloc((void**) &gpu_a, size);
13          cudaMalloc((void**) &gpu_b, size);
14          cudaMalloc((void**) &gpu_c, size);
15
16          /* initialise arrays, a and b */
```

```
17      ...
18
19      /* copy the arrays to the GPU */
20      cudaMemcpy (gpu_a, a, size, cudaMemcpyHostToDevice);
21      cudaMemcpy (gpu_b, b, size, cudaMemcpyHostToDevice);
```

In this code snippet we declare three arrays (a, b, and c) with N elements in Line 5. Subsequently, in Line 9, we define their corresponding storage locations (gpu_a, gpu_b and gpu_c) in the GPU. We then allocate space for them in the GPU by using the *cudaMalloc* call. Next, we initialise arrays a and b with values (code not shown), and then copy these arrays to the corresponding locations (gpu_a, and gpu_b) in the GPU using the CUDA function *cudaMemcpy*. It uses a flag called *cudaMemcpyHostToDevice*. In this case the *host* is the CPU and the *device* is the GPU.

The next operation is to add the vectors gpu_a, and gpu_b in the GPU. For this purpose, we need to write a *vectorAdd* function that can add the vectors. This function should take three arguments consisting of two input vectors, and an output vector. Let us for the time being assume that we have such a function with us. Let us show the code to invoke this function.

```
1  vectorAdd <<< N/32, 32 >>> (gpu_a, gpu_b, gpu_c);
```

We invoke the vectorAdd function with three arguments: gpu_a, gpu_b and gpu_c. Let us now look at the expression: $<<< N/32, 32 >>>$. This piece of code indicates to the GPU that we have $N/32$ blocks, and each block contains 32 threads. Let us now assume that the GPU magically adds the two arrays and saves the results in the array gpu_c in its physical memory space. The last step in the *main* function is to fetch the results from the GPU, and free space in the GPU. The code for it is as follows.

```
1  /* Copy from the GPU to the CPU */
2  cudaMemcpy (c, gpu_c, size, cudaMemcpyDeviceToHost);
3
4  /* free space in the GPU */
5  cudaFree (gpu_a);
6  cudaFree (gpu_b);
7  cudaFree (gpu_c);
8
9  } /* end of the main function */
```

Now, let us define the function *vectorAdd*, which needs to be executed on the GPU.

```
1  /* The GPU kernel */
2  __global__ void  vectorAdd ( int *gpu_a, int *gpu_b, int *gpu_c) {
3          /* compute the index */
4          int idx =  threadIdx.x + blockIdx.x * blockDim.x;
5
6          /* perform the addition */
7          gpu_c[idx] = gpu_a[idx] + gpu_b[idx];
8  }
```

Here, we access some built in variables that are populated by the CUDA runtime. In general, a grid and a block have three axes (x, y, and z). Since we assume only one axis in the blocks and the grid in this example, we only use the x axis. The variable $blockDim.x$ is equal to the number of threads in a block. If we would have considered 2D grids, then the dimension of a block would have been $blockDim.x \times blockDim.y$. $blockIdx.x$ is the index of the block, and $threadIdx.x$ is the index of the thread in the block. Thus, the expression $threadIdx.x + blockIdx.x * blockDim.x$ represents the index of the thread. Note that in this example, we associate each element of the arrays with a thread. Since the overhead of creation, initialisation, and switching of threads is small, we can adopt this approach in the case of a GPU. In the case of a CPU that has large overheads with creating and managing threads, this approach is not feasible. Once, we compute the index of the thread, we perform the addition in Line 7.

The GPU creates N copies of this kernel, and distributes it among N threads. Each of the kernels computes a different index in Line 4, and proceeds to perform the addition in Line 7. We showed a simple example. However, it is possible to write extremely complicated programs using the CUDA extensions to C/C++ replete with synchronisation statements, and conditional branch statements. The reader can consult the book by Farber [Farber, 2011] for an in-depth coverage of CUDA programming.

To summarise, let us show the entire GPU program. Note that we club the kernel of the GPU along with the code that is executed by the CPU into a single program. NVIDIA's compiler splits the single file into two binaries. One binary runs on the CPU and uses the CPU's instruction set, and the other binary runs on the GPU and uses the PTX instruction set. This is a classical example of a MPMD style of execution where we have different programs in different instruction sets, and multiple streams of data. Thus, we can think of the GPU's parallel programming model as a combination of SIMD, MPMD, and fine grained multithreading at the level of warps. We leave the readers with an artist's impression of a GPU (see Figure B.5).

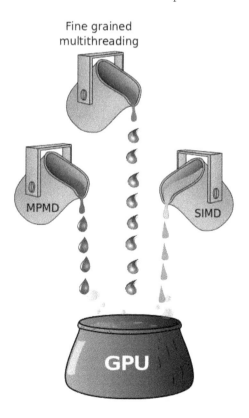

Figure B.5: Artist's impression of a GPU

```
1  #define N 1024
2
3  /* The GPU kernel */
4  __global__ void vectorAdd ( int *gpu_a, int *gpu_b, int *gpu_c) {
5      /* compute the index */
6      int idx =  threadIdx.x + blockIdx.x * blockDim.x;
7
8      /* perform the addition */
9      gpu_c[idx] = gpu_a[idx] + gpu_b[idx];
10 }
11 void main() {
12     /* Declare three arrays a, b, and c */
13     int a[N], b[N], c[N];
14
15     /* Declare the corresponding arrays in the GPU */
16     int size = N * sizeof(int);
17     int *gpu_a, *gpu_b, *gpu_c;
18
19     /* allocate space for the arrays in the GPU */
20     cudaMalloc((void**) &gpu_a, size);
21     cudaMalloc((void**) &gpu_b, size);
22     cudaMalloc((void**) &gpu_c, size);
23
24     /* initialise arrays, a and b */
25     ...
26
27     /* copy the arrays to the GPU */
28     cudaMemcpy (gpu_a, a, size, cudaMemcpyHostToDevice);
29     cudaMemcpy (gpu_b, b, size, cudaMemcpyHostToDevice);
30
31     /* invoke the vector add operation in the GPU */
32     vectorAdd <<< N/32, 32 >>> (gpu_a, gpu_b, gpu_c);
33
34     /* Copy from the GPU to the CPU */
35     cudaMemcpy (c, gpu_c, size, cudaMemcpyDeviceToHost);
36
37     /* free space in the GPU */
38     cudaFree (gpu_a);
39     cudaFree (gpu_b);
40     cudaFree (gpu_c);
41
42 } /* end of the main function */
```

Bibliography

[arm, a] The arm architecture with a focus on v7a and cortex-a8. `www.arm.com/files/pdf/ARM_Arch_A8.pdf`. Online: accessed on 21st Nov, 2013.

[arm, b] Arm cortex-m3 introduction. `www.arm.com/files/pdf/CortexM3_Uni_Intro.pdf`. Online: accessed on 21st Nov, 2013.

[nic,] Atm network interface. `http://en.wikipedia.org/wiki/File:ForeRunnerLE_25_ATM_Network_Interface_%281%29.jpg`. Online: accessed on 12th October, 2013.

[bak,] Bakhshali manuscript. `http://en.wikipedia.org/wiki/Bakhshali_manuscript/`. Online: accessed on 21st Nov, 2013.

[dis,] Compact disc. `http://openclipart.org/detail/104191/compact-disc-by-decosigner`. Online: accessed on 12th October, 2013.

[arm, c] Cortex -a15 mpcore tm tm revision: r3p2 technical reference manual. `www.arm.com`. Online: accessed on 21st Nov, 2013.

[ccl,] Creative commons share alike license 3.0. `http://creativecommons.org/licenses/by-sa/3.0/`. Online: accessed on 12th October, 2013.

[arm, d] Exploring the design of the cortex-a15 processor. `www.arm.com/files/pdf/at-exploring_the_design_of_the_cortex-a15.pdf`. Online: accessed on 21st Nov, 2013.

[gx8,] Gnu x86 assembler. `http://www.gnu.org`. Online: accessed on 21st Nov, 2013.

[har,] Hard disc – open clipart. `http://openclipart.org/detail/170369/hard-disk-by-ilnanny-170369`. Online: accessed on 12th October, 2013.

[fir,] Ieee 1394 standard. `http://standards.ieee.org/findstds/standard/1394-1995.html`. Online: accessed on 12th October, 2013.

[int,] Intel 64 and ia 32 architectures software developer manuals. `http://www.intel.com/content/www/us/en/processors/architectures-software-developer-manuals.html`.

[ind,] Interesting facts about india – my india, my pride – national portal of india. `http://knowindia.gov.in/myindia/myindia_frame.php?id=10`.

[mas,] Microsoft macro assembler 8.0 (masm) package. `http://www.microsoft.com/en-in/download/details.aspx?id=12654`. Online: accessed on 21st Nov, 2013.

[nas,] The netwide assembler. `http://www.nasm.us`. Online: accessed on 21st Nov, 2013.

[pci,] Pci express specifications. `http://www.pcisig.com/specifications/pciexpress`. Online: accessed on 12th October, 2013.

[red,] Red book (audio cd standard). `http://www.princeton.edu/~achaney/tmve/wiki100k/docs/Red_Book_(audio_CD_standard).html`.

[sat,] Sata specifications. `https://www.sata-io.org/technical-library`. Online: accessed on 12th October, 2013.

[uni,] The unicode standard. `http://www.unicode.org/standard/standard.html`. Online: accessed on 21st Nov, 2013.

[usb,] Usb specification. `http://www.usb.org/developers/docs/`. Online: accessed on 12th October, 2013.

[scs,] Www virtual library for scsi. `http://www.scsilibrary.com`. Online: accessed on 12th October, 2013.

[arm, 2000] (2000). *ARM Architecture Reference Manual* . ARM Limited.

[Abramovitch, 2001] Abramovitch, D. (2001). Magnetic and optical disk control: parallels and contrasts. In *American Control Conference, 2001. Proceedings of the 2001*, volume 1, pages 421–428 vol.1.

[Adve and Gharachorloo, 1996] Adve, S. V. and Gharachorloo, K. (1996). Shared memory consistency models: A tutorial. *computer*, 29(12):66–76.

[Adve et al., 2003] Adve, V., Lattner, C., Brukman, M., Shukla, A., and Gaeke, B. (2003). Llva: a low-level virtual instruction set architecture. In *Microarchitecture, 2003. MICRO-36. Proceedings. 36th Annual IEEE/ACM International Symposium on*, pages 205 – 216.

[Aho et al., 2006] Aho, A. V., Lam, M. S., Sethi, R., and Ullman, J. D. (2006). *Compilers, Principles, Techniques, and Tools*. Addison Wesley.

[Akkary et al., 2003] Akkary, H., Rajwar, R., and Srinivasan, S. T. (2003). Checkpoint processing and recovery: Towards scalable large instruction window processors. In *Microarchitecture, 2003. MICRO-36. Proceedings. 36th Annual IEEE/ACM International Symposium on*, pages 423–434. IEEE.

[Arvind and Maessen, 2006] Arvind, A. and Maessen, J.-W. (2006). Memory model= instruction reordering+ store atomicity. In *ACM SIGARCH Computer Architecture News*, volume 34, pages 29–40. IEEE Computer Society.

[Austin et al., 2002] Austin, T., Larson, E., and Ernst, D. (2002). SimpleScalar: An infrastructure for computer system modeling. *IEEE Computer*, 35(2):59–67.

[Baer, 2010] Baer, J.-L. (2010). *Microprocessor Architecture: from simple pipelines to chip multiprocessors*. Cambridge University Press.

[Balasubramonian et al., 2011] Balasubramonian, R., Jouppi, N. P., and Muralimanohar, N. (2011). Multicore cache hierarchies. *Synthesis Lectures on Computer Architecture*, 6(3):1–153.

[Bergstra and Middelburg, 2012] Bergstra, J. A. and Middelburg, C. A. (2012). *Instruction Sequences for Computer Science* . Atlantis.

[Blythe, 2008] Blythe, D. (2008). Rise of the graphics processor. *Proceedings of the IEEE*, 96(5):761–778.

[Boggs et al., 2004] Boggs, D., Baktha, A., Hawkins, J., Marr, D. T., Miller, J. A., Roussel, P., Singhal, R., Toll, B., and Venkatraman, K. (2004). The microarchitecture of the intel pentium 4 processor on 90nm technology. *Intel Technology Journal*, 8(1):1–17.

[Borrill, 1987] Borrill, P. (1987). Ieee 896.1: the futurebus. *Electronics and Power*, 33(10):628–631.

[Brent and Zimmermann, 2010] Brent, R. P. and Zimmermann, P. (2010). *Modern Computer Arithmetic*. Cambridge University Press.

[Brewer and Gill, 2008] Brewer, J. and Gill, M. (2008). *Nonvolatile Memory Technologies with Emphasis on Flash: A Comprehensive Guide to Understanding and Using Flash Memory Devices*. IEEE Press Series on Microelectronic Systems (Book 8). Wiley-IEEE Press.

[Brown et al., 2001] Brown, M. D., Stark, J., and Patt, Y. N. (2001). Select-free instruction scheduling logic. In *Microarchitecture, 2001. MICRO-34. Proceedings. 34th ACM/IEEE International Symposium on*, pages 204–213. IEEE.

[Burgess et al., 2011] Burgess, B., Cohen, B., Denman, M., Dundas, J., Kaplan, D., and Rupley, J. (2011). Bobcat: Amd's low-power x86 processor. *Micro, IEEE*, 31(2):16–25.

[Butler et al., 2011] Butler, M., Barnes, L., Sarma, D. D., and Gelinas, B. (2011). Bulldozer: An approach to multithreaded compute performance. *Micro, IEEE*, 31(2):6–15.

[Carpenter and Doran, 1986] Carpenter, B. E. and Doran, R. W. (1986). Turing's ACE Report of 1946 and Other Papers. Technical report, Cambridge.

[Carter, 1995] Carter, J. W. (1995). *Microprocessor Architecture and Microprogramming: A State Machine Approach*. Prentice Hall.

[Cavanagh, 2013] Cavanagh, J. (2013). *x86 Assembly Language and C Fundamentals*. CRC Press.

[Cheng and Hu, 1999] Cheng, Y. and Hu, C. (1999). *MOSFET Modeling and Bsim3 User's Guide*. Kluwer Academic Publishers, Norwell, MA, USA.

[Consortium et al., 2006] Consortium, H. T. et al. (2006). Hypertransport i/o link specification revision 3.00. *Document# HTC20051222-0046-0008*.

[Conway and Hughes, 2007] Conway, P. and Hughes, B. (2007). The amd opteron north bridge architecture. *Micro, IEEE*, 27(2):10–21.

[Cormen et al., 2009] Cormen, T. H., Leiserson, C. E., Rivest, R. L., and Stein, C. (2009). *Introduction to Algorithms*. MIT Press, third edition.

[Cover and Thomas, 2013] Cover, T. M. and Thomas, J. A. (2013). *Elements of Information Theory*. Wiley.

[Culler et al., 1998] Culler, D., Singh, J. P., and Gupta, A. (1998). *Parallel Computer Architecture: A Hardware/Software Approach*. The Morgan Kaufmann series in Computer Architecture Design. Morgan Kaufmann.

[Dally and Poulton, 1998] Dally, W. J. and Poulton, J. W. (1998). *Digital Systems Engineering*. Cambridge University Press.

[Danowitz et al., 2012] Danowitz, A., Kelley, K., Mao, J., Stevenson, J. P., and Horowitz, M. (2012). Cpu db: recording microprocessor history. *Communications of the ACM*, 55(4):55–63.

[Das, 2010] Das, L. B. (2010). *The X86 Microprocessors : Architecture and Programming (8086 to Pentium)*. Pearson.

[Downing and Meyer, 1997] Downing, T. and Meyer, J. (1997). *Java Virtual Machine*. O'Reilly Media.

[Durr et al., 2009] Durr, S., Fodor, Z., Frison, J., Hoelbling, C., Hoffmann, R., Katz, S. D., Krieg, S., Kurth, T., Lellouch, L., Lippert, T., Szabo, K. K., and Vulvert, G. (2009). Ab-initio determination of light hadron masses.

[Edler and Hill, 1999] Edler, J. and Hill, M. D. (1999). Dinero iv trace-driven uniprocessor cache simulator" http://www. cs. wisc. edu/markhill.

[Elsner and Fenlason, 1994] Elsner, D. and Fenlason, J. (1994). *Using as – The GNU Assembler*.

[Farber, 2011] Farber, R. (2011). *CUDA Application Design and Development*. Morgan Kaufmann.

[Farquhar and Bunce, 2012] Farquhar, E. and Bunce, P. J. (2012). *The MIPS Programmers Handbook* . Morgan Kaufmann.

[Gharachorloo et al., 1992] Gharachorloo, K., Adve, S. V., Gupta, A., Hennessy, J. L., and Hill, M. D. (1992). Programming for different memory consistency models. *Journal of parallel and distributed computing*, 15(4):399–407.

[Gibson, 2011] Gibson, J. R. (2011). *ARM Assembly Language an Introduction*. Lulu.

[Gilreath and Laplante, 2003] Gilreath, W. F. and Laplante, P. A. (2003). *Computer Architecture: A Minimalist Perspective*. Springer.

[gnu.org,] gnu.org. Gnu binutils. http://www.gnu.org/software/binutils.

[Gregg, 1998] Gregg, J. (1998). *Ones and zeros: understanding boolean algebra, digital circuits, and the logic of sets*. Wiley-IEEE Press.

[Guiady et al., 1999] Guiady, C., Falsafi, B., and Vijaykumar, T. N. (1999). Is sc+ ilp= rc? In *Computer Architecture, 1999. Proceedings of the 26th International Symposium on*, pages 162–171. IEEE.

[Gwennap, 2010] Gwennap, L. (2010). Sandy bridge spans generations. *Microprocessor Report*, 9(27):10–01.

[Halfhill, 2008] Halfhill, T. R. (2008). Intel's tiny atom. *Microprocessor Report*, 22(4):1.

[Hamacher et al., 2001] Hamacher, C., Vranesic, Z., and Zaky, S. (2001). *Computer Organization*. Mc-GrawHill.

[Hartstein et al., 2006] Hartstein, A., Srinivasan, V., Puzak, T. R., and Emma, P. G. (2006). Cache miss behavior: is it √2? In *Proceedings of the 3rd conference on Computing frontiers*, CF '06, pages 313–320.

[Henessey and Patterson, 2010] Henessey, J. and Patterson, D. (2010). *Computer Organization and Design: The Hardware/Software Interface*. Morgan Kaufmann.

[Hennessy and Patterson, 2012] Hennessy, J. L. and Patterson, D. A. (2012). *Computer architecture: a quantitative approach*. Elsevier.

[Hill et al., 1999] Hill, M. D., Jouppi, N. P., and Sohi, G. S. (1999). *Readings in Computer Architecture*. The Morgan Kaufmann series in Computer Architecture Design. Morgan Kaufmann.

[Hohl, 2009] Hohl, W. (2009). *ARM Assembly Language: Fundamentals and Techniques*. CRC Press.

[Hopcroft et al., 2006] Hopcroft, J. E., Motwani, R., and Ulmann, J. D. (2006). *Introduction to Automata Theory, Languages, and Computation*. Prentice Hall.

[Hughes et al., 2013] Hughes, J. F., Dam, A. V., Mcguire, M., Sklar, D. F., Foley, J. D., Feiner, S. K., and Akeley, K. (2013). *Computer Graphics: Principles and Practice*. Addison Wesley.

[Husson, 1970] Husson, S. S. (1970). *Microprogramming: Principles and Practices*. Prentice Hall.

[Hwang, 2003] Hwang, K. (2003). *Advanced computer architecture*. Tata McGraw-Hill Education.

[Hwu and Patt, 1987] Hwu, W.-M. W. and Patt, Y. N. (1987). Checkpoint repair for high-performance out-of-order execution machines. *Computers, IEEE Transactions on*, 100(12):1496–1514.

[INTEL, 2010] INTEL, I. (2010). Intel r 64 and ia-32 architectures software developer's manual.

[ITRS, 2011] ITRS (2011). *International Technology Roadmap for Semiconductors*. http://www.itrs.net/Links/2011ITRS/Home2011.htm.

[Jacob, 2009] Jacob, B. (2009). The memory system: you can't avoid it, you can't ignore it, you can't fake it. *Synthesis Lectures on Computer Architecture*, 4(1):1–77.

[Jacob et al., 2007] Jacob, B., Ng, S., and Wang, D. (2007). *Memory Systems: Cache, DRAM, Disk*. Morgan Kaufmann.

[Jerger and Peh, 2009] Jerger, N. E. and Peh, L.-S. (2009). On-chip networks. *Synthesis Lectures on Computer Architecture*, 4(1):1–141.

[Kahan, 1996] Kahan, W. (1996). Ieee standard 754 for binary floating-point arithmetic. *Lecture Notes on the Status of IEEE*, 754.

[Keleher et al., 1994] Keleher, P., Cox, A. L., Dwarkadas, S., and Zwaenepoel, W. (1994). Treadmarks: Distributed shared memory on standard workstations and operating systems. In *USENIX Winter*, volume 1994.

[Keltcher et al., 2003] Keltcher, C. N., McGrath, K. J., Ahmed, A., and Conway, P. (2003). The amd opteron processor for multiprocessor servers. *Micro, IEEE*, 23(2):66–76.

[Kohavi and Jha, 2009] Kohavi, Z. and Jha, N. K. (2009). *Switching and Finite Automata Theory*. Cambridge University Press.

[Koren, 2001] Koren, I. (2001). *Computer Arithmetic Algorithms*. CRC Press, second edition.

[Kreyszig, 2000] Kreyszig, E. (2000). *Advanced Engineering Mathematics*. Wiley, eigth edition.

[Krick et al., 2000] Krick, R. F., Hinton, G. J., Upton, M. D., Sager, D. J., and Lee, C. W. (2000). Trace based instruction caching. US Patent 6,018,786.

[Kumar, 2003] Kumar, V. R. (2003). *Microprocessor x86 Programming*. BPB.

[Lafore, 2002] Lafore, R. (2002). *Data Structures and Algorithms in Java*. Sams Publishing.

[Lin, 2011] Lin, M.-B. (2011). *Introduction to VLSI Systems: A Logic, Circuit, and System Perspective*. CRC Press.

[Lindholm et al., 2008] Lindholm, E., Nickolls, J., Oberman, S., and Montrym, J. (2008). Nvidia tesla: A unified graphics and computing architecture. *Micro, IEEE*, 28(2):39–55.

[Ling and Xing, 2004] Ling, S. and Xing, C. (2004). *Coding Theory: A First Course*. Cambridge University Press.

[Mano, 2007] Mano, M. M. (2007). *Computer Systems Architecture*. Pearson.

[Micheli, 1994] Micheli, G. D. (1994). *Synthesis and Optimization of Digital Circuits*. McGraw-Hill.

[Micheloni et al., 2010] Micheloni, R., Crippa, L., and Marelli, A. (2010). *Inside NAND Flash Memories*. Springer.

[Mitra, 1999] Mitra, T. (1999). Dynamic random access memory: A survey. *Department of Computer Science, State University of New York at Stony Brook*, 25.

[Muchnick, 1997] Muchnick, S. (1997). *Advanced Compiler Design and Implementation*. Morgan Kaufmann.

[Neubauer et al., 2007] Neubauer, A., Freudenberger, J., and Kuhn, V. (2007). *Coding Theory: Algorithms, Architectures and Applications*. Wiley-Blackwell.

[Owen and Steinman, 2008] Owen, J. and Steinman, M. (2008). North bridge architecture of amd's griffin microprocessor family. *Micro, IEEE*, 28(2):10–18.

[Parhami, 2009] Parhami, B. (2009). *Computer Arithmetic: Algorithms and Hardware Designs*. Oxford University Press.

[Patt and Patel, 2003] Patt, Y. and Patel, S. (2003). *Introduction to Computing Systems: From bits & gates to C & beyond*. McGraw-Hill.

[Paul, 1993] Paul, R. (1993). *SPARC Architecture, Assembly Language Programming and C*. Prentice Hall.

[Peterson et al., 1991] Peterson, C., Sutton, J., and Wiley, P. (1991). iwarp: a 100-mops, liw microprocessor for multicomputers. *Micro, IEEE*, 11(3):26–29.

[Petric et al., 2005] Petric, V., Sha, T., and Roth, A. (2005). *Reno: A rename-based instruction optimizer*, volume 33. IEEE Computer Society.

[Phelps and Parks, 2004] Phelps, A. M. and Parks, D. M. (2004). Fun and Games: Multi-Language Development. *Queue*, 1(10):46–56.

[Pratt, 1995] Pratt, V. (1995). Anatomy of the pentium bug. In *TAPSOFT'95: Theory and Practice of Software Development*, pages 97–107. Springer.

[Proakis and Salehi, 2007] Proakis, J. and Salehi, M. (2007). *Digital Communications*. McGrawHill.

[Quinn, 2003] Quinn, M. (2003). *Parallel Programming in C with OpenMP and MPI*. Tata McGrawHill.

[Qureshi et al., 2011] Qureshi, M. K., Gurumurthi, S., and Rajendran, B. (2011). Phase change memory: From devices to systems. *Synthesis Lectures on Computer Architecture*, 6(4):1–134.

[Radhakrishnan et al., 2007] Radhakrishnan, S., Chinthamani, S., and Cheng, K. (2007). The blackford north bridge chipset for the intel 5000. *Micro, IEEE*, 27(2):22–33.

[russell, 1978] russell, r. m. (1978). the cray-1 computer system. *communications of the acm*, 21(1):63–72.

[Sarangi et al., 2014] Sarangi, S. R., Ananthanarayanan, G., and Balakrishnan, M. (2014). Lightsim: A leakage aware ultrafast temperature simulator. In *ASPDAC*.

[Sarangi et al., 2006] Sarangi, S. R., Tiwari, A., and Torrellas, J. (2006). Phoenix: Detecting and recovering from permanent processor design bugs with programmable hardware. In *Proceedings of the 39th Annual IEEE/ACM International Symposium on Microarchitecture*, pages 26–37. IEEE Computer Society.

[Silberschatz et al., 2008] Silberschatz, A., Galvin, P. B., and Gagne, G. (2008). *Operating System Concepts*. Wiley, 8 edition.

[Sima et al., 1997] Sima, D., Fountain, T., and Karsuk, P. (1997). *Advanced Computer Architectures: A Design Space Approach*. Addison-Wesley.

[Sklar, 2001] Sklar, B. (2001). *Digital Communications: Fundamentals and Applications*. Prentice Hall.

[Smith and Sohi, 1995] Smith, J. E. and Sohi, G. S. (1995). The microarchitecture of superscalar processors. *Proceedings of the IEEE*, 83(12):1609–1624.

[Snir et al., 1995] Snir, M., Otto, S. W., Walker, D. W., Dongarra, J., and Huss-Lederman, S. (1995). *MPI: the complete reference*. MIT press.

[Sorin et al., 2011] Sorin, D. J., Hill, M. D., and Wood, D. A. (2011). A primer on memory consistency and cache coherence. *Synthesis Lectures on Computer Architecture*, 6(3):1–212.

[Srinivasan et al., 2004] Srinivasan, J., Adve, S. V., Bose, P., and Rivers, J. A. (2004). The case for lifetime reliability-aware microprocessors. In *Proceedings of the 31st annual international symposium on Computer architecture*, ISCA '04, pages 276–.

[Stallings, 2010] Stallings, W. (2010). *Computer Organization and Architecture: Designing for Performance*. Pearson.

[Stenstrom, 1990] Stenstrom, P. (1990). A survey of cache coherence schemes for multiprocessors. *Computer*, 23(6):12–24.

[Streetman and Banerjee, 2005] Streetman, B. and Banerjee, S. (2005). *Solid State Electronic Devices*. Prentice-Hall.

[Sze and Ng, 2006] Sze, S. M. and Ng, K. K. (2006). *Physics of semiconductor devices*. Wiley-Interscience.

[Tanenbaum, 2007] Tanenbaum, A. S. (2007). *Modern Operating Systems*. Prentice Hall, third edition.

[Tarjan et al., 2006] Tarjan, D., Thoziyoor, S., and Jouppi, N. P. (2006). Cacti 4.0. *HP laboratories, Technical report*.

[Taub and Schilling, 1977] Taub, H. and Schilling, D. L. (1977). *Digital integrated electronics*. McGraw-Hill New York.

[Verma et al., 2008] Verma, A. K., Brisk, P., and Ienne, P. (2008). Variable Latency Speculative Addition: A New Paradigm for Arithmetic Circuit Design. In *DATE*, pages 1250–1255.

[von Neumann, 1945] von Neumann, J. (1945). First Draft of a Report on the EDVAC. Technical report.

[Vranas et al., 2006] Vranas, P., Bhanot, G., Blumrich, M., Chen, D., Gara, A., Heidelberger, P., Salapura, V., and Sexton, J. C. (2006). The BlueGene/L Supercomputer and Quantum ChromoDynamics. In *Proceedings of the 2006 ACM/IEEE conference on Supercomputing*, SC '06, New York, NY, USA. ACM.

[Wakerly, 2000] Wakerly, J. F. (2000). *Digital design: principles and practices.* Prentice-Hall, Inc.

[Ware et al., 2010] Ware, M., Rajamani, K., Floyd, M., Brock, B., Rubio, J. C., Rawson, F., and Carter, J. B. (2010). Architecting for power management: the ibm® power7™ approach. In *High Performance Computer Architecture (HPCA), 2010 IEEE 16th International Symposium on*, pages 1–11. IEEE.

[Whitesitt, 2010] Whitesitt, J. E. (2010). *Boolean Algebra and its Applications.* Dover Books on Computer Science.

[Wikipedia,] Wikipedia. Dadda multiplier. `http://en.wikipedia.org/wiki/Dadda_multiplier`. Accessed on Oct 22nd, 2012.

[Yeager, 1996] Yeager, K. (1996). The mips r10000 superscalar microprocessor. *Micro, IEEE*, 16(2):28–41.

[Yeh and Patt, 1991] Yeh, T.-Y. and Patt, Y. N. (1991). Two-level adaptive training branch prediction. In *Proceedings of the 24th annual international symposium on Microarchitecture*, pages 51–61. ACM.

[Yeh and Patt, 1992] Yeh, T.-Y. and Patt, Y. N. (1992). Alternative implementations of two-level adaptive branch prediction. In *ACM SIGARCH Computer Architecture News*, volume 20, pages 124–134. ACM.

[Yeh and Patt, 1993] Yeh, T.-Y. and Patt, Y. N. (1993). A comparison of dynamic branch predictors that use two levels of branch history. *ACM SIGARCH Computer Architecture News*, 21(2):257–266.

[Yiu, 2009] Yiu, J. (2009). *The Definitive Guide to ARM Cortex-M3.* Newnes.

[Yiu, 2011] Yiu, J. (2011). *The Definitive Guide to ARM Cortex-M0.* Newnes.

[Yourst, 2007] Yourst, M. (2007). Ptlsim: A cycle accurate full system x86-64 microarchitectural simulator. In *ISPASS*, pages 23–34.

Index